W9-BZF-400

# Indian Ocean
## five island countries

Federal Research Division
Library of Congress
Edited by
Helen Chapin Metz
Research Completed
August 1994

On the cover: Traditional dhow seen among Indian
  Ocean islands

Third Edition, First Printing, 1995.

**Library of Congress Cataloging-in-Publication Data**

Indian Ocean : five island countries / Federal Research Division, Library of Congress ; edited by Helen Chapin
  Metz.—3rd ed.
    p. cm. — (Area handbook series, ISSN 1057–5294)
  (DA Pam ; 550–154)
    "Supersedes the 1982 edition of Indian Ocean : five
  island countries, edited by Frederica M. Bunge."—T.p.
  verso.
    "Research completed August 1994."
    Includes bibliographical references (pp. 343–72) and
  index.
    ISBN 0–8444-0857–3 (hc : alk. paper)
    1. Islands of the Indian Ocean—Handbooks, manuals,
  etc. I. Metz, Helen Chapin, 1928–  . II. Library of Congress. Federal Research Division. III. Series. IV. Series:
  DA Pam ; 550–154
DS349.8.I5  1995                                        95–16570
909'.09824–dc20                                            CIP

Reprinted without alteration on recycled acid-free paper.

Bernan
Lanham, Maryland
December 1995

# Foreword

This volume is one in a continuing series of books prepared by the Federal Research Division of the Library of Congress under the Country Studies/Area Handbook Program sponsored by the Department of the Army. The last two pages of this book list the other published studies.

Most books in the series deal with a particular foreign country, describing and analyzing its political, economic, social, and national security systems and institutions, and examining the interrelationships of those systems and the ways they are shaped by cultural factors. Each study is written by a multidisciplinary team of social scientists. The authors seek to provide a basic understanding of the observed society, striving for a dynamic rather than a static portrayal. Particular attention is devoted to the people who make up the society, their origins, dominant beliefs and values, their common interests and the issues on which they are divided, the nature and extent of their involvement with national institutions, and their attitudes toward each other and toward their social system and political order.

The books represent the analysis of the authors and should not be construed as an expression of an official United States government position, policy, or decision. The authors have sought to adhere to accepted standards of scholarly objectivity. Corrections, additions, and suggestions for changes from readers will be welcomed for use in future editions.

Louis R. Mortimer
Chief
Federal Research Division
Library of Congress
Washington, DC 20540–5220

# Acknowledgments

The authors wish to acknowledge the contributions of the writers of the 1982 edition of *Indian Ocean: Five Island Countries*, edited by Frederica M. Bunge. Their work provided general background for the present volume.

The authors are grateful to individuals in various government agencies and private institutions who gave of their time, research materials, and expertise in the production of this book. These individuals include Ralph K. Benesch, who oversees the Country Studies/Area Handbook program for the Department of the Army. The authors also wish to thank members of the Federal Research Division staff who contributed directly to the preparation of the manuscript. These people include Sandra W. Meditz, who reviewed all drafts and served as liaison with the sponsoring agency; Marilyn Majeska, who managed editing and book production; Andrea Merrill, who reviewed tables and figures; Barbara Edgerton and Izella Watson, who performed word processing; and Janie L. Gilchrist, David P. Cabitto, and Stephen C. Cranton, who prepared the camera-ready copy.

Also involved in preparing the text were Mimi Cantwell, who edited chapters; Beverly Wolpert, who performed the pre-publication editorial review; and Joan C. Cook, who compiled the index.

Graphics were prepared by David P. Cabitto, and Tim L. Merrill prepared map drafts, apart from the topography and drainage map prepared by Harriett R. Blood. David P. Cabitto and the firm of Greenhorne and O'Mara prepared the final maps. Special thanks are owed to Marty Ittner, who prepared the illustrations on the title page of all but one of the chapters, and David P. Cabitto, who did the cover art and art for one of the title pages.

Finally, the authors acknowledge the generosity of individuals, who allowed their photographs to be used in this study.

# Contents

|  | Page |
|---|---|
| **Foreword** | iii |
| **Acknowledgments** | v |
| **Preface** | xiii |
| **Introduction** | xvii |
| **Chapter 1.** Madagascar | 1 |

*Peter J. Schraeder*

| | |
|---|---|
| COUNTRY PROFILE | 3 |
| HISTORICAL SETTING | 9 |
| Precolonial Era, Prior to 1894 | 9 |
| Colonial Era, 1894–1960 | 12 |
| Independence, the First Republic, and the Military Transition, 1960–75 | 16 |
| The Second Republic, 1975–92 | 19 |
| The Third Republic, 1993– | 22 |
| PHYSICAL ENVIRONMENT | 23 |
| Topography | 23 |
| Climate | 28 |
| Flora and Fauna | 29 |
| SOCIETY | 30 |
| Population And Ethnicity | 30 |
| Language | 39 |
| Traditional Beliefs and Religion | 41 |
| Social Structure and Family | 46 |
| Education | 50 |
| Public Health | 53 |
| THE ECONOMY | 55 |
| Government Policy and Intervention | 55 |
| Structural Adjustment | 58 |
| National Accounts and Budget | 60 |
| Balance of Payments and Debt | 61 |
| Traditional Agriculture | 62 |
| Agricultural Production | 65 |

Industrial Development . . . . . . . . . . . . . . . . . . . . . . . . 68
Foreign Trade . . . . . . . . . . . . . . . . . . . . . . . . . . . . . . . 71
Transportation and Telecommunications . . . . . . . . 72
GOVERNMENT AND POLITICS . . . . . . . . . . . . . . . . . . . . . . 74
Constitution and Institutions of Governance . . . . . . 74
The *Fokonolona* and Traditional Governance . . . . . . . 77
Foreign Relations . . . . . . . . . . . . . . . . . . . . . . . . . . . . 79

**Chapter 2.** Mauritius . . . . . . . . . . . . . . . . . . . . . . . . . . . 89

*Anthony Toth*

COUNTRY PROFILE . . . . . . . . . . . . . . . . . . . . . . . . . . . . . . 91
HISTORICAL SETTING . . . . . . . . . . . . . . . . . . . . . . . . . . . 98
Early Settlement . . . . . . . . . . . . . . . . . . . . . . . . . . . . . 98
Rise of the Sugar Economy . . . . . . . . . . . . . . . . . . . . 100
British Colonial Rule . . . . . . . . . . . . . . . . . . . . . . . . . 102
Toward Independence . . . . . . . . . . . . . . . . . . . . . . . . 103
Independent Mauritius . . . . . . . . . . . . . . . . . . . . . . . . 105
PHYSICAL ENVIRONMENT . . . . . . . . . . . . . . . . . . . . . . . . 108
Geography . . . . . . . . . . . . . . . . . . . . . . . . . . . . . . . . . 108
Climate . . . . . . . . . . . . . . . . . . . . . . . . . . . . . . . . . . . 111
SOCIETY AND CULTURE . . . . . . . . . . . . . . . . . . . . . . . . . . 112
Population and Demography . . . . . . . . . . . . . . . . . . . 112
Ethnicity, Religion, and Language . . . . . . . . . . . . . . . 113
Education . . . . . . . . . . . . . . . . . . . . . . . . . . . . . . . . . . 115
Media . . . . . . . . . . . . . . . . . . . . . . . . . . . . . . . . . . . . 117
Health and Welfare . . . . . . . . . . . . . . . . . . . . . . . . . . 118
Role of Women . . . . . . . . . . . . . . . . . . . . . . . . . . . . . 118
ECONOMY . . . . . . . . . . . . . . . . . . . . . . . . . . . . . . . . . . . 120
Agriculture and Fishing . . . . . . . . . . . . . . . . . . . . . . 121
Industry and Commerce . . . . . . . . . . . . . . . . . . . . . . 123
Banking . . . . . . . . . . . . . . . . . . . . . . . . . . . . . . . . . . 124
Trade and Balance of Payments . . . . . . . . . . . . . . . . 125
Tourism . . . . . . . . . . . . . . . . . . . . . . . . . . . . . . . . . . 125
Labor . . . . . . . . . . . . . . . . . . . . . . . . . . . . . . . . . . . . 126
Transportation and Telecommunications . . . . . . . . 126
Water and Electricity . . . . . . . . . . . . . . . . . . . . . . . . 127
Budget and Public Finance . . . . . . . . . . . . . . . . . . . . 127
GOVERNMENT AND POLITICS . . . . . . . . . . . . . . . . . . . . . . 129
Structure of Government . . . . . . . . . . . . . . . . . . . . . . 129
Politics of the Republic of Mauritius . . . . . . . . . . . . . 131
Foreign Relations . . . . . . . . . . . . . . . . . . . . . . . . . . . 132

**Chapter 3.** Comoros . . . . . . . . . . . . . . . . . . . . . . . . . . . . . . . . . . 137
*Vincent Ercolano*
COUNTRY PROFILE. . . . . . . . . . . . . . . . . . . . . . . . . . . . . . . . . . 139
HISTORICAL SETTING. . . . . . . . . . . . . . . . . . . . . . . . . . . . . . 146
    Early Visitors and Settlers . . . . . . . . . . . . . . . . . . . . . . . 146
    French Colonization . . . . . . . . . . . . . . . . . . . . . . . . . . . . 148
    The Break with France. . . . . . . . . . . . . . . . . . . . . . . . . . . 150
    The Soilih Regime . . . . . . . . . . . . . . . . . . . . . . . . . . . . . 152
    The Abdallah Regime . . . . . . . . . . . . . . . . . . . . . . . . . . . 154
    The Issue of Mahoré . . . . . . . . . . . . . . . . . . . . . . . . . . . . 164
PHYSICAL ENVIRONMENT . . . . . . . . . . . . . . . . . . . . . . . . . . 168
SOCIETY AND CULTURE . . . . . . . . . . . . . . . . . . . . . . . . . . . . . 171
    Population . . . . . . . . . . . . . . . . . . . . . . . . . . . . . . . . . . . 171
    Society . . . . . . . . . . . . . . . . . . . . . . . . . . . . . . . . . . . . . . 172
    Status of Women. . . . . . . . . . . . . . . . . . . . . . . . . . . . . . . 176
    Religion and Education. . . . . . . . . . . . . . . . . . . . . . . . . . 177
    Public Health. . . . . . . . . . . . . . . . . . . . . . . . . . . . . . . . . 179
    Media. . . . . . . . . . . . . . . . . . . . . . . . . . . . . . . . . . . . . . . 180
ECONOMY . . . . . . . . . . . . . . . . . . . . . . . . . . . . . . . . . . . . . . . . 181
    Agriculture, Livestock, and Fishing . . . . . . . . . . . . . . 185
    Industry and Infrastructure . . . . . . . . . . . . . . . . . . . . . 187
    Transportation and Telecommunications . . . . . . . . 188
GOVERNMENT AND POLITICS . . . . . . . . . . . . . . . . . . . . . . . 190
    Political Dynamics. . . . . . . . . . . . . . . . . . . . . . . . . . . . . 192
    Foreign Affairs. . . . . . . . . . . . . . . . . . . . . . . . . . . . . . . . 195

**Chapter 4.** Seychelles . . . . . . . . . . . . . . . . . . . . . . . . . . . . . . 199
*Jean R. Tartter*
COUNTRY PROFILE. . . . . . . . . . . . . . . . . . . . . . . . . . . . . . . . . 201
HISTORICAL SETTING. . . . . . . . . . . . . . . . . . . . . . . . . . . . . . 207
    Crown Colony Status, 1903. . . . . . . . . . . . . . . . . . . . . . 209
    Steps Toward Independence, 1967–76 . . . . . . . . . . . 210
    Coup by René Supporters, 1977 . . . . . . . . . . . . . . . . . 212
PHYSICAL ENVIRONMENT . . . . . . . . . . . . . . . . . . . . . . . . . . 213
POPULATION . . . . . . . . . . . . . . . . . . . . . . . . . . . . . . . . . . . . . 216
    Ethnic Groups . . . . . . . . . . . . . . . . . . . . . . . . . . . . . . . . 217
    Languages. . . . . . . . . . . . . . . . . . . . . . . . . . . . . . . . . . . 217
SOCIAL ORGANIZATION. . . . . . . . . . . . . . . . . . . . . . . . . . . . 218
    Class and Social Structure. . . . . . . . . . . . . . . . . . . . . . 218
    Status of Women. . . . . . . . . . . . . . . . . . . . . . . . . . . . . . 219
RELIGION. . . . . . . . . . . . . . . . . . . . . . . . . . . . . . . . . . . . . . . . . 220

EDUCATION . . . . . . . . . . . . . . . . . . . . . . . . . . . . . . . . . . . . . . . . . 221
HEALTH AND WELFARE . . . . . . . . . . . . . . . . . . . . . . . . . . . . . . 223
THE ECONOMY . . . . . . . . . . . . . . . . . . . . . . . . . . . . . . . . . . . . . . 224
    Government Role . . . . . . . . . . . . . . . . . . . . . . . . . . . . . . . 225
    Budget . . . . . . . . . . . . . . . . . . . . . . . . . . . . . . . . . . . . . . . . 228
    Economic Development . . . . . . . . . . . . . . . . . . . . . . . . . 229
    Labor . . . . . . . . . . . . . . . . . . . . . . . . . . . . . . . . . . . . . . . . . 229
    Agriculture . . . . . . . . . . . . . . . . . . . . . . . . . . . . . . . . . . . . 231
    Fisheries . . . . . . . . . . . . . . . . . . . . . . . . . . . . . . . . . . . . . . 232
    Oil . . . . . . . . . . . . . . . . . . . . . . . . . . . . . . . . . . . . . . . . . . . 233
    Manufacturing . . . . . . . . . . . . . . . . . . . . . . . . . . . . . . . . 234
    Tourism . . . . . . . . . . . . . . . . . . . . . . . . . . . . . . . . . . . . . . 234
    Transportation and Telecommunications . . . . . . . . 235
    Foreign Trade . . . . . . . . . . . . . . . . . . . . . . . . . . . . . . . . 236
GOVERNMENT AND POLITICS . . . . . . . . . . . . . . . . . . . . . . 237
    Governmental System, 1979–93 . . . . . . . . . . . . . . . . 238
    Return to a Multiparty System . . . . . . . . . . . . . . . . . . 238
    Opposition Movements and Interest Groups . . . . . 240
    Information Media . . . . . . . . . . . . . . . . . . . . . . . . . . . . 243
    Legal System and Civil Rights . . . . . . . . . . . . . . . . . . 243
FOREIGN RELATIONS . . . . . . . . . . . . . . . . . . . . . . . . . . . . . . . 245

**Chapter 5.** Maldives . . . . . . . . . . . . . . . . . . . . . . . . . . . . . . 249
                 *Karl E. Ryavec*
COUNTRY PROFILE . . . . . . . . . . . . . . . . . . . . . . . . . . . . . . . . . 251
HISTORICAL SETTING . . . . . . . . . . . . . . . . . . . . . . . . . . . . . . 257
PHYSICAL ENVIRONMENT . . . . . . . . . . . . . . . . . . . . . . . . . . 262
    Physiography . . . . . . . . . . . . . . . . . . . . . . . . . . . . . . . . . . 262
    Climate . . . . . . . . . . . . . . . . . . . . . . . . . . . . . . . . . . . . . . . 263
SOCIETY . . . . . . . . . . . . . . . . . . . . . . . . . . . . . . . . . . . . . . . . . . . . 264
    Population . . . . . . . . . . . . . . . . . . . . . . . . . . . . . . . . . . . . 264
    Ethnic Groups and Language . . . . . . . . . . . . . . . . . . . 265
    Social Structure . . . . . . . . . . . . . . . . . . . . . . . . . . . . . . . 266
RELIGION . . . . . . . . . . . . . . . . . . . . . . . . . . . . . . . . . . . . . . . . . . 267
EDUCATION . . . . . . . . . . . . . . . . . . . . . . . . . . . . . . . . . . . . . . . . 269
HEALTH . . . . . . . . . . . . . . . . . . . . . . . . . . . . . . . . . . . . . . . . . . . . 271
    Health Conditions . . . . . . . . . . . . . . . . . . . . . . . . . . . . 271
    Health Care . . . . . . . . . . . . . . . . . . . . . . . . . . . . . . . . . . 271
ECONOMY . . . . . . . . . . . . . . . . . . . . . . . . . . . . . . . . . . . . . . . . . . 272
    Gross Domestic Product . . . . . . . . . . . . . . . . . . . . . . . 272
    Fishing . . . . . . . . . . . . . . . . . . . . . . . . . . . . . . . . . . . . . . 273

Tourism......................................... 274
Currency and Banking......................... 274
Budget......................................... 276
Employment..................................... 276
Transportation and Telecommunications ........ 277
Trade.......................................... 278
Economic Aid .................................. 279
GOVERNMENT AND POLITICS ...................... 279
Constitution................................... 279
Politics....................................... 280
Foreign Relations ............................. 282
Media.......................................... 282

**Chapter 6.** Strategic Considerations................... 285
*Thomas P. Ofcansky*
HISTORICAL INTEREST.............................. 287
MADAGASCAR...................................... 294
Security Concerns.............................. 294
Armed Forces in National Life ................. 296
The Military and the Government ............... 298
Forces Armées Populaires....................... 299
State Security Services ....................... 300
Training and Morale ........................... 301
Foreign Military Assistance.................... 302
Penal System .................................. 306
Human Rights .................................. 307
MAURITIUS ...................................... 308
Security Concerns.............................. 308
Armed Forces in National Life ................. 309
Police Agencies ............................... 310
Foreign Military Assistance.................... 312
Penal System .................................. 312
Human Rights .................................. 313
SEYCHELLES ..................................... 313
Security Concerns.............................. 313
Armed Forces in National Life ................. 315
Seychelles People's Defence Forces ............ 316
State Security Services ....................... 318
Training and Morale ........................... 319
Foreign Military Assistance.................... 319
Penal System .................................. 321

Human Rights.................................... 321
COMOROS........................................ 322
   Security Concerns ............................ 322
   The Military and the Government.............. 325
   Armed Forces ................................ 325
   State Security Services....................... 326
   Foreign Military Assistance ................... 326
   Penal System ................................ 327
   Human Rights................................ 327
MALDIVES...................................... 328
   Security Concerns ............................ 328
   Armed Forces in National Life ................ 329
   Penal System ................................ 330
   Human Rights................................ 330

**Appendix.** Tables ................................ 333

**Bibliography** ..................................... 343

**Glossary** ......................................... 373

**Index** ........................................... 379

**Contributors** .................................... 409

## List of Figures

1  Indian Ocean Countries: Geographic Setting, 1994 ...  xvi
2  Madagascar: Administrative Divisions, 1994 ..........  8
3  Madagascar: Topography and Drainage .............  26
4  Madagascar: Transportation System, 1994............  74
5  Mauritius: Administrative Divisions, 1994 ............  96
6  Comoros: Administrative Divisions, 1994.............  144
7  Seychelles: Main Islands and Island Groups, 1994.....  206
8  Maldives: Administrative Divisions, 1994 ............  256
9  Comoros, Madagascar, Maldives, Mauritius, and
       Seychelles: Strategic Airports and Ports, 1994 ......  292

# Preface

Few works offering a close look at the contemporary island societies of the Indian Ocean have been published in the English language. Even fewer works that place those societies in the context of their historical and geographic settings are to be found. This study, *Indian Ocean: Five Island Countries*, seeks to contribute in a modest way to fulfillment of the void, offering a compact and objective exposition of the dominant social, political, and economic institutions of the island countries and a view of their current problems and tensions. Analysis and interpretation by the authors must be judged, however, in the light of the scant nature of available research data in many subject areas.

With considerable justification, the reader may question the exclusion of Sri Lanka (the island nation formerly known as Ceylon, an important political force in the Indian Ocean) from other than the more general discussions in this study. That country's close proximity to, and long historical associations with, the Indian subcontinent and its early tutelage in self-rule under the British, beginning nearly two decades before independence, however, distinguish it quite clearly from the island countries in the southwestern Indian Ocean. Moreover, it has been treated already in a separate volume in the series. By the same token, the reader may question the inclusion of Maldives, insofar as, like Sri Lanka, it, too, lies close to the subcontinent in the northern Indian Ocean. Unlike Sri Lanka, however, Maldives appears nowhere else in the Country Study series, and in the view of the authors it warranted treatment here, especially as it shares some concerns of the island countries in the southwestern ocean. Réunion, although also a Mascarene Island like Mauritius, chose to become an integral part of metropolitan France, and thus is not included in this volume.

Measurements are given in the metric system; a conversion table is provided in the Appendix. The spelling of place-names generally follows that established by the United States Board on Geographic Names (BGN) in its latest available gazetteers for the area. Currency conversion factors appear in the Glossary, which is included for the reader's convenience. Country Profile data, ordinarily appearing in the front matter of books in this series, in this study are to be found with the relevant chapters.

The body of the text reflects information available as of July 1994. Certain other portions of the text, however, have been updated. The Introduction discusses significant events and trends that have occurred since the completion of research; the Country Profiles include updated information as available; and the Bibliography lists recently published sources thought to be particularly helpful to the reader

# Introduction

A VAST REGION, the Indian Ocean encompasses an area of about 73.4 million square kilometers, or roughly 14 percent of the earth's surface. The region has been defined variously, depending on whether the Antarctic Sea is included. Commonly, the Indian Ocean is thought to stretch from East Africa (or specifically from the southern tip of Africa at Cape Agulhas where it meets the Atlantic) to Tasmania (where it meets the Pacific), and from Asia to Antarctica.

Historically, the region has played a prominent commercial role in East-West trade since early times. For the colonial powers, particularly Britain and France, in the seventeenth, eighteenth, and nineteenth centuries until the construction of the Suez Canal in 1869, the islands of the Indian Ocean provided trading posts and refueling locations en route to their colonies in the East. More recently, the Indian Ocean was a focal point of East-West tension because it served as a route through which much oil from the Persian Gulf states passed in shipment to markets elsewhere.

By the mid-1990s, as a result of the breakup of the Soviet Union and the growing participation in international affairs of a number of Indian Ocean littoral states, such as India and South Africa, the balance of power and external influences in the region had altered markedly. In addition, the island nations that constitute the subject of this volume—Madagascar, Mauritius, Comoros, Seychelles, and Maldives—have experienced a growth in democratic institutions and economic development that has changed their relationships to outside powers. For example, the island states have tended to follow a non-aligned policy in their foreign relations and, reflecting their lack of defense capabilities, have sought to promote the Indian Ocean as a zone of peace, in which they include littoral states.

Despite their unique aspects, these island nations have certain features in common. For example, all have been colonies or protectorates of either Britain or France. All have gained their independence since 1965 (1960 in the case of Madagascar) and have been inclined (with the possible exception of Comoros) to institute rule based on the dominance of executive leadership, specifically based on the personality of one man. This has been true even though in several instances such rule may be under the guise of socialism. Those islands that adopted socialism are now moving toward greater privatization and a free-market system.

Traditionally, agriculture has been the economic basis of all these nations despite the limited land area available for this pursuit. As of the early 1990s, however, the nations were seeking to diversify their economies, stressing fisheries development, tourism, the establishment of export processing zones (EPZs) where raw materials are processed and textiles manufactured, and industrial development, or the creation of international commercial centers. Of these island states, only Madagascar has significant mineral and energy resources, although offshore exploration is taking place near several of the islands.

These island countries consist of multiethnic societies, often with several religious faiths, but some are more homogeneous than others. Notwithstanding this ethnic diversity, in a number of the countries human rights have tended to be limited, particularly with respect to the rights of women, workers, and opposition elements. As democratic institutions are strengthened and public opinion makes itself felt, most of the states are making progress in this regard.

## Madagascar

By far the largest of these island nations is Madagascar, which, with nearly 600,000 square kilometers, is somewhat smaller than Texas. Considered by the World Bank (see Glossary) as one of the world's poorest countries, Madagascar had a population estimated at 13.5 million in mid-1994. Nearly 80 percent of the country's population, which consists of some twenty ethnic groups, is engaged in the broad agricultural field, including fishing. After following a socialist path in the 1970s, Madagascar in the 1980s, with the advice of the World Bank and the International Monetary Fund (IMF—see Glossary), began liberalizing its economy by such measures as establishing an EPZ like that adopted by Mauritius. Madagascar traditionally had had some citizen participation in government through the *fokonolona* (village council) system; however, the country had been ruled almost singlehandedly by the president, Didier Ratsiraka, since 1975. As a result, pressures for greater political participation overtook economic reforms.

A 1992 referendum voted in a new constitution and resulted in multiparty elections in 1993. Opposition leader Albert Zafy was elected president; his party, the Comité des Forces Vives (Vital Forces Committee, known as Forces Vives), gained one-third of the National Assembly seats, with the remainder scattered among twenty-five parties. In August 1994, Prime Minister Francisque Ravony announced a new cabinet of twenty-four ministers, most of whom were reshuffled from the earlier government but who also reflected a somewhat broader representation of interests.

Madagascar's budget for 1995, presented to the National Assembly in December 1994, was an austerity budget designed to encourage the country's external funding sources. The government aimed to reach a 3.5 percent economic growth rate—the 1994 rate was only 1.29 percent compared with 2.1 percent in 1993—and to cut inflation from 32 percent in 1994 (the rate had been 13 percent in 1993) to 15 percent in 1995. In late 1994, the African Development Bank considered the steep increase in inflation as a potential source of social unrest.

Concurrently, the regime sought to decrease the budget deficit to 6.5 percent of gross domestic product (GDP—see Glossary) in 1995 from 6.76 percent in 1994. Measures to be taken entailed minimizing customs and tax exemptions, increasing tax collections, and eliminating price controls on certain products. In consequence, the government authorized a 15 percent increase in expenditures for the various ministries, apart from the fields of health and education, which were allowed a 20 percent increase. Despite these proposed solutions, the economy faced a troubled future because 1993 had seen a 13 percent decrease in investments as well as a decrease in production. In addition, the floating of the currency had resulted in a 50 percent devaluation of the Malagasy franc (for value of the Malagasy franc—see Glossary).

In January 1995, Ravony dismissed both the governor of the Central Bank of the Malagasy Republic and the minister of finance—the former because of his reckless policy concerning promissory notes and the latter as a result of his inability to control inflation. (The World Bank and the IMF had made the dismissal of the Central Bank governor a condition for their continued economic assistance.) Among the elements of the Malagasy economy in need of assistance are the country's infrastructure, particularly the railroad system, which suffered the impact of two major cyclones in 1994. Because of the shortage of investment capital to promote economic development in the EPZ, the International Finance Corporation (see World Bank entry in Glossary) in mid-1994 established the Madagascar Capital Development Fund of approximately US$1.1 million. The government also aims to increase tourism and develop its resources of coal and petroleum as well as shellfish. These moves, if implemented, should ease the problem of unemployment and underemployment, especially among young people—60 percent of the population is under age twenty-five.

To achieve economic progress, Madagascar has had to rely on foreign aid, particularly that from its former colonial power, France. Madagascar's major trading partner, France has not only provided bilateral aid and loans for specific projects but also canceled most of Madagascar's debt. Since South Africa's abandonment of apartheid, its relations with Madagascar have also grown apace, featuring a visit by then South African President Frederik Willem de Klerk in 1990 and the establishment of air and shipping ties as well as diplomatic relations in 1993. Both India and Australia have also sought to strengthen commercial relations with Madagascar.

Possibly in part because of its desire to promote foreign investment in the country, since 1993 Madagascar appears to have paid greater attention to human rights. The United States Department of State has indicated that once the 1993 election had occurred, the situation improved because of lack of violence between the Forces Vives (pro-Zafy) and the pro-Ratsiraka groups. Moreover, the government increased civilian control over the military forces and made use of combined commands of military, gendarmerie, and national police in implementing national security. Greater political stability continues to be essential in order to promote foreign investment.

## Mauritius

Mauritius, together with Rodrigues, constitutes part of the volcanic chain of the Mascarene Islands; collectively, the islands are less than half the size of Rhode Island. The country has a varied ethnic composition. The constitution recognizes four groups: Hindus representing about 52 percent of the population, a general category including Creoles and Europeans at about 29 percent, Muslims constituting about 16 percent, and Sino-Mauritians at about 3 percent. English is the island's official language, and both the government and the education system are patterned on the British model.

The economy in 1993 had a healthy growth rate of 5.5 percent, accompanied by an inflation rate of 10.5 percent. Agriculture represents the main economic activity; sugarcane, tea, fresh vegetables, and cut flowers are the main products. To diversify its economy, Mauritius established EPZs in 1971; export production centers on textiles and wearing apparel. The government also seeks to encourage tourism and to develop the private sector generally. Its economic development is such that the World Bank considers it close to becoming an upper-middle-income developing country. If it is to reach such a status, the economy needs to become more technologically oriented and capital-intensive as opposed to labor-intensive.

Such economic development is facilitated by the country's political system. Mauritius has a multiparty system, which it has maintained since independence, and the government represents a coalition of several parties. Mauritius became a republic in 1992, and the president, appointed by the prime minister and approved by the elected National Assembly, has a titular function. In a by-election for the legislature in late January 1995, two opposition candidates won. This result has been viewed as a warning to Prime Minister Aneerood Jugnauth of popular discontent with his government's policies; the government coalition only mustered 20 percent of the votes.

A member of the Commonwealth of Nations, Mauritius has good relations with the West, particularly France and Britain. Nonetheless, some tension exists with France over its claim to Tromelin Island, and with Britain and the United States over Britain's having allowed the United States to establish a military base on Diego Garcia, claimed by Mauritius. Mauritius also has good ties with a number of African, Arab, and Far Eastern nations.

Mauritius has been a leading exponent of the Indian Ocean zone of peace policy and in this and other instances has sought cooperation with other Indian Ocean island countries. For example, meetings of the Seychelles-Mauritius Joint Cooperation Commission occurred in late January and early February 1995 on Mahé Island, Seychelles. The discussions have led to greater bilateral cooperation in the fields of education, industry, and agriculture. In late March, Mauritius brought together delegations from six other members of the newly formed Indian Ocean Rim Association—Australia, India, Kenya, Oman, Singapore, and South Africa—to promote trade, industry, and economic cooperation. The conference dealt with such measures as standardizing customs procedures and promoting investment.

The growth of foreign investment is often considered to depend, among other factors, on a country's human rights record. With regard to Mauritius, the Department of State has indicated that civilians control the paramilitary special mobile police force used for internal security purposes. Trials are considered to be generally fair. However, the government controls all communications media, which it uses for political purposes; private individuals may not operate broadcasting stations. Workers' rights are limited. The government has taken some steps to improve the rights of women, but they continue to face "legal and societal discrimination."

## Comoros

Approximately the same size as Mauritius, Comoros belongs to an archipelago of four main islands of volcanic origin. Of these islands, Mahoré has continued its relationship with France and is not considered part of Comoros. Ethnically, the islands have a mixed population consisting of Arabs, African and Malayo-Indonesian peoples, and Creoles, who are descendants of French settlers. About 86 percent are Sunni Muslims, and Islam is the state religion. Arabic and French are official languages. Schools follow the French education system, but literacy is only about 50 percent.

The country is among the world's poorest, deriving its income primarily from agriculture. Comoros is the world's largest producer of ylang-ylang, used in perfume, and the world's second largest producer of vanilla; cloves are another major crop. Although markets for these products are somewhat unstable, in January 1995 Comoros announced major contracts for the purchase of cloves with the United Arab Emirates and probably with India, and a vanilla purchase contract with the United States. Because of the limited growing area, the islands must import most of their food. Efforts are underway to develop tourism and some forms of industry.

Economic development is linked with recent political steps that Comoros has taken. Comoros approved a new constitution in a referendum in June 1992, under which the president is elected by universal suffrage for a five-year term. The president in turn selects the ministers, the prime minister coming from the majority party in the Federal Assembly. The assembly is the elected body of the bicameral legislature; the Electoral College appoints the Senate. In October 1994, after much infighting among members of the ruling party, President Said Mohamed

Djohar named a new government, dismissing the previous prime minister, who had advocated the privatization of the national airlines, Air Comores. The airlines issue involved two of the president's sons-in-law. The previous prime minister was also unpopular for implementing a number of economic reforms demanded by the World Bank and the IMF.

In late September 1994, the IMF expressed its "disappointment" with the economic progress of Comoros, following the visit of an IMF mission to the island in late August and early September. In the first half of 1994, exports decreased 5 percent in volume compared with 1993; this decrease occurred in spite of the 33 percent devaluation of the Comoran franc (for value of the Comoran franc—see Glossary) in January 1994. Revenues were "disappointing" because of reduced trade and failure to recover customs duties due. Most IMF economic indicators had not been met, and arrears on external debt had been reduced only by one-third the targeted amount. As a result, the IMF recommended a freeze on 40 percent of budget amounts for the offices of the president, the prime minister, and the Federal Assembly as well as a freeze on hiring new government employees until personnel cuts had been made.

For its economic development, Comoros depended heavily on external sources, particularly France. Comoros had good relations with France and good regional relations with conservative Arab states and members of the Indian Ocean Commission. Therefore, it surprised many that in November 1994, while attending the Franco-African summit in Biarritz, Djohar announced the establishment of diplomatic relations with Israel. However, upon his return to Moroni the president amended his statement to indicate that diplomatic relations would be regularized only after a peace agreement had been signed among Israel, Syria, and Lebanon and the issue of Jerusalem had been resolved.

A source of friction in its relations with other countries is the government's human rights record. This record did not improve in 1994, according to the Department of State, and featured restrictions on the right of assembly and freedom of the press. Several persons were killed on Mohéli by security forces in June 1994 in an antigovernment demonstration. Furthermore, a number of persons involved in an abortive coup in September 1992 continued to be held incommunicado without charge or trial in early 1995. The regime closed the only nongovernment radio station in 1994 and on one occasion refused an opposition party the right to hold a rally. Although women have the vote, there are no women in the legislature or the cabinet. Unions have the right to bargain, but more than 75 percent of the labor force is unemployed, so collective bargaining does not, in fact, occur.

## Seychelles

Less than one-quarter the size of Comoros, Seychelles consists of an archipelago of 115 islands, most coralline and the rest granitic. The relatively homogeneous population of mixed European and African descent uses three official languages: Creole, English, and French, with a claimed literacy of 85 percent.

Seychelles has a comparatively high per capita GDP of US$5,900 and in the early 1990s was moving away from socialism toward a more liberal economy with greater privatization. Tourism is the major economic activity because the small area of cultivable land limits agriculture, and the small market limits industry. Fishing has considerable potential for diversifying the Seychellois economy. The government is encouraging the fisheries sector, and in August 1994 the Western Indian Ocean Tuna Organization held its meeting on Mahé, with representatives of Comoros, Mauritius, and Seychelles present as well as an observer from Madagascar. Among topics of discussion was the standardization of terms for granting fishing permits because French, Spanish, and Japanese ships conduct extensive fishing in the area. Seychelles alone had fifty-two licensing agreements in effect in early 1995, of which thirty-three were with European Union countries. Furthermore, the African Development Bank in December 1994 was engaged in restructuring the Seychelles state-owned tuna processing firm, Conserveries de l'Océan Indien, in order to make it eligible for privatization. In addition to tuna fishing, for which Victoria is one of the world's largest ports, Seychelles seeks to develop its shrimp industry and began commercial shrimp operations in 1993.

Furthermore, boasting of its good quality telecommunications system, its privatization of Victoria port in 1994, and new regulations to encourage the private sector, specifically the legal environment for investment, Seychelles is promoting itself as an international business center. A partial basis for such promotion lies in the country's good relations with Britain, France, and such littoral states as South Africa, India, and

Australia. Measures contemplated to further the private sector include the establishment of an EPZ and tax measures to reduce employer social security contributions for employees.

It is difficult to reconcile some of these proposed steps with the World Bank's 1993 report entitled *Poverty in Paradise* (Mark Twain had also referred to Seychelles as "paradise"). According to the report, "In 1993, almost 20 percent of the population were estimated to be living below the poverty line" of 900 Seychelles rupees (for value of the Seychelles rupee—see Glossary), or about US$195 per household per month. The World Bank criticized Seychelles's relatively low expenditure on education, especially secondary education, and the resultant lack of qualified workers in the education, health, finance, and construction fields. In spite of this criticism, the 1995 budget announced by the Ministry of Finance in late 1994 proposed a further 21 percent cut in the education budget, thereby exacerbating the situation with regard to qualified workers.

The relationship of the economy to the country's political system has been very close because Seychelles has followed a socialist form of government. Having gained its independence from Britain in 1976, Seychelles became a one-party socialist state under President France Albert René in 1977. After adopting a new constitution by referendum in 1992, Seychelles held its first multiparty elections in 1993. René was reelected, and his Seychelles People's Progressive Front (SPPF) won twenty-seven of the thirty-three seats in the People's Assembly (some election irregularities are considered to have taken place). As a result of political patronage, control of jobs, government contracts, and resources, the Department of State indicated that the SPPF dominated the country. Moreover, the president completely controlled the security apparatus, including the national guard, the army, the police, and an armed paramilitary unit.

In 1994 progress was made with regard to human rights under this controlled structure. However, the government has a "near monopoly on the media," and freedom of speech and press are limited by the ease with which law suits can be brought against journalists. In addition, because the leadership of both the SPPF and most opposition parties is white, despite the Creole popular majority, there is a perception that nonwhites lack a significant voice.

# Maldives

Maldives, smaller in area than Seychelles, includes some 1,200 coralline islands grouped in a double chain of nineteen atolls. The majority of these islands, which range from one to two square kilometers in area, are uninhabited. The people represent a homogeneous mixture of Sinhalese, Dravidian, Arab, Australasian, and African groups who speak a Dhivehi language. Sunni Muslims in faith, most Maldivians attend Quranic schools. Islam is the official religion, all citizens must be Muslims, and the practice of a faith other than Islam is forbidden. The country claims 98 percent literacy.

Ranked by the United Nations as one of the world's least developed countries, Maldives has a GDP based 17 percent on tourism; 15 percent on fishing, which is undergoing further development; and 10 percent on agriculture. Maldives' 1994 annual per capita income of US$620 is twice that of India. Maldives has some 17,000 foreign workers, many from India and Sri Lanka, most of whom are employed in resort hotels so that Maldivian Muslims need not serve alcoholic beverages.

Possibly in keeping with its more traditional culture, the country has a highly centralized presidential government, based on its 1968 constitution. Maumoon Abdul Gayoom, who has ruled since 1978, was reelected president for a five-year term in 1993. Members of the unicameral Majlis, or legislature, also serve five-year terms; forty are elected, and eight are appointed by the president. The president, who exercises control over most aspects of the country, also holds the posts of minister of defense and minister of finance. Political parties are officially discouraged as contrary to homogeneity. Maldives follows a nonalignment policy with regard to foreign affairs but as a member of the Commonwealth of Nations has particularly close relations with Britain.

The somewhat authoritarian nature of the government is reflected in the country's record on human rights. The Department of State has indicated that in 1994 Maldives restricted freedom of speech, press, and religion. Instances also occurred of arbitrary arrest and incommunicado detention of individuals as well as banishment to distant atolls. Although civil law exists, Islamic sharia law also applies and has limited the rights of women; for example, in accordance with Muslim practice, the testimony of one man is equivalent to that of two women. Nonetheless, in 1994 two women served in the Majlis and one in the cabinet. The rights of workers are also limited in that they may not form unions or strike. Freedom of the press was advanced somewhat in 1994 with the government's establishment of a Press Council designed to protect journalists.

*     *     *

The degree to which Madagascar, Mauritius, Comoros, Seychelles, and Maldives will separately and collectively promote democratic institutions, human rights, and economic development and diversification in the late 1990s remains to be seen. These island nations, with the exception of Maldives (which is located considerably to the northeast of the others), are already members of a common body, the Indian Ocean Commission, which seeks to promote commercial and social aspects of their relationship. The commission, or perhaps the larger Indian Ocean Rim Association, may broaden its concerns to include such areas as overall economic policy and defense matters. The amount of cooperation that may develop among these island states will depend to a great extent on the relative sense of stability and security of each of the nations involved.

May 31, 1995                                        Helen Chapin Metz

# Chapter 1. Madagascar

*National emblem of Madagascar*

# Country Profile

## Country

**Formal Name:** Republic of Madagascar.

**Short Name:** Madagascar.

**Term for Citizens:** Malagasy.

**Capital:** Antananarivo.

**Date of Independence:** June 26, 1960.

## Geography

**Size:** 587,040 square kilometers.

**Topography:** East coast has lowlands leading to steep bluffs and central highlands; Tsaratanana Massif in north with volcanic mountains; west coast with many protected harbors and broad plains; and southwest with plateau and desert region.

**Climate:** Two seasons: hot, rainy from November to April; cooler, dry season from May to October; southeastern trade winds dominate; occasional cyclones.

## Society

**Population:** July 1994 estimate 13,427,758. Annual growth rate 3.19 percent in 1994. Density 2.4 per square kilometer in 1994.

**Ethnic Groups:** Some twenty ethnic groups of which principal ones are central highlanders (Merina and related Betsileo) and *côtiers* of mixed Arab, African, Malayo-Indonesian ancestry. Other groups are Comorans, French, Indo-Pakistanis, and Chinese.

**Languages:** Malagasy belonging to Malayo-Polynesian language family; French also used extensively.

**Religion:** Estimated 55 percent hold indigenous beliefs; 40 percent Christian, evenly divided between Roman Catholics and Protestants; 5 percent Muslim.

**Education and Literacy:** Education compulsory for children ages six to fourteen; higher education available through University of Madagascar with six campuses. Literacy estimated at 80 percent in 1991.

**Health:** Economic decline has caused deterioration of medical services; 35 percent of population lacked adequate access to health services in early 1990s; infant mortality 114 per 1,000 in 1991. Major diseases malaria, schistosomiasis, tuberculosis, and leprosy as well as sexually transmitted diseases. Traditional medicine popular, especially in rural areas.

## Economy

**Gross Domestic Product (GDP):** Estimated at US$10.4 billion in 1993. Economic growth rate 1 percent in 1992.

**Gross National Product (GNP) per Capita:** US$210 in 1991; rated tenth poorest country in world by World Bank.

**Agriculture:** Constituted 33 percent of GDP in 1993, provided almost 80 percent of exports, and in 1992 employed almost 80 percent of labor force; 16 percent of cultivated land is irrigated. Major crops: coffee, vanilla, sugarcane, cloves, cocoa, rice, cassava, bananas, peanuts; widespread cattle raising; also extensive fishing.

**Industry, Mining, and Energy:** Responsible for 13 percent of GDP in 1993; major sectors food-processing, mining, and energy; and in export processing zones clothing manufacturing. Country has many minerals, but exploitation has been disappointing. Dependent on imported oil and local firewood for energy.

**Exports:** Estimated at US$311 million in 1992. Major exports coffee, vanilla, cloves, shellfish, and sugar. Main markets

France, United States, Germany, and Japan.

**Imports:** Estimated US$614 million in 1992. Major imports intermediate goods, capital goods, petroleum, consumer goods, food. Main suppliers France, Japan, and Germany.

**Balance of Payments:** External debt in November 1993 more than US$4 billion; debt has been rescheduled with Paris Club (see Glossary) and London Club (see Glossary).

**Currency and Exchange Rate:** 1 Malagasy franc (FMG) = 100 centimes; in May 1995, US$1.00 = FMG4,236.9.

**Inflation Rate:** Estimated at 20 percent in 1992.

**Fiscal Year:** Calendar year.

## Transportation and Telecommunications

**Highways:** About 4,000 kilometers of 40,000-kilometer road system asphalted in 1994.

**Railroads:** In 1994 some 1,095 kilometers of 1.000-meter gauge track in two separate systems: Antananarivo to Toamasina and Fianarantsoa to Manakara.

**Ports:** Fifteen major ports of which Toamasina, Mahajanga, and Antsiranana most important.

**Airports:** About 105 of total airports usable; of these thirty had permanent-surface runways in 1994.

**Telecommunications:** Telephone service sparse; most telephones located in Antananarivo. Two satellite ground stations provide excellent international links via International Telecommunications Satellite Organization (Intelsat) Indian Ocean satellite and Symphonie ground station with European telecommunications satellite. Seventeen government-owned amplitude modulation (AM) stations, three frequency modulation (FM) stations.

## Government and Politics

**Government:** Constitution approved August 19, 1992, by

national referendum. Constitution establishes separation of powers among executive, legislative, and judicial branches; multiparty political system; and protection of human rights and freedom of speech. President elected by universal suffrage for five-year period with two-term limit. Prime minister nominated by bicameral parliament composed of Senate and National Assembly, and approved by president. Supreme Court has eleven members and forms apex of other judicial bodies. Local government consists of twenty-eight regions with decentralized powers in economic field.

**Politics:** In first legislative elections of Third Republic in 1993, more than 120 political parties entered 4,000 candidates for 138 seats. Proportional representation list system encourages candidacies. Traditional village council (*fokonolona*) system supplements modern political system.

**Foreign Relations:** Good relations with many countries, particularly France and the West; in post-Cold War era, seeking diversified ties with East and West, including Arab countries and Far East.

## National Security

**Armed Forces:** Popular Armed Forces (including aeronaval forces—consisting of navy and air force), Presidential Guard. In 1994 army had about 20,000 personnel, navy about 500 including 100 marines, air force about 500.

**Military Budget:** In 1994 estimated at US$37.6 million.

**Major Military Units:** Army in 1994 had two battalions, one engineer regiment. Army equipment included twelve light tanks, reconnaissance vehicles, armored personnel carriers, and some towed artillery. Navy had one patrol craft and three landing craft. Air force had twelve combat aircraft.

**Paramilitary:** In 1994 about 7,500 gendarmerie, including maritime police.

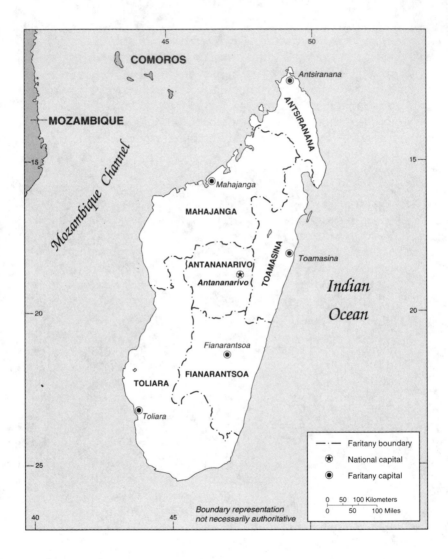

*Figure 2. Madagascar: Administrative Divisions, 1994*

THE REPUBLIC OF MADAGASCAR, formerly known as the Malagasy Republic and the Democratic Republic of Madagascar, has undergone significant socioeconomic and political changes during the nineteenth and twentieth centuries. Occupying a strategic location off the southeast coast of Africa, the island historically became the target of British and French imperial ambitions. Ultimately, the competition resulted in French colonization at the end of the nineteenth century. The country gained full independence from colonial rule on June 26, 1960. Philibert Tsiranana headed the conservative regime of the First Republic, superseded in 1975 by a Marxist-oriented military regime under Lieutenant Commander Didier Ratsiraka.

In the face of rising political dissent and socioeconomic decline that reached its height at the beginning of the 1990s, the Second Republic succumbed to the wave of democratization spreading throughout the African continent. On March 27, 1993, the inauguration of Albert Zafy as the third elected president of Madagascar since independence marked the beginning of the Third Republic.

## Historical Setting

### Precolonial Era, Prior to 1894

The ruins of fortifications built by Arab traders as far back as the ninth century underscore Madagascar's historical role as a destination for travelers from the Middle East, Asia, and Africa. Not until the beginning of the sixteenth century, however, did European ships flying Portuguese, Dutch, English, and French flags explore Madagascar's shoreline. Beginning in 1643, several French settlements emerged; the best known of these, Tôlanaro (formerly Faradofay) on the southeast coast, lasted for more than thirty years. The settlement survived in part because the colonists had taken pains to establish cordial relations with the Antanosy, the ethnic group inhabiting the area. Relations deteriorated later, however, and in 1674 a massacre of nearly all the inhabitants ended French colonization endeavors for more than a century; survivors fled by sea to the neighboring territory of Reunion.

This early checking of French imperial designs coincided with the spread of piracy into the Indian Ocean. In the absence of a significant naval power in waters remote from Europe, privateer vessels attacked ships of many nations for nearly forty years. The favorite hunting grounds were in the north in the Arabian Sea and Red Sea areas, but Madagascar was a popular hiding place where crews could recuperate and replenish supplies for another attack. By this time, the institution of slavery also had been implanted on the island. Madagascar became a source of slaves, not only for the neighboring islands of Mauritius and Rodrigues, but also for more distant points, including the Western Hemisphere.

Madagascar's social and political structure facilitated the slave trade. Within several small coastal kingdoms, stratified societies of nobles, commoners, and slaves gave allegiance to a single king or queen. For example, the Sakalava ethnic group dominated the western and northern portions of Madagascar in two separate kingdoms. Menabe, on the barren western grasslands, had its first capital at Toliara; Boina, in the northwest, included the port of Mahajanga. The towns became centers of trade where cattle and slaves, taken in war, were exchanged with European merchants for guns and other manufactured goods. These political domains were complemented by the Betsimisaraka kingdom along the east coast, and the southern coastal kingdoms dominated by the Mahafaly and the Antandroy ethnic groups.

The most powerful of Madagascar's kingdoms—the one that eventually established hegemony over a great portion of the island—was that developed by the Merina ethnic group. Before the Merina emerged as the dominant political power on the island in the nineteenth century, they alternated between periods of political unity and periods in which the kingdom separated into smaller political units. The location of the Merina in the central highlands afforded them some protection from the ravages of warfare that recurred among the coastal kingdoms. The distinction, recognized both locally and internationally, between the central highlanders (the Merina) and the *côtiers* (inhabitants of the coastal areas) would soon exert a major impact on Madagascar's political system (see Population and Ethnicity, this ch.). Organized like the coastal kingdoms in a hierarchy of nobles, commoners, and slaves, the Merina developed a unique political institution known as the *fokonolona* (village council). Through the *fokonolona*, village elders and other local notables were able to enact regulations and exert a measure of local control in such matters as public works and security.

Two monarchs played key roles in establishing Merina political dominance over Madagascar. The first, who ruled under the name of Andrianampoinimerina (r. 1797–1810), seized the throne of one of the Merina kingdoms in 1787. By 1806 he had conquered the remaining three kingdoms and united them within the former boundaries of Imerina, the capital established at the fortified city of Antananarivo. Radama I (r. 1810–28), an able and forward-looking monarch, succeeded to the throne in 1810 upon the death of his father. By adroitly playing off competing British and French interests in the island, he was able to extend Merina authority over nearly the entire island of Madagascar. Radama I first conquered the Betsileo ethnic group in the southern part of the central highlands and subsequently overpowered the Sakalava, an ethnic group that also sought at times to assert its hegemony over other groups. With the help of the British, who wanted a strong kingdom to offset French influence, Radama I modernized the armed forces. In 1817 the peoples of the east coast, facing an army of 35,000 soldiers, submitted with little or no protest; Radama then conquered the entire southeast as far as Tôlanaro. Particularly barren or impenetrable parts of the island escaped conquest, especially in the extreme south, but before his death Radama I succeeded in bringing the major and more hospitable portions of the country under Merina rule.

Radama I's interest in modernization along Western lines extended to social and political matters. He organized a cabinet and encouraged the Protestant London Missionary Society to establish schools and churches and to introduce the printing press—a move that was to have far-reaching implications for the country. The society made nearly half a million converts, and its teachers devised a written form of the local language, Malagasy, using the Latin alphabet. By 1828 several thousand persons, primarily Merina, had become literate, and a few young persons were being sent to Britain for schooling. Later the Merina dialect of Malagasy became the official language. Malagasy-language publications were established and circulated among the Merina-educated elite; by 1896 some 164,000 children, mainly Merina and Betsileo, attended the mission's primary schools. Along with new ideas came some development of local manufacturing. Much productive time was spent, however, in military campaigns to expand territory and acquire slaves for trade.

The reign of Radama I's wife and successor, Queen Ranavalona I (r. 1828–61), was essentially reactionary, reflecting her distrust of foreign influence. Under the oligarchy that ruled in her name, rivals were slain, numerous Protestant converts were persecuted and killed, and many Europeans fled the island. The ruling elite held all the land and monopolized commerce, except for the handful of Europeans allowed to deal in cattle, rice, and other commodities. Remunerations to the queen provided the French traders a supply of slaves and a monopoly in the slave trade. Enjoying particular favor owing to his remarkable accomplishments was French artisan Jean Laborde, who established at Mantasoa, near Antananarivo, a manufacturing complex and agricultural research station where he manufactured commodities ranging from silk and soap to guns, tools, and cement.

During the reign of Radama II (r. 1861–63), the pendulum once again swung toward modernization and cordial relations with Western nations, particularly France. Radama II made a treaty of perpetual friendship with France, but his brief rule ended with his assassination by a group of nobles alarmed by his pro-French stance. He was succeeded by his widow, who ruled until 1868, during which time she annulled the treaty with France and the charter of Laborde's company.

After 1868 a Merina leader, Rainilaiarivony, ruled the monarchy. To avoid giving either the French or the British a pretext for intervention, Rainilaiarivony emphasized modernization of the society and tried to curry British favor without giving offense to the French. He made concessions to both countries, signing a commercial treaty with France in 1868 and with Britain in 1877. Important social developments under his leadership included the outlawing of polygamy and the slave trade; the promulgation of new legal codes; the spread of education, especially among the Merina; and the conversion of the monarchy in 1869 to Protestantism.

## Colonial Era, 1894–1960

The French largely ended the attempts of Malagasy rulers to stymie foreign influence by declaring a protectorate over the entire island in 1894. A protectorate over northwest Madagascar, based on treaties signed with the Sakalava during the 1840s, had existed since 1882. But Queen Ranavalona III refused to recognize the 1894 effort to subordinate her king-dom to French rule. As a result, a French expeditionary force occupied Antananarivo in September 1895. A wave of antifor-eign, anti-Christian rioting ensued. In 1896 France declared Madagascar a French colony and deported the queen and the prime minister—first to Reunion, then to Algeria.

Nationalist sentiment against French colonial rule eventu-ally emerged among a small group of Merina intellectuals who had been educated by Europeans and exposed to Western intellectual thought. The group, based in Antananarivo, was led by a Malagasy Protestant clergyman, Pastor Ravelojoana, who was especially inspired by the Japanese model of modern-ization. A secret society dedicated to affirming Malagasy cul-tural identity was formed in 1913, calling itself Iron and Stone Ramification (Vy Vato Sakelika—VVS). Although the VVS was brutally suppressed, its actions eventually led French authori-ties to provide the Malagasy with their first representative voice in government.

Malagasy veterans of military service in France during World War I bolstered the embryonic nationalist movement. Throughout the 1920s, the nationalists stressed labor reform and equality of civil and political status for the Malagasy, stop-ping short of advocating independence. For example, the French League for Madagascar under the leadership of Ana-tole France demanded French citizenship for all Malagasy peo-ple in recognition of their country's wartime contribution of soldiers and resources. A number of veterans who remained in France were exposed to French political thought, most notably the anticolonial and pro-independence platforms of French socialist parties. Jean Ralaimongo, for example, returned to Madagascar in 1924 and became embroiled in labor questions that were causing considerable tension throughout the island.

Among the first concessions to Malagasy equality was the formation in 1924 of two economic and financial delegations. One was composed of French settlers, the other of twenty-four Malagasy representatives elected by the Council of Notables in each of twenty-four districts. The two sections never met together, and neither had real decision-making authority.

Only in the aftermath of World War II was France willing to accept a form of Malagasy self-rule under French tutelage. In the fall of 1945, separate French and Malagasy electoral col-leges voted to elect representatives from Madagascar to the Constituent Assembly of the Fourth Republic in Paris. The two delegates chosen by the Malagasy, Joseph Raseta and Joseph Ravoahangy, both campaigned to implement the ideal of the self-determination of peoples affirmed by the Atlantic Charter of 1941 and by the historic Brazzaville Conference of 1944.

Raseta and Ravoahangy, together with Jacques Rabemananjara, a writer long resident in Paris, had organized the Democratic Movement for Malagasy Restoration (Mouvement Démocratique de la Rénovation Malgache—MDRM), the foremost among several political parties formed in Madagascar by early 1946. Although Protestant Merina were well represented in the MDRM's higher echelons, the party's 300,000 members were drawn from a broad political base reaching across the entire island and crosscutting ethnic and social divisions. Several smaller MDRM rivals included the Party of the Malagasy Disinherited (Parti des Déshérités Malgaches), whose members were mainly *côtiers* or descendants of slaves from the central highlands.

The 1946 constitution of the French Fourth Republic made Madagascar a *territoire d'outre-mer* (overseas territory) within the French Union. It accorded full citizenship to all Malagasy parallel with that enjoyed by citizens in France. But the assimilationist policy inherent in its framework was incongruent with the MDRM goal of full independence for Madagascar, so Ravoahangy and Raseta abstained from voting. The two delegates also objected to the separate French and Malagasy electoral colleges, even though Madagascar was represented in the French National Assembly. The constitution divided Madagascar administratively into a number of provinces, each of which was to have a locally elected provincial assembly. Not long after, a National Representative Assembly was constituted at Antananarivo. In the first elections for the provincial assemblies, the MDRM won all seats or a majority of seats, except in Mahajanga Province.

Despite these reforms, the political scene in Madagascar remained unstable. Economic and social concerns, including food shortages, black-market scandals, labor conscription, renewed ethnic tensions, and the return of soldiers from France, strained an already volatile situation. Many of the veterans felt they had been less well treated by France than had veterans from metropolitan France; others had been politically radicalized by their wartime experiences. The blend of fear, respect, and emulation on which Franco-Malagasy relations had been based seemed at an end.

On March 29, 1947, Malagasy nationalists revolted against the French. Although the uprising eventually spread over one-third of the island, the French were able to restore order after reinforcements arrived from France. Casualties among the Malagasy were estimated in the 60,000 to 80,000 range (later reports estimated 11,000 casualties, of whom 180 were non-Malagasy). The group of leaders responsible for the uprising, which came to be referred to as the Revolt of 1947, never has been identified conclusively. Although the MDRM leadership consistently maintained its innocence, the French outlawed the party. French military courts tried the military leaders of the revolt and executed twenty of them. Other trials produced, by one report, some 5,000 to 6,000 convictions, and penalties ranged from brief imprisonment to death.

In 1956 France's socialist government renewed the French commitment to greater autonomy in Madagascar and other colonial possessions by enacting the *loi-cadre* (enabling law). The *loi-cadre* provided for universal suffrage and was the basis for parliamentary government in each colony. In the case of Madagascar, the law established executive councils to function alongside provincial and national assemblies, and dissolved the separate electoral colleges for the French and Malagasy groups. The provision for universal suffrage had significant implications in Madagascar because of the basic ethnopolitical split between the Merina and the *côtiers*, reinforced by the divisions between Protestants and Roman Catholics. Superior armed strength and educational and cultural advantages had given the Merina a dominant influence on the political process during much of the country's history. The Merina were heavily represented in the Malagasy component of the small elite to whom suffrage had been restricted in the earlier years of French rule. Now the *côtiers*, who outnumbered the Merina, would be a majority.

The end of the 1950s was marked by growing debate over the future of Madagascar's relationship with France. Two major political parties emerged. The newly created Social Democratic Party of Madagascar (Parti Social Démocrate de Madagascar— PSD) favored self-rule while maintaining close ties with France. The PSD was led by Philibert Tsiranana, a well-educated Tsimihety from the northern coastal region who was one of three Malagasy deputies elected in 1956 to the National Assembly in Paris. The PSD built upon Tsiranana's traditional political stronghold of Mahajanga in northwest Madagascar and rapidly extended its sources of support by absorbing most of the smaller parties that had been organized by the *côtiers*. In sharp contrast, those advocating complete independence from France came together under the auspices of the Congress Party for the Independence of Madagascar (Antokon'ny Kongresy Fanafahana an'i Madagasikara—AKFM). Primarily based in Antananarivo and Antsiranana, party support centered among the Merina under the leadership of Richard Andriamanjato, himself a Merina and a member of the Protestant clergy. To the consternation of French policy makers, the AKFM platform called for nationalization of foreign-owned industries, collectivization of land, the "Malagachization" of society away from French values and customs (most notably use of the French language), international nonalignment, and exit from the Franc Zone (see Glossary).

## Independence, the First Republic, and the Military Transition, 1960–75

After France adopted the Constitution of the Fifth Republic under the leadership of General Charles de Gaulle, on September 28, 1958, Madagascar held a referendum to determine whether the country should become a self-governing republic within the French community. The AKFM and other nationalists opposed to the concept of limited self-rule mustered about 25 percent of votes cast. The vast majority of the population at the urging of the PSD leadership voted in favor of the referendum. The vote led to the election of Tsiranana as the country's first president on April 27, 1959. After a year of negotiations between Tsiranana and his French counterparts, Madagascar's status as a self-governing republic officially was altered on June 26, 1960, to that of a fully independent and sovereign state. The cornerstone of Tsiranana's government was the signing with France of fourteen agreements and conventions designed to maintain and strengthen Franco-Malagasy ties. These agreements were to provide the basis for increasing opposition from Tsiranana's critics.

A spirit of political reconciliation prevailed in the early 1960s. By achieving independence and obtaining the release of the MDRM leaders detained since the Revolt of 1947, Tsiranana had co-opted the chief issues on which the more aggressively nationalist elements had built much of their support. Consistent with Tsiranana's firm commitment to remain attached to Western civilization, the new regime made plain its

*View of Antananarivo from the Royal Hill*
*Courtesy Brian Kensley*

intent to maintain strong ties to France and the West in the economic, defense, and cultural spheres. Not entirely sanguine about this prospect, the opposition initially concurred in the interest of consolidating the gains of the previous decade, and most ethnic and regional interests supported Tsiranana.

Similar to other African leaders during the early independence era, Tsiranana oversaw the consolidation of his own party's power at the expense of other parties. A political system that strongly favored the incumbent complemented these actions. For example, although the political process allowed minority parties to participate, the constitution mandated a winner-take-all system that effectively denied the opposition a voice in governance. Tsiranana's position was further strengthened by the broad, multiethnic popular base of the PSD among the *côtiers*, whereas the opposition was severely disorganized. The AKFM continued to experience intraparty rifts between leftist and ultranationalist, more orthodox Marxist factions; it was unable to capitalize on increasingly active but relatively less privileged Malagasy youth because the party's base was the Merina middle class.

A new force on the political scene provided the first serious challenge to the Tsiranana government in April 1971. The National Movement for the Independence of Madagascar (Mouvement National pour l'Indépendance de Madagascar—Monima) led a peasant uprising in Toliara Province. The creator and leader of Monima was Monja Jaona, a *côtier* from the south who also participated in the Revolt of 1947. The main issue was government pressure for tax collection at a time when local cattle herds were being ravaged by disease. The protesters

17

attacked military and administrative centers in the area, apparently hoping for support in the form of weapons and reinforcements from China. Such help never arrived, and the revolt was harshly and quickly suppressed. An estimated fifty to 1,000 persons died, Monima was dissolved, and Monima leaders, including Jaona and several hundred protesters, were arrested and deported to the island of Nosy-Lava.

Another movement came on the scene in early 1972, in the form of student protests in Antananarivo. A general strike involving the nation's roughly 100,000 secondary-level students focused on three principal issues: ending the cultural cooperation agreements with France; replacing educational programs designed for schools in France and taught by French teachers with programs emphasizing Malagasy life and culture and taught by Malagasy instructors; and increasing access for economically underprivileged youth to secondary-level institutions. By early May, the PSD sought to end the student strike at any cost; on May 12 and 13, the government arrested several hundred student leaders and sent them to Nosy-Lava. Authorities also closed the schools and banned demonstrations.

Mounting economic stagnation—as revealed in scarcities of investment capital, a general decline in living standards, and the failure to meet even modest development goals—further undermined the government's position. Forces unleashed by the growing economic crisis combined with student unrest to create an opposition alliance. Workers, public servants, peasants, and many unemployed urban youth of Antananarivo joined the student strike, which spread to the provinces. Protesters set fire to the town hall and to the offices of a French-language newspaper in the capital.

The turning point occurred on May 13 when the Republican Security Force (Force Républicaine de Sécurité—FRS) opened fire on the rioters; in the ensuing melee, between fifteen and forty persons were killed and about 150 injured. Tsiranana declared a state of national emergency and on May 18 dissolved his government, effectively ending the First Republic. He then turned over full power to the National Army under the command of General Gabriel Ramanantsoa, a politically conservative Merina and former career officer in the French army. The National Army had maintained strict political neutrality in the crisis, and its intervention to restore order was welcomed by protesters and opposition elements.

The Ramanantsoa military regime could not resolve rising economic and ethnic problems, and narrowly survived an attempted coup d'état on December 31, 1974. The fact that the coup was led by several *côtier* officers against a Merina military leader underscored the growing Merina/*côtier* polarization in the military. In an attempt at restoring unity, Ramanantsoa, on February 5, 1975, turned over power to Colonel Richard Ratsimandrava (a Merina with a less "aristocratic" background). Five days later, Ratsimandrava was assassinated, and a National Military Directorate was formed to restore order by declaring martial law, strictly censoring political expression, and suspending all political parties.

The political transition crisis was resolved on June 15, 1975, when the National Military Directorate selected Lieutenant Commander Didier Ratsiraka as head of state and president of a new ruling body, the Supreme Revolutionary Council (SRC). The choice of Ratsiraka allayed ethnic concerns because he was a *côtier* belonging to the Betsimisaraka ethnic group. In addition, Ratsiraka—a dedicated socialist—was perceived by his military peers as a consensus candidate capable of forging unity among the various leftist political parties (such as AKFM and Monima), students, urban workers, the peasantry, and the armed forces.

## The Second Republic, 1975–92

Ratsiraka was elected to a seven-year term as president in a national referendum on December 21, 1975, confirming the mandate for consensus and inaugurating Madagascar's Second Republic.

The guiding principle of Ratsiraka's administration was the need for a socialist "revolution from above." Specifically, he sought to radically change Malagasy society in accordance with programs and principles incorporated into the *Charter of the Malagasy Socialist Revolution*, popularly referred to as the "Red Book" (Boky Mena). According to this document, the primary goal of the newly renamed Democratic Republic of Madagascar was to build a "new society" founded on socialist principles and guided by the actions of the "five pillars of the revolution": the SRC, peasants and workers, young intellectuals, women, and the Popular Armed Forces. "The socialist revolution," explains the Red Book, "is the only choice possible for us in order to achieve rapid economic and cultural development in an autonomous, humane, and harmonious manner." The Red Book advocated a new foreign policy based on the principle of nonalignment, and domestic policies focused on renovating the *fokonolona*, decentralizing the administration, and fomenting economic development through rigorous planning and popular input.

Several early policies collectively decided by Ratsiraka and other members of the SRC set the tone of the revolution from above. The first major SRC decision was to bring the French-held sectors of the economy under government control. This "economic decolonization" was welcomed by nationalists, who long had clamored for economic and cultural independence from France. The government also lifted martial law but retained rigid press censorship. Finally, the SRC ordered the closure of an earth satellite tracking station operated by the United States as part of its commitment to nonaligned foreign relations.

Political consolidation proceeded apace following the addition of ten civilians to the SRC in January 1976. This act constituted the beginning of a civil-military partnership in that the SRC became more representative of the country's major political tendencies and ethnic communities. In March the Vanguard of the Malagasy Revolution (Antokin'ny Revolisiona Malagasy—Arema) was founded as the government party, and Ratsiraka became its secretary general. In sharp contrast to the single-party states created by other African Marxist leaders, Arema served as simply one (albeit the most powerful) member of a coalition of six parties united under the umbrella of the National Front for the Defense of the Revolution (Front National pour la Défense de la Révolution—FNDR). Membership in the FNDR, necessary for participation in the electoral process, was preconditioned on party endorsement of the revolutionary principles and programs contained in the Red Book.

Ratsiraka and Arema clearly dominated the political system. In the *fokonolona* elections held in March 1977, for example, Arema captured 90 percent of 73,000 contested seats in 11,400 assemblies. In June 1977, Arema won 220 out of a total of 232 seats in elections for six provincial general assemblies, and 112 out of a total of 137 seats in the Popular National Assembly. This trend toward consolidation was most vividly demonstrated by Rasiraka's announcement of his 1977 cabinet in which Arema members held sixteen of eighteen ministerial posts.

Yet, less than three years after taking power, Ratsiraka's regime was confronted with growing popular disenchantment.

As early as September 1977, antigovernment demonstrations erupted in Antananarivo because of severe shortages in foodstuffs and essential commodities. This trend intensified as the economy worsened under the weight of ill-conceived economic policies that gradually centralized government control over the key sectors of the economy, including banking and agriculture. Ratsiraka defiantly adopted authoritarian tactics in response to the evolving opposition, sending in the armed forces to stifle dissent and maintain order during student riots in May 1978. In the economic realm, however, Ratsiraka accepted the free-market reforms demanded by the International Monetary Fund (IMF—see Glossary) in order to ensure an infusion of foreign assistance vital to keeping the economy functioning. Whereas Ratsiraka's drift toward authoritarianism provided his enemies with political cannon fodder, his economic reforms led them to charge him with abandoning "scientific socialism" and alienated his traditional base of political supporters, as well.

The results of presidential elections within the de facto single-party framework that prevailed throughout the Second Republic clearly demonstrated Ratsiraka's declining political fortunes. Widespread initial enthusiasm for his socialist revolution from above secured him nearly 95 percent of the popular vote in the 1975 presidential elections, but support declined to 80 percent in 1982 and to only 63 percent in 1989. The year of 1989 marked a special turning point in that the fall of the Berlin Wall heralded the intellectual death of single-party rule in Eastern Europe and the former Soviet Union and similarly transformed electoral politics in Africa. In the case of Madagascar, increasingly vocal opposition parties denounced what they and international observers considered massive fraud in the 1989 presidential election, including Ratsiraka's refusal to update outdated voting lists that excluded the anti-Ratsiraka youth vote and the stuffing of ballot boxes at unmonitored rural polling stations. Massive demonstrations against Ratsiraka's inauguration led to violent clashes in Antananarivo that, according to official figures, left seventy-five dead and wounded.

Popular discontent with the Ratsiraka regime heightened on August 10, 1991, when more than 400,000 citizens marched peacefully on the President's Palace in order to oust the Ratsiraka government and create a new multiparty political system. Ratsiraka already faced an economy crippled by a general strike that had begun in May, as well as a divided and restless military whose loyalty no longer could be assumed. When the Presidential Guard opened fire on the marchers and killed and wounded hundreds, a crisis of leadership occurred.

The net result of these events was Ratsiraka's agreement on October 31, 1991, to support a process of democratic transition, complete with the formulation of a new constitution and the holding of free and fair multiparty elections. Albert Zafy, the central leader of the opposition forces and a *côtier* of the Tsimihety ethnic group, played a critical role in this transition process and ultimately emerged as the first president of Madagascar's Third Republic. The leader of the Comité des Forces Vives (Vital Forces Committee, known as Forces Vives), an umbrella opposition group composed of sixteen political parties that spearheaded the 1991 demonstrations, Zafy also emerged as the head of what became known as the High State Authority, a transitional government that shared power with the Ratsiraka regime during the democratization process.

A new draft constitution was approved by 75 percent of those voting in a national referendum on August 19, 1992. The first round of presidential elections followed on November 25. Frontrunner Zafy won 46 percent of the popular vote as the Forces Vives candidate, and Ratsiraka, as leader of his own newly created progovernment front, the Militant Movement for Malagasy Socialism (Mouvement Militant pour le Socialisme Malgache—MMSM), won approximately 29 percent of the vote. The remaining votes were split among a variety of other candidates. Because neither candidate obtained a majority of the votes cast, a second round of elections between the two frontrunners was held on February 10, 1993. Zafy emerged victorious with nearly 67 percent of the popular vote.

### The Third Republic, 1993–

The Third Republic officially was inaugurated on March 27, 1993, when Zafy was sworn in as president. The victory of the Forces Vives was further consolidated in elections held on June 13, 1993, for 138 seats in the newly created National Assembly. Voters turned out in low numbers (roughly 30 to 40 percent abstained) because they were being called upon to vote for the fourth time in less than a year. The Forces Vives and other allied parties won seventy-five seats. This coalition gave Zafy a clear majority and enabled him to chose Francisque Ravony of the Forces Vives as prime minister.

By the latter half of 1994, the heady optimism that accompanied this dramatic transition process had declined somewhat as the newly elected democratic government found itself confronted with numerous economic and political obstacles. Adding to these woes was the relatively minor but nonetheless embarrassing political problem of Ratsiraka's refusal to vacate the President's Palace. The Zafy regime has found itself under increasing economic pressure from the IMF and foreign donors to implement market reforms, such as cutting budget deficits and a bloated civil service, that do little to respond to the economic problems facing the majority of Madagascar's population. Zafy also confronts growing divisions within his ruling coalition, as well as opposition groups commonly referred to as "federalists" seeking greater power for the provinces (known as *faritany*) under a more decentralized government (see fig. 2). Although recently spurred by the desire of anti-Zafy forces to gain greater control over local affairs, historically Madagascar has witnessed a tension between domination by the central highlanders and pressures from residents of outlying areas to manage their own affairs. In short, the Zafy regime faces the dilemma of using relatively untested political structures and "rules of the game" to resolve numerous issues of governance.

## Physical Environment

### Topography

Madagascar can be divided into five geographical regions: the east coast, the Tsaratanana Massif, the central highlands, the west coast, and the southwest. The highest elevations parallel the east coast, whereas the land slopes more gradually to the west coast (see fig. 3).

The east coast consists of a narrow band of lowlands, about fifty kilometers wide, formed from the sedimentation of alluvial soils, and an intermediate zone, composed of steep bluffs alternating with ravines bordering an escarpment of about 500 meters in elevation, which gives access to the central highlands. The coastal region extends roughly from north of Baie d'Antongil, the most prominent feature on the east coast of the island formed by the Masoala Peninsula, to the far south of the island. The coastline is straight, with the exception of the bay, offering less in the way of natural harbors than the west coast. The Canal des Pangalanes (Lakandranon' Ampalangalana), an

800-kilometer-long lagoon formed naturally by the washing of sand up on the island by the Indian Ocean currents and by the silting of rivers, is a feature of the coast; it has been used both as a means of transportation up and down the coast and as a fishing area. The beach slopes steeply into deep water. The east coast is considered dangerous for swimmers and sailors because of the large number of sharks that frequent the shoreline.

The Tsaratanana Massif region at the north end of the island contains, at 2,880 meters, the highest point on the island and, north of this, the Montagne d'Ambre (Ambohitra), which is of volcanic origin. The coastline is deeply indented; two prominent features are the excellent natural harbor at Antsiranana (Diégo Suarez), just south of the Cap d'Ambre (Tanjon' i Bobaomby), and the large island of Nosy-Be to the west. The mountainous topography to the south, however, limits the potential of the port at Antsiranana by impeding the flow of traffic from other parts of the island.

The central highlands, which range from 800 to 1,800 meters in altitude, contain a wide variety of topographies: rounded and eroded hills, massive granite outcroppings, extinct volcanoes, eroded peneplains, and alluvial plains and marshes, which have been converted into irrigated rice fields. The central highlands extend from the Tsaratanana Massif in the north to the Ivakoany Massif in the south. They are defined rather clearly by the escarpments along the east coast, and they slope gently to the west coast. The central highlands include the Anjafy High Plateaux; the volcanic formations of Itasy (Lake Itasy itself is found in a volcanic crater) and the Ankaratra Massif, reaching a height of 2,666 meters; and the Ivakoany Massif in the south. The Isalo Roiniforme Massif lies between the central highlands and the west coast. Antananarivo, the national capital, is located in the northern portion of the central highlands at 1,468 meters above sea level. A prominent feature of the central highlands is a rift valley running north to south, located east of Antananarivo and including Lac Alaotra, the largest body of water on the island, having a length of forty kilometers. The lake is located 761 meters above sea level and is bordered by two cliffs, rising 701 meters to the west and 488 meters to the east, which form the walls of a valley resembling the rift valleys of East Africa. This region has experienced geological subsidence, and earth tremors are frequent here.

The west coast, composed of sedimentary formations deposited in several layers over time, is more indented than the east coast, especially in the northwest, thus offering a number of fine harbors sheltered from cyclones, such as the harbor at Mahajanga. Deep bays and well-protected harbors have attracted explorers, traders, and pirates from Europe, Africa, and the Middle East since ancient times; thus, the area has served as an important bridge between Madagascar and the outside world. Yet the broad alluvial plains found on the coast between Mahajanga and Toliara, which are believed to have great agricultural potential, are thinly inhabited and remain largely unexploited.

The southwest is bordered on the east by the Ivakoany Massif and on the north by the Isala Roiniforme Massif. It includes two regions along the south coast, the Mahafaly Plateau and the desert region occupied by the Antandroy people.

The Mananara and Mangoro rivers flow from the central highlands to the east coast, as does the Maningory, which flows from Lake Alaotra. Other rivers flowing east into the Indian Ocean include the Bemarivo, the Ivondro, and the Mananjary. These rivers tend to be short because the watershed is located close to the east coast. Owing to the steep elevations, they flow rapidly, often over spectacular waterfalls. The rivers flowing to the west coast and emptying into the Mozambique Channel tend to be longer and slower, because of the more gradual slope of the land. The major rivers on the west coast are the Sambirano, the Mahajamba, the Betsiboka (the port of Mahajanga is located at the mouth), the Mania, the North and South Mahavavy, the Mangoky, and the Onilahy. The Ikopa, which flows past Antananarivo, is a tributary of the Betsiboka. The Mangoky River has a basin area of some 50,000 square kilometers; the Ikopa River and the Betsiboka River have basin areas of 18,550 and 11,800 square kilometers, respectively. The principal river in the south, the Mandrare, has a basin area of some 12,435 square kilometers, but it runs dry during certain months in this desert region. Important lakes, aside from Alaotra, include Lake Kinkony in the northwest and Lake Ihotry in the southwest.

Madagascar has been called the "Great Red Island" because of the supposed preponderance of red lateritic soils. The red soils predominate in the central highlands, although there are much richer soils in the regions of former volcanic activity—Itasy and Ankaratra, and Tsaratanana to the north. A narrow band of alluvial soils is found all along the east coast and at the mouths of the major rivers on the west coast; clay, sand, and limestone mixtures are found in the west; and shallow or skeletal laterite and limestone are located in the south.

## Climate

The climate is dominated by the southeastern trade winds that originate in the Indian Ocean anticyclone, a center of high atmospheric pressure that seasonally changes its position over the ocean. Madagascar has two seasons: a hot, rainy season from November to April; and a cooler, dry season from May to October. There is, however, great variation in climate owing to elevation and position relative to dominant winds. The east coast has a subequatorial climate and, being most directly exposed to the trade winds, has the heaviest rainfall, averaging as much as 3.5 meters annually. This region is notorious not only for a hot, humid climate in which tropical fevers are endemic but also for the destructive cyclones that occur during the rainy season, coming in principally from the direction of the Mascarene Islands. Because rain clouds discharge much of their moisture east of the highest elevations on the island, the central highlands are appreciably drier and, owing to the altitude, also cooler. Thunderstorms are common during the rainy season in the central highlands, and lightning is a serious hazard.

Antananarivo receives practically all of its average annual 1.4 meters of rainfall between November and April. The dry season is pleasant and sunny, although somewhat chilly, especially in the mornings. Although frosts are rare in Antananarivo, they are common at higher elevations. During this time, the blue skies of the central highlands around Antananarivo are considered by many to be among the clearest and most beautiful in the world.

The west coast is drier than either the east coast or the central highlands because the trade winds lose their humidity by the time they reach this region. The southwest and the extreme south are semidesert; as little as one-third of a meter of rain falls annually at Toliara. Overall, surface water is most abundant along the east coast and in the far north (with the exception of the area around Cap d'Ambre, which has relatively little surface water). Amounts diminish to the west and south, and the driest regions are in the extreme south.

Madagascar suffers the impact of cyclones from time to time. From February 2–4, 1994, Madagascar was struck by Cyclone Geralda, the worst cyclone to come ashore on the island since 1927. The cyclone killed seventy people and destroyed enough property to leave approximately 500,000 homeless, including 30,000 in Antananarivo and 80,000 in Toamasina. The cyclone also significantly damaged the country's infrastructure, most notably coastal roads, railroads, and telecommunications, as well as agriculture. Damage has been estimated at US$45 million, and the World Bank's (see Glossary) International Development Association and various European organizations are engaged in financing the reconstruction. The Madagascar government will contribute US$6 million toward the infrastructure rehabilitation.

## Flora and Fauna

The island of Madagascar has been described as an "alternate world" or a "world apart" because of the uniqueness and rarity of many of its plant and animal species. Their characteristics are believed to reflect the island's origins as a part of Gondwanaland and its many millions of years of virtually total isolation following the breakup of the landmass. Thus, certain plants, including the "traveler's" tree (so called because its trunk holds potable water), are found both in Madagascar and on the South American continent, but not in Africa. Many of the most characteristic African species, particularly such large mammals as the elephant, rhinoceros, giraffe, zebra, and antelope and such beasts of prey as the lion and leopard, do not exist in Madagascar. In addition, the island has been spared the great variety of venomous snakes indigenous to the African continent. Although it is assumed that most life forms on the island had an African (or South American) origin, many millions of years of near-complete isolation have allowed old species—elsewhere extinct—to survive and new species unique to the island to evolve. Thus, a great number of plant, insect, reptile, and fish species are found only in Madagascar, and all indigenous land mammal species—sixty-six in all—are unique to the island.

Madagascar was once covered almost completely by forests, but the practice of burning the woods to clear the land for dry rice cultivation has denuded most of the landscape, especially in the central highlands. Rain forests are concentrated on the steep hillsides along a slender north-south axis bordering the east coast, from the Tsaratanana Massif in the north to Tôlan-aro in the south. Secondary growth, which has replaced the original forest and consists to a large extent of traveler's trees, raffia, and baobabs, is found in many places along the east coast and in the north. The vegetation of the central highlands and the west coast is for the most part savanna or steppe, and coarse prairie grass predominates where erosion has not exposed the orange-red lateritic soil. In the southwest, the vegetation is adapted to desert conditions.

The remaining rain forest contains a great number of unique plant species. The country has some 900 species of orchids. Bananas, mangoes, coconut, vanilla, and other tropical plants grow on the coasts, and the eucalyptus tree, brought from Australia, is widespread.

Wood and charcoal from the forests are used to meet 80 percent of domestic fuel needs. As a result, fuelwood has become scarce. The World Bank in 1990 launched an environmental program that has increased the planting of pine and eucalyptus to satisfy fuel needs.

## Society

### Population And Ethnicity

Madagascar has experienced steady population growth throughout the twentieth century. Since the first systematic census was undertaken by colonial authorities at the turn of the twentieth century, the population has grown from 2.2 million in 1900 to 7.6 million in 1975 (the last year that a census was undertaken) and to a population estimated by the IMF in mid-1993 at 11.86 million. It is expected that the population will approach 17 million by the end of the twentieth century, underscoring a more than fivefold increase in less than a hundred years. Moreover, the average rate of population growth itself has increased from 2.3 percent in 1975 to 3.1 percent over the 1980 to 1990 decade. This rate has made Madagascar one of the most rapidly growing countries in Africa, with a large youthful population—in 1992 nearly 55 percent of the population was under twenty years of age.

The increase in population is significantly influenced by Madagascar's increasingly healthy and youthful population. As a result of more extensive and accessible health care services, for example, Madagascar has witnessed a 36 percent decline in infant mortality from 177 per 1,000 live births in 1981 to 114 per 1,000 in 1991—the average for sub-Saharan Africa was 103. Moreover, as of 1991 a significant portion of the population (estimates range from 40 to 50 percent) was below fourteen years of age, and population density (per square kilometer) had risen to twenty (from roughly fourteen in 1981).

The urban population percentage has doubled since 1975, rising from 13 percent of the population to 26 percent in 1992. The annual urban population growth rate in the 1980s was 6.4 percent. Figures for Madagascar's foreign population in the early 1990s are lacking, but in 1988, such persons were estimated to include 25,000 Comorans, 18,000 French, 17,000 Indians, and 9,000 Chinese.

A unique blend of African and Asian landscapes and cultures is usually one of the first things recognized by first-time travelers to Madagascar. In the zebu cattle-raising regions of the south and west, for example, the savannas resemble those of East Africa. In the central highlands, however, irrigated and terraced rice fields evoke images of Southeast Asia. These contrasting images lie at the heart of an ongoing debate over the origins of the Malagasy people.

According to one theory, peoples from the Indonesian archipelago migrated along the coast of south Asia, across the Arabian Peninsula into the east coast of Africa and, finally, across the Mozambique Channel into present-day Madagascar. This movement occurred over several generations and, because of the gradual interaction between Asian and African populations, led to the arrival and eventual implantation of a distinct Malagasy people and culture. A second theory emphasizes the diversity of the peoples inhabiting Madagascar. Simply put, proponents argue that the Malagasy resulted from a series of migrations by different peoples over time. According to this theory, migrants from the Indonesian archipelago arrived first and eventually settled in the central highlands, followed by the arrival of African peoples as a result of normal migrational trends and the rise of the slave trade. Recent scholarship has suggested that perhaps the theories are complementary, with greater emphasis being placed on the first.

Scholars traditionally have described Madagascar as being divided into eighteen or twenty ethnic groups, each with its own distinct territory; political developments in the contemporary period are often described in terms of ethnic conflict. Yet ethnicity is potentially misleading in the Malagasy context because it connotes a more or less self-sufficient and unique cultural, socioeconomic, and historically united group that perceives itself as being different from other groups.

The population of Madagascar, however, is remarkably homogeneous in terms of language. Unlike most African countries, the vast majority speak the indigenous national Malagasy language. Moreover, despite significant variations, important cultural elements unify the Malagasy people and give them a "pan-islandic" identity. These include a system of kinship in which descent can be traced through either the paternal or the maternal line. The same kinship terms are used by all Malagasy. A second important element is the centrality of respect for the dead (*razana*) to the social, moral, and religious life of the people. Tombs and the ceremonies related to them are prominent features of both the Malagasy landscape and the way of life of the people. A third important feature is the division of Malagasy societies into three relatively rigid strata: nobles, commoners, and slaves (or descendants of slaves). Other common elements include the circumcision of children, the practice of astrology and divination, and certain concepts associated with authority, such as *hasina* (sacred, or life-giving, power), which legitimate the position of political and familial authorities.

Another potentially valuable method of analyzing Malagasy society is to differentiate between the so-called *côtiers*, or peoples living in coastal areas, and those who live in the central highlands. Indeed, scholars have noted in recent years that the salience of ethnic group identity has declined, while the division between the central highlands peoples and the *côtiers* continues to be of great importance in understanding social and political competition. Although many observers equate the term central highlander with the Merina ethnic group (once again suggesting the importance of ethnicity), it is important to note that the Betsileo people also live within this region, and the Merina themselves have settled in other regions of the country. Equally important, many *côtiers* do not live anywhere near the coast. In this sense, the central highlands/*côtier* split is best understood as the historical outcome of the domination of the Merina empire, the original center of which was Imerina (around the city of Antananarivo) and was located in the central highlands.

A true understanding of the character of Madagascar's population and historical development requires an appreciation of the inhabitants' shared characteristics, including language and kinship structure, as well as the central highlands/*côtier* split

*Royal tombs of kings and queens of Madagascar on Royal Hill;*
*audience hall in background*
*Courtesy Brian Kensley*

and other divisions based on geographical regions. These latter divisions coincide with the major geographical divisions of the island: east coast, west coast, central highlands, southwest, and the Tsaratanana Massif. Within these regions, the people have certain cultural similarities accentuated by the natural environment.

### Peoples of the East Coast

The Betsimisaraka constitute the second largest (14.9 percent) group of Madagascar's population and clearly are the most numerous on the east coast. They are divided into three subgroups: the northern Betsimisaraka, the Betanimena, and the southern Betsimisaraka. Their territory extends along the coast in a narrow band from the Bemarivo River in the north to the Mananjary River in the south, a distance of some 640 kilometers. The Betsimisaraka, whose name means "numerous and inseparable," have traditionally been traders, seafarers, and fishers, as well as cultivators of the tropical lowland areas. They trace their origins to the confederacy established by Ratsimilaho, allegedly the son of a British pirate and a Malagasy princess, who unified several small coastal states in the eighteenth century. The confederation continued after Ratsimilaho died in 1751, but it was much weakened by internal conflict and external pressure. The Betsimisaraka territory has included the important port city of Toamasina, as well as Fenerive and Maroansetra at the head of the Baie d'Antongil.

South of the Betsimisaraka are ethnic groups who trace their origins to Islamic traders of mixed Arab, African, and Malayo-Indonesian origin who settled on the coasts after the fourteenth century, and are known as Antalaotra ("people of the sea"). The Antambahoaka, whose name is translated as "the people," make up 0.4 percent of the population and live around the Mananjary River just south of the Betsimisaraka territory. They claim as their ancestor Raminia, a king who came from Mecca around the early fourteenth century, and are part of a larger group known as the Zafi-Raminia, or "descendants of Raminia"; some of this group migrated from the Mananjary region to become rulers of peoples to the south. Some scholars have speculated that the Zafi-Raminia may have formed part of the ruling class of the Merina, who came to dominate Madagascar in the nineteenth century. Their power and prestige derived from their willingness to use their knowledge of astrology, medicine, and divination to serve the courts of kings throughout Madagascar.

Another people descended from the Antalaotra, the Antaimoro ("people of the shore") constitute 3.4 percent of the population and also live south of the Betsimisaraka. The Antaimoro were apparently the last significant arrivals, appearing around the end of the fifteenth century, possibly from the Arabian Peninsula with a sojourn in Ethiopia or Somalia, just before the coming of the Europeans in the sixteenth century. They are the only Malagasy people before the nineteenth century to possess a system of writing, based on Arabic script. Their books, the *sorabe* (from the Arabic *sura*, meaning "writing," and the Malagasy *be*, meaning "big" or "great"), which were inscribed in ink on special paper made from beaten wood bark, dealt with astrology, divination, medicine, and historical chronicles. Like the Antambahoaka, the Antaimoro are noted throughout Madagascar for their knowledge of the supernatural and medicine.

Among a number of other groups around Farafangana, at the southern end of the Canal des Pangalanes, the most important are the Antaifasy ("people of the sands"), who constitute 1.2 percent of the population. To the south, the Antaisaka (5.3 percent of the population) are found in large numbers around the alluvial valley of the Mananara River. The Antanosy ("people of the island"), who live in the extreme southeastern part of the island around Tôlanaro, make up 2.3 percent of the population.

The peoples of the eastern escarpment separating the east coast from the central highlands are the Sihanaka ("people of the lake"), who represent 2.4 percent of the population; the Bezanozano (0.8 percent), living south of the Sihanaka; and the Tanala (3.8 percent). The Sihanaka live around Lake Alaotra and practice wet-rice cultivation in a manner similar to that of the Merina. The Bezanozano ("many little braids," referring to their hair style), the Tanala ("people of the forest"), and the inland Betsimisaraka practice slash-and-burn agriculture in the forests, cultivating dry rice, corn, yams, and other crops. Although the Merina conquered the Sihanaka, the Bezanozano, and the inland Betsimisaraka in the early nineteenth century, the southern Tanala remained independent up to the French occupation.

### Peoples of the West Coast

The peoples of the west coast, known as the Sakalava ("people of the long valley"), constitute 6.2 percent of the population. Their large territory of some 128,000 square kilometers extends in a broad band up the coast from the Onilahy River in the south to Nosy-Be in the north. The Sakalava were among the most dynamic and expansionist of the Malagasy peoples from the sixteenth to the early nineteenth centuries, when the Merina conquered them. During this period, Sakalava territory was divided into a number of kingdoms ruled by branches of the royal Maroserana clan. In the early eighteenth century, the kings of Menabe in the south and Boina in the north united these divisions into confederations.

The Sakalava, along with the Bara people of the southwest, are considered the most "African" of the Malagasy peoples. Specifically, several elements in Sakalava culture bear a strong resemblance to those of Africa, including the keeping of relics (such as pieces of bone) considered to have magical powers and the practice of spirit possession, in which a medium transmits the wishes of dead kings to the living. The Sakalava are also a pastoral people, and those who live in the hinterland keep large herds of zebu cattle that outnumber the human population.

The Sakalava are perhaps best known for the seafaring skills they developed throughout history. In the seventeenth century, they were potentially the first to receive firearms from Europeans in exchange for cattle and slaves and, thus, were in a position to force many of the other peoples of the island to pay them tribute. During the late eighteenth and early nineteenth centuries, large fleets of Sakalava outrigger canoes went on seasonal raids to capture slaves in the Comoro Islands and on the East African coast, causing much devastation. They also sought slaves in the central highlands of Madagascar. Because of the Merina conquest and subsequent French occupation at the end of the century, Sakalava fortunes declined somewhat. They have not increased in number as rapidly as many of the other Malagasy peoples, and their territories, still the largest of all the ethnic groups, have been encroached upon, particularly by the Tsimihety people to the east. A people known as the Makoa, the descendants of slaves brought from Africa by slave raiders, also live along the northwest coast and constitute about 1.1 percent of the population.

### Peoples of the Central Highlands

The Merina, whose name means "those from the country where one can see far" (an eloquent yet important reference to their control of the central highlands) are not only the most numerous of the Malagasy peoples, representing more than one-quarter of the total population (26.2 percent), but since the early nineteenth century have been the most organized in terms of social, economic, and political structure. During the nineteenth century, the Merina almost succeeded in unifying the entire island under a centralized administration. Although their influence declined somewhat during the French colonial period, especially after the unsuccessful Revolt of 1947, they are heavily represented among the country's socioeconomic and political elite. Merina territory originally consisted only of the lands encircling the current capital of Antananarivo, but as they expanded in the eighteenth and nineteenth centuries, it came to include most of the northern central highlands, now the province of Antananarivo. Many Merina have settled in other parts of the island as government officials, professionals, and traders, and all the major cities have sizable Merina populations.

The Merina are considered the most "Asian" of the Malagasy ethnic groups in terms of their physical characteristics and culture. Having relatively light complexions and straight black hair, as well as a way of life based on wet-rice cultivation, they are strongly reminiscent of the peoples of Southeast Asia. It has been suggested that the ancestors of the Merina may have preserved their Malayo-Indonesian characteristics through the practice of endogamy or intermarriage. Such a practice would have discouraged their marrying with African peoples even during their hypothesized sojourn on the East African coast, which may have lasted centuries. The plausibility of this thesis is supported by the fact that the Merina continue to practice endogamy, although it is also plausible that Merina ancestors may simply have migrated directly to Madagascar without settling first in Africa. The Merina are sensitive to physical differences and distinguish between people who are *fotsy* (white), with relatively light complexions and descended from the freeborn of the nineteenth-century Merina kingdom, and those who are *mainty* (black), descendants of slaves or captives from other parts of the island who are described as being more "African" in physical appearance. *Fotsy* and *mainty* are not always clearly distinguishable, even to the Merina themselves, but this racial distinction nonetheless divides Merina society into two distinct groups and contributes to its highly unequal nature.

The Betsileo, who constitute 12.1 percent of the population and live in the central highlands south of the Merina in a region of about 40,000 square kilometers, have a culture similar to that of their northern neighbors. They are reputedly the best farmers in Madagascar, building rice terraces on the slopes of steep hills similar to those of Indonesia or the Philippines. They were united in the late eighteenth century by King Andriamanalimbetany of Isandra, one of the four Betsileo royal principalities, but were incorporated into the Merina kingdom in 1830. The Betsileo share something of the privileged position of the Merina, constituting a significant portion of Madagascar's official, professional, and skilled artisan classes.

South of the Betsileo live the Bara (3.3 percent of the population), who are divided into five clans in the dry regions at the southern end of the central highlands. They keep large herds of zebu cattle and are the most pastoral people in Madagascar; they also have a reputation of being valiant warriors.

The Tsimihety (7.3 percent of the population), whose lands are located north of Imerina, illustrate rather strikingly the birth and development of a Malagasy people. Their name, "those who do not cut their hair," refers to the refusal of their forebears in the early eighteenth century to submit to the Sakalava custom of cutting their hair when the king died; rather, they migrated to the unsettled north-central region of the island. The Tsimihety are noted for the rapid expansion of their population and for their penchant for migration, expanding the boundaries of their territory and encroaching on the lands of neighboring peoples. Primarily raisers of cattle, they are divided into a large number of traditional clans with little political organization. They are described as the individualists of the island, desiring to live a life free of government control in the unsettled hinterlands.

### Peoples of the Tsaratanana Massif and the Southwest

The Antakarana, living on the Tsaratanana Massif and the northern tip of the island, make up 0.6 percent of the population. The topography of the region isolates them from the other Malagasy peoples. They are both cattle herders and tropical horticulturalists.

The major peoples of the arid southwest region are the Mahafaly and the Antandroy, making up 1.6 and 5.4 percent of the population, respectively. The Mahafaly occupy a region between the Onilahy River to the north and the Menarandra River to the south, encompassing an area of some 45,000 square kilometers. The Antandroy territory lies to the east, a desert area full of cacti and thorn bushes. Its terrain makes their name, translated as "people of the thorns," especially apt. Both peoples depend upon the raising of cattle. Limited cultivation is also practiced. The Antandroy region is especially poor, causing workers to migrate to other parts of the island to make a living. Along with cattle, the prickly pear cactus is vital to the people's livelihood. Its spiny growths have served as a source of water and nourishment and as a means of defense against outside invaders.

### Minorities

Madagascar is also inhabited by nonindigenous minorities who constitute roughly 1.7 percent of the population. Because of the status of France as the former colonial power, Madagascar is home to many former French colonial administrators and military officers. The country is also home to French professionals, businesspersons, managers of large plantations, and colons (small farmers) working their own holdings. Approximately 18,000 French citizens lived and worked in Madagascar in the early 1990s.

The Comorans (currently numbering 25,000) historically have constituted a second important nonindigenous population group, but their numbers decreased after racial riots in Mahajanga in December 1976 resulted in nearly 1,400 killed; in addition, some 20,000 were repatriated to the islands in the ensuing months. They have been concentrated in the northern part of Madagascar, along the coast, and prior to 1976 formed more than one-tenth of the populations of the port cities of Mahajanga and Antsiranana. Most of the Comorans, who adhere to the Muslim faith, have migrated from the island of Njazidja (Grande Comore); they typically work as unskilled laborers in the fields or on the docks of the ports.

Indo-Pakistanis (roughly numbering 17,000) represent a third nonindigenous minority group, and trace their origins to the regions of Gujerat or Bombay on the Indian subcontinent. Like the Comorans, they are for the most part Muslim. Despite living on the island for several generations (or even several centuries), the Indo-Pakistanis still maintain contact with their home areas in northwestern India and Pakistan. Historically, they have worked as merchants and small entrepreneurs and in the past have monopolized the wholesale and retail trade in textiles. They tend to be concentrated in the cities along the west coast.

The Chinese (numbering approximately 9,000) constitute a fourth major nonindigenous population group. Like the Indo-Pakistanis, they are engaged primarily in commerce but are found mostly along the east coast and around Antananarivo. They are more commonly found in the rural areas than the Indo-Pakistanis. They work as small traders and often marry Malagasy.

### Language

The Malagasy language—spoken throughout Madagascar by the entire population—is the only one in the African region that belongs to the Malayo-Polynesian language family. Linguists believe that it shares a common origin with, and is most closely related to Maanyan, a language spoken in southeast Borneo. Both Malagasy and Maanyan bear a close affinity with the languages of the western Indonesian archipelago, such as Malay, Javanese, Balinese, and the Minangkabau language of Sumatra.

The origins of the Malagasy language in southeast Asia are clearly demonstrated by common words and meanings shared with several of the Indonesian languages. For example, the Malagasy term *antalaotra* (people of the sea) echoes the Malay *laut* (sea). Even more geographically widespread and interesting affinities have been discovered. *Vahiny* means "stranger" in Malagasy, while *vahini* means "girl" in Tahitian Polynesian. Scholars suggest that the two words (assuming they share a common origin) reveal that the first Malayo-Indonesian settlers along the African coast, or Madagascar itself, were male and that women came later as guests or strangers to settlements already established.

Although different regional dialects of Malagasy exist, these are mutually intelligible, and the language is a significant basis of cultural unity. Words are formed from roots with basic meanings, which are combined with prefixes or suffixes to create derivatives. Many Malagasy words, particularly names (such as that of the Merina king, Andrianampoinimerina), are very long, but certain syllables, particularly the last, are lightly accented or not at all.

A number of foreign words are found in the Malagasy vocabulary. The names of the days of the week and the months of the year are taken from Arabic, and the names of animals are taken from a Swahili dialect of East Africa. A number of English and French words also entered the language in the nineteenth and twentieth centuries.

Before the nineteenth century, the only Malagasy people with a written language were the Antaimoro, keepers of the *sorabe*. By 1824–25, a written form of Malagasy using Roman characters was developed by members of the London Missionary Society working under the patronage of Merina King Radama I. The result was an almost perfectly consistent phonetic language that continues to be used throughout the country; the consonants are pronounced as in English and the vowels as in French, a compromise apparently promoted by Radama I. The completion of the alphabet enabled the missionaries to publish a Malagasy Bible and other books for their schools, and the possession of a written language was to prove decisive to the development of the Merina-dominated portion of Madagascar.

The colonial period witnessed the emergence of French as the dominant language of the island, and Malagasy was relegated to an inferior position, particularly in official and academic circles. Although the First Republic adopted an official policy of bilingualism (French and Malagasy), French continued to dominate until the inauguration of Ratsiraka and his promulgation of an official policy of Malagachization. Originally conceived by nationalists as the promotion of education in the national language, Malagachization also ultimately included the more radical denunciation of French culture and influence over the national economy and political system. Malagachization further entailed the creation of a common Malagasy language that partook of dialects from all the regions and peoples of the island rather than being primarily a Merina dialect, as remains the case with official Malagasy today. After 1982 the drive toward Malagachization increasingly faltered in favor of a continuing trend toward reembracing the concept of Madagascar's inclusion in the international francophone community. Indeed, French remains important, largely because of its international status and the fact that most of the leadership has been educated in French. Both Malagasy and French are used in official government publications.

## Traditional Beliefs and Religion

A firm belief in the existence of close ties between the living and the dead constitutes the most basic of all traditional beliefs and the foundation for Malagasy religious and social values. All the Malagasy peoples have traditionally accepted the existence of a supreme God, known commonly as Zanahary (Creator) or Andriamanitra (Sweet, or Fragrant, Lord). The dead have been conceived as playing the role of intermediary between this supreme God and humankind and are viewed as having the power to affect the fortunes of the living for good or evil. The dead are sometimes described as "gods on earth," who are considered the most important and authoritative members of the family, intimately involved in the daily life of the living members. At the same time, the *razana* (best defined as "ancestors") are the sources from which the life force flows and the creators of Malagasy customs and ways of life. The living are merely temporary extensions of the dead. Great hardship or trouble can result if the dead are offended or neglected.

The burial tomb, a prominent part of the island landscape in all regions, is the primary link between the living and the dead among the Malagasy. It is built with great care and expense, reflecting the privileged position of the dead, and is often more costly and substantial than the houses of the living. The land upon which a family tomb is situated—*tanindrazana* (land of the ancestors)—is inalienable, and social and economic practices are designed to guarantee that tomb lands are kept within the family. Anthropologists have described the Merina as living, in effect, in two localities: the place where one happens to work and keep one's household, and the *tanindrazana*, a locality of much deeper sentimental significance, the spiritual center where the family tomb is located. The two are usually separated by a considerable distance. Among some groups, whether one decides to be buried in the tombs of the father's or mother's family determines individual descent-group allegiance.

The tombs of the various peoples around the island differ somewhat in form. Merina tombs tend to be solid, stone structures, built partially underground, with a chamber in which the bodies of ancestors are kept on shelves, wrapped in silk shrouds. The traditional tombs of the Mahafaly in the southwest were built of stone but surmounted by intricately carved wooden posts depicting human and animal figures. More recent Mahafaly tombs, particularly those built by rich families, are often made of concrete, with glass windows, brightly painted designs and often remarkable depictions of airplanes, taxicabs, or other modern paraphernalia mounted on the roof. At one time, it was the custom of the Sakalava people living around the Morondava River on the west coast to decorate their tombs with carvings showing explicit sexual activity. These were meant to illustrate the life-giving force, or fertility, of the ancestors.

Among the Merina and Betsileo peoples of the central highlands, the custom of *famadihana* ("placing" or the "turning" of the dead) reaffirms the link between the living and the dead. This occurs when a person is taken from a temporary to a permanent tomb in the *tanindrazana*, and the remains are taken out of the tomb to be wrapped in new shrouds, or when a body is moved from one tomb to another. These ceremonies are costly, mainly because of the expense of providing food for a large number of relatives and guests. They represent for the peoples of the central highlands a time of communion with the

*Madagascar's capital, Antananarivo*
*Courtesy J.D. von Pischke*

*razana* and a means of avoiding or reducing guilt or blame. It is considered a serious transgression not to hold a *famadihana* when one is financially able to do so. The ceremony is presided over by an astrologer, but the chief participants are the close relatives of those persons whose remains are being moved or rewrapped. In this regard, the *famadihana* resembles in spirit a family reunion or the more austere ancestral ceremonies of China and Korea, where the spirits of ancestors are invited to a feast given by members of a family or lineage, rather than the funerals of the West, which are "final endings."

Although the *famadihana* does not occur outside the central highlands and the attitudes of the Merina and Betsileo toward the dead differ in certain significant respects, the idea of the dead as beings to be respected is universal in Madagascar. A number of different "souls" are recognized by the Malagasy. Among the Merina, these include the *fanahy,* a kind of essence which determines individual character and behavior; thus, an individual can have a good or a bad *fanahy*. Another is the soul of the person after death, the *ambiroa*, which is called to the tomb for the celebration of the *famadihana*, but which, over time, is believed to blend with the collective spirit of other ancestors. The *ambiroa* is believed to permeate the tomb building, the family household, and the hills and valleys of the *tanindrazana*, being in a sense omnipresent. Other concepts include the soul of a recently deceased person, the *lolo*, which is said to be harmless but feels homesick for its old surroundings and often appears in the form of a moth or a butterfly. The *angatra*, ghosts of the unknown dead, are often malevolent and frighten people at night. The emphases in the minds of the people, however, are not on the afterlife or on the experiences of the dead souls either as ghosts or in heaven or hell, but on the relationship of the dead with the living and the role of the former as bearers of power and authority.

The *ombiasy* and the *mpanandro* combine the functions of diviners, traditional healers, and astrologers. They originated among the Antaimoro and the Antambahoaka of the southwest coast, who were influenced by the Antalaotra. Among the Antandroy, it is the *ombiasy* who are often asked to eradicate a mistake made by neglecting a taboo. The Bara consult the *ombiasy* to look after the sick and dying. Family heads ask them when to begin certain agricultural tasks or when to marry or circumcise those entering adulthood. Merina families have their personal diviners who consult the stars; their advice is requested on all enterprises that are thought to involve dangers. They are paid a regular salary and additional fees for extra services. They set the auspicious day for a *famadihana*. Even a highly educated Merina would not think of building a house without consulting the *ombiasy* or the *mpanandro* for the favorable day to begin work. When a marriage is contemplated, both sets of parents will ask the *ombiasy* and the *mpanandro* whether the partners will be compatible.

The science of the *ombiasy* and the *mpanandro* is tied to the concept of *vintana*, which means fate ordained by the position of moon, sun, and stars. Accordingly, different values and different forces, either active or passive, are attributed to each fraction of time. Space, too, is thought to be affected by these forces, east being superior to west, and north being superior to south. Northeast therefore is believed to be the most favorable direction. People build their houses on the north-south axis and reserve the northeastern corner for prayers. Guests are seated on the northern side, and chickens are kept in the southwestern corner.

Fate is impersonal and cannot be changed, but certain aspects can be foretold and avoided. For divination the *ombiasy* use a system of Arabic origin in which fruit seeds or grains of corn are put into rows of eight. Various figure combinations indicate the future and what to do regarding sickness, love, business, and other enterprises. The *ombiasy* also sell talismans made of such objects as dried or powdered vegetables, glass beads, or animal teeth.

*Fady* are taboos on the use of certain substances, particularly foods, or on the performance, including the timing, of certain acts. They continue to regulate much of Malagasy life. Many are connected with *vintana*, while others express certain social values. For example, to deny hospitality to a stranger is *fady*, as is the act of refusing this hospitality. The concept of *fady* often also expresses a well-developed metaphorical sense. According to one *fady*, it is wrong to sit in the doorway of a house while the rice is sprouting, since the door of the house is compared to the "gateway" of birth and by blocking it, one might impede the "birth" of the rice. It is important to remember, however, that *fady*, particularly dietary prohibitions, vary widely among different ethnic groups, and from village to village within the same ethnic group. To be at home in a different locality, travelers must acquaint themselves with a large number of local variations.

Traditional beliefs are augmented by imported organized religions. Although exact figures on religious affiliations do not exist, it is estimated that approximately 55 percent of the total population adhere to traditional beliefs, and 40 percent are Christian, about evenly divided between Roman Catholics and Protestants, the remaining 5 percent being Muslim. Indeed, Protestant and Roman Catholic churches have found themselves competing for new adherents, most notably underscored by the fact that villages in the central highlands often have two churches, one Protestant and one Roman Catholic, that face each other at opposite ends of the village. The Roman Catholic church enjoys its largest support among the Betsileo people in the southern portion of the central highlands, and is also associated with former slaves and the *côtiers*. Protestantism enjoys its largest support among the Merina of the central highlands and, therefore, historically has been perceived as the

Christian affiliation of the upper classes. Despite the minority status of Christians, the Council of Christian Churches in Madagascar played a major role in arbitrating a resolution to the conflict resulting from the violence and general strikes in May and August 1991 (see The Second Republic, 1975–92, this ch.).

The nineteenth century witnessed a confrontation between Christianity and traditional religious beliefs, as Queen Ranavalona I expelled foreign missionaries and persecuted Christians, putting many of them to death. The tide reversed at her death, and at the beginning of the reign of Ranavalona II, the old *sampy*—idols or talismans endowed with supernatural powers to protect the kingdom—were destroyed, and Protestantism became the religion of the royal family. Yet opposition has given way in many cases to a kind of mutual assimilation. Christian missionaries were able to build on the Malagasy concept of a supreme God by using the term, "Andriamanitra," to refer to the biblical God and by choosing one of the traditional terms for soul, *fanahy,* to define its Christian counterpart. Although the supremacy of Christianity in the central highlands led to the demise of idol worship, Malagasy pastors have not challenged the strength of traditional beliefs in the power and authority of the *razana.* Christians have their dead blessed at a church before burying them according to the old ceremonies, and may invite the pastor to attend a *famadihana* and place a cross on top of the tomb. Christian belief in the power of a transcendent and somewhat distant God has blended with older beliefs in the closeness and intimacy of the dead as spiritual beings. Some Malagasy Christians will even say that the dead have become Christians themselves and continue to be the arbiters of right and wrong.

Exact figures are not available, but followers of the Sunni (see Glossary) and Shia (see Glossary) variants of Islam together constitute around 5 percent of the total population. Most are Comorans or Indo-Pakistanis; a small number are converted Malagasy. The majority are located in Mahajanga Province. A small minority of the Indian community practices Hinduism.

### Social Structure and Family

Traditional society is hierarchical in structure. Kinship groups are ranked precisely along a superior/inferior continuum, and individuals within these groups are ranked according to age, descent, and gender. This pervasive ranking reflects the perceived power of ancestors as the source of *hasina* (life-giving power), which is distributed unequally among individuals and family groups. Royal or noble persons are supposed to possess a greater amount of *hasina* than others, so that their descendants enjoy superior social status. Within families of any rank, elders possess greater *hasina* than the young, not only by virtue of their maturity and experience but also because they are perceived as closer to the dead and thus share in part of their power. Rulers do not rule alone but share their offices in effect with their ancestors, who are, in fact, more powerful and influential than the rulers themselves. Among the Sakalava, it is believed that the soul or spirit of a royal ancestor can take possession of a person in order to make known its commands to the living.

Social values are highly conservative, demonstrating an awareness of hierarchy and place that permeates the daily life of the people. Observers have noted, for example, that in Merina households each member of the family is expected to eat a meal in turn according to age; the youngest is served last. Family members are seated around the table in an arrangement that reflects age-rank, the father or grandfather occupying the "noble corner" (the northeast). Failure to honor the rank is considered a serious violation of *fady.* Children who eat before their elders can be severely punished. Within the village, the local notables and respected elders of kin groups, who are usually male, have preponderant influence in village affairs.

The society as a whole remains divided into a number of unequal social groups based entirely on descent. Among the Merina, Madagascar's dominant ethnic group, these are referred to as the *andriana* (nobles), the *hova* (commoners), and the *andevo* (slaves or, more properly, the descendants of slaves). The distinction between *andriana* and *hova* on the one hand and *andevo* on the other hand corresponds to the distinction between "whites" and "blacks" in Merina society. Among the Sakalava, royal clans descended from the Maroserana occupy the highest social position, followed by noble and commoner clans; the descendants of slaves again occupy the lowest status. Noble and commoner clans possess histories that define their relations to the king and their different social roles. The social hierarchy of the Malagasy people, however, is actually far more differentiated than this system might suggest, because within each "caste" constituent clans or kin groups are also arranged in a precise hierarchy of superior and inferior that is well known to all individuals.

Among the Merina, the Malagasy people most thoroughly studied by anthropologists, the population is divided into a number of *karazana* (large kin groups) that are defined in terms of the common land upon which the family tomb is located. They are hierarchically ranked and usually named after a single ancestor. Members of the same *karazana* are described as being "of one womb." The general practice is for individuals to marry within the *karazana* or even within the same subunit to which they belong. Although endogamy carries with it the taint of incest, intermarriage is preferred because, in this way, land (especially tomb land) can be kept within the kin unit rather than being inherited by outsiders. Preserving the boundaries of the kinship unit through intermarriage preserves the integrity of the all-important link between the living and the dead.

Below the level of the *karazana*, the Merina are divided into *fianakaviana* (family), which includes close relatives by blood and affiliation. The family is less defined by territory than by its role as the locus of feelings of loyalty and affection. Members of the same *fianakaviana* are *havana* (relatives) but with a strong emotional connotation. The ideal of *fihavanana* (amity, solidarity) is that *havana* should love and trust one another, rendering mutual aid and sharing each other's possessions. When a man moves to new lands, his relatives will often come after him to claim parcels of land to cultivate. Persons who are not *havana* are often considered untrustworthy. However, fictive kinship, described as "those who are kin because they are loved," is a widespread Malagasy institution drawing individuals into an intermediate status between strangers and kin. This system can be very useful in daily life, particularly outside the *tanindrazana.*

Descent among the Merina is neither strictly patrilineal nor matrilineal. Instead, the practice of endogamy enables the two families involved in a marriage to define the situation as one in which they each receive a new child. The husband and wife are equally deferential to both sets of in-laws. Although women have occupied social roles inferior to those of men in traditional society, they are not completely subject to the will of their husbands or parents-in-law, as has been the case in strictly patrilineal societies.

There is some choice of which tomb group an individual will join and, thus, in which tomb he or she will be buried. Tomb groups consist of closely related *fianakaviana* members who own and maintain a tomb in common. The heads of tomb groups are local notables or government officials, and each member contributes to the tomb's upkeep, often a heavy financial burden because the tomb buildings are large and in frequent need of repair. New tombs are built, and new tomb groups are formed with the passing of generations. Both social identity and relationship with the dead are determined by one's tomb group. The most unfortunate persons are those who, because they are strangers or because of some other disqualification, cannot be interred within a tomb.

The difference between former free persons and former slaves remains particularly significant, despite the formal abolition of slavery by the French in 1897. Persons of slave origin are generally poorer than other Merina and are expected to perform the most menial tasks and to be particularly deferential to others. One observer noticed among the Betsileo in a rural household that during a meal to which a number of men had been invited, two persons of slave origin had to use a common plate, while free persons had their own plates. Former slaves are also often stereotypically described as rude, uncultured, and ugly. Marriages between persons of slave origin and other Merina are rare. When they do occur, the offspring are considered part of the slave group and are denied a place in the tomb of the free parent's family. In fact, the parent of the offspring may also be denied entrance. Former slaves do not possess links to a *tanindrazana* and, thus, are apt to be more mobile than the descendants of free persons, because migration offers the possibility of escaping from the stigma of slave descent. It is estimated that as much as 50 percent of the population of Imerina is of slave origin, whereas the percentage for the Betsileo territory is much lower.

Although the Merina social and kinship pattern is to a great degree common to all the peoples of Madagascar, there are important variations based in part on different histories and on ecological variations between the rice-growing and pastoral regions of the country. The pastoral Bara and the Tsimihety, who are agriculturalists but place great cultural and sentimental significance on herds of zebu, base descent and inheritance on patrilineality more strictly than the Merina.

## Education

In traditional Madagascar, education was not seen as separate from the other spheres of life. It emphasized the importance of maintaining one's place in a hierarchical society, trained people in the proper observance of ritual and innumerable *fady* prohibitions, and, above all, taught respect for ancestors. Formal education in the modern sense first appeared when the missionary David Jones of the London Missionary Society established a school in Antananarivo in 1820. It was sponsored by King Radama I, and Jones's first students were children of the royal family. Literacy spread as a result of the schools the Imerina missionaries built; in 1835 an estimated 15,000 persons knew how to read and write the new Malagasy language. Despite significant retrenchment during the reign of Queen Ranavalona I, the missionary school system, including both Protestant and Roman Catholic institutions, continued to grow.

During the colonial period, the French established a system of public schools that was divided into two parts: elite schools, modeled after those of France and reserved for the children of French citizens (a status few Malagasy enjoyed); and indigenous schools for the Malagasy, which offered practical and vocational education but were not designed to train students for positions of leadership or responsibility. Middle-grade Malagasy civil servants and functionaries were trained at the *écoles régionales* (regional schools), the most important of which was the École le Myre de Villers in Antananarivo. Reforms of the public school system designed to give the Malagasy more educational opportunities were initiated after World War II. At independence in 1960, the country had a system of education almost identical to that of France.

Education is compulsory for children between the ages of six and fourteen. The current education system provides primary schooling for five years, from ages six to eleven. Secondary education lasts for seven years and is divided into two parts: a junior secondary level of four years from ages twelve to fifteen, and a senior secondary level of three years from ages sixteen to eighteen. At the end of the junior level, graduates receive a certificate, and at the end of the senior level, graduates receive the *baccalauréat* (the equivalent of a high-school diploma). A vocational secondary school system, the *collège professionnel* (professional college), is the equivalent of the junior secondary level; the *collège technique* (technical college), which awards the *baccalauréat technique* (technical diploma), is the equivalent of the senior level.

The University of Madagascar, established as an Institute for Advanced Studies in 1955 in Antananarivo and renamed in 1961, is the main institute of higher education. It maintains six separate, independent branches in Antananarivo, Antsiranana, Fianarantsoa, Toamasina, Toliara, and Mahajanga. (Prior to 1988, the latter five institutions were provincial extensions of the main university in Antananarivo.) The university system consists of several faculties, including law and economics, sciences, and letters and human sciences, and numerous schools that specialize in public administration, management, medicine, social welfare, public works, and agronomy. Official reports have criticized the excessive number of students at the six universities: a total of 40,000 in 1994, whereas the collective capacity is 26,000. Reform measures are underway to improve the success rate of students—only 10 percent complete their programs, and the average number of years required to obtain a given degree is eight to ten compared with five years for African countries. The *baccalauréat* is required for admission to the university. Madagascar also has teacher-training colleges.

The gradual expansion of educational opportunities has had an impressive impact on Malagasy society, most notably in raising the literacy level of the general population. Only 39 percent of the population could be considered literate in 1966, but the United Nations Children's Fund (UNICEF) estimated that this number had risen to 50 percent at the beginning of the 1980s and to 80 percent in 1991. Similarly, primary school enrollment is nearly universal, a significant increase from the lower figure of 65 percent enrollment in 1965 (Madagascar had 13,000 public primary schools in 1994); 36 percent of the relevant school-age population attends secondary school (there were 700 general education secondary schools and eighty *lycées* or classical secondary institutions); and 5 percent of the relevant school-age population attends institutions of higher learning. Despite these statistics, a 1993 UNICEF report considers the education system a "failure," pointing out that in contrast to the early 1980s when education represented approximately 33 percent of the national budget, in 1993 education constituted less than 20 percent of the budget, and 95 percent of this amount was devoted to salaries. The average number of years required for a student to complete primary school is twelve. Girls have equal access with boys to educational institutions.

The national education system often has been at the center of political debate. As is the case throughout Africa, educational credentials provide one of the few opportunities to obtain employment in a country with a limited private sector, and the distribution of educational resources has continued to be an issue with explosive political ramifications.

Historically, the system has been characterized by an unequal distribution of education resources among the different regions of the country. Because the central highlands had a long history of formal education beginning in the early nineteenth century, this region had more schools and higher educational standards than the coastal regions. The disparity continued to be a major divisive factor in national life in the years following independence. The Merina and the Betsileo peoples, having better access to schools, inevitably tended to be overrepresented in administration and the professions, both under French colonialism and after independence in 1960.

Adding to these geographical inequities is the continued lack of educational opportunities for the poorest sectors of society. For example, the riots that led to the fall of the Tsiranana regime in 1972 were initiated by students protesting official education and language policies, including a decision to revoke the newly established competitive examination system that would have allowed access to public secondary schools on the basis of merit rather than the ability to pay. Yet when the Ratsiraka regime attempted in 1978 to correct historical inequalities and make standards for the *baccalauréat* lower in the disadvantaged provinces outside the capital region, Merina students led riots against what they perceived as an inherently unfair preferential treatment policy.

The lack of access is compounded by an education system that still rewards those who are the most proficient in the French language, despite the fact that the country is officially bilingual. As of 1994, it was estimated that only between 20,000 and 30,000 citizens could be considered truly fluent in the French language and that another 2 million citizens have received, at best, a passive high school-level competence in the language. The vast majority (8 to 9 million) speak only Malagasy and, therefore, potentially find themselves at a distinct disadvantage in terms of future advancement. It is at least partially because of shortcomings in French-language abilities that approximately 90 percent of all first-year university students are refused entry into the second year.

A final challenge revolves around the growing gap between a declining government-sponsored public school system and an increasingly vibrant and growing private school system. The Ratsiraka regime's education policy of Malagachization strengthened this primarily two-tiered education system during the 1980s. The elite and the well-off middle class placed their children in private French-language schools, while the vast majority of the relatively poorer population had little choice but to enroll their children in increasingly disadvantaged public schools. By the 1991–92 academic year, only 5,870 students were enrolled in private French-sponsored grade schools and high schools (the most prestigious of the education system), while another 199,433 students were enrolled in the second tier of private Roman Catholic schools where teaching is also in French. An undetermined small number of students were enrolled in a third tier of private schools considered "mediocre" by French-language standards, but the vast majority (1,534,142) found themselves competing in the public school system.

## Public Health

Life expectancy at birth has gradually improved from an average of 37.5 years for men and 38.3 years for women in 1966 to an average of fifty-two years for men and fifty-five years for women in 1990 (for a combined average of fifty-four). Malaria remains the most serious tropical disease, although eradication campaigns against mosquitoes waged since 1948 initially resulted in spectacular declines in incidence and a dramatic decrease in the island's mortality rate during a twenty-year period. Indeed, in some regions, especially the central highlands, these campaigns were almost completely successful, although malaria continues to be prevalent in the coastal regions, especially the east coast. As prevention practices faltered during the late 1970s and throughout the 1980s, the mosquito staged a comeback. The effect on a population with a significantly reduced resistance to malaria was devastating. For example, the Malagasy Ministry of Health reported 490,000 cases and 6,200 deaths from malaria in 1985, but these figures rose—to 760,000 cases and 11,000 deaths—in 1987.

As of 1994, other serious diseases included schistosomiasis, tuberculosis, and leprosy. The prevalence of schistosomiasis, a parasitic ailment that spreads primarily through the passing of human wastes into ponds, irrigation canals, and slow-moving streams, reflects the continued lack of adequate sewerage facilities, especially in the rural areas. Occasional outbreaks of bubonic plague occur in urban areas, the most recent of them in 1990. Yet Madagascar has been spared many of the diseases common in tropical countries, such as trypanosomiasis, cholera, brucellosis, and yellow fever.

The occurrence of sexually transmitted diseases (STDs) has increased during the 1980s and the 1990s. It is estimated that 287 of 100,000 inhabitants have gonorrhea, and 220 of 100,000 have syphilis. According to data collected from 9,574 inhabitants treated for STDs in 1987, the breakdown by type of disease was as follows: gonorrhea (38 percent); syphilis (33 percent); trichomoniasis (20 percent); and candidiasis (8 percent). According to data compiled by the World Health Organization, only three cases of acquired immune deficiency syndrome (AIDS) were reported in the 1990–92 period, and six cases in 1993, earning Madagascar a 0.0 "case rate" (reported cases per 100,000 population).

The government has committed itself to the principle that good health is a right of each Malagasy citizen, and has made significant strides in the area of health care. A number of new hospitals and medical centers were built in various parts of the country during the 1970s and the first part of the 1980s. However, about two-thirds of the population reside at least five kilometers from a medical center, resulting in the May 1993 finding of UNICEF that 35 percent of the population lacked adequate access to health services.

Economic decline has led to a deterioration in medical services during the late 1980s and the early 1990s. In 1976, of the national budget, 9.2 percent was allocated to health care; this percentage dropped to 6.6 percent in 1981, 4.5 percent in 1990, and 2 percent in 1994. For example, as of 1993, according to UNICEF, the country had only one physician per 17,000 people. Important regional differences also exist. For example, in some provinces the ratio was as low as one physician for 35,000 persons. For the entire island, in 1993 a total of 234 medical centers were under the direction of one doctor, and the remaining 1,728 centers were under the direction of paramedics, midwives, nurses, health aides, or sanitarians. For those unable to obtain modern medical treatment, traditional medicine—the use of herbs or the exorcism of malicious spirits—remains popular.

Additional factors contributing to health problems include overcrowding (in some areas five to eight persons live in a room fourteen meters square), contagious diseases such as the plague, and inadequate garbage disposal facilities. Infant mortality has risen from sixty-eight per 1,000 births in 1975 to 109 per 1,000 in 1980 and 114 per 1,000 in 1991. Malnutrition, diarrheal diseases, respiratory infections, and malaria are major causes of infant deaths. Madagascar had a serious malaria epidemic in 1990 causing the death of tens of thousands; efforts are underway for annual antimalarial campaigns, especially in the Anjafy High Plateaux.

## The Economy

### Government Policy and Intervention

Over the years, successive French colonial and independence-era governments have sought to modernize Madagascar's economy. Despite such efforts, the majority of Malagasy in 1994 continued to earn their livelihoods in ways fundamentally unchanged from those of their ancestors—small-scale farms supporting traditional irrigated rice cultivation, dryland farming of cassava and other foods, zebu cattle herding, or the raising of cash crops.

The first modern land use projects were established by French settlers or Creole immigrants from the Mascarene Islands in the nineteenth and twentieth centuries. They introduced cash crops such as coffee, sugarcane, vanilla, cloves, and sisal for export. They also built small-scale mines to exploit the island's graphite, chromite, and uranium resources. To facilitate the processing and marketing of these commodities, the immigrants established a number of financial and commercial enterprises and built a small, modern railroad system. They then brought some Malagasy into this modern sector of the economy, either as wage laborers and sharecroppers on the foreign-owned plantations, or as low-level employees in the civil service or business enterprises. The foreign owners and managers, however, retained almost all of the benefits from these operations.

After independence the Tsiranana regime did little to change the French domination of the modern sector of the economy, despite increasing outrage at this continued economic dependence. This anger, together with growing concern over an unequal distribution of wealth that left the southern and western parts of the island in relative poverty, caused the ouster of Tsiranana in 1972 and a shift in economic policy. The new military regime led by Ramanantsoa cut most ties with France and began to Malagachize the economy. Slow progress toward this goal, however, helped to precipitate the end of the Ramanantsoa regime in mid-1975. Only with the rise of Ratsiraka to the presidency later that year did the takeover of formerly French-dominated enterprises begin in earnest.

Ratsiraka's policy of "revolution from above" went beyond confiscating or buying out foreign firms and turning them over to Malagasy ownership; he intended to socialize the economy by nationalizing major enterprises. The state acquired majority or minority ownership in nearly all large financial, transportation, marketing, mining, and manufacturing enterprises. Firms left under private control were required to buy and sell at state-controlled prices, and the state closely monitored the repatriation of profits. In the rural sector, Ratsiraka aimed to establish local farming cooperatives. Almost as important as this institutional reform was the regime's intention, announced in an economic plan for the 1978–80 period, to increase dramatically the level of government capital investment in all sectors of the economy in order to improve the availability of goods and services to all.

By the start of the 1980s, however, Ratsiraka's attempt to fashion viable socialist institutions and to stimulate the economy through increased investment had failed to improve economic production and welfare. Economic growth throughout the 1970s had not kept pace with the expanding population. Despite the availability of significant agricultural and mineral resources, the economy was less productive than at the start of the decade when the average per capita income was already among the lowest in the world. The only apparent effect of the enhanced level of investment, which reached all-time highs in the 1978–80 period, was to put the country deeply in debt to foreign creditors and, therefore, pave the way for a series of structural adjustment agreements signed with the IMF and the World Bank during the 1980s and the early 1990s. Such agreements were necessary because as a 1993 World Bank study pointed out, between 1971 and 1991 the per capita income of Malagasy dropped 40 percent; to return to its 1971 level by

*Cut-out embroidered tablecloths for sale in a village on the island*
*of Nosy-Be*
*Courtesy Brian Kensley*

2003, Madagascar would require a 6 percent annual growth
rate.

Eventually admitting that adoption of the socialist model of
economic centralization and state control was a mistake, the
Ratsiraka regime in 1980 initiated a return to a more classic liberal economic model that the Zafy regime wholeheartedly
adopted following its inauguration in 1993. The post-1980 Ratsiraka and Zafy regimes have overseen the privatization of parastatals (see Glossary), the disbanding of agricultural marketing
boards, the ratification of more liberal investment codes favor-
ing foreign investment, the privatization of the banking industry, diversification of traditional, primary-product exports, and
greater investment in food production. The Zafy regime has
made reinvigoration of the Malagasy economy its number-one
priority.

The major aims of the Zafy regime's agricultural policy are fivefold. The government seeks to make the country self-sufficient with regard to rice by expanding production through such measures as increased irrigation. It is also attempting to improve the quality of the major export crops—cloves, coffee, and vanilla—but to limit their quantities because of restrictions on world demand. The regime is trying to develop new export crops such as cashews, palm oil, shellfish, and soybeans and to diversify consumer food products through introducing rainfed crops such as corn and sorghum. In addition, the government is endeavoring to improve agricultural research and breeding facilities.

## Structural Adjustment

The structural adjustment requirements of the World Bank and the IMF were and remain critical to understanding the liberalization policies of the Ratsiraka and Zafy regimes. In 1980 severe balance of payments deficits led the Ratsiraka regime to seek the first of ten IMF standby and related agreements to be signed during the 1980s. The last series of agreements of the decade included one in 1988 using IMF trust funds and one in 1989 that expired in 1992. Throughout the 1980s, Madagascar also drew four times on the IMF and received four adjustment loans from the World Bank for industrial rehabilitation (1985—US$60 million), agricultural reform (1986—US$60 million), trade and industry adjustment (1987—US$100 million), and public-sector reform (1988—US$127 million).

The granting of these standby and related agreements was linked to a coordinated set of structural adjustment requirements designed to foster the liberal, export-oriented economy favored by the IMF and the World Bank. For example, an IMF standby agreement signed on July 9, 1982 to cover the 1982–83 period released 51 million in special drawing rights (SDRs—see Glossary) only after the Ratsiraka regime agreed to reduce both the current account deficit and the budget deficit, devalue the Malagasy franc (FMG—for value, see Glossary), limit domestic credit expansion, avoid any new short- or medium-term foreign borrowing, and limit public-sector salary increases. Among the major measures required by later agreements were a ceiling on rice imports, increases in producer prices of rice and coffee, and a further devaluation of the Malagasy franc. Despite a reputation for reneging on commitments to reform, formerly Marxist Ratsiraka ironically became known as one of the IMF's "star pupils" in Africa.

According to its agreement with the IMF, Madagascar was to limit its deficit to 5 percent of gross domestic product (GDP— see Glossary) in 1989–92. It succeeded in doing so until 1991 when production dropped, inflation increased, and tax income decreased because of political disturbances. Since then the government has not acted on the increased budget deficit, which was scheduled to be 6.2 percent of GDP in 1994, causing dissatisfaction on the part of World Bank officials.

Economic reform was stalled by the economic and political turmoil associated with the downfall of Ratsiraka and his replacement by the popularly elected Zafy regime in 1992. Although publicly critical of the IMF and World Bank during the 1993 election campaign, Zafy, who is a strong proponent of a liberal, free-market economy, initiated negotiations with these financial institutions to resume Madagascar's structural adjustment programs (and thereby gain access to more than US$1 billion in blocked development funds). However, negotiations throughout the first half of 1994 were tense as Zafy sought to avoid conditions that, no matter how logical from the macroeconomic perspective of long-term reform and development, would constitute political suicide.

General principles of reform that the World Bank considered necessary included macroeconomic stability, which implied moderate rates of inflation and of exchange; foreign trade and financial policy modifications that allowed the convertibility of the current account and liberalized import regulations; and the elimination of barriers to economic activity, such as eliminating obstacles to foreign investment and to participation in the export processing zones (EPZs). The World Bank's reform principles also involved encouraging the private sector by privatizing the parastatals, as well as concentrating government investment on infrastructure programs and the development of human resources by improving education, including technical education, and health facilities, including family planning to limit population growth. Among the specific reforms demanded by the World Bank were the revision of the 1994 budget, a new timetable for proposed privatization of parastatals, further reforms of the public sector, and the restructuring of terms for marketing agricultural products, most notably vanilla.

The IMF echoed these demands and added several more. These included allowing the Malagasy franc to float freely on the international currency market, restructuring the National Bank for Rural Development, privatizing the National Bank for Trade Development, and forcing all banks to maintain reserves of 10 percent of all deposits. To avoid pressures from the World Bank, the government sought funds from other sources. Considerable furor developed in the spring of 1994, when it became known that without the knowledge of the minister of finance, who was supposed to authorize such transactions, or the prime minister, but with the agreement of president Zafy and the president of the National Assembly, Richard Andriamanjato, the governor of the Central Bank of the Malagasy Republic, Raoul Ravelomanana, had signed promissory notes to several European banks committing Madagascar to repay loans of US$2 million. In short, the Zafy regime must balance the need for international funds (and the conditions that accompany their disbursement) with the need to maintain popular support if Zafy intends to seek a second term in office.

## National Accounts and Budget

Economists note that Madagascar's economy severely deteriorated from the 1960s to the late 1980s, particularly as a result of the misguided economic policies of the Ratsiraka regime. Whereas the growth rate in the GDP rose at an average of 2.9 percent in real terms during the 1960s, during the 1970s and the early 1980s this figure declined to 0.2 percent, compared with 2.6 percent population growth. Real GDP rebounded in the latter half of the 1980s, reaching a high of 4 percent in 1989. GDP increased at 1.1 percent per year in the 1980s and at 1 percent in 1992, but the economic output was unable to keep pace with population growth. This can be seen in Madagascar's economic ranking relative to other countries. In terms of gross national product (GNP—see Glossary) per capita, for example, the country declined from a World Bank ranking of the thirtieth poorest country in the world in 1979 (GNP per capita of US$290) to the tenth poorest in 1991 (GNP per capita of US$210).

Going beyond the traditional indicators of GDP and GNP per capita, however, Madagascar is doing better than might be thought. For example, according to the *Human Development Report* published by the United Nations Development Programme (UNDP) in 1993, Madagascar ranked 128th in the world (and seventeenth in Africa) in terms of "human development." This category represents a composite score of several indicators of development, such as life expectancy and literacy. The UNDP report further notes that, despite a slight drop in the early 1990s, Madagascar's human development steadily advanced during the decades of the 1970s and the 1980s.

The Zafy regime tried to balance the need for economic growth with a desire to enhance social welfare after the turbulent transition period of the early 1990s by putting together a Public Investment Program for 1994–96. The priorities of the US$326 million budget are clearly demonstrated by the breakdown of investments according to four broad categories: infrastructure (US$160 million—49 percent), with transportation receiving the largest share of US$87 million; producing sector (US$79 million—24 percent), with US$53.5 million of this devoted to agriculture; social assistance, including education, health care, and social assistance (US$52.2 million—16 percent); and public administration (US$32.4 million—10 percent). An overriding interest in development as opposed to security is clearly demonstrated by the relatively small amount of investment funds (US$2 million—0.6 percent) allocated to the Malagasy Armed Forces. Finally, the percentage of investment funds slated for each of the individual regions suggests an awareness of the need to favor those that historically have been neglected. The breakdown of investments by region in order of importance is as follows: Antsiranana (28 percent), Toliara (21 percent), Mahajanga (18 percent), Toamasina (15 percent), Antananarivo (10 percent), and Fianarantsoa (9 percent).

## Balance of Payments and Debt

The deterioration of the Malagasy economy that peaked in the 1980s is clearly demonstrated by the evolution of balance of payments problems and a growing debt burden (see table 2, Appendix). In 1980 Madagascar experienced a trade deficit of US$328 million and a service deficit of US$286 million, the combination of which contributed to a record current account deficit of US$568 million for the year. After nearly a decade of implementing the structural adjustment demands of the IMF and the World Bank, the Ratsiraka regime reduced the current account deficit to US$128 million in 1989. Among the economic trends contributing to this were a sharp reduction in imports and significant increases in bilateral and multilateral foreign assistance. Progress in reducing the current account deficit was reversed at the beginning of the 1990s, however, because of disruptions caused by the transition to democracy.

A rising debt burden constitutes the most notable indicator of Madagascar's fiscal dilemmas. Whereas as late as 1978 Madagascar had only accumulated US$293.5 million in debt, massive borrowing on the international market during a three-year span led in 1981 to the quadrupling of this figure to US$1.37 billion. By the end of the decade, this figure had nearly tripled to US$3.94 billion. Even worse, Madagascar's external debt exceeded annual GNP after 1986, reaching its height in 1988 when external debt as a percentage of GNP exceeded 160 percent.

The downfall of the Ratsiraka regime and the turbulence associated with the subsequent period of democratic transition exacerbated the debt crisis and presented the Zafy regime with one of its greatest economic challenges. As of November 1993, Madagascar's external debt was estimated to exceed US$4 billion, with an outstanding initial debt of US$295 million and rescheduled debt of US$625 million being owed to Paris Club (see Glossary) members. Whereas the outstanding initial debt was owed primarily to France (US$138 million) and Japan (US$126 million), several countries were owed the majority of outstanding rescheduled debt, including France (US$182 million), Italy (US$96 million), Japan (US$84 million), Spain (US$76 million), and Germany (US$55 million). Approximately US$77 million was also owed to commercial banks in the London Club (see Glossary), including the Arab Intercontinental Bank (US$31 million), Chase Manhattan Bank of Paris (US$9.5 million), Banque Nationale de Paris (US$7.5 million), and Banque Nationale d'Algérie (US$7.2 million).

## Traditional Agriculture

Traditional farming methods vary from one ethnic group or location to another, according to population density, climate, water supply, and soil. The most intensive form of cultivation is practiced among the Betsileo and Merina groups of the central highlands, where population densities are the highest. At the other extreme are the extensive slash-and-burn methods of brush clearing and shifting cultivation in the south and the east.

The Betsileo are probably the most efficient traditional rice farmers. They construct rice paddies on narrow terraces ascending the sides of steep valleys in the southern portion of the central highlands, creating an intricate landscape reminiscent of Indonesia or the Philippines. The irrigation systems use all available water, which flows through narrow canals for considerable distances. Some of the rice paddies cover no more than a few square meters. Only those surfaces that cannot be irrigated are planted in dryland crops.

In parts of the central highlands, two rice crops a year can be grown, but not on the same plot. The Betsileo use a variety of local species that can be sown at different times, employing irrigation to grow some varieties in the dry season and waiting for the rainy season to plant others. The fields surrounding the typical Betsileo village often represent a checkerboard of tiny plots in different stages of the crop cycle.

The cultivation cycle begins with the repair of irrigation and drainage canals and plowing, which is performed with a long-handled spade or hoe. Manure or fertilizer is then spread over the field. If the supply of manure or artificial fertilizer is limited, only the seedbeds are fertilized. After fertilizing, family and neighbors join in a festive trampling of the fields, using cattle if available. Occasionally, trampling takes the place of plowing altogether. If the rice is to be sown broadcast, it may be done on the same day as trampling. In the more advanced areas, the seedlings are raised in protected seedbeds and transplanted later.

Rice-farming techniques among the Merina resemble those of the Betsileo but are usually less advanced and intensive. The Merina territory includes some areas where land is more plentiful, and broader areas permit less laborious means of irrigation and terracing. Although rice is still the dominant crop, more dryland species are grown than in the Betsileo region, and greater use is made of the hillsides and grasslands.

In the forested areas of the eastern coast, the Betsimisaraka and Tanala peoples also practice irrigated rice culture where possible. The dominant form of land use, however, is shifting cultivation by the slash-and-burn method, known as *tavy*. The smaller trees and brush are cut down and left to dry, then burned just before the rainy season. The cleared area is usually planted with mountain rice and corn. After two or three years of cultivation, the fields are usually left fallow and are gradually covered by secondary vegetation known as *savoka*. After ten or twenty years, the area may be cultivated again.

Because the slash-and-burn method destroys the forest and other vegetation cover, and promotes erosion, it has been declared illegal. Government assistance is offered to those cultivators who prepare rice paddies instead, and those practicing *tavy* are fined or, in extreme cases, imprisoned. Despite the penalties, and much to the chagrin of forestry agents, *tavy* continues to be practiced. Even those who cultivate wet paddies often practice *tavy* on the side. The crop cycle for *tavy* is shorter than for irrigated rice, and generations of experience have taught that it is one of the only forms of insurance against the droughts that occur about every three years. Moreover, the precipitous slopes and heavy, irregular rains make it difficult to maintain affordable and controllable irrigation systems.

A similar system of shifting cultivation is practiced in the arid, sparsely populated regions of the extreme south and southwest. The dry brush or grassland is burned off, and drought-resistant sorghum or corn is sown in the ashes. In the Antandroy and some Mahafaly areas, however, the main staples of subsistence—cassava, corn, beans, and sorghum—are also grown around the villages in permanent fields enclosed by hedges.

Dry-season cultivation in empty streambeds is practiced largely on the western coast and in the southwest and is called *baiboho*. The crops are sown after the last rising of the waters during the rainy seasons, and after the harvest fresh alluvial deposits naturally replenish the soil. Lima beans (known as Cape peas) are raised by this system on the Mangoky River system delta, along with tobacco and a number of newer crops.

The traditional livestock-raising peoples are the Bara, Sakalava, and other groups of the south and the west, where almost every family owns some zebu cattle. The common practice is to allow the animals to graze almost at will, and the farmers take few precautions against the popular custom of cattle stealing. These farmers are also accustomed to burning off the dry grass to promote the growth of new vegetation for animal feed. The cattle generally are slaughtered only for ceremonial occasions, but these are so frequent that the per capita meat consumption among the cattle herders is very high.

Fishing is popular as a sideline by farmers who supplement their farm produce with fish from freshwater rivers, lakes, and ponds. Perhaps two-thirds of the total yearly catch is consumed for subsistence; transportation costs to the capital make the price of marketed fish prohibitively expensive to other domestic consumers. The introduction of tilapia fish from the African mainland in the 1950s increased inland aquaculture. Many families, particularly in the central highlands, have established fish ponds to raise carp, black bass, or trout. The breeding of fish in rice fields, however, requires sophisticated water control and a strong guard against dynamiting, poisoning, and poaching, which remain chronic problems.

## Agricultural Production

The 1984–85 agricultural census estimated that 8.7 million people live in the rural areas and that 65 percent of the active population within these areas lives at the subsistence level. The census also noted that average farm size was 1.2 hectares, although irrigated rice plots in the central highlands were often 0.5 hectares. Only 5.2 percent (3 million hectares) of the country's total land area of 58.2 million hectares is under cultivation; of this hectarage, fewer than 2 million hectares are permanently cultivated. Agriculture is critical to Madagascar's economy in that it provides nearly 80 percent of exports, constituting 33 percent of GDP in 1993, and in 1992 employed almost 80 percent of the labor force. Moreover, 50.7 percent (300,000 square kilometers) of the total landmass of 592,000 square kilometers supports livestock rearing, while 16 percent (484,000 hectares) of land under cultivation is irrigated.

The government significantly reorganized the agricultural sector of the economy beginning in 1972. Shortly after Ratsiraka assumed power, the government announced that holdings in excess of 500 hectares would be turned over to landless families, and in 1975 it reported that 500,000 hectares of land had been processed under the program. The long-range strategy of the Ratsiraka regime was to create collective forms of farm management, but not necessarily of ownership. By the year 2000, some 72 percent of agricultural output was to come from farm cooperatives, 17 percent from state farms, and only 10 percent from privately managed farms. Toward this end, the Ministry of Agricultural Production coordinated with more than seventy parastatal agencies in the areas of land development, agricultural extension, research, and marketing activities. However, these socialist-inspired rural development policies, which led to a severe decline in per capita agricultural output during the 1970s, were at the center of the liberalization policies of the 1980s and the structural adjustment demands of the IMF and the World Bank.

The evolution of rice production—the main staple food and the dominant crop—offers insight into some of the problems associated with agricultural production that were compounded by the Ratsiraka years. Rice production grew by less than 1 percent per year during the 1970–79 period, despite the expansion of the cultivated paddy area by more than 3 percent per year. Moreover, the share of rice available for marketing in the rapidly growing urban areas declined from 16 or 17 percent of the total crop in the early 1970s to about 11 or 12 percent during the latter part of the decade. As a result, Madagascar became a net importer of rice beginning in 1972, and by 1982 was importing nearly 200,000 tons per year—about 10 percent of the total domestic crop and about equal to the demand from urban customers.

The inefficient system of agricultural supply and marketing, which since 1972 increasingly had been placed under direct state control, was a major factor inhibiting more efficient and expanded rice production. From 1973 to 1977, one major parastatal agency, the Association for the National Interest in Agricultural Products (Société d'Intérêt National des Produits Agricoles—SINPA), had a monopoly in collecting, importing, processing, and distributing a number of commodities, most notably rice. Corruption leading to shortages of rice in a number of areas caused a scandal in 1977, and the government was forced to take over direct responsibility for rice marketing. In 1982 SINPA maintained a large share in the distribution system for agricultural commodities; it subcontracted many smaller parastatal agencies to handle distribution in certain areas. The decreasing commercialization of rice and other commodities continued, however, suggesting that transportation bottlenecks and producer prices were undermining official distribution channels.

To promote domestic production and reduce foreign imports of rice, the Ratsiraka regime enacted a series of structural adjustment reforms during the 1980s. These included the removal of government subsidies on the consumer purchase price of rice in 1984 and the disbanding of the state marketing monopoly controlled by SINPA in 1985. Rice growers responded by moderately expanding production by 9.3 percent during the latter half of the 1980s from 2.18 million tons in 1985 to 2.38 million tons in 1989, and rice imports declined dramatically by 70 percent between 1985 and 1989. However, the Ratsiraka regime failed to restore self-sufficiency in rice production (estimated at between 2.8 million and 3.0 million tons), and rice imports rose again in 1990. In 1992 rice production occupied about two-thirds of the cultivated area and produced 40 percent of total agricultural income, including fishing, which was next with 19 percent, as well as livestock raising and forestry (see table 3, Appendix).

In February 1994, Cyclone Geralda hit Madagascar just as the rice harvesting was about to start and had a serious impact on the self-sufficiency goal. In addition, the southern tip of Madagascar suffered from severe drought in late 1993, resulting in emergency assistance to 1 million people from the United Nations (UN) World Food Program (WFP). This WFP aid was later transformed into a food-for-work program to encourage development.

Other food crops have witnessed small increases in production from 1985 to 1992. Cassava, the second major food crop in terms of area planted (almost everywhere on the island) and probably in quantity consumed, increased in production from 2.14 million tons in 1985 to 2.32 million tons in 1992. During this same period, corn production increased from 140,000 tons to 165,000 tons, sweet potato production increased from 450,000 tons to 487,000 tons, and bananas dropped slightly from 255,000 tons to 220,000 tons.

Several export crops are also important to Madagascar's economy. Coffee prices witnessed a boom during the 1980s, making coffee the leading export crop of the decade; in 1986 coffee earned a record profit of US$151 million. Prices within the coffee market gradually declined during the remainder of the 1980s, and earnings reached a low of US$28 million in 1991 although they rebounded to US$58 million in 1992. Cotton traditionally has been the second major export crop, but most output during the early 1980s was absorbed by the local textile industry. Although cotton output rose from 27,000 tons in 1987 to 46,000 tons in 1988, once again raising the possibility of significant export earnings, the combination of drought and a faltering agricultural extension service in the southwest contributed to a gradual decline in output to only 20,000 tons in 1992.

Two other export crops—cloves and vanilla—have also declined in importance from the 1980s to the 1990s. Indonesia, the primary importer of Malagasy cloves, temporarily halted purchases in 1983 as a result of sufficient domestic production, and left Madagascar with a huge surplus. A collapse in international prices for cloves in 1987, compounded by uncertain future markets and the normal cyclical nature of the crop, has led to a gradual decline in production from a high of 14,600 tons in 1991 to 7,500 tons in 1993. Similarly, the still state-regulated vanilla industry (state-regulated prices for coffee and cloves were abolished in 1988–89) found itself under considerable financial pressure after 1987 because Indonesia reentered the international market as a major producer, and synthetic competitors emerged in the two major markets of the United States and France. As a result, vanilla production has declined from a high of 1,500 tons in 1988 and 1989 to only 700 tons in 1993.

The fisheries sector, especially the export of shrimp, is the most rapidly growing area of the agricultural economy (see table 4, Appendix). This production is making up for lost revenues and potential structural decline within the ailing coffee, vanilla, and clove trade. Since 1988 total fish production has expanded nearly 23 percent from 92,966 tons to 114,370 tons in 1993. The export of shrimp constituted an extremely important portion of this production, providing export earnings of US$48 million in 1993. It is estimated by Aqualma, the major multinational corporation in the shrimp industry, that expansion into roughly 35,000 hectares of swampland on the country's west coast may allow for the expansion of production from the current 6,500 tons and US$40 million in revenues to nearly 75,000 tons and US$400 million in revenues by the end of the 1990s. The prospects are also good for promoting greater levels of fish cultivation in the rice paddies, and exports of other fish products, most notably crab, tuna, and lobster, have been rising.

Livestock production is limited in part because of traditional patterns of livestock ownership that have hampered commercialization. Beef exports in the early 1990s decreased because of poor government marketing practices, rundown slaughtering facilities, and inadequate veterinary services. Approximately 99 percent of cattle are zebu cattle. In 1990 the Food and Agriculture Organization of the UN estimated that Madagascar had 10.3 million cattle, 1.7 million sheep and goats, and some 21 million chickens.

## Industrial Development

After registering a negative average annual growth rate of −2.8 percent from 1981 to 1986, industrial development improved from 1987 to 1991 with a positive, albeit small, average annual growth rate of 1.1 percent. As of 1993, it was esti-

*Traffic on a street in Antananarivo*
*Courtesy J.D. von Pischke*

mated that industrial output was responsible for 13 percent of GDP, and that the food-processing, mining, and energy sectors contributed 65 percent of the manufacturing portion of this total.

The establishment of EPZs and the passage of a new investment code in 1990 contributed to an expansion of industrial output (see table 5, Appendix). Despite the implications of the title, the EPZs do not require registered companies to establish themselves in specific geographic zones but merely constitute entities that fall under a specific fiscal code. The EPZs are financially attractive in that registered companies only pay one tax on profits (*impôt sur les bénéfices*) and another on revenues from capital transfers (*impôt sur les revenus de capitaux mobiliers*), and, in the case of the former, receive an exemption of as much as the first fifteen years of operation. From 1990 to 1993, 100 new companies had established themselves in the EPZs, creating more than 17,500 jobs and generating more than US$113 million in foreign investments. The majority of these firms were distributed among three economic sectors—clothing (48 percent), handicrafts (13 percent), and agro-processing (9 percent). Only 14 percent were owned by Malagasy; the remainder were owned by French (55 percent), Mauritian (16 percent), South African (4 percent), or other nationals (11 percent). Another 7,000 jobs and US$70 million in investments were generated by more than 160 new companies taking advantage of the new investment code. The creation by the International Finance Corporation (IFC—see Glossary) in June 1994 of the US$2.6 million Madagascar Capital Development Fund is designed to encourage Malagasy firms to establish themselves in the EPZs.

Madagascar contains a wide variety of minerals, but most of the deposits exist in scattered and relatively inaccessible locations. The government nationalized all mineral deposits in 1975, bringing mineral exploitation under the National Military Office for Strategic Industries (Office Militaire National pour les Industries Stratégiques). In 1990 a new mining investment code that encouraged private investment and exploitation was implemented, but the results have been disappointing. Several companies, including most recently Royal Dutch Shell, which disbanded its operations in early 1994, have sought unsuccessfully to find petroleum.

In another venture, in August 1993, a Swiss enterprise, International Capital and Securities Exchange, obtained the right to explore and mine for gold over a twenty-five-year period. French government sources estimate Madagascar's gold production at about three to four tons of gold annually and its potential yield double that. In 1992, however, as a result of smuggling, only thirty-seven kilograms of gold were officially exported.

Madagascar has reserves of bauxite, chromite, graphite, limestone, mica, nickel, and limestone. The exploitation of these minerals varies. More than 108,000 tons of chromium ores and concentrates, mostly in Andriamena in the central area and near Befandriana Avaratra in the north central area (Madagascar is the world's tenth largest producer), and 10,600 tons of graphite were successfully extracted in 1992. In contrast, the production of ilmenite ore, used in the manufacture of titanium, ceased in 1977 (although a joint Malagasy-Canadian firm is expected to resume production beginning in

1995). In the southeast, approximately 100 million tons of bauxite deposits at Manantenima are at present unexploited. A variety of other minerals are mined on a small scale, including agate, beryl, quartz, garnet, amazonite, amethyst, moonstone, tourmaline, citrine, and a number of abrasives and feldspars.

Madagascar depends completely on foreign imports to satisfy its oil needs, but it also refines some petroleum for export. Two-thirds of all electricity demand is met by production from seven hydroelectric power plants that serve Antananarivo, Antsirabe, and the Andriamena chrome mine; the remaining one-third is met by thermal stations. Many plants have their own small diesel or steam generators. Energy needs are also met by firewood and charcoal, which has contributed to the precarious nature of the country's forests and serious erosion problems, and by the bagasse from sugarcane used in sugar production; two power stations using bagasse as fuel and a solar energy plant are planned. Reserves of 100 million tons of coal are found primarily near Sakoa in the southwest, although fewer than 10,000 tons are used on an annual basis. The government seeks to expand domestic coal use.

Another area that the government has begun to develop is that of tourism, which has good potential in view of Madagascar's exotic flora and fauna, and some 5,000 kilometers of beaches. In early 1989, the regime launched a tourism plan that was designed to bring in 100,000 tourists annually by 1995. Thus far, however, the greatest number of tourists attracted has been 52,900 in 1990, compared with 250,000 on the much smaller island of Mauritius. To achieve its goal, Madagascar needs additional infrastructure in the way of transportation, accommodations, and other facilities, as well as a greater sense of security on the part of foreigners—in 1993 gendarmes shot two German researchers in error, causing Germany, which was Madagascar's second largest tourist source, to boycott the island.

## Foreign Trade

As of 1992, 81.1 percent (US$311 million) of Madagascar's total exports of US$383.5 million were to the industrialized West. Four countries served as the primary destination of Malagasy goods: France (30.4 percent), the United States (13.3 percent), Germany (10.1 percent) and Japan (7.5 percent) (see table 6, Appendix). In contrast, only 51 percent (US$313.2 million) of Madagascar's total imports of US$614.1 million in 1992 came from the industrialized West (a sharp decline from 78.7 percent in 1980), and only France remained a significant partner (providing 29.9 of Madagascar's imports). Whereas Japan and Germany were responsible for 4.3 and 3.9 percent of Madagascar's imports, respectively, the United States contributed a meager 1.1 percent. Russia remains marginal in terms of both imports and exports (less than 1 percent), and, along with the other former communist countries, has never constituted a major trading partner of Madagascar. In aggregate terms, Madagascar's exports to the industrialized West dropped slightly from US$316 million in 1980 to US$311 million in 1992.

Two trends in trade with the developing world stand out. First, Madagascar slightly increased the percentage of goods exported to other southern countries from 14.3 percent in 1980 to 18.8 percent in 1992. Other African countries were the major market for Malagasy goods (11.0 percent) in 1992, Asia came in second (7.1 percent), and the Middle East and Latin America together imported only 0.5 percent. In aggregate terms, Madagascar's exports to the developing south expanded from US$57.5 million in 1980 to US$72.3 million in 1992.

A second, more noticeable shift occurred in terms of Madagascar's imports from other southern countries, increasing from US$55 million in 1980 to US$301 million in 1992. In sharp contrast to regional patterns related to exports, Madagascar imported the majority of its goods from Asia (15.5 percent) and the Middle East (8.5 percent). Other African countries were the source of only 6.1 percent of Madagascar's imports, and Latin America registered the negligible total of 2.1 percent. A burgeoning trade deficit that exceeded US$230 million in 1992 remains one of the biggest trade problems confronting Malagasy policy makers.

## Transportation and Telecommunications

The expansion of the economy is hindered by an inadequate transportation system that deteriorated throughout the 1980s (see fig. 4). Only 4,000 kilometers (10 percent) of an estimated 40,000-kilometer road network are asphalted (no all-weather road links the capital with the southern and northern extremes of the island), and the state-controlled railroad consists of 1,095 kilometers of track in two limited (and separate) railroad systems. The first connects the capital of Antananarivo with the port city of Toamasina, the rice-producing area of

Lake Alaotra, and the town of Antsirabe; the second connects the regional capital of Fianarantsoa with the coastal town of Manakara.

The country's ports and airports fare better than the land or rail network. Madagascar has fifteen major ports along the 4,828-kilometer coastline, of which Toamasina, Mahajanga, and Antsiranana are the most important. The air network revolves around the main international airport, Ivato-Antananarivo. The country technically contains 211 airfields, but only approximately 50 percent are usable, and only thirty maintain permanent-surface runways. Whereas the national airline, Air Madagascar, is two-thirds owned by the government (Air France owns the remaining one-third), twelve airports (including Ivato-Antananarivo) were taken over in 1990 by a private company, Aéroports de Madagascar.

In 1994 Madagascar's telecommunications system was sparse, serving only commercial users and residents of large towns and cities. Almost 60 percent of the country's 27,200 telephones were located in Antananarivo in 1989. Figures for that year showed that the country averaged only three telephones per 1,000 inhabitants, and service was limited to government offices, large companies, and a few wealthy families in urban areas. The telecommunications system deteriorated appreciably during the 1980s so that Madagascar had fewer telephones in 1994 than in 1975. Two satellite ground stations near the capital provide excellent international links via the International Telecommunications Satellite Organization's (Intelsat's) Indian Ocean satellite and the Symphonic ground station, working with a European telecommunications satellite.

Broadcast services are thinly scattered countrywide. The entire country has only seventeen mediumwave amplitude modulation (AM) radio stations—a powerful transmitter in the capital and sixteen low-power repeaters in other cities. A government-owned, AM shortwave station broadcasting in French and Malagasy on five frequencies reaches listeners in remote locations and in neighboring countries. In addition, Radio Nederlands has a powerful station in western Madagascar that relays programs throughout Africa and the Indian Ocean on shortwave frequencies. Antananarivo and two other cities each have a single frequency modulation (FM) station. Thirty-seven low-power television transmitters broadcast for three and a half hours daily in urban areas.

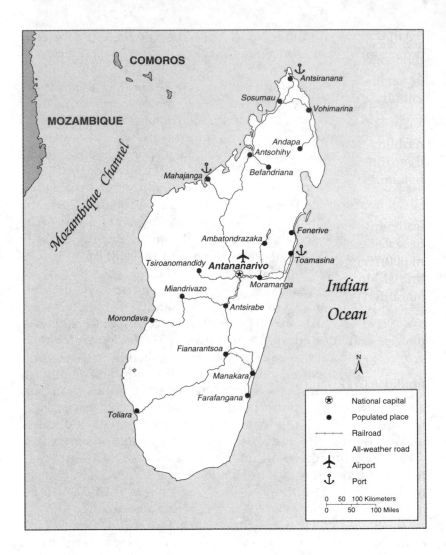

*Figure 4. Madagascar: Transportation System, 1994*

## Government and Politics

### Constitution and Institutions of Governance

The Third Republic received its first expression of popular support and legitimacy on August 19, 1992, when the constitutional framework constructed by the National Conference was approved by more than 75 percent of those voting in a popular referendum (the constitution took effect on September 12). On this date, the people overwhelmingly approved a new constitution consisting of 149 articles that provided for the separation of powers among the executive, legislative, and judicial branches of government; the creation of a multiparty political system; and the protection of individual human rights and freedom of speech.

The power of the executive branch is divided between a president who is elected by universal suffrage and a prime minister from the parliament who is nominated by his/her peers but who must be approved by the president. If the nominee for prime minister does not achieve an absolute majority of support within the parliament, the president may choose a candidate from the parliament who will serve for one year. As captured in the Malagasy concept *ray aman-dreny* (father and mother of the nation), enshrined in Article 44 of the constitution, the president serves as the symbol of national unity. The president also is the recognized leader of foreign policy and constitutes by far the single most powerful political person within the country. All presidential decrees must be counter signed, however, and the president is bound by the constitutional reality that the prime minister is responsible for the functioning of the government.

The president is elected for a five-year period and is limited to two terms in office. In the event that no candidate wins a simple majority of the popular vote, a run-off election is held between the two leading candidates within a period of two months. The most important unwritten law regarding the executive branch revolves around the *côtier*/central highlands distinction. If a *côtier* is elected president, it is understood that a Merina will fill the position of prime minister, and vice versa. In the case of the first national elections held under the Third Republic, for example, the elected president—Zafy—who is a *côtier*, chose a prime minister—Francisque Ravony—from the ranks of the Merina (although several of the Merina elite were not entirely happy with the choice because Ravony is only half Merina).

The constitution provides for a bicameral parliament composed of a Senate and a National Assembly (Assembleé Nationale). The Senate represents territorial groups and serves as the consultative chamber on social and economic issues. Two-thirds of its members are chosen by an Electoral College, and the remaining one-third are chosen by the president. Envisioned elections for 1994 had not been held as of June 1994. The National Assembly consists of 138 deputies elected by universal suffrage using a proportional representation list-system. Both senators and deputies serve for four years. The June 16, 1993, elections resulted in about half the deputies elected being members of the Forces Vives. The remainder belonged to six parties, of which the largest had fifteen deputies and the smallest nine deputies. The parliament as a whole operates with a variety of classic parliamentary measures, such as a vote of no confidence, that enable it to serve as a check on the power of the executive.

A new system of local governance under the constitution is known as the Decentralized Territorial Authorities (Collectivités Territoriales Décentralisées). According to the decentralization law adopted by the National Assembly in March 1994, twenty-eight regions (*faritra*), more than 100 departments (*fileovana*), and fewer than 1,000 communes (*faribohitra*) have been created. Certain urban communes, such as the cities of Antananarivo, Nosy-Be, and Sainte Marie, will function as departments. Envisioned as regional vehicles for popular input in which members are elected by universal suffrage, these authorities have yet to be implemented; their exact role in the policy-making process remains ill-defined, but it is contemplated that the national government will handle such areas as foreign affairs, defense, public security, justice, currency, and broad economic planning and policy, leaving economic implementation to the decentralized bodies. However, the Zafy regime is confident that, once functioning, these regional boards will take the political initiative away from the so-called federalist opposition, which has been seeking to shift power away from the central government to the regions.

A strong, independent judiciary is also enshrined in the 1992 constitution. An eleven-member Supreme Court serves as the highest arbiter of the laws of the land. Other judicial bodies include the Administrative and Financial Constitutional Court, the Appeals Courts, tribunals, and the High Court of Justice. The creation of this complex system indicates the desire of the constitutional framers for a society built upon the rule of law. Indeed, the constitution explicitly outlines the fundamental rights of individual citizens and groups (most notably freedom of speech) and guarantees the existence of an independent press free from government control or censorship.

The creation of a truly free and fair multiparty system is the centerpiece of the new constitutional order. In sharp contrast to the Ratsiraka era, when political parties could only exist under the ideological umbrella of the FNDR, democratization of the political system has led to the proliferation of political parties of all ideological stripes. In the first legislative elections held under the Third Republic in 1993, for example, more than 120 political parties fielded at least 4,000 candidates for a total of 138 legislative seats. Despite constitutional guarantees concerning the rights of citizens to form political parties without fear of government retribution, parties that call for ethnic or religious segregation or demonstrably endanger national unity are subject to being banned.

The electoral system is designed to promote and facilitate widespread popular participation. In fact, it is argued that the proportional representation list-system (including the rule of the largest remainder) for electing deputies actually encourages large numbers of candidates to take part. All resident citizens eighteen years of age or older can vote in elections, but candidates must be at least twenty-one years of age to participate. Electoral registers are usually revised during a two-month period beginning in December, and the country is divided into sixty-eight constituencies for electoral purposes. Although there was a four-month gap between the end of the first presidential elections and the first legislative elections held under the Third Republic in 1993, legislative elections are supposed to be held no less than two months after the end of presidential elections. The next presidential elections are scheduled for 1998.

## The *Fokonolona* and Traditional Governance

Madagascar has a tradition of limited village self-rule associated with the institution of the *fokonolona*—a village council composed of village elders and other local notables. After having been alternately suppressed and encouraged by the French colonial authorities, authorities officially revived the *fokonolona* in 1962 in an attempt to involve local communities in plans for rural economic and social development. The perceived usefulness of the *fokonolona* derived from its traditional role of maintaining order in the village and providing social and economic assistance.

In 1973 the Ramanantsoa military regime furthered the self-rule concept by establishing self-governing bodies at the local level. Government functionaries who were formerly appointed were to be replaced by elected officials. Yet it was not until 1975, under the leadership of Ratsiraka, that the *fokonolona* was given constitutional recognition as the "decentralized collective of the state" responsible for economic, social, cultural, and municipal development at the local level. Despite his best intentions, during Ratsiraka's rule the *fokonolona* was still far from an idealized self-governing institution. Its governing bodies were dominated, as in the past, by conservative elders, and participation by youth was either minimal or not encouraged by elders. Under the Zafy regime the *fokonolona* will continue to offer policy guidance at the local level, but it has been superseded by the Decentralized Territorial Collectives.

The *fokonolona* often is characterized as one of the most characteristic Malagasy social institutions. It is, in fact, not a "pan-Malagasy" cultural element but an institution that evolved among the Merina and was implanted in other parts of the country by both the Merina and the French. Even among the neighboring Betsileo, it is considered something of a foreign implantation. Nonetheless, the *fokonolona* offers aid to members in need (such as when a child is born or a funeral is held), undertakes village projects (such as the repair of rice fields or village buildings after a cyclone), coordinates mutual aid at planting and harvest time, and occasionally chastises—or ostracizes—those considered wrongdoers.

The *fokonolona* ties individuals together in a network of mutual obligations. Its meetings bring together in a cooperative setting people of different kinship groups within a village, and the common use of fictive kinship terms promotes the creation of an atmosphere of amity and solidarity (*fihavanana*), necessary for sincere cooperation. The *fokonolona*, however, traditionally has not been a democratic institution despite its town-meeting character, because its meetings tend to be dominated by influential local notables. Local political power remains a function of age and membership in a high-status kinship group; in some cases, the descendants of slaves (*andevo*) attend *fokonolona* meetings, but their influence is marginal.

At *fokonolona* meetings, it is possible to see one of Madagascar's most striking cultural expressions, the *kabary* (discourse), a lengthy speech in which a speaker uses flowery and poetic language to make a critical point in a most indirect fashion. The people will listen silently from beginning to end. Those who disagree will not express their opinion but will counter with a speech that at first seems to support the first speaker but that actually contains a hidden counterproposal. Speakers may express their views by telling jokes. If people laugh or if they simply act according to the second speaker's proposal, the first has lost. Rarely if ever does an open confrontation between speakers occur.

## Foreign Relations

Close Franco-Malagasy ties formed the cornerstone of Madagascar's foreign policy in the early independence years, as witnessed by the signing of fourteen agreements and conventions with France. An Economic and Financial Cooperation Agreement signed in June 1960 specified and regulated Madagascar's status as a member of the Franc Zone. Other economic agreements ensured the sanctity of existing French economic interests and, therefore, continued strong levels of French influence over Madagascar's economy. The Malagasy role was largely limited to the impact of decision makers in the upper echelons of government and input at the grass-roots level by small-scale farmers producing for subsistence or export. Other sectors by and large remained the domain of French trading conglomerates, large-scale agriculturalists, or Chinese and Indian intermediaries.

In the realm of security, defense agreements underscored France's willingness to provide strategic protection for Madagascar. France was allowed access to military bases and installations in Madagascar. These included the natural harbor of Antsiranana at the northern end of the island and the Ivato airfield near Antananarivo. France also enjoyed complete freedom of movement in the island's airspaces and coastal waters. In return for these benefits, France provided military aid, technical assistance, and training for Malagasy security forces.

French influence was equally strong in the cultural realm. The country's intellectual elite was French-speaking, and many prominent Malagasy studied in French *lycées* and acquired degrees from French universities. Newspapers and periodicals published in French as well as Malagasy circulated in Antananarivo and other major cities. French was the language of instruction for higher education, and many teachers were French. At secondary and higher levels, the curriculum was modeled closely on that of France.

The strengthening of ties with France was complemented by a desire to enhance links with other Western countries, including Britain, Italy, Switzerland, the Federal Republic of Germany (West Germany), and most notably the United States. In October 1963, the Tsiranana regime consented to the construction of a National Aeronautics and Space Administration (NASA) satellite tracking station near the old airport outside the capital. In return, the United States initiated a modest foreign assistance program that guaranteed private investment in the island's economy and made available a number of fellowships to students from Madagascar. Madagascar also established diplomatic links with other newly emerging nations, particularly former French colonies in Africa, and strengthened relationships with Asian countries, most notably Japan, India, and Indonesia.

A significant shift occurred in Madagascar's foreign policy after the downfall of the Tsiranana regime in 1972. In a series of diplomatic moves that three years later were embraced by the Ratsiraka regime as the cornerstones of the Second Republic, the Ramanantsoa regime pronounced Madagascar's commitment to nonalignment, anti-imperialism, anticolonialism, and antiracism in international affairs. In the context of the privileged Franco-Malagasy relationship, these themes translated into harsh rhetoric concerning the necessity of revoking the "slavery agreements" of the Tsiranana regime, followed by the uncompensated nationalization of all French banks and insurance firms in June 1975, contributing to the dramatic cooling of diplomatic relations. Moreover, in June 1976, the Ratsiraka regime laid claim to small, rocky, French-held islands around Madagascar, including the Glorieuses (claimed concurrently by Comoros), Juan de Nova, Europa, Bassas da India, and Tromelin (also claimed by Mauritius). Originally administered as part of French-ruled Madagascar, these possessions were split off just prior to independence in 1960 and include some minor military facilities.

Diplomatic links also soured with other Western powers, such as Britain, which closed its embassy in 1975. In the case of the United States, the immediate cause of strained ties was the Ratsiraka regime's decision to close the NASA tracking station. Another source of friction was the frequent verbal assaults by the Ratsiraka regime against the United States military presence at Diego Garcia Island. The Malagasy position was that, in accordance with a UN resolution passed in 1971, the Indian Ocean should be a demilitarized, nuclear-free zone of peace. Nonetheless, trade relations remained essentially unaffected,

*Presidential Palace, Antananarivo*
*Courtesy J.D. von Pischke*

and diplomatic relations continued, albeit at the reduced level of chargés d'affaires.

The most dramatic development was the strengthening of ties with Eastern Europe and with other communist regimes. After establishing diplomatic links with the Soviet Union in October 1972—followed one month later by the establishment of ties with China and the Democratic People's Republic of Korea (North Korea)—ties were enhanced in the economic, cultural, and politico-military realms. Soviet development assistance was directed toward the fields of agriculture, medicine, science, and technology, and scholarships were provided to at least 2,000 Malagasy students to study in the Soviet Union. A new Malagasy-Soviet Intergovernmental Commission on Economic and Technical Cooperation and Trade facilitated these links. The Soviet Union was particularly interested in promoting security ties with the Ratsiraka regime. In addition to providing military advisers and technical advice, the former Soviet Union became the primary source of military equipment for the Malagasy Armed Forces, including providing access to MiG–21 Fishbed jet fighters, and aided in the construction of a series of sealane intercept stations along Madagascar's west coast astride the Mozambique Channel. These stations were eventually dismantled in 1983 after protests by the West.

Relationships with other communist countries developed in a variety of fields. Whereas Cuba provided technical assistance within the educational realm, China funded the construction of roads between Moramanga and Toamasina, and built a new sugar factory near Morondava. The Ratsiraka regime was especially impressed by North Korean leader Kim Il Sung and his ideology of national self-reliance known as *juche* (or *chuch'e*), hosting an international conference on this topic in Antananarivo in 1976. North Korean assistance was fairly extensive in the fields of agriculture and irrigation. The North Koreans were most noted, however, for their training of Ratsiraka's presidential security unit and the construction of a presidential bunker at Iavohola.

New directions in foreign policy were equally pronounced in Madagascar's relationships with other developing countries and its positions in a variety of international forums. In addition to breaking ties with Israel and South Africa, the Ramanantsoa/Ratsiraka regimes strengthened links with Libya, the Palestine Liberation Organization, and liberation movements in southern Africa and the Western Sahara. Madagascar also joined the Nonaligned Movement, became more active in the Organization of African Unity (OAU), and took positions in the UN that favored the communist states, including abstaining on a resolution that denounced the Soviet Union's invasion of Afghanistan in 1979 and supporting Vietnam's invasion of Cambodia in 1978. In conjunction with his Cuban and Soviet allies, Ratsiraka even tried to broker an end to rising tensions between Marxist Ethiopia and Marxist Somalia just prior to the outbreak of the Ogaden War in 1977–78.

Despite some alarmist projections that the communist countries would replace the West and turn Madagascar into a Soviet satellite, the changes in Madagascar's foreign policies represented a short-term shift rather than a true break with the past. The Ratsiraka regime had gained little in the form of economic assistance from its friendly relations with the Soviet Union and other communist countries—aid from these sources constituted less than 1 percent of all bilateral assistance from 1977 to 1980—and was confronted with the harsh realities of economic decline. As a result, an increasingly pragmatic Ratsiraka sought to reaffirm and strengthen Madagascar's foreign policy relationships with the West. Indeed, relations with the West appeared to be on the upswing at the beginning of the 1980s, whereas those with the communist countries were more or less static—despite the similarity of views on a wide range of international issues routinely reaffirmed by the spokespersons of Madagascar and of communist countries. As was the case with other self-proclaimed Marxist regimes during the 1970s and the 1980s, Ratsiraka pursued politico-military links with the Soviet Union while seeking to maintain economic ties with the West.

Diplomatic overtures to France served as the logical starting point for achieving a balance in Madagascar's foreign policy relationships. As early as 1977, Ratsiraka provided assurances concerning compensation for French firms nationalized during the mid-1970s in order to foster greater official and private investment in Madagascar. France responded positively, as demonstrated by the tremendous increase in foreign assistance from US$38.4 million in 1979 to US$96.4 million in 1982. Indeed, as of the early 1980s, France remained Madagascar's most important foreign policy partner. It was the principal source of foreign assistance and the most valuable trading partner. The dispute over French control of neighboring islands, although unresolved, had little if any ill effect on Franco-Malagasy relations, mainly because the Ratsiraka regime no longer publicly pressed this issue in international forums. (The motion asking France to cede the islands had been adopted by the UN General Assembly by a ninety-seven to seven vote in 1979 with thirty-six abstentions.)

The diversification of ties, thereby avoiding dependence on any single power, served as another cornerstone of Madagascar's foreign policy initiatives during the 1980s. Relations were fully restored with Washington in November 1980 when United States Ambassador Fernando E. Rondon assumed his post for the first time since his predecessor had been recalled during the summer of 1975. Receiving the new envoy, Ratsiraka expressed the hope that "fruitful, loyal, and lasting cooperation" would develop between the two countries and that there would be "no further misunderstandings" as a result of differing opinions on international issues. Other major events included the reopening of the British embassy in 1979, Ratsiraka's visits with President Ronald Reagan in Washington in 1982 and 1983, the opening of a World Bank office in Antananarivo in 1983, and the strengthening of links with other industrialized countries, most notably Japan.

The levels of foreign assistance provided by the West demonstrate the success of Ratsiraka's diplomatic initiatives (see table 7, Appendix). Bilateral aid from the West constituted only US$36.3 million one year after Ratsiraka had taken power in 1975. Four years after the beginning of the foreign policy changes initiated by the Ramantsoa regime, this amount increased to US$168.1 million in 1982, to US$217.6 million in 1988, and to US$365.5 million in 1991. Similarly, multilateral assistance from Western financial institutions, such as the IMF and the European Common Market (European Union), increased from US$34.1 million in 1976 to US$80.6 million in 1982, to US$108.9 million in 1988, and to US$191.4 million in 1991.

Equally important, Ratsiraka's policies led to a diversification of Madagascar's sources of foreign assistance. Although France in 1991 still provided approximately 43 percent (US$157.0 million) of Madagascar's bilateral foreign assistance, in 1988 it had provided approximately 50 percent (US$108.5 million). The amount marked a significant decline from almost total dependence in 1970 when nearly 90 percent of all Western assistance was provided by France. Noteworthy, however, was France's provision of US$655.4 million of the total US$1,334.5 million multilateral aid that Madagascar received between 1985 and 1990. In addition, France gave Madagascar loan assistance for such projects as telecommunications, transportation, and banking, and canceled US$715 million in debts that the Madagascar government owed France. In 1993 Madagascar received about US$167 million in aid from France compared with about US$152 million in aid received from France in 1992. Whereas the United States provided US$71.0 million in multilateral aid in 1991, Japan and Germany extended US$56.8 million and US$30.3 million respectively.

United States direct development aid has become increasingly important for Madagascar and has risen from about US$10 million in 1990 to US$13.5 million in 1991 (US$28 million was authorized but could not be used because of strikes and the disrupted political and economic situation), US$40 million in 1992, and US$40.6 million in 1993. Of the 1993 total, US$20.4 million was earmarked for environmental protection and US$10 million for the private sector.

The growing partnership with the West was cemented by dramatic changes in the international system and in Madagascar's domestic political system. The fall of the Berlin Wall in 1989 signaled the beginning of a process eventually leading to the downfall of communist regimes and trading partners in Eastern Europe, the fragmentation of the Soviet Union, and the increasing international isolation of North Korea and Cuba as pariah regimes. Furthermore, this international trend facilitated the rise of popular pressures for a multiparty democracy in Madagascar, eventually leading to the downfall of Ratsiraka's Second Republic and its replacement in 1993 with a democratically inspired Third Republic under the leadership of Zafy.

The cornerstone of Madagascar's foreign policy in the post-Cold War era is the continued diversification of ties, with an emphasis on promoting economic exchanges. In addition to establishing formal diplomatic ties with the Republic of Korea (South Korea) in May 1993, negotiations were initiated to restore diplomatic links with Israel and South Africa. In each of these cases, diplomatic links are perceived as the precursor to lucrative trading agreements. For example, one month after establishing diplomatic ties with South Korea, Madagascar hosted a South Korean trade mission that included representatives of six major South Korean companies: Daewoo, Dong Yong Electronics, Hyundai, Kolon, Peace Industries, and Samsung. As underscored by Prime Minister Ravony, one of the most critical challenges facing Madagascar is the restructuring of its embassies and foreign policy to "objectives of economic redeployment" in the post-Cold War era. Of particular interest to Madagascar, in view of their proximity and commercial potential, are relations and trade with India, Mauritius, Australia, and South Africa.

The benefits associated with changes in the international environment have an impact on Madagascar's domestic political system. Similar to other newly installed African democracies at the beginning of the 1990s, the Zafy regime confronts the challenge of consolidating still-fragile democratic practices and governing institutions in a significantly changed international environment. Although such potential benefits associated with the end of the Cold War as a renewed focus on economic as opposed to military investments have been heralded by Western observers, the leaders of African countries, including Madagascar, rightfully wonder if their countries will be further marginalized as former benefactors either turn inward or toward more lucrative economic markets in Asia and Latin America. Equally important, the Zafy regime faces balancing rising public demands to receive immediately the fruits of democratization with the harsh reality of the political constraints of a democratic system. Indeed, democratization has not proved to be a quick panacea for resolving such issues as the necessity of overhauling and privatizing largely inert and bloated state-operated economic enterprises, and has even led to the emergence of new problems, most notably federalist demands for greater regional autonomy. Nonetheless, Madagascar's political elite clearly seems committed to the continued reform and strengthening of multiparty democracy, as well as the expansion of the country's role as a leader in both regional and international forums.

\* \* \*

The amount of scholarship devoted to Madagascar in the English language is small but growing, and complements a larger body of literature in the French language and a smaller body of research in the Malagasy language. For the most up-to-date analyses by francophone scholars, see a special 1993 edition of *Politique Africaine* devoted to Madagascar.

Several works offer a useful introduction to the society, economics, and especially the politics of Madagascar. One of the earliest and most useful introductions in English is Virginia Thompson and Richard Adloff, *The Malagasy Republic: Madagascar Today*. A more recent introduction, Maureen Covell's *Madagascar: Politics, Economics, and Society*, is especially relevant for understanding the Marxist policies of the Ratsiraka era. Pierre Vérin's *Madagascar* provides the standard French introduction and includes a useful bibliographic essay.

Several scholars have distinguished themselves as specialists on Madagascar, and their works serve as helpful introductions to each of their discipline's treatment of Madagascar. In the field of anthropology, Maurice Bloch has written several seminal works, most notably *Placing the Dead: Tombs, Ancestral Villages, and Kinship Organization in Madagascar* and *From Blessing to Violence: History and Ideology in the Circumcision Ritual of the Merina of Madagascar*. In the field of history, Mervyn Brown's *Madagascar Rediscovered: A History from Early Times to Independence* provides a good overview of the early history of Madagascar. Raymond K. Kent's *Early Kingdoms in Madagascar, 1500–1700* outlines the historical development of various Malagasy kingdoms. In the field of economics, Frederic L. Pryor's *Poverty, Equity, and Growth in Malawi and Madagascar* is valuable in exploring the equity versus growth dilemma as applied to Madagascar. Paul A. Dorosh's *Macroeconomic Adjustment and the Poor: The Case of Madagascar* offers important insights into the impact of national economic policies and their effect on rural populations.

A variety of bulletins and journals are useful for staying apprised of political and economic developments in Madagascar. The separate economic and political monthly bulletins of the *Africa Research Bulletin* contain brief references. Also recommended are the annual country surveys in the *Africa Contemporary Record: Annual Survey and Documents* and the *Annuaire des Pays de l'Océan Indien.* However, the *Indian Ocean Newsletter* constitutes the most informative weekly source of up-to-date information on political, and to a lesser degree, economic developments in the African countries and islands in or around the Indian Ocean, including Madagascar. The annual country profiles and the quarterly reports of the Economist Intelligence Unit are vital for understanding trends in the Malagasy economy. (For further information and complete citations, see Bibliography.)

# Chapter 2. Mauritius

STELLA CLAVISQUE MARIS INDICI

*National emblem of Mauritius*

# Country Profile

## Country

**Formal Name:** Republic of Mauritius.

**Short Name:** Mauritius.

**Term for Citizens:** Mauritian(s).

**Capital:** Port Louis.

**Date of Independence:** March 12, 1968 (from Britain).

## Geography

**Size:** Approximately 1,865 square kilometers.

**Topography:** Includes Rodrigues Island, some 600 kilometers east, and some uninhabited coralline islands; Mauritius and Rodrigues part of volcanic chain of Mascarene Islands. Mauritius part of broken ring of mountain ranges (about 18 percent) encircling central tableland (about 25 percent), with low-lying coastal plains (about 46 percent) and coral reefs offshore. Numerous rivers and streams.

**Climate:** Below about 400-meter level, humid, subtropical climate. Above that level more temperate. Two seasons: hot and wet summer, November through April, including cyclones December through March; cool and dry winter, May through October. Overall average 200 centimeters of rain annually.

## Society

**Population:** In mid-1993 estimated at 1,106,516 with population growth rate of 0.95 percent. Density more than 537 inhabitants per square kilometer.

**Ethnic Groups:** Constitution recognizes four population categories: Hindus (about 52 percent in 1989), general population (about 29 percent in 1989), Muslims (about 16 percent in 1989), and Sino-Mauritians (about 3 percent in 1989). Ancestors of Hindus and Muslims came from Indian subcontinent; most Sino-Mauritians from Hunan; general category represents all others, including Europeans, Creoles.

**Languages:** English (official), Creole, French, Hindi, Bhojpuri, and Tamil.

**Religion:** In 1990 Hindu (49 percent), Christian (27 percent Roman Catholic, 0.5 percent Protestant), Muslim (16 percent, of which 95 percent Sunni), and other (7.5 percent).

**Education:** Follows British system, free through postsecondary level. University of Mauritius and other postsecondary institutions exist. Overall literacy in 1990: 80 percent; 85 percent for males and 75 percent for females.

**Health:** Government health services accessible to most of population. In 1994 life expectancy at birth estimated at: 70.5 years overall, 74.6 for females, 66.6 years for males. In 1994 infant mortality 18.4 per 1,000 live births.

## Economy

**Gross Domestic Product:** 1993 estimate US$8.6 billion, with growth rate of 5.5 percent, and inflation rate of 10.5 percent.

**Agriculture:** Sugar major crop covering more than 90 percent of cultivated land; more than 500,000 tons annually exported under Lomé Convention. Other products: tea, fresh vegetables, tobacco, cut flowers; livestock raising and fishing.

**Industry:** Industrial development accelerated by establishment of export processing zones (EPZs) in 1971; textiles and wearing apparel main products; efforts at diversification since 1991. Tourism and construction other major industries.

**Exports:** 1992 EPZ exports estimated at US$1.3 billion; major markets Britain, France, United States, and Germany.

**Imports:** 1992 imports estimated at US$1.6 billion; major products: manufactured goods, capital equipment, food, petroleum products, chemicals; major sources: France, South

Africa, Britain, and Japan.

**Balance of Payments:** 1992 trade deficit US$370 million.

**Currency and Exchange Rate:** 1 Mauritian rupee (MauR) = 100 cents. August 1995 exchange rate US$1.00 = MauR14.43.

**Fiscal Year:** July 1–June 30.

**Fiscal Policy:** 1992–94 development plan stressed private sector and free market, aimed at 6 percent annual growth rate.

## Transportation and Telecommunications

**Highways:** In 1984 out of 1,800 kilometers 1,640 paved.

**Ports:** Port Louis.

**Airports:** Two of four airports have permanent-surface runways.

**Telecommunications:** Good, small system using mainly microwave radio relay; more than 48,000 telephones; two radio stations; four television stations; one Indian Ocean International Telecommunications Satellite Corporation (Intelsat) earth station.

## Government and Politics

**Government:** Patterned on British system; political party with majority support in National Assembly chooses prime minister, who selects cabinet. National Assembly has elected representatives from twenty three-member constituencies and one two-member district on Rodrigues. Also eight seats for "best losers": two each for Hindus, Muslims, Chinese, and general population. Mauritius became republic in 1992; president appointed by prime minister and approved by assembly has titular function. Supreme Court heads judicial system, based on Napoleonic Code and English common law. Local government not specified in 1968 constitution, but all councils elected.

**Politics:** Numerous political parties of which government consists of coalition of Militant Socialist Movement (MSM), Mauritian Militant Movement (MMM), and several others; opposition led by Mauritian Labor Party (MLP) and Mauritian Social Democratic Party (PMSD).

**Foreign Relations:** Member of Commonwealth of Nations; has particularly strong relations with Britain, France, India, and, since 1990, South Africa. Mauritius supports Indian Ocean zone of peace; has tension with France over claim to Tromelin Island, 550 kilometers northwest. Some strain in relations with United States because of United States base on Diego Garcia Island. Growing trade relations with Hong Kong, Japan, and China. Member of Organization of African Unity.

## National Security

**Defense Forces:** National Police Force, including paramilitary Special Mobile Force, Special Support Unit, and National Coast Guard.

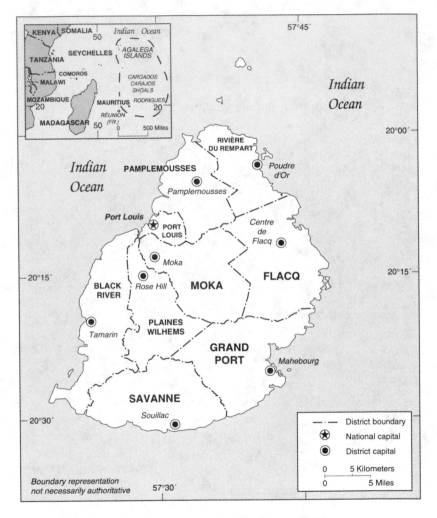

*Figure 5. Mauritius: Administrative Divisions, 1994*

96

THE REPUBLIC OF MAURITIUS is a democratic and prosperous country whose entire population has ancestral origins elsewhere: Europe, Africa, India, and China. Until recently, the country's economy was dominated by the production and export of sugar, a legacy of its French and British colonial past. After independence in 1968, government-directed diversification efforts resulted in the rapid growth of tourism and a manufacturing sector producing mainly textiles for export.

During French colonial rule, from 1767 to 1810, the capital and main port, Port Louis, became an important center for trade, privateering, and naval operations against the British. In addition, French planters established sugarcane estates and built up their fortunes at the expense of the labor of slaves brought from Africa. The French patois, or colloquial language, which evolved among these slaves and their freed descendants, referred to as Creole, has become the everyday language shared by most of the island's inhabitants. French is used in the media and literature, and the Franco-Mauritian descendants of the French settlers continue to dominate the sugar industry and economic life of modern Mauritius.

The British captured the island in 1810 and gave up sovereignty when Mauritius became independent in 1968. During this period, the French plantation aristocracy maintained its economic, and, to a certain degree, its political prominence. The British abolished slavery but provided for cheap labor on the sugar estates by bringing nearly 500,000 indentured workers from the Indian subcontinent. The political history of Mauritius in the twentieth century revolves around the gradual economic and political empowerment of the island's Indian majority.

Mauritian independence was not gained without opposition and violence. Tensions were particularly marked between the Creole and Indian communities, which clashed often at election time, when the rising fortunes of the latter at the expense of the former were most apparent. Nonetheless, successive governments have, with varying success, attempted to work out a peaceful modus vivendi that considers the concerns of the island's myriad communities.

These varied interests have contributed to a political culture that is occasionally volatile and highly fluid, characterized by shifting alliances. A notable lapse from democratic practices, however, occurred in 1971. The Mauritius Labor Party (MLP)-led coalition government of Sir Seewoosagur Ramgoolam, faced with the radical and popular challenge of the Mauritian Militant Movement (Mouvement Militant Mauricien—MMM) and its allies in the unions, promulgated the Public Order Act, which banned many forms of political activity. This state of emergency lasted until 1976. The resilience and stability of Mauritian society, however, were demonstrated by the fact that an MMM-led government eventually gained power through the ballot box in 1982.

Despite many differences, the major political parties have worked successfully toward the country's economic welfare. For this reason, Mauritius has evolved from a primarily agricultural monocrop economy marked by high unemployment, low salaries, and boom-or-bust cycles to one dominated by manufacturing, tourism, and expanding financial services. As Mauritius faces the future, it can look back on its dazzling economic performance in the 1980s and attempt to build on that success by continuing its tradition of political stability, foresight, and prudent development planning.

## Historical Setting

### Early Settlement

Although there is no evidence of human habitation on Mauritius before the early seventeenth century, Phoenicians probably visited the island about 2,000 years ago, and Malays and Arabs stopped on the island in subsequent centuries. The Portuguese charted the waters surrounding the island, which they called Ilha do Cirne (Island of the Swan), in the early sixteenth century. In 1638 the Dutch began colonizing the island, which they named after Maurice of Nassau, the *stadthouder* (head of state) of Holland. The island's first governor, Cornelius Simonsz Gooyer, presided over a small population of Dutch convicts and slaves from Indonesia and Madagascar, who sought to export ambergris, ebony, and other resources. After twenty years, the colony failed, as did a second settlement established in 1664. Poor administration and harsh conditions forced the Dutch to withdraw permanently by 1710. In addition to presiding over the extinction of the dodo bird and leaving behind perhaps some runaway slaves, swarms of rats, and ravaged ebony forests, the Dutch introduced a plant that was to be prominent in the island's future—sugarcane.

French efforts to colonize the area were more successful. Around 1638 they had taken the islands of Rodrigues and Reunion, and in 1715 an expedition of the French East India Company claimed Mauritius for France. The company established a settlement named Île de France on the island in 1722. The company ruled until 1764, when, after a series of inept governors and the bankruptcy of the company, Mauritius became a crown colony administered by the home government. One exception among the early company governors was Mahé de la Bourdonnais, who is still celebrated among Mauritians. During his tenure from 1735 to 1746, he presided over many improvements to the island's infrastructure and promoted its economic development. He made Mauritius the seat of government for all French territories in the region, built up Port Louis, and strengthened the sugar industry by building the island's first sugar refinery. He also brought the first Indian immigrants, who worked as artisans in the port city.

Under French government rule, between 1764 and 1810, Port Louis gained prestige and wealth. The island's population increased, and its planters grew rich. Agricultural prosperity was achieved by exploiting cheap slave labor. Between 1767 and 1797, the population reached 59,000 inhabitants, including 6,200 whites, 3,700 free persons, and 49,100 slaves; the population in each category more than doubled during the period. Although the island's elite culture was distinctly French, its social structure became more complex as the population grew. Port Louis, open to free trade after the demise of the French East India Company, saw a major increase in shipping, especially from Europe and North America. For example, from 1786 to 1810 almost 600 ships from the United States called on Mauritius, and the United States established a consulate in Port Louis in 1794. Privateering was an even greater boon to the economy.

News of the French Revolution reached Mauritius in 1790, prompting settlers unhappy with royal administration to establish more representative forms of government: a colonial assembly and municipal councils. When a squadron arrived three years later, however, to enforce the new French government's abolition of slavery, the settlers turned the squadron back. Napoleon sent a new governor to the island in 1803, resulting in the dissolution of the assembly and councils. The waning of French hegemony in the region permitted a British force of 10,000, carried from the Indian subcontinent by a fleet of seventy ships, to land on Mauritius in 1810. The French capitulated to the British, but the British agreed to leave in place existing legal and administrative structures. The 1814 Treaty of Paris awarded the island, together with the Seychelles and Rodrigues islands, to Britain. English became the official language, but French and Creole dominated. Few British immigrants came to the colony.

The plantation-owning Mauritians of French origin (Franco-Mauritians) resisted British attempts to eradicate slavery. Finally, after much investigation, petitioning, and subterfuge, the authorities abolished slavery in 1835. Plantation owners won several concessions from the government, however, including a payment of 2.1 million pounds sterling and laws obliging freed slaves to remain on their former owner's land as "apprentices" for six years. Widespread desertions by "apprentices" forced the abolition of the laws in 1838, two years before schedule, and created a severe labor shortage.

### Rise of the Sugar Economy

Under the British, Mauritius was no longer a free port. To compensate for the resulting loss in trade, the government encouraged sugar production. In 1825 Britain equalized the duty on sugar from all of its colonies, providing a strong stimulus for Mauritians to produce more sugar. Production leaped from 11,000 tons in 1825 to 21,000 tons in 1826; by 1854 production exceeded 100,000 tons. By the mid-nineteenth century, Mauritius had reached the apex of its importance in the world sugar market: it was Britain's main sugar-producing colony and produced 9.4 percent of the world's sugarcane between 1855 and 1859. Although overall production would continue to rise into the twentieth century, declines in world prices and a massive increase in production in other countries robbed Mauritius of its dominant role in subsequent years. Nonetheless, as sugar increased in economic importance, the percentage of food crop production dropped accordingly, and landownership became concentrated in large, profitable estates.

Indentured workers from India replaced slaves as a source of cheap labor for the sugar plantations. Between 1834 and 1910 (the last year of arrivals), 451,776 Indians migrated to Mauritius, the majority arriving before 1865. Because 157,639

*Statue of Mahé de la Bourdonnais, an early governor appointed by the
French East India Company, in Port Louis, the capital
Courtesy Mari G. Borstelmann*

of these Indians left, the island had a net gain of 294,137 Indians during the period. Most workers came from Bengal and Madras, under contract to work for at least ten years for low wages under harsh conditions. At the end of their contracts, workers supposedly had the option of returning home, but plantation owners often succeeded in eliminating this choice. Many plantation owners punished workers with beatings, hunted down those who ran away and imprisoned them, and unjustly withheld pay. In 1878 a labor law regularized the pay system, and in 1917 the indenture system formally ended. Moreover, a 1922 law permitted workers to choose their places of work.

By 1871 more than 68 percent of the population was Indian, of which more than 25 percent had been born in Mauritius. In 1931 the proportion of Indians in the population was the same, but more than 93 percent of them were natives. By contrast, Mauritius had no immigration from Africa. The freed slaves and their Creole offspring left the plantations to become fishers, dockworkers, and civil servants and formed about 20 percent of the population in 1931. A number of Chinese immigrated during the nineteenth century, and this group made up about 2 percent of the population in 1931.

Starting in the 1860s, the island's sugar economy declined in the face of varied pressures. As sugar beet production and sugarcane production in other countries increased, world prices declined. The opening of the Suez Canal in 1869 shifted trade routes away from the Indian Ocean. And, in addition to regularly occurring droughts and cyclones, a deadly malaria epidemic killed more than 40,000 people between 1867 and 1869. The Franco-Mauritian plantation owners responded in several ways. They cut costs by centralizing sugar production in fewer factories. Furthermore, to increase the profitability of their operations, from the 1870s to about 1920 the planters sold the less productive portions of their landholdings. The process was known as the *grand morcellement,* and it permitted many Indians who could put together enough capital to become small landowners. This meant that for the first time, sugar was produced on small plots with free labor. Between 1864 and 1900, according to one scholar, Indians purchased 24 million rupees worth of land. The Indian rupee became the island's official currency in 1876. By 1921 Indians owned about 35 percent of the island's cultivated land.

## British Colonial Rule

Colonial rule amounted to a thin layer of British administrative and judicial officials attempting to preside over an assertive and powerful Franco-Mauritian elite. Although many members of this elite derived their status and wealth from owning plantations, some were senior police officials and magistrates. Below the Franco-Mauritians on the ladder of social status were the Creoles, descendants of African slaves, some of mixed white descent, who tended to be francophone and generally supportive of the Franco-Mauritians. In the nineteenth century, Indians were at the bottom of the social ladder until their economic opportunities broadened.

In 1831 the British introduced a constitution that provided for a Council of Government whose seven members were nominated by the governor. In an effort to win the support of the Franco-Mauritians, who wanted a greater voice in government, Governor John Pope-Hennessy expanded the council to include ten elected members from nine electoral districts in the constitution of 1886. The franchise was limited to wealthy property owners, who constituted a scant 2 percent of the adult population. Elected municipal councils also appeared in the nineteenth century, first in Port Louis and then in four other major towns. The British established district councils at the end of the nineteenth century. By 1907 the Creole middle class, led by Dr. Eugene Laurent, formed Liberal Action (Action Libérale), which sought to open up political and economic opportunities for themselves. Although it won Port Louis in the 1911 elections against the Oligarchs, Liberal Action dissolved shortly thereafter.

The Indo-Mauritians, who included both Hindus and Muslims, became active in the early twentieth century, thanks in part to the work of a lawyer from India named Manilal Maganlall Doctor. Sent to Mauritius in 1907 at the behest of Mohandas Gandhi (known as Mahatma Gandhi), Manilal was a tireless and eloquent proponent of Indian rights. He sought to inculcate a sense of self-respect in the community by teaching Mauritian Indians about their heritage, and he defended them in the courts against unscrupulous employers. Manilal also founded the *Hindustani,* a newspaper that expressed the concerns of the Indian community.

In 1926 the first Indo-Mauritians were elected to the government council. This small victory, however, did not lead to better conditions in the community. Despite incremental improvements in contracts, wages, and working conditions on the sugar plantations and in processing plants, the work was as hard and daily life as precarious as they had been 100 years earlier. In addition, the boom-or-bust nature of the world sugar economy meant that only the upper classes were insulated from hardship during periods of low world demand. Dissatisfaction on the part of Indian workers and small planters sparked widespread rioting on Mauritius in 1937 and 1943, and a strike in 1938.

During this period, Indian and Creole Mauritians formed several organizations aimed at improving labor laws and introducing political reforms. Dr. Maurice Curé, a noted Creole politician, founded the MLP in 1936. The party attracted urban Creole workers and rural Indian farmers. Another important group was the Indian Cultural Association, and a notable member of this group was Seewoosagur Ramgoolam, who would become the country's first prime minister.

## Toward Independence

After World War II, the pace of constitutional reform quickened as Britain began to loosen its grip on its colonies. In Mauritius this transformation was presided over by Donald

Mackenzie Kennedy, governor from 1942 to 1949. A consultative committee, which for the first time included representatives of all Mauritian communities, made suggestions for a new constitution. In addition to providing for a Legislative Council that was more representative, the new constitution expanded the franchise in 1947 to all adults able to write their names in any of the island's languages. In the 1948 election, eleven of the nineteen candidates winning seats in the Legislative Council were Hindu. However, Governor Mackenzie Kennedy assured the dominance of British and Franco-Mauritian interests by nominating twelve conservatives to the body—some seats were appointed and others elected. This tactic was repeated after the 1953 election by Sir Hilary Blood, the new governor.

A new constitution in 1958 included several changes that increased political participation. It provided for suffrage to adults over twenty-one years of age and divided the country into forty single-member constituencies that elected representatives to the Legislative Council. Also, to assure representation of more constituencies, the constitution allowed the governor to appoint to the council "best losers," candidates whose support was not quite enough to win their races. In the 1959 election, the MLP won twenty-three seats, the Independent Forward Block (IFB) five, the Committee for Muslim Action (Comité d'Action Musulmane—CAM) five, the Mauritian Party (Parti Mauricien—PM) three, and Independents three. The governor awarded best-loser seats to the PM and to Chinese candidates.

After negotiations among the major parties in 1961, the British decided that the winning party's leader in the 1963 election would become premier. In addition, the Legislative Council would become the Legislative Assembly, and the Executive Committee would become the Council of Ministers. The new government would be responsible for all but the island's defense, internal security, and foreign affairs. Although the PM leader, Gaetan Duval, put up strong competition, the MLP, under Ramgoolam, won the election with nineteen seats. Leery that a Hindu victory would jeopardize its economic position, the Creole community expressed unease and opposition in May 1965 riots that left several dead.

A constitutional conference held in London in 1965, with members of all political parties present, decided that the island should become independent from Britain as soon as general elections returned a party in favor of such a notion. Some parties, however, opposed independence. The Franco-Mauritian community and many of the island's Creoles backed the Mauritian Social Democratic Party (Parti Mauricien Social Démocrate—PMSD, formerly the PM), which strongly advocated continued "free association" with Britain. The PMSD representatives walked out of the constitutional conference when it became apparent that one price for independence would be the incorporation of the Chagos Archipelago (formerly administered from Mauritius) into the planned British Indian Ocean Territory (BIOT) along with portions of Seychelles. Other conferees, represented by the CAM, feared that their constituents would be placed at a disadvantage. In the end, the CAM joined the MLP and the IFB to form the winning coalition in the decisive general election of August 7, 1967. A Commonwealth of Nations observer team was satisfied that the highly participatory election was fair. The winning coalition took thirty-nine of the sixty-two seats in the assembly.

## Independent Mauritius

On August 22, 1967, Prime Minister Ramgoolam moved that the assembly request independence according to arrangements made previously with Britain. The new nation came into being on March 12, 1968, as an independent member of the Commonwealth.

Over the years, some elections have been marked by ethnic discord; voting in 1948, 1953, 1959, and 1967, for example, was split roughly along ethnic lines. The Indo-Mauritian majority gained progressively at the expense of other groups as suffrage was extended. More significant was the ethnic rioting in 1964 and 1968. In May 1964, Hindu and Creole communities clashed in the village of Trois Boutiques, outside Souillac. One police officer and one Franco-Mauritian were killed. In early 1968, just six weeks before independence, violence between Creoles and Muslims in the nation's capital left at least twenty-five people dead and hundreds injured before British troops quelled the fighting.

Most Mauritians deplored these outbreaks of violence, and the government responded to both by declaring a state of emergency. One consequence of the unrest was an amendment to the constitution in 1969 extending the first parliament to 1976. Another effect was the entry of the PMSD into the ruling coalition, and the departure of the IFB to form a small opposition party.

Social and economic conditions after World War II contributed to the political conflicts. As the provision of health, education, pension, and other public welfare services expanded, expectations began to rise. The eradication of malaria and parasitic diseases in the 1940s and 1950s improved the life expectancy of the poor and helped fuel a population increase of 3 percent per year. Family planning measures reduced the population growth rate in the 1960s and 1970s, but the labor force continued to increase rapidly. Registered unemployment stood at more than 12 percent of the work force on the eve of independence.

The unemployed, especially the youth, rallied behind a new political party, the MMM, formed in 1969. Its organizers were Paul Bérenger (a Franco-Mauritian), Dev Virahsawmy (a Telegu speaker), and Jooneed Jeerooburkhan (a Muslim). They appealed to poor and working-class Mauritians of all backgrounds with their radical program of socialist change. An early show of strength for the party was a by-election victory in the prime minister's district in 1970. With widespread union support, the MMM called a number of debilitating strikes in 1971, demanding better benefits for workers and elections by 1972, the year previously mandated. Four PMSD members made attempts on the lives of Virahsawmy and Bérenger in November 1971. The authorities placed many of the party's leadership and rank and file in jail under the Public Order Act of 1971. The government also banned political meetings, suspended twelve unions, and closed *Le Militant*, the MMM newspaper. The government extended the state of emergency until 1976, proscribing most political opposition.

The MMM succeeded in placing the issue of job creation high on the list of priorities for the country's first economic development plan, covering 1971–75. The plan called for additional jobs in manufacturing and in agriculture outside sugar production. It also initiated a program called Work for All (Travail pour Tous), which created the Development Works Corporation (DWC) to hire laborers for public construction and relief projects. These policies, high sugar prices, growth in tourism, and the success of the newly created export processing zones (EPZs) helped reduce the unemployment rate to 7 percent by 1976.

The slow economic progress enabled the MMM to make significant gains in the closely fought 1976 general elections; the party won 40 percent of the vote and thirty-four of the seventy assembly seats. Part of the MMM's success came from the lowering of the voting age to eighteen in 1975, which allowed the party to garner the youth vote across ethnic lines. In addition, the ruling coalition hurt itself by nominating incompetent and corrupt candidates, failing to win the support of trade unions, and maintaining unpopular positions regarding the Chagos Archipelago and the United States military presence on Diego Garcia. (The MMM favored returning to Mauritian sovereignty the Chagos Archipelago, of which Diego Garcia was a part.)

The MLP and the PMSD, both of which had declined in popularity since the previous election, formed a coalition government to lock the MMM out of power. This government was plagued by internal division: MLP chief whip Harish Boodhoo broke off to form the Mauritian Socialist Party (Parti Socialiste Mauricien—PSM). In addition, the government suffered from political corruption scandals, poor economic performance, and the destructive effects of cyclones each year from 1979 to 1981. These and other factors were instrumental in the 1982 electoral victory of a new MMM-PSM coalition. In a concession to Hindu political sensibilities, Anerood Jugnauth was named prime minister. Paul Bérenger served as minister of finance. Faced with the realities of governing the country, including heavy obligations to the International Monetary Fund (IMF—see Glossary) and the World Bank (see Glossary), the government backed away from the radical policies the MMM espoused when it was in opposition. It succeeded in expanding regional cooperation abroad and worked at modest nationalization and job creation at home. The ruling coalition broke up in less than a year, however, and new elections were held in August 1983.

Prime Minister Jugnauth founded a new party, the Militant Socialist Movement (Mouvement Socialiste Militant), subsequently renamed the Mauritian Socialist Movement (Mouvement Socialiste Mauricien—MSM) after combining with the PSM. The MSM joined during the 1983 election with the MLP and the PMSD to win comfortably. In 1984 some MLP members fell out with the government after several MLP ministers were dismissed. Those MLP members who stayed in the ruling coalition, called the Alliance, formed the Assembly of Mauritian Workers (Rassemblement des Travaillistes Mauriciens—

RTM). In December 1985, however, the government suffered several setbacks that would trouble it for many months to come: MMM municipal election victories; the death of Ramgoolam, a close adviser to Jugnauth and a respected figure in national politics; and a drug scandal involving four Alliance deputies caught with twenty-one kilograms of heroin at the Amsterdam airport. In a surprising electoral victory in 1987, the Alliance retained power, thanks in large part to Jugnauth's handling of the economy. The MMM, under the leadership of Dr. Prem Nababsing, won twenty-one seats and was allotted three best-loser seats.

Beginning with the PMSD's defection in August 1988, the Alliance began to unravel. The MSM thwarted the growing political threat posed by a resurgent MLP by forging an alliance with the MMM, built in part on the promise of making Mauritius a republic. The MSM/MMM coalition won a convincing victory in September 1991 and quickly passed changes in the constitution that led to the declaration of Mauritius as a republic in March 1992.

## Physical Environment

### Geography

The island of Mauritius lies about 800 kilometers east of Madagascar between longitudes 57°18' and 57°49' east, and latitudes 19°59' and 20°32' south. Pearl-shaped, it is sixty-one kilometers long and forty-six kilometers wide at the extremes and has a total land area of some 1,865 square kilometers—about the size of Rhode Island. Mauritian territory also incorporates the island of Rodrigues, some 600 kilometers to the east, which is 119 square kilometers in area. Two tiny dependencies to the north of Mauritius, the Agalega Islands and the Cargados Carajos Shoals (also known as the St. Brandon Rocks), are unpopulated (see fig. 5). Nonetheless, their location permits the nation's exclusive economic zone (EEZ—see Glossary) to cover about 1.2 million square kilometers of the Indian Ocean. Just off the Mauritian coast lie some twenty uninhabited islands. Mauritius and France both claim sovereignty over Tromelin, 483 kilometers to the northwest. Mauritius sought to regain sovereignty, lost just before independence in 1968, over the Chagos Archipelago (1,931 kilometers to the northeast), which includes the Diego Garcia atoll.

*Mountain view in Mauritius*
*Courtesy Mari G. Borstelmann*

Mauritius and Rodrigues are part of the Mascarene Islands, a chain of volcanic islands that include Reunion, the nation's nearest neighbor at 145 kilometers to the southwest and governed as an overseas territory (*département*) of France. The islands are perched on submarine ridges, including the Mascarene Plateau, which runs for some 3,000 kilometers in an arc bowed outward the African mainland, and the Rodrigues Fracture Zone, which ripples eastward and connects this underwater platcau with the massive Mid-Indian Ridge.

Mauritius is relatively young geologically, having been created by volcanic activity some 12 million years ago. There has been no active volcano on the island for more than 100,000 years. The island consists of a broken ring of mountain ranges, some 600 to 800 meters above sea level, encircling a central tableland that slopes from a level of 300 meters in the north to 600 meters in the southwest. The mountains are surrounded by low-lying, sometimes hilly, coastal plains, except in the southwest where the drop-off is precipitous. The mountains are steepest toward the center of the island and are probably the tips of the eroded original shield volcano. The sea has built up a ring of coral reefs around most of the 160 kilometers of coastline, which form many shallow lagoons, white coral sand beaches, and dunes. Two of the best harbors are Port Louis and Mahébourg. Politically, the island is divided into eight administrative divisions called districts and one municipality where the capital, Port Louis, is located.

Lowland plains and gently undulating slopes cover about 46 percent of the total land area. Low-lying plains make up most of the Pamplemousses, Rivière du Rempart, and Flacq districts; southern Grand Port District; the heavily populated northwestern section of Plaines Wilhems District from Beau Bassin to Quatre Bornes and to the sea; and smaller areas around Chemin Grenier. These areas are planted with sugarcane and mixed vegetable crops. The districts of Port Louis and Black River and the more hilly interior plains leading up to the tableland support tea, rice, and sugarcane cultivation and include areas of savanna and scrub forest.

The central tableland covers about a quarter of the island. A large plateau spans most of the districts of Moka, eastern Plaines Wilhems, and western Grand Port, where mostly sugarcane and vegetables are harvested, except around Curepipe and Vacoas, where tea is grown. The southern part of the tableland—in the districts of Black River, Savanne, and southern Plaines Wilhems—is much smaller and heavily dissected with a diverse topography. It contains tea and forest plantations, including reserves of indigenous trees.

Mountains cover about 18 percent of the terrain. The Moka-Long Mountain Range is situated in the northwest near Port Louis, and its highest peak is Pieter Both (823 meters). The Rivière Noire Mountains and Savanne Mountains are in the west and southwest, where Mont Piton of the Petite Rivière Noire (828 meters) is the highest point on the island. The mountains are broken into four ridges that produce deep valleys, gorges, and waterfalls. The Grand Port Range lies in the east, and to its north are the isolated Mont Blanche (520 meters) and Fayences Mountain (425 meters).

Rivers and streams dot the island; many of them are formed in the crevices between land created by new and old lava flows. Drainage radiates from the central tableland to the sea, and many rivers are steeply graded with rapids and falls. Torrential flows are common during storms and cyclones. Marshes and ponds lie in the tableland and on the coastal plain, but the country has only two natural lakes, both crater lakes. The largest of several man-made reservoirs is the Mare aux Vacoas.

Rodrigues Island was formed earlier than Mauritius, but in a similar fashion. It sits lengthwise on an east-west axis, along which runs a spine-like mountain range some 600 meters above sea level. The north-south spurs of these mountains cut deep crevices into the terrain.

The other dependencies of Mauritius are coralline rather than volcanic islands. The two Agalega islands are connected by a sandbar and covered with coconut palms. The Cargados Carajos Shoals are a group of more than twenty islands, none more than one square kilometer in area, which are primarily fishing stations.

## Climate

Mauritius has two kinds of climate. Below the 400-meter level on most of the windward (southeastern) side of the island and below 450 meters on the leeward side, a humid, subtropical climate prevails. Above these altitudes, the climate is more temperate, but there is no sharp break, and variations in exposure, altitude, and distance from the sea produce a wide range of patterns. The island has two seasons. The hot and wet summer lasts from November through April. February is the warmest month with temperatures averaging 27°C in the lowlands and 22°C on the plateau. Cyclones occur from December through March, and the storms, which come from the northeast, have caused much destruction on the island over the years. For example, Cyclone Hollanda hit Mauritius February 10, 1994, leaving 1,400 persons homeless, and damaging 60 percent of the electrical system and 50 percent of the telephone network, as well as destroying between 20 and 30 percent of the sugarcane plantations. The overall cost of this cyclone was estimated at US$81 million.

Winter, lasting from May through October, is cool and dry, influenced by the steady southeasterly trade winds. July is the coolest month and has average temperatures of 22°C in the lowlands and 16°C in the plateau. Rainfall is abundant, ranging from 90 centimeters per year in the western lowlands to 500 centimeters in the tableland—an average of 200 centimeters per year overall. Nonetheless, the high rate of evaporation and uneven distribution necessitate irrigation. Humidity is frequently above 80 percent.

Mauritius has fertile soil that supports a variety of vegetation. All but 1 percent of the native hardwood forests that once covered most of the island have been cut down, threatening the survival of several bird species. Sugarcane is now the dominant crop, covering half the arable land, but other cash and food crops are grown as well. Coral reefs and marine life off the northwest coast have been hurt by pollution, mainly from large hotels. To prevent the destruction caused by rapid and poorly planned development and in response to foreign criticism for its lack of environmental protection, the government established the Ministry of the Environment in 1990. In July 1991, the legislature passed the Environmental Protection Act, which requires an environmental impact assessment for all new projects. The ministry has also established standards for existing industry, followed by inspections. Steps are being taken to induce the construction industry to shift from the use of coral sand (in the early 1990s, the building trade used 600,000 tons of coral sand annually) to basaltic sand. Marine parks are being zoned to protect coral and marine life, and a sewerage master plan is being developed to prevent the discharge of untreated sewage into the ocean. Solid waste management is upgrading the handling of waste, and the principle of "the polluter must pay" is being introduced.

## Society and Culture

### Population and Demography

The estimated population of Mauritius in July 1993 was 1,106,516 with a population growth rate of 0.95 percent for 1993. According to the 1990 census, the population was 1,065,988, of whom 34,292 lived on Rodrigues and 170 on outer islands. The country's population density, more than 537 inhabitants per square kilometer, is one of the highest in the world. The majority of the island's inhabitants are young; some 58.6 percent were under the age of twenty-nine in 1990. The capital, Port Louis, is the largest city, with a population of 142,645. Other large metropolitan areas, in descending order, are Beau Bassin-Rose Hill, Vacoas-Phoenix, Curepipe, and Quatre Bornes. In 1991 the population was relatively evenly divided between those residing in rural and urban areas.

The rate of population increase grew to between 3 percent and 4 percent in the 1950s, resulting, in large part, from the elimination of malaria, higher living standards, and improved health care. Worried that such high growth rates would impede the island's development and tax its resources, the government and private groups instituted extensive family planning efforts.

Family planning services were centralized under the administration of the Maternal and Child Health Care Division of the Ministry of Health in 1972, and together with the non-governmental Action Familiale, which promoted natural techniques of birth control, reduced the country's birthrate significantly. The rate dropped to around 2 percent in the 1960s, and fell to 1.1 percent in 1973. In the 1980s, the rate fell below 1 percent. According to a Ministry of Health publication, the following methods of birth control were used in 1985: birth control pills, 40 percent; barrier methods, 21 percent; natural methods, 16 percent; intrauterine device (IUD), 10 percent; tubal ligation, 8 percent; Depo Provera, 5 percent. Abortion is illegal, but a Mauritian family planning official has estimated that there is one abortion for every live birth. The crude birthrate in 1991 was 20.7 births per 1,000 population, and the crude death rate stood at 6.6 per 1,000.

## Ethnicity, Religion, and Language

The forebears of the various ethnic groups composing Mauritian society arrived as settlers, slaves, indentured laborers, and immigrants. Although the country's past contains dark chapters of inequality and exploitation, modern Mauritian history has been remarkable for its relatively smooth and peaceful transition from colonial rule and the rule of large plantation owners to multiparty democracy.

"Harmonious separatism" is the way in which one writer characterizes communal relations in Mauritius. The term, however, does not preclude the existence of tensions. Ethnicity, religion, and language have been important factors in shaping the way Mauritians relate to each other in the political and social spheres. And despite the fact that sectarian factors are less of a determining factor in people's social and political behavior, they remain an important clue to the people's past and self-identity.

The 1968 constitution recognized four population categories: Hindus, Muslims, Sino-Mauritians, and the general population. According to a 1989 estimate, of a total population of 1,080,000, Hindus constituted about 52 percent (559,440); the general population, about 29 percent (309,960); Muslims, about 16 percent (179,280); and Sino-Mauritians, about 3 percent (31,320).

The ancestors of the Hindu and Muslim populations came predominantly from the Indian subcontinent, and, from the censuses of 1846 to 1952, were classified as "Indo-Mauritians." The ancestral language of most Hindus is Hindi or Bhojpuri, with a minority of Tamil or Telegu speakers. Hindu immigrants brought with them the caste system. Upon arrival on the island, many members of lower castes upgraded their status to join the Vaish middle caste. Although the caste system was not supported by the occupational structure as in India, minority members of the high Brahmin and Khsatriya castes sometimes joined with the Vaish to exclude lower castes from top civil service and political jobs. For the most part, however, the caste system is not an important factor in social organization and, if anything, lingers mainly as a basis for choosing spouses. Most of the Hindu population adheres to the orthodox rituals of the Sanatanist branch of the religion. These Hindus observe their rituals in rural community centers called *baitkas*. The Arya Samajists adhere to a reform branch of Hinduism popular with the lower classes and instrumental in the Indo-Mauritian community's political and cultural development in the early years of the twentieth century.

The Muslim population is approximately 95 percent Sunni and Hindi-speaking. Other languages include Bhojpuri, Gujarati, Urdu, and Arabic. The principal place of worship is the Jummah Mosque in Port Louis, but there are many smaller mosques in the towns and villages. Among the Shia (see Glossary) minority, some have their origins in different parts of India, others are adherents of the Agha Khan from East Africa, and still others are Ahmadists from the Punjab.

The earliest Chinese immigrants to the island came from the Canton region and spoke Cantonese, but most Sino-Mauritians descend from Mandarin-speaking settlers from Hunan. Some adhere to Buddhism and other Chinese religions, but many converted to Roman Catholicism in the twentieth century.

Unlike members of these specific population categories, those grouped under the general population rubric do not share close ethnic and cultural bonds. Members of the general population have in common only the fact that they do not belong to the other three groups. This category includes Franco-Mauritians, other European immigrants, and Creoles. The Creoles are ethnically diverse, some with black African ancestry, others of mixed descent, and still others from parts of Asia. They share a common language, which is a patois based on French, and the Roman Catholic religion.

In the past, a close association existed between certain occupations and ethnic groups. Although these patterns persist, they are changing. The Chinese, for example, predominate in commerce, as store owners and assistants, and in the restaurant and casino businesses. Hindus form the majority of agricultural workers, and members of the Muslim and Creole populations are artisans. African Creoles tend to be dockworkers, fishers, transportation workers, or service employees. Franco-Mauritians dominate the sugar industry and own most of the hotels, banks, and manufacturing industries. The civil service attracts educated members of all groups.

Mauritian society is noteworthy for its high degree of religious tolerance. Mauritians often share in the observances of religious groups other than their own. In part as a result of the multiplicity of religions, Mauritius has more than twenty national holidays. In addition, the government grants subsidies to all major religious groups according to their membership. According to the 1990 census, 49 percent of the population was Hindu, 27 percent Roman Catholic, 16 percent Muslim, and 0.5 percent Protestant; 7.5 percent belonged to other groups.

Language is perhaps the most complex and perplexing aspect of the Mauritian social mosaic. This intricacy derives from the number of languages spoken, combined with the uses to which they are put and the sociopolitical connotations they bear. Philip Baker and Peter Stein, scholars studying language use in Mauritius, have found that English is associated with "knowledge," French with "culture," Creole with "egalitarianism," and other languages with "ancestral heritage." Consequently, although Creole is the most widely spoken language in the country, French predominates in the media, and English is the official language of government and school instruction.

The growing use of Creole by non-Creole Mauritians reflects a widespread movement away from ethnically based language use. Among Muslims and Sino-Mauritians, for example, Creole is the principal language. According to the 1983 census, the top five languages were: Creole, 54.1 percent; Bhojpuri, 20.4 percent; Hindi, 11.5 percent; French, 3.7 percent; and Tamil, 3.7 percent. These figures indicate the principal language used in the home. Most Mauritians, however, speak several languages.

## Education

The education system in Mauritius, patterned after the British model, has improved greatly since independence. It has been free through the secondary level since 1976 and through the postsecondary level since 1988. The government has made an effort to provide adequate funding for education, occasionally straining tight budgets. In 1991–92, reflecting the trend of earlier budgets, the government allocated 13 percent (Mauritian rupee—MauR; see Glossary—1.5 billion) for education, culture, and art. Nonetheless, facilities in rural areas tend to be less adequate than those in Port Louis and other cities. Literacy in 1990 for the population over fifteen years of age on the island of Mauritius was 80 percent overall, 85 percent for males, and 75 percent for females.

In 1979 the government established a new unit in the Ministry of Education and Cultural Affairs to oversee and coordinate teaching resources at some 900 private preschools. The increasing participation of women in the labor force necessitated the expansion of the preschool system. The government established public preschools in 1984. Primary education (standard 1–6) is compulsory, and 6,507 teachers taught 137,491 students in 283 schools in 1990, representing an estimated 92 percent of children in that age-group. During the same period at the secondary level (forms 1–6), 3,728 teachers taught 78,110 students in 124 schools. As in the British system, students must pass standardized exams at several stages to be able to continue their studies. About 50 to 60 percent of primary students pass the exam for admission to secondary school. In 1986, 60.7 percent of the form 5 students taking the School Certificate exam passed; not all went on to form 6. In the same year, 53.7 percent of the form 6 students taking the Higher School Certificate exam passed. In addition to government schools, there are many private primary and secondary schools, but statistical data on these are lacking.

The country's principal institution of higher education is the University of Mauritius, where 1,190 students were enrolled in 1991. Other postsecondary institutions include the Mauritius Institute of Education for teacher training; the Mauritius College of the Air, which broadcasts classes; and the Mahatma Gandhi Institute. Of the several hundred Mauritians studying abroad each year, most go to Britain, France, and India. In addition, 1,190 students were enrolled at eleven vocational training centers, and 690 were taking courses at three technical institutions and five handicraft training centers in 1991.

From standard 4 onward, English is the sole language of instruction. Before that, teachers use Creole and Bhojpuri when teaching English to those students who do not already know it. From standard 3 onward, French is a required course. Students may also take classes in several Asian languages.

The government of Mauritius regards education as a sphere of utmost importance in its move toward the "second stage" of economic development, namely becoming a newly industrialized country. Therefore, at a donors' meeting in Paris in November 1991, the minister of education presented an ambitious Education Master Plan for the years 1991–2000. The plan calls for expanding education at all levels, from preprimary through university, through the establishment of new schools and the improvement of existing facilities, especially technical and vocational education; the latter is an area that to date has not provided the technical skills required by island industries. Despite the population's 95 percent literacy rate for those under thirty years of age, government officials have been concerned at the high dropout rate, especially at the secondary level. University places are also being increased to 5,000, and new courses of study are being introduced. The donor response to the plan was very favorable. The World Bank pledged US$20 million, the African Development Bank US$15 million, and other donors an additional US$14 million.

## Media

The news media in Mauritius, especially the press, are lively and free. During the 1970s, the government attempted to impose some restrictions, particularly on those newspapers opposed to its policies, but fierce opposition led to the climination of the laws.

There were five French dailies (the two principal ones being *L'Express* and *Le Mauricien*) and two small Chinese dailies with a combined circulation of more than 80,000 in 1993. Several weekly, biweekly, and monthly papers and magazines are also published, some of them in English. Most of the printed media are in the hands of political parties, religious organizations, or private firms.

The government controls the Mauritius Broadcasting Corporation (MBC), which regulates television and radio broadcasting. Mauritius has two television and two radio stations, which broadcast in twelve languages. About 50 percent of MBC broadcasts are in French, 25 percent in Hindi or Bhojpuri, 14 percent in English, and 11 percent in other languages. Most

Mauritians also receive French television broadcasts from Reunion.

## Health and Welfare

Government-funded health services and facilities are widespread and accessible to most of the population, although facilities are concentrated in urban centers. According to data from the Ministry of Economic Planning and Development, between 1972 and 1987 the number of doctors per 100,000 population increased from twenty-seven to eighty. The number of hospital beds decreased from 328 to 285 per 100,000 population in the same period. In 1992 Mauritius had 3,094 hospital beds, and 1,090 physicians (including 152 specialists). Life expectancy at birth in 1994 on the island of Mauritius was 74.6 years for females and 66.6 years for males, for an overall life expectancy of 70.5 years. In 1994 infant mortality stood at 18.4 per 1,000 live births. In its 1991–92 national budget, the government allocated 7.7 percent (about US$57.9 million) to health care.

Malaria, tuberculosis, and other diseases prevalent in pre-World War II years have been brought under control by successful public health measures. The major causes of death in 1990, in descending order, were diseases of the circulatory system, diseases of the respiratory system, and cancer. With growing affluence and changes in social conditions, drug abuse has become a problem. By 1993 all the population had easy access to potable water. Nutritional standards are high; the daily per capita caloric intake in 1987 was 2,680, or 124 percent of the United Nations (UN) Food and Agriculture Organization recommended requirement.

In the early 1980s, forty social welfare centers and thirty village centers provided training in nutrition and maternal and child health care, as well as recreational facilities and courses in home economics and dressmaking. The government provides services, including board and lodging, to the elderly and the infirm. Family welfare allowances are also available for the poor. The Central Housing Authority and the Mauritius Housing Corporation provide funding for low-income housing.

## Role of Women

As in other industrializing countries, the role of women is changing rapidly. A major force for change has been the rapid influx of women into the many jobs created in the 1980s in the export processing zones (EPZs—see Industry and Commerce,

*Opera house, Port Louis*
*Courtesy Mari G. Borstelmann*

this ch.). Although low-paying for the most part, the jobs allow women formerly confined to the roles of mother and wife to gain a certain degree of personal and social freedom. One woman, in a 1993 *National Geographic* article, said:

> For a Mauritian woman, to work is to be free. Before, a girl could not leave home until her parents found a husband for her, and then she moved into her husband's family's home and spent the rest of her life having babies. I met my husband at work, and it was my decision to marry him. Now we live in our own house.

The government has taken measures to promote equality of the sexes by repealing discriminatory laws dealing with inheritance and emigration. In 1989 the government appointed equal opportunity officers in the principal ministries to deal with women's issues. Reports by the Ministry of Women's Rights and Family Welfare and others indicate, however, that violence against women is prevalent. The increased employment of women has created the need for more child-care services and for more labor-saving devices in the home.

## Economy

The Mauritian economy has undergone remarkable transformations since independence. From a poor country with high unemployment exporting mainly sugar and buffeted by the vagaries of world demand, Mauritius has become relatively prosperous and diverse, although not without problems.

The 1970s were marked by a strong government commitment to diversify the economy and to provide more high-paying jobs to the population. The promotion of tourism and the creation of the EPZs did much to attain these goals. Between 1971 and 1977, about 64,000 jobs were created. However, in the rush to make work, the government allowed EPZ firms to deny their workers fair wages, the right to organize and strike, and the health and social benefits afforded other Mauritian workers. The boom in the mid-1970s was also fueled by increased foreign aid and exceptional sugar crops, coupled with high world prices.

The economic situation deteriorated in the late 1970s. Petroleum prices rose, the sugar boom ended, and the balance of payments deficit steadily rose as imports outpaced exports; by 1979 the deficit amounted to a staggering US$111 million. Mauritius approached the IMF and the World Bank for assistance. In exchange for loans and credits to help pay for imports, the government agreed to institute certain measures, including cutting food subsidies, devaluing the currency, and limiting government wage increases.

By the 1980s, thanks to a widespread political consensus on broad policy measures, the economy experienced steady growth, declining inflation, high employment, and increased domestic savings. The EPZ came into its own, surpassing sugar as the principal export-earning sector and employing more workers than the sugar industry and the government combined, previously the two largest employers. In 1986 Mauritius had its first trade surplus in twelve years. Tourism also boomed, with a concomitant expansion in the number of hotel beds and air flights. An aura of optimism accompanied the country's economic success and prompted comparisons with other Asian countries that had dynamic economies, including Hong Kong, Singapore, Taiwan, and the Republic of Korea (South Korea).

The economy had slowed down by the late 1980s and early 1990s, but the government was optimistic that it could ensure the long-term prosperity of the country by drawing up and implementing prudent development plans. According to Larry W. Bowman, an expert on Mauritius, four development aims of the country into the 1990s will be "modernizing the sugar sector, expanding and diversifying manufacturing infrastructure, diversifying agriculture, and developing tourism." In addition, because of the threats to agriculture resulting from Europe's Common Agricultural Policy and the potential effects on textiles of the General Agreement on Tariffs and Trade (GATT), Mauritius hopes to transform itself into a center for offshore banking and financial services. A stock exchange opened in Port Louis in 1989. Another sector needing attention is that of housing because increased family incomes have raised the demand for housing. Overall, Mauritius had a 1993 gross domestic product (GDP—see Glossary) estimated at US$8.6 billion, with a growth rate of 5.5 percent, and a 1993 inflation rate of 10.5 percent.

## Agriculture and Fishing

### Sugar

In 1990 the government initiated a five-year plan costing MauR7.3 billion to bolster the sugar industry. Sugarcane covers 45 percent of the total area of Mauritius and more than 90 percent of the cultivated land. Production has remained steady at between 600,000 and 700,000 tons since the mid–1960s. The exception occurs when severe cyclones or droughts cause a decline in the cane harvest.

Nineteen large estates account for about 55 percent of the 76,000 hectares planted in cane and range in size from about 730 hectares to 5,500 hectares. (Land in Mauritius is also measured in an archaic French unit, the *arpent*.) Mauritian firms own fifteen of these plantations; the British multinational Lonrho owns two and controls a Mauritian firm that owns another; and the Mauritian government owns one estate. Some 35,000 small growers (with plots ranging from less than one hectare to about 400 hectares) tend the remainder of the crop and send their harvest for processing to the large planters, each of whom owns a sugar factory.

Since 1951 the production of sugar has been encouraged by marketing arrangements with consuming countries (principally Britain), which have guaranteed prices and markets for the Mauritian crop. The government has acquired a portion of this reliable sugar income through a sugar export tax. By the mid-1980s this tax had evolved into a steeply progressive one, with producers of under 1,000 tons of cane paying no tax, producers of 1,000 to 3,000 tons paying 15.75 percent, and producers of more than 3,000 tons paying 23.625 percent. This tax provided 13 percent of the government's revenues in 1986. However, complaints mainly by the large miller/planters and severe economic pressures on the sugar industry prompted the government in 1993 to reduce the tax in each category by 9.4 percent. This move met opposition by many who claimed the large growers were being given favorable treatment.

Since 1975 Mauritius has had an export quota of about 500,000 tons per year under the Sugar Protocol of the Lomé Convention (see Glossary), the largest share of all nineteen signatories. The guaranteed price in 1991 was nearly twice the world free-market price. In 1992 the country exported 597,970 tons of sugar; of this amount, Britain received 498,919 tons.

Since 1984 the Mauritius Sugar Authority, operating under the Ministry of Agriculture, has advised the government regarding sugar policy. In addition, the authority acts as a nexus between the government and the numerous organizations involved in sugar production. These organizations include parastatal, producers', and workers' organizations, as well as extension and research bodies. The private Mauritius Sugar Syndicate, which has offices in London and Brussels, handles all aspects of domestic and foreign sugar marketing, including transportation, finance, insurance, and customs duties. The Mauritius Sugar Industry Research Institute (MSIRI) conducts research in such areas as plant breeding, entomology, and food-crop agronomy.

### Tea

As part of its agricultural diversification efforts, the government supported the large-scale production of tea in the late 1960s. Second to sugar in exports, tea covered 2,870 hectares in 1991. The Tea Development Authority (TDA) owned and managed three-fourths of this land, which it leased to tenant growers. Although tea thrives at the island's higher elevations, production has been hindered by high costs, including labor, and fluctuations in world prices. Since 1986 the government has subsidized tea production to compensate for low prices. In the same year, it established the Mauritius Tea Factories Company to manage four factories that had been run by the TDA.

Tea production reached 8,115 tons in 1985, its highest level, only to decline steadily to 5,918 tons in 1991. Export earnings have declined from MauR104 million in 1986 to MauR83 million in 1991. The government is considering other uses for its tea-planted land in the face of continuing economic pressures.

### Other Crops

Mauritius produces enough potatoes and fresh vegetables to meet domestic demand. The government subsidizes the production of some crops. The area under cultivation for food crops was 5,494 hectares in 1991; total production was 64,090 tons. Between 1987 and 1989, food crops suffered from poor weather, including cyclones, disease, and lack of land for tenant farmers. Tobacco covered 623 hectares in 1991, and production amounted to 876 tons. British American Tobacco processed the entire crop for domestic consumption. Cut flowers have proved to be a very successful crop, beginning in the late 1980s, and efforts are also being made to produce tropical fruits for export.

### Livestock

Although self-sufficient in poultry and pork, Mauritius had to import 80 percent of its dairy products and 90 percent of its beef in 1991. The following are figures for livestock production in 1991: beef, 544 tons; goat and mutton, 178 tons; pork, 906 tons; poultry, 13,250 tons; and milk, 10,800,000 liters.

### Fishing

Declines in local fishing catches in the early 1980s prompted the government to institute programs aimed at ensuring self-sufficiency in fish. The programs included the construction of fishing wharves and the purchase of new vessels. In 1990 the total catch amounted to 13,985 tons, which included fish caught by foreign vessels for the tuna canning industry.

## Industry and Commerce

### Export Processing Zones

Industrial development in Mauritius expanded rapidly after 1971, when the government established EPZs. In return for tax benefits, duty-free imports of raw materials and machinery, and other inducements, the owners of EPZ enterprises agree to export all their products. In the first year of operation, nine EPZ firms employing 644 persons accounted for 1 percent of export earnings. In 1992 a total of 568 EPZ enterprises employing 89,949 persons produced such items as flowers, furniture, jewelry, and leather goods. The EPZ rate of growth of employment and foreign exchange earnings slowed in the 1980s and early 1990s. However, the value of EPZ exports in 1993 set a record of MauR15.8 billion.

Textiles are the main EPZ product, accounting for 89 percent of jobs and 83 percent of exports. With regard to wearing apparel, Mauritius benefits from preferential treatment in the European Community (EC—see Glossary) under the Lomé Convention. Hong Kong, the source of 22 percent of all foreign investment, is the largest foreign investor in the textile sector. Other countries participating include France, Britain, and Germany. Two foreign firms dominate the textile industry: Socota and Woventex. In a 1991 policy paper, the government urged diversification of EPZ industries and pledged to give priority to nonclothing industries such as electronics.

### Construction

The construction industry's contribution to GDP grew from 5.3 percent in 1987 to about 7.6 percent in 1992, thanks to investment in housing, roads, hotels, factories, and a new airport terminal. Average annual real growth in the construction sector between 1989 and 1992 has been around 10 percent. In 1992 an estimated 10,600 persons were employed in the industry, accounting for about 3.7 percent of total employment.

## Banking

The Bank of Mauritius, established in 1966, is the country's central bank. Twelve commercial banks (eight of them foreign-owned) operate in the country; the three major ones are the State Commercial Bank, Barclays, and the Mauritius Commercial Bank. Other financial institutions include the Mauritius Housing Corporation, the State Finance Corporation, and the Development Bank of Mauritius. The national currency is the Mauritius rupee (MauR), whose March 1993 exchange rate with the United States dollar was 16.68:1.

## Trade and Balance of Payments

The success of the EPZs has meant that sugar, the traditional leader in exports, has been replaced by manufactured goods. Although the level of sugar exports has remained relatively flat (rising to MauR5.3 billion in 1992 from MauR4.3 billion in 1987), EPZ exports have risen from MauR6.6 billion in 1987 to MauR13.5 billion in 1992. Most exports went to Britain (35 percent in 1991), followed by France (19 percent), the United States (11 percent), and Germany (11 percent).

Manufactured goods accounted for 34 percent of imports in 1991, followed by machinery and transportation equipment (25 percent), food (11 percent), and fuels (8 percent). In the same year, France was the main supplier of imported goods (13 percent), followed by South Africa (12 percent), Britain (7 percent), and Japan (7 percent). Other sources of imports are Germany, India, China, Hong Kong, and Taiwan.

The country's geographic isolation, reliance on imported fuel, food, and manufactured goods, and its limited export base have combined to create persistent visible balance of trade deficits in the late 1980s and early 1990s. Imports outpaced exports by MauR1.1 billion in 1987, and the trade deficit grew to an estimated MauR5.8 billion in 1992.

## Tourism

The attractive climate and numerous beaches of Mauritius have been among the features that have attracted record numbers of tourists each year since 1984. Some 300,000 tourists visited in 1991, earning the country MauR3.9 million in foreign exchange; in 1993 the number rose to 375,000 tourists, bringing in MauR5.3 million in foreign exchange. In 1993 Mauritius had eighty-five hotels with 10,980 beds and an occupancy rate for the larger hotels of 68.5 percent; tourism employs more than 11,000 people.

The three principal sources of tourists in 1993 were Reunion (26 percent), France (21 percent), and South Africa (11 percent). Tourism increased by 10 percent in 1993 over 1992—Mauritius has concentrated on developing a quality tourist industry rather than on appealing to the mass market. Most investors in tourism are Mauritian; South Africans, French, British, and Germans also invest in tourism.

## Labor

One of the government's economic successes in the late 1980s was job creation, largely through the growth of EPZ enterprises. Between 1983 and 1989, total employment rose by 55 percent. Manufacturing employment increased about 16,000 per year between 1985 and 1988, but only by 3,500 annually in the 1988 to 1992 period. Women account for about 65 percent of EPZ employees and 34 percent of total employment, representing 158,900 women. The rapid growth of manufacturing jobs has created labor shortages in the agricultural and manufacturing sectors; as a result, Chinese guest workers have been brought in by some textile factories. The total number of employed in 1992 was 282,400, and the number of unemployed was estimated at 10,300; as of 1993, unemployment was negligible (about 9,000 persons), and Mauritius could boast of full employment. Some 38 percent worked in manufacturing (27 percent in clothing firms), 20 percent in government services, and 15 percent in agriculture. As it enters the stage of becoming a newly industrialized country, Mauritius needs to use its labor force more effectively, shifting workers from less productive to more productive sectors. This transition requires the government to promote labor mobility, as well as greater technological skills and training (see Education, this ch.).

In 1991 a total of 287 registered unions and nine federations represented 107,400 workers. Unions are free to organize; however, the Industrial Relations Act (IRA) of 1973 restricts some of their activities, including the right to strike. The IRA also created the National Remuneration Board, composed of government ministers, union leaders, and employer representatives, to resolve wage disputes brought to its attention. This board, however, cannot institute hearing procedures, and most wage settlements take their lead from the annual settlement between the government and public-sector employees. Civil servants are unionized but have no right to strike. Collective bargaining is limited to the stronger labor unions, such as the dockworkers' union.

## Transportation and Telecommunications

The island's network of surfaced roads covered 1,880 kilometers in 1992. In that same year, approximately 150,000 vehicles were registered. Port Louis and other urban centers have heavy traffic congestion. Railroads have been abandoned, but an extensive bus network exists, and the government is considering the construction of a monorail network. Port Louis, the sole commercial port, is large and was recently modernized. In 1992 it handled some 3.5 million tons of cargo, about 70 percent of which was in containers. The government's Sir Seewoosagur Ramgoolam International Airport at Plaisance is modern, having undergone an expansion costing MauR450 million in the early 1990s. In 1992 it handled 950,000 passengers, half of whom were carried by the national carrier, Air Mauritius. In the same year, 34,000 tons of freight passed through the airport, and the average number of daily arriving and departing flights was twenty-nine. Air Mauritius plans to expand its fleet of three Boeing 727s by adding three Airbus A340-300s, expected for delivery in 1994.

Communications facilities in Mauritius are well developed, including modern postal, facsimile, and telex services. In 1992 the telephone network had a capacity of 100,000 lines. International direct dialing was instituted in 1987. Also serving the country are two radio stations, four television stations, and one International Telecommunications Satellite Organization earth station.

## Water and Electricity

Imported oil is the largest source of energy for the island; consumption reached 530,000 tons in 1992. In an attempt to reduce its dependence on imported oil, the government has invested in alternative sources of energy. Most of the hydroelectric potential of the country's rivers has been exploited. (The most recent hydroelectric station, Champagne, came online in 1985.) Therefore, the prime focus has been on using a waste product of the sugar industry, bagasse, which also is less damaging to the environment, in generating electricity. Two bagasse-fired plants were proposed, and studies for them were funded by the World Bank in 1992. In 1991 electric power production amounted to 737.2 million kilowatt-hours.

## Budget and Public Finance

Whereas successive governments have differed on questions such as social welfare spending, labor policy, and privatization, they have maintained remarkable unanimity in passing budgets and promulgating policies aimed at strengthening the national economy. Faced with growing budget deficits in the late 1970s, for example, Mauritius implemented a Structural Adjustment Program in 1979–80 drawn up principally by the IMF and the World Bank. The program has been relatively successful; budget deficits fell from 12.6 percent of GDP in 1981–82 to below 2 percent of GDP in the early 1990s. (Deficits during fiscal years (FY—see Glossary) 1988–89 and 1989–90 rose above 30 percent of GDP, however, in large part because of increases in government salaries.) In May 1991, Mauritius paid all its debt to the IMF ahead of schedule, a rare accomplishment for a developing country.

Revenues during FY 1991–92 amounted to MauR10.9 billion; government estimates showed 90 percent coming from tax revenues and 10 percent from non-tax revenues and grants. Expenditures for the year amounted to MauR11.8 billion, of which MauR2.6 billion went to public debt service; MauR1 billion to social security; MauR1.5 billion to education, arts, and culture; and MauR778 million to health. In 1993 the government was set to reform the tax system in order to widen the tax base and reduce evasion.

The budget for the FY 1994–95 came to MauR17.8 billion, of which MauR1.3 billion was designated for foreign and domestic debt repayment. Revenue was estimated at MauR15 billion, of which MauR2.7 billion came from direct taxes, MauR9.6 billion from indirect taxes, MauR1.5 billion or 2.2 percent of gross national product (GNP—see Glossary) from a budget deficit, and the remainder from foreign support and miscellaneous sources. The budget contained some new provisions to encourage investment and savings; it abolished foreign currency controls and eliminated the tax on sugar products. Budgetary appropriations in 1994–95 included MauR2.4 billion for education (almost double the 1991–92 amount), MauR208 million to train middle management (compared with MauR90 million the previous year), MauR138 million for industry, and MauR327 million to build 2,000 houses for low-income families. The FY 1993–94 budget had stressed health, allocating MauR1.2 billion to this area and MauR552 million for road construction, as well as appropriations for lengthening by 780 meters the runway at Sir Seewoosagur Rangoolam International Airport and providing 75,000 new telephone lines.

These budgetary appropriations fell within the broader framework of the 1992–94 development plan, released in April 1993. The plan emphasized the role of the private sector and of the free market as opposed to public-sector bodies and state controls. The plan aimed at an overall annual growth rate of 6 percent: 4.9 percent in agriculture, 10.5 percent in construction, 7.7 percent in the EPZ, 6.5 percent in financial and business services, 9 percent in tourism, and 9.5 percent in utilities (electricity, gas, and water). Specific plan allocations were the following: agriculture MauR1.85 billion, airport MauR1.28 billion, education MauR1.02 billion, environment MauR1.89 billion, health MauR602 million, housing MauR7.86 billion, industry MauR219 million, roads MauR1.39 billion, Rodrigues and other islands MauR658 million, social services MauR124 million, telecommunications MauR866 million, tourism MauR257 million, water MauR951 million, and youth and sports MauR152 million.

# Government and Politics

## Structure of Government

The 1968 constitution proclaims that Mauritius is a "democratic state" and that the constitution is the supreme law of the land. It guarantees the fundamental rights and freedoms of the people, including the right to hold private property and to be free from racial or other discrimination. Fundamental rights can only be suspended during wars or states of emergency, which must be duly declared by the parliament and reviewed every six months.

The political structure is patterned to a large extent on the British system. As in Britain, the political party that can gain support from a majority in parliament chooses the prime minister, who, along with the cabinet, wields political power.

The National Assembly (Assemblée Nationale or parliament), the country's prime law-making body, consists of representatives elected from twenty three-member constituencies and one two-member district on Rodrigues. In addition, unlike the British system, eight assembly seats are apportioned to the "best losers" among the nonelected candidates, according to their ethno-religious affiliation—two each for Hindus, Muslims, Chinese, and the general population. An attempt must be made to distribute these seats proportionally to the major political parties, which are expressly referred to in the constitution. The sixty seats from the constituencies, together with the eight best-loser seats and the two seats representing Rodrigues, constitute the seventy-member parliament or National Assembly.

Parliament may remain in office for a maximum of five years, unless it is dissolved by a vote of no-confidence or an act of the prime minister. A constitutional amendment, however, provided that the first assembly reckon its term from 1971, a de facto term of eight years. The assembly is responsible for all legislation and appropriations and may amend the constitution by either a two-thirds or three-quarters majority, depending on the part of the constitution in question. A largely titular governor general presided over parliament in the name of the British monarch from independence in 1968 until March 12, 1992, when Mauritius declared itself a republic. Since then a president, appointed by the prime minister and ratified by the parliament, has assumed the role of the governor general.

The constitution also provides for three important commissions—the Judicial and Legal Service Commission, the Public Services Commission, and the Police Service Commission—as well as an ombudsman. The commissions oversee the appointment of government officials; the ombudsman investigates official misconduct.

The country's legal system is based on the Napoleonic Code and English common law. The Supreme Court heads the judicial system and has the power to interpret the constitution and to judge the constitutionality of legislation brought to its attention. Appointed by the prime minister and president, the chief justice helps select five other judges on the court. The Supreme Court also serves as the Court of Criminal Appeal and the Court of Civil Appeal. Mauritius continues to refer legal and constitutional matters of undeterminable jurisdiction to Britain's Privy Council. Lower courts having original jurisdiction over various kinds of cases include the Intermediate Court, the Industrial Court, and ten district courts.

The constitution does not specify the form of local government. Port Louis has a city council, whereas the four townships—Beau Bassin-Rose Hill, Curepipe, Quatre Bornes, and Vacoas-Phoenix—each have a municipal council. There are district councils for Pamplemousses-Rivière du Rempart, Moka-Flacq, and Grand Port-Savanne; 124 village councils; and five parish councils on Rodrigues. All councils are elected bodies, but the cabinet occasionally—over much opposition—has suspended municipal elections because of political unrest. In the August 30, 1992, village elections, villages each elected twelve village councillors, who then were grouped into four district councils. In seven of the 124 villages, the candidates were unopposed. In the remaining villages, 3,577 persons ran for 1,404 seats. The election turnout represented 68 percent of eligible voters. Local governments depend on the central government for more than 70 percent of their revenues, and only the municipal councils have the power to levy their own taxes.

## Politics of the Republic of Mauritius

Mauritius became the twenty-ninth republic under the British Commonwealth on March 12, 1992. Even during the transition period, the varied and lively social and political forces of the country manifested themselves. The former governor general, Sir Veerasamy Ringadoo, a Hindu, was appointed first president for three months to appease Hindu voters. On July 1, in accordance with an electoral pact between the ruling parties, the MSM and the MMM, the MMM obtained the post of president for Cassam Uteem, a Muslim and former deputy leader of the party. His appointment aroused widespread opposition from MSM politicians and from the island's Hindu majority, the source of much MSM support. Critics feared that Uteem, formerly minister of industry and industrial technology, would unduly politicize his office and promote a strongly pro-Muslim agenda. Upon taking office, Uteem tried to assuage these misgivings by stating that he would look after the interests of all Mauritians, regardless of religion, ethnicity, or politics. He also said that he would play an active (not merely ceremonial), impartial role in the political life of the country.

Although the MLP and PMSD suffered heavy electoral losses in the September 1991 general election and were faced with internal weakness, they attempted to act as an assertive and contentious opposition. The PMSD lost its veteran leader Sir Gaetan Duval at the end of 1991 after his retirement. The MLP's leader, Dr. Navin Ramgoolam, has been attacked by his own political allies for his inexperience in high office and frequent overseas travels. The opposition was quick to criticize the prime minister, Sir Anerood Jugnauth, for issuing a new MR20 bank note with the image of the prime minister's wife in mid-1992. In addition, the opposition and the ruling coalition have taken each other to court over charges of fraud in the 1991 election.

A particularly acrimonious row developed over Ramgoolam's absence from parliament beginning in July 1992 in order to pursue a law degree in London. The speaker of the National Assembly claimed that the MLP leader violated rules relating to absences by members of parliament. The case was referred to the Supreme Court. The Ramgoolam affair not only has prompted grumbling within the MLP but also has highlighted the tension within the ruling coalition, namely, the continuing friction between Paul Bérenger, external affairs minister and secretary general of the MMM, and Prime Minister Jugnauth. Bérenger criticized Jugnauth for calling the National Assembly out of recess while Ramgoolam was out of the country, claiming that the prime minister was merely creating another pretext for stripping the MLP leader of his seat.

Matters came to a head in August 1993 when the prime minister dismissed Bérenger because of his continuing criticism of government policy. The ouster led to a split in the MMM between members of the party who remained allied with the government of MSM Prime Minister Jugnauth, led by Deputy Prime Minister Prem Nababsing, and those MMM parliamentary members who supported Bérenger and went into opposition. Bérenger declined to become opposition leader, although his group was the largest single opposition element; he allowed the leader of the Labor Party, Navin Ramgoolam, to continue as opposition leader. In April 1994, Bérenger and Navin Ramgoolam reached an electoral agreement according to which the two groups were to cooperate.

## Foreign Relations

The orientation of Mauritius toward other countries is influenced by its location, resources, colonial past, domestic politics, and economic imperatives. Mauritius has particularly strong relations with Britain, France, India, and since 1990 with South Africa. A member of the Commonwealth, Mauritius recognized Queen Elizabeth II as head of state until it became a republic in 1992. Mauritius enjoys warm political relations and important economic ties with Britain, and receives significant development and technical assistance.

France, another former colonial power, provides Mauritius with its largest source of financial aid, and also promotes the use of the French language in Mauritius. In addition to trade, in which France has traditionally been Mauritius's largest supplier as well as its largest or second largest customer, particularly of textiles, France provides Mauritius with numerous kinds of assistance. For example, France has helped computerize the island's government ministries, has performed road feasibility studies and highway maintenance, has undertaken livestock services and the construction of a cannery, and has loaned Mauritius US$60 million to construct a large diesel-electric power station in western Mauritius, completed in 1992. Other French-sponsored infrastructure projects have included the French firm Alcatel's supply and installation of 30,000 additional telephone lines, a contract awarded in December 1988, and a five-year project scheduled to begin construction in January 1995 by SCAC Delmas Vieljeux (SCV) to create a ninety-hectare free-port area and attendant facilities at Port Louis. The intent is that the free port should serve as a means for attracting African trade under the Preferential Trade Area for Eastern and Southern Africa.

An area of tension between France and Mauritius relates to the latter's claim to Tromelin Island, some 550 kilometers northwest of Mauritius, which France retained when Mauritius received its independence. Tromelin had been governed by France from Mauritius during the colonial period, and Mauritius for a number of years has raised the question of the return of the one-square-kilometer island where France has a meteorological observation station. When French president François Mitterrand visited Mauritius (along with Madagascar, Comoros, and Seychelles) in 1990, Mauritius raised its claim; despite several subsequent discussions, the matter has not been resolved.

Mauritius acknowledges the legitimacy of France's military interests even though it supported the UN Indian Ocean Zone of Peace (IOZP) Resolution (adopted in 1971) calling for the demilitarization of the region. French military interests include the neighboring island of Reunion, a French *département* and headquarters for a military detachment. France has also provided the Special Mobile Force of Mauritius with MauR2.8 million worth of military equipment and training.

India, which has deep social and historical links with a large portion of the population of Mauritius, is the country's second largest source of foreign assistance. India has devoted a large share of aid to cultural ventures, such as the Mahatma Gandhi Institute, a library and language school opened in 1976.

Apart from traditional cultural and trade relations of Mauritius with India, the two countries have exchanged visits by their leading officials in recent years; have engaged in numerous joint ventures, particularly in the textiles area; and have signed cooperation agreements in various spheres. For example, in 1990 cooperation agreements were concluded in the fields of agriculture; oceanography; maritime resources, including the exploitation of Mauritius's EEZ; science and technology; drug trafficking; and sports and youth affairs. India has provided Mauritius with technical expertise, such as computer and high sensing technology, radio and telecommunications, further expansion of Mauritius's telephone lines from 60,000 to 100,000 lines over a three-year period beginning in 1991, and the creation of a science center and planetarium.

In the early 1990s, Mauritius saw the new South Africa as a partner, particularly in an economic sense, and was willing to forget charges that in 1989 South Africans had engaged in drug trafficking to Mauritius and had sought to assassinate Prime Minister Jugnauth. A South African trade bureau was approved in 1990; a health cooperation agreement was concluded in 1991 whereby Mauritians requiring complex medical procedures could obtain them in South African hospitals; and President Frederik Willem de Klerk visited Mauritius in November 1991. The two countries initiated diplomatic relations at the consular level in March 1992, and a South African resort chain began activities in Mauritius in late 1992.

Mauritius has sought to increase cooperation among its fellow island entities. In 1982 the country forged an agreement that created the Indian Ocean Commission (IOC), whose members include Mauritius, Madagascar, Seychelles, Comoros, and Reunion (represented by France). IOC members have met regularly to discuss social and economic relations, and in 1989 the IOC established its secretariat in Mauritius. Mauritius has particularly close cooperation with Seychelles in the fields of agriculture, education, energy, fishing, and transportation.

Relations between the United States and Mauritius have been dominated by questions of trade and sovereignty over Diego Garcia Island, a British possession that is the site of a United States military base. Exports from Mauritius, mostly textiles, have grown from US$28 million in 1982 to US$120 million in 1987. United States import quotas have restricted the level of Mauritian exports to the United States, however. Mauritian imports from the United States have increased from US$11 million in 1986 to US$48 million in 1991.

The question of Diego Garcia is a complex one. Mauritius ceded control over the Chagos Archipelago (including Diego Garcia) to Britain in exchange for 3 million pounds sterling in 1965 as one tacit precondition for independence. Despite UN objections to British control of the islands, Britain leased Diego Garcia to the United States in 1966 for fifty years. The United

States established a major military base on the island, including anchorage facilities for large numbers of ships, an airfield capable of handling B–52s, and a satellite communications facility. After a period of relative indifference to the fate of the Chagos Archipelago following its cession, Mauritian governments since the late 1980s have called for its return to Mauritian sovereignty. There was no indication in 1994 that Britain or the United States was willing to acquiesce. Differences of opinion notwithstanding, between 1982 and 1987 the United States provided Mauritius with US$56.2 million in aid, mainly for development.

Mauritius has limited but growing trade relations with the industrializing countries of Asia, particularly Hong Kong and Japan. It also has close relations with China. Although it belongs to the Organization of African Unity (OAU) and has been an opponent of apartheid, Mauritius has closer links to South Africa than to any other country on the continent. These relations are based in large part on the economic exigency of obtaining mainly manufactured goods more cheaply from the closest developed country.

In addition to membership in the OAU, UN, and Commonwealth, Mauritius belongs to the Nonaligned Movement. It has received assistance from the World Bank, the IMF, and the European Development Bank.

\* \* \*

For an excellent overview of the history, society, economy and foreign relations of Mauritius, see Larry W. Bowman's *Mauritius: Democracy and Development in the Indian Ocean*. The best in-depth account of the country's pre-independence history, with special attention to the twentieth century, is *Modern Mauritius* by Adele Smith Simmons. Particularly useful for detailed and current economic and political information are publications of the Economist Intelligence Unit: the annual *Country Profile: Mauritius, Seychelles* and the quarterly *Country Report: Madagascar, Mauritius, Seychelles, Comoros*.

Other useful works include *Mauritius: Development of a Plural Society* by A.R. Mannick; *The Economic and Social Structure of Mauritius* by J.E. Meade, et al.; and the World Bank publication, *Mauritius: Managing Success*. Updates of mainly economic news appear in *Africa Economic Digest* and *Marchés tropicaux et méditerranéens*. (For further information and complete citations, see Bibliography.)

# Chapter 3. Comoros

*National emblem of Comoros*

## Country

**Formal Name:** Federal Islamic Republic of the Comoros.

**Short Name:** Comoros.

**Term for Citizens:** Comorans (or Comorians).

**Capital:** Moroni.

**Date of Independence:** July 6, 1975 (from France).

## Geography

**Size:** Variously given as 1,862 to 2,170 square kilometers.

**Topography:** Archipelago consists of four main islands, all of volcanic origin. Njazidja (Grande Comore), the largest, has two volcanoes with a plateau connecting them; its thin soil cannot hold water. Nzwani (Anjouan) has three mountain chains and deeper soil cover. Mwali (Mohéli), the smallest, has central mountain chain and some rain forest. Mahoré (Mayotte) continues its relationship with France and is not included as part of Comoros.

**Climate:** Marine tropical, with two seasons: hot and humid from November to April, with northeastern monsoon and possible cyclones; rest of year cooler and dryer. Average annual rainfall 2,000 millimeters.

## Society

**Population:** 1991 census, excluding Mahoré, 446,817. Population density varies among islands, ranging from 1991 high of 470 persons per square kilometer on Nzwani to 120 persons per square kilometer on Mwali. Population growth rate estimated at 3.55 percent in 1994.

**Ethnic Groups:** Arabs, descendants of Shirazi settlers; African groups: Cafres and Makoa; Malayo-Indonesian peoples: Oimatsaha, Antalotes, and Sakalava; and Creoles, descendants of French settlers.

**Languages:** Arabic (official), French (official), and Comoran dialect related to Swahili.

**Religion:** Sunni Muslim, 86 percent; Roman Catholic, 14 percent.

**Education and Literacy:** Education compulsory for ages seven through fifteen; about 75 percent of primary-school-age children enrolled in 1993 in schools following French educational system. No university but postsecondary education available. Adult literacy in 1993 only 50 percent.

**Health:** Health care and most health facilities in poor condition. Malaria endemic; 80 to 90 percent of population affected. Scarcity of safe drinking water and child malnutrition are problem areas. 1994 estimate of life expectancy at birth fifty-eight years. Infant mortality rate estimated at eighty per 1,000 live births in 1994.

## Economy

**Gross National Product per Capita:** Estimated at US$400 in 1994 following January devaluation of Comoran franc. One of world's poorest countries, Comoros became eligible in 1991 for International Development Association's Special Program of Assistance.

**Agriculture:** Including fishing, provided about 40 percent of gross domestic product (GDP) in 1994 and involved 80 percent of labor force. Almost all meat and vegetables and much of rice must be imported. Main cash crops ylang-ylang essence for perfume, vanilla, and cloves, all subject to fluctuating demand. Various agricultural development projects underway with foreign aid. Livestock raising limited; fishing being expanded.

**Industry:** Provided 5 percent of GDP in 1994. Most industries entailed processing cash crops or handicrafts. Efforts underway to develop tourism, which, with other services, provided 25 percent of GDP in 1994.

**Exports:** Ylang-ylang (world's largest producer), vanilla (world's second largest producer), cloves. Exports estimated at US$21 million in 1992; major markets United States and France.

**Imports:** Basic foodstuffs, petroleum, construction materials. Imports estimated at US$60 million in 1992; major sources: France and Belgium-Luxembourg.

**Currency and Exchange Rate:** One Comoran franc (CF) = 100 centimes. In June 1995, US$1.00 = CF363.98.

**Inflation:** Estimated at 15 percent in 1994.

**Fiscal Year:** Calendar year.

## Transportation and Telecommunications

**Roads:** 750 kilometers of roads along coasts, of which 210 kilometers paved.

**Airports:** Daily flights to islands carried most passenger traffic; four airports with permanent-surface runways; airstrips on all islands. Air Comores is national carrier.

**Ports:** Mutsamudu on Nzwani and Moroni on Njazidja have artificial harbors. Almost all freight carried by sea.

**Telecommunications:** Moroni has international telecommunications; estimated 3,000 telephones in few existing towns in 1987. Two radio broadcast stations, one amplitude modulation (AM), one frequency modulation (FM).

## Government and Politics

**Government:** Constitution approved in referendum on June 7, 1992. Islam is state religion. President elected by universal suffrage for five-year term; president nominates ministers to form twelve-member Council of Government; prime minister belongs to majority party in legislature. Bicameral legislature: Federal Assembly elected for four-year terms; Senate appointed by Electoral College. Supreme Court and judiciary independent branch.

**Politics:** More than twenty political parties active in 1994. Most recent election in December 1993, with voting irregularities. Incumbent ruling coalition declared selves winners with twenty-two of forty-two seats. Opposition parties refused to participate in legislature.

**Foreign Relations:** Close relationships traditionally with France and recently with conservative Persian Gulf states and to lesser extent with South Africa. Good regional relations with Madagascar, Mauritius, and Seychelles in Indian Ocean Commission. Also developing relations with China and Japan.

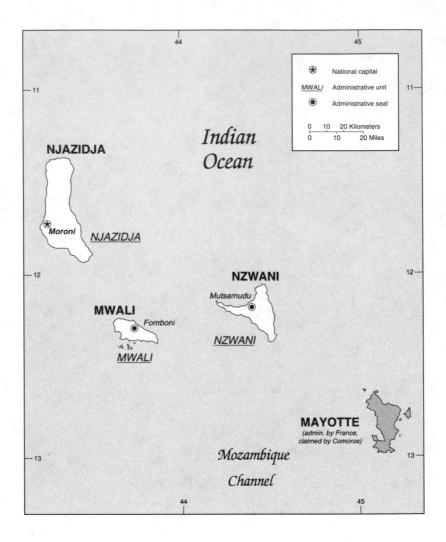

*Figure 6. Comoros: Administrative Divisions, 1994*

THE FEDERAL ISLAMIC REPUBLIC of the Comoros is an archipelago situated in the western Indian Ocean, about midway between the island of Madagascar and the coast of East Africa at the northern end of the Mozambique Channel. The archipelago has served in past centuries as a stepping stone between the African continent and Madagascar, as a southern outpost for Arab traders operating along the East African coast, and as a center of Islamic culture. The name "Comoros" is derived from the Arabic *kamar* or *kumr*, meaning "moon," although this name was first applied by Arab geographers to Madagascar. In the nineteenth century, Comoros was absorbed into the French overseas empire, but it unilaterally proclaimed independence from France on July 6, 1975.

Comoros has had a troubled and uncertain course as an independent state. Mahoré, or Mayotte, the easternmost of the archipelago's four main islands, including Njazidja (formerly Grande Comore), Mwali (formerly Mohéli), and Nzwani (formerly Anjouan), remains under French administration, a majority of its voters having chosen to remain tied to France in referendums held in 1974 and 1976 (see Physical Environment, this ch.). By the mid-1990s, the integration of Mahoré into Comoros remained an official objective of the Comoran government, but it had taken a back seat to more pressing concerns, such as developing a viable national economy. Meanwhile, the Mahorais were making the most of their close relationship with France. They accepted large amounts of developmental aid and took an intense interest in French political events. Although South Africa played a major role in the Comoran economy in the 1980s, by the early 1990s France was the island republic's foremost patron, providing economic aid, political guidance, and national security.

Comoros is densely populated and dedicates only limited amounts of land to food production. Thus, it depends heavily on imports of rice, vegetables, and meat. Its economy is based on the production of cash crops, principally ylang-ylang (perfume essence), vanilla, and cloves, all of which have experienced wild price swings in recent years, thus complicating economic planning and contributing to a burgeoning trade deficit. A growing dependence on foreign aid, often provided to meet day-to-day needs for food, funds, and government operations, further clouds economic prospects. Comoros suffers the ills of a developing nation in particularly severe form: food shortages and inadequate diets, poor health standards, a high rate of population growth, widespread illiteracy, and international indebtedness.

The country has endured political and natural catastrophes. Less than a month after independence, the government of the first Comoran president, Ahmed Abdallah, was overthrown; in 1978 foreign mercenaries carried out a second coup, overthrowing the radical regime of Ali Soilih and returning Abdallah to power. Indigenous riots in Madagascar in 1976 led to the repatriation of an estimated 17,000 Comorans. The eruption of the volcano, Kartala, on Njazidja in 1977 displaced some 2,000 people and possibly hastened the downfall of the Soilih regime. Cyclones in the 1980s, along with a violent coup that included the assassination of President Abdallah in 1989 and two weeks of rule by European mercenaries, rounded out the first fifteen years of Comoran independence.

In the early 1990s, the omnipresent mercenaries of the late 1970s and 1980s were gone, and the winding down of civil conflict in southern Africa, in combination with the end of the Cold War, had reduced the republic's value as a strategic chess piece. However, as in the 1970s and 1980s, the challenge to Comorans was to find a way off the treadmills of economic dependency and domestic political dysfunction.

## Historical Setting

### Early Visitors and Settlers

Little is known of the first inhabitants of the archipelago, although a sixth-century settlement has been uncovered on Nzwani by archaeologists. Historians speculated that Indonesian immigrants used the islands as stepping stones on the way to Madagascar prior to A.D. 1000. Because Comoros lay at the juncture of African, Malayo-Indonesian, and Arab spheres of influence, the present population reflects a blend of these elements in its physical characteristics, language, culture, social structure, and religion. Local legend cites the first settlement of the archipelago by two families from Arabia after the death of Solomon. Legend also tells of a Persian king, Husain ibn Ali, who established a settlement on Comoros around the beginning of the eleventh century. Bantu peoples apparently moved to Comoros before the fourteenth century, principally from the coast of what is now southern Mozambique; on the island of Nzwani they apparently encountered an earlier group of inhabitants, a Malayo-Indonesian people. A number of chieftains bearing African titles established settlements on Njazidja and Nzwani, and by the fifteenth century they probably had contact with Arab merchants and traders who brought the Islamic faith to the islands.

A watershed in the history of the islands was the arrival of the Shirazi Arabs in the fifteenth and sixteenth centuries. The Shirazi, who originated from the city of Shiraz in what is now Iran, were Sunni (see Glossary) Muslims adhering to the legal school of Muhammad ibn Idris ash Shafii, an eighth-century Meccan scholar who followed a middle path in combining tradition and independent judgment in legal matters. The Shirazi Arabs traveled and traded up and down the East African coast and as far east as India and Maldives. A legend is recounted on Comoros and on the East African coast of seven Shirazi brothers who set sail in seven ships, landed on the coast of northwest Madagascar and on Njazidja and Nzwani, and established colonies in the fifteenth century. The Shirazi, who divided Njazidja into eleven sultanates and Nzwani into two, extended their rule to Mahoré and Mwali, although the latter in the nineteenth century came under the control of Malagasy rulers. The Shirazi built mosques and established Islam as the religion of the islands. They also introduced stone architecture, carpentry, cotton weaving, the cultivation of a number of fruits, and the Persian solar calendar. By the sixteenth century, the Comoros had become a center of regional trade, exporting rice, ambergris, spices, and slaves to ports in East Africa and the Middle East in exchange for opium, cotton cloth, and other items.

The first Europeans to visit the islands were the Portuguese, who landed on Njazidja around 1505. The islands first appear on a European map in 1527, that of Portuguese cartographer Diogo Roberos. Dutch sixteenth-century accounts describe the Comoros' sultanates as prosperous trade centers with the African coast and Madagascar. Intense competition for this trade, and, increasingly, for European commerce, resulted in constant warfare among the sultanates, a situation that persisted until the French occupation. The sultans of Njazidja only occasionally recognized the supremacy of one of their number as *tibe,* or supreme ruler.

By the early seventeenth century, slaves had become Comoros' most important export commodity, although the market for the islands' other products also continued to expand, mainly in response to the growing European presence in the region. To meet this increased demand, the sultans began using slave labor themselves, following common practice along the East African coast.

Beginning in 1785, the Sakalava of the west coast of Madagascar began slaving raids on Comoros. They captured thousands of inhabitants and carried them off in outrigger canoes to be sold in French-occupied Madagascar, Mauritius, or Reunion to work on the sugar plantations, many of which French investors owned. The island of Mahoré, closest of the group to Madagascar, was virtually depopulated. Comoran pleas for aid from the French and the other European powers went unanswered, and the raids ceased only after the Sakalava kingdoms were conquered by the Merina of Madagascar's central highlands. After the Merina conquest, groups of Sakalava and Betsimisaraka peoples left Madagascar and settled on Mahoré and Mwali.

Prosperity was restored as Comoran traders again became involved in transporting slaves from the East African coast to Reunion and Madagascar. Dhows carrying slaves brought in huge profits for their investors. On Comoros, it was estimated in 1865 that as much as 40 percent of the population consisted of slaves. For the elite, owning a large number of slaves to perform fieldwork and household service was a mark of status. On the eve of the French occupation, Comoran society consisted of three classes: the elite of the Shirazi sultans and their families, a middle class of free persons or commoners, and a slave class consisting of those who had been brought from the African coast or their descendants.

## French Colonization

France's presence in the western Indian Ocean dates to the early seventeenth century. The French established a settlement in southern Madagascar in 1634 and occupied the islands of Reunion and Rodrigues; in 1715 France claimed Mauritius (Île de France), and in 1756 Seychelles. When France ceded Mauritius, Rodrigues, and Seychelles to Britain in 1814, it lost its Indian Ocean ports; Reunion, which remained French, did not offer a suitable natural harbor. In 1840 France acquired the island of Nosy-Be off the northwestern coast of Madagascar, but its potential as a port was limited. In 1841 the governor of Reunion, Admiral de Hell, negotiated with Andrian Souli, the

Malagasy ruler of Mayotte, to cede Mayotte to France. Mahoré offered a suitable site for port facilities, and its acquisition was justified by de Hell on the grounds that if France did not act, Britain would occupy the island.

Although France had established a foothold in Comoros, the acquisition of the other islands proceeded fitfully. At times the French were spurred on by the threat of British intervention, especially on Nzwani, and at other times, by the constant anarchy resulting from the sultans' wars upon each other. In the 1880s, Germany's growing influence on the East African coast added to the concerns of the French. Not until 1908, however, did the four Comoro Islands become part of France's colony of Madagascar and not until 1912 did the last sultan abdicate. Then, a colonial administration took over the islands and established a capital at Dzaoudzi on Mahoré. Treaties of protectorate status marked a transition point between independence and annexation; such treaties were signed with the rulers of Njazidja, Nzwani, and Mwali in 1886.

The effects of French colonialism were mixed, at best. Colonial rule brought an end to the institution of slavery, but economic and social differences between former slaves and free persons and their descendants persisted. Health standards improved with the introduction of modern medicine, and the population increased about 50 percent between 1900 and 1960. France continued to dominate the economy. Food crop cultivation was neglected as French *sociétés* (companies) established cash crop plantations in the coastal regions. The result was an economy dependent on the exporting of vanilla, ylang-ylang, cloves, cocoa, copra, and other tropical crops. Most profits obtained from exports were diverted to France rather than invested in the infrastructure of the islands. Development was further limited by the colonial government's practice of concentrating public services on Madagascar. One consequence of this policy was the migration of large numbers of Comorans to Madagascar, where their presence would be a long-term source of tension between Comoros and its giant island neighbor. The Shirazi elite continued to play a prominent role as large landowners and civil servants. On the eve of independence, Comoros remained poor and undeveloped, having only one secondary school and practically nothing in the way of national media. Isolated from important trade routes by the opening of the Suez Canal in 1869, having few natural resources, and largely neglected by France, the islands were poorly equipped for independence.

In 1946 the Comoro Islands became an overseas department of France with representation in the French National Assembly. The following year, the islands' administrative ties to Madagascar were severed; Comoros established its own customs regime in 1952. A Governing Council was elected in August 1957 on the four islands in conformity with the *loi-cadre* (enabling law) of June 23, 1956. A constitution providing for internal self-government was promulgated in 1961, following a 1958 referendum in which Comorans voted overwhelmingly to remain a part of France. This government consisted of a territorial assembly having, in 1975, thirty-nine members, and a Governing Council of six to nine ministers responsible to it.

## The Break with France

Politics in the 1960s were dominated by a social and economic elite—largely descendants of the precolonial sultanate ruling families—which was conservative and pro-French. During Comoros' period of self-government as an overseas department, there were two main conservative political groupings: the Parti Vert (Green Party), which later became known as the Comoros Democratic Union (Union Démocratique des Comores—UDC), and the Parti Blanc (White Party), later reconstituted as the Democratic Assembly of the Comoran People (Rassemblement Démocratique du Peuple Comorien—RDPC). Dr. Said Mohamed Cheikh, president of the Parti Vert and of the Governing Council, was, until his death in 1970, the most important political leader in the islands. The Parti Blanc, under Prince Said Ibrahim, provided the opposition, endorsing a progressive program that included land reform and a loosening of the monopoly on Comoran cash crops enjoyed by the foreign-owned plantation *sociétés*. The second most powerful member of the Parti Vert, Ahmed Abdallah, a wealthy plantation owner and representative to the French National Assembly, succeeded Cheikh as president of the Governing Council soon after Cheikh died.

Well into the 1960s, the two established parties were concerned primarily with maintaining a harmonious relationship with France while obtaining assistance in economic planning and infrastructure development. Given this consensus, politically active Comorans often based their allegiance on personal feelings toward the doctor and the prince who led the two main parties and on whatever patronage either party could provide.

The independence movement started not in the Comoro Islands but among Comoran expatriates in Tanzania, who founded the National Liberation Movement of Comoros (Mouvement de la Libération Nationale des Comores—Molinaco) in 1962. Molinaco actively promoted the cause of Comoran independence abroad, particularly in the forum of the Organization of African Unity (OAU), but not until 1967 did it begin to extend its influence to the islands themselves, engaging in largely clandestine activities. The Socialist Party of Comoros (Parti Socialiste des Comores—Pasoco), established in 1968, was largely supported by students and other young people.

A growing number of politically conscious Comorans, resenting what they perceived as French neglect of the Comoro Islands, supported independence. Independence-minded Comorans, especially younger ones, were energized by dramatic events across the Mozambique Channel on the African mainland. Tanganyika had gained its independence from Britain in 1961 and soon adopted a government based on "African socialism." Zanzibar, another long-time British colony, became independent in 1963 and overthrew the ruling Arab elite in a violent revolution the following year; the island state then merged with Tanganyika to form the new nation of Tanzania. Meanwhile, nationalists were beginning uprisings in the Portuguese colony of Mozambique.

Abdallah, although a conservative politician, saw independence as a "regrettable necessity," given the unsatisfactory level of French support and the growing alienation of an increasingly radicalized younger generation. The violent suppression of a student demonstration in 1968 and the death of Said Mohammed Cheikh in 1970 provided further evidence of the erosion of the existing order. In 1972 leaders of the Parti Vert (now the UDC) and the Parti Blanc (now the RDPC) agreed to press for independence, hoping at the same time to maintain cordial relations with France. A coalition of conservative and moderate parties, the Party for the Evolution of Comoros (Parti pour l'Évolution des Comores), was in the forefront of the independence effort. The coalition excluded Pasoco, which it perceived as violently revolutionary, but it cooperated for a time with Molinaco. During 1973 and 1974, the local government negotiated with France, and issued a "Common Declaration" on June 15, 1973, defining the means by which the islands would gain independence. Part of the backdrop of the negotiations was a pro-independence riot in November 1973 in Moroni in which the buildings of the Chamber of Deputies were burned. A referendum was held on December 22, 1974. Voters supported independence by a 95 percent majority, but 65 percent of those casting ballots on Mahoré chose to remain as a French department (see The Issue of Mahoré, this ch.).

Twenty-eight days after the declaration of independence, on August 3, 1975, a coalition of six political parties known as the United National Front overthrew the Abdallah government, with the aid of foreign mercenaries. Some observers claimed that French commercial interests, and possibly even the French government, had helped provide the funds and the matériel to bring off the coup. The reasons for the coup remain obscure, although the belief that France might return Mahoré to Comoros if Abdallah were out of power appears to have been a contributing factor. Abdallah fled to Nzwani, his political power base, where he remained in control with an armed contingent of forty-five men until forces from Moroni recaptured the island and arrested him in late September 1975. After the coup, a three-man directorate took control. One of the three, Ali Soilih, was appointed minister of defense and justice and subsequently was made head of state by the Chamber of Deputies on January 3, 1976. Four days earlier, on December 31, 1975, France had formally recognized the independence of Comoros (minus Mahoré), but active relations, including all aid programs, which amounted to more than 40 percent of the national budget, remained suspended.

## The Soilih Regime

Originally an agronomist, Ali Soilih had become politically active as a supporter of RDPC leader Said Ibrahim in 1970. Lasting from January 1976 to May 1978, his rule was marked by continued hostility between France and Comoros. The main issues were the status of Mahoré (particularly after France held a second referendum on the island, on February 7, 1976, in which 99.4 percent of the voters endorsed continued status as a French department) and a radical reform program designed to break the hold of traditional values and French influence on Comoran life. Soilih envisioned accomplishing his revolution in three phases, beginning with independence from France. The second phase, a "social revolution," would abolish such customs as the wearing of veils, the costly *grand mariage* (great

wedding; in Swahili *ndola nkuu*), and traditional funeral ceremonies. Comoran citizens, including young women, would be
mobilized to serve in revolutionary militia and army units in an
attempt to create something resembling the Red Guards of
China's Cultural Revolution of the late 1960s (see Society, this
ch.). The third phase would decentralize government administration by establishing thirty-four local *moudirias,* or provinces.
These would serve not only as administrative centers but would
also provide post and telephone service and consumer goods
for localities of about 9,000 people on the model of the Chinese people's communes.

Soilih emphasized the central role of young people in the
revolution, lowering the voting age to fourteen. He mobilized
Comoran youth into a special revolutionary militia (the Commando Moissy), which, particularly in the villages, launched
violent attacks on conservative elders in Red Guard style (see
Comoros, ch. 6).

After the withdrawal of French financial subsidies, the treasury was soon emptied, and in a move having budgetary as well
as ideological implications, some 3,500 civil servants were dismissed in 1977. Soilih made a more than symbolic break with
the past in 1976 by burning French government archives,
which had been kept since the acquisition of Mahoré 135 years
before. Tanzanian officers trained the Comoran Armed Forces,
and the Democratic People's Republic of Korea (North Korea),
Saudi Arabia, and other countries provided limited aid.

Soilih, who described himself as a devout Muslim, advocated
a secular state and limitations on the privileges of the muftis, or
Muslim jurists who interpret Islamic law. These reforms, which
were perceived as attacks on Comoran traditions, combined
with a deepening economic crisis to erode support for his government. Several attempts were made on Soilih's life, and in a
referendum held in October 1977, only 55 percent of the voters supported a new constitution proposed by his government.
Attacks by the Moissy on real and imagined political opponents
escalated; raids on mosques were common; a number of refugees fled to Mahoré. The eruption of Kartala in April 1977 and
the influx of refugees from Madagascar following a massacre of
resident Comorans there exacerbated the situation. In March
1978, some fishers in the town of Iconi, south of Moroni, were
killed after protesting the government's policy on compulsory
sale of their catch to the state. Severe food shortages in 1976–
77 required the government to seek aid internationally and

forced the young nation to divert its already limited export earnings from economic development to purchases of rice and other staples.

Popular support had dwindled to such a level that when a mercenary force of fifty, consisting largely of former French paratroopers, landed at Itsandra Beach north of the capital on May 12, 1978 the regular armed forces offered no resistance. The mercenaries were led by French-born Bob Denard (an alias for Gilbert Bourgeaud, also known as Said Mustapha M'Hadjou) a veteran of wars of revolution, counterrevolution, and separatism from Indochina to Biafra. (Ironically, Denard had played a role in the 1975 coup that had enabled Soilih to come to power.) Most Comorans supported the coup and were happy to be free of Soilih's ineffective and repressive regime. The deposed head of state was killed under mysterious circumstances on May 29, 1978. The official explanation was that he had attempted to escape.

## The Abdallah Regime

Following a few days of provisional government, the two men who had financed the coup, former president Ahmed Abdallah (himself the victim of the 1975 coup) and former vice president Mohamed Ahmed, returned to Moroni from exile in Paris and installed themselves as joint presidents. Soon after, Abdallah was named sole executive.

The continued presence of the mercenaries impeded Abdallah's early efforts to stabilize Comoros. Denard seemed interested in remaining in Comoros, and he and his friends were given financially rewarding appointments with the new government. In reaction to Denard's involvement with Abdallah, the OAU revoked Comoros' OAU membership, Madagascar severed diplomatic relations, and the United Nations (UN) threatened economic sanctions against the regime. France also exerted pressure for Denard to leave, and in late September—temporarily, as it developed—he departed the islands.

Abdallah consolidated power, beginning with the writing of a new constitution. The document combined federalism and centralism. It granted each island its own legislature and control over taxes levied on individuals and businesses resident on the island (perhaps with an eye to rapprochement with Mahoré), while reserving strong executive powers for the president. It also restored Islam as the state religion, while acknowledging the rights of those who did not observe the Muslim

*Port at Moroni, Njazidja, capital of Comoros*
*Friday mosque and port, Moroni*
*Courtesy Mari G. Borstelmann*

faith. The new constitution was approved by 99 percent of Comoran voters on October 1, 1978. The Comorans also elected Abdallah to a six-year term as president of what was now known as the Federal Islamic Republic of the Comoros.

Although Abdallah had been president when Comoros broke away from France in 1975, he now moved to establish a relationship much more to France's liking. Upon Denard's departure, he gave a French military mission responsibility for training Comoros' defense force. He also signed an agreement with France to allow its navy full use of Comoran port facilities.

Making the most of Comoros' new presidential system, Abdallah induced the nation's National Assembly to enact a twelve-year ban on political parties, a move that guaranteed his reelection in 1984. In 1979 his government arrested Soilih regime members who had not already left or been killed during the 1978 coup. Four former ministers of the Soilih government disappeared and allegedly were murdered, and about 300 other Soilih supporters were imprisoned without trial. For the next three years, occasional trials were held, in many cases only after France had insisted on due process for the prisoners.

Although the restoration of good relations with France represented a sharp break with the policies of the previous regime, Abdallah built on Soilih's efforts to find new sources of diplomatic and economic support. Thanks in large part to aid from the European Community (EC—see Glossary) and the Arab states, the regime began to upgrade roads, telecommunications, and port facilities. The government also accepted international aid for programs to increase the cultivation of cash crops and food for domestic consumption. Abdallah endeavored to maintain the relations established by Soilih with China, Nigeria, and Tanzania, and to expand Comoros' contacts in the Islamic world with visits to Libya and the Persian Gulf states.

Despite international assistance, economic development was slow. Although some Comorans blamed the French, who had yet to restore technical assistance to pre-1975 levels, others suspected that Abdallah, who owned a large import-export firm, was enriching himself from development efforts with the assistance of Denard, who continued to visit Comoros.

Opposition to the Abdallah regime began to appear as early as 1979, with the formation of an exile-dominated group that became known as the United National Front of Comorans-Union of Comorans (Front National Uni des Komoriens-Union des Komoriens—FNUK-Unikom). In 1980 the Comoran ambassador to France, Said Ali Kemal, resigned his position to form another opposition group, the National Committee for Public Safety (Comité National de Salut Public). A failed coup in February 1981, led by a former official of the Soilih regime, resulted in arrests of about forty people.

In regard to Mahoré, Abdallah offered little more than verbal resistance to a 1979 decision of the French government to postpone action on the status of the island until 1984. At the same time, he kept the door open to Mahoré by writing a large measure of autonomy for the component islands of the republic into the 1978 constitution and by appointing a Mahorais as his government's minister of finance. Having established an administration that, in comparison with the Soilih years, seemed tolerable to his domestic and international constituencies, Abdallah proceeded to entrench himself. He did this through domestic and international policies that would profoundly compromise Comoros' independence and create the chronic crisis that continued to characterize Comoran politics and government in 1994.

## The Undermining of the Political Process

In February 1982, Comoros became a one-party state. The government designated Abdallah's newly formed Comoran Union for Progress (Union Comorienne pour le Progrès—UCP) as the republic's sole political party. Although unaffiliated individuals could run for local and national office, the only party that could organize on behalf of candidates henceforth would be the UCP. In March 1982 elections, all but one of Abdallah's handpicked UCP candidates won. UCP candidates likewise dominated the May 1983 National Assembly elections, and opposition candidates attempting to stand for election in balloting for the three islands' legislative councils in July were removed from the lists by the Ministry of Interior. Abdallah himself was elected to a second six-year term as head of state in September 1984, winning more than 99 percent of the vote as the sole candidate. During the National Assembly elections of March 22, 1987, the Abdallah regime arrested 400 poll watchers from opposition groups. A state radio announcement that one non-UCP delegate had been elected was retracted the next day.

Abdallah also kept opponents from competing with him in the arena of legitimate politics by reshuffling his government and amending the 1978 constitution. As part of what one observer wryly called the process of "remov[ing] his most avid successors from temptation," Abdallah pushed through a constitutional amendment in 1985 that abolished the post of prime minister, a move that made the president both head of state and head of the elected government. The amendment also diminished the status of Ali Mroudjae, the erstwhile prime minister and a likely future candidate for president. Another 1985 amendment took away many of the powers of the president of the National Assembly, including his right to become interim head of state in the event of the incumbent's death. The amendment transferred the right of succession to the president of the Supreme Court, an appointee of the head of state. Feeling the effect of this second amendment was assembly president Mohamed Taki, another man generally regarded as presidential timber.

Mroudjae's subsequent career in the Abdallah government illustrated the way in which Abdallah used frequent reshufflings of his cabinet to eliminate potential challengers. Mroudjae's next job was to share duties as minister of state with four other people; he was removed from the government altogether in another reshuffle four months later.

Looking to the end of his second (and, according to the constitution, final) term as head of state, Abdallah created a commission in 1988 to recommend changes to the constitution. These changes, among other things, would permit him to run yet again in 1990. A referendum on revisions to the constitution was scheduled for November 4, 1989.

A weak, divided, and opportunistic opposition facilitated Abdallah's efforts to undermine the political process. The character of Comoran politics ensured that opposition would be sustained by an unwieldy group of strong personalities. As the personal stock of these would-be leaders rose and fell, coalitions coalesced and just as quickly fell apart in a process that engendered distrust and cynicism. The ban on opposition political organizations at home—brutally upheld, when necessary, by the Presidential Guard (Garde Présidentielle—GP) and the Comoran military—further undercut efforts to organize against the head of state. The French government's displeasure at intrigues of Comoran exiles in Paris also complicated opposition efforts.

Given the absence of an ideological basis for resisting the regime, it was also not surprising that some opposition leaders were willing to ally themselves with the head of state if such a move appeared likely to advance them personally. For example, Mouzaoir Abdallah, leader of the opposition Union for a Democratic Republic in Comoros (Union pour une République Démocratique aux Comores—URDC), appeared with the president at independence day celebrations in July 1988 amid rumors that the URDC chief was being considered for a reconstituted prime minister's office. In September 1988, another opposition leader, Said Hachim, agreed to join the commission considering revisions to the constitution.

The credibility of Abdallah's opponents was also damaged by the efforts of one opposition leader, former ambassador to France Said Ali Kemal, to recruit mercenaries to help overthrow the Abdallah government. Arrested in Australia in late 1983, six of the mercenaries gave testimony discrediting Kemal.

### Mercenary Rule

Abdallah complemented his political maneuvers by employing a GP officered by many of the same mercenaries who had helped him take power in 1978. Denard led this force, and also became heavily involved in Comoran business activities, sometimes acting in partnership with President Abdallah or as a front for South African business interests, which played a growing role in the Comoran economy during the Abdallah regime.

Although Denard had made a ceremonial departure from Comoros following the 1978 coup, by the early 1980s he was again openly active in the islands. The GP, whose numbers were reported to range from 300 to 700 members, primarily indigenous Comorans, were led by about thirty French and Belgian mercenaries, mostly comrades of Denard's in the post-World War II conflicts that accompanied the decolonization of Africa and Asia. Answerable only to the president, the GP operated outside the chain of command of the French-trained 1,000-member Comoran Armed Forces, a situation that caused resentment among the regular military, Comoran citizens, and other African states.

The GP's primary missions were to protect the president and to deter attempts to overthrow his government. During the July 1983 elections to the three islands' legislative councils, the GP beat and arrested demonstrators protesting the republic's single-party system. During elections to the National Assembly in March 1987, the GP—which had become known as *les affreux*, "the frighteners"—replaced several hundred dissident poll watchers who had been arrested by the army. On March 8,

1985, one of the most serious attempts to overthrow the Abdallah government began as a mutiny by about thirty Comoran troops of the GP against their European officers. The disaffected guards had formed ties to the Democratic Front (Front Démocratique—FD), one of the more nationalistic of the republic's many banned political parties. The mutiny was quickly squelched; three of the rebellious guards were killed, and the rest were taken prisoners.

President Abdallah used the uprising as an opportunity to round up dissidents, primarily FD members, whose leadership denied involvement in the coup attempt. Later in 1985, seventy-seven received convictions; seventeen, including the FD's secretary general, Mustapha Said Cheikh, were sentenced to life imprisonment at hard labor. Most of the prisoners were released in 1986 following Amnesty International charges of illegal arrests, torture, and other abuses. France had also exerted pressure by temporarily withholding new aid projects and purchases of Comoran vanilla.

Perhaps the most notorious action of the GP on behalf of the Abdallah government occurred in November 1987. After an apparent attempt by dissidents to free some political prisoners, an event quickly labeled a coup attempt by the Abdallah regime, the GP arrested fourteen alleged plotters and tortured seven of them to death. Officials of the Comoran government apparently were not allowed to participate in the prisoners' interrogation. President Abdallah was on a state visit to Egypt at the time.

With Abdallah's acquiescence and occasional participation, Denard and the other GP officers used their connections to the head of state to make themselves important players in the Comoran economy. Denard was a part owner of Établissements Abdallah et Fils, Comoros' largest import-export firm, whose primary owner was President Abdallah. Denard also owned and operated a highly profitable commercial shuttle between South Africa and Comoros, and owned Sogecom, a private security firm with contracts to protect South African hotels being built in the islands.

The GP officers, sympathetic to South Africa's apartheid government, established themselves as a conduit of South African investment and influence in Comoros. An official South African trade representative conceded that a number of his country's investment projects, including a 525-hectare experimental farm, housing, road construction, and a medical evacuation program, were brokered and managed by guard officers at the mercenaries' insistence.

The GP also arranged for South African commercial aircraft to fly in the Middle East and parts of Africa under the aegis of the Comoran national airline, in contravention of international sanctions against South Africa. Furthermore, the GP provided for South African use of Comoran territory as a base for intelligence gathering in the Mozambique Channel and as a staging area for the shipment of arms to rightist rebels in Mozambique. The GP was widely understood to be funded by South Africa, at the rate of about US$3 million per year.

### Comoros as Client State: The Economics of Abdallah

President Abdallah generally put his personal interests ahead of national interests in making economic policy. The result was the creation of a client state whose meager and unpredictable cash crop earnings were supplemented with increasing infusions of foreign aid.

Throughout the 1980s, export earnings from Comoros' four main cash crops—vanilla, ylang ylang, cloves, and copra—experienced a wrenching sequence of booms and collapses because of weather and market factors, or else steadily dwindled. The regime's principal form of response was to apply the president's considerable diplomatic skills to developing an extensive network of governments and international organizations willing to extend loans and donate aid. The main suppliers were France, South Africa, the EC, the conservative Arab states, the World Bank (see Glossary) and related organs, and regional financial institutions such as the Arab Bank for Economic Development in Africa and the African Development Bank. Some assistance went to projects of indisputable value, such as efforts to create independent news media and improve telephone communications with the outside world. Much of the aid, however, was questionable—for example, loans and grants to help the republic meet the payroll for its oversized civil service. Other more plausible projects, such as the protracted development of a seaport at the town of Mutsamudu, construction of paved ring roads linking each island's coastal settlements, and the building of power stations, nonetheless tended to be instances of placing the cart before the horse. That is, capital-intensive improvements to infrastructure had not been coordinated with local development projects; hence, little, if any, domestic commerce existed to benefit from road networks, electrical power, and world-class port facilities. The importation of huge quantities of building materials and construction equipment provided immediate benefits to import-export firms in the islands, of which Établissements Abdallah et Fils was the largest. In the meantime, the projects were of little immediate use to Comorans and were likely to go underused for years to come.

Throughout the Abdallah period, rice imports drained as much as 50 percent of Comoran export earnings. Projects to increase food self-sufficiency, as one observer noted, "fail[ed] to respond to the largesse" provided by international sponsors such as the European Development Fund and the International Fund for Agricultural Development. The president joined with vanilla growers in resisting international pressure to divert vanilla-producing land to the cultivation of corn and rice for domestic consumption. He also declined to heed World Bank advice to impose tariffs and domestic taxes on imported rice. Abdallah's import-export firm was heavily involved in vanilla exports, as well as in the importation of Far Eastern rice at three times its price at the source.

Abdallah's firm, whose co-owners included Denard and Kalfane and Company, a Pakistani concern, also profited from managing the importation of materials used by South African firms in developing tourist hotels. Little of the material used in building these resorts was of Comoran origin. Also, once completed, the resorts would be almost entirely owned and managed by non-Comorans. Although tourism, mainly by South Africans who were unwelcome in other African resorts, was widely considered the only promising new industry in Comoros, Abdallah guided its development so that resorts benefited few Comorans other than himself and his associates.

Under Abdallah's tutelage, the Comoran economy finished the 1980s much as it had started the decade—poor, underdeveloped, and dependent on export earnings from cash crops of unpredictable and generally declining value. The critical difference, with enormous implications for the republic's capacity to have some say in its own destiny, was its new status as a nation abjectly in debt. By 1988, the last full year of the Abdallah regime, 80 percent of annual public expenditures were funded by external aid (see Economy, this ch.).

### *The Demise of Abdallah, 1989*

Only weeks before the violent end of the Abdallah regime in late 1989, one observer noted that "Comoros is still run like a village, with a handful of tough men in charge and supported by foreign aid." As Comorans prepared for a November 4, 1989, referendum on constitutional changes that would enable President Abdallah to run for a third term in 1990, human rights remained in precarious condition, and the only avenue of economic advancement for most islanders—the civil service—faced cutbacks at the urging of the World Bank and the International Monetary Fund (IMF—see Glossary). Even those who would keep their government jobs, however, were not guaranteed economic security. As often occurred whenever export earnings slid, civil servants had not been paid since midsummer.

The official result of the referendum was a 92.5 percent majority in favor of the amendments proposed by Abdallah, which now created "the conditions for a life presidency," warned one opposition leader. Balloting was marked by the now customary manipulation by the government. Opposition groups reported that polling places lacked private voting booths, government officials blocked the entry of opposition poll watchers, and the army and police removed ballot boxes before voting ended. Reaction to these abuses was unusually angry. In Njazidja voters smashed ballot boxes rather than have them carted away by the army; the governor's office was set on fire in Nzwani, and a bomb was found outside the home of the minister of finance in Moroni. More than 100 people were arrested following the election, and in subsequent weeks the international media described a deteriorating situation in the islands; the head of state claimed that France "authorizes terrorism in the Comoros," and leaders of the banned opposition in bold public statements questioned the legitimacy of the referendum.

President Abdallah was shot to death on the night of November 26–27, reportedly while asleep in his residence, the Beit el Salama (House of Peace). At first his death was seen as a logical outcome of the tense political situation following what was, in effect, his self-appointment as head of state for life. The recently dismissed head of the Comoran military was duly blamed for the murder.

Evidence emerged subsequently that Abdallah's assassination resulted from the late president's proposed actions with regard to the GP. In September 1989, Abdallah had engaged a French military consultant, who determined that the GP should be absorbed into the regular army. Following consultations among Abdallah, the French government, and South Africa's Ministry of Foreign Affairs, a decision was made to expel Denard and his fellow officers of the GP by the end of 1989. Denard and his second in command were seen walking with Abdallah only hours before he died. Although the mercenary initially blamed the assassination on the Comoran army, he later conceded that he was in Abdallah's office when the president was killed, but called the shooting "an accident due to the general state of mayhem" in the Beit el Salama (see Political Dynamics, this ch.).

Two days later, on November 29, the real reasons for the assassination emerged when Denard and the GP seized control of the government in a coup. Twenty-seven police officers were killed, hundreds of people were arrested, and all journalists were confined to their hotels. The mercenaries disarmed the regular army, ousted provisional president Haribon Chebani, who as chief of the Supreme Court had succeeded Abdallah, and installed Mohamed Said Djohar, who just three days earlier had become chief of the Supreme Court, as Comoros' third president in less than a week.

The immediate reaction of the republic's two main supporters, France and South Africa, was to isolate Denard. South Africa, admitting years of funding of the GP, cut off all aid. France began a military build-up on Mahoré and likewise suspended aid. On December 7, anti-Denard demonstrations by about 1,000 students and workers were violently broken up by the protests. By then the islands' school system had shut down, and the civil service had gone on strike. Faced with an untenable situation, Denard surrendered to French forces without a fight on December 15. Along with about two dozen comrades, he was flown to Pretoria and put under house arrest. The French government later announced that Denard would remain in detention in South Africa pending the outcome of a French judicial inquiry into Abdallah's death. In February 1993, he returned to France, where he was initially arrested, tried, and exonerated of involvement in the death of Abdallah.

## The Issue of Mahoré

One of the touchiest issues in the negotiations between Comoros and France over independence in the early 1970s had been whether the 1974 referendum would be considered for the Comoros archipelago as a whole or on an island-by-island basis. Opposition to independence on Mahoré was organized by the Mayotte Popular Movement (Mouvement Populaire Mahorais—MPM), an organization that had been founded in the 1960s by Zeina M'Dere, a spokeswoman for Mahoré shop-keepers, mostly women, who had been affected economically when the colonial capital was moved from the Mahoré town of Dzaoudzi to Moroni on Njazidja in 1962.

The reasons behind Mahoré's 65 percent vote against independence were several. First, the people of Mahoré considered themselves culturally, religiously, and linguistically distinct from those of the other three islands; they felt that their long association with France (since 1841) had given their island a distinct Creole character like that of Reunion or Seychelles. Second, given Mahoré's smaller population, greater natural resources, and higher standard of living, the Mahorais thought that their island would be economically viable within a French union and ought not to be brought down to the level of the other three poorer islands. Third, most Mahorais apparently felt that Mahoré's future within a Comoran state would not be a comfortable one, given a perception of neglect that had begun with the much resented transfer of the capital.

In France and among conservatives on Reunion, the 1974 vote on Mahoré in favor of continued association with France was greeted with great enthusiasm. Comoran leaders, in contrast, accused the MPM and its leader, Marcel Henri, of fabricating the illusion of Mahorais "uniqueness" to preserve the power of Mahoré's non-Muslim, Creole elite. The issue poisoned Comoran relations with France, particularly because the Indian Ocean lobby, whose leaders included Reunion's deputy to the French National Assembly, Michel Debré, pushed for a "Mayotte française" (French Mayotte). Apparently leaning toward the interpretation that the December 1974 referendum was an island-by-island plebiscite, the French legislature voted in June 1975 to postpone independence for six months and hold a second referendum. The Abdallah government responded by declaring independence unilaterally on July 6, 1975, for all Comoro Islands, including Mahoré. France reacted by cutting off financial aid, which provided 41 percent of the national budget. Fearing a Comoran attempt to assert control of Mahoré forcibly, France sent members of the Foreign Legion from Reunion and a fleet of three vessels to patrol the waters around the island on July 6-7. On November 12, 1975, the UN General Assembly passed a resolution giving

Comoros UN membership and recognized its claims to Mahoré, which France opposed.

French policy toward Mahoré had been, in the words of one observer, "to cultivate a more or less honest majority for reunification among the uncooperative Mahorais," particularly after the forthrightly anti-French regime of Ali Soilih ended in 1978. By contrast, the Mahorais' objective appeared to be full departmental status such as that of Reunion, where residents enjoyed full rights as French citizens. In a 1976 referendum, the Mahorais expressed dissatisfaction with their status as an overseas territory. France then created a new classification for Mahoré— territorial community (*collectivité territoriale*)—under which Mahoré was administered by a prefect appointed by the French government. Local government consisted of a popularly elected seventeen-member General Council. The island was entitled to send elected representatives to Paris, one each to the National Assembly and the Senate. The French franc served as the currency of the island. This status still applied in 1994.

After it appeared that Mahoré would not be tempted by the federalist design of Ahmed Abdallah's 1978 constitution to join the Republic of the Comoros, the National Assembly in Paris decided in 1979 to prolong the existence of the *collectivité territoriale* until a 1984 plebiscite, resolving meanwhile to study the situation and consult with the islanders. In late 1984, with an overwhelming vote to remain associated with France in the offing, the French government postponed the plebiscite indefinitely. By mid-1994, it had still not been held, the Mahorais apparently still eager to remain part of France and as disinclined as ever to reunite with the three troubled islands to their immediate west.

Although many politically conservative French relished the Mahorais' popular vow that *nous resterons français pour rester libre* ("we will remain French to remain free"), the Mahoré situation caused some discomfort for France internationally. Every year, resolutions calling on France to relinquish Mahoré to Comoros passed with near unanimity in the UN, and the OAU likewise issued annual condemnations. Although Comoran official distaste for the situation became more muted in the 1980s and 1990s, the Comoran government continued to draw French attention to the issue. In May 1990, newly elected president Said Mohamed Djohar called for peaceful dialogue and French review of Mahoré's status. But feeling obligated not to change

*Woman grinding coconuts,
a staple food
Courtesy
Mari G. Borstelmann*

*Women and children in
front of houses on Mwali
Courtesy
Mari G. Borstelmann*

the Mahorais' status against their will, the French could do little. Anti-Comoran riots and demonstrations, and the formation of an anti-immigrant paramilitary group on Mahoré in response to the presence of illegal Comoran immigrants, were also sources of embarrassment to France.

The economy of Mahoré in some ways resembles that of Comoros. Rice, cassava, and corn are cultivated for domestic consumption; ylang-ylang and vanilla are the primary exports. The main imports, whose value far outstrips that of exports, are foodstuffs, machinery and appliances, transport equipment, and metals. Construction, primarily of French-funded public works, is the only industrial activity.

A five-year development plan (1986–91) focused on large-scale public projects, principally construction of a deepwater port at Longoni and an airport at the capital, Dzaoudzi. The plan and its two main projects were later extended through 1993. Despite Mahoré's great natural beauty, tourism has been inhibited by a dearth of hotel rooms and the island's isolated location.

Under French administration, Mahoré generally enjoyed domestic peace and stability, although tensions appeared to be rising by the early 1990s. In the summer of 1991, the relocation of people from their homes to allow the expansion of the airport met with vociferous protests, mostly by young people. The protests soon grew into violent demonstrations against the local government's administration of the island. Paramilitary attacks on Comoran immigrants occurred in June 1992, and a February 1993 general strike for higher wages ended in rioting. Security forces from Reunion and France were called in to restore order.

## Physical Environment

The Comoros archipelago consists of four main islands aligned along a northwest-southeast axis at the north end of the Mozambique Channel, between Mozambique and the island of Madagascar (see fig.6). Still widely known by their French names, the islands are officially called by their Swahili names by the Comoran government. They are Njazidja (Grande Comore), Mwali (Mohéli), Nzwani (Anjouan), and Mahoré (Mayotte). The islands' distance from each other—Njazidja is some 200 kilometers from Mahoré, forty kilometers from Mwali, and eighty kilometers from Nzwani—and a lack of good harbor facilities make transportation and communication difficult. The islands have a total land area of 2,236 square kilometers (including Mahoré) and claim territorial waters that extend 320 kilometers offshore.

Njazidja is the largest island, sixty-seven kilometers long and twenty-seven kilometers wide, with a total area of 1,146 square kilometers. The most recently formed of the four islands in the archipelago, it is also of volcanic origin. Two volcanoes form the island's most prominent topographic features: La Grille in the north, with an elevation of 1,000 meters, is extinct and largely eroded; Kartala in the south, rising to a height of 2,361 meters, last erupted in 1977. A plateau averaging 600 to 700 meters high connects the two mountains. Because Njazidja is geologically a relatively new island, its soil is thin and rocky and cannot hold water. As a result, water from the island's heavy rainfall must be stored in catchment tanks. There are no coral reefs along the coast, and the island lacks a good harbor for ships. One of the largest remnants of Comoros' once-extensive rain forests is on the slopes of Kartala. The national capital has been at Moroni since 1962.

Nzwani, triangular shaped and forty kilometers from apex to base, has an area of 424 square kilometers. Three mountain chains—Sima, Nioumakele, and Jimilime—emanate from a central peak, Mtingui (1,575 meters), giving the island its distinctive shape. Older than Njazidja, Nzwani has deeper soil cover, but overcultivation has caused serious erosion. A coral reef lies close to shore; the island's capital of Mutsamudu is also its main port.

Mwali is thirty kilometers long and twelve kilometers wide, with an area of 290 square kilometers. It is the smallest of the four islands and has a central mountain chain reaching 860 meters at its highest. Like Njazidja, it retains stands of rain forest. Mwali's capital is Fomboni.

Mahoré, geologically the oldest of the four islands, is thirty-nine kilometers long and twenty-two kilometers wide, totaling 375 square kilometers, and its highest points are between 500 and 600 meters above sea level. Because of greater weathering of the volcanic rock, the soil is relatively rich in some areas. A well-developed coral reef that encircles much of the island ensures protection for ships and a habitat for fish. Dzaoudzi, capital of Comoros until 1962 and now Mahoré's administrative center, is situated on a rocky outcropping off the east shore of the main island. Dzaoudzi is linked by a causeway to Île Pamanzi, which at ten square kilometers in area is the largest of several islets adjacent to Mahoré. Islets are also scattered in the coastal waters of Njazidja, Nzwani, and Mwali.

Comoran waters are the habitat of the coelacanth, a rare fish with limblike fins and a cartilaginous skeleton, the fossil remains of which date as far back as 400 million years and which was once thought to have become extinct about 70 million years ago. A live specimen was caught in 1938 off southern Africa; other coelacanths have since been found in the vicinity of the Comoro Islands.

Several mammals are unique to the islands themselves. The macao, a lemur found only on Mahoré, is protected by French law and by local tradition. Another, Livingstone's fruit bat, although plentiful when discovered by explorer David Livingstone in 1863, has been reduced to a population of about 120, entirely on Nzwani. The world's largest bat, the jet-black Livingstone fruit bat has a wingspan of nearly two meters. A British preservation group sent an expedition to Comoros in 1992 to bring some of the bats to Britain to establish a breeding population. Humboldt's flycatcher is perhaps the best known of the birds native to Comoros.

Partly in response to international pressures, Comorans in the 1990s have become more concerned about the environment. Steps are being taken not only to preserve the rare fauna, but also to counteract degradation of the environment, especially on densely populated Nzwani. Specifically, to minimize the cutting down of trees for fuel, kerosene is being subsidized, and efforts are being made to replace the loss of the forest cover caused by ylang-ylang distillation for perfume. The Community Development Support Fund, sponsored by the International Development Association (IDA—a World Bank affiliate—see Glossary) and the Comoran government, is working to improve water supply on the islands as well.

The climate is marine tropical, with two seasons: hot and humid from November to April, the result of the northeastern monsoon, and a cooler, drier season the rest of the year. Average monthly temperatures range from 23°C to 28°C along the coasts. Although the average annual precipitation is 2,000 millimeters, water is a scarce commodity in many parts of Comoros. Mwali and Mahoré possess streams and other natural sources of water, but Njazidja and Nzwani, whose mountainous landscapes retain water poorly, are almost devoid of naturally occurring running water. Cyclones, occurring during the hot and wet season, can cause extensive damage, especially in coastal areas. On the average, at least twice each decade houses, farms, and harbor facilities are devastated by these great storms.

## Society and Culture

Comoran society and culture reflect the influences of Islam and the traditions of East Africa. The former provides the basis for religion and law; the East African influence is evident in the language, a Swahili dialect, and in a number of pre-Islamic customs. Western, primarily French, influences are also prevalent, particularly in the modern educational sector, the civil service, and cultural affairs.

### Population

The most recent official census by the Comoran government, conducted in 1991, put the islands' population, exclusive of Mahoré, at 446,817. Official counts put the population of Mahoré at 67,167 in 1985 and 94,410 in 1991—a 40 percent increase in just six years.

Average population density in Comoros was 183 persons per square kilometer in 1980. This figure concealed a great disparity between the republic's most crowded island, Nzwani, which had a density of 470 persons per square kilometer in 1991; Njazidja, which had a density of 250 persons per square kilometer in 1991; and Mwali, where the 1991 population density figure was 120 persons per square kilometer. Overall population density increased to about 285 persons per square kilometer by 1994. Mahoré's population density went from 179 persons per square kilometer in 1985 to 251 per square kilometer in 1991.

By comparison, estimates of the population density per square kilometer of the Indian Ocean's other island microstates ranged from 241 (Seychelles) to 690 (Maldives) in 1993. Given the rugged terrain of Njazidja and Nzwani, and the dedication of extensive tracts to agriculture on all three islands, population pressures on Comoros are becoming increasingly critical. A similar situation obtains on Mahoré.

The age structure of the population of Comoros is similar to that of many developing countries, in that the republic has a very large proportion of young people. In 1989, 46.4 percent of the population was under fifteen years of age, an above-average proportion even for sub-Saharan Africa. The population's rate of growth was a very high 3.5 percent per annum in the mid-

1980s, up substantially from 2.0 percent in the mid-1970s and 2.1 percent in the mid-1960s.

In 1983 the Abdallah regime borrowed US$2.85 million from the IDA to devise a national family planning program. However, Islamic reservations about contraception made forthright advocacy and implementation of birth control programs politically hazardous, and consequently little was done in the way of public policy (see Status of Women, this ch.).

The Comoran population has become increasingly urbanized in recent years. In 1991 the percentage of Comorans residing in cities and towns of more than 5,000 persons was about 30 percent, up from 25 percent in 1985 and 23 percent in 1980. Comoros' largest cities were the capital, Moroni, with about 30,000 people, and the port city of Mutsamudu, on the island of Nzwani, with about 20,000 people. Mahoré's capital, Dzaoudzi, had a population of 5,865 according to the 1985 census; the island's largest town, Mamoudzou, had 12,026 people.

Migration among the various islands is relatively small. Natives of Njazidja often settle in less crowded Mwali, and before independence people from Nzwani commonly moved to Mahoré. In 1977 Mahoré expelled peasants from Njazidja and Nzwani who had recently settled in large numbers on the island. Some were allowed to reenter starting in 1981 but solely as migrant laborers.

The number of Comorans living abroad has been estimated at between 80,000 and 100,000; most of them live in Tanzania, Madagascar, and other parts of East Africa. The number of Comorans residing in Madagascar was drastically reduced after anti-Comoran rioting in December 1976 in Mahajanga, in which at least 1,400 Comorans were killed. As many as 17,000 Comorans left Madagascar to seek refuge in their native land in 1977 alone. About 40,000 Comorans live in France; many of them had gone there for a university education and never returned. Small numbers of Indians, Malagasy, South Africans, and Europeans live on the islands and play an important role in the economy.

## Society

The Comoran people are a blend of African, Arab, and Malayo-Indonesian elements. A few small communities, primarily in Mahoré, speak *kibushi*, a Malagasy dialect. The principal Comoran Swahili dialect, written in Arabic script, is related to the Swahili spoken in East Africa but is not easily intelligible to

East African Swahili speakers. Classical Arabic is significant for religious reasons, and French remains the principal language with which the Republic of the Comoros communicates with the rest of the world.

A number of ethnically distinguishable groups are found: the Arabs, descendants of Shirazi settlers, who arrived in significant numbers in the fifteenth century; the Cafres, an African group that settled on the islands before the coming of the Shirazi; a second African group, the Makoa, descendants of slaves brought by the Arabs from the East African coast; and three groups of Malayo-Indonesian peoples—the Oimatsaha, the Antalotes, and the Sakalava, the latter having settled largely on Mahoré. Intermarriage has tended to blur the distinctions among these groups, however. Creoles, descendants of French settlers who intermarried with the indigenous peoples, form a tiny but politically influential group on Mahoré, numbering no more than about 100 on that island. They are predominantly Roman Catholic and mainly cultivate small plantations. In addition, a small group of people descended in part from the Portuguese sailors who landed on the Comoro Islands at the beginning of the sixteenth century are reportedly living around the town of Tsangadjou on the east coast of Njazidja.

Shirazi Arab royal clans dominated the islands socially, culturally, and politically from the fifteenth century until the French occupation. Eleven such clans lived on Njazidja, where their power was strongest, and their leaders, the sultans or sharifs, who claimed to be descendants of the Prophet Muhammad, were in a continual state of war until the French occupation. Two similar clans were located on Nzwani, and these clans maintained vassals on Mahoré and Mwali after the Sakalava wiped out the local nobles in the late eighteenth and early nineteenth centuries. Although the clan system was weakened by the economic and social dislocations of the colonial era, the descendants of clan nobles continue to form a major portion of the educated and propertied classes. The pre-independence rivalry of Said Mohamed Cheikh and Prince Said Ibrahim, leaders, respectively, of the conservative Parti Vert and the Parti Blanc, was interpreted by some as a revival of old clan antagonisms. Yet many descendants of nobles live in poverty and apparently have less influence socially and politically on Nzwani than on Njazidja.

The present-day elite, although composed in part of those of noble ancestry who took advantage of the opportunities of the cash crop economy established by the French, is mainly defined in terms of wealth rather than caste or descent. This focus on wealth is not unusual, considering that the original Shirazi settlers themselves were traders and that the precolonial sultans were actively involved in commerce. Conspicuous consumption continues to mark the lifestyle of the elite.

Especially well regarded are those individuals who hold the *grand mariage*, often after a lifetime of scrimping and saving. This wedding ceremony, which can cost as much as the equivalent of US$20,000 to US$30,000, involves an exchange of expensive gifts between the couple's families and feasts for an entire village. Although the gift giving and dancing that accompany the *grand mariage* have helped perpetuate indigenous arts in silversmithing, goldsmithing, folk song, and folk dance, the waste involved has disastrous consequences for an economy already short on domestic resources. A ban or curb on the *grand mariage* was on the agenda of many reformers in the period preceding the radical regime of Ali Soilih, who himself had taken the almost unheard-of step of declining to participate in the ritual. However, the efforts of the Soilih government to restrict the custom aroused great resentment, and it was restored to its preeminent place in Comoran society almost immediately after Soilih was deposed in 1978.

Although its expense limits the number of families that can provide their sons and daughters a *grand mariage*, the ritual is still used as a means of distinguishing Comoran society's future leaders. Only by participating in the ceremony is a Comoran man entitled to participate in his village's assembly of notables and to wear the *mharuma*, a sash that entitles him to enter the mosque by a special door. Few, if any, candidates win election to the National Assembly without a *grand mariage* in their pasts. For these reasons in particular, critics of traditional Comoran society condemn the *grand mariage* as a means of excluding people of modest resources from participating in the islands' political life.

Those who can afford the pilgrimage to Mecca are also accorded prestige. The imams who lead prayers in mosques form a distinct elite group.

Despite the weakening of the position of the Shirazi elite, one observer reports that in many subtle ways old distinctions persist. The descendants of slaves, formally emancipated in 1904, are mostly sharecroppers or squatters, working the land that belonged to their ancestors' former owners, although

*Grand mosque, Nzwani*
*Courtesy Brian Kensley*

some have gone abroad as migrant laborers (a greatly restricted option since Madagascar's expulsion of thousands of Comorans in the late 1970s). Men of "freeborn" families choose "freeborn" wives, holding, if possible, a *grand mariage*, but if they take second wives, these women often are of slave ancestry.

## Status of Women

Among men who can afford it, the preferred form of marriage appears to be polygyny with matrilocal residence. Although the first marriage is formally initiated with the *grand mariage* when possible, subsequent unions involve much simpler ceremonies. The result is that a man will establish two or even more households and will alternate residence between them, a reflection, most likely, of the trading origins of the Shirazi elite who maintained wives at different trading posts. Said Mohamed Djohar, elected president in 1990, had two wives, one in Njazidja and the other in Nzwani, an arrangement said to have broadened his appeal to voters. For men, divorce is easy, although by custom a divorced wife retains the family home.

Islamic law recognizes only male ownership and inheritance of land. In Comoros, however, certain landholdings called *magnahouli* are controlled by women and inherited through the female line, apparently in observance of a surviving matriarchal African tradition.

Despite their lower economic status, women married to farmers or laborers often move about more freely than their counterparts among the social elite, managing market stands or working in the fields. On Mwali, where traditional Islamic values are less dominant, women generally are not as strictly secluded. Women constituted 40.4 percent of the work force in 1990, a figure slightly above average for sub-Saharan Africa.

Girls are somewhat less likely than boys to attend school in Comoros. The World Bank estimated in 1993 that 67 percent of girls were enrolled in primary schools, whereas 82 percent of boys were enrolled. In secondary school, 15 percent of eligible Comoran girls were in attendance, in comparison with about 19 percent of eligible boys.

Although the 1992 constitution recognizes their right to suffrage, as did the 1978 constitution, women otherwise play a limited role in politics in Comoros. By contrast, in Mahoré female merchants sparked the movement for continued association with France, and later, for continued separation from the Republic of the Comoros (see The Issue of Mahoré, this ch.).

Comoros accepted international aid for family planning in 1983, but it was considered politically inexpedient to put any plans into effect. According to a 1993 estimate, there were 6.8 births per woman in Comoros. By contrast, the figure was 6.4 births per woman for the rest of sub-Saharan Africa (see Population, this ch.).

In one of Comoran society's first acknowledgments of women as a discrete interest group, the Abdallah government organized a seminar, "Women, Family, and Development," in 1986. Despite participants' hopes that programs for family planning and female literacy would be announced, conference organizers stressed the role of women in agriculture and family life. Women fared slightly better under the Djohar regime. In February 1990, while still interim president, Djohar created a cabinet-level Ministry of Social and Women's Affairs, and appointed a woman, Ahlonkoba Aithnard, to head it. She lasted until a few weeks after Djohar's election to the presidency in March, when her ministry was reorganized out of existence, along with several others. Another female official, Situ Mohamed, was named to head the second-tier Ministry of Population and Women's Affairs, in August 1991. She lost her position—and the subministry was eliminated—hardly a week later, in one of President Djohar's routine ministerial reshufflings. Djohar made another nod to women in February 1992, when he invited representatives of an interest group, the Women's Federation, to take part in discussions on what would become the constitution of 1992. Women apparently organized and participated in a large demonstration critical of French support of the Djohar regime in October 1992, following government suppression of a coup attempt.

## Religion and Education

Islam and its institutions help to integrate Comoran society and provide an identification with a world beyond the islands' shores. As Sunni Muslims, the people follow religious observances conscientiously and strictly adhere to religious orthodoxy. During the period of colonization, the French did not attempt to supplant Islamic customs and practices and were careful to respect the precedents of Islamic law as interpreted by the Shafii school (one of the four major legal schools in Sunni Islam, named after Muhammad ibn Idris ash Shafii, it stresses reasoning by analogy). Hundreds of mosques dot the islands.

Practically all children attend Quranic school for two or three years, starting around age five; there they learn the rudiments of the Islamic faith and some classical Arabic. When rural children attend these schools, they sometimes move away from home and help the teacher work his land.

France established a system of primary and secondary schools based on the French model, which remains largely in place. Comoran law requires all children to complete nine years of schooling between the ages of seven and sixteen. The system provides six years of primary education for students ages seven to twelve, followed by seven years of secondary school. In recent years, enrollment has expanded greatly, particularly at the primary level. About 20,750 pupils, or roughly 75 percent of primary-school-age children were enrolled in 1993, up from about 46 percent in the late 1970s. About 17 percent of the secondary-school-age population was enrolled, up from an estimated 7 percent fifteen to twenty years earlier. Teacher-student ratios also improved, from 47:1 to 36:1 in the primary schools and from 26:1 to 25:1 in secondary schools. The increased attendance was all the more significant given the population's high percentage of school-age children. Improvement in educational facilities was funded in 1993 by loans from the Organization of the Petroleum Exporting Countries (OPEC) and the African Development Bank. Despite the spread of education, adult literacy in 1993 has been estimated at no better than 50 percent.

Comoros has no university, but postsecondary education, which in 1993 involved 400 students, is available in the form of teacher training, agricultural education training, health sciences, and business. Those desiring higher education must study abroad; a "brain drain" has resulted because few university graduates are willing to return to the islands. Teacher training and other specialized courses are available at the M'Vouni School for Higher Education, in operation since 1981 at a site near Moroni. Few Comoran teachers study overseas, but the republic often cannot give its teachers all the training they need. Some international aid has been provided, however, to further teacher training in the islands themselves. For example, in 1987 the IDA extended credits worth US$7.9 million to train 3,000 primary and 350 secondary school teachers. In 1986 the government began opening technology training centers offering a three-year diploma program at the upper secondary level. The Ministry of National Education and Professional Training is responsible for education policy.

As elsewhere in Comoran society, political instability has taken a toll on the education system. Routinely announced reductions in force among the civil service, often made in response to international pressure for fiscal reform, sometimes result in teacher strikes. When civil service cutbacks result in canceled classes or examinations, students have at times taken to the streets in protest. Students have also protested, even violently, against government underfunding or general mismanagement of the schools—the World Bank stated in 1994 that the quality of education resulted in high rates of repetition and dropouts such that many students needed fourteen years to complete the six-year primary cycle.

## Public Health

After independence in 1975, the French withdrew their medical teams, leaving the three islands' already rudimentary health care system in a state of severe crisis. French assistance was eventually resumed, and other nations also contributed medical assistance to the young republic. Despite improvements in life expectancy and the infant mortality rate, Comoros in 1994 continued to face public health problems characteristic of developing countries.

Life expectancy at birth was estimated at fifty-six years in 1990, up from fifty-one years in 1980. The crude birthrate was forty-eight per 1,000 and the crude death rate, twelve per 1,000 according to 1989 statistics. All three of these figures were close to the averages for sub-Saharan Africa. The rate of infant mortality per 1,000 live births was eighty-nine in 1991, down from 113 in 1980. The 1990 average rate for sub-Saharan Africa was 107.

Malaria is ubiquitous in the islands, with 80 to 90 percent of the population said to be affected by the disease. Other prevalent maladies include tuberculosis, leprosy, and parasitic diseases. In 1989 about half of all children one year old or younger had been immunized against tuberculosis, diphtheria, pertussis, tetanus, polio, and measles, a proportion roughly comparable to the rate of immunization among other states in sub-Saharan Africa. Per capita daily caloric intake in 1988 was 2,046, about average for sub-Saharan Africa but only a little better than 90 percent of daily requirements. Children are most often the victims of malnutrition. Their generally poor diets are deficient in protein in part because local custom discourages the feeding of fish to children. The scarcity of safe drinking water—available to about one in three Comorans—makes intestinal parasites a problem and compounds malnutrition, with children again being the main victims.

The World Bank estimated that in 1993 Comoros had one physician per 6,582 Comorans, a marked improvement over the ratio of one to 13,810 reported in 1983. Comparable data for sub-Saharan Africa as a whole were not available; however, it appeared that Comorans enjoyed a more favorable ratio than many of their neighbors in East Africa and the Indian Ocean.

Despite improvements in life expectancy, infant mortality, and the number of physicians, the overall quality of care remains poor. About 80 percent of the population lives within one hour's walk of a health facility, usually headed by a trained nurse, but paramedical staff are in short supply, and many health facilities are in poor condition. Some international medical aid has been provided, mostly by France and the World Health Organization (WHO).

Although Comoros lacks homegrown narcotics, the islands are used as a transit site for drugs coming mainly from Madagascar. In view of international concern about drug trafficking, in 1993 France began providing technical expertise in this field to Comoros. In addition, the World Bank in a 1994 report pointed out the "high prevalence of sexually transmitted diseases and the low use of condoms" as a significant health threat with regard to the spread of acquired immune deficiency syndrome (AIDS), which already affected the islands. However, in the period prior to 1990 and extending through 1992, the WHO reported that Comoros had a very low incidence of AIDS—a total of three cases with no case reported in 1992, or an overall case rate of 0.1 per 100,000 population.

## Media

As recently as the early 1980s Comoros had no national media. State-run Radio Comoros, transmitting from Njazidja, was not strong enough to send clear signals to the republic's other two islands. In 1984 France agreed to provide Radio Comoros with funding for an FM (frequency modulation) transmitter strong enough to broadcast to all three islands, and in 1985 made a commitment to fund a national newspaper after a United Nations Educational, Scientific, and Cultural

Organization (UNESCO) study revealed that Comoros was the only UN member lacking print and electronic media. A state-owned newspaper, *Al Watwany*, began operations in July 1985, first as a monthly and soon afterward as a weekly. An independent weekly, *L'Archipel*, began publishing in 1988. A news agency, Agence Comores Presse, is now based in Moroni, and France has provided funds for establishing a national television service. In 1989 Comoros had an estimated 61,000 radios and 200 television sets.

In addition to national broadcasts on FM in Comoran Swahili and French, Radio Comoros in 1994 broadcast internationally on the shortwave band in Swahili, Arabic, and French. An independent commercial FM radio station, Radio Tropique FM, began broadcasting in 1991, although it and its director, political activist Ali Bakar Cassim, have both been the object of government ire over the station's readiness to criticize the Djohar regime.

During the independent media's brief career, its representatives occasionally have been rounded up along with other critics of the government during the republic's recurrent bouts of political crisis. However, outlets such as Radio Tropique FM and *L'Archipel*, which is noted for its satirical column, "Winking Eye," continue to provide independent political commentary.

## Economy

During the colonial period, the French and local leading citizens established plantations to grow cash crops for export. Even after independence, French companies, such as Société Bambao and Établissements Grimaldi—and other concerns, such as Kalfane and Company and, later, President Abdallah's Établissements Abdallah et Fils—dominated the Comoran economy. These firms diverted most of their profits overseas, investing little in the infrastructure of the islands beyond what was needed for profitable management of the plantations, or what could benefit these businesses' associates or related concerns. A serious consequence of this approach has been the languishing of the food-crop agricultural sector and the resultant dependence on overseas food imports, particularly rice. In 1993 Comoros remained hostage to fluctuating prices on the international market for such crops as vanilla, ylang-ylang, and cloves.

Comoros is one of the world's poorest countries; its per capita gross national product (GNP—see Glossary) was estimated at US$400 in 1994, following the January devaluation of the Comoran franc. Although GNP increased in real terms at an average annual rate of 3.1 percent during the 1980s, rapid population growth effaced these gains and caused an average annual decrease in per capita GNP of 0.6 percent. Gross domestic product (GDP—see Glossary) grew in real terms by 4.2 percent per year from 1980 to 1985, 1.8 percent from 1985 to 1988, and 1.5 percent in 1990. In 1991, because of its balance of payments difficulties, Comoros became eligible for the IDA's Special Program of Assistance for debt-distressed countries of sub-Saharan Africa.

The economy is based on private ownership, frequently by foreign investors. Nationalization, even during the Soilih years, has been limited. Soilih did expropriate the facilities of a foreign oil company, but only after the government of Madagascar took over the company's plants in that country. The Abdallah government, despite its openness to foreign participation in the economy, nationalized the Société Bambao and another French-capitalized firm, the Comoran Meat Company (Société Comorienne des Viandes—Socovia), which specialized in sales of meat and other foods in the islands. The nationalization was short-lived, however, because Socovia and other government-held enterprises were either liquidated or privatized as part of economic restructuring efforts in 1992.

Following the Abdallah regime's rapprochement with France in 1978, the Comoran economy became increasingly dependent on infusions of French aid, along with assistance from other governments and international organizations. By 1990, the year Comoros concluded negotiations with the IMF for an economic restructuring program, the republic's total external public debt was US$162.4 million, an amount equal to about three-quarters of GNP. The government delayed implementing the structural adjustment plan and was directed by the World Bank and the IMF to do so by September 1992. The plan recommendations entailed discharging about 2,800 of 9,000 civil servants, among other unpopular measures. The IMF granted Comoros a new credit for US$1.9 million in March 1994 under the Structural Adjustment Facility. For the period 1994-96, Comoros sought an economic growth rate of 4 percent, as well as an inflation rate of 4 percent for 1995–96. The growth rate for 1994, however, was estimated only at 0.7 percent and the inflation rate at 15 percent. Meanwhile, in a move designed to encourage private enterprise and reduce unem-

*Village on Njazidja*
*Market on Mwali*
*Courtesy Mari G. Borstelmann*

ployment, in May 1993 the UN Development Programme had given Comoros a credit of US$2 million for programs in these areas. In January 1994, the European Development Fund (EDF) granted 1.3 million European Currency Units (ECUs— see Glossary) to Comoros to develop small businesses. Comoros also received 5.7 million French francs from the French Aid and Cooperation Fund for agriculture and rural development.

The results of foreign aid to Comoros have been mixed at best. The purposes of the aid ranged from helping the government cover its payroll for such huge, seemingly endless projects as expanding the seaport at Moroni and developing a new port at Mutsamudu on Nzwani. Neither project had shown much promise by mid-1994. Meanwhile, the islands have been unable to develop local resources or create the infrastructure needed for economic development. The few successes include the creation of national news media and limited improvements in public health, education, and telecommunications. Developmental assistance from the United States, which totaled US$700,000 in fiscal year (FY—see Glossary) 1991, was administered by CARE, the nongovernmental organization, and focused primarily on reforestation, soil conservation, and sustainable development in agriculture.

The overall effect of the republic's dependence on aid has been perennial trade deficits accompanied by chronic budget deficits. In 1992 total exports had a value of US$21 million, and total imports were valued at US$50 million. In 1991 receipts totaled about US$34.7 million (CF9.7 trillion; CF— Comoran franc; for value of the Comoran franc—see Glossary) whereas expenditures totaled about US$93.8 million (CF26.2 trillion). The shortfall, which equaled about 170 percent of receipts, was financed by international grants and loans, by drawing upon existing lines of credit, and by debt rescheduling.

In 1991 France received 55 percent of Comoran exports, followed by the United States (19 percent) and Germany (16 percent). The main export products were vanilla, ylang-ylang, and cloves. The republic's primary suppliers were France (56 percent of imports), the Belgium-Luxembourg economic union (11 percent), and Japan (5 percent). Imports consisted of basic foodstuffs (rice and meat), petroleum, and construction materials.

Comoros has officially participated in the African Franc Zone (Communauté Financière Africaine—CFA; see Glossary) since 1979. The CFA franc was devalued by 50 percent on January 12, 1994, causing the exchange rate to become 100 CFA francs for one French franc. Subsequently, the Comoran franc was devalued so that instead of being directly aligned with the CFA franc, seventy-five Comoran francs equaled one French franc.

The banking system consists of the Central Bank of Comoros (Banque Centrale des Comores) established in 1981; the Bank for Industry and Commerce (Banque pour l'Industrie et le Commerce—BIC), a commercial bank established in 1990 that had six branches in 1993 and is a subsidiary of the National Bank of Paris-International (Banque Nationale de Paris-Internationale); BIC Afribank, a BIC subsidiary; and the Development Bank of Comoros (Banque de Développement des Comores), established in 1982, which provides support for small and midsize development projects. Most of the shares in the Development Bank of Comoros are held by the Comoran government and the central bank; the rest are held by the European Investment Bank and the Central Bank for Economic Cooperation (Caisse Centrale de Coopération Économique—CCCE), a development agency of the French government. All of these banks have headquarters in Moroni.

A national labor organization, the Union of Comoran Workers (Union des Travailleurs des Comores), also has headquarters in Moroni. Strikes and worker demonstrations often occur in response to political crises, economic restructuring mandated by international financial organizations, and the failure of the government—occasionally for months at a time—to pay civil servants.

## Agriculture, Livestock, and Fishing

Agriculture supported about 80 percent of the population and supplied about 95 percent of exports in the early 1990s. Two agricultural zones are generally defined: the coastal area, which ranges in elevation from sea level to 400 meters and which supports cash crops such as vanilla, ylang-ylang, and cloves; and the highlands, which support cultivation of crops for domestic consumption, such as cassava, bananas, rain-fed rice, and sweet potatoes. As the population increased, food grown for domestic use met fewer and fewer of Comorans' needs. Data collected by the World Bank showed that food production per capita fell about 12 percent from 1980 to 1987. The republic imports almost all its meat and vegetables; rice imports alone often account for up to 30 percent of the value of all imports.

Comoros is the world's principal producer of ylang-ylang essence, an essence derived from the flowers of a tree originally brought from Indonesia that is used in manufacturing perfumes and soaps. Ylang-ylang essence is a major component of Chanel No. 5, the popular scent for women. The republic is the world's second largest producer of vanilla, after Madagascar. Cloves are also an important cash crop. A total of 237 tons of vanilla was exported in 1991, at a price of about CF19 per kilogram. A total of 2,750 tons of cloves was exported in 1991, at a price of CF397 per kilogram. That year forty-three tons of ylang-ylang essence were exported at a price of about CF23,000 per kilogram. The production of all three commodities fluctuates wildly, mainly in response to changes in global demand and natural disasters such as cyclones. Profits—and, therefore, government receipts—likewise skyrocket and plummet, wreaking havoc with government efforts to predict revenues and plan expenditures. Stabex (Stabilization of Export Earnings— see Glossary), a system of the EC, provides aid to Comoros and other developing countries to mitigate the effects of fluctuations in the prices of export commodities.

Long-term prospects for the growth and stabilization of the markets for vanilla and ylang-ylang did not appear strong in the early 1990s. Vanilla faced increased competition from synthetic flavorings, and the preferences of perfume users were moving away from the sweet fragrance provided by ylang-ylang essence. Copra, the dried coconut meat that yields coconut oil, once an important Comoran export, had ceased to be a significant factor in the economy by the late 1980s, when the world's tastes shifted from high-fat coconut oil toward "leaner" substances such as palm oil. Although clove production and revenues also experienced swings, in the early 1990s cloves did not appear to face the same sorts of challenges confronting vanilla and ylang-ylang. Most Comoran vanilla is grown on Njazidja; Nzwani is the source of most ylang-ylang.

Numerous international programs have attempted to reduce the country's dependence on food imports, particularly of rice, a major drain on export earnings. Organizations initiating these rural development programs have included the EDF, the International Fund for Agricultural Development (IFAD), the World Food Program, the Arab Bank for Economic Development in Africa, the UN Food and Agriculture Organization, and the governments of France and the United States. Despite these international efforts, which numbered as many as seventeen in 1984, food production per capita actually declined in Comoros during the 1980s. The major clove and vanilla growers, whose plantations occupy the islands' fertile coastal lands, generally resisted these restructuring efforts, as did rice-importing firms, including the country's largest, Établissements Abdallah et Fils.

Crowded onto the mountain slopes by the cash-crop plantations, food-crop farmers have caused deforestation and the erosion of the highlands' thin, fragile soil. In response, aid providers have dedicated an increasing amount of agricultural assistance to reforestation, soil restoration, and environmentally sensitive means of cultivation. For example, all United States agricultural aid in 1991 (US$700,000) was directed to such projects, as was a US$4 million loan from the IFAD to help initiate a small producers' support program on Nzwani.

The livestock sector is small—some 47,000 cattle, 120,000 goats, 13,000 sheep, and 4,000 asses in 1990. Comoros continues to import most domestically consumed meat.

Since the latter part of the 1980s, Comoros has made headway in developing fisheries as a source of export earnings. In 1988 the government concluded a three-year agreement with the EC by which forty French and Spanish vessels would be permitted to fish in Comoran waters, primarily for tuna. In return, Comoros would receive ECU300,000, and ECU50,000 would be invested in fisheries research. In addition, fishing vessel operators would pay ECU20 per ton of tuna netted. Although the deep waters outside the islands' reefs do not abound in fish, it has been estimated that up to 30,000 tons of fish could be taken per year from Comoran waters (which extend 320 kilometers offshore). The total catch in 1990 was 5,500 tons. Japan has also provided aid to the fishing industry. Fisheries development is overseen by a state agency, the Development Company for Small-Scale Fisheries of Comoros (Société de Développement de la Pêche Artisanale des Comores).

## Industry and Infrastructure

Industrial activities are responsible for only a tiny portion of Comoran economic activity—about 5 percent of GDP in 1994. Principal industries are those that involve processing cash crops for export: preparing vanilla and distilling ylang-ylang into perfume essence. These activities were once controlled almost entirely by French companies, but as they closed unprofitable plantations, individual farmers set up many small, inefficient distilleries. Comorans also produce handicrafts for export. Other industries are small and geared to internal markets: sawmills, printing, carpentry, and the production of shoes, plastics, yogurt, handicrafts (such as the jewelry exchanged as part of the *grand mariage*), and small fishing boats. Several factors provide major obstacles to the growth of industry: the islands' geographically isolated position, their distance from each other, a scarcity of raw materials and skilled labor, and the high cost of electricity (energy is produced by hydropower, imported petroleum, and wood products) and transportation. Value added in industry slowly declined throughout the 1980s.

Perhaps the primary outcome of South African penetration of the Comoran economy during the Abdallah regime was the development of tourism. Although South African investors built or renovated several hotels during the 1980s (with assistance from the South African and Comoran governments), only one resort, the 182-room Galawa Beach on Njazidja, was operating by late 1992. About 100 other hotel rooms are available on the islands. Political instability, a declining South African interest in the islands as the apartheid regime was disassembled and other tropical tourism venues became more welcoming, and the need to import most construction materials and consumable supplies inhibited the growth of tourism, despite the islands' physical beauty. Nonetheless, in large part thanks to Galawa Beach, which had been closed during 1990, tourism increased from 7,627 visitors in 1990 to about 19,000 in 1992. Most of these tourists were Europeans, primarily French.

### Transportation and Telecommunications

The relative isolation of the Comoro Islands had made air traffic a major means of transportation. One of President Abdallah's accomplishments was to make Comoros more accessible by air. During his administration, he negotiated agreements to initiate or enhance commercial air links with Tanzania and Madagascar. The Djohar regime reached an agreement in 1990 to link Moroni and Brussels by air. By the early 1990s, commercial flights connected Comoros with France, Mauritius, Kenya, South Africa, Tanzania, and Madagascar. The national airline is Air Comores. Daily flights link

*Nzwani factory that distils
oil from lemongrass
Courtesy Brian Kensley*

the three main islands, and air service is also available to Mahoré; each island has airstrips. In 1986 the republic received a grant from the French government's CCCE to renovate and expand Hahaya airport, near Moroni. Because of the absence of regularly scheduled sea transport between the islands, nearly all interisland passenger traffic is by air.

More than 99 percent of freight is transported by sea. Both Moroni on Njazidja and Mutsamudu on Nzwani have artificial harbors. There is also a harbor at Fomboni, on Mwali. Despite extensive internationally financed programs to upgrade the harbors at Moroni and Mutsamudu, by the early 1990s only Mutsamudu was operational as a deepwater facility. Its harbor can accommodate vessels of up to eleven meters' draught. At Moroni, ocean-going vessels typically lie offshore and are loaded or unloaded by smaller craft, a costly and sometimes dangerous procedure. Most freight continues to be sent to Kenya, Reunion, or Madagascar for transshipment to Comoros. Use of Comoran ports is further restricted by the threat of cyclones from December through March. The privately operated Comoran Navigation Company (Société Comorienne de Navigation) is based in Moroni and provides services to Madagascar. )

Roads serve the coastal areas, rather than the interior, and the mountainous terrain makes surface travel difficult. In 1987 the total length of roads in Comoros was about 750 kilometers, including both paved and dirt roads.

In large part thanks to international aid programs, Moroni has international telecommunications service. Telephone service, however, is largely limited to the islands' few towns. Some 3,000 telephones were in use in 1991.

## Government and Politics

The Constitution of the Federal Islamic Republic of the Comoros was approved by referendum on June 7, 1992. It replaced the constitution of 1978, as amended in 1982 and 1985. Among the general principles enumerated in the preamble are the recognition of Islam as the state religion and respect for human rights as set forth in the UN Universal Declaration of Human Rights. All citizens are declared equal before the law.

The president is elected by direct universal suffrage to a five-year term and is limited to two terms. All persons over the age of eighteen who possess full civil and political rights may vote.

The president may be elected to no more than two terms. The president is both head of state and head of government. The president nominates ministers to form the Council of Government, which had twelve members in the latter half of 1994. The ministries are routinely reshuffled, merged, eliminated, and resurrected. In 1994 the Council of Government consisted of : the prime minister, who also served as minister of civil service, and the ministers of Economy, Plan, Industry, and Handicrafts; Equipment, Energy, Urbanization, and Housing; Finance and Budget; Foreign Affairs and Cooperation; Information, Culture, Youth, Sports, and Posts and Telecommunication; Islamic Affairs and Justice; National Education and Technical and Professional Teaching; Public Health; Rural Development, Fisheries, and the Environment; Social Affairs, Work, and Employment; and Transportation and Tourism. The president also nominates governors for each of the three islands for five-year terms. If the presidency becomes vacant, the president of the Supreme Court serves as interim president until an election can be held.

The constitution provides for a bicameral legislature. The forty-two members of the "lower" house, the Federal Assembly, represent electoral wards for four-year terms. The Federal Assembly meets for two forty-five-day sessions per year, in April and October. The upper house, the Senate, has fifteen members, five from each island, who are chosen by an Electoral College. The post of prime minister is held by a member of the party holding a majority of seats in the Federal Assembly. The number of political parties may be regulated by federal law. In 1994 more than twenty political parties were active. Areas subject to federal legislation include defense, communications, law, international trade, federal taxation, economic planning, and social services.

As a federal republic, Comoros assigns autonomy to the three constituent islands in matters that, in accordance with the constitution, do not come within the purview of the national government. Each island has a council whose members are elected to represent electoral wards for four-year terms. Normally, each council meets twice yearly, in March and December, for a fifteen-day session (see Political Dynamics, this ch.).

The judiciary is considered independent of the executive and legislature. The Supreme Court examines constitutional issues and supervises presidential elections. The high court also arbitrates when the government is accused of malpractice. The Supreme Court normally consists of at least seven members: two chosen by the president, two elected by the Federal Assembly, and three chosen by the respective island councils. Former presidents also may serve on the high court.

## Political Dynamics

In the immediate aftermath of the Abdallah assassination and subsequent events of late 1989, a limited amount of political healing occurred in Comoros. Denard and his fellow mercenaries were expelled, although the fate of their vast financial holdings in the islands remained unclear. With the South African government temporarily out of the picture, French officials now oversaw the police and the army, and the remnants of the GP were under the watchful eye of French paratroopers. Among those released in a general amnesty for political prisoners was Mustapha Said Cheikh, leader of the opposition FD who had been imprisoned for four years for alleged involvement in the unsuccessful March 1985 coup. He was quickly proposed as a possible presidential candidate. Also suggested was Mohamed Taki, one-time National Assembly president whose power had been diminished by Abdallah's constitutional maneuvers; he had subsequently gone into exile in France, where his entourage reportedly included two mercenary bodyguards. Also announcing for the presidency was Said Ali Kemal, who had been living in quiet exile in Paris since being exposed as the sponsor of Australian mercenaries who had plotted to overthrow the Abdallah government in 1983. In late December 1989, members of the formerly banned opposition, along with President Djohar, decided to form a provisional "national unity" government and to hold a multiparty presidential election in 1990.

In an awkward but somehow effective campaign to keep himself in power, Djohar spent much of the early 1990s playing a political shell game with the opposition. He moved election dates backward and forward and sanctioned irregularities, giving his opponents little choice but to condemn the balloting as invalid. Djohar began this strategy within weeks of his installation as interim president, rescheduling the presidential election set for January 14, 1990, to February 18. Djohar's decision was met with demonstrations and violence that marked an abrupt end to the post-Abdallah period of national unity, hardly three weeks after Bob Denard had been expelled from the country. The February 18 balloting broke down shortly after the polls opened. The government was accused of widespread fraud, including issuing multiple voting cards to some voters and opening the polls to voters who looked well below the minimum age of eighteen.

Elections were rescheduled for March 4, 1990, with a runoff on March 11; Djohar was the official victor, claiming 55 percent of the vote over runner-up Mohamed Taki's 45 percent. Djohar had run under the banner of the Union Comorienne pour le Progrès (Udzima—Comoran Union for Progress), basically a recycled version of Ahmed Abdallah's old UCP, whereas Taki had represented the National Union for Comoran Democracy (Union Nationale pour la Démocratie Comorienne—UNDC). As would be the case in other Comoran elections in the 1990s, the sole major issue appeared to be the character and ability of the incumbent president rather than any matter of public policy or ideology. The Supreme Court certified the results of the election, despite strong evidence that the Ministry of Interior had altered the vote count, especially in the first round, to favor Djohar at Taki's expense.

In March 1992, with two of the government's Udzima ministers having broken away to form a new party and conflict among the remaining Udzima ministers growing, Djohar headed off the complete collapse of his government by convening a multiparty constitutional convention. He scheduled a referendum on the new document in May, with general elections in June and balloting for local offices in July. After one postponement, the referendum was held on June 7. The Constitution of 1992 passed with about 74 percent of the vote, despite intensive campaigning against it by the FD and Udzima, which by this point opposed President Djohar. Among the new document's elements were articles calling for a bicameral legislature and a limit on presidential tenure to two five-year terms.

The legislative elections, postponed several times, finally were held on November 22 and 29, 1992. They were preceded in late September by an attempted coup by junior army officers, allegedly with the support of opposition politicians. Possible motives for the coup were an unpopular restructuring program mandated by the World Bank, which entailed sharp reductions in the number of civil servants, and President Djohar's ambiguous threat on September 10 that his main opponents would "not be around for the elections." Djohar used the coup attempt as an opportunity to jail six military men and six opposition leaders "under conditions of extreme illegality," according to the Comoran Association for Human Rights (Association Comorienne des Droits Humains—ACDH).

Although a trio of French public officials sent to observe the balloting judged the election generally democratic, President Djohar's most prominent and determined opponents spent the voting days either in hiding or in jail. Two of the most important of the republic's twenty-four political parties, Udzima and the UNDC, boycotted the election. Given the president's own lack of party support, he spent most of 1993 cobbling together one government after another; at one point, in late spring 1993, he formed two governments in the space of three weeks.

The events of a single day in July 1993 perhaps summed up the near-term prospects of politics in Comoros. On July 23, heeding demands that he call legislative elections (he had dissolved parliament on June 18 because of its inability to agree on a candidate for prime minister and because of the lack of a government majority) or else face the prospect of "other forms of action" by the opposition, Djohar scheduled voting for late October. That same day, his government arrested two opposition leaders for public criticism of the president.

The scheduled elections were again postponed—for the fourth time—until December 1993. On November 17, 1993, Djohar created a new National Electoral Commission, said to be appropriately representative of the various political parties. Meanwhile Djohar had established a new progovernment party, the Rally for Democracy and Renewal (Rassemblement pour la Démocratie et le Renouveau—RDR). In the first round of elections on December 12, which featured twenty-four parties with 214 candidates for forty-two seats, various voting irregularities occurred, including the failure to issue voting cards to some 30 percent of eligible voters. The government announced that Djohar's party had won twenty-one seats with three seats remaining to be contested. Most opposition parties stated that they would not sit in the assembly and also refused to participate in the postponed second-stage elections, which were supervised by the Ministry of Interior and the gendarmerie after the National Electoral Commission disintegrated. As a result, the RDR gained a total of twenty-two seats, and Djohar appointed RDR secretary general Mohamed Abdou Madi as prime minister.

Denouncing the proceedings, on January 17, 1994, thirteen opposition parties formed a combined Forum for National

Recovery (Forum pour le Redressement National—FRN). The Udzima Party began broadcasting articles about Comoros appearing in the *Indian Ocean Newsletter*, including criticisms of the RDR. In consequence, its radio station, Voix des Îles (Voice of the Islands), was confiscated by the government in mid–February 1994—in September 1993, the radio station belonging to Abbas Djoussouf, who later became leader of the RDR, had been closed. Tensions increased, and in March 1994 an assassination attempt against Djohar occurred. At the end of May, civil service employees went on strike, including teachers, and violence erupted in mid-June when the FRN prepared to meet.

## Foreign Affairs

Comoros' most significant international relationship is that with France. The three years of estrangement following the unilateral declaration of independence and the nationalistic Soilih regime were followed during the conservative Abdallah and Djohar regimes by a period of growing trade, aid, cultural, and defense links between the former colony and France, punctuated by frequent visits to Paris by the head of state and occasional visits by the French president to Moroni. The leading military power in the region, France has detachments on Mahoré and Reunion, and its Indian Ocean fleet sails the waters around the islands. France and Comoros signed a mutual security treaty in 1978; following the mercenary coup against Abdallah in 1989, French troops restored order and took responsibility for reorganizing and training the Comoran army. With Mahoré continuing to gravitate politically and economically toward France, and Comoros increasingly dependent on the French for help with its own considerable social, political, and economic problems, the issue of Mahoré diminished somewhat in urgency.

The close relationship Comoros developed with South Africa in the 1980s was much less significant to both countries in the 1990s. With the reform of its apartheid government, South Africa no longer needed Comoros as evidence of its ostensible ability to enjoy good relations with a black African state; the end of the Cold War had also diminished Comoros' strategic value to Pretoria. Although South Africa continued to provide developmental aid, it closed its consulate in Moroni in 1992. After the 1989 coup and subsequent expulsion of South African-financed mercenaries, Comoros likewise turned away from South Africa and toward France for assistance with its security needs.

The government has fostered close relationships with the more conservative (and oil-rich) Arab states, such as Saudi Arabia and Kuwait. It frequently received aid from those countries and the regional financial institutions they influenced, such as the Arab Bank for Economic Development in Africa and the Arab Fund for Economic and Social Development. In October 1993, Comoros joined the League of Arab States, after having been rejected when it applied for membership initially in 1977.

Regional relations generally are good. In 1985 Madagascar, Mauritius, and Seychelles agreed to admit Comoros as the fourth member of the Indian Ocean Commission (IOC), an organization established in 1982 to encourage regional cooperation. In 1993 Mauritius and Seychelles had two of the five embassies in Moroni, and Mauritius and Madagascar were connected to the republic by regularly scheduled commercial flights.

Comoros also hosts an embassy of China, which established relations during the Soilih regime. The Chinese had long been a source of aid and apparently wished to maintain contact with Comoros to counterbalance Indian and Soviet (later Russian) influence in the Indian Ocean. Comoran relations with Japan are also significant because Japan is the second largest provider of aid, consisting of funding for fisheries, food, and highway development. The United States established diplomatic relations in 1977 but in September 1993 closed it embassy in Moroni. The two countries enjoy friendly relations.

In November 1975, Comoros became the 143d member of the UN. In the 1990s, the republic continued to represent Mahoré in the UN. Comoros is also a member of the OAU, the EDF, the World Bank, the IMF, the IOC, and the African Development Bank.

Comoros has thus cultivated relations with various nations, both East and West, seeking to increase trade and obtain financial assistance. In 1994, however, it was increasingly facing the need to control its expenditures and reorganize its economy so that it would be viewed as a sounder recipient of investment. Comoros also confronted domestically the problem of the degree of democracy the government was prepared to grant to its citizens, a consideration that related to its standing in the world community.

\*      \*      \*

The reader seeking recent works on the history, politics, and society of Comoros also needs to consult a number of publications that cover the republic as one of many African or Indian Ocean countries. These include *Africa Analysis, Africa Contemporary Record, Africa Events, Africa Research Bulletin,* and *Africa South of the Sahara.* Other periodically issued sources include the annual country-by-country *Amnesty International Report* and the newsletters *Africa Confidential* and *Indian Ocean Newsletter.* Whereas the *Times* of London, *New York Times,* and *Washington Post* report Comoros' more serious upheavals, more regular coverage is provided by *Le Monde.* Useful social and economic data can be obtained from World Bank publications. One such publication in particular, *Social Indicators of Development,* an annual, provides country-by-country tables of data on indicators of poverty and resources and expenditures. Books such as Thierry Flobert's 1976 work, *Les Comores: Évolution juridique et socio-politique,* the World Bank 1979 publication *The Comoros: Problems and Prospects of a Small, Island Economy,* and Malyn Newitt's *The Comoro Islands: Struggle Against Dependency in the Indian Ocean* provide useful background despite their growing datedness. (For further information and complete citations, see Bibliography.)

# Chapter 4. Seychelles

FINIS CORONAT OPUS

*National emblem of Seychelles*

## Country

**Formal Name:** Republic of Seychelles.

**Short Name:** Seychelles.

**Term for Citizens:** Seychellois.

**Capital:** Victoria.

**Date of Independence:** June 29, 1976 (from Britain).

## Geography

**Size:** Approximately 444 square kilometers.

**Topography:** Archipelago consists of 115 islands, of which some forty are granitic, within ninety kilometers of Mahé, and remainder coralline, stretching over 1,200 kilometers from northeast to southwest. Major islands are Mahé, Praslin, and La Digue. Granitic islands have hills up to 940 meters high, some narrow coastal plains, and coral reefs on east coasts. Coralline islands are flat with no fresh water.

**Climate:** Tropical with high humidity but breezy. Cooler weather brought by southeast monsoon from late May to September; northwest monsoon from March to May brings warmer weather. Mean average annual rainfall in Mahé 2,880 millimeters at sea level and 3,550 millimeters on slopes.

## Society

**Population:** July 1994 estimate 72,113 with population growth rate of 0.8 percent.

**Ethnic Groups:** Relatively homogeneous population of mixed European and African descent.

**Languages:** Official languages: Creole (first), English (second),

French (third).

**Religion:** Roman Catholics (90 percent), Anglicans (7 percent), evangelical Protestants (1 percent), and other (2 percent).

**Education:** Free, required attendance grades one through nine. Initial instruction in Creole, English added in grade three, French in grade six. Participation in one-year National Youth Service program at age fifteen generally needed to enter Seychelles Polytechnic or to begin work. No higher education on island. Overall claimed literacy in 1991: 85 percent.

**Health:** Free government health services for all citizens. In 1994 life expectancy at birth estimated at: overall 69.7 years, 73.4 for females, 66.1 years for males. Infant mortality in 1994 estimated at 11.7 per 1,000 live births.

## Economy

**Gross Domestic Product:** 1992 estimate US$407 million, with growth rate of 4 percent, and inflation rate of 3.3 percent (1993 inflation rate 4 percent). 1992 per capita GDP of US$5,900. In 1980s socialist France Albert René government created many parastatals; in early 1990s moving toward more liberal economy and privatization.

**Labor Force:** In 1991 government employed 38 percent of labor, parastatals employed 26 percent, and private sector 36 percent. Independent trade unions allowed since November 1993.

**Tourism:** Major source of economic activity, including tourism-related services; provides 50 percent of GDP, but imported food and materials for tourism cost 70 percent of tourism income. In 1993 more than 116,000 tourists, mainly from Europe, South Africa.

**Agriculture:** Only 400 hectares cultivable on islands. Some vegetables and fruit grown, but most food, including rice, imported. Market for traditional crops, copra and cinnamon, has decreased; tea grown for local consumption. Fishing (tuna and shrimp particularly) encouraged; population eats eighty-five kilograms seafood per capita annually.

**Industry:** Very limited because of small market, lack of raw materials; mostly food processing, handicrafts for tourists.

**Exports:** 1992 estimate US$47 million. Major products canned and frozen fish, copra, cinnamon bark. Major markets Britain, France, Reunion.

**Imports:** 1992 estimate US$192 million. Major items include manufactured goods, food, petroleum products, transportation equipment and machinery. Major sources: Bahrain, South Africa, Britain, Singapore, and France.

**Balance of Payments:** Visible trade always in deficit, but tourism helps compensate for excess of imports.

**Currency and Exchange Rate:** 1 Seychelles rupee (SRe) = 100 cents. August 1995 exchange rate US$1.00 = SRe4.25.

**Fiscal Year:** Calendar year.

## Transportation and Telecommunications

**Highways:** 302 kilometers in 1994, of which 202 hard surfaced.

**Ports:** Mahé.

**Airports:** Eight of fourteen have hard-surfaced runways.

**Telecommunications:** Good, small system using mainly satellite communications to outside world and direct radio communications with adjacent islands and African coastal countries; some 13,000 telephones in 1994; two amplitude modulation (AM) stations, no frequency modulation (FM) station; two television stations; one Indian Ocean International Telecommunications Satellite Organization (Intelsat) earth station. In 1992 Seychellois had some 38,000 radios and 10,900 television sets.

## Government and Politics

**Government:** Between 1979 and 1993, governed under single-party socialist system. New constitution was approved in referendum June 1992; multiparty elections in July 1993 in which President René and Seychelles People's Progressive Front (SPPF) victorious. President selects cabinet. People's Assembly includes twenty-two elected representatives from constituencies and eleven other members. SPPF holds twenty-seven seats, New Democratic Party of James Mancham five seats, and United Opposition Party (a coalition) one seat. Legal system consists of magistrates' courts, Supreme (or trial) Court, and Court of Appeal.

**Politics:** Various political parties of which government party, SPPF, holds clear majority.

**Foreign Relations:** Member of Commonwealth of Nations; has pragmatic foreign policy of "positive nonalignment." Member of Organization of African Unity, Indian Ocean Commission, and Nonaligned Movement.

## National Security

**Defense Forces:** All services under army; total forces of 800 persons in 1994, including 300 in Presidential Guard. Army has one infantry battalion and two artillery elements. Paramilitary forces include national guard of 1,000 persons, coast guard estimated at 300 members including 100-member air wing and eighty marines. Defense budget in 1993 estimated at US$15.9 million.

THE REPUBLIC OF SEYCHELLES, one of the world's smallest nations, comprises 115 islands, including a central granitic group and more than seventy widely scattered coral islands. Most of the population is a relatively homogeneous mixture of European and African descent and lives on the main granitic island of Mahé. Before the opening of commercial airline links in 1971, Seychelles had a plantation economy heavily dependent on exports of copra and cinnamon. Tourism has since become the most important sector of economic life.

Claiming jurisdiction over more than 1 million square kilometers of productive fishing grounds, Seychelles has profited from the fees and commercial activity produced by foreign fishing fleets, from the export of fresh and frozen fish of its domestic fishing fleet, and from a tuna cannery operated jointly with French interests. Although Seychelles is vulnerable to fluctuations in the world economy, per capita income is high by developing country standards. Its citizens benefit from a modern social welfare system and free health care and schools.

The nation was a French possession until 1814. In that year, the British took control, administering it first as a dependency of Mauritius and after 1903 as a crown colony (see Glossary). Seychelles was granted independence on June 29, 1976. In June 1977, a coup brought to power a leftist government with France Albert René as president and his party, the socialist-oriented Seychelles People's United Party (SPUP) as ruling group. From 1977 through 1991, the René government dominated political life and controlled all phases of the economy. Dissent was forbidden, and opposition figures were forced to flee the country. In 1992 a multiparty system was restored, and in July 1993, after a new constitution was approved by referendum, the nation held free elections. René's Seychelles People's Progressive Front (SPPF—the new name of the SPUP following the 1979 constitution) won easily, defeating the Democratic Party (DP) of former president James Mancham and a coalition of smaller opposition parties.

## Historical Setting

Although known and visited by traders from the Persian Gulf area and East Africa in earlier times, the Seychelles Archipelago first appeared on European maps at the beginning of the sixteenth century after Portuguese explorers sighted the islands during voyages to India. Recorded landings did not occur until 1609, however, when members of the British East India Company spent several days on Mahé and other nearby islands. A French expedition from Mauritius reached the islands in 1742, and during a second expedition in 1756 the French made a formal claim to them. The name "Seychelles" honors the French minister of finance under King Louis XV. Settlement began in 1778 under a French military administration but barely survived its first decade. Although the settlers were supposed to plant crops only to provision the garrison and passing French ships, they also found it lucrative to exploit the islands' natural resources. Between 1784 and 1789, an estimated 13,000 giant tortoises were shipped from Mahé. The settlers also quickly devastated the hardwood forests—selling them to passing ships for repairs or to shipyards on Mauritius. In spite of reforms to control the rapid elimination of trees, exploitation of the forest continued for shipbuilding and house building and later for firing cinnamon kilns, ultimately destroying much of the original ecology.

Possession of the islands alternated between France and Britain several times during the French Revolution and the Napoleonic wars. France ceded Seychelles—which at that time included the granitic group and three coral islands—to Britain in 1814 in the Treaty of Paris after rejecting a British offer to take French holdings in India in place of Seychelles. Because Britain's interest in the islands had centered mainly on halting their use as a base for French privateering, its main concern was to keep the islands from becoming burdens. Britain administered Seychelles as a dependency of Mauritius, from which they received little attention and few services.

The first European settlers were French who had been living on Mauritius, Reunion, or in French settlements in India. Many lived in conditions of poverty quite similar to those of their African slaves, who from early on greatly outnumbered the remainder of the population. After the abolition of slavery in the islands in 1834, many settlers left, taking their slaves with them. Later, large numbers of Africans liberated by the British navy from slaving ships on the East African coast were released on Seychelles. Small numbers of Chinese, Malaysians, and Indians moved to the islands, usually becoming small traders and shopkeepers. Intermarriage among all groups except the Indians was common, however, and left so few families of pure descent that by 1911 the practice of categorizing residents according to race was abandoned.

Before 1838 most Seychellois worked on white-owned estates as slaves, producing cotton, coconut oil, spices, coffee, and sugarcane, as well as sufficient food crops to support the population. After the abolition of slavery, they became agricultural wage laborers, sharecroppers, fishers, or artisans, settling as squatters where they liked. Labor-intensive field crops rapidly gave way to crops that required relatively little labor, including copra, cinnamon, and vanilla. Only those industries related to processing the cash crops or exploiting natural resources developed. As a result, the increasing population quickly came to depend on imports for most basic necessities, including food and manufactured goods.

## Crown Colony Status, 1903

Political development proceeded very slowly. From 1814 until 1903, when the islands became a crown colony, they were granted increasing administrative autonomy from Mauritius. In 1888 separate nominated administrative and executive councils were established for Mauritius and Seychelles. Thus, for the first time, some landed white Seychellois were allowed to serve in official advisory positions. In 1897 the administrator of Seychelles was given the powers of a colonial governor, although it was not until 1903 that the islands were separated from Mauritius. When Seychelles became a separate colony, the other islands of the archipelago, except for Coetivy and the Farquhar Islands, were added to the original group acquired by Britain in 1814. Coetivy was transferred from Mauritius in 1908 and the Farquhars in 1922 after World War I.

Widespread involvement of Seychellois in their own political affairs began in 1948 after World War II, when Britain granted suffrage to approximately 2,000 adult male property owners, who then elected four members to the Legislative Council that advised the governor. The winning candidates were drawn from a group known as the Seychelles Taxpayers' and Producers' Association (STPA), which represented the landed strata of society—known colloquially as the *grands blancs* (great whites). The STPA defended its members' interest in matters of crop marketing and other issues and was the principal political force in the nation until the early 1960s, when representatives of the small new urban professional and middle class began to win seats.

Two parties emerged to represent this new constituency: the DP, led by James Mancham, and the SPUP, led by France Albert René. Both men were London-educated lawyers who had returned to Seychelles determined to improve local conditions and to develop popularly based local politics.

Although community rivalries and the differing styles of the two leaders were important in attracting followers, the two parties also differed in substantive ways. The SPUP called itself socialist, favored worker-oriented policies, and pressed for complete independence from Britain and a nonaligned foreign policy. The pressure for independence was intensified after Britain in 1965 removed Île Desroches, the Aldabra Islands, and the Farquhar Islands from Seychelles and made them part of the British Indian Ocean Territory. The DP took a more laissez-faire capitalist approach and wanted to continue the association with Britain and to allow British and United States bases on the islands.

### Steps Toward Independence, 1967–76

Continuous and mounting demands for an increased share in running the colony's affairs prompted Britain to enact a series of constitutions for Seychelles, each of which granted important new concessions. In 1967 Britain extended universal suffrage to the colony and established a governing council to run it, the majority of whose members for the first time were elected. That year almost 18,000 Seychellois voted, and the DP emerged in control of the council. In 1970 Britain set up a ministerial form of government and gave Seychellois the responsibility to administer all but external affairs, internal security, the civil service, and the government's broadcasting service and newspaper. The DP won ten seats, and the SPUP won five in the Legislative Assembly. Mancham became the islands' chief minister and René, the leader of the opposition.

The opening of an international airport on the east coast of Mahé in 1971 improved contact with the outside world. Before this most journeys to and from Seychelles had involved long voyages on bimonthly steamers running between East Africa and India and often required inconvenient transits in Mombasa and Bombay. Air service had been available only on a restricted basis at an airstrip used by the United States in building a satellite station on Mahé. The end of the islands' relative isolation triggered tourism and concomitant booms in foreign capital investment and the domestic construction industry. Within a few years, the construction of the international airport changed the economy from a traditional agricultural and fishing one into one in which services accounted for the major portion of employment and gross domestic product (GDP— see Glossary). The two parties differed on the ways to manage the new tourist industry and to apportion its benefits. The SPUP favored controlling the growth of tourism and at the same time developing the entire economy, whereas the SDP wanted to stimulate the rapid growth of tourism and to establish the islands as an international financial center.

Independence from Britain was the dominant issue between the two parties in the early 1970s, however. The SPUP insisted on cutting the colony's ties with Britain, whereas Mancham argued for even closer association. But when it became plain that the independence issue was popular and Britain showed no interest in retaining close relations, the SDP also shifted to a pro-independence policy. Moreover, the disfavor with which African and Asian nations viewed colonialism had put the SDP into disrepute in the region. The SDP won the election campaign in 1974, but the election provoked angry controversy. The SPUP charged that the results had been rigged; because of the way constituencies had been demarcated, the SDP won thirteen of the fifteen seats with only 52.4 percent of the vote, lending credibility to the charges. Thereafter, relations between the two parties, already personalized and bitter, worsened steadily.

Despite their differences, the two parties formed a coalition under Mancham to lead Seychelles to independence. Five members from each party were added to the Legislative Assembly in an attempt to equalize political representation. One year later, Britain granted the colony complete independence, and on June 29, 1976, the Republic of Seychelles became a sovereign nation, with Mancham as president and René as vice president. As a gesture of goodwill, Britain returned Île Desroches, the Aldabra Islands, and the Farquhar Islands. In addition, Britain made a series of grants to the new nation to smooth the transition to an independent economy. Both parties agreed to support the coalition government until elections were held in 1979.

## Coup by René Supporters, 1977

On June 4–5, 1977, sixty supporters of the SPUP who had been training in Tanzania staged a coup and overthrew Mancham while he was in London. René, who denied knowing of the plan, was then sworn in as president and formed a new government.

A year later, the SPUP combined with several smaller parties and redesignated itself the Seychelles People's Progressive Front (SPPF), or simply the Front. A new constitution adopted in 1979 stipulated that the SPPF be the sole recognized party. The constitution provided for a strong executive headed by the president and a legislature of twenty-three elected and two appointed members.

In the first election, held in June 1979, René was the single candidate for president. He won with 98 percent of the vote. The results were viewed as a popular endorsement of the socialist policies pursued by the government in the two years following the coup. The SPPF proceeded with its program to set minimum wage levels, raise government salaries, improve housing and health facilities, broaden educational opportunities, increase social security coverage, and generate employment in agriculture and fisheries. The lives of most Seychellois were enhanced, and most citizens appeared to favor the government's policies.

The decision to turn the nation into a one-party state based on socialist ideology, as well as certain initiatives of the government, caused some bitterness, especially among the upper and middle classes. Censorship of the media and control over public expression were unpopular. A number of groups attempted to oust the René government between 1978 and 1987. The most notable was a group of mercenaries who tried to enter the country in 1981 disguised as tourists from South Africa. The mercenaries were exposed as they came through customs at the international airport, but most of them, including their leader, Colonel Michael "Mad Mike" Hoare, escaped after commandeering an Air India passenger plane to South Africa. Although the South African government prosecuted and jailed some of the mercenaries for air hijacking, Hoare testified that South African military and intelligence officials were involved in the coup attempt. During this period, the Seychelles government received support from Tanzania, which deployed troops to the islands to strengthen the government's hand.

Mancham and other exiled opposition figures based principally in London formed several groups that sought to turn international opinion against the René government, stigmatizing it as antidemocratic, procommunist, and pro-Soviet. As part of its efforts to stifle opposition, the government embarked on a campaign in 1987 to acquire parcels of land owned by dissident Seychellois living abroad. The takeovers were not subject to legal challenge, but the amount of compensation—in the form of bonds payable over twenty years—could be appealed in court. The government's authoritarianism finally brought it under growing pressure from its chief patrons—Britain and France. Finally, in 1991 René and the SPPF consented to liberalize the political system, inviting opposition leaders to return to Seychelles and help rewrite the constitution to permit multiparty politics.

## Physical Environment

The archipelago consists of 115 islands and thirty prominent rock formations scattered throughout a self-proclaimed exclusive economic zone (EEZ—see Glossary) of more than 1.35 million square kilometers of ocean (see fig. 7). Some forty islands are granitic and lie in a ninety-kilometer radius from Mahé, the main island. The remaining islands are coralline, stretching over a 1,200-kilometer radius from Île aux Vaches in the northeast to the Aldabra Atoll in the southwest. The islands are all small—the aggregate land area is only 444 square kilometers, about two-and-a-half times the size of Washington, D.C.

Mahé is twenty-five kilometers long and no more than eight kilometers wide. It contains the capital and only city, Victoria, an excellent port. Victoria lies approximately 1,600 kilometers east of Mombasa, Kenya; 2,800 kilometers southwest of Bombay; 1,700 kilometers north of Mauritius; and 920 kilometers northeast of Madagascar. The only other important islands by virtue of their size and population are Praslin and La Digue, situated about thirty kilometers to the northeast of Mahé.

The granitic islands are the peaks of the submarine Mascarene Plateau, a continental formation theorized to be either a part of Africa separated when Asia began to drift away from the original single continent of Gondwanaland, or the remnants of a microcontinent that existed up to the beginning of the Tertiary Period, approximately 50 million years ago. The granitic islands are characterized by boulder-covered hills and mountains as high as 940 meters rising abruptly from the sea.

Elsewhere, narrow coastal plains extend to the base of the foot-hills. Extensively developed coral reefs are found mainly on the east coasts because of the southwest trade winds and equatorial current. Ninety-nine percent of the population is located on the granitic islands, and most are on Mahé.

The coralline islands differ sharply from the granitic in that they are very flat, often rising only a few feet above sea level. They have no fresh water, and very few have a resident popula-tion. Many, like Île aux Vaches, Île Denis, the Amirante Isles, Platte Island, and Coetivy Island, are sand cays upon which extensive coconut plantations have been established. Some of the coralline islands consist of uplifted reefs and atolls covered with stunted vegetation. Several of these islands have been important breeding grounds for turtles and birds, as well as the sites of extensive guano deposits, which formerly constituted an important element of the Seychellois economy but now for the most part are depleted. The Aldabra Islands, the largest coralline atoll with an area greater than Mahé, are a sanctuary for rare animals and birds.

The uniqueness of the Seychelles ecology is reflected in the US$1.8 million project of the Global Environment Trust Fund of the World Bank (see Glossary) entitled Biodiversity Conser-vation and Marine Pollution Abatement, which began in 1993. The World Bank study for this project states that the islands contain, out of a total of 1,170 flowering plants, "at least sev-enty-five species of flowering plants, fifteen of birds, three of mammals, thirty of reptiles and amphibians, and several hun-dred species of snails, insects, spiders and other invertebrates" found nowhere else. In addition, the waters contain more than 900 kinds of fish, of which more than one-third are associated with coral reefs. Specific examples of unique birds are the black paradise flycatcher, the black parrot, the brush warbler, and a flightless rail.

As a result of extensive shipping to Seychelles that brings needed imports and the discharge of commercial tuna fishing, the waters are becoming polluted. Furthermore, goats brought to the Aldabra Islands are destroying much of the vegetation on which giant turtles, including two species unique to Sey-chelles (the green and the hawksbill), feed or seek shade.

Seychelles began addressing the conservation problem in the late 1960s by creating the Nature Conservancy Commis-sion, later renamed the Seychelles National Environment Com-mission. A system of national parks and animal preserves

*Fisherman holding hawksbill turtle, Aldabra Islands; shell is used to make tortoiseshell objects.
Courtesy Brian Kensley*

*Giant land tortoises, Aldabra Islands
Courtesy Brian Kensley*

covering 42 percent of the land area and about 26,000 hectares of the surrounding water areas has been set aside. Legislation protects wildlife and bans various destructive practices. In Seychelles' 1990–94 National Development Plan, an effort was made to include in the appropriate economic sectors of the development plan environment and natural resources management aspects.

Also connected with ecology is a World Bank project dealing with the environment and transportation. Launched in 1993 with a loan of US$4.5 million, it is designed to improve the infrastructure of Seychelles with regard to roads and airports or airstrips so as to encourage tourism as a source of income, while simultaneously supporting environmental programs in resource management, conservation, and the elimination of pollution.

The climate of Seychelles is tropical, having little seasonal variation. Temperatures on Mahé rarely rise above 29° C. or drop below 24° C. Humidity is high, but its enervating effect is usually ameliorated by prevailing winds. The southeast monsoon from late May to September brings cooler weather, and the northwest monsoon from March to May, warmer weather. High winds are rare inasmuch as most islands lie outside the Indian Ocean cyclone belt; Mahé suffered the only such storm in its recorded history in 1862. Mean annual rainfall in Mahé averages 2,880 millimeters at sea level and as much as 3,550 millimeters on the mountain slopes. Precipitation is somewhat less on the other islands, averaging as low as 500 millimeters per year on the southernmost coral islands. Because catchment provides most sources of water in Seychelles, yearly variations in rainfall or even brief periods of drought can produce water shortages. Small dams have been built on Mahé since 1969 in an effort to guarantee a reliable water supply, but drought can still be a problem on Mahé and particularly on La Digue.

## Population

According to a July 1994 estimate, the nation's population was 72,113—double what it had been in 1951. The growth rate of 0.8 percent annually had slackened from the 2.1 percent rate recorded in the late 1970s. The infant mortality rate in 1994 was estimated at 11.7 per 1,000 live births. There were twenty-two births per 1,000 population annually and only seven deaths per 1,000; the outward migration rate of seven per 1,000 helped stem population growth.

About 90 percent of all Seychellois live on Mahé; most of the remainder live on Praslin (6,000) and La Digue (1,800). The population of the outer coralline group is only about 400, mostly plantation workers gathering coconuts for copra. To restrict population growth on Mahé, the government has encouraged people to move to Praslin and other islands where water is available.

The birthrate has declined by one-third from thirty-two per 1,000 in 1974 and is relatively lower than most African and Asian countries. By 1980 about one-third of all Seychellois women of reproductive age were reported to be using some form of contraception, which is considered unusually high compared with other African and Asian countries. Death rates are exceptionally low, in part because of the young age structure, but also because of the availability of free medical services to all segments of society, and the healthy climate and living conditions. The average life expectancy at birth in 1994 was 66.1 years for males and 73.4 for females.

## Ethnic Groups

The population is a relatively homogeneous one of mixed European and African descent, and most citizens consider themselves as Seychellois, possessors of a unique culture and society. Contrary to other Indian Ocean island nations, the Asian population is relatively small; it consists almost entirely of Indians and Chinese. However, the intermixing of the Indian and Chinese communities with the larger society is greater than was common elsewhere. Some twenty *grand blanc* planter families, descendants of the original French settlers, represent a separate group but under the socialist government no longer command the power and social prestige they once had. About 2,000 foreign workers and their families lived in Seychelles in the early 1990s.

## Languages

Creole, the mother tongue of 94 percent of the nation in 1990, was adopted as the first official language of the nation in 1981. English is the second language and French the third, all of them officially recognized. The increased emphasis on Creole is designed to facilitate the teaching of reading to primary-level students and to help establish a distinct culture and heritage. Opponents of the René government thought it a mistake to formalize Creole, which had no standardized spelling system. They regarded it as a great advantage for Seychellois to be bilingual in French and English; treating Creole as a language of learning would, they feared, be at the expense of French and English.

Creole in Seychelles developed from dialects of southwest France spoken by the original settlers. It consists basically of a French vocabulary with a few Malagasy, Bantu, English, and Hindi words, and has a mixture of Bantu and French syntax. Very little Seychelles Creole literature exists; development of an orthography of the language was completed only in 1981. The government-backed Kreol Institute promotes the use of Creole by developing a dictionary, sponsoring literary competitions, giving instruction in translation, and preparing course materials to teach Creole to foreigners.

More than one-third of Seychellois can use English, and the great majority of younger Seychellois can read English, which is the language of government and commerce. It is the language of the People's Assembly, although speakers may also use Creole or French. The principal journals carry articles in all three languages.

Although discouraged by the René regime as a colonialist language, French continues to carry prestige. It is the language of the Roman Catholic Church and is used by older people in correspondence and in formal situations. Some 40 percent of television transmissions are in French—beamed by satellite to an earth station provided by the French government—and most Seychellois can speak and understand the language.

## Social Organization

### Class and Social Structure

Several indexes of social status operate. The first is color. Although almost all Seychellois are so racially mixed as to defy classification, light skin remains a status feature because authority in Seychelles traditionally has been vested in a white plantation owner or manager, or later in British officials. Skin color, according to anthropologist Burton Benedict, is distinguished in Seychelles by the terms *blanc* (white), *rouge* (red), or *noir* (black), all of which are applied relatively depending on the speaker's own pigmentation. Economic achievement and material possessions are equally important signs of social status.

According to Benedict, Seychellois are highly status conscious and are anxious to improve their social positions. Possessions, particularly land and substantial homes, are important indicators of status and prestige. Fine clothing, cars, jewelry, and watches are similarly regarded. A willingness to spend freely is, among men, a means to impress others.

Persons with light skin enjoy greater prestige, but the skin shade does not reliably determine social status or position of power in society. Lighter-skinned persons find it easier to advance to managerial or supervisory positions. It is considered advantageous to marry a lighter-skinned person, although a wealthier man of dark skin or a darker-skinned woman with property may not experience such discrimination. Social tensions based on race are almost unknown, and persons of differing racial types mix freely in schools, business, and social gatherings.

A feature of the Seychellois social system is the prevalence of sexual relationships without formal marriage. Most family units take the form of de facto unions known as living *en ménage*. One result of this practice is that nearly three-fourths of all children born in the islands are born out of wedlock. Most of these children are, however, legally acknowledged by their fathers.

The institutionalization of *en ménage* unions as alternatives to legal marriage can be attributed to several factors. The expense of socially required wedding festivities, trousseaus, and household furnishings can exceed a year's income for a laborer. Widely separated economic status of partners, a mother's wish to retain the earning potential of her son, or a previous marriage by one partner may be impediments to marriage. The difficulty and expense of divorce also tend to discourage a legal relationship. Although frowned upon by the church and civil authorities, *en ménage* unions are generally stable and carry little stigma for either partner or for their children. Among women of higher status, prevailing standards of social respectability require that they be married to the men with whom they are living. Sexual fidelity is not as likely to be demanded of husbands, who often enter into liaisons with lower-class women.

## Status of Women

Women enjoy the same legal, political, economic, and social rights as men. Women form nearly half of the enrollment at the prestigious Seychelles Polytechnic, the highest level of education on the islands. In 1994 two women held cabinet posts—

the minister of foreign affairs, planning, and environment and the minister of agriculture and marine resources—and women filled other major positions. In the early 1990s, many SPPF branch leaders were women, although in government as a whole women were underrepresented. According to a Department of State human rights report for 1993, "The Geneva-based Inter-Parliamentary union cited Seychelles as having the world's highest percentage of female representation in its parliament (at 45.8 percent of the total delegates)."

Seychellois society is essentially matriarchal. Mothers tend to be dominant in the household, controlling most current expenditures and looking after the interests of the children. Men are important for their earning ability, but their domestic role is relatively peripheral. Older women can usually count on financial support from family members living at home or contributions from the earnings of grown children.

## Religion

Some 90 percent of the population was Roman Catholic as of 1992. The initial white settlers in Seychelles were Roman Catholics, and the country has remained so, despite ineffective British efforts to establish Protestantism in the islands during the nineteenth century. The nation has been a bishopric since 1890, and mission schools had a virtual monopoly on education until the government took over such schools in 1944. Sunday masses are well attended, and religious holidays are celebrated throughout the nation both as opportunities for the devout to practice their faith and as social events. Practicing Catholicism, like speaking French, confers a certain status by associating its adherents with the white settlers from France.

Approximately 7 percent of Seychellois are Anglicans—most coming from families converted by missionaries in the late nineteenth and early twentieth centuries. Evangelical Protestant churches are active and growing, among them Pentecostals and Seventh-Day Adventists. Some 2 percent of the population are adherents of other faiths, including Hinduism, Buddhism, and Islam. No temples or mosques, however, exist on the islands. No restrictions are imposed on religious worship by any of the denominations.

Although clergy and civil authorities disapprove, many Seychellois see little inconsistency between their orthodox religious observance and belief in magic, witchcraft, and sorcery. It is common to consult a local seer—known as a *bonhomme de*

*Palm forest on Mahé*
*Courtesy Brian Kensley*

*bois* or a *bonne femme de bois*—for fortune-telling or to obtain protective amulets or charms, called *gris-gris,* to bring harm to enemies.

## Education

Until the mid–1800s, little formal education was available in Seychelles. Both the Roman Catholic and Anglican churches opened mission schools in 1851. The missions continued to operate the schools—the teachers were monks and nuns from abroad—even after the government became responsible for them in 1944. After a technical college opened in 1970, a supply of locally trained teachers became available, and many new schools were established. Since 1981 a system of free education has been in effect requiring attendance by all children in grades one to nine, beginning at age five. Ninety percent of all children also attend nursery school at age four.

The literacy rate for school-aged children had risen to more than 90 percent by the late 1980s. Many older Seychellois had not been taught to read or write in their childhood, but adult education classes helped raise adult literacy from 60 percent to a claimed 85 percent in 1991.

Children are first taught to read and write in Creole. Beginning in grade three, English is used as a teaching language in certain subjects. French is introduced in grade six. After completing six years of primary school and three years of secondary school, at age fifteen students who wish to continue attend a National Youth Service (NYS) program. Students in the NYS live at an NYS village at Port Launnay on the northwest coast of Mahé, wearing special brown and beige uniforms. In addition to academic training, the students receive practical instruction in gardening, cooking, housekeeping, and livestock raising— one of the aims of the program is to reduce youth unemployment. They are expected to produce much of their own food, cook their own meals, and do their own laundry. Self-government is practiced through group sessions and committees.

From the time the NYS program was instituted in 1981, it met with heated opposition and remained highly unpopular. Students spend the entire period away from home, with parental visits permitted only at designated times at intervals of several months. Many consider the quality of education to be inferior; indoctrination in the socialist policies of the SPPF is part of the curriculum. Nevertheless, failure to attend the NYS makes it difficult to proceed to more advanced study. In 1991 the NYS program was reduced from two years to one year. The total enrollment in that year was 1,394, with roughly equal numbers of boys and girls. Those who leave school but do not participate in the NYS can volunteer for a government-administered six-month work program, receiving a training stipend below the minimum wage.

After completing their NYS program, students may attend Seychelles Polytechnic (1,600 students in 1991) for pre-university studies or other training. In 1993, responding to popular pressure, the government eliminated the requirement of NYS participation in order to enter the Polytechnic. However, it strongly encouraged students to complete NYS before beginning to work at age eighteen. The largest number of students were in teacher training (302), business studies (255), humanities and science (226), and hotels and tourism (132). No opportunities for higher education are available on the islands. Instead, university and higher professional courses are usually pursued through various British, United States, and French scholarship programs.

Seychelles has received funds for developing its educational programs from several multinational sources. These include a grant from the Organization of the Petroleum Exporting

Countries (OPEC) in 1988 and a US$9.4 million loan from the African Development Bank in November 1991.

## Health and Welfare

Health and nutritional conditions are remarkably good, approaching those of a developed country. The favorable projections of life expectancy are attributable in large degree to a salubrious climate, an absence of infectious diseases commonly associated with the tropics (such as malaria, yellow fever, sleeping sickness, and cholera), and the availability of free medical and hospital services to all Seychellois.

The National Medical Service operated by the Ministry of Health provides free medical treatment to all citizens. The principal medical institution is the 421-bed Victoria Hospital, which has medical, surgical, psychiatric, pediatric, and maternity departments. Five other hospitals and clinics have a combined 113 beds in general wards, and a psychiatric hospital has sixty beds. In addition, a total of twenty-five outpatient clinics exist on Mahé, Praslin, and La Digue. Most of the forty-eight doctors and ten dentists come from overseas; few Seychellois who go abroad for training return to practice medicine.

Improvements in prenatal and postnatal care since the late 1970s have brought the infant mortality rate down from more than fifty per 1,000 live births in 1978 to an estimated 11.7 in 1994, a rate comparable to that of Western Europe. Some 90 percent of protein in the diet is derived from fish, which, along with lentils, rice, and fruits, gives most families access to a reasonably nutritious diet. Nevertheless, many prevailing health problems, especially among children, result from poverty, limited education, poor housing, polluted water, and unbalanced diets.

Local threats to health include intestinal parasites such as hookworm and tapeworm. Venereal diseases are widespread, and local programs to contain their spread have been described as ineffective. Dengue fever epidemics—although not fatal—have periodically struck large segments of the population, causing severe discomfort and unpleasant aftereffects. Alcoholism is a serious problem, and narcotic use—mainly of marijuana and heroin—is beginning to appear among the young. In late November 1992, the Ministry of Health confirmed the first case of acquired immune deficiency syndrome (AIDS); a year previously the ministry had announced that twenty people tested positive for the human immunodeficiency virus (HIV).

Under the social security law, employers and employees contribute to a national pension program that gives retirees a modest pension. Self-employed persons contribute by paying 15 percent of gross earnings. The government also has a program to provide low-cost housing, housing loans, and building plots, although the program is said to reflect favoritism on behalf of SPPF supporters.

## The Economy

A notable feature of the Seychelles economy was the high per capita GDP of US$5,900 in 1992, some fifteen times the average of sub-Saharan Africa. Total GDP was estimated at US$407 million in 1992. Economic growth, which had proceeded at a strong 5 to 6 percent annually since the mid-1980s, resumed in 1992 at an estimated rate of 4 percent.

The major source of economic activity is the tourist industry and tourist-related services in terms of employment, foreign earnings, construction, and banking. Although earnings from the tourism sector are impressive, providing about 50 percent of GDP, they are offset by the need to import large amounts of food, fuels, construction materials, and equipment, costing some 70 percent of tourism income. Gross tourism foreign exchange earnings in 1993 were SRe607 million (for value of the Seychelles rupee—see Glossary). Moreover, the possibilities for expanding tourism are limited, and it is vulnerable to unpredictable shifts in demand, as occurred in 1991 when the Persian Gulf War contributed to a sharp decline from 103,900 tourists in 1990 to 90,000 in 1991. By 1993 there was a strong recovery in the tourist trade, bringing more than 116,000 visitors.

Hoping to avoid overdependence on tourism, the government has attempted to diversify economic activity by encouraging new industries and revitalizing traditional exports. Production of food and other items is being emphasized to reduce the heavy burden of imports needed to sustain tourism. Development of the nation's marine resources remains a principal governmental goal, pursued by expanding indigenous coastal fisheries and by profiting from fees and services provided to foreign fishing fleets operating in Seychelles' EEZ. Small traditional fishing accounted for less than 3 percent of

GDP in the early 1990s but provided jobs for about 1,500 persons and growing foreign-exchange earnings.

Seychelles' traditional marketings of copra and cinnamon bark had declined to an insignificant level by 1991. The government's goal of achieving 60 percent self-sufficiency in food has not been realized, although its efforts have resulted in increases in fruit, vegetable, meat (mainly chicken and pork), and tea production.

Parastatal (mixed government and private) companies proliferated in many sectors of the economy under the René regime. State-owned and parastatal companies accounted for more than half the country's GDP and about two-thirds of formal employment. The parastatals enjoyed mixed success, and by 1992 the government had begun to divest itself of selected enterprises.

Seychelles traditionally has run a large trade deficit because of the need to import nearly all manufactured and most agricultural commodities. Much of the gap has been covered by revenues from the tourism sector and to a lesser extent by remittances from Seychellois workers abroad and by overseas loans and grants.

Seychelles has been relatively successful in containing inflation. The retail price index, which includes some goods and services whose prices are set by the government, rose by 3.3 percent in 1992 and 4.0 percent in 1993. The generally stable price environment has resulted in part from wage discipline, the weakness in world oil prices, and a policy of importing from countries with low prices, including South Africa, whose currency has depreciated steadily against the Seychelles rupee.

To support its anti-inflationary strategy, the government has pursued a liberal exchange-rate policy. Since 1979 the rupee has been pegged to the International Monetary Fund's (IMF—see Glossary) special drawing right (SDR—see Glossary). The rupee's relative stability has contributed to the stability of domestic prices.

## Government Role

Under the socialist policies of President René, the government has taken a leading role in developing the national economy. Since 1978, the Ministry of Planning and Development has drawn up very detailed "rolling" five-year development plans, which are updated and extended every year. The Ministry of Finance is responsible for economic decisions and budgetary policy. A separate Monetary Authority supervises the banking system and manages the money supply. Although foreign banks operate branches in Seychelles, the government owns the two local banks—the Development Bank of Seychelles, which mobilizes resources to fund development programs, and the Seychelles Savings Bank, a bank for savings and current accounts.

The expansion of parastatal companies since 1979, when the first such institution was created, has had primary economic significance. By 1988 the number of parastatals had reached thirty-five, but in 1994 there were indications that the government's more liberal economic policy would probably reduce the role and number of parastatals. Among the most important organizations of the public sector is the Seychelles National Investment Corporation, whose role is to promote economic development in areas neglected by private enterprise or to become a major stockholder in private companies that encounter economic difficulties. The most powerful of the state enterprises is the Seychelles Marketing Board (SMB), which is the sole importer of key commodities, exercises controls over other imports, and regulates prices, production, and distribution of most goods and services.

The state-owned Seychelles Timber Company has responsibility for reforestation and for operating the government sawmill at Grande Anse. The Fishing Development Company controls industrial tuna fishing and the tuna cannery operated as a joint venture with France. Air Seychelles, a parastatal, flies both international and interisland routes, making a critical contribution to the tourist industry. The Islands Development Company (IDC) was established in 1980 to develop agriculture, tourism, and guano production on ten of the outlying islands—guano deposits have since been depleted. A hotel complex on Île Desroches is among the projects conducted by the IDC. Opened in 1988, the Desroches resort is managed by another parastatal, Islands Resorts. A US$12 million shrimp farming project on Coetivy Island remained in the final development stage in 1992. The high initial investment and heavy transport costs raised doubts about its viability, although a study has indicated that about 8 tons of shrimp could be caught annually in the area.

Despite the government's strong involvement in the economy, it has never imposed a policy of forced nationalization. Rather, the government encourages foreign investment, prefer-

*Victoria, Mahé, capital of Seychelles*
*Courtesy Brian Kensley*

ably as joint ventures. Concurrently with the political liberalization in 1992, the government has attempted to strengthen the private sector, announcing measures to attract investment and planning to divest some state-owned companies. Among companies scheduled for privatization are the agro-industrial division of the SMB and Stationery, Printing, and Computer Equipment, to be sold as three separate enterprises. A parastatal holding 65 percent of Seychelles hotel assets reportedly is ready to sell some hotels or to privatize their management. Private investors nevertheless remain cautious because of the continued high level of state economic control.

## Budget

The government budget for 1993 foresaw total expenditures of SRe1,335.6 million consisting of SRe1,078.7 million in current expenditures, SRe232.5 million in capital expenditures, and SRe24.4 million in net lending. The proposed spending was 6 percent higher than the 1992 level. Total revenues were budgeted at SRe1,186.1 million in 1993, consisting of SRe1,122.6 million in current revenues and SRe63.5 million in grants. The projected deficit for 1993 was SRe149.5 million, compared with a 1992 budget deficit of SRe94.5 million. The 1994 budget projected a 6 percent decrease in expenditures, leading to a surplus of SRe64 million rather than a deficit. The 1994 budget also relaxed import controls and set forth a five-year development plan to increase private-sector economic participation, increase employment and foreign-exchange earnings, reduce taxation and the inflation rate, and improve social welfare. Interest on the public debt consumed more than 18 percent of current expenditures.

Among other leading components of 1993 current outlays were education (10.7 percent), health (7.0 percent), transportation and tourism (5.6 percent), and subsidies to parastatals (4.3 percent). Defense spending was cut by 35 percent between 1992 and 1993—from 7.8 percent to 5.0 percent of the total budget. The government's contribution to the SPPF—SRe9.6 million in 1991 and 1992—was eliminated in 1993.

The main revenue sources were a trade tax that included taxes on imports (50 percent of total revenues estimated for 1993) and a business tax based on profits (12.4 percent of total revenue). Various fees, charges, dividends and interest, rents, and Social Security Fund transfers made up most of the remaining budget receipts. The government's program of social services, defense spending, and new parastatals had generated growing budget deficits that peaked at 20 percent of GDP in the recession year of 1986. Austerity in public spending and new taxes had resulted in some improvement; by 1992 the deficit was limited to 4.4 percent of GDP but was expected to rise to 6.5 percent in 1993. The continued excess of spending over receipts, combined with lower foreign assistance levels, remains a worrisome problem.

## Economic Development

The government has detailed its economic development targets in successive five-year plans. The plan for 1985–89 emphasized tourism, agriculture, and fisheries. It proposed to improve the balance of payments by achieving 60 percent self-sufficiency in food and by stimulating tourism. Improved productivity, increased exports, and a lowering of the unemployment level were additional aims. The 1990–94 plan stressed the need to attract foreign investment and the need for greater food self-sufficiency. A ten-year plan for protecting the environment was supported by a pledge of US$40 million from World Bank donors. The total projected investment was SRe4,206 million in constant 1989 prices, of which 26 percent would be funded by the public sector. It was not expected, however, that the investment goals would be realized. Capital spending was aimed at improved living standards—water supplies, waste disposal, and housing. Tourism and related investments were also regarded as priorities.

An ambitious government initiative is the East Coast Development Plan to reclaim land on Mahé for residential and commercial construction. Some 800 new homes are to be built to ease the housing shortage among ordinary Seychellois. In addition, part of the area will be reserved for luxury housing and tourist facilities. In 1993 the government announced that it would seek private-sector investment to help complete this major project.

## Labor

The government is the nation's largest employer, providing jobs for 38 percent of the wage-earning labor force in 1991. The parastatal sector employed a further 26 percent, leaving only 36 percent of workers in the private sector. The total labor force was about 29,600 in 1991; some 19 percent were domestic workers, self-employed, or family workers. The remainder were in formal wage employment. Hotel and restaurant workers formed the largest single category (14.1 percent), followed by transportation (13.8 percent), manufacturing (11.2 percent), public administration (10.9 percent), and agriculture (9.1 percent).

The government establishes official minimum wages depending upon job classification, although most jobs are paid at well above the rates set. Average monthly earnings as of mid-1992 were about SRe2,750 in the government and parastatal sectors and SRe2,260 in the private sector. The differential was caused by high 1992 salary increases for government and parastatal workers amounting to 12.3 percent and 14.3 percent, respectively, which the private sector could not match. The Central Bank of Seychelles has noted that wage inflation, which averaged 10.8 percent for the entire labor force, greatly exceeded the retail price inflation of 3.3 percent and could not be justified by corresponding productivity gains. The bank feared that the government's salary awards would add to existing pressures on the country's cost base, its external competitiveness, and its external accounts.

The sole labor union is the National Workers' Union (NWU), which is controlled by the SPPF. All workers are members because a percentage of their social security contributions are earmarked for union dues. Workers can elect their own shop stewards, but candidates are screened by the NWU executive secretariat, which can dismiss any elected shop steward. Workers can strike only with the permission of the SPPF Central Committee. Nevertheless, two labor disputes occurred in the changed 1992 political environment. Workers in the main electrical generating plant organized a brief shutdown, winning increased allowances in their compensation packages, and stevedores struck for better conditions and higher compensation. To avoid disruption at a critical time for the industrial fisheries sector, the government essentially met the stevedores' demands.

In November 1993, the National Assembly passed the Trade Union Industrial Act, which gave Seychellois workers the right to join and to form their own unions. Any such unions, however, may not compete with the overall NWU. One independent union was formed in late 1993.

In addition to approving collective bargaining agreements and reviewing private wage scales, the Ministry of Employment and Social Affairs can enforce employment conditions and benefits. With many free or subsidized public services, notably education and health, even workers at the low end of the pay scale can sustain their families at a basic level. Even so, many families rely on two or more incomes to deal with the high price structure.

The government has set a legal work week of forty or thirty-five hours, depending on the occupation. With overtime, the work week may not exceed sixty hours. Workers are entitled to a thirty-minute break each day and twenty-one days of paid annual leave. Comprehensive occupational health and safety regulations are enforced through regular workplace visits.

## Agriculture

The Ministry of Agriculture and Marine Resources in 1993 gave up the management of five state-owned farms, which were divided into small plots and leased to individuals. In addition, the agricultural sector consisted of state farms of the Seychelles Agricultural Development Company (Sadeco) and the outer islands managed by the IDC; three other large holdings producing mainly coconuts, cinnamon, and tea; about 250 families engaged in full-time production of foodstuffs; and an estimated 700 families working on a part-time basis. Many households cultivate gardens and raise livestock for home consumption.

The total cultivable area of the islands is only about 400 hectares. Although rainfall is abundant, wet and dry seasons are sharply defined. Better irrigation and drainage systems are needed to improve food crops. The government has taken various measures to reduce dependency on imported foods, including deregulating production and marketing and reducing the trade tax on fertilizers and equipment. As a result, vegetable and fruit production climbed from 505 tons in 1990 to 1,170 tons in 1992. This increase failed to be matched by a commensurate decrease in imports of fruits and vegetables, which reached 3,471 tons in 1992. Local consumption had apparently increased, and substitution between imported and domestic foodstuffs was possible only to a limited degree. In most cases, imported produce is significantly cheaper in spite of air freight, import taxes, and other costs, necessitating a high import markup by the SMB to prevent disruption of domestic production. Neither rice, a dietary staple, nor other grains can be grown on the islands.

The expansion of livestock production is hampered by encroachment of housing and other development on agricultural land as well as by increased labor and animal feed costs. The number of cattle slaughtered in 1992 (329 head) was virtually unchanged from five years earlier. The slaughter of pigs (4,598) was about 45 percent higher than 1987, and chicken production (439,068) had risen by 60 percent.

The two traditional export crops of copra—dried coconut meat from which an oil is produced—and cinnamon have declined greatly because of the high cost of production and pressure from low-cost competitors on the international market. Vanilla, formerly important, is produced on a very small scale. Tea grown on the misty slopes of Mahé is a more recent plantation crop, serving mainly the local market.

## Fisheries

The fisheries sector is divided into two distinct categories: traditional fishing by a domestic fleet of some 400 vessels; and industrial tuna fishing by foreign vessels, which began to develop in the mid-1970s and has emerged as a major revenue source. The domestic inshore fleet consists mainly of open boats equipped with inboard or outboard engines, operating within a radius of sixteen to forty-eight kilometers of the main islands. Domestic offshore operations on banks surrounding the Mahé group and the Amirantes Isles are conducted by handlines from larger boats with sleeping quarters. Most of the catch is frozen. The fish division of the SMB bought and distributed fish landed on the three main islands to avoid serious price fluctuations. An export trade in the local catch developed after the opening of the international airport made possible deliveries to Europe and other markets.

Local consumption of fish traditionally has been high, and has been estimated at eighty-five kilograms per capita annually in the early 1990s. The local catch is also an important menu item at the tourist hotels. The domestic fisheries catch reached 5,734 tons in 1992, about 10 percent of which was accounted for by a new industrial fishing venture, the *Pêcheur Breton* mothership-dory enterprise.

Beyond 100 kilometers from the Seychelles coasts, fishing is conducted by some fifty-five French and Spanish purse seiners based at Victoria. (The Spanish vessels briefly shifted their base to Mombasa in 1992 but returned when the Seychelles government reduced its port charges.) Some 160,000 tons of tuna were transshipped through Victoria in 1992, of which 45,000 tons were reported by the vessels' owners to have been fished within Seychelles' EEZ. The Seychelles authorities had no way of verifying these claims.

In 1991 Seychelles, Mauritius, and Madagascar formed the Tuna Fishing Association to promote their interests. In addition, a series of three-year agreements granted European Community (EC—see Glossary) vessels the right to fish in the Seychelles EEZ. The fourth such agreement, signed in early 1993, was expected to generate US$13.5 million annually. The islands' economy also benefits from the resulting business activity at Victoria in the form of port services, stevedoring, and ship chandling. The Seychelles government had leased one purse seiner to profit more directly from the tuna industry, and is building ten seiners, but the project has encountered financial difficulties.

In 1992 the Seychelles Fishing Authority issued 292 licenses to long-lines fishing vessels mainly from Taiwan and the Republic of Korea (South Korea). These vessels make few calls at Victoria, offloading their catches onto motherships in mid-ocean. Seychelles is unable to carry out naval and air surveillance of possible illegal fishing, especially in more remote parts of the EEZ. There is a strong presumption, however, that unauthorized use is being made of its fishing grounds.

The tuna canning plant opened in 1987, with 70 percent of its capital of Seychelles origin and 30 percent invested by a French cooperative; the plant is designed to process 8,000 to 10,000 tons of fish a year. It employs 425 people, mostly women, and has brought a rapid growth of export earnings, reaching US$12.3 million by 1991. The net gain in balance of payments was less because the operation required some imports, notably the cans, which could not be produced domestically.

## Oil

Seychelles depends on imported petroleum to meet its domestic power requirements. Following the increase in oil prices in 1990, fuel accounted for nearly 8.6 percent of the nation's import bill, exclusive of reexports. The possibility of commercially exploitable offshore oil led to the granting of exploration rights in 1977 to a consortium headed by Amoco Oil Company. Amoco later bought out its partners and acquired additional exploration rights but ceased drilling in 1986 when all of its test wells proved dry.

The government embarked on a new program to interest oil companies in exploration in 1985 with technical assistance from Norway in preparing feasibility studies. In 1987 the British Enterprise Oil Company and the United States Texaco Corporation obtained rights for areas south and west of Mahé. After completing promising seismic studies, Enterprise announced plans to begin drilling in 1995. The Seychelles government retains rights to participate in joint development of the concession if commercial quantities of oil are found. In August 1990, Ultramar Canada, Inc. stated that it had an agreement to search 10,200 square kilometers of seabed northeast of Mahé.

## Manufacturing

Owing to the small size of the local market and the lack of raw materials, manufacturing occurs on a very limited scale. As of 1991, only 2,563 persons were employed in a total of eighty-eight enterprises, twelve of them parastatals. Most employed fewer than ten people, and only five firms employed as many as 100. A number are import-substitution industries (see Glossary), the largest of which is a brewery and soft drink plant. Other firms include cigarette, clothing, paint, plastics, and furniture factories, cinnamon and coconut processing plants, and some handicrafts catering to the tourist industry. To encourage foreign interest in the manufacturing sector, the government has developed a new investment code guaranteeing full repatriation of profits and capital, protection against nationalization, free import of capital goods, and other incentives. The government reserves the right, however, to require that the state share an interest in larger-scale industrial activities.

## Tourism

Tourism is the most important nongovernment sector of the economy. About 15 percent of the formal work force is directly employed in tourism, and employment in construction, banking, transportation, and other activities is closely tied to the tourist industry. Foreign-exchange gross earnings from tourism were SRe607 million in 1993. The direct contribution of the tourism sector to GDP was estimated at 50 percent, and it provides about 70 percent of total foreign-exchange earnings. Although difficult to measure, the import content of tourism expenditures is high, so net tourism earnings are significantly lower.

The tourist industry was born with the completion of the international airport in 1971, advancing rapidly to a level of 77,400 arrivals in 1979. After slackening in the early 1980s, growth was restored through the introduction of casinos, vigorous advertising campaigns, and more competitive pricing. After a decline to 90,050 in 1991 because of the Persian Gulf War, the number of visitors rose to more than 116,000 in 1993. In 1991 France was the leading source of tourists, followed by Britain, Germany, Italy, and South Africa. Europe provided 80 percent of the total tourists and Africa—mostly South Africa and Reunion—most of the remainder. European tourists are considered the most lucrative in terms of length of stay and per capita spending.

Under the 1990–94 development plan, which emphasizes that the growth of tourism should not be at the expense of the environment, the number of beds on the islands of Mahé, Praslin, and La Digue is to be limited to 4,000. Increases in total capacity are to be achieved by developing the outer islands. To avoid future threats to the natural attractions of the islands, 150,000 tourists per year are regarded as the ultimate ceiling. The higher cost of accommodations and travel, deficiencies in services and maintenance of facilities, and a limited range of diversions handicap Seychelles in attracting vacationers at the expense of other Indian Ocean tourist destinations.

## Transportation and Telecommunications

Cars and buses are the principal means of transportation; Seychelles has no railroads. The total road network as of 1994 was 302 kilometers, of which 202 kilometers were hard surfaced. Road conditions on the island of Mahé are for the most part excellent. Vehicle registrations consist of 4,072 private cars, 216 buses, 1,105 commercial vehicles, and 102 motorcycles. Between 1983 and 1986, car imports were prohibited to conserve foreign exchange. Under a quota system subsequently introduced, vehicle imports were allowed to rise to 1,070 in 1989.

Mahé has an international airport and a good harbor. A government ferry service links Mahé to the nearby islands of Praslin and La Digue. Private vessels serve some smaller islands, but in the more remote islands service is less frequent and is primarily for loading copra and delivering supplies. In April 1994,

Seychelles Shipping Line was founded to provide additional international service.

Seychelles has fourteen airports or airstrips, eight with hard-surfaced runways. The state airline, Air Seychelles, was converted from an interisland to an international carrier in 1983 to offset the effects of termination of air service by British Airways. In 1989 it purchased a Boeing 767, followed in 1993 by a Boeing 757 on a lease-purchase arrangement. The larger 767 flies to northern European cities, such as London, Frankfurt, and Zurich, and the 757 provides service to Johannesburg, Nairobi, Bahrain, Dubayy, Singapore, Rome, Paris and Madrid. The airline also has four de Havilland DHC–6 Twin Otters and one Pilatus Britten-Norman Islander. In addition, five international carriers serve the airport on Mahé. Air Seychelles' share of international traffic was 35 percent in 1992, which it hoped to expand to more than 40 percent.

Seychelles has an air traffic control center covering some 2.6 million square kilometers between the east coast of Africa and the Indian subcontinent. The center opened in June 1991 and has taken over some of the responsibilities that Somalia handled; it serves seventeen international airlines.

Seychelles has good telecommunications links with all parts of the world by satellite and telephone service on the islands of Mahé, Praslin, and La Digue. Direct radio communications link the outer islands to Mahé and to African coastal countries. Some 13,000 telephone lines were in use as of 1994, along with more than 200 telex and facsimile machines. In 1994 some 40,000 radios and 13,000 television sets could receive programs of the government-owned Seychelles Broadcasting Corporation. With the help of three relay stations, television signals are available to between 75 and 80 percent of the population. The television stations carry foreign programming beamed to an Indian Ocean International Telecommunications Satellite Organization (Intelsat) earth station. There are two amplitude modulation (AM) radio stations, one government and the other a missionary system licensed to broadcast both local and international religious programs.

### Foreign Trade

Seychelles has experienced recurrent foreign-exchange problems because of its limited export potential and fluctuations in tourist traffic. Growing national income has been accompanied by pressures for increased imports of manufactured consumer goods that cannot be produced domestically. In 1991 the government took measures to restrain imports, and in 1992 it imposed surcharges on luxury goods, in addition to taking other actions to restrict domestic spending.

Until 1987 the nation's principal export was fresh and frozen fish, followed by high-quality copra, for which Pakistan, the leading importer, paid premium prices. Cinnamon bark and shark fins were the only other exports of consequence. Reexports, mainly of tourist-related duty-free items and petroleum products for aircraft and ships, were considerably higher than earnings from merchandise exports. From 1987 onward, canned tuna dominated the islands' export trade. With a value of SRe64.1 million, canned tuna constituted 73 percent of all domestic exports in 1991. Fresh and frozen fish exports brought SRe17.7 million, but copra and cinnamon had shrunk to insignificant levels.

France had been the principal destination of Seychelles exports for many years, sometimes absorbing more than 60 percent of the islands' products. In 1991 the Seychelles trade pattern shifted sharply in favor of Britain (52.7 percent of total exports), followed by France (22.8 percent), and Reunion (13.6 percent). Both Reunion and Mauritius are leading customers for frozen fish.

Seychelles imports a broad range of foods, manufactured goods, machinery, and transportation equipment. The largest single category is petroleum fuels and lubricants, although much of this is reexported through servicing of ships and aircraft. Seychelles' main suppliers in 1991 were Bahrain, South Africa, Britain, Singapore, and France. Because of its high import dependence, the country's visible trade is always heavily in deficit. In 1991 its total of domestic exports and reexports (SR258 million) was only 28 percent of total imports (SR910 million). Gross receipts from tourism usually cover some 60 percent of imports but fall short of bridging the gap in the balance of payments. In 1993 Seychelles joined the Preferential Trade Area for Eastern and Southern Africa, which should improve its trade because of greater currency convertibility, particularly with Mauritius.

## Government and Politics

Between 1979 and 1993, Seychelles was governed under a single-party socialist system. President René, who had assumed power in a military coup d'état in 1977, had been the sole candidate in the presidential elections of 1979, 1984, and 1989, each time winning an affirmative vote of more than 90 percent.

The SPPF agreed to relinquish its monopoly of power in December 1991 when a party congress approved René's proposal to allow other political groups to be registered (see Return to a Multiparty System, this ch.). Groups receiving sufficient popular support were permitted to take part in revising the constitution. A first effort to produce a new constitution failed in a referendum in November 1992, but after further negotiations constitutional changes were approved the following June. Multiparty elections followed in July 1993 in which René and the SPPF were again victorious.

## Governmental System, 1979–93

Under the constitution that took effect in 1979, all political activity, in particular that regarding the formulation and debate of policy, was conducted under the auspices of the SPPF, or Front. The party constitution was attached as a supplement to the national constitution. The president, as head of state and commander in chief of the armed forces, was nominated by the national congress of the SPPF and stood for election on a yes-no basis. All Seychellois aged seventeen or older could vote. The president served a five-year term and could be elected no more than three times in succession.

The constitution provided few checks on executive powers. The president appointed a cabinet without review by the People's Assembly. The latter consisted of twenty-three members elected for four-year terms from twenty-three constituencies, plus two members named by the president to represent the inner and outer islands. The president appointed the chair of the assembly. The SPPF selected candidates for assembly seats. In some constituencies, only one candidate was nominated, but in others the voters could choose from as many as three SPPF nominees. The legislature exercised no independent role, simply enacting into law bills proposed by the executive branch. Debates on issues occurred and were reported in the media, but criticism of the president or the government was not tolerated.

## Return to a Multiparty System

Several factors contributed to the shift away from single-party rule. Political changes in the former Soviet Union and Eastern Europe, and a movement toward multiparty systems in

Africa, left Seychelles conspicuously out of step with trends in the rest of the world. Britain and France trimmed their foreign aid programs, tying future aid to progress on the political front. Exiled Seychelles political figures were active in drawing attention to the autocratic features of the Seychelles system (see Opposition Movements and Interest Groups, this ch.). In addition, domestic opposition to domination by the SPPF had become increasingly open by 1991. The Roman Catholic Church, the business community, and even a few figures in the SPPF had begun to express dissatisfaction. Embryonic local government had been introduced by combining the role of local party branch leaders and district councillors, but this step failed to satisfy sentiment for a more open and democratic system.

On December 3, 1991, at a special congress of the SPPF, President René announced that, beginning in January 1992, political groupings of at least 100 members would be permitted to register and that multiparty elections for a commission to participate in drafting a new constitution would be held six months later. In April 1992, former president James Mancham returned from Britain to lead the New Democratic Party (NDP), which tended to represent the commercial and wealthy in the election campaign. Six additional parties were also registered. In the voting for the constitutional commission, the SPPF gained 58.4 percent of the votes and the NDP, 33.7 percent. None of the other parties gained enough to be represented, although the most successful of these, the Seychellois Party (Parti Seselwa) led by Wavel Ramkalanan and calling for restoring free enterprise, was granted one seat on the commission. As a prelude to the constitutional conference, in September 1992 the government ended the eleven-year state of emergency declared after the 1981 attempted mercenary coup.

During the subsequent constitutional conference, the NDP delegation withdrew, objecting to closed sessions and claiming that the SPPF was forcing through an undemocratic document that reinforced the wide powers of the current president. The SPPF members, who constituted a quorum, continued the commission's work, and the draft constitution was submitted for popular referendum in November 1992.

The vote in favor of the new constitution was 53.7 percent, well short of the 60 percent needed for acceptance. The NDP campaigned for rejection of the draft, claiming that it would perpetuate domination by the president. The draft stipulated that half of the assembly seats would be allocated by proportional representation based on the presidential election results, thus guaranteeing the president a majority. The Roman Catholic Church also objected to the legalization of abortion called for in the document.

In January 1993, the constitutional commission reconvened to resume negotiations on a new draft constitution. The proceedings were conducted more openly, live television coverage was permitted, and interest groups could submit proposals. The new constitution, which had the support of both the SPPF and the NDP, was approved by 73.9 percent of the voters in a second referendum held on June 18, 1993. The text emphasized human rights and the separation of executive, legislative, and judicial powers. The presidency was again limited to three terms of five years each. The constitution provided for a leader of the opposition to be elected by the National Assembly. The assembly consisted of thirty-three members, twenty-two of them elected and eleven designated by proportional representation.

In the first election under the new constitution, held on July 23, 1993, René was again elected president with 60 percent of the vote. Mancham of the NDP received 37 percent, and Philippe Boullé of the United Opposition Party, a coalition of the smaller parties, received 3 percent. Of the elective seats for the National Assembly, SPPF candidates won twenty-one and the NDP, one. Of the total thirty-three seats in the assembly, twenty-seven went to the SPPF, five to the NDP, and one to the United Opposition Party.

Although Seychelles security forces intimidated some anti-SPPF candidates in 1992, no coercion was reported during the 1993 voting. Fears of loss of jobs and benefits are believed to have played a part in the SPPF victory, however.

## Opposition Movements and Interest Groups

Most domestic critics of the government had been silenced by harassment or had been forced into exile during the period of one-party rule from 1977 to 1991. Opposition groups, about which little information is available, included the Movement for Resistance (Mouvement pour la Résistance), Seychelles Liberation Committee, and Seychelles Popular Anti-Marxist Front. Government control over the press and radio and television broadcasts also made it difficult for any opposition views to be heard, although newspapers printed by exiles were smuggled in from abroad or received by fax. The Roman Catholic and

*Typical early twentieth-century house, Mahé*
*Street scene, suburbs of Victoria*
*Courtesy Brian Kensley*

Anglican churches were allowed to comment on social and political issues during broadcasts of religious services, which each was allowed on alternate Sundays. The Roman Catholic bishop exercised a degree of influence and was regarded as one of the few checks against abuse by the René regime.

Until 1992 the Seychelles government tolerated no manifestation of domestic opposition, and opposition figures were forced to carry on their anti-SPPF campaigns from abroad, mainly in London. One exile leader, Gérard Hoarau, head of the Seychelles National Movement, was assassinated in 1985 in a crime that the British police were unable to solve.

The leading member of the exile community, however, was Mancham, former head of the Seychelles Democratic Party who was overthrown as president in 1977. In April 1992, Mancham returned to Seychelles to revive his political movement. Since 1989 Mancham had mounted what he called a "fax revolution" from London, designed to stir up opposition by sending facsimile messages to the 200 fax machines in Seychelles. His program, entitled the Crusade for Democracy, was intended to restore democracy to Seychelles peacefully. Data transmitted by fax included accounts of human rights violations in Seychelles and charges of corruption of the René regime. René's government made it illegal to circulate a seditious fax in Seychelles, but fax owners eluded this regulation by photocopying the original before turning it in to the police. René then sought to counter the criticism through a government media campaign, but in so doing he admitted the existence of an opposition in Seychelles. The end result was that he was obliged to give way and allow multiparty democracy to exist. René recognized Mancham as official Leader of the Opposition, and Mancham received a salary as a government employee with various perquisites.

A third opposition leader was Anglican clergyman Wavel Ramkalanan. In a 1990 radio sermon, Ramkalanan denounced violations of human rights by the René government. Although forced off the air, he continued to distribute copies of his sermons charging government corruption. Ramkalanan formed the Parti Seselwa when the government lifted its political ban but obtained only a 4.4 percent return in the 1992 election for delegates. The Parti Seselwa and five other newly registered parties allied themselves with Mancham's NDP but later broke away to form the United Opposition Party, charging Mancham with being too willing to compromise with René and the SPPF.

The Roman Catholic Church continued to wage opposition to the René regime. In early 1993, the Roman Catholic bishop appeared before the constitutional commission several times to complain about past human rights violations by the René government. He also demanded that the new constitution adopt a ban on abortion and provide for religious education in the schools.

### Information Media

During the rule of René and the SPPF through 1991, political expression was tightly controlled. The only daily newspaper was the government-owned *Seychelles Nation*, which had an estimated circulation of 4,000. Published by the Department of Information and Telecommunications, it has a government bias and does not present independent views. *L'Écho des Îles*, a Roman Catholic weekly that touches on current events, is not subject to censorship and often carries views critical of the government. Its circulation is about 2,000. After the political liberalization of 1992, several opposition journals appeared and were allowed to publish without government harassment. Foreign publications are imported and sold without interference.

The state-owned Seychelles Broadcasting Corporation (SBC), previously closely controlled, was granted autonomous status in 1992. Television and radio continued to show a pro-SPPF bias but began to broadcast material critical of the government in their news. Party political broadcasts were permitted, and SBC coverage of the campaigns and constitutional deliberations was followed closely.

### Legal System and Civil Rights

The three-tiered judicial system consists of magistrates' or small claims courts, the Supreme (or trial) Court, and the Court of Appeal. The Court of Appeal hears appeals from the Supreme Court in both civil and criminal cases. The Supreme Court has jurisdiction of first instance as well as acting as an appeals court from the magistrates' courts. The system is based on English common law, with influences of the Napoleonic Code (e.g., in tort and contract matters), and customary law. Criminal cases are heard in magistrates' courts or the Supreme Court depending on the seriousness of the charge. Juries are called only in cases of murder or treason. Normal legal protections are extended to defendants. They include public trials, the right of the accused to be present, and the accused's right to confront witnesses, to appeal, to qualify for bail in most cases, and to be represented by counsel, on a *pro bono* basis if indigent. Judges from other Commonwealth countries—mostly African or Asian—are employed on a contract basis. Judges remain independent from influence by the executive in spite of occasional government pressure.

Under the penal code, a detained person must be brought before a magistrate within forty-eight hours. Before repeal of the Public Security Act in 1992, persons could be detained indefinitely on security charges. The president still has broad personal powers to detain persons regarded as security threats. Since 1989 only a few brief detentions have been reported, all under the Public Security Act.

Much progress in human rights has occurred since political freedoms were restored in 1992. Both military and police engaged in physical harassment of members of opposition parties before the 1992 election of constitutional delegates, but later elections were free of intimidation. The government's control of jobs, housing, and land enables it to reward supporters and discourage dissent. Legislation still on the books in 1994 brings the risk of prosecution and imprisonment for publishing defamatory material against the president or for publishing or possessing publications banned by the government for security reasons. The close association of the armed forces with the SPPF represents a further threat to the full exercise of political rights. In an attempt to mollify domestic and foreign critics, René removed the deputy secretary general of the SPPF as chief of staff of the defense forces in 1992.

The number of crimes and other offenses reported in 1990 was 4,564, of which 35 percent involved violations of traffic ordinances. Thefts, burglaries, housebreaking, and other forms of stealing made up most of the remaining 1,559 offenses. There were five cases of homicide; thirteen cases of rape and indecent assault; 634 aggravated or common assaults; 287 offenses against property such as trespass and arson; and 403 incidents of disorderly conduct. The general trend appears to be downward, although the sharpest decline is in vehicular offenses. Theft in tourist hotels is said to be on the rise. Juvenile delinquency—linked to boredom and isolation—is a growing problem.

Official statistics are not available on sentencing or the prison population. The United States Department of State described living conditions at the Police Bay prison as spartan but said that in 1993 both the SPPF and opposition members drafting the constitution had been allowed to visit and found conditions satisfactory. Weekly family visits are allowed, and inmates have access to printed materials.

## Foreign Relations

Officials characterize the nation's foreign policy as one of "positive nonalignment," under which the country pursues an active and independent course in the conduct of its international relations. Seychelles is a member of the United Nations (UN) and a number of related agencies, including the IMF. It is also a member of the Commonwealth, which has assisted it in transition to multiparty democracy; the Organization of African Unity (OAU); and the Nonaligned Movement. In 1984 Seychelles became linked with Mauritius and Madagascar in the Indian Ocean Commission (IOC); later joined by Comoros and France on behalf of Reunion, the IOC seeks to promote economic cooperation in the region and expand interisland trade.

Although the René government often has sided with the more radical members and causes of the Nonaligned Movement, neither the positions taken nor the radical rhetoric in which they were expressed have been allowed to interfere with essentially pragmatic decisions directly affecting the nation's interests. Seychelles is particularly active in promoting the concept of the Indian Ocean as a zone of peace, campaigning for the removal of all foreign powers and bases in the region. It is committed to seeking the end of the United States naval presence on Diego Garcia, an island territory of Britain situated about 1,900 kilometers east of Mahé. In a spirit of solidarity with the more radical states of the nonaligned spectrum, Seychelles has pursued political ties with the German Democratic Republic (East Germany), Libya, Cuba, Iraq, and the Democratic People's Republic of Korea (North Korea). It has supported the former Soviet Union on such controversial issues as its invasion of Afghanistan.

Seychelles also seeks to strengthen its relations with the littoral nations of the Indian Ocean. Such states include other island governments such as those of French-administered Reunion, and independent Maldives and Mauritius as well as more distant nations such as India, Bangladesh, Tanzania, and Kenya. India has been a source of funding for Seychelles projects, and in October 1990 René paid his third visit to the country following the first meeting of the Indo-Seychelles Joint Commission. The body has continued to meet biennially to discuss common trade, investment, and communications matters. In addition, the navies of the two countries cooperate. In February 1992, the Seychelles minister of education visited Bangladesh to expand bilateral cooperation in education, literacy programs, and rural development. Relations with the Tanzanian government were especially close during the early years of the René regime. Tanzanians had helped train and equip the initiators of the coup that brought René to power, and Tanzanian advisers had helped establish and train the Seychelles People's Liberation Army. With both Tanzania and Kenya, Seychelles has discussed sharing labor resources and with Tanzania, the sharing of its EEZ, tourism promotion, and air flights.

In a practical sense, Seychelles' links with the countries of the West have been much more significant than its political kinship with more radical developing countries. Seychelles has succeeded in attracting relatively large amounts of aid; foreign assistance per capita was US$223 annually in 1975–79, US$295 in 1980–85, and US$331 in 1985–90. France has been the leading donor, providing US$53.9 million in bilateral assistance between 1982 and 1990, in addition to contributions through the World Bank and the EC. Loans placed through the Seychelles Development Bank and direct investments are also important. Examples of projects France has funded for Seychelles included in 1990 assistance to the television station to promote broadcasting in French and provision of devices to improve airport security. Britain has been second in total aid, supplying US$26.1 million in the 1982–90 period. Australia has extended modest amounts of aid, primarily in the form of education and training programs, as part of its efforts to become more fully engaged in the Indian Ocean region. Before the Soviet Union broke up in 1990, it was a significant contributor, granting such aid as fuel oil to assist in patrolling the EEZ. The relative prosperity of the islands has brought a decline in aid from most sources. The British aid level had fallen to about US$1.5 million annually in 1991.

In addition to Peace Corps volunteers working in Seychelles, United States assistance, which earlier amounted to US$3.3 million annually, was US$1.3 million in fiscal year (FY— see Glossary) 1993. The preeminent feature of United States-Seychelles relations over the preceding thirty years was the

United States Air Force satellite tracking station situated on Mahé on land leased from Seychelles at US$4.5 million annually as of 1993. The Seychelles economy benefits by a further US$5 to US$6 million annually in local spending linked to the station. The facility's complement consists of four uniformed air force personnel, about seventy-five civilian contract personnel who operate the equipment, and some 175 Seychellois employees. United States naval vessels periodically pay calls at Victoria. Restrictions on British and United States ships carrying nuclear weapons had not been enforced since 1983.

Furthermore, Seychelles has sought to promote economic relations, particularly with countries from which it might receive loan assistance. For example, it obtained a US$1 million loan for elementary education in December 1988 from the OPEC Fund for International Development. In August 1990, Seychelles signed an agreement on economic and technological cooperation with China.

The Seychelles government condemned apartheid policies in South Africa and joined in the voting in the OAU for trade sanctions. Although René declared that his government would take steps to reduce Seychelles' reliance on South African products, South Africa's relatively low prices and short delivery times have in fact brought South Africa a growing share of Seychelles' trade. In 1991 South Africa accounted for 13.5 percent of total imports. Numerous factors combined to curtail tourism from South Africa in the early 1980s—the René government's hostility, the apparent South African involvement in the 1981 coup attempt, a reduction in air links, and the recession in South Africa. Beginning in 1988, however, tourist arrivals began to increase dramatically, climbing to 13,570 in 1993.

As negotiations proceeded to convert to a multiracial political system in Pretoria, Seychelles modified its hostile political stance, agreeing to enter into commercial and consular relations in April 1992. South Africa also agreed in August 1992 to pay compensation of US$3 million for the abortive 1981 coup. In November 1993 the two countries agreed to establish relations at the ambassadorial level.

\*     \*     \*

*The Seychelles: Unquiet Islands* by Marcus F. Franda is an indispensable introduction to the islands' history and society, covering political developments until 1982. An important sociological study, based on fieldwork in 1974–75, is *Men,*

*Women, and Money in Seychelles* by Marion and Burton Benedict. James R. Mancham's *Paradise Raped: Life, Love, and Power in the Seychelles* provides helpful political background up to 1983. The quarterly reports and annual profile by the Economist Intelligence Unit provide a record of current political and economic developments. The annual reports of the Central Bank of Seychelles contain assessments of the performance of the various sectors of the economy and future prospects. Because relatively little is published on the Seychelles, the reader must rely on such publications as *Africa Economic Digest, Africa Report, New African, Africa Contemporary Record, Economist, Indian Ocean Newsletter, Marchés tropicaux et méditerranéens,* and *Africa Research Bulletin.* The United States Department of State's annual *Country Reports on Human Rights Practices* contains brief but useful appraisals of political and social conditions in Seychelles. (For further information and complete citations, see Bibliography.)

# Chapter 5. Maldives

*National emblem of Maldives*

## Country

**Formal Name:** Republic of Maldives.

**Short Name:** Maldives.

**Term for Citizens:** Maldivian(s).

**Capital:** Male.

**Date of Independence:** July 26, 1965 (from Britain).

## Geography

**Size:** Approximately 298 square kilometers.

**Topography:** Includes some 1,200 coral islands grouped in double chain of twenty-seven atolls. Most atolls are ring-shaped coral reefs supporting five to ten inhabited islands and twenty to sixty uninhabited islands. Average size of islands one to two kilometers and height of 1.5 meters above sea level.

**Climate:** Relatively high humidity but sea breezes stir air. Dry season of northeast monsoon December through March; rainy season of southwest monsoon April through October. Annual rainfall 2,540 millimeters in north, 3,810 millimeters in south.

## Society

**Population:** July 1994 estimate 252,077, with a growth rate of 3.6 percent. High birthrate of 44 per 1,000 in 1994.

**Ethnic Groups:** A homogeneous mixture of Sinhalese, Dravidian, Arab, Australasian, and African groups; also small group of Indian traders.

**Languages:** Maldivian Dhivehi is common language with loanwords from Arabic, Hindi, and Tamil.

**Religion:** Sunni Muslim apart from Shia Muslim Indian traders.

**Education:** Primary (one through five), secondary (six through ten), and higher secondary (eleven and twelve); attendance noncompulsory. Most students attend private Quranic schools that charge fees in contrast to free government schools. No university but some vocational education. Overall literacy claimed as 98.2 percent in 1991.

**Health:** Waterborne and tropical diseases prevalent because of inadequate drinking water supply. In 1994 life expectancy at birth estimated at: overall 64.7 years, 66.1 for females, 63.2 years for males. In 1994 infant mortality 53.8 per 1,000 live births.

## Economy

**Gross National Product (GNP):** Ranked by United Nations as one of world's twenty-nine least developed countries, World Bank estimated 1991 GNP at US$101 million and per capita income at US$460, with annual growth rate of 6 percent in 1993.

**Agriculture:** Accounted for almost 10 percent of gross domestic product (GDP) in 1990 and employed about 7 percent of labor force. Major products coconuts, cassava, corn, taro, and sweet potatoes. Most food imported.

**Fishing:** Provided 15 percent of GDP in 1992 and employed 22 percent of labor force; extensive fishing fleet of domestically built boats; 1992 catch record 82,000 tons. Modernization and refrigeration projects underway.

**Tourism:** In 1992 represented 17 percent of GDP and major source of foreign exchange. In 1992 had 235,852 tourists, mainly from Germany, Italy, Britain, and Japan.

**Exports:** Fish and fish products, clothing accessories; main markets Britain, United States, and Sri Lanka.

**Imports:** Foodstuffs, petroleum products, consumer goods; sources India, Sri Lanka, Singapore, and Britain.

**Balance of Payments:** 1992 trade deficit US$110.5 million; current account deficit US$33.2 million.

**Currency and Exchange Rate:** 1 rufiyaa (Rf) = 100 laari. June 1995 exchange rate US$1.00 = Rf11.77.

**Fiscal Year:** Calendar year.

## Transportation and Telecommunications

**Ports:** Male, Gan; merchant fleet of some twelve vessels.

**Airports:** Two with permanent-surface runways: Male and Gan; Air Maldives is national airline.

**Telecommunications:** (1994) Minimal domestic and international facilities; 8,500 telephones; two amplitude modulation (AM) stations, one frequency modulation (FM) station; one television station; one Indian Ocean International Telecommunications Satellite Organization (Intelsat) earth station.

## Government and Politics

**Government:** Highly centralized presidential system of government, based on 1968 constitution as revised. Islam is official religion. President is elected for renewable five-year term by legislature, or Majlis. Majlis is a unicameral legislature whose members serve five-year terms; combination of elected and appointed members. Muslim sharia law applies to civil and criminal cases; judges appointed by president; courts under minister of justice.

**Politics:** No organized political parties, but various political factions exist. Maumoon Abdul Gayoom reelected president in 1993; also holds posts of minister of defense and minister of finance.

**Foreign Relations:** Member of Commonwealth of Nations; has particularly close relations with Britain but seeks to maintain cordial relations with all states. Founder of South Asian Association for Regional Cooperation (see Glossary) in 1985.

## National Security

**Defense Forces:**  No armed forces but National Security Service of 1,800 members perform army, police, and maritime duties.

MALDIVES IS AN ISOLATED nation and is among the smallest and poorest countries in the world. In olden times, the islands provided the main source of cowrie shells, then used as currency throughout Asia and parts of the East African coast. Moreover, historically Maldives has had a strategic importance because of its location on the major marine routes of the Indian Ocean. Maldives' nearest neighbors are Sri Lanka and India, both of which have had cultural and economic ties with Maldives for centuries. Although under nominal Portuguese, Dutch, and British influences after the sixteenth century, Maldivians were left to govern themselves under a long line of sultans and occasionally sultanas.

Maldives gained independence in 1965. The British, who had been Maldives' last colonial power, continued to maintain an air base on the island of Gan in the southernmost atoll until 1976. The British departure in 1976 almost immediately triggered foreign speculation about the future of the air base; the Soviet Union requested use of the base, but Maldives refused.

The greatest challenge facing the republic in the early 1990s was the need for rapid economic development and modernization, given the country's limited resource base in fishing and tourism. Concern was also evident over a projected long-term rise in sea level, which would prove disastrous to the low-lying coral islands.

## Historical Setting

Maldivians consider the introduction of Islam in A.D. 1153 as the cornerstone of their country's history. Islam remains the state religion in the 1990s. Except for a brief period of Portuguese occupation from 1558–73, Maldives also has remained independent. Because the Muslim religion prohibits images portraying gods, local interest in ancient statues of the pre-Islamic period is not only slight but at times even hostile; villagers have been known to destroy such statues recently unearthed.

Western interest in the archaeological remains of early cultures on Maldives began with the work of H.C.P. Bell, a British commissioner of the Ceylon Civil Service. Bell was shipwrecked on the islands in 1879, and he returned several times to investigate ancient Buddhist ruins. Historians have established that by the fourth century A.D. Theravada Buddhism originating from Ceylon (present-day Sri Lanka) became the dominant religion of the people of Maldives. Some scholars believe that the name "Maldives" derives from the Sanskrit *maladvipa*, meaning "garland of islands." In the mid-1980s, the Maldivian government allowed the noted explorer and expert on early marine navigation, Thor Heyerdahl, to excavate ancient sites. Heyerdahl studied the ancient mounds, called *hawitta* by the Maldivians, found on many of the atolls. Some of his archaeological discoveries of stone figures and carvings from pre-Islamic civilizations are today exhibited in a side room of the small National Museum on Male.

Heyerdahl's research indicates that as early as 2,000 B.C. Maldives lay on the maritime trading routes of early Egyptian, Mesopotamian, and Indus Valley civilizations. Heyerdahl believes that early sun-worshipping seafarers, called the Redin, first settled on the islands. Even today, many mosques in Maldives face the sun and not Mecca, lending credence to this theory. Because building space and materials were scarce, successive cultures constructed their places of worship on the foundations of previous buildings. Heyerdahl thus surmises that these sun-facing mosques were built on the ancient foundations of the Redin culture temples.

The interest of Middle Eastern peoples in Maldives resulted from its strategic location and its abundant supply of cowrie shells, a form of currency widely used throughout Asia and parts of the East African coast since ancient times. Middle Eastern seafarers had just begun to take over the Indian Ocean trade routes in the tenth century A.D. and found Maldives to be an important link in those routes. The importance of the Arabs as traders in the Indian Ocean by the twelfth century A.D. may partly explain why the last Buddhist king of Maldives converted to Islam in the year 1153. The king thereupon adopted the Muslim title and name of Sultan Muhammad al Adil, initiating a series of six dynasties consisting of eighty-four sultans and sultanas that lasted until 1932 when the sultanate became elective. The person responsible for this conversion was a Sunni (see Glossary) Muslim visitor named Abu al Barakat. His venerated tomb now stands on the grounds of Hukuru Mosque, or *miski*, in the capital of Male. Built in 1656, this is the oldest mosque in Maldives. Arab interest in Maldives also was reflected in the residence there in the 1340s of the well-known North African traveler Ibn Battutah.

In 1558 the Portuguese established themselves on Maldives, which they administered from Goa on India's west coast. Fifteen years later, a local guerrilla leader named Muhammad Thakurufaan organized a popular revolt and drove the Portuguese out of Maldives. This event is now commemorated as National Day, and a small museum and memorial center honor the hero on his home island of Utim in South Tiladummati Atoll.

In the mid-seventeenth century, the Dutch, who had replaced the Portuguese as the dominant power in Ceylon, established hegemony over Maldivian affairs without involving themselves directly in local matters, which were governed according to centuries-old Islamic customs. However, the British expelled the Dutch from Ceylon in 1796 and included Maldives as a British protected area. The status of Maldives as a British protectorate was officially recorded in an 1887 agreement in which the sultan accepted British influence over Maldivian external relations and defense. The British had no presence, however, on the leading island community of Male. They left the islanders alone, as had the Dutch, with regard to internal administration to continue to be regulated by Muslim traditional institutions.

During the British era from 1887 to 1965, Maldives continued to be ruled under a succession of sultans. The sultans were hereditary until 1932 when an attempt was made to make the sultanate elective, thereby limiting the absolute powers of sultans. At that time, a constitution was introduced for the first time, although the sultanate was retained for an additional twenty-one years. Maldives remained a British crown protectorate until 1953 when the sultanate was suspended and the First Republic was declared under the short-lived presidency of Muhammad Amin Didi. This first elected president of the country introduced several reforms. While serving as prime minister during the 1940s, Didi nationalized the fish export industry. As president he is remembered as a reformer of the education system and a promoter of women's rights. Muslim conservatives in Male eventually ousted his government, and during a riot over food shortages, Didi was beaten by a mob and died on a nearby island.

Beginning in the 1950s, political history in Maldives was largely influenced by the British military presence in the islands. In 1954 the restoration of the sultanate perpetuated the rule of the past. Two years later, Britain obtained permission to reestablish its wartime airfield on Gan in the southernmost Addu Atoll. Maldives granted the British a 100-year lease on Gan that required them to pay £2,000 a year, as well as some forty-four hectares on Hitaddu for radio installations. In 1957, however, the new prime minister, Ibrahim Nasir, called for a review of the agreement in the interest of shortening the lease and increasing the annual payment. But Nasir, who was theoretically responsible to then sultan Muhammad Farid Didi, was challenged in 1959 by a local secessionist movement in the southern atolls that benefited economically from the British presence on Gan (see Maldives, Armed Forces in National Life, ch. 6). This group cut ties with the Maldives government and formed an independent state with Abdulla Afif Didi as president. The short-lived state (1959–62), called the United Suvadivan Republic, had a combined population of 20,000 inhabitants scattered in the atolls then named Suvadiva—since renamed North Huvadu and South Huvadu—and Addu and Fua Mulaku. In 1962 Nasir sent gunboats from Male with government police on board to eliminate elements opposed to his rule. Abdulla Afif Didi fled to the then British colony of Seychelles, where he was granted political asylum.

Meanwhile, in 1960 Maldives allowed Britain to continue to use both the Gan and the Hitaddu facilities for a thirty-year period, with the payment of £750,000 over the period of 1960 to 1965 for the purpose of Maldives' economic development.

On July 26, 1965, Maldives gained independence under an agreement signed with Britain. The British government retained the use of the Gan and Hitaddu facilities. In a national referendum in March 1968, Maldivians abolished the sultanate and established a republic. The Second Republic was proclaimed in November 1968 under the presidency of Ibrahim Nasir, who had increasingly dominated the political scene. Under the new constitution, Nasir was elected indirectly to a four-year presidential term by the Majlis (legislature). He appointed Ahmed Zaki as the new prime minister. In 1973 Nasir was elected to a second term under the constitution as amended in 1972, which extended the presidential term to five years and which also provided for the election of the prime minister by the Majlis. In March 1975, newly elected prime minister Zaki was arrested in a bloodless coup and was banished to a remote atoll. Observers suggested that Zaki was becoming too popular and hence posed a threat to the Nasir faction.

During the 1970s, the economic situation in Maldives suffered a setback when the Sri Lankan market for Maldives' main export of dried fish collapsed. Adding to the problems was the British decision in 1975 to close its airfield on Gan in line with its new policy of abandoning defense commitments east of the Suez Canal. A steep commercial decline followed the evacuation of Gan in March 1976. As a result, the popularity of Nasir's government suffered. Maldives's twenty-year period of authoritarian rule under Nasir abruptly ended in 1978 when he fled to Singapore. A subsequent investigation revealed that he had absconded with millions of dollars from the state treasury.

Elected to replace Nasir for a five-year presidential term in 1978 was Maumoon Abdul Gayoom, a former university lecturer and Maldivian ambassador to the United Nations (UN). The peaceful election was seen as ushering in a period of political stability and economic development in view of Gayoom's priority to develop the poorer islands. In 1978 Maldives joined the International Monetary Fund (IMF—see Glossary) and the World Bank (see Glossary). Tourism also gained in importance to the local economy, reaching more than 120,000 visitors in 1985. The local populace appeared to benefit from increased tourism and the corresponding increase in foreign contacts involving various development projects. Despite coup attempts in 1980, 1983, and 1988, Gayoom's popularity remained strong, allowing him to win three more presidential terms. In the 1983, 1988, and 1993 elections, Gayoom received more than 95 percent of the vote. Although the government did not allow any legal opposition, Gayoom was opposed in the early 1990s by Islamists (also seen as fundamentalists) who wanted to impose a more traditional way of life and by some powerful local business leaders.

Whereas the 1980 and 1983 coup attempts against Gayoom's presidency were not considered serious, the third coup attempt in November 1988 alarmed the international community. About eighty armed Tamil mercenaries landed on Male before dawn aboard speedboats from a freighter. Disguised as visitors, a similar number had already infiltrated Male earlier. Although the mercenaries quickly gained the nearby airport on Hulele, they failed to capture President Gayoom, who fled from house to house and asked for military intervention from India, the United States, and Britain. Indian prime minister Rajiv Gandhi immediately dispatched 1,600 troops by air to restore order in Male. Less than twelve hours later, Indian paratroopers arrived on Hulele, causing some of the mercenaries to flee toward Sri Lanka in their freighter. Those unable to reach the ship in time were quickly rounded up. Nineteen people reportedly died in the fighting, and several taken hostage also died. Three days later, an Indian frigate captured the mercenaries on their freighter near the Sri Lankan coast. In July 1989, a number of the mercenaries were returned to Maldives to stand trial. Gayoom commuted the death sentences passed against them to life imprisonment.

The 1988 coup had been headed by a once prominent Maldivian businessperson named Abdullah Luthufi, who was operating a farm on Sri Lanka. Ex-president Nasir denied any involvement in the coup. In fact, in July 1990 President Gayoom officially pardoned Nasir in absentia in recognition of his role in obtaining Maldives' independence.

## Physical Environment

### Physiography

Maldives consists of approximately 1,200 coral islands grouped in a double chain of twenty-seven atolls. Composed of live coral reefs and sand bars, these atolls are situated atop a submarine ridge 960 kilometers long that rises abruptly from the depths of the Indian Ocean and runs from north to south. Only near the southern end of this natural coral barricade do two open passages permit safe ship navigation from one side of the Indian Ocean to the other through the territorial waters of Maldives. For administrative purposes, the Maldives government organized these atolls into nineteen administrative divisions (see fig. 8; Government and Politics, this ch.).

Most atolls consist of a large, ring-shaped coral reef supporting numerous small islands. Islands average only one to two square kilometers in area, and lie between one and 1.5 meters above mean sea level. The highest island is situated at three meters above sea level. Maldives has no hills or rivers. Although some larger atolls are approximately fifty kilometers long from north to south, and thirty kilometers wide from east to west, no individual island is longer than eight kilometers.

Each atoll has approximately five to ten inhabited islands; the uninhabited islands of each atoll number approximately twenty to sixty. Several atolls, however, consist of one large, isolated island surrounded by a steep coral beach. The most notable example of this type of atoll is the large island of Fua Mulaku situated in the middle of the Equatorial Channel.

The tropical vegetation of Maldives comprises groves of breadfruit trees and coconut palms towering above dense scrub, shrubs, and flowers. The soil is sandy and highly alkaline, and a deficiency in nitrogen, potash, and iron severely limits agricultural potential. Ten percent of the land, or about 2,600 hectares, is cultivated with taro, bananas, coconuts, and other fruit. Only the lush island of Fua Mulaku produces fruits such as oranges and pineapples, partly because the terrain of Fua Mulaku is higher than most other islands, leaving the groundwater less subject to seawater penetration. Freshwater floats in a layer, or "lens," above the seawater that permeates the limestone and coral sands of the islands. These lenses are shrinking rapidly on Male and on many islands where there are resorts catering to foreign tourists. Mango trees already have been reported dying on Male because of salt penetration. Most residents of the atolls depend on groundwater or rainwater for drinking purposes. Concerns over global warming and a possible long-term rise in sea level as a result of the melting of polar ice are important issues to the fragile balance between the people and the environment of Maldives in the 1990s.

## Climate

The temperature of Maldives ranges between 24°C and 33°C throughout the year. Although the humidity is relatively high, the constant sea breezes help to keep the air moving. Two seasons dominate Maldives' weather: the dry season associated with the winter northeast monsoon and the rainy season brought by the summer southwest monsoon. The annual rainfall averages 2,540 millimeters in the north and 3,810 millimeters in the south.

The weather in Maldives is affected by the large landmass of the Indian subcontinent to the north. The presence of this landmass causes differential heating of land and water. Scientists also cite other factors in the formation of monsoons, including the barrier of the Himalayas on the northern fringe of the Indian subcontinent and the sun's northward tilt, which shifts the jet stream north. These factors set off a rush of moisture-rich air from the Indian Ocean over the subcontinent, resulting in the southwest monsoon. The hot air that rises over the subcontinent during April and May creates low-pressure areas into which the cooler, moisture-bearing winds from the Indian Ocean flow. In Maldives, the wet southwest monsoon lasts from the end of April to the end of October and brings the worst weather with strong winds and storms. In May 1991, violent monsoon winds created tidal waves that damaged thousands of houses and piers, flooded arable land with seawater, and uprooted thousands of fruit trees. The damage caused was estimated at US$30 million.

The shift from the moist southwest monsoon to the dry northeast monsoon over the Indian subcontinent occurs during October and November. During this period, the northeast winds contribute to the formation of the northeast monsoon, which reaches Maldives in the beginning of December and lasts until the end of March. However, the weather patterns of Maldives do not always conform to the monsoon patterns of the Indian subcontinent. Rain showers over the whole country have been known to persist for up to one week during the midst of the dry season.

## Society

### Population

Based on the 1990 census, the population was 213,215. The country's population in mid-1994 was estimated at 252,077. The high 1994 birthrate of 44 per 1,000 will lead to a population of more than 300,000 by the year 2000 and 400,000 by 2020. Although the high population growth rate is a serious problem, Maldives lacks an official birth control policy. The population growth rate also poses problems for the country's future food supply because the dietary staple of rice is not grown in the islands and must be imported.

The largest concentration of Maldives' population is in Male, a small island of approximately two square kilometers, whose 1990 population of 55,130 represented slightly more than 25 percent of the national total. Giving meaningful average population density is difficult because many of Maldives' approximately 1,200 islands are uninhabited. Of the approximately 200 inhabited islands in 1988, twenty-eight had fewer than 200 inhabitants, 107 had populations ranging from 200 to 500, and eight had populations between 500 and 1,000. A government study in the mid-1980s listed twenty-five places with a population of more than 1,000. Maldives has few towns besides the capital of Male. Villages comprise most of the settlements on the inhabited islands. The 1990 census recorded an average population density for Maldives of 706 persons per square kilometer.

The first accurate census was held in December 1977 and showed 142,832 persons residing in Maldives, an increase of 37 percent over a 1967 estimate. The next census in March 1985 showed 181,453 persons, consisting of 94,060 males and 87,393 females. This pattern has continued in Maldives, with the 1990 census listing 109,806 males and 103,409 females.

Despite rapid population growth, family planning programs in Maldives did not begin in a well-funded and planned manner until the UN implemented several programs in the 1980s. These programs focused on improving health standards among the islanders, including family planning education emphasizing the spacing of births and raising the customary age of marriage among adolescents. Abortion is not a legally accepted method for child spacing in Maldives. In the mid-1980s, a World Health Organization (WHO) program monitored the extent and use of various contraceptive methods over a four-year period. As of the early 1990s, the government had taken no overt actions toward limiting the number of children per couple or setting target population goals.

## Ethnic Groups and Language

The contemporary homogeneous mixture of Sinhalese, Dravidian, Arab, Australasian, and African ethnicity in Maldives results from historical changes in regional hegemony over marine trade routes. Clarence Maloney, an anthropologist who conducted fieldwork in Maldives in the 1970s, determined that an early Dravidian-speaking substratum of population from Kerala in India had settled in the islands, leaving its legacy in the language and place-names. This group was subsequently displaced by Dhivehi-speakers who arrived from Sri Lanka and whose language became the official one. Arabs compose the last main group to arrive beginning in the ninth century. However, a rapidly disappearing endogamous subgroup of persons of African origin called the Ravare or Giraavaru also existed. In 1970, facing the loss of their home island in Male Atoll because of erosion, the Ravare moved to Hulele. But a few years later, the community of 200 people was transferred to Male to permit the expansion of the airport on Hulele.

The only distinct ethnic minority is found in Male among the trading community of Indians, who settled there in the

1800s. Several hundred in number, they are also a religious minority, belonging to the Shia (see Glossary) branch of Islam. In addition, a small number of Sri Lankans have come to Maldives in recent years to work in the tourist resorts because Maldivians, as devout Muslims, refuse to work in facilities serving alcoholic beverages. This situation has created some resentment on the part of local Maldivians facing unemployment.

The language Maldivian Dhivehi belongs to the Indo-European language family. Derived from Elu, an archaic form of Sinhalese (the language of Sri Lanka), it has numerous loanwords from Arabic, from Hindi—which is used in trade with Indian merchants—and from Tamil. It has contributed one word, "atoll," to international usage. In Dhivehi, the numbers from one to twelve are of Sinhalese origin, and after twelve, Hindi. The names of the days are Sinhalese and Hindi. The names of persons are Arabic.

Dhivehi is spoken throughout the atolls. Dialect differences are pronounced in the four southernmost atolls, however. The traditional script, Thaana, is written from right to left. This locally invented script contains twenty-four letters, the first nine of which are forms of the Arabic numerals. In 1977 a romanized script was introduced to be used along with Thaana for official correspondence, but since 1979 the requirement is no longer mandatory.

## Social Structure

Maldives was a caste society well into the 1920s. Modernization efforts, however, have helped make Maldives more homogeneous in the early 1990s. Traditionally, a significant gap has existed between the elite living on Male and the remainder of the population inhabiting the outer islands—those atolls distant from Male. President Gayoom's development philosophy has centered on decreasing this gap by raising the standard of living among the 75 percent of Maldivians who live in the outer atolls as well as making Maldives more self-sufficient. Fortunately, social tensions that might have affected these two distinct societies were lessened by the isolation of the outer islands. The geographical advantage of having many islands, for example, has enabled Maldives to limit the impact of tourism to special resorts.

Male, the traditional seat of the sultans and of the nobility, remains an elite society wielding political and economic power. Members of the several traditionally privileged ruling families;

government, business, and religious leaders; professionals; and scholars are found there. Male differs from other island communities also because as many as 40 percent of its residents are migrants.

The island communities outside Male are in most cases self-contained economic units, drawing meager sustenance from the sea around them. Islanders are in many instances interrelated by marriage and form a small, tightly knit group whose main economic pursuit is fishing. Apart from the heads of individual households, local influence is exerted by the government appointed island *khatib*, or chief. Regional control over each atoll is administered by the *atolu verin*, or atoll chief, and by the *gazi*, or community religious leader. Boat owners, as employers, also dominate the local economy and, in many cases, provide an informal, but effective, link to Male's power structure.

The family is the basic unit of society. Roughly 80 percent of Maldivian households consist of a single nuclear family composed of a married couple and their children rather than an extended family. Typically, unmarried adults remain with relatives instead of living alone or with strangers. The man is usually the head of the family household, and descent is patrilineal. Women do not accept their husbands' names after marriage but maintain their maiden names. Inheritance of property is through both males and females.

As Muslims, men may have as many as four wives, but there is little evidence to suggest that many have more than one. Islamic law, as practiced in Maldives, makes divorce easy for men and women. Divorce rates are among the highest in the world. According to the 1977 census, nearly half the women over the age of thirty had been married four times or more. Half of all women marry by the age of fifteen. About 60 percent of men marry at age twenty or later.

The status of women has traditionally been fairly high, as attested to in part by the existence of four sultanas. Women do not veil, nor are they strictly secluded, but special sections are reserved for women in public places, such as stadiums and mosques.

## Religion

With the exception of Shia members of the Indian trading community, Maldivians are Sunni Muslims; adherence to Islam, the state religion since the twelfth century, is required for citizenship. The importance of Islam in Maldives is further evident in the lack of a secular legal system. Instead, the traditional Islamic law code of sharia, known in Dhivehi as *sariatu*, forms the basic law code of Maldives as interpreted to conform to local Maldivian conditions by the president, the attorney general, the Ministry of Home Affairs, and the Majlis. On the inhabited islands, the *miski*, or mosque, forms the central place where Islam is practiced. Because Friday is the most important day for Muslims to attend mosque, shops and offices in towns and villages close around 11 a.m., and the sermon begins by 12:30 p.m. Most inhabited islands have several mosques; Male has more than thirty. Most mosques are whitewashed buildings constructed of coral stone with corrugated iron or thatched roofs. In Male, the Islamic Center and the Grand Friday Mosque, built in 1984 with funding from the Persian Gulf states, Pakistan, Brunei, and Malaysia, are imposing elegant structures. The gold-colored dome of this mosque is the first structure sighted when approaching Male. In mid-1991 Maldives had a total of 724 mosques and 266 women's mosques.

Prayer sessions are held five times daily. *Mudimu*, the mosque caretakers, make the call, but tape recordings rather than the human voice are often used. Most shops and offices close for fifteen minutes after each call. During the ninth Muslim month of Ramadan, Muslims fast during the daylight hours. Therefore, cafés and restaurants are closed during the day, and working hours are limited. The exact occurrence of Ramadan varies each year because it depends on the lunar cycle. Ramadan begins with the new moon and ends with the sighting of the next new moon.

The isolation of Maldives from the historical centers of Islam in the Middle East and Asia has allowed some pre-Islamic beliefs and attitudes to survive. Western anthropologist Maloney during his 1970s fieldwork in Maldives reports being told by a Muslim cleric that for most Maldivians Islam is "largely a matter of observing ablutions, fasting, and reciting incomprehensible Arabic prayer formulas." There is a widespread belief in jinns, or evil spirits. For protection against such evils, people often resort to various charms and spells. The extent of these beliefs has led some observers to identify a magico-religious system parallel to Islam known as *fandita*, which provides a more personal way for the islanders to deal with either actual or perceived problems in their lives.

# Education

Only primary and secondary education, neither of which is compulsory, is offered in Maldives. Students seeking higher education must go abroad to a university. Maldives has three types of schools: Quranic schools, private Dhivehi-language primary schools, and English-language primary and secondary schools. Schools in the last category are government-supported and are the only ones equipped to teach the standard curriculum. In 1992 approximately 20 percent of government revenues went to finance education, a significant increase over the 1982 expenditure of 8.5 percent. Part of the reason for this large expenditure results from recent increases in the construction of modern school facilities on many of the islands. In the late 1970s, faced with a great disparity between the quality of schooling offered in the islands and in Male, the government undertook an ambitious project to build one modern primary school in each of the nineteen administrative atolls. The government in Male directly controls the administration of these primary schools. Literacy is reportedly high; the claimed 1991 adult literacy rate of 98.2 percent would give Maldives the highest rate in South Asia and the Indian Ocean region.

In Maldives primary education comprises classes one through five, enrolling students in the corresponding ages six through ten. Secondary education is divided between classes six through ten, which represent overall secondary education, and classes eleven and twelve, which constitute higher secondary education. In 1992 Maldives had a total of 73,642 pupils in school: 32,475 in government schools and 41,167 in private schools.

Traditionally, education was the responsibility of religious leaders and institutions. Most learning centered on individual tutorials in religious teachings. In 1924 the first formal schools opened in Male. These schools were call *edhuruge*, and served as Quranic schools. *Edhuruge* were only established on two other islands at this time. The basic Quranic primary school on the islands in the 1990s is the *makthab*, dating from the 1940s. Quranic primary schools of a slightly larger scale, in terms of curriculum, enrollment, and number of teachers, are called *madhrasaa*. During the 1940s, a widespread government campaign was organized to bring formal schooling to as many of the inhabited islands as possible. Enthusiastically supported by the islanders, who contributed a daily allotment of the fish catch to support the schools, many one-room structures of coral and lime with thatched roofs were constructed. The *mak-thab* assumed the functions of the traditional *edhuruge* while also providing a basic curriculum in reading, writing, and arithmetic. But with the death of reformist president Didi and the restoration of the sultanate in the early 1950s, official interest in the development of education in the atolls waned.

Throughout the 1960s, attention to education focused mainly on the two government schools in Male. In 1960 the medium of instruction changed from Dhivehi to English, and the curriculum was reorganized according to the imported London General Certificate of Education. In the early 1990s, secondary education was available only in Male's English-medium schools, which also had preschool and primary-level offerings.

As of the early 1990s, education for the majority of Maldivian children continues to be provided by the *makthab*. In 1989 there were 211 community and private schools, and only fifty government schools. The results of a UN study of school enrollment in 1983 showed that the total number in the new government primary schools on the atolls was only 7,916, compared with 23,449 in private schools. In Male the number of students attending government schools was 5,892, with 5,341 in private schools. Throughout the 1980s, enrollment continued to rise as more government-sponsored schools were constructed in the atolls. In 1992 the first secondary school outside Male opened on Addu Atoll.

In 1975 the government, with international assistance, started vocational training at the Vocational Training Center in Male. The training covered electricity, engine repair and maintenance, machinery, welding, and refrigeration. Trainees were chosen from among fourth- and fifth-grade students. In the atolls, the Rural Youth Vocational Training Program provided training designed to meet local needs in engine repair and maintenance, tailoring, carpentry, and boat building. On the island of Mafuri in Male Atoll, a large juvenile reformatory also offered vocational training. Established by the Ministry of Home Affairs in 1979, the reformatory provided training courses in electrical and mechanical engineering, carpentry, welding, and tailoring, as well as a limited primary school academic curriculum.

International organizations enabled the creation of the Science Education Center in 1979, and an Arabic Islamic Education Center opened in 1989. Japanese aid enabled the founding of the Maldives Center for Social Education in 1991. In the latter half of 1993 work began on the Maldives Institute of Technical Education to help eliminate the shortage of skilled labor.

## Health

### Health Conditions

Life expectancy at birth in Maldives in 1994 was 63.2 years for males, 66.1 for females, and 64.7 overall. The death rate was estimated at seven per 1,000 in 1994. Infant mortality was estimated at 53.8 per 1,000 live births in 1994, a dramatic decrease from the rate of 120 per 1,000 in the 1970s. Nutrition is an important factor affecting health. In the 1980s, the daily average intake of calories was estimated at 1,781.

Waterborne and tropical communicable diseases are prevalent as the result of an inadequate drinking water supply. In Maldives the freshwater table is shallow and easily contaminated by organic and human waste. To combat these problems, the Male Water Supply and Sewerage Project was launched in 1985. Its completion in 1988 allowed sewer pipes to collect sewage for pumping into the sea. However, in the outer islands no such sewerage systems exist. The government has promoted the construction of ferro-cement rainwater tanks in recent years to help ensure safe drinking water in the outer islands. Major diseases include gastroenteritis, typhoid, and cholera. Malaria, tuberculosis, filariasis, eye infections, poliomyelitis, venereal diseases, and leprosy are also reported. Since the late 1970s, a number of disease-eradication projects have been organized with assistance from the World Health Organization.

### Health Care

In Maldives the Ministry of Health is responsible for the delivery of health services. Despite government efforts, a major constraint facing the health sector in the early 1990s is a shortage of skilled personnel and health facilities. The WHO reported in 1989 that the population per physician was 7,723. However, when the ratio for Male was separated from that for the atolls, the acute shortage of physicians for the majority of Maldivians became even more obvious. Whereas the population per doctor in Male in 1989 was 2,673, in the atolls it was 35,498. These ratios were derived from a 1989 total of sixteen physicians: twelve in Male and four in the atolls. Also, in 1989 the only dentist was located in Male.

Maldives' medical establishment in the early 1990s consisted of the Male Central Hospital, four regional hospitals, two in the north and two in the south, and twenty-one primary health care centers. The Central Hospital maintains ninety-five beds, and the four regional hospitals have a combined total of sixty-one beds. In 1992 thirty physicians and seventeen medical specialists worked in the Central Hospital. Furthermore, the government opened the Institute for Health Sciences in 1992, and the 200-bed Indira Gandhi Memorial Hospital was scheduled to open in 1994.

Each administrative atoll has at least one health center staffed by community health workers. Most of the inhabited islands also have traditional medical practitioners. However, it was reported in the early 1990s that the atoll hospitals and health centers could only treat minor illnesses. Routine operations could be performed only in Male Central Hospital, which had Russian physicians.

To provide better health facilities in the outer islands, the United Nations Children's Fund (UNICEF), in collaboration with the Maldives government, outfitted two boats to be used by mobile health teams. In 1985 two mobile health teams were dispatched from Male, one to the north and one to the south. Each team included a primary health care worker, a nurse, a family health worker, a malaria fieldworker, three community health workers, and a government official. The services they provided included immunization, communicable disease control, family health, nutrition, and health education. In the late 1980s, a third team was added.

## Economy

### Gross Domestic Product

In the early 1990s, Maldives was ranked by the UN as one of the world's twenty-nine least developed countries. The World Bank estimated Maldives' gross national product (GNP—see Glossary) in 1991 at US$101 million and its per capita income at US$460. The 1993 estimated real growth rate was 6 percent. Between 1980 and 1991, GNP was estimated to increase at an average annual rate of 10.2 percent.

President Gayoom's development philosophy centers on increasing Maldives' self-sufficiency and improving the standard of living of residents of the outer islands. In 1994 a considerable gap continued to exist between the general prosperity of the inhabitants of Male and the limited resources and comparative isolation of those living on the outer islands. The Third National Development Plan (1991–93) reflected these objectives and aimed to improve overall living standards, to reduce the imbalance in population density and socioeconomic progress between Male and the atolls, and to achieve greater self-sufficiency for purposes of future growth.

The fishing and tourist industries are the main contributors to the gross domestic product (GDP—see Glossary). In 1992 the fishing industry provided approximately 15 percent of total GDP. Revenues from tourism were comparable to 80 percent of visible export receipts in 1992, contributing approximately 17 percent of GDP. The country had no known mineral resources, and its cropland—small and scattered over the approximately 200 inhabited islands—was inadequate to sustain a burgeoning population. Agriculture employed a little more than 7 percent of the labor force in 1990 in the limited production of coconuts, cassava, taro, corn, sweet potatoes, and fruit, and accounted for almost 10 percent of GDP. These basic foodstuffs represented only 10 percent of domestic food needs, with the remainder being imported.

## Fishing

Formerly, Maldives shipped 90 percent of its fishing catch of tuna in dried form to Sri Lanka. However, because Sri Lanka cut back its imports of such fish, in 1979 Maldives joined with the Japanese Marubeni Corporation to form the Maldives Nippon Corporation that canned and processed fresh fish. Also in 1979 the Maldivian government created the Maldives Fisheries Corporation to exploit fisheries resources.

Maldives has an extensive fishing fleet of boats built domestically of coconut wood, each of which can carry about twelve persons. In 1991 there were 1,258 such pole and line fishing boats and 352 trawlers. Based on a US$3.2 million loan from the International Development Association (IDA—see Glossary), most of the boats have been mechanized in the course of the 1980s. Although the addition of motors has increased fuel costs, it has resulted in doubling the fishing catch between 1982 and 1985. Moreover, the 1992 catch of 82,000 tons set a record—for example, in 1987 the catch was 56,900 tons.

Progress has also been made as a result of fisheries development projects undertaken by the World Bank. Harbor and refrigeration facilities have been improved, leading to a fourfold increase in earnings from canned fish between 1983 and 1985. Further construction of fisheries refrigeration installations and related facilities such as collector vessels were underway in 1994, with funding both from Japan and the World Bank.

## Tourism

Because of its clear waters, distinctive corals, and sandy white beaches, Maldives has many features to attract tourists. As a result, tourism by 1989 had become the country's major source of foreign exchange, surpassing fishing. In 1992 tourism income constituted 17 percent of GDP. Furthermore, tourism is expected to increase as the government infrastructure improvement projects in the areas of transportation, communications, sanitation, water supply, and other support facilities are put into place.

Since the 1970s, approximately fifty resorts, mostly consisting of thatched bungalows, have been built on many uninhabited islands on Male Atoll. In 1990 a dozen new resorts were under construction on Maldives. In the following year, 196,112 tourists visited Maldives, primarily from Germany, Italy, Britain, and Japan in that order.

Tourist facilities have been developed by private companies and in 1991 consisted of sixty-eight "island resorts" with nearly 8,000 hotel beds. Tourists are not allowed to stay on Male so as not to affect adversely the Muslim life-style of the indigenous people. Wilingili Island has also been off limits for tourist accommodation since 1990 to allow for population overflow from Male to settle there.

## Currency and Banking

The Maldivian unit of currency is the rufiyaa (Rf—see Glossary). Introduced in 1981, the rufiyaa replaced the Maldivian rupee. The rufiyaa is divided into 100 laari. The January 1994 dollar exchange rate was US$1 = Rf11.1 rufiyaa. The rufiyaa has been steadily declining in value against the dollar. The 1993 estimated inflation rate in consumer prices was 15 percent.

Established in 1981, the Maldives Monetary Authority was the nation's first central bank. In 1974 the first bank estab-

*The sandy beaches of Maldives make tourism a major source of income. Courtesy Gloria Garcia*

lished in Maldives was a branch of the State Bank of India. A branch of the Habib Bank of Pakistan was established in 1976, and the Bank of Ceylon also opened two branches. The first commercial bank established in Maldives was the Bank of Maldives, Limited. It opened in 1982 as a joint venture between the government and the International Finance Investment and Credit Bank of Bangladesh; by 1993 it was 100 percent state-owned.

## Budget

The fiscal system in Maldives has been described as rudimentary; the country has no income tax. Tax revenues are derived from customs duties, a tourist/airport tax, and property taxes. Major sources of nontax revenues are derived from the State Trading Organization, rentals of islands to tourist resorts, and boat licensing fees.

Maldives has experienced a budget deficit since the 1980s, when more accurate accounting data became available. Government revenues in 1984 totaled Rf205.4 million. In 1992 government revenues rose to Rf1.02 billion, whereas expenditures totaled Rf1.5 billion. Of these expenditures, education received Rf223 million, atoll development projects Rf362 million, security Rf117 million, and health Rf111 million.

## Employment

In 1992 the fishing industry employed about 22 percent of the labor force, making it the largest single source of employment in Maldives. However, a high level of disguised unemployment existed on a seasonal basis as a result of climatic conditions.

Despite its importance as a source of government revenue, tourism provides few meaningful employment opportunities to Maldivians. Tourism accounts for only about 6 percent of the country's labor force. Because most Maldivians have no education beyond primary school, most lack the required knowledge of foreign languages to cater to foreign tourists. As a result, non-Maldivians fill most of the best jobs in the tourist industry. Indigenous employment on the resort islands is also discouraged by the government's efforts to limit contact between Maldivians and Westerners to prevent adverse influence on local Islamic mores. Also, the low season for tourists, the time for rainy monsoons from late April to late October, coincides with the low season for the fishing industry.

After fishing, the largest source of employment is in the industrial sector, including mining, manufacturing, power, and construction. Although this sector also accounted for nearly 22 percent of the labor force in 1990, most employment was in traditional small-scale cottage industries. Women are mainly employed in these activities, such as coir rope making from coconut husks, *cadjan* or thatch weaving from dried coconut palm leaves, and mat weaving from indigenous reeds. The ancient task of cowrie-shell collecting for export is another occupation in which only women participate. In the early 1990s, a small number of modern industries were operating, mostly fish canning and garment making.The largest garment factories are Hong Kong-owned and occupy abandoned hangars and other maintenance buildings at the former British air station on Gan. They employ about 1,500 local women who are bused in and about 500 young Sri Lankan women who reside at the site working the nightshift.

Other forms of employment in 1990 were minor. Government administration accounted for about 7 percent of workers; transportation and communications, 5 percent; trade, 3 percent; and mining of coral, 1 percent.

### Transportation and Telecommunications

Maldives has two airports with permanent-surface runways more than 2,440 meters long, one located adjacent to Male on Hulele Island, known as Male International Airport, and the other on Gan Island in the southernmost Addu Atoll, which is scheduled to become an international airport. Since 1981, after the runway was widened and expanded, the airport on Hulele has been able to handle direct charter flights from Europe. The airport on Gan is used only for domestic traffic. Two additional domestic airports cater to foreign tourists. One on Kadu Island in Haddummati Atoll opened in 1986, and the other on Hanimadu Island in South Tiladummati Atoll opened in 1990. A further domestic airport on Kodedu Island was scheduled to open in 1994.

In 1974 the government created Air Maldives, which had one eighteen-seat airplane. In the early 1990s, Air Maldives flew between Hulele and Gan three days a week, and between Hulele and Kadu twice a week. A twenty-seat seaplane operated by Inter Atoll Air also flew scheduled and chartered flights between Hulele and many of the resorts. In addition, Hummingbird Helicopters (Maldives) and Seagull Airways each operated four helicopters for interisland flights. Another firm, Maldives Air Services, coordinated all air services on the ground.

Maldives has an active merchant shipping fleet used for import and export purposes, including ten cargo vessels, one container ship, and one oil tanker. The government-owned Maldives National Ship Management, Limited, is the largest of several Maldivian shipping firms.

Male, the only port that can handle international traffic, has been improved by the First Male Port Development Project completed in late 1992. The Second Male Port Development Project, partly financed by a loan from the Asian Development Bank, began in late 1993 and is scheduled for completion in 1996.

The fishing *dhoni* is the traditional all-purpose vessel in Maldives. Although *dhonis* have sails, most are also engine-powered. *Dhonis* are used mainly within the sheltered waters of each atoll. Travel through the open sea from one atoll to another is usually by *vedis*, larger, square-shaped wooden cargo boats.

The primary form of road traffic in Maldives is the bicycle. Motorcycles are the most common form of motor vehicle, of which 4,126 were registered in 1992. Passenger cars on Male are primarily status symbols for the Maldivian elite; however, the larger inhabited islands and resort islands have limited taxi services for transporting people to and from wharves and airfields. In 1992 there were 691 registered passenger cars, and 379 trucks and tractors.

Modern communications are minimal in Maldives. Most people use citizen-band radios on the islands and in boats (see Media, this ch.). Telephone service between Male and the islands is limited. However, most of the resort islands can be contacted directly by telephone, and administrative atoll offices are linked both to Male and to each other by radio-telephone. Modernization efforts of the government have resulted in a steady increase in the number of telephones. The 1984 number of 1,060 telephones increased in 1992 to 8,523. There is good international telephone service through a satellite ground station in Male.

### Trade

Based on IMF reports, Maldives's trade deficit increased to US$110.5 million in 1992 from US$82.6 million in 1991. The current account deficit also increased to US$33.2 million in 1992 from US$9.0 million in 1991. Principal food commodities imported were rice, wheat flour, and sugar. The main imported manufactured goods were petroleum products and various consumer goods. Imports in 1991 came primarily from India, Sri Lanka, Singapore, and Britain in that order.

Principal exports consisted of frozen, dried, and salted skipjack tuna; canned fish; dried sharkfins; and fish meal. Maldives also exported apparel and clothing accessories from its small manufacturing sector. Exports were destined mainly to Britain, the United States, and Sri Lanka in descending order.

### Economic Aid

Before the 1980s, Maldives received limited assistance from certain UN specialized agencies. Much of the external help came from Arab oil-producing states, notably Saudi Arabia, Kuwait, and the United Arab Emirates, for use on an ad hoc basis rather than as part of comprehensive development planning. With local impetus in the 1980s from the developmental commitment of the Gayoom presidency to raise the standard of living in the outer islands, Maldives received an annual average of US$15.5 million in external assistance in the form of grants and loans. For example, in 1988 bilateral donors accounted for approximately 73 percent of disbursements; the UN, 20 percent; other multilateral sources, 5 percent; and nongovernmental organizations, about 2 percent.

Foreign aid in 1992 was approximately US$11.6 million and came from international agencies such as the World Bank and the Asian Development Bank and individual countries, particularly Japan—in 1991 Japan was Maldives's largest aid donor. Other than humanitarian aid, loans and grants went for such purposes as education, health, transportation, fisheries, and harbor development. As a result of the severe damage caused by the 1991 monsoon, Maldives received relief aid from India, Pakistan, the United States, and a number of other countries.

## Government and Politics

### Constitution

Government organization is based on the 1968 constitution, as revised in 1970, 1972, and 1975. The document provides the basis for a highly centralized, presidential form of government. Its philosophical frame of reference is derived from Islam; thus the distinction between secular and religious authority is often academic. The constitution vests final authority for the propagation of Islam in the president, who in turn is empowered to appoint all judges who interpret and apply the sharia in the adjudication of civil and criminal cases. In Maldives, therefore, the courts are not independent of the executive branch, but rather are under the minister of justice, who is appointed by the president.

Constitutional provisions regarding the basic rights of the people are broadly phrased. They refer to freedom of speech and assembly, equality before the law, and the right to own property, but these rights are to be exercised within the framework of the sharia. In 1990 younger members of the recently expanded president's Consultative Council called for the repeal or amendment of Article 38 in the penal code, which allows the jailing or banishment "for any gesture, speech or action that instills malice or disobedience in the minds of Maldivians against lawfully formed government."

The president is elected for a renewable five-year term by the Majlis, or legislature. The election must be formalized through confirmation in a popular referendum. The chief executive is assisted by a cabinet, or Council of Ministers, whose members serve at his pleasure. The post of prime minister, which had existed under the sultan and in the early years of the republic, was eliminated in 1975 by President Ibrahim Nasir because of abuses of the office. Cabinet ministers need not be members of the Majlis. The legislature is unicameral, with members elected for five-year terms by citizens aged twenty-one and above, or appointed by the president. Eight of its forty-eight members are appointed by the president, and the rest are chosen popularly, two from Male and two from each of the nineteen administrative atolls.

## Politics

The presidential and Majlis elections are held on a nonpartisan basis because there are no organized political parties in the country. Candidates run as independents on the basis of personal qualifications.

Although in 1994 Maldives had no organized political competition in the Western sense, partisan conflict occurred behind the scenes. Battles were intensely fought on the basis of factional or personal alliances among elite circles. For more than twenty years, until late 1978, the dominant faction had been led by former President Nasir, who ran the government with a firm hand and who seldom appeared in public. His sudden departure from Maldives, subsequently revealed as connected with malfeasance, ended a political era.

Transition was smooth under the new leadership group presided over by Maumoon Abdul Gayoom, a former cabinet member and diplomat who took office on November 11, 1978, after a peaceful election. The new president pledged to administer the country in a fair and more open manner by restoring civil rights, by establishing rapport at the grass-roots level, and by remedying the long neglect of popular welfare in the outer islands. However, criticism of alleged nepotism and corruption has continued through the 1980s and early 1990s.

Gayoom's presidential cabinet, including his relatives in key positions, is considered a "kitchen cabinet" of traditional power holders that exert a strong influence against democratic reforms on a weak but relatively popular president. Events in the spring of 1990 tended to confirm that Gayoom's announced support for democratic reform was not being honored throughout the governmental power structure. In April, three pro-reform members of the Majlis received anonymous death threats. A few months later, all publications not sanctioned by the government were banned, and some leading writers and publishers were arrested. These actions followed the emergence of several politically outspoken magazines, including *Sangu* (Conch Shell). The circulation of this magazine increased from 500 in February 1990 to 3,000 in April.

Gayoom reshuffled the cabinet in May 1990, dismissing his brother-in-law, Ilyas Ibrahim, as minister of state for defense and national security. Ibrahim had left the country suddenly, apparently before being called to account for embezzlement and misappropriation of funds. Gayoom placed him under house arrest when he returned in August 1990. He was cleared by an investigatory commission in March 1991 and appointed minister of atolls' administration. In April 1991, President Gayoom established a board to investigate charges of malfeasance against government officials. As a result of Gayoom's increasing assertion of his power in the early 1990s, by 1992 he had assumed the duties of both minister of defense and minister of finance, posts he still held in August 1994 as well as that of governor of the Maldives Monetary Authority. Gayoom was reelected to a fourth five-year term as president in national elections in 1993. His principal rival, Ilyas Ibrahim, was sentenced to fifteen years' banishment after being found guilty of "treason" because of his attempts to win the presidency.

## Foreign Relations

Maldives has traditionally sought to maintain a status independent of the great powers while simultaneously preserving cordial relations with all members of the world community. The purposes of this stance are to receive additional aid and to keep the Indian Ocean area at peace. An instance of Maldives' nonalignment was its refusal of a Soviet offer of US$1 million in October 1977 as rental for the former British air base on Gan, which Britain evacuated in 1976. Historically, Maldives has had close relations with Britain, its former colonial power, and has been a full member of the British Commonwealth since 1985.

Maldives participates in a variety of international organizations. It joined the UN in 1965 and the World Bank and the IMF in 1978. In connection with its concern over the security of the Indian Ocean area, Maldives became a founder of the South Asian Association for Regional Cooperation (SAARC— see Glossary) in 1985. It has been a member of the Colombo Plan designed to promote economic and social development in Asia and the Pacific since 1963. In 1990 the fifth SAARC annual conference was held in Male. Maldives is also a member of the Asian Development Bank.

Although a Muslim nation, Maldives has remained apart from most of the problems associated with the Islamist (also seen as fundamentalist) movement in the Middle East. Maldives falls within India's sphere of influence and in 1976 signed an agreement demarcating the maritime boundary between the two countries. It has also received military assistance from India, such as the sending of 1,600 military personnel in 1988 at President Gayoom's request to repel a group of invading mercenaries.

## Media

The major daily newspaper in Maldives is *Haveeru* (North Side) in Male with a circulation of 2,500. *Aafathis*, another daily in Dhivehi and English, has a circulation of 300. Maldives also has a number of weekly and monthly publications as well as several news agencies and publishers.

Censorship exists in Maldives although on a smaller scale than before President Gayoom took office in 1978. Nevertheless, open dissent against the government is not tolerated. For example, in early 1990 the Consultative Council discussed freedom of speech in the press. But when publications critical of the government appeared in the spring of 1990, all publications that lacked government sanction were banned. Also, leading writers and publishers have been arrested.

Hindi-language films, newspapers, and magazines from India are popular. For eleven hours each day, the government radio station Voice of Maldives, established in 1962, broadcasts to the entire country in Dhivehi and English. Maldivians in 1992 had 28,284 radio receivers to pick up such broadcasts. In 1978 government-run Television Maldives was established. During the week, its one channel broadcasts for five hours a day, with an extended weekend service. However, it can only be received (by the 6,591 Maldivians with television sets in 1992) within a thirty-kilometer radius of Male. Maldives also receives broadcasts by the British Broadcasting Corporation, Radio Australia, and Radio Beijing.

Given the censorship that exists, the media play only a limited role in promoting greater democracy. A major question facing Maldives is the way in which democracy will be defined in view of the contrast between a South Asian kinship system and its egalitarian Western-style parliamentary elections.

*　　*　　*

The best recent work that provides a wealth of information on Maldives' physical environment is the relevant section of *Maldives and Islands of the East Indian Ocean, A Travel Survival Kit,* by Robert Willox. Additional insight into contemporary travel and ways of life in the outer islands is provided by Thor Heyerdahl in *The Maldive Mystery.*

Maldives's history is outlined according to official governmental views in *Maldives: A Historical Overview.* More candid descriptions are provided by both the above-mentioned work by Heyerdahl and Clarence Maloney's *People of the Maldive Islands.* Maloney's work is also an excellent source for information on modern Maldivian society, based as it is on the fieldwork of an anthropologist. Additional sources of information on Maldivian society include the United Nations Educational, Scientific, and Cultural Organization (UNESCO) report *Status of Women: Maldives,* and the official Maldives publication *Maldives: Social Development.* A wealth of contemporary data on all aspects of Maldives's social development can be found in

"Maldives: Physical and Social Geography," in *The Far East and Australasia, 1993*.

The best source for a concise, yet scholarly description of the history and contemporary position of Islam in Maldives may be found in volume six of *The Encyclopedia of Islam*. Both the history and current situation of education in Maldives are detailed in the UNESCO report, *Innovation in Primary School Construction*, by M. Luthfi and H. Zubair. The recent series of reports on health conditions and care in Maldives by the World Health Organization, such as the 1989 *Twenty-Four Monthly Report on Technical Aspects of Programme Implementation*, is an excellent source for the study of health.

The Maldivian economy is outlined in the official *Maldives: An Economic Brief*, and *Maldives: Year Book 1988*. Additional relevant data are contained in the *World Factbook, 1994*, and the Europa *The Far East and Australasia, 1994*. Useful periodicals include the *Indian Ocean Newsletter, Keesing's Contemporary Archives*, and *Africa Research Bulletin*. (For further information and complete citations, see Bibliography).

# Chapter 6. Strategic Considerations

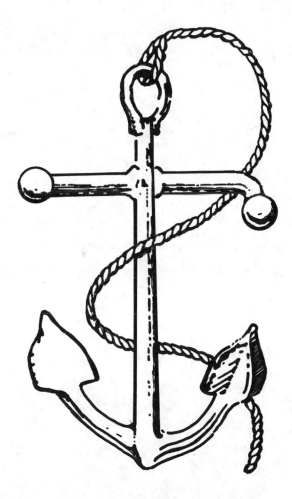

*Anchor, symbolizing naval power in the Indian Ocean*

HISTORICALLY, the western Indian Ocean has played a vital role in international politics. In ancient times, maritime commerce attracted numerous nations to the region, including Ceylon (Sri Lanka), China, Egypt, India, Indonesia, and Persia (Iran). During the period of European colonial empires, Portugal, the Netherlands, Britain, and France sought to safeguard their respective strategic and commercial interests by protecting the lines of communication and providing external defense and internal security to Madagascar, Mauritius, Comoros, Seychelles, and Maldives. After 1945 Cold War considerations provoked competition between the United States and the former Soviet Union for access to strategically important air and naval bases in the western Indian Ocean and for the loyalties of the area's indigenous governments. Britain and France also maintained a military and political presence in the region throughout much of the Cold War. Moscow ended its military presence in the western Indian Ocean after communism collapsed in the Soviet Union, but the United States has continued its interest in the region. The post-Cold War era also has provided traditional powers such as France and emerging regional states such as India, South Africa, and Australia with an opportunity to increase their activities in the western Indian Ocean.

Madagascar, Mauritius, Comoros, Seychelles, and Maldives have also pursued their own national security objectives in the region. Apart from providing internal stability, indigenous security forces have sought to protect the exclusive economic zones (EEZs—see Glossary) claimed by all five countries and to prevent the use of the western Indian Ocean as a transshipment point for illegal drugs.

## Historical Interest

The Indian Ocean has a long maritime history. Since approximately 2500 B.C., traders, adventurers, and explorers from Ceylon, China, Egypt, India, Indonesia, and Persia conducted oceangoing commerce and at times maintained maritime empires in the Indian Ocean. Additionally, many peoples who lived in the Red Sea and Persian Gulf regions relied on the Indian Ocean for their livelihoods. In the mid-1800s, the most notable local power was Oman. The sultan of Oman moved his capital from Muscat to Zanzibar in 1841 and established a trading empire along the East African coast based largely on ivory and slaves. In the wake of these activities, Asians began to migrate into the western Indian Ocean. As early as 500 B.C., however, Dravidians and Sinhalese from India and Ceylon had settled in the Maldive Islands. By A.D. 1000, Malayo-Indonesians had established communities in Madagascar.

The emergence of the great European maritime empires marked a historical watershed in the Indian Ocean. In the sixteenth century, the Portuguese, Dutch, French, and British quickly gained control over much of the region, using sophisticated ships and maritime strategies and exploiting local rivalries to gain allies and territory. These activities signaled the beginning of the use of the Indian Ocean as a theater where European maritime nations competed for power and influence. This rivalry spawned many extraregional wars and alliances, many of which caused instability in the region's islands.

One of the most important personalities during the early European period was Alfonso d'Albuquerque, governor of Portugal's Indian Ocean possessions from 1508 to 1515. Rather than devoting his energies to territorial conquest, he used naval power to control trade routes. D'Albuquerque established a network of bases in the Indian Ocean; constructed forts at the entrances to the Red Sea, the Persian Gulf, and the Strait of Malacca; and concluded alliances with economically powerful rulers on the African and Asian coasts. These tactics enabled Portugal to dominate commercial activity in the Indian Ocean from 1511 to 1641.

From the seventeenth century until the opening of the Suez Canal in 1869, Europe and North America relied on the western Indian Ocean and its islands for transporting Eastern goods and spices. As this shorter route quickly supplanted the longer Cape of Good Hope route and steam gradually replaced sail, the region's strategic importance diminished. The islands of Madagascar, Mauritius, Comoros, Seychelles, and, to a lesser extent, Maldives, all of which had been important way stations for international shipping, became remote colonial outposts.

The Suez Canal enabled Britain to consolidate its hegemony over the Indian Ocean, but it also opened the way for other European nations into the area. The stronger European powers not only challenged British mastery over the Indian Ocean but also began a scramble for colonies. The French established a presence in the Horn of Africa and Madagascar, both of which protected the route to their Southeast Asia empire. The Italians, Germans, and Portuguese planted colonies along the East African coast. Russia viewed the Suez Canal as a means of creating a network of warm water ports, but Japan's 1904 victory over the Russian fleet ended this dream. Over the next several years, Japan and the United States posed a growing naval challenge to Britain's dominance in the Indian Ocean. Nevertheless, British seapower remained preeminent throughout the region.

During World War I, the Indian Ocean aroused international interest as the British and the Germans battled one another for control of various colonies. These nations also sought to protect shipping routes from the Persian Gulf and India, via the Suez Canal, to Europe. Despite the area's importance, Madagascar, Mauritius, Comoros, Seychelles, and Maldives managed to escape the ravages of World War I.

The western Indian Ocean, especially Madagascar, played a more significant role in World War II. On May 5, 1942, the British defeated pro-Vichy French troops and then occupied Diégo Suarez. This action denied an important naval base to Japan, which undoubtedly would have used the facility to threaten British maritime communications along East Africa with the Middle East. After occupying Majunga, Tamatave, and Tananarive (now Antananarivo), the British established a military administration over Madagascar that functioned until mid-1943. Apart from these activities, German submarines harassed Allied shipping throughout the western Indian Ocean.

The most notable wartime event in the region occurred at the 1942 Battle of the Java Sea. The Japanese destroyed the British Royal Navy elements that participated, marking the end of British hegemony over the Indian Ocean. Nonetheless, in the absence of a strong contending naval power, Britain retained nominal control of sizable portions of the Indian Ocean, even though it lacked the ability and resources to reassert its former maritime dominance. France confined its activities mainly to the western Indian Ocean. Politically, World War II weakened British and French holds over their respective colonial empires. The rising tide of nationalism that swept through Africa and Asia accelerated demands for independence on the part of all the western Indian Ocean islands.

During the postwar period, several factors affected the strategic importance of the Indian Ocean. The onset of the Cold War increased superpower activity throughout the region. By

1964 the United States had developed ballistic missile submarines that could hit industrial targets in the Soviet Union from the Arabian Sea. Moscow perceived this as a prelude to a similar buildup in the Indian Ocean. This perception was compounded by Washington's announcement that it intended to deploy some ballistic missile submarines to the Pacific Ocean and to build a very low frequency communications station— designed for submarine contact—in western Australia.

As British power in the region weakened, London and Washington sought ways to uphold the interests of both nations. In 1965 the British government told a Mauritian delegation that the island's independence was contingent on the sale of the Chagos Archipelago and the transfer of sovereignty to Britain. On November 8, 1965, the British government created the Crown Colony (see Glossary) of the British Indian Ocean Territory (BIOT). The BIOT consisted of the Chagos Archipelago, earlier administered from the British Crown Colony of Mauritius; and the Aldabra Islands, the Farquhar Islands, and Île Desroches, previously administered from the British Crown Colony of Seychelles. In 1966 Britain leased the approximately eighteen-square-kilometer island of Diego Garcia in the Chagos Archipelago to the United States for a fifty-year period until the year 2016, with a twenty-year extension available if neither London nor Washington opposed continuation. For political and security reasons, the British government resettled the indigenous population of 1,200 who lived on Diego Garcia in Mauritius and Seychelles, giving them US$8 million in compensation. The controversy surrounding these actions never has disappeared; even in 1994, the Mauritian government periodically attempted to reassert its sovereignty over the Chagos Archipelago, especially Diego Garcia.

The closure of the Suez Canal during the June 1967 Arab-Israeli War increased the importance of Madagascar, Comoros, Seychelles, and, to a lesser extent, Mauritius. Shippers had to transport their goods around the Cape of Good Hope, and each of these islands had the potential to command the Cape route. The islands retained their significance after the canal reopened in 1975 because many of the supertankers built to carry petroleum over the longer route were now too large to pass through the canal.

In early 1968, the strategic situation in the Indian Ocean changed again when the British government announced its intention to withdraw all its military forces from east of the

Suez Canal by 1971. Two months after this declaration, the Soviet Union deployed four warships to the Indian Ocean, and arranged for them to call at ports on the Indian subcontinent, the Persian Gulf, and the East Africa coast. After 1969 Soviet naval units regularly visited the region. Throughout the 1970s, Moscow also succeeded in gaining access to several countries, such as Madagascar and Seychelles, and increasing the number of Soviet intelligence, research, and fishing vessels operating in the Indian Ocean. As a result, the number of Soviet naval craft in the area often exceeded those of the United States.

The British pullback from east of Suez also led to an increased United States military presence in the Indian Ocean. In 1972 a new agreement allowed the United States to build a naval communications facility on Diego Garcia for British and United States use. Also, in 1972 the United States naval element, Commander in Chief Pacific (CINCPAC), extended its operational area to cover most of the Indian Ocean. In 1976 the United States transformed Diego Garcia into a naval support facility with deep-water docks and an expanded runway (see fig. 9).

For the next several decades, the United States and the Soviet Union competed with one another for strategic superiority in the Indian Ocean. After the Soviet invasion of Afghanistan in December 1979, President Jimmy Carter announced his intention to use military force to prevent any foreign power (i.e., the Soviet Union) from controlling the Persian Gulf region. The United States enhanced its ability to respond quickly to any military contingency by increasing its military presence in the Indian Ocean. After the downfall of Iran's imperial government in 1979, the United States deployed a second carrier task force to the area to join the one already on station. Additionally, the United States government concluded a series of military access agreements with Egypt, Kenya, Oman, and Somalia, and arranged to conduct joint military exercises with these countries. On March 1, 1980, President Carter also authorized the creation of the Rapid Deployment Joint Task Force, later reorganized as the United States Central Command (USCENTCOM), whose area of responsibility includes Afghanistan, Bahrain, Djibouti, Egypt, Ethiopia, Iran, Iraq, Jordan, Kenya, Kuwait, Oman, Pakistan, Qatar, Saudi Arabia, Somalia, Sudan, the United Arab Emirates, and Yemen.

During the 1980s, the Indian Ocean continued to provoke competition between Washington and Moscow. The United

States increased its presence on Diego Garcia by building new airfield facilities and an air force satellite detection and tracking station, initiating Strategic Air Command (SAC) operations, improving navigational aids, and increasing anchorages and moorings for pre-positioned warehouse ships stationed permanently at the island.

From Moscow's perspective, its Soviet Indian Ocean Squadron performed a defensive mission against the United States, and promoted Soviet foreign policy in the region. Apart from access to naval facilities in Seychelles, Mauritius, and Reunion, the Soviet Union also conducted long-range maritime surveillance flights over much of the Indian Ocean. Despite this activity, Moscow avoided a military confrontation with Washington in the Indian Ocean, largely because it lacked modern, high-performance aircraft carriers and the ability to defend long sea and air lines of communication to and from the region.

France also remained active in the Indian Ocean during the Cold War years. Until 1973, the headquarters of the French forces was in Madagascar. After Antananarivo severed military relations with Paris, French forces operated from Reunion, Comoros, and Djibouti. Throughout much of the 1980s and the early 1990s, France maintained the second largest naval fleet in the Indian Ocean. In addition, France maintains 5,000 troops and a small number of fighter aircraft in Djibouti.

## Madagascar

### Security Concerns

Madagascar faces no external threat. During the 1980s, however, Madagascar experienced periods of tension with South Africa. Although it had the capabilities to launch an air or amphibious attack, South Africa never threatened Madagascar, largely because it feared international condemnation. Relations between the two countries gradually improved after Frederik Willem de Klerk became South Africa's president in 1989.

Since independence, several internal threats against the Malagasy government have emerged. This domestic instability reflects the growing restiveness of opposition elements and popular frustration with the government's inability to resolve the political, economic, and social problems confronting the island. Also, the Malagasy armed forces repeatedly have acted against the government for failing to preserve law and order.

The first serious challenge to the government occurred on April 1–2, 1971, when more than 1,000 armed members of the left-wing National Movement for the Independence of Madagascar (Mouvement National pour l'Indépendance de Madagascar—Monima) attacked five military posts in Tuléar Province. Government forces quickly restored order and imprisoned Monima's leader, Monja Jaona. According to a government communiqué, Monima casualties included forty-five killed, nine wounded, and 847 held for questioning; security forces suffered one killed and eleven wounded. According to Jaona, the revolt was directed against the local administration, which had failed to provide disaster relief to the province after it had experienced a drought, followed by floods caused by cyclones. Also at issue were government pressures for tax collection at a time when local cattle herds were being ravaged by disease.

In early 1972, what began as a student protest against French cultural domination of the island's schools quickly spread to a call for a general strike to protest poor economic conditions. Within days antigovernment protests arose both in the capital and in the provinces. On May 13, 1972, elements from the Republican Security Force (Force Républicaine de Sécurité—FRS) opened fire on a group of rioters in Antananarivo, killing between fifteen and forty and injuring about 150. The government also declared a state of national emergency. On May 18, 1972, President Philibert Tsiranana dissolved his government and turned over power to the army, under the command of General Gabriel Ramanantsoa. The army, which had remained neutral throughout the general strike, quickly restored order by placing military officers in control of the six provinces and establishing a new, multiethnic cabinet. In November 1972, after a national referendum, Ramanantsoa became the new head of state.

Continued political and economic instability doomed the Ramanantsoa regime. On December 31, 1974, the armed forces launched an unsuccessful coup attempt. On February 5, 1975, Ramanantsoa, hoping to promote political unity, handed over the government to the former minister of interior, Colonel Richard Ratsimandrava. On February 11, 1975, several members of the Mobile Police Group (Groupe Mobile de Police—GMP) assassinated Ratsimandrava. The government responded by declaring martial law, imposing censorship, and suspending political parties. Also, General Gilles Andriamahazo formed the National Military Directorate, consisting of nineteen military officers from all branches of service and from all over the island. On June 15, 1975, Didier Ratsiraka, who had a seat on the National Military Directorate, became head of state and president of the new ruling body, the Supreme Revolutionary Council.

The next major internal threat surfaced in the mid-1980s, when about 6,000 members of various Chinese martial arts Kung-Fu associations battled the Tanora Tonga Saina (TTS), which acted as Ratsiraka's private presidential security force. Problems started in September 1984, when Ratsiraka banned the practice of martial arts. After several clashes between Kung-Fu adherents and the TTS, a larger confrontation occurred on December 4, 1984, when Kung-Fu groups attacked TTS headquarters in Behorika and killed more than 100 TTS members. Kung-Fu demonstrations continued for the next few years. Finally, on July 31, 1986, army units supported by twelve armored cars and helicopters demolished Kung-Fu headquarters in Antananarivo, and killed the movement's leader and about 200 of his followers.

Cycles of escalating political unrest and increased governmental repression led to at least three failed coup attempts in 1989, 1990, and 1992. Moreover, general strike demonstrations organized by a prodemocracy opposition coalition called Comité des Forces Vives (Vital Forces Committee, known as Forces Vives) occurred in Antananarivo and several other Malagasy towns. Following the near paralysis of the economy and demonstrations at the presidential palace during which government forces opened fire on civilians, opposition leaders announced the formation of a transitional government of national unity. Eventually, presidential elections, held between November 1992 and February 1993, resulted in a victory for Forces Vives leader Albert Zafy over Ratsiraka.

### Armed Forces in National Life

Madagascar has a rich military history. During the early nineteenth century, the Merina kings relied on the army to extend their control through most of Madagascar. A small permanent force of career soldiers formed the backbone of the royal army. Periodic levies of freepersons augmented these core units. Theoretically, military service was obligatory for all males, but conscription laws excused sons of members of the ruling class and barred slaves from serving in the army. All soldiers shared in the spoils of war as the Merina expanded and consolidated their control over the island.

During the 1820s, the army's size increased to about 14,000 professional soldiers. Britain, hoping to counter French influence in Madagascar, furnished new weapons, ammunition, uniforms, and technical assistance to the army. The British also helped reorganize and train the army.

Increasing French interest in Madagascar prompted numerous clashes with the island's indigenous forces. Between 1883 and 1885, France launched several attacks on Madagascar. To end hostilities, the Merina recognized French control over Diégo Suarez, agreed to pay an indemnity, and allowed a French resident at Antananarivo to control the country's foreign relations. In 1894 France declared a protectorate over the island, but the Malagasy refused to acknowledge French authority. After a French expeditionary force occupied the capital in September 1895, Queen Ranavalona III recognized the protectorate.

The Menalamba ("red togas," also given as "red cloth" and "red shawls"—armed guerrilla bands) revolt broke out between 1895 and 1899, however, among Merina conservatives against the institutions and agents of a repressive state-church society. Some observers also have suggested that the revolt was an attempt to overthrow the newly established colonial government. France reacted to this unrest by exiling the queen and the former prime minister to Algeria and by declaring Madagascar a French colony. The new French governor, General Joseph Gallieni, eventually pacified the country and carried out many reforms, including the abolition of slavery.

During the French period, which lasted from 1896 to 1960, the Malagasy could be conscripted into the colonial forces. During World War I and World War II, several thousand Malagasy served in France, North Africa, and other combat zones. After 1945 many Malagasy started agitating for independence. In March 1947, the Merina, who regarded themselves as Madagascar's genuine rulers, and some *côtiers* (literally coastal people, an ethnic group), staged an uprising against the French. The island's colonial governor responded by unleashing a reign of terror against the rebels. Estimates of the numbers of Malagasy who died in the revolt ranged from 11,000 to 80,000 (relatively few French soldiers died during the fighting). Notwithstanding these losses, France retained its influence in Madagascar, even after the island gained its independence.

During the postcolonial period, the Malagasy armed forces reflected the French heritage. Military personnel continued to receive training in France and to use French-manufactured weapons. Moreover, with the exception of a brief period in the late 1970s, French military advisers continued to serve in Madagascar.

## The Military and the Government

After he came to power in 1975, Ratsiraka promised to create a "socialist revolution." As part of this policy, Ratsiraka enlarged and reorganized the security forces to make them appropriate for a "people's army" in a "socialist revolutionary" state. In 1975 he renamed the National Army the People's Armed Forces (Forces Armées Populaires—FAP) and expanded its mission. Henceforth, the FAP engaged in civic-action programs and spread ideological education in the countryside. Between 1975 and 1980, the FAP doubled in size.

This reorganization diluted the power of the former National Army, which owed little loyalty to Ratsiraka. To prevent the FAP from challenging his authority, Ratsiraka started transferring able and experienced officers from troop command responsibilities to more senior, but less powerful, positions. Invariably, the new posts were in the inspector general's section of the Office of the President and in various Ministry of Defense committees that studied how the FAP could best facilitate national development.

Despite these changes, the FAP contributed little to the country's "socialist revolution" although it remained a potentially important political player. Nevertheless, Ratsiraka, relying on manipulation and intimidation, retained almost absolute control of the armed forces until the growth of the prodemocracy movement in the early 1990s. Prodemocracy and antidemocracy factions emerged in the FAP and many other government security services. Clashes among these factions added to the political turmoil sweeping through Madagascar, eventually dooming the Ratsiraka regime.

After the FAP was formed in 1975, the cost of maintaining the military establishment became a greater burden on the national budget. The FAP itself annually assessed the military's needs, in conjunction with the Ministry of Defense, which then sent budget recommendations to Ratsiraka. After the Cold War ended and foreign military assistance declined, the Malagasy defense budget also decreased from more than US$101 million

*People's Armed Forces troops*
*of Madagascar*
*Courtesy*
*Thomas P. Ofcansky*

in 1979 to about US$36 million in 1991 (see table 8, Appendix).

## Forces Armées Populaires

In 1994 the FAP numbered about 21,000. Madagascar's president is commander in chief of the FAP. There is no reserve force. Males aged eighteen to fifty are subject to conscription for eighteen months of military or civil service. The majority of conscripts belong to the relatively poor *côtiers* because exceptions to the conscription law allow influential or prosperous persons to avoid military service. The officer corps remains a promising career for most Malagasy. The FAP is divided into two operational services, the army and the aeronaval forces. The former is responsible for land operations and ground-based air defense; however, its primary role has been to defend state institutions and the president from armed opposition. The latter conducts air, naval, and amphibious operations.

The 20,000-member army, which is deployed as a coastal and internal security force, consisted in 1994 of two battalions and one engineer regiment. Because Madagascar lacks an indigenous arms production industry, the army imports all its equipment. The army weapons system includes Soviet PT–76 light tanks, various reconnaissance vehicles, and United States

M–3A1 half-track armored personnel carriers (see table 9, Appendix). The army also has air defense guns, artillery pieces, mortars, and rocket launchers.

The mission of the aeronaval forces' 500-member air component includes combat, transport, and maritime patrol duties. The air force maintains its headquarters at Ivato, near Antananarivo, and operates from bases at Antalaha, Antsohihy, Arivoniamamo, Diégo Suarez, Fianarantsoa, Fort Dauphin, Majunga, Nosy-Be, Tamatave, and Tuléar. The air force consists of one fighter squadron, a transport squadron, and a helicopter squadron. In addition, the air force has liaison aircraft and trainer aircraft.

The 500-member Malagasy navy includes 100 marines and lacks a seagoing capability. It performs a coastal patrol mission from bases at Diégo Suarez, Tamatave, Fort Dauphin, Tuléar, and Majunga. The naval inventory consists of one patrol boat and three amphibious craft.

## State Security Services

Madagascar has five state security services in addition to the FAP: the National Gendarmerie, the FRS, the Civil Police, the Civil Service, and the Antigang Brigade. With the exception of the National Gendarmerie, all these units are outside the FAP chain of command.

A 7,500-member National Gendarmerie operates within the Ministry of Defense. This organization maintains public order, preserves security at the village level, protects government facilities, pursues criminals, and prevents cattle rustling. National Gendarmerie units are stationed throughout the island. The organization's equipment inventory includes automatic weapons, armored cars, and aircraft. The National Gendarmerie also operates a maritime police contingent with five patrol craft.

Shortly after becoming president, Tsiranana created the 700-member FRS to safeguard his personal security and to act as an antiriot unit. By 1972 the FRS, which eventually became the GMP, included about 1,000 personnel. In late 1981, Ratsiraka established and commanded a similar organization called the Presidential Security Regiment (Régiment de Sécurité Présidentielle—Reser), or simply the Presidential Guard. Initially, North Korean instructors trained this 1,200-member unit, whose personnel belonged to Ratsiraka's Betsimisaraka ethnic group. The Presidential Guard has a bunker at Iavoloha near Antananarivo; the guard includes the Mahajamba Regiment, which specializes in riot control. In the late 1980s, the French assumed responsibility for training the Presidential Guard.

A 3,000-member Civil Police force is attached to the Ministry of Interior. Most Civil Police personnel serve in the island's cities. The head of each prefecture commands at least a small contingent. Like the National Gendarmerie, the Civil Police often overreact during times of civil strife, thus earning the enmity of protesters. Since the late 1980s, however, both organizations have attempted to improve their image.

The Civil Service is a paramilitary force that serves as a reserve element of the defense forces. Its operations are nonmilitary in nature and often involve working in rural and social development programs. Potential draftees serve in the Civil Service as an alternative to regular military duty.

During his early days as president, Ratsiraka created a 300-member intelligence and political investigation unit known as the General Directorate of Information and Documentation, Internal and External (Direction Générale de l'Information et de la Documentation, Intérieure et Extérieure—DGIDIE). This organization, whose personnel were trained originally by German Democratic Republic (GDR—East Germany) and then by French advisers, has unlimited arrest and detention powers. To perform its duties, the DGIDIE relies on a vast network of informers to ferret out dissenters, currency violators, and potential political opponents of the president. Over the years, the DGIDIE has been accused of violating human rights, engaging in corrupt practices, and imprisoning foreign nationals accused of spying.

In February 1989, the French helped Madagascar establish an Antigang Brigade. This unit, which reports to the Ministry of Interior, is responsible for combatting hijackers, terrorists, and dangerous criminals. French security advisers train the brigade.

## Training and Morale

Prior to independence, the French conducted all military training. In 1966 the Malagasy government, with French assistance, established the Military Academy (Académie Militaire) at Antsirabe. This school trains officers for the armed forces, the National Gendarmerie, and the Civil Service. In 1967 the first students enrolled in a three-year program that included courses in military and civic affairs. Students specialize in arts or sciences. A few foreign officers, usually from francophone African countries, also study at the Military Academy.

The May 1972 student strikes affected the Military Academy, which temporarily suspended examinations after students complained about the curriculum. Over the next several weeks, academy officials agreed to consider modernizing course material, examinations, entry requirements, and general educational policies.

In addition to training officers at the Military Academy, the Malagasy government annually selects a small number of officer candidates to attend the French Military Academy at St. Cyr. Also, until military relations were severed in the mid-1970s, Malagasy and French units participated in joint annual exercises.

During the Cold War, hundreds, if not thousands, of FAP personnel received military training from several Soviet-bloc countries, including the former Soviet Union, the former GDR, Cuba, and the Democratic People's Republic of Korea (North Korea). Beginning in the mid-1980s, France resumed training limited numbers of Malagasy military personnel. The United States also started an International Military Education and Training (IMET) program that sought to enhance the FAP's professional skills and reduce dependence on East European countries. By the early 1990s, the United States had expanded the IMET program to include management and technical training with emphasis on construction engineering skills and medical courses.

Historically, morale in the armed forces has been good, if for no other reason than that the military provides job security in a country plagued by high unemployment. However, many *côtiers* who have been conscripted to serve in the ranks resent the lack of opportunity and the Merina domination of the officer corps. Also, with the decline of foreign military assistance since the end of the Cold War, poor morale has become a problem in many FAP units.

### Foreign Military Assistance

Since independence, the Malagasy armed forces have relied on numerous countries for military assistance. Historically, France has been the most powerful and most influential of Madagascar's military allies, despite the rift between the two countries in the 1970s. Other nations that have provided military assistance to Madagascar include the former Soviet Union, North Korea, the former Federal Republic of Germany (West Germany), and the United States.

On June 27, 1960, the day after independence, Paris and Antananarivo signed an accord that empowered France to protect Madagascar and to establish military bases on the island. France also gained freedom of movement in Madagascar's airspace and coastal waters. A joint Franco-Malagasy defense command—consisting of the island's president, the French ambassador, and the commander of France's Third Overseas Zone, the southwestern Indian Ocean—managed the security relationship between the two countries. France also agreed to transfer about 4,500 Malagasy personnel who had been serving in the French forces to Madagascar's newly established armed forces.

French officers and French-trained Merina officers dominated the Malagasy armed forces. Additionally, the presence of French officers in Madagascar helped to maintain professionalism and noninvolvement of the military in politics. President Tsiranana, with French support, tried to offset Merina domination in the officer corps by sending promising *côtier* military personnel to France for training and assigning them to important positions upon their return to Madagascar.

Apart from these activities, France also equipped the Malagasy armed forces. During the first five years of independence, France provided military aid worth approximately US$5 million annually, which included technical assistance, training, and nearly all the arms and equipment for the Malagasy armed forces. France also maintained about 2,500 troops at Diégo Suarez and Antsirabe; by 1972 this number had grown to approximately 4,000. A general with the title of senior commander of French Forces in the southern Indian Ocean was in charge of these troops, as well as of French forces on Reunion and Comoros. His forces included a marine parachute regiment, a Foreign Legion regiment, and several internal security units. French air units, based primarily at Ivato airfield, had helicopters and transport aircraft, and naval units operated three destroyer-size vessels, a tanker, a logistical support ship, and escort vessels.

Franco-Malagasy military relations changed radically in the early 1970s. Ramanantsoa's government demanded the withdrawal of French military forces from Antananarivo and announced that it would allow France to have access to the

Diégo Suarez naval base only on a renewable basis. By 1975 the French government, which opposed the tenuous nature of this proposed new relationship, had withdrawn all its military units from Madagascar.

Beginning in the mid-1980s, Franco-Malagasy relations improved. Between 1982 and 1988, for example, 783 Malagasy officers enrolled in various military courses in France. In 1989 France financed the formation of the Antigang Brigade. On April 5, 1990, France announced that it had donated eight Auverland jeeps fitted with weapons, two ambulances, military engineering equipment, accessories for service vehicles, and 8,290 air force and navy uniforms. France also supplied the Malagasy gendarmes with equipment and a variety of other technical and material aid.

The democratization movement again altered the nature of the Franco-Malagasy military relationship. On August 15, 1991, French president François Mitterrand ordered the withdrawal of French military advisers who were in charge of the personal security of Malagasy president Ratsiraka. This action occurred after the Presidential Guard opened fire and killed thirty-one demonstrators at a prodemocracy rally. Relations between the two countries improved after Zafy was elected president in early 1993, and French security technicians provided him with an independent communications system.

Former West Germany was another important source of military assistance in the immediate postindependence era. By 1964 Bonn had furnished approximately US$1.6 million of military assistance, including thirty jeeps and five coastal patrol boats. Additionally, fifty-five Malagasy naval personnel were studying at military schools in West Germany.

During the Ratsiraka era, the FAP gradually abandoned its almost total reliance on France for equipment and training, and looked to several communist nations for foreign military assistance. During the 1975–82 period, the FAP acquired artillery, small arms, and ammunition from North Korea and the People's Republic of China; two landing craft from North Korea; three Mi–8 helicopters, twelve MiG–21 jet fighter aircraft, and two An–26 transport aircraft from the former Soviet Union. North Korea also provided four MiG–17s on long-term loan, and about ninety military advisers who furnished crew and maintenance support for these aircraft. Approximately 130 Soviet technicians maintained the MiG–21s and the An–26s. FAP personnel received training from Cuban, Romanian,

*Malagasy armored personnel carrier*
*Malagasy armored scout car*
*Courtesy Thomas P. Ofcansky*

Soviet, and Chinese instructors. As Ratsiraka's radicalism waned, Madagascar distanced itself from these countries. The collapse of the Soviet Union signaled the end of Madagascar's reliance on the communist world for military assistance.

Since 1960 the United States and Madagascar have maintained diplomatic relations. Because of Ratsiraka's radicalism and Madagascar's relations with the communist world, however, the two countries did not establish a military relationship until the mid-1980s. In 1984 the United States initiated an IMET program (see Training and Morale, this ch.). The following year, one Malagasy officer attended the Naval War College and another studied at the Army Command and General Staff College; in addition, six mid-level officers enrolled in advanced engineering, infantry, field artillery, and communications courses. Also, in fiscal year (FY—see Glossary) 1985, the United States approved a Military Assistance Program (MAP) for Madagascar, which included funds for medical supplies and Caterpillar earth-moving and road-building equipment. In July 1988, the United States provided US$1.2 million worth of military engineering equipment to Madagascar's Department of Military Engineering for National Development. Madagascar and the United States also cooperated on several military development projects such as construction of roads, schools, and health centers for the FAP. The FY 1989 MAP provided for maintenance support for the Malagasy Air Force's C–47 Dakota fleet. In the late 1980s, Washington earmarked US$200,000 for a civic-action project designed to build low-cost housing. In 1987 a "Seabee" battalion deployed to Manjakandriana to give a two-month training course to fifty-two men of the Third Regiment of the Malagasy Army's Development Force. By the early 1990s, the United States had confined its military aid objectives to developing Madagascar's military engineering capability, supporting the air force's transport aircraft, and providing managerial and technical training to the armed forces.

## Penal System

The Malagasy penal code is based primarily on French penal codes and procedures and has been somewhat influenced by Malagasy customary law. The Malagasy penal code affords the accused most of the rights and protections granted under French and Western laws. The most severe punishments are death and forced labor for life.

Madagascar has three levels of courts. Lower courts are responsible for civil and criminal cases carrying limited fines and sentences. The Court of Appeals includes a criminal court for cases carrying sentences of five years or more. The Supreme Court functions as the highest court in the country. A separate and autonomous Constitutional High Court (also known as the Administrative and Financial Constitutional Court) reviews laws, decrees, and ordinances. It monitors elections and certifies their results. A military court has jurisdiction over all cases that involve national security.

Madagascar has a nationwide prison system. Both men and women sentenced to long terms normally serve their time at the Central Prison (Maison Centrale) in Antananarivo. Each province has a central prison for inmates serving sentences of less than five years. At the seats of various courts, there also are at least twenty-five lesser prisons for individuals serving terms of less than two years and for prisoners awaiting trial. Courts at the local (subprefecture) level maintain jails for lesser offenders serving sentences of up to six months.

Conditions in Malagasy prisons are harsh. Cells built for one often house up to eight prisoners. Family members of prisoners need to augment the inadequate daily food rations. Prisoners without relatives often go for several days without food. Inmates also suffer from numerous medical problems that are not usually treated, including malnutrition, infections, malaria, and tuberculosis. Children of women prisoners normally live in prisons with their mothers. Female inmates sometimes engage in prostitution in collusion with guards.

## Human Rights

By developing country standards, Madagascar has a moderately good human rights record. However, numerous human rights violations, largely committed during the Ratsiraka regime, have caused concern among international humanitarian agencies. In the late 1970s, the government enacted the law Information against X for Plotting and Attacking State Security, under which anyone can be arrested without warrant and held indefinitely without trial. The law also enables the security forces to arrest, search, or seize property. Under the French penal code, arrest is limited to forty-eight hours, but in Madagascar the arrest time is extended to fifteen days and is renewable indefinitely. The authorities do not release information about the status of the detainees, who often may be real or suspected opponents of the government. Many individuals in custody are beaten, tortured, or deprived of medical care.

In the 1990s, Madagascar's human rights record became more controversial. During the prodemocracy unrest of the early 1990s, the Malagasy government acted against the opposition. In July 1991, for example, government troops abducted and briefly detained four Forces Vives leaders who had been nominated as provisional government ministers. On August 10, 1991, the Presidential Guard fired on a crowd of some 300,000 people marching on the President's Palace to call for Ratsiraka's resignation. At least thirty demonstrators were killed and 200 wounded. On October 23, 1991, security forces killed at least twelve people and wounded about seventy during a prodemocracy demonstration in the capital.

In 1992 government violence continued to claim victims throughout the country. On March 31, 1992, the authorities killed eight and wounded thirty-one people when hundreds of pro-Ratsiraka demonstrators tried to force their way into the National Forum's debate on a new constitution. In October 1992, government troops killed eight people during a clash with a pro-Ratsiraka group that was trying to close the Antsiranana airport.

Madagascar has, however, taken steps to improve its human rights record. In December 1990, the government abolished press censorship; by mid-1991, the state-owned Malagasy Radio-Television allowed opposition figures to appear on a weekly discussion program. The DGIDIE director, a former judge appointed in mid-1990, worked to prevent abuses against prisoners held in custody. Legal safeguards against arbitrary arrest and detention are not always followed, however, especially in rural areas. Most Western observers maintain that Madagascar's human rights record will probably improve as a result of the country's commitment to democratization and increasing civilian control over the military.

## Mauritius

### Security Concerns

Mauritius faces no external security threat. At least since 1980, Mauritius has not experienced significant, large-scale political violence. Several assassination attempts have been made against Prime Minister Anerood Jugnauth, but these actions were by disaffected individuals rather than any antigovernment group.

## Armed Forces in National Life

Traditionally, the armed forces have played a minimal role in Mauritian national life. In 1859 the British colonial government established the first Mauritian Police Force, with a separate unit for Port Louis. An 1893 ordinance expanded the police force, which by 1899 numbered 700 personnel, 300 of whom were stationed in Port Louis and the remainder at eight other locations. The officer corps included one inspector general and seven inspectors, and the other ranks had twelve sub-inspectors. With the exception of about 100 police who carried Martini Henry rifles, the police force was unarmed. Europeans, Creoles, and Indians served in the police. Initial recruitment into the police was for a period of not more than three years. The colonial government allowed men of good character to reenlist for a further five years.

Except during 1942, when a Japanese attack seemed imminent, World War II had little impact on Mauritius although Mauritians fought in North Africa and the Middle East. Additionally, the Royal Mauritius Regiment, a small part-time home defense volunteer unit, deployed to Madagascar to safeguard lines of communication. This regiment became involved in a mutiny in Madagascar caused by tensions among British, Franco-Mauritians, and Creoles in the military.

After the British garrison withdrew from Mauritius in 1960, the authorities created the paramilitary Special Mobile Force (SMF), with six officers and 146 enlisted personnel to maintain internal security. The separate regular police force was divided into special divisions, including criminal investigation, riot control, traffic control, immigration and passports, and water police.

On at least two occasions during the last few years before independence, the SMF required British assistance to maintain internal security. On May 10, 1965, political grievances caused armed clashes between the Hindu and Creole communities. After the governor declared a state of emergency, a company of 2d Battalion, Coldstream Guards, flew from Aden to Mauritius to help keep the peace. These troops remained on the island until July 1965.

On January 22, 1968, the governor again requested British soldiers to help maintain order. The authorities feared that politically motivated violence between the capital's "Istanbul" Muslim gang and the rival "Texas" Creole gang in Port Louis would spread to the rest of the island. Troops from B Company of 1st Battalion, The King's Shropshire Light Infantry, deployed to Mauritius from Malaysia, and worked with the police and the SMF to restore peace.

With independence in 1968, almost all internal security duties became the responsibility of the Mauritian government. Under the terms of a joint defense agreement announced on March 11, 1968, however, the British government agreed to help Mauritius combat any internal security threat and to train local security and police forces. This agreement remained in effect until 1975. During the early 1970s, the Mauritian regime used the SMF to jail opposition politicians and trade union members. By the 1980s, however, such practices had stopped.

## Police Agencies

Since independence, Mauritius has refrained from establishing an army, largely because of the cost of maintaining such a force. Instead, the security establishment includes the National Police Force, which consists of a regular armed police of about 4,000 personnel, the paramilitary 1,300-member SMF, and the 240-member Special Support Unit (SSU), all of which are responsible for internal security. In 1994 the SMF had six rifle elements, two mobile elements, one engineer company, and support troops. A Special Constabulary and a small Anti-Drug and Smuggling Unit operate under police jurisdiction.

Mauritius lacks a traditional military budget. Expenditures for the various police defense forces in FY 1994 are estimated at MauR 207.2 million (for value of the Mauritian rupee—see Glossary), or about US$11.3 million.

The National Police Force reports to a police commissioner, who in turn comes under the jurisdiction of the Ministry of Internal Security. For all intents and purposes, however, Prime Minister Jugnauth commands the police. Equipment used by all these organizations includes small arms, rifles, riot-control gear such as clubs and shields, and tear gas canisters. The transportation inventory includes Land Rovers, light scout cars, and at least two helicopters. Recruitment is by voluntary enlistment from all ethnic communities. Training is usually conducted in Mauritius; however, some officers have trained in foreign military academies such as the Royal Military Academy at

Sandhurst in Britain. In 1990 the Mauritian government approved the construction of a Police Academy at Vacoas.

In addition, at least two security organizations report to the prime minister's office. In 1982 the Mauritian government established the National Investigation Unit (NIU), which had been known as the State Service, to monitor internal security developments and the activities of foreign embassies and certain foreign visitors. This organization includes up to 200 full-time agents, all of whom are recruited from the regular police force, and 3,000 informers scattered throughout the country. In 1989, after an unsuccessful attempt on his life, Jugnauth ordered the establishment of a 100-member Very Important Persons Security Unit.

Mauritius maintains a small air patrol to undertake maritime surveillance, to perform search and rescue missions, and to patrol the country's EEZ. The aircraft inventory includes two specially configured Dornier-228s, which were operated by Indian crews until the first Mauritians were trained.

The mission of the 500-member National Coast Guard (NCG) is to ensure the safety of Mauritian fishers, prevent smuggling, and protect the marine environment. The NCG inventory includes two Soviet-built surveillance craft, the CGS Rescuer, and the CGS Retriever. Both vessels carry cannons with 1,000-meter-plus precise-target air or marine-surface strike capability. In March 1993, the NCG purchased a 210-ton Indian-built seaward defense boat. This vessel is armed with two Bofors 40/60 guns and carries a thirty-two-member crew. Acquisition of this boat improved the NCG's coastal surveillance capability. An Indian naval officercommands the NCG; an unknown number of NCG personnel have received training from Indian naval instructors.

On March 25–26, 1994, the Mauritian government announced that it had awarded a US$14.6 million contract to the Chilean navy's Naval Docks and Yards (Astilleros y Maestranzas de la Armada) yard for construction of an Offshore Patrol Vessel (OPV). The vessel will be armed with a turret-mounted, automatic, 40mm cannon on the foredeck and several 12.7mm or smaller-caliber machine guns on flexible mountings. The NCG will use the OPV to protect its fisheries and EEZ, perform search and rescue, fight fires, contain pollution, and serve as a mobile emergency command center. Chile will deliver the vessel in March 1996. Mauritius has an option to buy a second OPV.

## Foreign Military Assistance

Historically, Mauritius has received little foreign military assistance. In January 1990, the former Soviet Union presented Mauritian authorities with two patrol boats, each of which can carry a twenty-member crew. An eight-member Soviet training team rovided the NCG a ninety-day orientation training program on the use of these vessels. A five-member Soviet mechanic and engineer team remained in Mauritius for one year to service the patrol boats.

Since independence, France, Britain, and India have provided an array of equipment and training to various Mauritian police units. Following two assassination attempts against Jugnauth in 1988 and 1989, for example, India provided a security adviser, J.N. Taimini, to help Mauritius upgrade its security services. France also has provided security assistance to bolster Jugnauth's personal bodyguard. In March 1990, the British donated a modern explosives detector to the SMF. Often, these nations have competed with one another. In June 1991, France withdrew two military cooperation agents after Mauritius granted India a contract for communications and broadcasting equipment for the SMF.

Since the late 1980s, the United States has become more active in Mauritius. In FY 1988 Washington initiated an IMET program to increase the SMF's defensive capabilities. Since then, the IMET program has sought to enhance the country's ability to protect its EEZ and combat narcotics trafficking by offering training in small boat maintenance and coastal patrol.

## Penal System

Laws governing the Mauritian penal system are derived partly from old French codes and from English law. The judicial system consists of the Supreme Court, presided over by the chief justice and five other judges who also serve as judges of the Court of Appeal, the Industrial Court, and ten district courts. Final appeal can be made to the Queen's Privy Council in Britain; approximately 50 percent of the Supreme Court rulings referred to the Privy Council have been reversed. Mauritius has no military courts. The prison system consists of four facilities: a prison, a rehabilitation center, a youth institution, and an industrial school. The daily average prison population is 700.

## Human Rights

The Mauritian government has a history of respecting basic human rights. The constitution protects political and civil rights, including freedom of speech and of the press. In 1991 the government enacted the Public Gathering Act, which prevents indefinite detention without charge or trial. During the early 1990s, there were no reports of political or other extra-judicial killings or disappearances. Various Mauritian media reports have alleged that the police have mistreated or killed criminal suspects; however, follow-up investigations have failed to confirm any consistent pattern of abuse.

# Seychelles

## Security Concerns

Seychelles confronts no external security threat. During the Cold War, however, Seychelles faced several threats from foreign powers interested in the country's strategic position astride the Indian Ocean's oil-tanker lanes. In particular, during the late 1970s and early 1980s, President France Albert René feared South African aggression. On at least two occasions, he accused South Africa of trying to overthrow his regime. Both incidents involved Colonel Michael "Mad Mike" Hoare, a mercenary who allegedly had been acting on behalf of the South African government. The first coup attempt occurred in November 1979, when René announced that he had foiled a plot "sponsored from abroad with the cooperation of mercenaries standing ready in Durban." The authorities arrested but later released eighty coup plotters. Although a South African connection could not be ruled out, some Western observers believed the affair was French inspired.

The second, more serious coup attempt occurred on November 25, 1981, when a group of forty-five European mercenaries, led by Colonel Hoare, arrived at Mahé International Airport on a commercial flight from Swaziland to overthrow the René regime. The Seychellois authorities quickly thwarted the coup attempt, known as Operation Anvil, and the mercenaries hijacked an Air India plane and forced the captain to fly them to Durban, South Africa. As soon as the aircraft arrived, the South African police arrested all the mercenaries. Several of the mercenaries, including Colonel Hoare, served time in jail for their involvement in Operation Anvil. On May 7, 1985, Colonel Hoare was freed under a general presidential pardon.

Seychellois-South African relations began to improve in the aftermath of Operation Anvil, following what appeared to be a secret agreement. In exchange for the release of South African prisoners in Seychelles, the South African government promised to refrain from future actions against the René regime, help guarantee Seychellois security, and provide an indemnity payment to Seychelles. In July 1992, Pretoria announced that it would pay Victoria, the capital of Seychelles, about 8 million rand in compensation for Operation Anvil. On November 8, 1993, the two countries established diplomatic relations at the ambassadorial level.

In 1986 another coup attempt against the René regime occurred, supposedly involving the United States, France, and Britain. In addition to this foreign connection, the plot, known as Operation Distant Lash, included thirty mercenaries and some 350 partisans in Seychelles. The figurehead of this coup attempt was Minister of Defense Ogilvy Berlouis, who reportedly was groomed to be the country's new pro-Western president. Security forces thwarted the attempt, however, subsequently arresting Berlouis and forcing several officers of the Seychellois army, the Seychelles People's Liberation Army (SPLA), to resign.

In July 1987, British police uncovered yet another plot to overthrow the René regime and to abduct leading members of the African National Congress (ANC), the South African opposition movement that maintained an office in London. The authorities eventually arrested four men and charged them with conspiracy to kidnap the ANC members; the charges were later withdrawn because of insufficient evidence.

Since independence, numerous internal threats against the Seychellois government have arisen. After overthrowing James Mancham's regime on June 5, 1977, René quickly established a socialist one-party state, censored the rival newspaper, and abolished religious fee-paying schools. René also created an army and a large security apparatus for the first time in the country's history.

As a result of such controversial policies, popular resentment against the René regime grew and thousands of Seychellois went into exile to form opposition groups to overthrow René. In April 1978, some of James Mancham's followers unsuccessfully tried to overthrow the government when René was on a state visit to North Korea and China. The Movement for Resistance (Mouvement pour la Résistance), which sought to restore democracy in Seychelles, indicated that about 100 of its members had financed the November 1981 coup attempt. The Seychelles Liberation Committee, established in 1979 by exiles in Paris, also wanted to remove René and abolish his one-party state. The Seychelles National Movement maintained that it was a broad-based opposition group with followers in Seychelles, Britain, and Australia. The Seychelles Popular Anti-Marxist Front (SPAMF) declared that it had unsuccessfully tried to persuade the South African government to support a SPAMF coup attempt against René. Most Western observers believed that, notwithstanding the November 1981 coup attempt, these exile organizations had little chance of effecting a change of government in Seychelles, largely because they had few supporters in the country and minimal resources. With the end of the Cold War and the successful transition to multiparty politics in Seychelles through elections in 1993, the external and internal threats against the René regime have dissipated.

## Armed Forces in National Life

Prior to 1977, Seychelles had no armed forces. Instead, there was a small police force modeled along British lines. René believed that the Seychelles People's Defence Forces (SPDF), which he created in 1977, would help preserve the country's revolution and advance socialism. Although the armed forces have been largely loyal to René, on at least one occasion, the SPLA staged a mutiny against the René regime. On August 17–18, 1982, some eighty-eight noncommissioned officers and enlisted personnel seized the Victoria radio station and port, police stations, telegraph facilities, and the Union Vale army camp. The mutineers demanded a change in the composition and ideological orientation of the René regime, the expulsion of all Tanzanian military advisers, and an improvement in the living conditions of the ordinary soldier. Within thirty-six hours, loyalist forces, supported by approximately 400 Tanzania People's Defence Force (TPDF) personnel, crushed the mutiny and recaptured all key installations. In April 1983, the government concluded a secret court martial of the mutineers. Since then, the armed forces have acquiesced in the goals and policies of the René regime.

## Seychelles People's Defence Forces

The SPDF consists of the SPLA, the Seychelles People's Navy, and the Seychelles People's Air Force. In December 1992, the government amalgamated the Seychelles People's Navy and the Seychelles People's Air Force to form the 250-member Seychelles Coast Guard (since increased to 300 members). Each service commander reports to the armed forces chief of staff, who is responsible to the commander in chief, René. The president also retains the minister of defense portfolio. The Defence Forces Council, which is chaired by the armed forces chief of staff, manages the SPDF.

The 1,000-member SPLA includes the 800-member army and the 300-member Presidential Guard. The army consists of one infantry battalion and two artillery elements. The SPDF also consists of the 300-member Seychelles Coast Guard, which includes the 100-member air wing and eighty marines. The army possesses six BRDM reconnaissance vehicles, armored personnel carriers, three D–130 122mm towed artillery pieces, six M–43 82mm mortars, ten SA–7 surface-to-air missiles, and an unknown number of RPG–7 rocket launchers. The SPLA's mission includes defending the nation's territorial integrity and, when necessary, assisting the People's Militia in preserving domestic law and order. Because much of its equipment is in need of maintenance, the army has minimal capabilities. Western observers believe that the army would be ineffective against a professional military force.

The 100-member air wing of the coast guard operates one Britten-Norman BN–2A Maritime Defender and a Cessna 152 trainer. The Britten-Norman, donated by the British government in 1980, patrols the EEZ, which extends over an area of almost 1 million square kilometers. It normally works with the patrol boats from the navy wing of the coast guard, searching for vessels engaged in smuggling and illegal fishing. The aircraft also conducts light transport, search and rescue, and medical evacuation missions. The air wing is the most effective service with equipment in good operating condition.

The navy wing of the coast guard, based in Port Victoria, owns one Italian Andromache, one Soviet Zoroaster, two Soviet Zhuk inland patrol boats, and one amphibious landing craft. The navy wing patrols the country's EEZ and conducts anti-drug and search and rescue missions, and marine pollution containment. The navy wing's effectiveness is extremely limited, largely because it rarely has more than two of its vessels

*Cadets of Madagascar Military Academy, Antsirabe*
*Motorcycle force of Madagascar gendarmerie*
*Courtesy Thomas P. Ofcansky*

operational at one time. In 1994 the government asked the United States to fund a two-year US$400,000 Coast Guard Development Program. The United States refused because of lack of funds.

## State Security Services

The People's Militia has existed since the beginning of the René regime. On June 10, 1977, the president called for volunteers to register for training in the People's Militia, which was to guard against a countercoup by James Mancham. By the early 1990s, the 1,000-member People's Militia consisted largely of untrained and unfit volunteers. Its mission is to defend the country from external aggression and to preserve the revolution. In June 1989, René assumed overall control of the People's Militia; the chief of staff is responsible for running it on a day-to-day basis. The People's Militia is divided into five military regions (north, central, west, south Mahé, and Praslin). Most Western observers consider the People's Militia a totally ineffective force.

The national police, which is organized along British lines and commanded by a police commissioner, includes a regular 500-member unit and a sixty-member paramilitary mobile unit. Members of the force normally are unarmed, but mobile unit personnel are equipped with modern weapons, including 7.62mm rifles. For operational and administrative purposes, Seychelles is divided into the Central Police Division, which comprises the capital; North Police Division; South Police Division; and Praslin/La Digue Police Division. A senior police officer commands each of these formations. Seychelles maintains a total of seventeen police stations in all divisions. The police organization includes headquarters, Criminal Investigation Department (CID), Special Force (Police Mobile Unit), general duties, and special branch. A commandant manages the police training school at Praslin. This school provides fifteen-week and refresher training courses for recruits, two-week supervisory officers' courses, two-week promotion courses, and four-week basic courses. Each district also has field training. Most Western observers agree that the national police forces are under strength and poorly paid. As a result, they have limited military value.

President France Albert René maintains a 300-member Presidential Guard for his own protection. This unit, which includes an unknown number of European mercenaries, has high-quality personnel and weapons. The army of 800 members in 1994 includes the Presidential Guard, supplemented by an infantry battalion and two artillery elements.

Information about Seychelles defense spending is limited. The 1991 defense expenditures, which were decided by René, amounted to about US$16 million. Estimated defense expenditures for 1993 are thought to be comparable.

## Training and Morale

Historically, with the exception of the air wing, the armed forces have been poorly trained and suffered from low morale. Beginning in the late 1980s, the government began to establish a military training infrastructure. On May 16, 1987, the first noncommissioned officers (NCOs) passed through a three-month refresher course at the SPDF NCO Training School. At the graduation ceremony, Chief of Staff James Michel told the NCOs that a new career development program would give each of them "an equal opportunity to develop his career and rise up the promotion scale to the highest ranks." On May 7, 1988, the SPDF, supported by the People's Militia, conducted a simulated offensive at the Grand Police Military Training Center. The troops covered offensive and defensive military tactics, weapons training, field communications and engineering, first aid, map reading, and other military subjects. On June 2, 1990, officials opened the Seychelles Defence Academy, which provided training courses for the SPDF, the People's Militia, and the police. Despite these efforts, the SPLA and the navy wing have failed to improve their capabilities. Personnel still suffer from low morale, poor qualifications, and ineffective combat skills.

The air wing, however, shows a relatively high degree of professionalism. All pilots receive training in the Cessna 152 before moving on to the Britten-Norman. After acquiring the requisite number of flying hours and the necessary commercial licenses, most pilots are seconded to the national airline, Air Seychelles. Some pilots are assigned to the Seychelles government, which operates one Cessna Citation and one Cessna Caravan II as passenger and light transport aircraft.

## Foreign Military Assistance

Seychelles traditionally received foreign military assistance from numerous nations, including Tanzania, India, the former Soviet Union, North Korea, and the United States. Of these, Tanzania has been Seychelles' most important military ally. The two countries initiated military relations shortly after René established the People's Militia; twelve Tanzanian military advisers arrived in Seychelles to help train the militia. By 1980 the TPDF maintained an estimated 140-member contingent in Seychelles, including a thirty-member training team. After the expulsion of French technicians in 1979, Tanzania reinforced its presence in Seychelles. In June 1979, Seychellois military units participated in a joint exercise with TPDF and Malagasy units. On November 26, 1981, the day after Colonel Hoare's coup attempt failed, 400 TPDF personnel started patrolling Mahé International Airport and the coast to prevent a return of Hoare's mercenaries. According to some Western observers, the intervention of Tanzanian military personnel during the August 1982 SPDF mutiny probably saved the René regime.

India has been one of René's oldest military allies. On June 5, 1982, India gave Seychelles two Chetak helicopters as a Liberation Day gift for the People's Air Force; after one crashed, Bombay provided another. By the early 1990s, the Indian presence in Seychelles included a colonel who managed the Seychelles Defence Academy, and two police advisers.

Between 1979 and 1990, the former Soviet Union provided an array of military aid to Seychelles, including small arms, ammunition, SA–7 surface-to-air missiles, artillery, patrol boats, and petroleum. Additionally, the former Soviet Union deployed an unknown number of Soviet military and technical advisers to Seychelles. By December 1990, changing political conditions in Moscow forced the former Soviet Union to terminate its military aid program and withdraw all its advisers from Seychelles. In exchange for aid provided, the former Soviet Union hoped to gain access to Seychelles naval ports. René did allow Soviet warships to make port calls, but he never signed a formal access agreement with Moscow.

By 1983 North Korea had deployed a fifty- to sixty-member military advisory team to Seychelles. These personnel assumed responsibility for training the SPLA. Unconfirmed reports also indicated that the North Koreans instructed the Presidential Guard. By 1988, according to Michel, the North Koreans had left Seychelles.

The United States provided security assistance to Seychelles to retain access to the United States Air Force Satellite Tracking station at La Misère. Aid activities focused on the IMET program, civic action, and coastal security. Since FY 1984, a small number of Seychellois military personnel have attended

IMET courses in technical and professional areas such as communications and studied at infantry and command and staff level military schools. Other training includes basic infantry, naval, and coast guard operations courses. During the early 1990s, the United States hoped to expand its security assistance to the Seychelles to include air-sea rescue, explosives ordinance disposal, and military working dog training.

Since the end of the Cold War, Seychelles increasingly has relied on India and the United States for foreign military assistance. France also has provided some maintenance aid to the Seychellois coast guard. Some Western observers maintain that, with the establishment of diplomatic relations, South Africa could initiate a military aid program in Seychelles within a few years.

### Penal System

The Seychellois penal system is based on English common law and Napoleonic civil law. The judiciary system includes the magistrates' (or small claims) courts, the Supreme (or trial) Court, and the Court of Appeal. The president also exercises quasi-judicial powers, especially in national security cases. Seychellois law requires that military personnel be tried by court martial unless the president decrees otherwise.

The courts often sentence criminals to the Grand Police Camp, a high security prison run by the army on Mahé Island. Amnesty International reports that prison authorities often require prisoners to perform excessively strenuous labor.

### Human Rights

From 1977 to 1993, Seychelles was an authoritarian, one-party, socialist state. The country's 1979 constitution failed to provide for basic human rights, including them instead in a preamble as a goal of the Seychellois people. René has also intimidated dissidents and opponents by threatening to invoke the Public Security Act, which allows for indefinite detention in security cases. Moreover, he often exiles opponents or orders the confiscation of their property. Over the years, numerous credible reports indicate that the police beat prisoners. Invariably, the government dismisses complaints against police officers charged with such practices. By the early 1990s, the Seychellois human rights record had improved somewhat as the government adopted a less belligerent attitude toward dissidents and opposition groups. In June 1993, a referendum was held on the new constitution, and in July 1993 multiparty elections were held for the National Assembly and the presidency.

## Comoros

### Security Concerns

Comoros faces no external threats. During the 1970s and 1980s, however, various groups of European mercenaries, all supposedly supported by foreign powers, played a significant role in Comoran domestic politics.

Since independence the Comoran government has contended with several internal threats. This domestic instability reflects the weakness of the island's central government, the unpopularity of its rulers, and the presence of European mercenaries. On July 6, 1975, the Comoran Chamber of Deputies approved a unilateral declaration of independence from France, named Ahmed Abdallah as president, and constituted itself as the National Assembly. On August 3, 1975, a group of prominent citizens, radicals, and technocrats overthrew the Abdallah regime. These individuals replaced the National Assembly with a National Executive Council, led by Prince Said Mohammed Jaffar. In January 1976, Ali Soilih succeeded Jaffar as president.

Soilih embarked immediately on a revolutionary program, based on Maoist and Islamic philosophies, that sought to develop an economically self-sufficient and ideologically progressive state. In addition to alienating France, which terminated its aid and technical assistance programs to Comoros, Soilih's policies aroused resentment among the island's traditional leaders. To make matters worse, Soilih established his version of Mao's Red Guards, known as the Commando Moissy. These vigilantes, trained by Tanzanian military advisers, further alienated Comoran society by acting as a repressive political police. Growing popular discontent resulted in four unsuccessful coup attempts against the Soilih regime during its two-and-a-half-year existence.

On May 12–13, 1978, a fifty-member European mercenary unit, hired by Ahmed Abdallah in France and led by French Colonel Robert Denard, finally overthrew Soilih. Two weeks later, security personnel killed Soilih, allegedly while he was trying to escape from house arrest. Ahmed Abdallah and his former deputy, Mohamed Ahmed, then became co-presidents. Although it initially experienced some opposition because of

*Diégo-Suarez, near Antsiranana, site of Malagasy port and naval base*
*Courtesy Thomas P. Ofcansky*

the role played by Denard and his mercenaries in the coup, the new government eventually gained popular support. Its popularity rested on its ability to restore relations with France, which resumed economic, military, and cultural aid to the islands, and to gain assistance from the European Community and several Arab countries, including Saudi Arabia, Iraq, and Kuwait. On October 22, 1978, Abdallah was elected to a six-year term as president.

Despite the influx of foreign aid, political conditions in Comoros remained unsettled, largely because Abdallah failed to establish a government that adequately represented people on the outlying islands of Njazidja (Grande Comore), Nzwani (Anjouan), and Mwali (Mohéli). Moreover, Abdallah frequently used repressive methods against his real and imagined adversaries. In this turbulent atmosphere, opponents of Abdallah's regime made at least four unsuccessful attempts to overthrow his government.

In February 1981, loyal Presidential Guard (Garde Présidentielle—GP) units crushed an army mutiny on the main island of Njazidja, and the authorities subsequently arrested about 150 people. In December 1983, another plot surfaced after the arrest of a group of British mercenaries in Australia. According to the Comoran government, they had planned to overthrow Abdallah on behalf of a former Comoran diplomat, Said Ali Kemal. A March 1985 plot against Abdallah by the GP also failed and resulted in seventeen people being sentenced to forced labor for life and fifty others being imprisoned. In November 1987, French mercenaries and South African military advisers based in Comoros reportedly thwarted a coup by a small number of GP and armed forces personnel.

In late November 1989, the Abdallah regime finally fell after members of the GP, which included several European advisers under Colonel Denard's command, assassinated the president. As outlined in the constitution, the Supreme Court president, Said Mohamed Djohar, became interim head of state, pending a presidential election. Denard and his associates, however, engineered a coup attempt against Djohar, disarmed the army, and killed at least twenty-seven police. Growing French and South African pressure forced Colonel Denard to leave Comoros for South Africa. In April 1990, the Comoran government announced that France would maintain a military team on the islands for two years to train local security forces.

Despite the presence of French troops and a general amnesty for all political prisoners, Comoros continued to suffer from internal instability. On August 18–19, 1990, armed rebels unsuccessfully tried to overthrow Djohar by attacking various French installations on the island of Njazidja. A small group of European mercenaries allegedly supported the coup attempt and believed that the Djohar regime would fall if they could force the French to withdraw from the islands. The authorities detained more than twenty people in connection with the uprising. Another coup attempt occurred on September 26, 1992, when Lieutenant Said Mohamed and 100 Comoran army personnel tried to overthrow Djohar. According to plotters, the coup's purpose was "to ensure state security and to put in place a true democracy." Troops loyal to Djohar quickly crushed this coup attempt. Since then, political instability has continued to plague Comoros for several reasons. In part, there is opposition to Djohar, and, despite two democratic legislative elections, clear majorities are lacking in the National Assembly, leading to considerable internal political maneuvering. Moreover, economic hardships contribute to unrest.

## The Military and the Government

Until independence, Comoros had no armed forces. Since then, the government has maintained a small military establishment, which, by international standards, possesses minimal capabilities. Despite the lack of a strong military tradition, however, the armed forces have played a significant role in the country's political life. In particular, the GP, which is the best trained and best armed of all security services, has repeatedly intervened in politics and eventually controlled Comoros. Such activities understandably have attracted considerable attention, especially because the GP includes European mercenaries in its ranks and in senior positions. Over the years, numerous reports, some of them unconfirmed, suggested that foreign powers such as France, Britain, or South Africa provided these mercenaries with money and weapons. By the early 1990s, most Western observers believed that as long as French military forces remained in the islands, the Comoran armed forces were unlikely to maintain a high political profile.

Little information exists about Comoran defense economics. In 1987, the most recent year for which figures were available, the government budgeted about 910 million Comoran francs (Cf; for value of the Comoran franc—see Glossary) for defense expenditures.

## Armed Forces

The national army, the Comoran Armed Forces (Forces Armées Comoriennes—FAC), maintains a personnel strength of approximately 700 to 800 men. The FAC inventory includes an array of small arms and light military vehicles. A small military aviation element operates a Cessna 402B and an AS–350B Écureuil. The aircraft are used for Very Important Persons (VIP) transport. Comoros lacks a navy. Most military training occurs in Comoros; however, a small number of army personnel have received some foreign training, primarily in France and the United States. Historically, army morale has been low, largely because of the GP's predominance and influence. After taking control of the country in December 1989, France dissolved the Comoran army and devised a multiyear plan to organize a new Comoran Armed Forces.

## State Security Services

The 600-member GP reports to the president's office. After members of the GP assassinated President Abdallah in November 1989, however, the GP, under Colonel Denard's command, controlled the country. France assumed responsibility for Comoran security the following month, and immediately announced that the GP would be limited to a ceremonial role with a reduced number of troops. The 500-member National Police Force (Force de Police Nationale) is headquartered in Moroni, with detachments in the other islands.

## Foreign Military Assistance

Since independence, Comoros has received foreign military assistance from Tanzania, France, South Africa, and the United States. Only France and the United States continued to provide military aid to Comoros as of mid-1994.

Tanzania hoped to limit Western influence in Comoros by providing military aid to President Soilih. It was able to deploy about 100 military advisers to the islands to train the army and the Commando Moissy, but Tanzania lacks the resources to make a significant long-term impact on the Comoran Armed Forces.

Historically, France has been the most important military player in Comoros, largely because it has strategic interests in the Indian Ocean and military installations on the islands of Reunion and Mayotte. Even before independence, France and Comoros signed a defense agreement in 1973; five years later, the two nations concluded a technical military assistance agreement. After the Soilih regime fell in 1978, French military advisers replaced European mercenaries and guaranteed Comoran security. On November 10, 1978, the two governments signed a military agreement that provided French training for Comoran Armed Forces and French military assistance in case of an attack on the islands. By January 1985, seventy-six Comoran military personnel had received training in France, and the French military had stationed twenty-three advisers in Comoros.

After the assassination of President Abdallah, France deployed 140 troops from the 21st Marine Paratroop Regiment and fifty officers and warrant officers from the Military Assistance and Instruction Detachment. According to a December 16, 1989, statement by President Djohar, the latter unit was supposed to remain on the islands for one to two years to train and to reorganize the Comoran Armed Forces. In August 1994, France continued to maintain a military presence in Comoros.

During the late 1980s, South Africa and Comoros maintained a discreet but significant military relationship. The South African government constructed a radio-monitoring station on the islands. Also, according to the *Indian Ocean Newsletter*, Comoros was a transshipment point for arms from South Africa to Iran and to the Mozambican National Resistance (Resistência Nacional Moçambicano—Renamo) rebel movement in Mozambique. South Africa also funded the GP, under Colonel Denard's command. In late 1989, South Africa severed its connection to the GP and Colonel Denard, thereby allowing France to become the dominant foreign military power on the islands.

Since the late 1980s, the United States has maintained a small IMET program in Comoros. Initially, five to six Comoran officers received basic military training and English language instruction in the United States. In 1989 the IMET program was expanded to include professional military education and technical training courses for a small number of Comoran military personnel. By the early 1990s, the IMET program complemented the ongoing French effort to reorganize the Comoran armed forces. However, the United States embassy in Comoros closed in September 1993.

## Penal System

The Comoran legal system rests on Islamic law and an inherited French legal code. Village elders or civilian courts settle most disputes. The judiciary is independent of the legislature and the executive. The Supreme Court acts as a Constitutional Council in resolving constitutional questions and supervising presidential elections. As High Court of Justice, the Supreme Court also arbitrates cases in which the government is accused of malpractice. The Supreme Court consists of two members selected by the president, two elected by the Federal Assembly, and one by the council of each island.

## Human Rights

In the African context, Comoros' human rights record is above average. However, in early 1979, Comoran authorities arrested some 300 supporters of Soilih's regime and imprisoned them without trial in Moroni. Four of Soilih's former ministers also disappeared. For the next two years, arrests, shootings, and disappearances continued. Under pressure from France, some trials were held, but many Comorans remained political prisoners, despite protests from Amnesty International and other humanitarian organizations. The Abdallah regime also restricted freedom of speech, press, association, citizens' rights to change their government, women's rights, and workers' rights. After Abdallah's death in late 1989, the country's human rights record improved. The European mercenaries who ruled the island ordered only a few arrests and released nearly all political prisoners who had been detained after the 1985 and 1987 coup attempts.

This trend continued until March 1990, when Djohar became president of Comoros. Those who opposed his regime were subjected to various human rights violations. For example, after an unsuccessful August 18–19, 1990, coup attempt, the authorities detained twenty-four people without trial in connection with the uprising. In October 1990, the security forces killed Max Veillard, the leader of the coup. The following year, after efforts to remove him from the presidency for negligence failed, Djohar ordered the arrest of several Supreme Court judges and declared a state of emergency. Another failed coup attempt on September 26, 1992, prompted the authorities to detain more than twenty people, including former Minister of Interior Omar Tamou. Police held these detainees incommunicado and reportedly tortured some of them. The Comoran Association for Human Rights (Association Comorienne des Droits Humains), which had been established in May 1990, also accused the Djohar regime of executing without trial individuals suspected of supporting armed opposition groups. In 1994 groups such as Amnesty International continued to monitor the human rights situation in Comoros, and to speak out against the Djohar regime.

# Maldives

## Security Concerns

Since independence Maldives has faced no external threats but has experienced three major internal threats. In May 1980, President Maumoon Abdul Gayoom disclosed details of an abortive coup against his regime. According to Gayoom, former president Ibrahim Nasir, supported by nine British ex-Special Air Services mercenaries, masterminded the plot. Nasir denied this allegation, but in April 1981 the authorities sentenced Ahmed Naseem, former deputy minister of fisheries and brother-in-law of Nasir, to life imprisonment for plotting to overthrow Gayoom. Attempts to extradite Nasir from Singapore failed. In July 1990, Gayoom pardoned Nasir in absentia, ostensibly because of his role in the independence struggle. In 1983 Gayoom faced another unsuccessful coup attempt.

The most serious challenge to Gayoom occurred in November 1988, when former Maldivian businessperson Abdullah Luthufi led a seaborne mercenary force of about 150 Sri Lankan Tamil separatists who invaded Maldives and attempted to seize key government installations. Gayoom asked the Indian government for assistance, and Bombay deployed a 1,600-member contingent to Maldives. This unit quickly suppressed the coup attempt and restored order. In September 1989, Gayoom commuted to life imprisonment the death sentences imposed on twelve Sri Lankans and four Maldivians who participated in the coup attempt. A few weeks later, India withdrew its remaining 160 troops from Maldives. By the early 1990s, internal security had improved, largely because Gayoom had embarked on a democratization program.

## Armed Forces in National Life

For hundreds of years, Maldives had not experienced security problems and therefore had no need for a military establishment. In 1956, however, Maldives allowed Britain to establish a Royal Air Force base on Gan, an island in Addu atoll. As part of a 1965 accord, the British gained access to Gan until 1986, but budgetary retrenchment forced them to pull out in 1976. In 1977 Maldives rejected a request by the former Soviet Union to lease the Gan facilities. By the early 1980s, Maldives maintained only one security unit, the National Security Service (NSS). This organization, which numbered fewer than 1,000 personnel, performed army, police, and maritime duties. Its mission includes preserving internal security and patrolling the country's territorial waters for illegal fishing and smuggling. After the 1988 coup attempt, the government expanded the NSS to about 1,500 personnel; by 1990, the NSS had grown to approximately 1,800 personnel.

## Penal System

Maldivians follow the sharia or Islamic law. Occasionally, the courts order convicted criminals to be flogged. Usually, however, punishment is limited to fines, compensatory payment, house arrest, imprisonment, or banishment to a remote island. The country's judicial system includes a High Court and eight lesser courts in Male. The High Court handles politically sensitive cases and acts as a court of appeal. Each of the lesser courts deals with cases that involve debt, theft, or property claims. All-purpose courts exist on other islands. Maldives has no jury trials; Islamic law judges conduct trials, which are open to the public. The president appoints all judges and has the final word in all legal cases.

## Human Rights

Maldives has a fairly good human rights record, but individual freedoms are restricted in areas such as speech and press, religion, the right of citizens to change their government, and women's and workers' rights. Other problems include arbitrary arrest, incommunicado detention, and lack of an independent judiciary. Despite Gayoom's commitment to democratization, Western observers believe that these problems will continue to mar the country's human rights record.

Notwithstanding the end of the Cold War, the Indian Ocean island countries undoubtedly will continue to maintain a degree of strategic importance for nations such as France, South Africa, and India. It is unlikely that any of these nations will intervene militarily in any of the region's islands. It also is unlikely that any of the islands will experience significant internal security problems in the near future. As a result of dwindling foreign military assistance, the security forces on each of the islands probably will undergo some reorganization or downsizing in the years ahead. Consequently, by the turn of the century, the military capabilities of each of the Indian Ocean islands will be far less than they are today.

\*     \*     \*

Historically, various foreign and indigenous armed forces have played a significant role in Indian Ocean life. Available military literature focuses mainly on Madagascar. Useful historical works for this country include *The Rising of the Red Shawls: A Revolt in Madagascar, 1895–1899* by Stephen D.K. Ellis and two works of Samuel Pasfield Oliver: *Examples of Military Operations in Madagascar by Foreign Powers and Native Campaigns, 1642–1881* and *French Operations in Madagascar, 1883–1885.* Two of the more important studies about Madagascar's role in World War II are *Into Madagascar* and *The King's African Rifles in Madagascar,* both by Kenneth Cecil Gander Dower.

Several essential works for the postindependence period include Mike Hoare's *The Seychelles Affair,* Anthony Mockler's *The New Mercenaries: The History of the Hired Soldier from the Congo to the Seychelles,* and Philip M. Allen's *Security and Nationalism in the Indian Ocean: Lessons from the Latin Quarter Islands.*

For material about the strategic importance of the Indian Ocean, see *The Politics of Intrusion: The Super Powers and the Indian Ocean* by Kim C. Beazley and Ian Clark. Other works of interest include Monoranjan Bezboruah's *U.S. Strategy in the Indian Ocean: The International Response,* Vijay Kumar Bhasin's *Super Power Rivalry in the Indian Ocean,* and *The Indian Ocean: Its Political, Economic, and Military Importance* edited by Alvin J. Cottrell and R.M. Burrell.

Material about the military aspects of the Indian Ocean and its islands exists in a variety of periodical sources, including the *Indian Ocean Newsletter, African Defence Journal, Africa Research Bulletin,* and *Africa Confidential.* Other useful publications are *New African, Africa Events, Africa News, Focus on Africa,* and the *Journal of Modern African Studies.* Two International Institute for Strategic Studies annuals, *The Military Balance* and *Strategic Survey,* are essential for understanding the evolution of Indian Ocean security forces. The same is true of three annuals: *Africa Contemporary Record, Africa South of the Sahara,* and *SIPRI World Armaments and Disarmament.* The last is published by the Stockholm International Peace Research Institute. (For further information and complete citations, see Bibliography).

# Appendix

Table
1 Metric Conversion Coefficients and Factors
2 Madagascar: Balance of Payments, Selected Years, 1984–92
3 Madagascar: Production of Major Crops, Selected Years, 1986–92
4 Madagascar: Fish Production, 1992, 1993, and 1994
5 Madagascar: Industries Within the Export Processing Zones, 1989, 1991, and 1993
6 Madagascar: Direction of Trade, Selected Years, 1984–92
7 Madagascar: Foreign Assistance, Selected Years, 1979–91
8 Security Forces of Indian Ocean Island Countries, 1994
9 Major Equipment of Madagascar Armed Forces, 1994

### Table 1. *Metric Conversion Coefficients and Factors*

| When you know | Multiply by | To find |
|---|---|---|
| Millimeters ...................... | 0.04 | inches |
| Centimeters ........ ............. | 0.39 | inches |
| Meters........................... | 3.3 | feet |
| Kilometers ....................... | 0.62 | miles |
| Hectares ........................ | 2.47 | acres |
| Square kilometers .................. | 0.39 | square miles |
| Cubic meters ..................... | 35.3 | cubic feet |
| Liters ........................... | 0.26 | gallons |
| Kilograms ....................... | 2.2 | pounds |
| Metric tons ...................... | 0.98 | long tons |
| ...................... | 1.1 | short tons |
| ...................... | 2,204.0 | pounds |
| Degrees Celsius (Centigrade) ........ | 1.8 and add 32 | degrees Fahrenheit |

### Table 2. *Madagascar: Balance of Payments, Selected Years, 1984–92*[1] (in millions of United States dollars)

|  | 1984 | 1986 | 1988 | 1990 | 1992 |
|---|---|---|---|---|---|
| Merchandise exports, f.o.b.[2] ....... | 337 | 323 | 284 | 319 | 328 |
| Merchandise imports, f.o.b. ........ | −360 | −331 | −319 | −566 | −466 |
| Trade balance ................. | −23 | −8 | −34 | −248 | −138 |
| Export of services ............... | 58 | 80 | 131 | 209 | 178 |
| Import of services ............... | −306 | −365 | −443 | −450 | 411 |
| Net private transfers ............. | −1 | 21 | 38 | 49 | 88 |
| Net public transfers ............. | 78 | 132 | 158 | 188 | 148 |
| Current account balance ........ | −193 | −141 | −149 | −251 | −136 |
| Direct and portfolio investment .... | n.a.[3] | n.a. | n.a. | 22 | 21 |
| Other capital ................... | −23 | 22 | −22 | −40 | −109 |
| Capital account balance ......... | −23 | 22 | −22 | −18 | −88 |
| Errors and omissions ............ | n.a. | n.a. | 53 | −9 | −52 |
| Changes in reserves (− means increase) .............. | −25 | −62 | −39 | 3 | 1 |

[1] Figures may not add to totals because of rounding.
[2] f.o.b.—free on board.
[3] n.a.—not available.

Source: Based on information from Economist Intelligence Unit, *Country Profile: Madagascar, 1994–95*, London, 1994, 28.

*Table 3. Madagascar: Production of Major Crops, Selected Years,*
*1986–92*
(in thousands of tons)

| Crop | 1986 | 1988 | 1990 | 1992 |
|---|---|---|---|---|
| Bananas ....................... | 225 | 260 | 220 | 220 |
| Cassava ....................... | 2,421 | 2,200 | 2,292 | 2,320 |
| Cloves ......................... | 7 | 12 | 10 | 11 |
| Cocoa ......................... | 2 | 3 | 4 | 3 |
| Coffee ......................... | 59 | 66 | 85 | 80 |
| Corn .......................... | 153 | 156 | 155 | 165 |
| Cotton (seed) .................. | 50 | 46 | 32 | 26 |
| Peanuts ....................... | 33 | 30 | 30 | 32 |
| Rice (paddy) ................... | 2,230 | 2,235 | 2,420 | 2,200 |
| Sisal .......................... | 20 | 20 | 20 | 18 |
| Sugar (raw) .................... | 102 | 122 | 2,000 | 1,724 |
| Sweet potatoes ................. | 467 | 485 | 486 | 487 |
| Tobacco ....................... | 5 | 4 | 4 | 4 |
| Vanilla (prepared) .............. | 1 | 2 | 9 | 7 |

Source: Based on information from Economist Intelligence Unit, *Country Profile: Mada-*
*gascar, 1994–95, London,* 1994, 13.

*Table 4. Madagascar: Fish Production, 1992, 1993, and 1994*
(in tons)

| | 1992 | 1993 | 1994[1] |
|---|---|---|---|
| Crabs ................................. | 960 | 1,200 | 1,500 |
| Lobsters ............................. | 460 | 570 | 650 |
| Shrimp .............................. | 7,890 | 8,600 | 10,100 |
| Tuna ................................. | 9,000 | 11,000 | 11,500 |
| Other ................................ | 57,900 | 66,000 | 68,000 |
| Freshwater fishing ...................... | 25,000 | 27,000 | 28,000 |
| Total production ....................... | 101,210 | 114,370 | 119,750 |

[1] Forecast.

Source: Based on information from Economist Intelligence Unit, *Country Report: Mada-*
*gascar, Mauritius, Seychelles* [London], No. 2, 1994, 26.

*Table 5. Madagascar: Industries Within the Export Processing Zones, 1989, 1991, and 1993*

| | 1989 | | 1991 | | 1993 | |
|---|---|---|---|---|---|---|
| | Persons Employed | Capital Invested[1] | Persons Employed | Capital Invested[1] | Persons Employed | Capital Invested[1] |
| Agro-processing . . . . . . . . . . . . . . . . . . | 0 | 0 | 588 | 10,248 | 1,062 | 17,789 |
| Textiles and clothing . . . . . . . . . . . . . . | 5,464 | 12,487 | 6,456 | 21,041 | 18,965 | 66,985 |
| Hides and skins . . . . . . . . . . . . . . . | 148 | 958 | 200 | 915 | 423 | 4,420 |
| Wood manufacturers . . . . . . . . . . . . | 0 | 0 | 750 | 20,726 | 829 | 21,315 |
| Electronics . . . . . . . . . . . . . . . . | 0 | 0 | 51 | 119 | 237 | 1,513 |
| Chemical . . . . . . . . . . . . . . . | 0 | 0 | 28 | 427 | 44 | 777 |
| Watchmaking . . . . . . . . . . . . . | 0 | 0 | 226 | 2,739 | 226 | 2,739 |
| Other . . . . . . . . . . . . . . . . | 0 | 0 | 332 | 5,901 | 1,362 | 11,550 |
| Promotion of export processing zones (EPZs) . . . . . . . . . . . . . | 66 | 111,660 | 66 | 111,660 | 66 | 111,660 |
| TOTAL . . . . . . . . | 5,678 | 125,105 | 8,697 | 173,776 | 23,214 | 238,748 |

[1] In millions of Malagasy francs (for value of the Malagasy franc—see Glossary).

Source: Based on information from Economist Intelligence Unit, *Country Report: Mauritius, Madagascar, Seychelles* [London], No. 2, 1994, 27.

*Table 6. Madagascar: Direction of Trade, Selected Years, 1984–92[1]*
(in millions of United States dollars)

| | 1984 | 1986 | 1988 | 1990 | 1992 |
|---|---|---|---|---|---|
| **Exports** | | | | | |
| Industrialized countries | | | | | |
| France .................. | 107.4 | 104.2 | 95.1 | 111.3 | 116.8 |
| Germany[2] .............. | 38.8 | 24.3 | 20.8 | 25.6 | 38.6 |
| Japan ................. | 36.7 | 35.0 | 31.4 | 20.0 | 28.7 |
| Russia[3] ................ | 2.7 | 6.6 | 7.0 | 2.3 | 2.7 |
| United States ........... | 67.4 | 48.2 | 33.7 | 107.7 | 50.9 |
| Other .................. | 47.9 | 59.7 | 39.2 | 76.1 | 73.3 |
| Total industrialized countries ............ | 300.9 | 278.1 | 227.1 | 342.8 | 311.0 |
| Developing countries | | | | | |
| Africa .................. | 7.2 | 11.5 | 23.0 | 36.7 | 42.2 |
| Asia .................... | 15.2 | 22.3 | 12.1 | 22.3 | 27.1 |
| Europe ................. | 9.8 | 1.1 | 8.2 | 2.7 | 1.0 |
| Latin America ........... | 0.1 | 0.1 | —[4] | 0.6 | 0.3 |
| Middle East ............. | 0.1 | — | 3.9 | 0.1 | 1.7 |
| Other .................. | — | — | 0.1 | 0.2 | 0.2 |
| Total developing countries ............ | 32.4 | 34.9 | 47.2 | 62.4 | 72.3 |
| Total exports .......... | 333.3 | 313.0 | 274.4 | 404.7 | 383.5 |
| **Imports** | | | | | |
| Industrialized countries | | | | | |
| France ................. | 126.9 | 113.2 | 124.9 | 184.4 | 183.5 |
| Germany .............. | 17.5 | 24.9 | 30.5 | 34.8 | 23.9 |
| Japan ................. | 10.2 | 22.3 | 23.3 | 36.5 | 26.5 |
| Russia ................. | 8.3 | 37.2 | 32.9 | 3.1 | 3.8 |
| United States ........... | 42.9 | 37.9 | 13.2 | 13.1 | 6.7 |
| Other .................. | 44.8 | 34.2 | 40.6 | 72.1 | 68.8 |
| Total industrialized countries ............ | 250.6 | 269.8 | 265.4 | 344.1 | 313.2 |
| Developing countries | | | | | |
| Africa .................. | 1.8 | 7.6 | 7.7 | 31.2 | 37.4 |
| Asia .................... | 92.3 | 42.1 | 44.9 | 86.2 | 95.3 |
| Europe ................. | 1.6 | 16.7 | 19.6 | 11.4 | 12.9 |
| Latin America ........... | 1.8 | 2.7 | 2.7 | 13.4 | 13.0 |

### Table 6. Madagascar: Direction of Trade, Selected Years, 1984–92[1]
#### (in millions of United States dollars)

| | 1984 | 1986 | 1988 | 1990 | 1992 |
|---|---|---|---|---|---|
| Middle East .............. | 132.6 | 0.3 | 20.1 | 30.3 | 52.0 |
| Other .................. | 48.2 | 0.5 | 3.7 | 74.7 | 90.4 |
| Total developing countries ............ | 278.3 | 69.3 | 98.7 | 247.2 | 301.0 |
| Total imports .......... | 528.9 | 339.6 | 363.9 | 590.3 | 614.1 |

[1] Forecast.
[2] West Germany before 1991.
[3] Soviet Union before 1992.
[4] — means negligible.

Source: Based on information from International Monetary Fund, *Direction of Trade Statistics Yearbook, 1986*, Washington, 1986, 262–63; and *Direction of Trade Statistics Yearbook, 1993*, Washington, 1993, 262–63.

### Table 7. Madagascar: Foreign Assistance, Selected Years, 1979–91
#### (in millions of United States dollars)

| | 1979 | 1982 | 1985 | 1988 | 1991 |
|---|---|---|---|---|---|
| Bilateral assistance | | | | | |
| France ..................... | 38.4 | 96.4 | 47.4 | 108.5 | 157.0 |
| Germany[1] .................. | 2.1 | 12.6 | 16.3 | 14.3 | 30.3 |
| Italy ....................... | 0.2 | 1.6 | 2.6 | 3.7 | 21.6 |
| Japan ..................... | 21.0 | 28.3 | 11.6 | 42.8 | 56.8 |
| Switzerland ................ | 5.8 | 6.8 | 4.8 | 25.8 | 15.3 |
| United States .............. | 3.0 | 15.0 | 17.0 | 13.0 | 71.0 |
| Other ..................... | 7.8 | 7.4 | 5.7 | 9.5 | 13.5 |
| Total bilateral assistance ..... | 78.3 | 168.1 | 105.4 | 217.6 | 365.5 |
| Multilateral assistance | | | | | |
| African Development Fund .... | —[2] | 2.0 | 7.2 | 8.7 | 17.7 |
| European Economic Community ............... | 15.8 | 21.6 | 17.8 | 30.6 | 17.3 |
| International Development Association ................. | 12.6 | 33.1 | 58.4 | 51.0 | 106.0 |
| Other ..................... | 12.5 | 23.9 | 11.7 | 18.6 | 50.4 |
| Total multilateral assistance .. | 40.9 | 80.6 | 95.1 | 108.9 | 191.4 |
| Other ...................... | 13.8 | 15.0 | 0.0 | 2.7 | 0.0 |
| TOTAL ..................... | 133.0 | 263.7 | 200.5 | 329.2 | 556.9 |

[1] West Germany before 1991.
[2] — means negligible.

Source: Based on information from Organisation for Economic Co-operation and Development, *Geographical Distribution of Financial Flows to Developing Countries*, Paris, 1991.

*Table 8. Security Forces of Indian Ocean Island Countries, 1994*

| Country | Personnel |
|---|---|
| **Madagascar** | |
| People's Armed Forces (Forces Armées Populaires—FAP) | |
| Army | 20,000 |
| Aeronaval force | 1,000 |
| National Gendarmerie | 7,500 |
| Civil Police | 3,000 |
| Mobile Police Group | 1,000 |
| Presidential Guard | 1,200 |
| **Mauritius** | |
| Special Mobile Force (SMF) | 1,300 |
| Police | 4,000 |
| Special Support Unit | 240 |
| National Coast Guard | 500 |
| Very Important Persons Security Unit | 100 |
| **Seychelles** | |
| Seychelles People's Defence Forces | |
| Seychelles People's Liberation Army | 800 |
| Coast Guard (includes 100-member air wing and 80 marines) | 300 |
| People's Militia | 1,000 |
| Police | 560 |
| Presidential Guard | 300 |
| **Comoros** | |
| Comoran Armed Forces | 700–800 |
| National Police Force | 500 |
| Presidential Guard | 600[1] |
| **Maldives** | |
| National Security Service | 1,800 |

[1] Undergoing reorganization.

Source: Based on information from *The Military Balance, 1994–1995*, London, 230–32.

## Table 9. Major Equipment of Madagascar Armed Forces, 1994

| Type and Description | Country of Origin | In Inventory |
|---|---|---|
| **Light tanks** | | |
| PT–76 . . . . . . . . . . . . . . . . . . . . . . . . . . . | Soviet Union | 12 |
| **Reconnaissance** | | |
| BRDM–2 armored cars . . . . . . . . . . . . . . . | -do- | 35 |
| M–8 armored scout cars . . . . . . . . . . . . . . | United States | 8 |
| M–3A1 armored scout cars . . . . . . . . . . . . | -do- | 20 |
| FV–701 Ferret scout cars . . . . . . . . . . . . . | Britain | 10 |
| **Armored personnel carriers** | | |
| M–3A1 . . . . . . . . . . . . . . . . . . . . . . . . . . | United States | 30 |
| **Towed artillery** | | |
| ZIS–3 76mm . . . . . . . . . . . . . . . . . . . . . . | Soviet Union | 12 |
| M–101 105mm . . . . . . . . . . . . . . . . . . . . | United States | n.a. |
| D–30 122mm . . . . . . . . . . . . . . . . . . . . . . | Soviet Union | 12 |
| **Recoilless guns** | | |
| M–40A1 106mm . . . . . . . . . . . . . . . . . . . | United States | n.a.[1] |
| **Mortars** | | |
| M–37 82mm . . . . . . . . . . . . . . . . . . . . . . | Soviet Union | n.a. |
| M–43 120mm . . . . . . . . . . . . . . . . . . . . . | -do- | 8 |
| **Air defense guns** | | |
| ZPU–4 14.5mm . . . . . . . . . . . . . . . . . . . . | -do- | 50 |
| 37mm Type 55 . . . . . . . . . . . . . . . . . . . . . | -do- | 20 |
| **Fighter/ground attack aircraft** | | |
| MiG–21FL Fishbed . . . . . . . . . . . . . . . . . . | -do- | 8 |
| MiG–17F Fresco . . . . . . . . . . . . . . . . . . . . | -do- | 4 |
| **Transport** | | |
| An–26 Curl . . . . . . . . . . . . . . . . . . . . . . . | -do- | 4 |
| Yak–40 Codling . . . . . . . . . . . . . . . . . . . . | -do- | 2 |
| BN–2 Defender . . . . . . . . . . . . . . . . . . . . | Britain | 3 |
| C–212 Aviocar . . . . . . . . . . . . . . . . . . . . . | Spain | 2 |
| **Helicopters** | | |
| Mi–8 Hip . . . . . . . . . . . . . . . . . . . . . . . . . | Soviet Union | 6 |
| **Liaison** | | |
| Cessna 310R . . . . . . . . . . . . . . . . . . . . . . | United States | 1 |
| Cessna 337 . . . . . . . . . . . . . . . . . . . . . . . | -do- | 3 |
| PA–23 Aztec . . . . . . . . . . . . . . . . . . . . . . | -do- | 1 |
| **Training** | | |
| Cessna 172 . . . . . . . . . . . . . . . . . . . . . . . | -do- | 4 |
| **Patrol craft, inshore** | | |
| Malaika PR–48 . . . . . . . . . . . . . . . . . . . . | France | 1 |
| **Amphibious** | | |
| Toky (Batram design) | | |
| Landing ship, medium . . . . . . . . . . . . . | -do- | 1 |

*Table 9. Major Equipment of Madagascar Armed Forces, 1994*

| Type and Description | Country of Origin | In Inventory |
|---|---|---|
| Landing ship, assault ................. | unknown | 1 |
| EDIC-type landing craft, tank ........... | France | 1 |

[1] n.a.—not available.

Source: Based on information from *The Military Balance, 1994–1995*, London, 1994, 230–31.

# Bibliography

## Chapter 1

Althabe, Gérard. "Les manifestations paysannes d'avril 1971," *Revue française d'études politiques africaines* [Dakar, Senegal], 78, June 1972, 70–77.

Andriamirado, Sennen. *Madagascar aujourd'hui*. Paris: Éditions J.A., 1978.

Andriamparany, L.M., J. Ratsimandrava, and J.F. Giovannetti. "Setting Up a Bibliographic Data-Base from National Inventory of Scientific and Technical Literature—The Cidst Experience in Madagascar," *International Library Review*, 23, No. 4, 1991, 345–56.

Anizon, A. *Production de l'habitat à Antananarivo*. Paris: Harmattan, 1988.

Archer, Robert. *Madagascar depuis 1972: La marche d'une révolution*. Paris: Harmattan, 1976.

Attenborough, David. *Journeys to the Past: Travels in New Guinea, Madagascar, and the Northern Territory of Australia*. Guildford, United Kingdom: Lutterworth Press, 1981.

"L'attitude des églises malgaches face à la situation politique," *Revue française d'études politiques africaines* [Dakar, Senegal], 72, December 1971, 85–89.

Baré, J.F. *Pouvoir des vivants, langage des morts: Idéologiques Sakalava*. Paris: François Maspero, 1977.

Baré, J.F. *Sable rouge*. Paris: Harmattan, 1980.

Battistini, René. *Géographie de Madagascar*. Paris: EDIGEF, SEDES, 1986.

Bavoux, Claude, and Claudine Bavoux. "Le coût social des dernières politiques linguistiques," *Politique africaine: Madagascar* [Paris], 52, December 1993, 76–88.

Bavoux, Claudine. *Islam et métissage—Les musulmans créolophones à Madagascar: Les indiens sunnites Sourti de Tamatave*. Paris: Harmattan, 1990.

Beaujard, P. "Rice From Heaven. Rice from the Earth: Ideology, the Political System, and Rice Production in the Tanala Kingdoms of Ikongo (Southeastern Coast of Madagascar)," *Études rurales* [Montrouge, France], No. 99–1, 1985, 389–402.

Berg, Elliot. "The Liberalization of Rice Marketing in Madagascar," *World Development* [Oxford], 17, May 1989, 719–28.

Berg, Gerald M. "Sacred Acquisition: Andrianampoinimerina at Ambohimanga, 1777–1790," *Journal of African History* [London], 29, No. 2, 1988, 191–211.

Berg, Gerald M. "The Sacred Musket: Tactics, Technology, and Power in Eighteenth-Century Madagascar," *Comparative Studies in Society and History* [London], 27, April 1985, 261–79.

Blardone, G. "Development Strategy and Structural Adjustments—Alternative to IMF Policy: Application to Madagascar and Tanzania," *Canadian Journal of Development Studies* [Ottawa], 13, No. 3, 1992, 433–42.

Bloch, Maurice. *From Blessing to Violence: History and Ideology in the Circumcision Ritual of the Merina of Madagascar.* New York: Cambridge University Press, 1986.

Bloch, Maurice. "The Implications of Marriage Rules and Descent: Categories for Merina Social Structure," *American Anthropologist*, 73, No. 1, February 1971, 164–77.

Bloch, Maurice. "Marriage Amongst Equals: An Analysis of the Marriage Ceremony of the Merina of Madagascar," *Man: The Journal of the Royal Anthropological Institute* [London], 13, No. 1, March 1978, 21–33.

Bloch, Maurice. "The Moral and Tactical Meaning of Kinship Terms," *Man: The Journal of the Royal Anthropological Institute* [London], 6, No. 1, March 1971, 79–87.

Bloch, Maurice. *Placing the Dead: Tombs, Ancestral Villages, and Kinship Organization in Madagascar.* New York: Seminar Press, 1971.

Bloch, Maurice. *Ritual, History, and Power: Selected Papers in Anthropology.* Atlantic Highlands, New Jersey: Athlone Press, 1989.

Bloch, Maurice. "Social Implications of Freedom for Merina and Zafimaniry Slaves." Pages 269–97 in Raymond K. Kent (ed.), *Madagascar in History: Essays from the 1970s.* Albany, California: Foundation for Malagasy Studies, 1979.

Bloch, Maurice. "Tombs and Conservatism among the Merina of Madagascar," *Man: The Journal of the Royal Anthropological Institute* [London], 3, No. 1, March 1968, 94–104.

Bouillon, Antoine. *Madagascar, le colonisé et son âme: Essai sur le discours psychologique colonial.* Paris: Harmattan, 1981.

Bradt, Hilary. *Madagascar.* Cincinnati: Seven Hills, 1989.

Brown, Mervyn. *Madagascar Rediscovered: A History from Early Times to Independence.* Hamden, Connecticut: Archon Books, 1979.

Cadoux, Charles. "La constitution de la troisième république," *Politique africaine* [Paris], 52, December 1993, 58–66.

Campbell, Gwyn. "The Adoption of Autarky in Imperial Madagascar, 1820–1835," *Journal of African History* [London], 28, No. 3, 1987, 395–411.

Campbell, Gwyn. "Currency Crisis, Missionaries, and the French Takeover in Madagascar, 1861–1895," *International Journal of African Historical Studies,* 21, No. 2, 1988, 273–89.

Campbell, Gwyn. "An Industrial Experiment in Precolonial Africa: The Case of Imperial Madagascar, 1825–1861," *Journal of Southern African Studies* [London], 17, No. 3, 1991, 525–59.

Campbell, Gwyn. *Missionaries and Fanompoana in Late Nineteenth-Century Madagascar.* Johannesburg, South Africa: African Studies Institute, University of the Witwatersrand, 1987.

Campbell, Gwyn. "Missionaries, Fanompoana, and the Menalamba Revolt in Late 19th-Century Madagascar," *Journal of Southern African Studies* [London], 15, No. 1, 1988, 54–73.

Campbell, Gwyn. "Slavery and Fanompoana: The Structure of Forced Labour in Imerina (Madagascar), 1790–1861," *Journal of African History* [London], 29, No. 3, 1988, 163–86.

Campbell, Gwyn. "The State and Pre-Colonial Demographic History: The Case of Nineteenth-Century Madagascar," *Journal of African History* [London], 32, No. 3, 1991, 415–45.

Chaigneau, Pascal. *Rivalités politiques et socialisme à Madagascar.* Paris: CHEAM, 1985.

Chazan-Gillig, Suzanne. *La société sakalave: Le Menabe dans la construction nationale malgache, 1947–1972.* Paris: Éditions de l'Orstom, 1991.

Covell, Maureen. *Madagascar: Politics, Economics, and Society.* New York: Frances Pinter, 1987.

Dahl, Otto Chr. *Migration from Kalimantan to Madagascar.* Oslo: Institute for Comparative Research in Human Culture, Norwegian University Press, 1991.

Deleris, Ferdinand. *Ratsiraka: Socialisme et misère à Madagascar.* Paris: Harmattan, 1986.

Deschamps, Hubert. *Histoire de Madagascar.* (4th ed.) Paris: Éditions Berger-Levrault, 1972.

Deschamps, Hubert, and Suzanne Vianès. *Les malgaches du sud-est.* Paris: Presses universitaires de France, 1959.

Desjeux, Dominique. *La question agraire à Madagascar: Administration et paysannat de 1895 à nos jours.* Paris: Harmattan, 1979.

*Direction of Trade Statistics Yearbook, 1986.* Washington: International Monetary Fund, 1986.

*Direction of Trade Statistics Yearbook, 1993.* Washington: International Monetary Fund, 1993.

Dorosh, Paul A. *Macroeconomic Adjustment and the Poor: The Case of Madagascar.* Ithaca, New York: Cornell Food and Nutrition Policy Program, 1990.

DuBois, Robert. *Olombelona: Essai sur l'existence personnelle et collective à Madagascar.* Paris: Harmattan, 1978.

Duncan, Alex, and John Howell (eds.). *Structural Adjustment and the African Farmer.* Portsmouth, New Hampshire: Heinemann, 1992.

Durufle, Gilles. *L'ajustement structurel en Afrique: Sénégal, Côte d'Ivoire, Madagascar.* Paris: Karthala, 1988.

Economist Intelligence Unit. *Country Profile: Madagascar* (annuals 1986–1987 through 1994–1995). London: 1986–94.

Economist Intelligence Unit. *Country Report: Madagascar, Mauritius, Seychelles, Comoros* [London], Nos. 1–4, 1986–92.

Economist Intelligence Unit. *Country Report: Madagascar, Mauritius, Seychelles* [London], Nos. 1–4, 1993.

Economist Intelligence Unit. *Country Report: Madagascar, Mauritius, Seychelles* [London], Nos. 1–2, 1994.

Ellis, Stephen D.K. *The Rising of the Red Shawls: A Revolt in Madagascar, 1895–1899.* Cambridge: Cambridge University Press, 1985.

Ellis, Stephen D.K. *Un complot colonial à Madagascar: L'affaire Rainandriamampandry.* Paris: Karthala, 1990.

Fanomezantsoa, Anselme. "Le régicide ambigu ou mouvement de 1991 vu de Tamatave," *Politique africaine* [Paris], 52, December 1993, 40–49.

Feeley-Harnik, Gillian. "Divine Kingship and the Meaning of History among the Sakalava of Madagascar," *Man: The Journal of the Royal Anthropological Institute* [London], 13, No. 3, September 1978, 402–17.

Feeley-Harnik, Gillian. *A Green Estate: Restoring Independence in Madagascar.* Washington: Smithsonian Press, 1991.

Feeley-Harnik, Gillian. "The Political Economy of Death: Communication and Change in Malagasy Colonial History," *American Ethnologist,* 11, 1984, 1–19.

Fujisaka, Sam. *Agroecosystem and Farmer Practices and Knowledge in Madagascar's Central Highland: Toward Improved Rice-Based System Research.* Manila: International Rice Research Institute, 1990.

Georges, C. "Resistance and Initiative in Madagascar," *International Review of Education* [Dordrecht, The Netherlands], 39, Nos. 1–2, 1993, 102–8.

Gow, Bonar A. *Madagascar and the Protestant Impact.* New York: Holmes and Meier, 1980.

Greenaway, D., and C. Milner. "Industrial Incentives, Domestic Resource Costs, and Resource Allocation in Madagascar," *Applied Economics* [London], 22, No. 6, 1990, 805–21.

Guilcher, André, and René Battistini. *Madagascar: Géographie régionale.* Paris: Centre de documentation universitaire, 1967.

Heseltine, Nigel. *Madagascar.* New York: Praeger, 1971.

Hewitt, Adrian. "Madagascar." Pages 86–112 in Alex Duncan and John Howell (eds.), *Structural Adjustment and the African Farmer.* Portsmouth, New Hampshire: Heinemann, 1992.

Hugon, Philippe. "L'évolution économique de Madagascar de la 1$^{re}$ à la 2$^e$ république," *Revue française d'études politiques africaines* [Dakar, Senegal], 143, November 1977, 26–57.

Huntington, Richard. *Gender and Social Structure in Madagascar.* Bloomington: Indiana University Press, 1987.

Jarosz, L. "Women as Rice Sharecroppers in Madagascar," *Society and Natural Resources,* 4, No. 1, 1991, 53–63.

Jolly, Alison. *Madagascar.* Tarrytown, New York: Pergamon Press, 1984.

Jolly, Alison. *A World Like Our Own: Men and Nature in Madagascar.* New Haven: Yale University Press, 1980.

Jolly, Alison, Philippe Oberle, and Roland Albignac (eds.) *Madagascar.* New York: Pergamon Press, 1984.

Kent, Raymond K. *Early Kingdoms in Madagascar, 1500–1700.* New York: Holt, Rinehart, and Winston, 1970.

Kent, Raymond K. *From Madagascar to the Malagasy Republic.* Westport, Connecticut: Greenwood Press, 1976.

Kent, Raymond K. "The Possibilities of Indonesian Colonies in Africa with Special Reference to Madagascar." Pages 93–105 in *Mouvements de populations dans l'Océan Indien.* Paris: Honoré Champion, 1979.

Kent, Raymond K. (ed.). *Madagascar in History: Essays from the 1970s.* Albany, California: Foundation for Malagasy Studies, 1979.

Koenig, Jean-Paul. *Malagasy Customs and Proverbs.* Serbrooke, Quebec, Canada: Naaman, 1984.

Kottak, Conrad P. *Madagascar: Society and History.* Durham: Carolina Academic Press, 1986.

Kottak, Conrad P. *The Past in the Present: History, Ecology, and Cultural Variation in Highland Madagascar.* Ann Arbor: University of Michigan Press, 1980.

Kottak, Conrad P. "Social Groups and Kinship Calculation among the Southern Betsileo," *American Anthropologist,* 73, No. 1, February 1971, 178–92.

Lambek, Michael. "Taboo as Cultural Practice among Malagasy Speakers," *Man: The Journal of the Royal Anthropological Institute* [London], 27, 1992, 245–66.

Larson, Pier M. *Slavery in Central Madagascar: Imerina During the Nineteenth Century.* Madison: University of Wisconsin Press, 1987.

Leisinger, K.M. "Multinational Companies and Agricultural Development: A Case Study of Taona Zina in Madagascar," *Food Policy* [Gloucester, United Kingdom], 12, No. 3, 1987, 227–41.

Little, Henry William. *Madagascar: Its History and People.* Westport, Connecticut: Negro Universities Press, 1970.

Lombard, Jacques. *Le royaume Sakalava du Menabe, 17ᵉ–20ᵉ: Essai d'analyse d'un système politique à Madagascar.* Paris: Éditions de l'Orstom, 1988.

"Madagascar: La malgachisation en question," *Revue française d'études politiques africaines* [Dakar, Senegal], 85, January 1973, 29–32.

"Malagasy: The Road to Socialism," *Africa* [London], 109, September 1980, 28–33.

Mangold, Max. *A Pronouncing Dictionary of Malagasy Place Names.* Hamburg, Germany: H. Buske, 1982.

Meldrum, Andrew. "Madagascar: Trouble in Paradise," *Africa Report*, 39, No. 2, March–April 1994, 61–63.

*Mouvements de populations dans l'Océan Indien: Actes du 4e Congres de l'Association Historique Internationale de l'Océan Indien et du 14e Colloque de la Commission Internationale d'Histoire Maritime à Réunion, 1972.* Paris: Champion, 1979.

Mukonoweshuro, Eliphas G. "State Resilience and Chronic Political Instability in Madagascar," *Canadian Journal of African Studies* [Toronto], 24, No. 3, 1990, 376–98.

Murphy, Dervla. *Muddling Through in Madagascar.* New York: Overlook Press, 1990.

Oberlé, Philippe. *Tananarive et l'Imerina: Description historique et touristique.* Antananarivo: 1976.

Organisation for Economic Co-operation and Development. *Geographical Distribution of Financial Flows to Developing Countries.* Paris: 1981.

Ottino, Paul. *L'étrangère intime: Essai d'anthropologie de la civilisation de l'ancien Madagascar.* Paris: Éditions des archives contemporaines, 1986.

Paillard, Yvan Georges. "Demographic Research on Madagascar at the Beginning of the Colonial Period and Ami Documents," *Cahiers d'études africaines* [Paris], 37, No. 1–2, 1987, 17–42.

Paillard, Yvan-Georges. "The First and Second Malagasy Republics: The Difficult Road of Independence." Pages 298–354 in Raymond K. Kent (ed.), *Madagascar in History: Essays from the 1970s.* Albany, California: Foundation for Malagasy Studies, 1979.

Pavageau, Jean. *Jeunes paysans sans terre, l'exemple malgache: Une communauté villageoise en période révolutionnaire.* Paris: Harmattan, 1981.

Pearson, Mike Parker. "Tombs and Monumentality in Southern Madagascar: Preliminary Results of the Central Androy Survey," *Antiquity* [Gloucester, United Kingdom], 11, 1992, 941–48.

Poirier, Jean. "Les groupes ethniques de Madagascar," *Revue française d'études politiques africaines* [Dakar, Senegal], 100, April 1974, 31–40.

Poirier, Jean. "Problèmes de la mise en place des couches ethniques et des couches culturelles à Madagascar." Pages 51–59 in *Mouvements de populations dans l'Océan Indien*. Paris: Champion, 1979.

Price, Arnold H. (ed.). *Missionary to the Malagasy: The Madagascar Diary of the Rev. Charles T. Price, 1875–1877*. New York: P. Lang, 1989.

Pryor, Frederic L. "Changes in Income Distribution in Poor Agricultural Nations: Malawi and Madagascar," *Economic Development and Cultural Change*, 39, 1990, 23–45.

Pryor, Frederic L. *Malawi and Madagascar*. New York: Oxford University Press, 1990.

Pryor, Frederic L. *Poverty, Equity, and Growth in Malawi and Madagascar*. New York: Oxford University Press, 1991.

Rabenoro, Césaire. *Les relations extérieures de Madagascar: De 1960 à 1972*. Paris: Harmattan, 1986.

Rabetafika, Roger. *Réforme fiscale et révolution socialiste à Madagascar*. Paris: Harmattan, 1990.

Rabevazaha, C. "Control of Development by the People: Regional Planning and Basic Needs in Madagascar," *International Labour Review* [Geneva], 110, July/August 1981, 439–52.

Raison, Jean Pierre. "Une esquisse de géographie électorale malgache," *Politique africaine* [Paris], 52, December 1993, 67–75.

Raison, Jean Pierre. *Les hautes terres de Madagascar et leurs confins occidentaux: Enracinement et mobilité des sociétés rurales*. Paris: Karthala, 1984.

Raison-Jourde, Françoise. *Bible et pouvoir à Madagascar au XIXe siècle: Invention d'une identité chrétienne et construction de l'état, 1780–1880*. Paris: Karthala, 1991.

Raison-Jourde, Françoise. *Les souverains de Madagascar: L'histoire royale et ses résurgences contemporaines*. Paris: Karthala, 1983.

Raison-Jourde, Françoise. "Une transition achevée ou amorcée?" *Politique africaine* [Paris], 52, December 1993, 6–18.

Rajoelina, Patrick. *Madagascar, la grande île.* Paris: Harmattan, 1989.

Rajoelina, Patrick. *Quarante années de la vie politique de Madagascar, 1947–1987.* Paris: Harmattan, 1988.

Rakotondrabe, Daniela T. "Essai sur les non-dits du discours fédéraliste," *Politique africaine* [Paris], 52, December 1993, 50–57.

Ramahatra, Olivier. *Madagascar: Une économie en phase d'ajustement.* Paris: Harmattan, 1989.

Razafindrakoto, André. "Educational Reform and Decentralization: An Example from Madagascar." Pages 201–11 in *Educational Reforms: Experiences and Prospects.* Paris: United Nations Educational, Scientific, and Cultural Organization, 1979.

Razafindratandra, Yvan. "Le régime malgache de zone franche," *Politique africaine* [Paris], 52, December 1993, 19–21.

Richardson, Freida. *Madagascar's Miracle Story.* Hazlewood, Missouri: Word Aflame Press, 1989.

Ruud, Jorgen. *Taboo: A Study of Malagasy Customs and Beliefs.* Oslo: Oslo University Press, 1960.

Serre-Ratsimandisa, Georges. "Théorie et practique du 'Fokonolona' moderne à Madagascar." *Canadian Journal of African Studies* [Toronto], 12, No. 1, 1978, 37–58.

Sharp, Lesley A. "Possessed and Dispossessed Youth: Spirit Possession of School Children in Northwest Madagascar," *Culture, Medicine, and Psychiatry* [Dordrecht, The Netherlands], 14, No. 3, 1990, 339–64.

Sharp, Lesley A. *The Possessed and the Dispossessed: Spirits, Identity, and Power in a Madagascar Migrant Town.* Berkeley: University of California Press, 1993.

Shuttleworth, Graham. "Policies in Transition: Lessons from Madagascar," *World Development* [Oxford], 17, 1989, 397–408.

Smith, F. Graeme. *Triumph in Death: The Story of the Malagasy Martyrs.* Phillipsburg, New Jersey: Presbyterian and Reformed Publishing, 1987.

Southall, Aidan. "Ideology and Group Composition in Madagascar," *American Anthropologist,* 73, No. 1, February 1971, 144–63.

Spacensky, Alain. *Madagascar: 50 ans de vie politique.* Paris: Nouvelles éditions latines, 1970.

Steedman, Charles. *Do Telecommunications and Air/Sea Transport Problems Limit Madagascar's Exports?* Ann Arbor: Center for Research on Economic Development, University of Michigan, 1993.

Stevens, Rita. *Madagascar.* New York: Chelsea House, 1988.

Szal, Richard. *An Agrarian Crisis in Madagascar?* Geneva: International Labour Office, 1987.

Szal, Richard. "Is There an Agrarian Crisis in Madagascar?" *International Labour Review* [Geneva], 127, No. 6, 1988, 735–60.

Thompson, Virginia, and Richard Adloff. *The Malagasy Republic: Madagascar Today.* Stanford: Stanford University Press, 1965.

Turcotte, Denis. *La politique linguistique en Afrique francophone: Une étude comparative de la Côte d'Ivoire et de Madagascar.* Quebec: Presse de l'Université Laval, 1981.

Urfer, Sylvain. "Quand les églises entrent en politique," *Politique africaine* [Paris], 52, December 1993, 31–39.

Vérin, Pierre. *The History of Civilization in North Madagascar.* Brookfield, Vermont: Ashgate, 1986.

Vérin, Pierre. *Madagascar.* Paris: Karthala, 1990.

Wilson, Peter J. *Freedom by a Hair's Breath: Tsimihety in Madagascar.* Ann Arbor: University of Michigan Press, 1992.

Wilson, Peter J. "Sentimental Structure: Tsimihety Migration and Descent," *American Anthropologist,* 73, No. 1, February 1971, 193–208.

(Various issues of the following publications also were used in the preparation of this chapter: *Africa Research Bulletin* [Oxford, United Kingdom]; and *Indian Ocean Newsletter* [Paris]).

# Chapter 2

*Action Plan for the Sugar Industry, 1985–1990.* Port Louis: Mauritius Sugar Authority, 1985.

Alladin, Ibrahim M. *Economic Miracle in the Indian Ocean: Can Mauritius Show the Way?* Rose Hill, Mauritius: Éditions de l'Océan Indien, 1993.

Alladin, Ibrahim M. *Education and Neocolonialism: A Study of Educational Development in Mauritius.* New York: Lang, 1990.

Anand, J.P. "Mauritius," *IDSA (Institute for Defence Studies and Analyses) Journal* [New Delhi], 11, October–December 1978, 165–82.

*Aneerood Jugnauth: Le premier ministre du changement.* Port Louis: Nouveau Militant, 1982.

Baker, Kenneth. *Trade Unionism in Mauritius.* Port Louis: J.E. Felix, Acting Government Printer, 1946.

Barnwell, P.J. *Visits and Despatches: Mauritius, 1598–1948.* Port Louis: Standard Printing Establishment, 1948.

Barnwell, P.J., and Auguste Toussaint. *A Short History of Mauritius.* London: Longmans, Green, 1949.

Benedict, Burton. *Indians in a Plural Society: A Report on Mauritius.* London: Her Majesty's Stationery Office, 1961.

Benedict, Burton. *Mauritius: Problems of a Plural Society.* London: Pall Mall, 1965.

Bissoonoyal, Basdeo. *A Concise History of Mauritius.* Bombay: Bharatiya Vidya Bhavan, 1963.

Bissoonoyal, Basdeo. *The Truth About Mauritius.* Bombay: Bharatiya Vidya Bhavan, 1968.

Bowman, Larry W. *Mauritius: Democracy and Development in the Indian Ocean.* Boulder, Colorado: Westview Press, 1991.

Callikan, D., and M.K. Gundooa (eds.). *The Mauritius Handbook.* Port Louis: Government Printing Office, 1989.

Chandrasekhar, Sripati. *The Population of Mauritius: Fact, Problem, and Policy.* La Jolla, California: Population Review Books, 1990.

Dassyne, Rajen, Mahmood A. Mansour, Kishone Mundile, and Palma Veerapcn. *Regards sur le monde rural mauricien.* Port Louis: ENDA-Océan Indien, 1981.

Dinan, Monique. *The Mauritian Kaleidoscope: Languages and Religions.* Port Louis: Best Graphics, 1986.

Economist Intelligence Unit. *Country Profile: Mauritius, Seychelles* (annuals 1986–1987 through 1994–1995). London: 1986–94.

Economist Intelligence Unit. *Country Report: Madagascar, Mauritius, Seychelles, Comoros* [London], Nos. 1–4, 1986–92.

Economist Intelligence Unit. *Country Report: Madagascar, Mauritius, Seychelles* [London], Nos. 1–4, 1993.

Economist Intelligence Unit. *Country Report: Madagascar, Mauritius, Seychelles* [London], Nos. 1–2, 1994.

Fanchette, Régis, and Pierre Argo. *Maurice: A l'aube de l'an 2000s.* Rose Hill, Mauritius: Éditions de l'Océan Indien, 1992.

Fanchette, Régis, and Pierre Argo. *Mauritius: Stepping into the Future.* Rose Hill, Mauritius: Éditions de l'Océan Indien, 1988.

Gulhati, Ravi, and Raj Nallari. *Successful Stabilization and Recovery in Mauritius.* Washington: World Bank, 1990.

Hazareesingh, K. (ed.). *Selected Speeches of Seewoosagur Ramgoolam.* London: Macmillan, 1979.

Hazareesingh, K. (ed.). *History of Indians in Mauritius.* London: Mauritius, 1975.

Hollingsworth, Derek. *They Came to Mauritius.* London: Oxford University Press, 1965.

Houbert, Jean. "Mauritius: Independence and Dependence," *Journal of Modern African Studies* [Cambridge], 19, No. 1, 1981, 75–105.

Houbert, Jean. "Mauritius: Politics and Pluralism at the Periphery," *Annuaire des Pays de l'Océan Indien* [Aix-en-Provence], 9, 1982–83, 225–65.

Jones, P., and B. Andrews. *A Taste of Mauritius.* London: Macmillan, 1982.

Jugnauth, Aneerood. *Peace, Development, and Self-Reliance, 1982–1985.* Rose Hill, Mauritius: Éditions de l'Océan Indien, 1986.

Lamusse, Roland. *The Breakthrough in Export Processing Industrialization in Mauritius.* Boston: African-American Issues Center, 1986.

Latham-Koenig, Alfred. "Mauritius: Political Volteface in the 'Star of the Indian Ocean'," *Round Table* [London], 290, April 1984, 166–73.

Lehembre, B. *L'Île Maurice.* Paris: Karthala, 1984.

Leymarie, Philippe. "L'Île Maurice: La constitution manipulée," *Revue française d'études politiques africaines* [Paris], 8, No. 96, 1973, 24–27.

Leymarie, Philippe. "La presse de l'Île Maurice et de l'Île de la Réunion," *Revue française d'études politiques africaines* [Paris], 8, No. 88, 1973, 74–89.

McCarry, John. "Mauritius: Island of Quiet Success," *National Geographic,* April 1993, 116–32.

Mahta, Shiv Rattan. *Social Development in Mauritius: A Study on Rural Modernization in an Island Community.* New Delhi: Wiley Eastern, 1981.

Mannick, A.R. *Mauritius: Development of a Plural Society.* Nottingham, United Kingdom: Spokesman, 1979.

Mannick, A.R. *Mauritius: The Politics of Change.* Mayfield, United Kingdom: Dodo, 1989.

Mauritius. Ministry of Information. *The Mauritius Handbook.* Port Louis: 1989.

*Mauritius: Managing Success.* Washington: World Bank, 1989.

Meade, J.E., et al. *The Economic and Social Structure of Mauritius.* London: Frank Cass, 1968.

Napal, D. *British Mauritius, 1810–1948.* Port Louis: Hart Publishing, 1984.

Ramdoyal, Ramesh Dutt. *The Development of Education in Mauritius, 1710–1976.* Reduit: Mauritius Institute of Education, 1977.

Ramgoolam, Seewoosagur. *Our Freedom.* New Delhi: Vision Books, 1982.

Ramgoolam, Seewoosagur. *Our Struggle: 20th Century Mauritius.* New Delhi: Vision Books, 1982.

Rivière, Lindsay. *Historical Dictionary of Mauritius.* Metuchen, New Jersey: Scarecrow Press, 1982.

Sambasiva Rao, Goparaju. *A Sociolinguistic Survey of Mauritius.* Mysore, India: Central Institute of Indian Languages, 1989.

Scott, Robert. *Limuria: The Lesser Dependencies of Mauritius.* London: Oxford University Press, 1961.

Selvon, Sydney. *Ramgoolam.* Port Louis: Éditions de l'Océan Indien, 1986.

Shillington, Kevin. *Jugnauth.* London: Macmillan, 1991.

Simmons, Adele Smith. *Modern Mauritius: The Politics of Decolonization.* Bloomington: Indiana University Press, 1982.

"Spécial Maurice," *Marchés tropicaux et méditerranéens* [Paris], No. 2463, January 22, 1993, 204–30.

Titmiss, Richard M., and Brian Abel-Smith assisted by Tony Lynes. *Social Policies and Population Growth in Mauritius*. London: Methuen, 1961.

Toussaint, Auguste. *Bibliography of Mauritius, 1502–1924*. Port Louis: Esclapon, 1956.

Toussaint, Auguste. *History of Mauritius*. London: Macmillan, 1977.

Toussaint, Auguste. *Port Louis: A Tropical City.* London: George Allen and Unwin, 1973.

Virashawmy, Raji. *State Policies and Agriculture in Africa: The Case of Mauritius*. Addis Ababa: Institute of Development Research, 1984.

Walker, Iain. *Zaffer Pe Senze: Ethnic Identity and Social Change Among the Ilois in Mauritius*. Vacoas: KMLI, 1986.

Wright, Carol. *Mauritius*. Newton Abbot: David and Charles, 1974.

(Various issues of the following publications also were used in the preparation of this chapter: *Africa Analysis* [London]; *Africa Confidential* [London]; *Africa Economic Digest* [London]; *Africa Events* [London]; *Africa Research Bulletin* (Political, Social, and Cultural Series) [Oxford, United Kingdom]; *African Business* [London]; Foreign Broadcast Information Service, *Daily Report: Sub-Saharan Africa; Indian Ocean Newsletter* [Paris]; *Indian Ocean Review* [Perth]; *Journal of Mauritius Studies* [Moka]; *Marchés tropicaux et méditerranéens* [Paris]; *Mauritian International* [London]; and *New African* [London]).

# Chapter 3

*Africa Contemporary Record: Annual Survey and Documents, 1983–84*. (Ed., Colin Legum.) New York: Africana, 1984.

*Africa Contemporary Record: Annual Survey and Documents, 1984–85*. (Ed., Colin Legum.) New York: Africana, 1985.

*Africa Contemporary Record: Annual Survey and Documents, 1985–86*. (Ed., Colin Legum.) New York: Africana, 1986.

*Africa Contemporary Record: Annual Survey and Documents, 1986–87*. (Ed., Colin Legum.) New York: Africana, 1987.

*Africa Contemporary Record: Annual Survey and Documents, 1987–88*. (Eds., Colin Legum and Marion E. Doro.) New York: Africana, 1988.

*Africa Contemporary Record: Annual Survey and Documents, 1988–89.* (Eds., Colin Legum and Marion E. Doro.) New York: Africana, 1989.

*African South of the Sahara, 1994.* (23d ed.) London: Europa, 1993.

*Africa's Development Challenges and the World Bank: Hard Questions, Costly Choices.* Boulder, Colorado: Lynne Rienner, 1988.

Amnesty International. *Amnesty International Report, 1993.* London: 1993.

Baum, Dan. "The Comoros Connection," *Africa Report,* 34, No. 1, January–February 1989, 49.

Bouvet, Henri. *Les problèmes de formation aux Comores.* Paris: Institut national des langues et civilisations orientales, 1985.

Boxhall, Peter. "Arabian Seafarers in the Indian Ocean," *Asian Affairs* [London], 20, 1989, 287–95.

Carver, Richard. "Called to Account: How African Governments Investigate Human Right Violations," *African Affairs* [London], No. 89, July 1990, 391–415.

Charpantier, Jean. "Le pouvoir d'Ali Soilih Ngazidja, 1975–1978," *L'Afrique et l'Asie moderne* [Paris], No. 157, 1988, 70–89.

Charpantier, Jean. "Le régime d'Ali Soilih Moroni, 1975–1978: Analyse structurelle (première partie)," *Le mois en Afrique: Études politiques, économiques, et sociologiques africaines* [Paris], Nos. 219–220, 1984, 32–50.

Charpantier, Jean. "Le régime d'Ali Soilih Moroni, 1975–1978: Analyse structurelle (deuxième partie)," *Le mois en Afrique: Études politiques, économiques, et sociologiques africaines* [Paris], Nos. 221–222, 1984, 3–22.

Charpantier, Jean. "Le régime d'Ali Soilih Moroni, 1975–1978: Analyse structurelle (troisième partie)," *Le mois en Afrique: Études politiques, économiques et sociologiques africaines* [Paris], Nos. 223–224, 1984, 29–47.

Church, R.J. Harrison. "The Comoros." Pages 277–88 in *Africa South of the Sahara, 1994.* (23d ed.) London: Europa, 1993.

Comoros. *Constitution.* Moroni: 1992.

*Contes et mythes de Madagascar et des Comores.* Paris: Institut national des langues et civilisations orientales, 1987.

*Culture des îles et développement.* Paris: UNESCO, 1991.

Damir, Ben Ali. *Traditions d'une ligne royale des Comores*. Paris: Harmattan, 1985.

Davis, Bruce E. "Quality of Life in Small Island Nations in the Indian Ocean," *Human Ecology*, 14, No. 4, 1986, 453–71.

Decracne, Philippe. "L'Archipel des Comores face à la montée des périls," *L'Afrique et l'Asie moderne* [Paris], No. 159, 1988–89, 52–61.

*Documents comoriens* (annual). Paris: Institut national des langues et civilisations orientales, 1982–93.

*Education in Sub-Saharan Africa: Policies for Adjustment, Revitalization, and Expansion*. Washington: World Bank, 1988.

*Études sur les Comores et l'Islam en l'honneur de Paul Guy*. Paris: Institut national des langues et civilisations orientales, 1985.

Flobert, Thierry. *Les Comores: Évolution juridique et sociopolitique*. (Travaux et mémoires de la Faculté de Droit et de Science Politique d'Aix-Marseilles.) Aix-marseilles: Centre d'études et de recherches sur les sociétés de l'Océan Indien, 1976.

Gaspart, Claude. "The Comoro Islands since Independence: An Economic Appraisal," *Civilisations* [Brussels], 29, Nos. 3–4, 1979, 293–311.

Griffin, Michael. "The Perfumed Isles," *Geographical Magazine* [London], No. 58, October 1986, 524–27.

Griffin, Michael. "The Politics of Isolation," *Africa Report*, 33, No. 1, January–February 1988, 52–55.

Harrison, Selig S., and K. Subrahmanyam (eds.). *Superpower Rivalry in the Indian Ocean: Indian and American Perspectives*. London: Oxford University Press, 1989.

Hartley, Aidan. "Paradise Lost," *Africa Report*, 35, No. 2, March–April 1990, 37–40.

Martin, B.G. "Arab Migrations to East Africa in Medieval Times," *International Journal of African Historical Studies*, 7, No. 3, 1974, 367–90.

Martin, Jean. "L'affranchissement des esclaves de Mayotte, décembre 1846–juillet 1847," *Cahiers des études africaines* [Paris], 16, Nos. 1–2, 1976, 207–33.

Martin, Jean. "Les débuts du protectorat et la révolte servile de 1891 dans l'Île d'Anjouan," *Revue française d'histoire d'outre-mer* [Paris], 60, No. 218, 1973, 45–85.

Moines, Jacques. "Océan Indien et progressisme," *L'Afrique et l'Asie moderne* [Paris], No. 123, 1979, 3–23.

Mukonoweshuro, Eliphas G. "The Politics of Squalor and Dependency: Chronic Political Instability and Economic Collapse in the Comoro Islands," *African Affairs* [London], No. 89, October 1990, 555–77.

Newitt, Malyn. "The Comoro Islands in Indian Oceans Trade Before the 19th Century," *Cahiers des études africaines* [Paris], 23, Nos. 1–2, 1983.

Newitt, Malyn. *The Comoro Islands: Struggle Against Dependency in the Indian Ocean.* Boulder, Colorado: Westview Press, 1984.

Ostheimer, John M. "Political Development in Comoros," *African Review* [Dar-es-Salaam], 3, No. 3, 1973, 491–506.

Ottenheimer, Martin. "The Use of Comorian Documents," *History in Africa*, 12, 1985, 349–55.

Rais, Rasul B. *The Indian Ocean and the Superpowers: Economic, Political, and Strategic Perspectives.* Totowa, New Jersey: Barnes and Noble, 1987.

"Rediscovering the Islands of the Moon," *The Courier* (UNESCO) [Paris], 42, March 1989, 31–32.

Richmond, Edmun B. *Language Teaching in the Indian Ocean: Policy and Pedagogy in Three Developing Nations: A Study of the Formation of National Language Policies in Comoros, Mauritius, and Seychelles.* Lanham: University Press of America, 1983.

Robineau, Claude. "Jeunesse, religion des révolutions: L'expérience comorienne (1975–1978)," *Cahier des sciences humaines* [Paris], 21, Nos. 2–3, 1985, 187–96.

Rozika, Jill. "After the Decade," *Africa Report*, 30, No. 5, September–October 1985, 75–81.

Saint Alban, Cédric. "Les partis politiques comoriens entre la modernité et la tradition," *Revue française d'études politiques africaines* [Dakar, Senegal], 8, No. 94, 1973, 76–88.

Sasseen, Jane. "Out of Africa (France's Assiduously Cultivated Links with Its Former Colonies in Africa Brought Little Return)," *International Management* (European ed.), 47, May 1992, 69–70.

Schultz, Patrick. "Le statut constitutionnel et administratif de Mayotte," *Penant: Revue de droit des pays d'Afrique* [Paris], 96, Nos. 790–791, January–July 1986, 97–128.

Shepherd, George W., Jr. *The Trampled Grass: Tributary States and Self-Reliance in the Indian Ocean Zone of Peace.* New York: Praeger, 1987.

"Status of Women in 99 Countries: Population Crisis Committee Briefing Paper," *American Journal of Public Health*, 78, October 1988, 1325.

*Sub-Saharan Africa, from Crisis to Sustainable Growth: A Long-Term Perspective Study.* Washington: World Bank, 1989.

Terrill, W. Andrew. "The Comoro Islands in South African Regional Strategy," *Africa Today*, 33, No. 2, 2d/3d quarters 1986, 59–70.

United States. Department of State. Bureau of Public Affairs. *Background Notes: Comoros.* (Department of State Publication No. 8963.) Washington: GPO, 1992.

Vasilyev, R. "Winds of Change Over the Comoro Islands," *International Affairs* [Moscow], No. 10, 1976, 105–09.

Venter, Denis. "The Comorian Comitragedy: Final Curtain on Abdallahism?," *Africa Insight* [Johannesburg], 20, No. 3, 1990, 141–50.

Watremez, Emmanuel. "The Satirical Press in Francophone Africa," *Index on Censorship* [London], 21, No. 10, October 1992, 34–36.

Welch, Claude E., Jr. "The Organisation of African Unity and the Promotion of Human Rights," *Journal of Modern African Studies* [London], 29, December 1991, 535–55.

Willox, Robert. *Maldives and Islands of the East Indian Ocean: A Travel Survival Kit.* Berkeley, California: Lonely Planet, 1990.

World Bank. *African Development Indicators.* Washington: 1992.

World Bank. *African Economic and Financial Data.* Washington: 1989.

World Bank. *The Comoros: Problems and Prospects of a Small, Island Economy.* Washington, 1979.

World Bank. *Social Indicators of Development, 1993.* Baltimore: Johns Hopkins University Press, 1993.

(Various issues of the following publications also were used in the preparation of this chapter: *Africa Analysis* [London]; *Africa Confidential* [London]; *Africa Events* [London]; *Africa Research Bulletin* [Oxford, United Kingdom]; *Le Monde* [Paris]; *New York Times*, *Times* [London], and *Washington Post*).

## Chapter 4

Anand, J.P. "The Seychelles Group: A Profile," *IDSA (Institute for Defence Studies and Analyses) Journal* [New Delhi], 11, January–March 1979, 287–302.

Belling, L.N. *Seychelles: Island of Love.* Boulogne: Delroise, 1971.

Benedict, Burton. *People of the Seychelles.* London: Her Majesty's Stationery Office, 1966.

Benedict, Marion, and Burton Benedict. *Men, Women, and Money in the Seychelles.* Berkeley: University of California Press, 1982.

Bradley, J.T. *History of Seychelles.* Victoria: Clarion Press, 1940.

Central Bank of Seychelles. *Annual Report.* Victoria: 1984–93.

Chloros, A.G. *Codification in a Mixed Jurisdiction: The Civil and Commercial Law of Seychelles.* Amsterdam, New York: North Holland, 1977.

Cohen, Robin (ed.). *African Islands and Enclaves.* Beverly Hills, California: Sage, 1983.

Commonwealth Observer Group. *The Presidential and National Assembly Elections in Seychelles, 20–23 July, 1993.* London: Commonwealth Secretariat, 1993.

Economist Intelligence Unit. *Country Profile: Mauritius, Seychelles* (annuals 1986–1987 through 1994–1995). London: 1986–94.

Economist Intelligence Unit. *Country Report: Madagascar, Mauritius, Seychelles, Comoros* [London], Nos. 1–4, 1986–92.

Economist Intelligence Unit. *Country Report: Madagascar, Mauritius, Seychelles* [London], Nos. 1–4, 1993.

Economist Intelligence Unit. *Country Report: Madagascar, Mauritius, Seychelles* [London], Nos. 1–2, 1994.

Filliot, Jean-Michel. *Les Seychelles et la révolution française.* Paris: ORSTOM, Institut français de recherche scientifique pour le développement en coopération: Ministère de la coopération et du développement, 1989.

Franda, Marcus F. *Quiet Turbulence in the Seychelles: Tourism and Development.* (American Field Staff Reports, Asia Series, No. 10.) Hanover, New Hampshire, 1979.

Franda, Marcus F. *The Seychelles: Unquiet Islands.* Boulder, Colorado: Westview Press, 1982.

Gavshon, Arthur. "A Tilt to the West?" *Africa Report,* 28, No. 6, November–December 1983, 56–59.

Hoare, Mike. *The Seychelles Affair.* New York: Bantam Press, 1986.

International Monetary Fund. *Seychelles: Recent Economic Developments.* Washington: 1983.

Kaplinsky, Raphael. "Prospering at the Periphery: A Special Case—The Seychelles." Pages 195–216 in Robin Cohen (ed.), *African Islands and Enclaves.* Beverly Hills, California: Sage, 1983.

Koechlin, Bernard (ed.). *Les Seychelles et l'Océan Indien.* Paris: Harmattan, 1984.

Lee, C. *Seychelles: Political Castaways.* London: Hamish Hamilton, 1976.

Leymarie, Phillipe. "Les Seychelles: Les `indépendantistes contre le tourisme sauvage,'" *Revue française d'études politiques africaines* [Paris], 8, No. 95, 1973, 21–23.

Lionnet, Guy. *The Seychelles.* Harrisburg: Stackpole, 1972.

Mancham, James R. *Island Spendour.* London: Methuen, 1984.

Mancham, James R. *Paradise Raped: Life, Love, and Power in the Seychelles.* London: Methuen, 1983.

Mees, C.C. *The Fishermen of Seychelles: Results of a Socio-economic Study of Seychelles Fishing Community.* Mahé: Seychelles Fishing Authority, 1990.

Moines, Jacques. "Les Seychelles: Beaucoup de bruit autour d'un si petit pays," *L'Afrique et l'Asie moderne* [Paris], No. 2, 1977, 39–51.

Moines, Jacques. "Seychelles: Éléments de la situation," *L'Afrique et l'Asie moderne* [Paris], No. 166, Fall 1990, 18–33.

Mukonoweshuro, Eliphas G. "'Radicalism' and the Struggle for Affluence in the Seychelles," *Scandinavian Journal of Development Alternatives* [Stockholm], 10, March–June 1991, 139–71.

Nwulia, Moses D.E. *The History of Slavery in Mauritius and the Seychelles, 1810–1875.* Rutherford, New Jersey: Fairleigh Dickinson University Press, 1981.

Ostheimer, John M. (ed.). *The Politics of the Western Indian Ocean Islands.* New York: Praeger, 1975.

René, France Albert. *Seychelles: The New Era.* Victoria: Ministry of Education and Information, 1982.

Rowe, J.W.F. *Report on the Economy of the Seychelles and Its Future Development.* Mahé: Government Printer, 1959.

Seychelles. Central Statistical Office. *Seychelles Handbook*. Mahé: 1976.

Seychelles. Management and Information Systems Division. *1987 Census Report*. Victoria: 1991.

Seychelles. Management and Information Systems Division. *The Population of Seychelles: 1987–2012*. Victoria: 1992.

Seychelles. Ministry of Planning and External Relations. *National Development Plan, 1990–94*. Victoria: 1990.

United States. Department of State. *Country Reports on Human Rights Practices for 1991*. (Report submitted to United States Congress, 102d, 2d Session, Senate, Committee on Foreign Relations, and House of Representatives, Committee on Foreign Affairs.) Washington: GPO, 1992.

United States. Department of State. *Country Reports on Human Rights Practices for 1992*. (Report submitted to United States Congress, 103d, 1st Session, Senate, Committee on Foreign Relations, and House of Representatives, Committee on Foreign Affairs.) Washington: GPO, 1993.

United States. Department of State. *Country Reports on Human Rights Practices for 1993*. (Report submitted to United States Congress, 103d, 2d Session, Senate, Committee on Foreign Relations, and House of Representatives, Committee on Foreign Affairs.) Washington: GPO, 1994.

Vine, Peter. *Seychelles*. (2d ed.) London: Immel, 1992.

(Various issues of the following publications also were used in the preparation of this chapter: *Africa Analysis* [London]; *Africa Confidential* [London]; *Africa Economic Digest* [London]; *Africa Events* [London]; *Africa Report*; *Africa Research Bulletin* (Political, Social, and Cultural Series) [Oxford, United Kingdom]; *African Business* [London]; Foreign Broadcast Information Service, *Daily Report: Sub-Saharan Africa*; *Economist* [London]; *Indian Ocean Newsletter* [Paris]; *Indian Ocean Review* [Perth]; *Marchés tropicaux et méditerranéens* [Paris]; and *New African* [London]).

# Chapter 5

Abeysinghe, Arilya. "Development, Underdevelopment and Dependent Development in Atoll Environments of Selected Indian Ocean and South Pacific Basin Countries," *Scandina-*

*vian Journal of Development Alternatives* [Stockholm], 6, December 1987, 125–42.

Adeney, M., and Carr, W.K. "The Maldives Republic." In John M. Ostheimer (ed.), *The Politics of the Western Indian Ocean Islands.* New York: Praeger, 1975.

Butany, W.T. *Report on Agricultural Survey and Crop Production.* Rome: United Nations Development Programme, 1974.

Chawla, Subash. *The New Maldives.* Colombo, Sri Lanka: Diana, 1986.

*The Encyclopedia of Islam.* Leiden, the Netherlands: E.J. Brill, 1993.

*The Far East and Australasia, 1993.* (24th ed.) London: Europa, 1992.

*The Far East and Australasia, 1994.* (25th ed.) London: Europa, 1993.

Farmer, B.H. "Maldives: Physical and Social Geography." Pages 543–50 in *The Far East and Australasia, 1993.* (24th ed.) London: Europa, 1993.

Haaland, Gunnar. *Evolution of Socio-economic Dualism in the Maldives.* Bergen, Norway: Michelsen Institute, DERAP (Development Research and Action Program), 1987.

Heyerdahl, Thor. *The Maldive Mystery.* London: Allen and Unwin, 1986.

Lateef, K. *An Introductory Economic Report.* Washington: World Bank, 1980.

Luthfi, M., and Zubair, H. *Innovation in Primary School Construction: Maldives Community Schools.* Bangkok: UNESCO Regional Office for Education in Asia and the Pacific, 1987.

*The Maldive Islands: Monograph on the History, Archaeology, and Epigraphy.* Colombo: Government Printer, 1940.

Maldives. Department of Information and Broadcasting, *The Constitution of the Republic of Maldives.* (Unofficial translation; Trans., Ibrahim Hilmy Didi.) Male: 1975.

Maldives. Department of Information and Broadcasting. *Maldives: Development Cooperation.* Male: 1989.

Maldives. Department of Information and Broadcasting. *Maldives: An Economic Brief.* Male: 1985.

Maldives. Department of Information and Broadcasting. *Maldives: A Historical Overview.* Male: 1985.

Maldives. Department of Information and Broadcasting. *Maldives: Social Development.* Male: 1985.

Maldives. Department of Information and Broadcasting. *Maldives: Year Book, 1988.* Male: 1988.

Maloney, Clarence. *People of the Maldive Islands.* Bombay: Orient Longman, 1980.

Maniku, Hassan Ahmed. *Changes in the Topography of the Maldives.* Maldives: Forum of Writers on the Environment, 1990.

Maniku, Hassan Ahmed. *The Maldives: A Profile.* Male: Department of Information and Broadcasting, 1977.

Munch-Peterson, N.F. *Background Paper for Population Needs Mission.* Rome: United Nations Development Programme, 1981.

Phadnis, Urmila, and Ela Dutt Luithui. "The Maldives Enter World Politics," *Asian Affairs,* 8, January–February 1981, 166–79.

Phadnis, Urmila, and Ela Dutt Luithui. *Maldives: Winds of Change in an Atoll State.* New Delhi: South Asian, 1985.

Reynolds, C.H.B. *Linguistic Strands in the Maldives.* London: School of Oriental and African Studies, 1978.

Reynolds, C.H.B. *The Maldive Islands.* London: Royal Central Asian Society, 1974.

Smallwood, C.A. *Visit to the Maldive Islands.* London: Royal Central Asian Society, 1961.

UNESCO Principal Regional Office for Asia and the Pacific. *Status of Women: Maldives.* Bangkok: 1989.

Webb, Paul A. *Maldives: People and Environment.* Male: Department of Information and Broadcasting, 1989.

Williams, Freda Britt. *Island World of Maldives.* Male: Media Transasia (for Ministry of Tourism, Maldives), 1988.

Willox, Robert. *Maldives and Islands of the East Indian Ocean: A Travel Survival Kit.* Berkeley, California: Lonely Planet, 1990.

World Health Organization. Office of the WHO Representative to Maldives. *Twenty-Four Monthly Report on Technical Aspects of Programme Implementation.* Male: 1989.

(Various issues of the following publications also were used in the preparation of this chapter: *Africa Research Bulletin* [Oxford, United Kingdom]; *Indian Ocean Newsletter* [Paris]; and *Keesing's Contemporary Archives* [Marlow, United Kingdom].)

# Chapter 6

*Africa South of the Sahara, 1994.* (23d ed.) London: Europa, 1993.

Allen, Philip M. *Security and Nationalism in the Indian Ocean: Lessons from the Latin Quarter Islands.* Boulder, Colorado: Westview Press, 1987.

Archer, Robert. *Madagascar depuis 1972: La marche d'une révolution.* Paris: Harmattan, 1976.

Banerjee, B.N. *Indian Ocean: A Whirlpool of Unrest.* New Delhi: Paribus, 1988.

Beazley, Kim C., and Ian Clark. *The Politics of Intrusion: The Super Powers and the Indian Ocean.* Sydney: Alternative Publishing, 1979.

Bezboruah, Monoranjan. *U.S. Strategy in the Indian Ocean: The International Response.* New York: Praeger, 1977.

Bhasin, Vijay Kumar. *Super Power Rivalry in the Indian Ocean.* New Delhi: Chand, 1981.

Bowman, Larry W., and Ian Clark (eds.). *The Indian Ocean in Global Politics.* Boulder, Colorado: Westview Press, 1981.

Braun, Dieter. *The Indian Ocean: Region of Conflict or "Peace Zone"?* New York: St. Martin's Press, 1983.

Chauliac, G. "Contribution à l'étude médico-militaire de l'expédition de Madagascar en 1895," *Bulletin de Madagascar* [Tananarive], No. 240, May 1966, 411–41; No. 241, June 1966, 507–51; and No. 242, July 1966, 624–40.

Chellapermal, A. *The Problem of Mauritius Sovereignty over the Chagos Archipelago and the Militarization of the Indian Ocean.* Perth: University of Western Australia, 1984.

Chipman, John. *French Military Policy and African Security.* (Adelphi Papers No. 201.) London: International Institute for Strategic Studies, 1985.

Chipman, John. *French Power in Africa.* Oxford: Blackwell, 1989.

Clayton, Anthony. *France, Soldiers, and Africa.* London: Brassey's, 1988.

Clayton, Anthony. "Hazou, Fazou, Tazou—Forest, Fire, and Fever: The French Occupation of Madagascar." Pages 83–103 in A. Hamish Ion and E.J. Errington (eds.), *Great Powers and Little Wars: The Limits of Power.* Westport, Connecticut: Praeger, 1993.

Cohen, Robin (ed.). *African Islands and Enclaves.* Beverly Hills, California: Sage, 1983.

Condamy, Charles Auguste Louis François. *Une méthode de guerre coloniale: La conquête du Ménabé à Madagascar, 1897–1900.* Paris: Charles-Lavauzelle, 1906.

Condamy, Charles Auguste Louis François. *L'insurrection dans le sud Madagascar (1904–1905).* Paris: Fournier, 1914.

Copson, Raymond. "East Africa and the Indian Ocean: A 'Zone of Peace'?" *African Affairs* [London], 76, No. 304, July 1977, 339–58.

Cottrell, Alvin J. *Sea Power and Strategy in the Indian Ocean.* Beverly Hills, California: Sage, 1981.

Cottrell, Alvin J., and R.M. Burrell (eds.). *The Indian Ocean: Its Political, Economic, and Military Importance.* New York: Praeger, 1972.

Domingo, F.R. *Les mauriciens dans la deuxième guerre mondiale.* Rose Hill, Mauritius: Éditions de l'Océan Indien, 1983.

Dowdy, William L., and Russell B. Todd (eds.). *The Indian Ocean: Perspectives on a Strategic Arena.* Durham: Duke University Press, 1985.

Dower, Kenneth Cecil Gander. *Into Madagascar.* London: Penguin Books, 1943.

Dower, Kenneth Cecil Gander. *The King's African Rifles in Madagascar.* Nairobi: East Africa Command, 1943.

Duchesne, Jacques Charles René Achille. *L'expédition de Madagascar.* Paris: Charles-Lavauzelle, 1896.

Ellis, Stephen D.K. "The Political Elite of Imerina and the Revolt of the Menelamba: The Creation of a Colonial Myth in Madagascar, 1895–1898," *Journal of African History* [Cambridge], 21, No. 2, 1980, 219–34.

Ellis, Stephen D.K. *The Rising of the Red Shawls: A Revolt in Madagascar, 1895–1899.* Cambridge: Cambridge University Press, 1985.

Escare, Alain. "Les militaires et le pouvoir à Madagascar de 1960 à 1975," *Les mois en Afrique* [Paris], 18, Nos. 211–212, 1983, 48–53.

Esoavelomandroso, F.V. "Rainilaiarivony and the Defence of Malagasy Independence at the End of the Nineteenth Century." Pages 228–51 in Raymond K. Kent (ed.), *Madagascar in*

*History: Essays from the 1970s.* Albany, California: Foundation for Malagasy Studies, 1979.

Fuglestad, F., and J. Simensen (eds.). *Norwegian Missions in African History, 2: Madagascar.* Oslo: Norwegian University Press, 1986.

Gaudusson, Jean du Bois de. "Madagascar: A Case of Revolutionary Pragmatism." Pages 101–21 in John Markakis and Michael Waller (eds.), *Military Marxist Regimes in Africa.* London: Frank Cass, 1986.

Harrison, Selig S., and K. Subrahmanyam (eds.). *Superpower Rivalry in the Indian Ocean: Indian and American Perspectives.* London: Oxford University Press, 1989.

Hoare, Mike. *The Seychelles Affairs.* New York: Bantam Press, 1986.

Hooker, Richard. "Japan's Lost Opportunity in the War," *Yale Review,* 35, No. 1, September 1945, 30–39.

*The Indian Ocean as a Zone of Peace.* New York: International Peace Academy, 1986.

"Indian Ocean—Zone of Peace or Superpower Battleground?" *Commonwealth Journal* [London], December–January 1979/80, 2–9.

Ion, A. Hamish, and E.J. Errington (eds.). *Great Powers and Little Wars: The Limits of Power.* Westport, Connecticut: Praeger, 1993.

Jawatkar, K.S. *Diego Garcia in International Diplomacy.* Bombay: Popular Prakashan, 1983.

Julis, G., and A. Guillotin. "La présence militaire de la France en Afrique," *Cahiers du Communisme* [Paris], 64, No. 10, October 1988, 68–76.

Kaushik, Devendra. *The Indian Ocean: A Strategic Dimension.* New Delhi: Vikas, 1983.

Kaushik, Devendra. *Indian Ocean: Towards a Zone of Peace.* New Delhi: Vikas, 1972.

Keegan, John (ed.). *World Armies.* (2d ed.) Detroit: Gale Research, 1983.

Kent, Raymond K. (ed.). *Madagascar in History: Essays from the 1970s.* Albany, California: Foundation for Malagasy Studies, 1979.

Khan, J. "Diego Garcia: The Militarization of an Indian Ocean Island." Pages 165–93 in Robin Cohen (ed.), *African Islands and Enclaves.* Beverly Hills, California: Sage, 1983.

Knight, Edward Frederick. *Madagascar in War Time.* London: Longmans, Green, 1896.

Kombo, Marcelino. "The Day Seychelles Routed Mercenaries," *Africa* [London], No. 125, January 1982, 36–38.

Kruger, F.H. "The Siege of Antsirabe," *Antananarivo Annual* [Antananarivo], 5, 1896, 484–90.

Kurian, George Thomas (ed.). *World Encyclopedia of Police Forces and Penal Systems.* New York: Facts on File, 1989.

Larus, Joel. "Diego Garcia: The Military and Legal Implications of America's Pivotal Base in the Indian Ocean." Pages 435–51 in William L. Dowdy and Russell B. Todd (eds.), *The Indian Ocean: Perspectives on a Strategic Area.* Durham: Duke University Press, 1985.

L'Estrac, J.C. de. "Diego Garcia: Mauritius Battles a Superpower to Reclaim a Cold War Hostage," *Parliamentarian* [London], 72, No. 4, October 1991, 267–70.

Little, Douglas. "Cold War and Colonialism in Africa: The United States, France, and the Madagascar Revolt of 1947," *Pacific Historical Review,* 59, No. 4, 1990, 527–52.

Lyautey, Maréchal. *Dans le sud de Madagascar: Pénétration militaire, situation politique et économique (1900–1902).* Paris: Charles-Lavauzelle, 1903.

McAteer, William. *Rivals in Eden: A History of the French Settlement and British Conquest of the Seychelles Islands: 1742–1818.* Lewes: Book Guild, 1991.

McNamera, Francis Terry. *France in Black Africa.* Washington: National Defense University, 1989.

Mancham, James R. *Paradise Raped: Life, Love, and Power in the Seychelles.* London: Methuen, 1983.

Markakis, John, and Michael Waller (eds.). *Military Marxist Regimes in Africa.* London: Frank Cass, 1986.

Maude, Francis Cornwallis. *Five Years in Madagascar, with Notes on the Military Situation.* London: Chapman and Hall, 1895.

*The Military Balance, 1994–1995.* London: International Institute for Strategic Studies, 1994.

Mockler, Anthony. *The New Mercenaries: The History of the Hired Soldier from the Congo to the Seychelles.* New York: Paragon House, 1987.

Monro, A.G.F. "Madagascar Interlude," *Army Quarterly* [London], 53, No. 2, January 1947, 209–19.

Ogunbadejo, Oye. "Diego Garcia and Africa's Security," *Third World Quarterly* [London], 4, No. 1, January 1982, 104–20.

Oliver, Samuel Pasfield. *Examples of Military Operations in Madagascar by Foreign Powers and Native Campaigns, 1642–1881.* London: Harrison and Sons, 1885.

Oliver, Samuel Pasfield. *French Operations in Madagascar, 1883–1885.* London: Harrison and Sons, 1886.

Oliver, Samuel Pasfield. *The True Story of the French Dispute in Madagascar.* London: T. Fisher Unwin, 1885.

Paillard, Yvan-Georges, and Jean Boutonne. "Espoirs et deboires de l'immigration européenne à Madagascar sous Gallieni: L'expérience de colonisation militaire," *Revue française d'histoire d'outre-mer* [Paris], 65, No. 3, 1978, 333–51.

Poulose, T.T. (ed.). *Indian Ocean Power Rivalry.* New Delhi: Young Asia, 1974.

Raison-Jourde, Françoise. "Une rébellion en quête de statut: 1947 à Madagascar," *Revue de la bibliothèque nationale* [Paris], No. 34, 1989, 24–32.

Ranchot, A. *Expédition de Madagascar en 1895.* Paris: Société d'éditions géographiques, maritimes et coloniales, 1930.

Remnick, Richard B. "The Soviet Naval Presence in the Indian Ocean and Western Security." Pages 83–105 in W.J. Wilson (ed.), *U.S. Strategic Interests in the Gulf Region.* Boulder, Colorado: Westview Press, 1987.

Rennell of Rodd. *British Military Administration in Africa During the Years 1941–1947.* London: His Majesty's Stationery Office, 1948.

Rennemo, O. "The Menalamba Uprising in the Norwegian Mission Districts." Pages 126–44 in F. Fuglestad and J. Simensen (eds.), *Norwegian Missions in African History, 2: Madagascar.* Oslo: Norwegian University Press, 1986.

Rogers, Stanley. *The Indian Ocean.* London: Harrap, 1932.

Rosenthal, Eric. *Japan's Bid for Africa, Including the Story of the Madagascar Campaign.* Johannesburg: Central News Agency, 1944.

Rowlands, David J. "The Dress of 1st Battalion, 5th (Northumberland) (Fusiliers) Regiment of Foot in Mauritius 1856, and the Indian Mutiny 1857–59," *Journal of the Society for Army Historical Research* [London], 64, No. 260, 1986, 212–17.

Shepherd, George W., Jr. *The Trampled Grass: Tributary States and Self-Reliance in the Indian Ocean Zone of Peace.* New York: Praeger, 1987.

Sidhu, K.S. *The Indian Ocean: A Zone of Peace.* New Delhi: Harman, 1983.

*SIPRI Yearbook of World Armaments and Disarmament.* (Stockholm International Peace and Research Institute.) New York: Humanities Press, 1994.

Stockman, Jim. "Madagascar 1942—Part I: Prelude to Assault," *British Army Review,* 82, April 1986, 74–79.

Stockman, Jim. "Madagascar 1942—Part II: The Battle," *British Army Review,* 83, August 1986, 64–72.

*Strategic Survey 1993–94.* London: International Institute for Strategic Studies, 1994.

Tahtinen, Dale R. *Arms in the Indian Ocean: Interests and Challenges.* Washington: American Enterprise Institute for Public Policy Research, 1977.

Terrill, W. Andrew. "The Comoro Islands in South African Regional Strategy," *Africa Today,* 33, No. 2, 2d/3d quarters 1986, 59–70.

Thomson, Alvin. "The Role of Firearms and the Development of Military Techniques in Merina Warfare, c. 1785–1828," *Revue française d'histoire d'outre-mer* [Paris], 61, No. 224, 1974, 417–35.

Toussaint, Auguste. *History of the Indian Ocean.* Chicago: University of Chicago Press, 1961.

Tronchon, Jacques. *L'insurrection malagache de 1947.* Paris: Karthala, 1986.

Wall, Patrick. *The Indian Ocean and the Threat to the West.* London: Stacey International, 1975.

Wilson, W.J. (ed.). *U.S. Strategic Interests in the Gulf Region.* Boulder, Colorado: Westview Press, 1987.

(Various issues of the following publications also were used in the preparation of this chapter: *Africa Report; Africa Confidential* [London]; *African Defence Journal* [Paris]; *Africa News; Africa Research Bulletin* [Oxford, United Kingdom]; *Asian Defence Jour-*

*nal* [Kuala Lumpur]; *Cahiers des études africaines* [Paris]; *Focus on Africa* [London]; *Horn of Africa; Journal of Modern African Studies* [Cambridge]; *Keesing's Contemporary Archives* [Harlow, United Kingdom]; *New African* [London]; *New York Times; Round Table* [London]; *Strategic Analysis* [New Delhi]; and *United States Naval Institute Proceedings*.)

# Glossary

CFA—Communauté Financière d'Afrique (African Financial Community). The CFA covers those African countries whose currencies are linked with the French franc at a fixed rate of exchange.

Comoran franc (CF)—One Comoran franc = 100 centimes; in June 1995, US$1.00 = CF363.98.

crown colony—A colony of the British Commonwealth over which the crown maintains some control, as through appointment of the governor.

European Community (EC)—*See* European Union.

European Currency Unit (ECU)—Standard currency unit of the European Union (*q.v.*); in April 1995, ECU1 = US$0.75.

European Union (EU)—Formerly the European Community, it was established by the Maastricht Treaty of December 1991 to expand European cooperation from economic and commercial into monetary, security, and judicial matters. It officially came into being at the end of 1993.

exclusive economic zone (EEZ)—A wide belt of sea and seabed adjacent to the national boundaries where the state claims preferential fishing rights and control over the exploitation of mineral and other natural resources. Madagascar claims a 150-nautical-mile exclusive economic zone. Mauritius, Comoros, Seychelles, and Maldives all claim 200 nautical miles. Boundary situations with neighboring states sometimes prevent the extension of the exclusive economic zones to the full limits claimed.

fiscal year (FY)—Same as the calendar year for all except Mauritius, in which it runs from July 1 to June 30.

Franc Zone—A monetary union among countries whose currencies are linked to the French franc. Members are France and its overseas appendages and fourteen African countries, including Comoros.

gross domestic product (GDP)—A value measure of the flow of domestic goods and services produced by an economy over a period of time, such as a year. Only output values of goods for final consumption and intermediate production are assumed to be included in the final prices. GDP is sometimes aggregated and shown at market prices, meaning that indirect taxes and subsidies have been eliminated; the result is GDP at factor cost. The word "gross" indicates that deductions for depreciation of physical assets have not been made. *See also* gross national product.

gross national product (GNP)—Gross domestic product (*q.v.*) plus the net income or loss stemming from transactions with foreign countries. GNP is the broadest measurement of the output of goods and services by an economy. It can be calculated at market prices, which include indirect taxes and subsidies. Because indirect taxes and subsidies are only transfer payments, GNP is often calculated at factor cost, removing indirect taxes and subsidies.

import substitution—The replacement of imports by domestically produced goods, often supported by tariffs or import quotas, and motivated by foreign-exchange considerations.

International Development Association (IDA)—*See* World Bank.

International Finance Corporation (IFC)—*See* World Bank.

International Monetary Fund (IMF)—Established along with the World Bank (*q.v.*) in 1945, the IMF is a specialized agency affiliated with the United Nations and is responsible for stabilizing international exchange rates and payments. The main business of the IMF is the provision of loans to its members (including industrialized and developing countries) when they experience balance of payments difficulties. These loans frequently carry conditions that require substantial internal economic adjustments by the recipients, most of which are developing countries.

Lomé Convention—The first Lomé Convention (Lomé I) came into force in 1976. Lomé II came into effect in 1981, Lomé III in 1985, and Lomé IV in 1990. The convention covers economic relations between the members of the European Economic Community (EEC) and their former colonies in Africa, the Caribbean, and the Pacific (ACP). The convention allows most ACP exports to enter the EEC duty-free or at special rates and, among other things, provides funds through the Stabex system (*q.v.*) to offset adverse fluctuations in the prices of ACP exports.

London Club—An informal group of commercial banks that come together to negotiate a debt rescheduling agreement with a country. The group has two committees, an economics committee that develops economic data projections and a negotiating committee. Committee members usually come from the five principal banks that hold the largest amounts of a country's debt.

Malagasy franc (FMG)—1 Malagasy franc (franc malgache—FMG) = 100 centimes; in May 1995, US$1.00 = FMG4,236.9.

Mauritian rupee (MauR)—1 Mauritian rupee = 100 cents; in August 1995, US$1.00 = MauR14.43.

parastatal—A semi-autonomous, quasi-governmental, state-owned enterprise.

Paris Club—The informal name for a consortium of Western creditor countries (Belgium, Britain, Canada, France, Germany, Italy, Japan, the Netherlands, Sweden, Switzerland, and the United States) that have made loans or guaranteed export credits to developing nations and that meet in Paris to discuss borrowers' ability to repay debts. Paris Club deliberations often result in the tendering of emergency loans to countries in economic difficulty or in the rescheduling of debts. Formed in October 1962, the organization has no formal or institutional existence. Its secretariat is run by the French treasury. It has a close relationship with the International Monetary Fund (*q.v.*), to which all of its members except Switzerland belong, as well as with the World Bank (*q.v.*) and the United Nations Conference on Trade and Development (UNCTAD). The Paris Club is also known as the Group of Ten (G–10).

rufiyaa (Rf)—Maldives currency; 1 rufiyaa = 100 laari; in June 1995, US$1.00 = Rf11.77.

Seychelles rupee (SRe)—1 Seychelles rupee = 100 cents; in August 1995, US$1.00 = SRe4.25.

Shia (from Shiat Ali, the Party of Ali)—A member of the smaller of the two great divisions of Islam. The Shia supported the claims of Ali and his line to presumptive right to the caliphate and leadership of the Muslim community, and on this issue they divided from the Sunni (*q.v.*) in the major schism within Islam. Later schisms have produced further divisions among the Shia over the identity and number of imams. Most Shia revere Twelve Imams, the last of whom is believed to be hidden from view.

South Asian Association for Regional Cooperation (SAARC)—Comprises the seven nations of South Asia: Bangladesh, Bhutan, India, Maldives, Nepal, Pakistan, and Sri Lanka; founded as South Asian Regional Cooperation (SARC) organization at a meeting of foreign ministers in New Delhi on August 1–2, 1983; a second organizational meeting of foreign ministers was held in Thimphu in May 1985; inaugural meeting of heads of state and government in Dhaka on December 7–8, 1985. The goal is to effect economic, technical, and cultural cooperation and to provide a forum for discussions of South Asian political problems.

special drawing rights (SDRs)—Monetary units of the International Monetary Fund (*q.v.*) based on a basket of international currencies including the United States dollar, the German deutsche mark, the Japanese yen, the British pound sterling, and the French franc.

Stabex system—A system of export earnings stabilization set up by the European Community (EC—*q.v.*) in accordance with the African, Caribbean, and Pacific (ACP) states. The system helps developing countries withstand fluctuations in the price of their agricultural products by paying compensation for lost export earnings.

Sunni—The larger of the two great divisions of Islam. The Sunni, who rejected the claims of Ali's line, believe that they are the true followers of the sunna, the guide to proper behavior set forth by Muhammad's personal deeds and utterances. *See also* Shia.

World Bank—Informal name used to designate a group of four affiliated international institutions: the International Bank for Reconstruction and Development (IBRD), International Development Association (IDA), International Finance Corporation (IFC), and Multilateral Investment Guarantee Agency (MIGA). The IBRD, established in 1945, has the primary purpose of providing loans to developing countries for productive projects. The IDA, a legally separate loan fund but administered by the staff of the IBRD, was set up in 1960 to furnish credits to the poorest developing countries on much easier terms than those of conventional IBRD loans. The IFC, founded in 1956, supplements the activities of the IBRD through loans and assistance specifically designed to encourage the growth of productive private enterprises in the less developed countries. The MIGA, founded in 1988, insures private foreign investment in developing countries against various noncommercial risks. The president and certain senior officers of the IBRD hold the same positions in the IFC. The four institutions are owned by the governments of the countries that subscribe their capital. To participate in the World Bank group, member states must first belong to the International Monetary Fund (IMF—*q.v.*).

# Index

Aafathis, 282

Abdallah, Ahmed, 150, 151, 322; arrested, 152; assassination of, 146, 162–63, 324, 326; economic activities of, 156, 160, 162; exiled, 152; import-export firm of, 156; as president, 154, 156, 322, 323

Abdallah government (Comoros), 154–64; manipulation in, 157–58; opposition to, 156–57, 158–59, 160, 323–24; overthrown, 146, 152, 322, 323–24; women under, 177

abortion: in Maldives, 265; in Mauritius, 113; in Seychelles, 240

ACDH. See Comoran Association for Human Rights

acquired immune deficiency syndrome (AIDS): in Comoros, 180; in Madagascar, 54; in Seychelles, 223–24

Action Familiale (Mauritius), 113

Action Libérale. See Liberal Action

aeronaval forces of Madagascar, 299, 300; bases of, 300; missions of, 300; number of personnel in, 300

Aéroports de Madagascar, 73

Afghanistan: Soviet invasion of, 293

Africa: exports to, 72; influence of, on Comoros, 146

African Development Bank, xix, xxiv; aid to Comoros from, 161, 178, 196; education aid from, 117, 223

African Franc Zone (Communauté Financière Africaine—CFA), 184–85

African National Congress (ANC), 314

Africans: in Comoros, xxii; in Maldives, xxvi, 265

Agalega Islands (Mauritius), 108, 111

Agence Comores Presse, 181

agricultural: cooperatives, 56; policy, 58; production, 65–68

agricultural products (see also under individual crops): cassava, 67; cinnamon, 207, 209, 225, 231, 232, 237; cloves, xxii, 55, 58, 67–68, 145, 149, 161, 181, 184, 185, 186, 187; coffee, 55, 58, 67; of Comoros, 145; copra, 161, 186, 207, 209, 225, 231, 232, 237; cotton, 67; diversification of, 58; exports of, 65, 123, 184; flowers, xxi, 123; food crops, 185; of Madagascar, 55, 58, 62–64, 65–67; of Maldives, 273; of Mauritius, xxi, 110; rice, 62–64, 65–67; of Seychelles, 231, 232; sugarcane, xxi, 55, 97, 99, 100, 110, 112, 121; tea, xxi, 110, 122–23, 231, 232; tobacco, 123; vanilla, xxii, 55, 58, 67, 68, 145, 149, 161, 181, 184, 185, 186, 187, 209, 232; vegetables, xxi; ylang-ylang, xxii, 145, 149, 161, 181, 184, 185, 186

agricultural research, 12

agriculture, xviii; of Betsileo, 62–63; budget for, 61; cash crops, 55, 58; in Comoros, xxii, 185–87; employment in, 65, 212, 273; income from, xxii; in Madagascar, xviii, 21, 55, 58, 61, 62–65; on Mahoré, 168; in Maldives, xxvi, 273; in Mauritius, xxi, 121–21, 129; of Merina, 63–64; in Seychelles, 211, 212, 231–32; slash-and-burn, 62, 63–64

Ahmed, Mohamed: as president, 154, 322

AIDS. See acquired immune deficiency syndrome

Air Comores, xxiii, 188

air force: of Madagascar, 300; of Seychelles, 316

Air France, 73

Air Madagascar, 73

Air Maldives, 277

Air Mauritius, 127

air patrol (Mauritius), 311

airports: in Comoros, 188–90; on Hulele, 265; on Mahé, 210, 211; on Mahoré, 168; in Madagascar, 73; in Maldives, 277; in Mauritius, 127; in Seychelles, 210, 211, 216, 235, 235, 236

Air Seychelles, 226, 236

Aithnard, Ahlonkoba, 177

AKFM. See Congress Party for the Independence of Madagascar

al Adil, Muhammad, 258
al Barakat, Abu, 258
Aldabra Islands (Seychelles), 214
Alliance government (Mauritius), 107, 108
*Al Watwany*, 181
Ambohitra. *See* Montagne d'Ambre
Amirantes Isles (Seychelles), 214; fishing off, 232
Amnesty International, 160, 328
Amoco Oil Company, 233–34
ANC. *See* African National Congress
Andriamahazo, Gilles, 295–96
Andriamanalimbetany, 37
Andriamanjato, Richard, 16, 60
Andrianampoinimerina, 11; unification of Madagascar under, 11
Anglican Church: mission schools of, 221; in Seychelles, 220, 242
Anjafy High Plateaux (Madagascar), 24
Anjouan. *See* Nzwani
Ankaratra Massif (Madagascar), 24
Antaifasy people (Madagascar), 35
Antaimoro people (Madagascar), 34–35; language of, 40; literature of, 34, 40; as percentage of Madagascar population, 34
Antaisaka people (Madagascar), 35
Antakarana people (Madagascar), 38
Antalaotra people (Madagascar), 34
Antalote people (Madagascar), 173
Antambahoaka people (Madagascar), 34
Antananarivo (Madagascar): climate in, 28; French occupation of, 13; investment in, 61; location of, 24; protests in, 18, 21
Antandroy people (Madagascar), 10, 38
Antanosy people (Madagascar), 9, 35
Antigang Brigade (Madagascar), 300, 301, 304
Antokon'ny Kongresy Fanafahana an'i Madagasikara. *See* Congress Party for the Independence of Madagascar
Antsiranana (Madagascar): French control of, 297, 303; harbor at, 27, 79; investment in, 61; port of, 24, 73
Aqualma (Madagascar), 68
Arab Bank for Economic Development in Africa: aid to Comoros from, 161, 186, 196
Arab Fund for Economic and Social Development, 196

Arabic Islamic Education Center (Maldives), 270
Arabic language, 114; broadcasts in, 181; classical, 173, 178
Arab Intercontinental Bank: loans from, 62
Arabs: clans, 173; in Comoros, xxii, 173; influence of, on Comoros, 146; in Maldives, xxvi, 265; Shirazi, 147, 149, 173
Arab states: aid to Comoros from, 156, 161, 323; aid to Maldives from, 279; relations of, with Comoros, 196
Arab traders: in Comoros, 145, 147; in Madagascar, 9; in Maldives, 258–59; in Mauritius, 98; in Seychelles, 207
archaeological research: in Maldives, 257–58; on Nzwani, 146
Arema. *See* Vanguard of the Malagasy Revolution
armed forces of Comoros, 325–26; aviation unit, 325; Commando Moissy, 153; French control of, 192; matériel of, 325; morale, 325–26; mutiny in, 324; number of personnel in, 325; political role of, 325; under Soilih, 153; training, 325
armed forces of Madagascar (*see also* aeronaval forces; army), 296–300; budget for, 61, 298–99; civic-action projects of, 298, 306; conscription of, 299; ethnic tensions in, 19; factions in, 298; matériel of, 299–300; modernization of, 11; morale of, 301–2; number of personnel in, 299; officers in, 299; reorganization of, 298; role of, 299; training of, 301–6
armed forces of Maldives, 329–30
armed forces of Mauritius, 309–10
armed forces of Seychelles, 314, 315, 316–18; created, 315; matériel of, 316; mercenaries in, 318; morale of, 319; mutiny in, 315; training of, 246, 319
army of Comoros: mutiny in, 324; Tanzanian advisers in, 326
army of Madagascar: matériel of, 299–300; number of personnel in, 299; role of, 299; rule by, 18–19
army of Seychelles, 318–19; number of personnel in, 318
Asia: trade with, 72, 135
Asian Development Bank, 278, 282; aid

to Maldives from, 279

Assembly of Mauritian Workers (Rassemblement des Travaillistes Mauriciens—RTM), 107–8

Association Comorienne des Droits Humains. *See* Comoran Association for Human Rights

Association for the National Interest in Agricultural Products (Société d'Intérêt National des Produits Agricoles—SINPA) (Madagascar), 66

Atlantic Charter (1941), 14

Atokin'ny Revolisiona Malagasy. *See* Vanguard of the Malagasy Revolution

Australasian people: in Maldives, xxvi, 265

Australia, 287; in Indian Ocean conference, xxi; relations of, with Madagascar, 85; relations of, with Seychelles, xxv; trade of, with Madagascar, 85


Bahrain: trade of, with Seychelles, 237

Baie d'Antongil (Madagascar), 23

Baker, Philip, 115

balance of payments: in Comoros, 182; deficits, 58., 120; in Madagascar, 58, 61–62; in Mauritius, 120, 125

balance of power, xvii

Bangladesh: relations of, with Seychelles, 245, 246

Bank for Industry and Commerce (Banque pour l'Industrie et le Commerce—BIC) (Comoros), 185

banking: in Comoros, 185; in Madagascar, 21, 60; in Maldives, 274–75; in Mauritius, 124; in Seychelles, 224

Bank of Ceylon, 276

Bank of Maldives, Limited, 276

Bank of Mauritius, 124

Banque Centrale des Comores. *See* Central Bank of Comoros

Banque de Développement des Comores. *See* Development Bank of Comoros

Banque Nationale d'Algérie, 62

Banque Nationale de Paris, 62

Banque Nationale de Paris-Internationale. *See* National Bank of Paris-International

Banque pour l'Industrie et le Commerce. *See* Bank for Industry and Commerce

Bantu people (Comoros), 146–47

Bara people (Madagascar), 37–38; livestock of, 64; as percentage of Madagascar population, 37; social structure of, 49

Barclays Bank, 124

Battle of the Java Sea (1942), 289

Beau Bassin-Rose Hill (Mauritius), 112; government of, 130

Belgium: trade with, 184

Bell, H.C.P., 257–58

Bemarivo River (Madagascar), 27

Bérenger, Paul, 106, 107, 132; assassination attempt on, 106

Berlouis, Ogilvy, 314

Betanimena people (Madagascar), 33

Betsiboka River (Madagascar), 27

Betsileo people (Madagascar), 11, 32, 37; agriculture of, 62–63; attitudes of, toward dead, 43; education of, 52; occupations of, 37; as percentage of Madagascar population, 37; religion of, 45; slave descendants among, 49

Betsimisaraka kingdom (Madagascar), 10

Betsimisaraka people (Madagascar), 33, 35, 148; etymology of, 34; origins of, 34; as percentage of Madagascar population, 33

Bexanozano people (Madagascar), 35

Bhojpuri language: broadcasts in, 117; as language of instruction, 116–17; in Mauritius, 114, 115

BIC. *See* Bank for Industry and Commerce

BIC Afribank (Comoros), 185

Biodiversity Conservation and Marine Pollution Abatement, 214

BIOT. *See* British Indian Ocean Territory

birth control. *See* family planning

black market: in Madagascar, 142

Black River District (Mauritius), 110

Blood, Sir Hilary, 104

Boina kingdom (Madagascar), 10

Boky Mena (Red Book). *See* *Charter of the Malagasy Socialist Revolution*

Boodhoo, Harish, 107

Boullé, Philippe, 240

Bourdonnais, Mahé de la, 99

Bourgeaud, Gilbert. *See* Denard, Bob

Bowman, Larry W., 121

Brazzaville Conference (1944), 14
Britain, 288; aid from, to Seychelles, 211, 246; air base of, in Maldives, 257, 260, 261, 277, 282, 329; and attempted coups in Seychelles, 314; education in, 116, 222; exploration by, 9, 287, 288; investment by, 124; matériel from, 297, 312; Mauritius awarded to, 100, 148; military interests of, 287, 325; military intervention by, 11, 309–10; military presence of, 259–60, 290–93; military training provided by, 312; occupation of Maldives by, 259; occupation of Rodrigues by, 148; relations of, with Madagascar, 80, 83; relations of, with Maldives, xxvi, 257, 282; relations of, with Mauritius, xxi, 132; relations of, with Seychelles, xxiv, 213; Seychelles awarded to, 100, 148; tourists from, 235, 274; trade of, with Maldives, 279; trade of, with Mauritius, 125; trade of, with Seychelles, 237
British American Tobacco, 123
British Broadcasting Corporation, 283
British East India Company, 208
British Indian Ocean Territory (BIOT), 105, 210, 290
British rule: of Madagascar, 289; of Mauritius, 97, 102–5; of Seychelles, 148, 207, 208
Brunei: aid from, to Maldives, 268
Buddhism, 114, 258; in Seychelles, 220
budget. *See* under government budget

Cafre people (Comoros), 173
Caisse Centrale de Coopération Économique. *See* Central Bank for Economic Cooperation
CAM. *See* Committee for Muslim Action
Canal des Pangalanes (Lakandranon' Ampalangalana) (Madagascar), 23–24
Cantonese language, 114
Cap d'Ambre (Tanjon' i Bobaomby) (Madagascar), 24
Cargados Crajos Shoals (Mauritius), 108, 111
Carter, Jimmy, 293
Cassim, Ali Bakar, 181
Catholic Church, Roman: French language in, 218; mission schools of, 221; in Seychelles, 240, 242, 243

Catholics, Roman: in Comoros, 173; conflicts of, with Protestants, 15; in Madagascar, 45; in Mauritius, 114, 115; in Seychelles, 220
CCCE. *See* Central Bank for Economic Cooperation
censorship: in Madagascar, 19, 20, 295; in Maldives, 282, 283; in Seychelles, 212
Central Bank for Economic Cooperation (Caisse Centrale de Coopération Économique—CCCE) (France), 185
Central Bank of Comoros (Banque Centrale des Comores), 185
Central Bank of Seychelles, 230
Central Bank of the Malagasy Republic, xix, 60
central highlands of Madagascar, 23, 24, 33; climate of, 28; conflict of, with *côtiers*, 32, 75; elevation of, 24; peoples of, 36–38; schools in, 52
Central Housing Authority (Mauritius), 118
Ceylon, 287
Ceylon Civil Service, 257
CFA. *See* African Franc Zone
Chagos Archipelago, 107, 108, 135
*Charter of the Malagasy Socialist Revolution* (Red Book), 19–20
Chase Manhattan Bank of Paris: loans from, 62
Chebani, Haribou, 164
Cheik, Said Mohamed, 150, 173; death of, 151
Cheikh, Mustapha Said, 160, 192
Chemin Grenier (Mauritius), 110
children: child-care for, 120; diets of, 179–80; immunization of, 179
Chile, 311
China, 287
China, People's Republic of: assistance to Madagascar from, 82, 196; economic relations of, with Seychelles, 247; matériel from, 304; military training by, 306; relations of, with Comoros, 156, 196; relations of, with Madagascar, 81; relations of, with Mauritius, 135; trade of, with Mauritius, 125
China, Republic of (Taiwan): trade with, 125
Chinese people: languages of, 115; in

Madagascar, 39; in Mauritius, 101, 104, 113, 114, 126, 129; occupations of, 115; as percentage of population in Mauritius, 101–2, 113; in Seychelles, 208, 217
Christians: in Madagascar, 45, 46
chromium: in Madagascar, 70
cinnamon, 207, 209, 232
Civil Police (Madagascar). *See* police (Madagascar)
civil rights: in Seychelles, 243–44
civil servants: in Comoros, 149, 153, 182; in Madagascar, 18
civil service: of Comoros, 161, 162, 179, 195; of Maldives, 276; of Seychelles, 229
Civil Service (militia) (Madagascar), 300, 301
climate: of Comoros, 170–71; cyclones, 28, 111, 170–71, 216; of Madagascar, 28–29; of Maldives, 263–64; of Mauritius, 111; monsoons, 263, 264; rainfall, 28, 111, 216, 263, 264; seasons, 28, 111, 170, 263; of Seychelles, 216; temperature, 111, 170, 216, 263
cloves, xxii, 55, 58, 67–68, 145, 149, 161, 181, 184, 185, 186, 187
coast guard (Mauritius), 311
coast guard (Seychelles), 316–18; air wing, 316, 319; navy wing, 316–18
coastline: of Madagascar, 23, 24
Coetivy Island (Seychelles), 214
Cold War, 287, 289–94
Collectivités Territoriales Décentralisees. *See* Decentralized Territorial Authorities
Colombo Plan, 282
Comité d'Action Musulmane. *See* Committee for Muslim Action
Comité des Forces Vives (Vital Forces Committee—Forces Vives) (Madagascar), 22, 296; in elections of 1993, xix, 22, 76
Comité National de Salut Public. *See* National Committee for Public Safety
Commando Moissy (Comoros), 153, 322, 326
Committee for Muslim Action (Comité d'Action Musulmane—CAM) (Mauritius): in elections of 1959, 104
Common Agricultural Policy, 121
Common Declaration (1973) (Como-

ros), 151–52
Commonwealth of Nations: Maldives in, xxvi, 282; Mauritius in, xxi; Seychelles in, 245
Communauté Financière Africaine. *See* African Franc Zone
communications. *See* telecommunications
Community Development Support Fund, 170
Comoran Association for Human Rights (Association Comorienne des Droits Humains—ACDH), 194
Comoran Meat Company (Société Comorienne des Viandes—Socovia), 182
Comoran Navigation Company (Société Comorienne de Navigation), 190
Comorans: in France, 172; in Madagascar, 39, 46, 172; religion of, 46; in Tanzania, 172
Comoran Swahili, 171, 172; broadcasts in, 181
Comoran Union for Progress (Union Comorienne pour le Progrès—UCP), 157, 193, 195
Comoros: archaeological research in, 146; etymology of, 145; in Indian Ocean Commission, 134; integration of Mahoré into, 145; land area of, 169; location of, 145, 168; migration from, 149
Comoros Democratic Union (Union Démocratique des Comores—UDC), 150; platform of, 150
Congress Party for the Independence of Madagascar (Antokon'ny Kongresy Fanafahana an'i Madagasikara—AKFM), 16; platform, 16; political base of, 17
Conserveries de l'Océan Indien, xxiv
Constituent Assembly of the Fourth Republic (France): representatives from Madagascar to, 13–14
constitutional convention (Comoros), 193
constitutional convention (Seychelles), 239
constitution of Comoros (1961), 150
constitution of Comoros (1978), 154–56, 190; amendments to, 158; women under, 176

constitution of Comoros (1992), xxii, 190–92, 193; human rights under, 190; Islam under, 190; judiciary under, 191–92; legislature under, xxii, 191; president under, xxii, 190; prime minister under, xxii; women under, 176

constitution of Madagascar (1992), xviii, 74–77; approved, 22, 75; executive branch under, 75; individual rights under, 76; legislature under, 75–76; president under, 75; prime minister under, 75

constitution of Maldives (1932), 259

constitution of Maldives (1968), xxvi, 279–80; amendments to, 260; rights under, 280

constitution of Mauritius (1831), 102

constitution of Mauritius (1958), 104

constitution of Mauritius (1968), 129–31; legislature under, 129–30; president under, 130; rights under, 129

constitution of Seychelles (1967), 210

constitution of Seychelles (1970), 210

constitution of Seychelles (1979), 212, 321, 238; legislature under, 238; president under, 238

constitution of Seychelles (1993), xxv, 207, 238, 240

construction: in Mahoré, 168; in Mauritius, 112, 124, 129; in Seychelles, xxv, 211, 224

consultative committee (Mauritius), 104

copra, 161, 186, 207, 209, 217, 232, 237

corruption: in Madagascar, 66

*côtiers*, (Madagascar) 10; conflict of, with Merina, 15, 19, 32, 75; political affiliations of, 17; religion of, 45

Council of Christian Churches (Madagascar), 46

Council of Government (Comoros), 191

Council of Government (Mauritius), 102

Council of Ministers (Mauritius), 104

coups d'état (Comoros): of 1975, 146, 152, 154, 322; of 1978, 146, 322; of 1989, 146, 164

coups d'état (Maldives): of 1975, 260

coups d'état (Seychelles): of 1977, 207, 212–13, 237, 242

coups d'état, attempted (Comoros), 322, 324; of 1981, 157; of 1983, 324; of 1985, 160, 324; of 1987, 324; of 1989, 324; of 1990, 324, 328; of 1992, xxiii, 193–94, 324–25, 328

coups d'état, attempted (Madagascar): of 1974, 19, 295; of 1989, 296; of 1990, 296; of 1992, 296

coups d'état, attempted (Maldives): of 1980, 261, 328–29; of 1983, 261, 329; of 1988, 261, 261–62, 282, 329

coups d'état, attempted (Seychelles), 212; mercenaries in, 212, 313–14; of 1977, 314; of 1978, 314–15; of 1979, 313; of 1981, 212, 313, 320; of 1986, 314; of 1987, 314

courts: of Comoros, 191–92, 327; of Madagascar, 76, 307; of Maldives, 280, 330; of Mauritius, 130, 312; of Seychelles, 243, 321

Creole language: as language of instruction, 116–17, 221; literature, 218; in Mauritius, 97, 100, 114, 115; popular view of, 115; in Seychelles, xxiv, 217–18; structure of, 218

Creole people: in Comoros, xxii, 173; in Mauritius, xx, 97, 101, 102, 103, 105, 114, 309; occupations of, 115; political affiliations of, 105; religion of, 114, 173; social status of, 102, 103; tensions of, with Indians, 97, 309

crime: in Seychelles, 244

Crusade for Democracy (Seychelles), 242

Cuba: assistance to Madagascar from, 82; military training by, 302, 304; relations of, with Seychelles, 245

Curé, Maurice, 103

Curepipe (Mauritius), 112; government of, 130

currency: of Comoros, xxiii, 184–85; of Madagascar, xix, 58; of Maldives, 257, 258, 274; of Mauritius, 102, 120, 124; of Seychelles, 225

current account: deficit, 58, 61–62, 279; in Madagascar, 58, 61–62; in Maldives, 278

customs duties: in Madagascar, xix

Cyclone Geralda, 29, 67

Cyclone Hollanda, 111

cyclones: in Comoros, 146, 170–71, 186, 190; in Madagascar, 28, 29; in Mauritius, 111, 121, 123; in Seychelles, 216

d'Albuquerque, Alfonso, 288

Debré, Michel, 165

debt. *See* foreign debt

Decentralized Territorial Authorities (Collectivités Territoriales Décentralisées), 76, 78

Defence Forces Council, 316

defense spending: in Comoros, 325; in Madagascar, 61; in Seychelles, 228, 319

de Gaulle, Charles, 16

de Hell, Admiral, 148

de Klerk, Frederik Willem, 134, 294

Democratic Assembly of the Comoran People (Rassemblement Démocratique du Peuple Comorien—RDPC), 150; platform of, 150

Democratic Front (Front Démocratique—FD) (Comoros), 160

Democratic Movement for the Malagasy Restoration (Mouvement Démocratique de la Rénovation Malgache—MDRM): outlawed, 15; platform of, 14; political base of, 14

Democratic Party (DP) (Seychelles), 207, 210; platform of, 210, 211

democracy movement, 9, 238–40, 304, 308

demonstrations. *See* political demonstrations

Denard, Bob, 154; and assassination of Abdallah, 164, 324; in coups, 154, 164, 322, 323, 324; economic activities of, 156, 160, 162; expelled, 164, 192, 324; in Presidential Guard, 159, 327; rewards for, 154; withdrawal of, 154

Department of Information and Telecommunications (Seychelles), 243

Department of Military Engineering for National Development (Madagascar), 306

Development Bank of Comoros (Banque de Développement des Comores), 185

Development Bank of Mauritius, 124

Development Bank of Seychelles, 226

Development Company for Small-Scale Fisheries of Comoros (Société de Développement de la Pêche Artisanale des Comores), 187

Development Works Corporation (DWC) (Mauritius), 106

Dhivehi language, 266; broadcasts in, 283; as language of instruction, 269, 270; newspapers in, 282

Didi, Abdulla Afif, 260

Didi, Muhammad Amin: death of, 259; overthrown, 259; as president, 259; as prime minister, 259; reforms under, 259

Didi, Muhammad Farid, 260

Diego Garcia, 108, 290; United States military base on, xxi, 107, 80, 245, 290, 293–94

Diégo Suarez. *See* Antsiranana

diet: in Comoros, 146, 179–80; in Maldives, 271; in Mauritius, 118; in Seychelles, 223, 232

Direction Générale de l'Information et de la Documentation, Intérieure et Extérieure. *See* General Directorate of Information and Documentation, Internal and External

discrimination: in Seychelles, xxv

district councils (Mauritius), 103

divorce: in Comoros, 176; in Maldives, 267; in Seychelles, 219

Djohar, Said Mohamed, xxii–xxiii, 164, 166, 324

Djohar government (Comoros), xxiii, 324; women under, 177

Djoussouf, Abbas, 195

Doctor, Manilal Maganlall, 103

DP. *See* Democratic Party

Dravidian people (Maldives), xxvi, 265

drought: in Madagascar, 67; in Mauritius, 121

drug abuse: in Mauritius, 118; in Seychelles, 223

drug trafficking, 287; in Comoros, 180; in Mauritius, 108, 134, 310, 312

Duval, Gaetan: in elections of 1963, 104

DWC. *See* Development Works Corporation

Dzaoudzi (Comoros), 169; population of, 172

East Coast Development Plan (Seychelles), 229

east coast of Madagascar, 23–24, 33; climate of, 28; elevation of, 23; peoples of, 33–35; topography of, 23

East Germany. *See* German Democratic Republic

EC. *See* European Community

École le Myre de Villers, 50
economic development: in Comoros, xxii, xxiii, 156; in Madagascar, 20; in Maldives, 272–73; in Mauritius, xxi, 106; in Seychelles, 229
economic growth: in Comoros, 182; in Madagascar, xix; in Mauritius, xx, 120; in Seychelles, 224
economic planning (*see also under individual plans*): in Madagascar, 20; in Maldives, 273; in Mauritius, 106
economic policy: of Madagascar, 55–58; of Seychelles, 226–28
economic reform: in Comoros, xxiii; in Madagascar, 21, 59
economy (Comoros), 181–88; South Africa in, 159, 188; structural adjustment, 182, 193
economy (Madagascar), xviii, 55–72; French domination of, 55–56; government control of, 20; government intervention in, 55–58; under Ratsiraka, 20, 56, 60; structural adjustment, 56, 58–60, 66; under Tsiranana, 18, 18; under Zafy, 57
economy (Maldives), 261, 272–77
economy (Mauritius), xx, 120–26; diversification of, 120; structural adjustment, 128
economy (Seychelles), 224–35; diversification of, 224; government role in, 225–28
education (*see also* schools) (Comoros), 178–79; abroad, 178; higher, 178; loans for, 178, 184; quality of, 178
education (*see also* schools) (Madagascar), 50–53; access to, 51, 52; budget for, 51, 61; French, 50; for girls, 52; investment in, 59; language of, 52–53; spread of, 12
education (*see also* schools) (Maldives), 269–71; abroad, 269; aid for, 270–71; budget for, 269; language of, 269; reforms in, 259
education (*see also* schools) (Mauritius), 106, 115–17; budget for, 116, 128; foreign, 116; importance of, 117
education (*see also* schools) (Seychelles), 221–23; abroad, 79, 81; access to, 212; aid for, 222; budgets for, 228; of girls, 219; government spending on, xxv; languages of, 221, 79; workers in, xxv

Education Master Plan, 117
EEZ. *See* exclusive economic zone
Egypt, 287, 293
elections in Comoros, 190, 325; abuse of, 162; for National Assembly, 157; of 1957, 150; of 1958, 150; of 1978, 323; of 1982, 157; of 1983, 157, 159; of 1987, 157, 159; of 1989, 162; of 1990, 192–93; of 1992, 193, 194; of 1993, 194
elections in Madagascar, 21, 75; for *fokonolona*, 20; of 1975, 19, 21; of 1977, 20; of 1982, 21; of 1989, 21; of 1992, 22, 296; of 1993, xviii, 77, 296; for National Assembly, xix, 22, 76; for National Representative Assembly, 14; Ratsiraka in, 21; voter turnout in, 22
elections in Maldives, 280; of 1983, 261; of 1988, 261; of 1993, 261
elections in Mauritius, 105; of 1911, 103; of 1948, 104; of 1959, 104; of 1963, 104; of 1967, 105; of 1976, 107; of 1983, 107; of 1987, 108; of 1991, 108, 131; of 1995, xxi; observers in, 105
elections in Seychelles: irregularities in, xxv; in 1974, 211; in 1979, 212, 237; in 1984, 237; in 1989, 237; in 1993, xxv, 207, 237, 240
Electoral College (Comoros), xxii
electric power: hydro, 71, 127; in Madagascar, 71; in Mauritius, 127
elite class: in Comoros, 148, 149, 173–74; education of, 53; in Madagascar, 15, 36; in Maldives, 266–67; markers of, 174; in Mauritius, 102; Merina as, 15
Elizabeth II, 132
employment: in agriculture, 65, 212, 273; in civil service, 277; in construction, 124; in fishing, 212, 225, 277; in industry, 277; in Maldives, 273, 276–77; in manufacturing, 234; in Mauritius, 120, 124, 125, 126; in mining, 277; in service sector, 211; in Seychelles, 212, 224, 229–31; in telecommunications, 277; in tourism, 125, 224, 234, 277; in trade, 276; in transportation, 276
English language: broadcasts in, 117, 283; as language of instruction, 115, 116–17, 221, 270; in Mauritius, xx, 100, 115; newspapers in, 282; popular view of, 115; in Seychelles, xxiv, 217, 218

Enterprise Oil Company (British), 234
Environmental Protection Act (1991) (Mauritius), 112
EPZs. *See* export processing zones
Établissements Abdallah et Fils (Comoros), 160, 162, 181, 187
Établissements Grimaldi (French), 181
ethnic diversity, xviii
ethnic groups (*see also under individual groups*): in Comoros, xxii; in Madagascar, xviii, 30–39; in Maldives, 265–66; marriage between, 208–9; in Mauritius, xx, 97, 105, 113–15; occupations of, 115; in Seychelles, 208, 217; tensions among, 14, 19, 31–32, 97, 105; violence among, 105
ethnic minorities: in Madagascar, 38–39
European Common Market, 84
European Community (EC): aid to Comoros from, 156, 161, 323; in Seychelles EEZ, 233
European Development Bank: Mauritius in, 135
European Development Fund: aid to Comoros from, 162, 184, 186
European Investment Bank
Europeans: in Comoros, 172; in Mauritius, xx, 114, 309; in Seychelles, 217; trade with, 10, 147
Evangelical Protestant churches: in Seychelles, 220
exchange rate: in Comoros, 185; in Maldives, 274; in Mauritius, 124; in Seychelles, 225
exclusive economic zone (EEZ), 287; of Mauritius, 108, 134, 312; of Seychelles, 213, 224, 233, 246
Executive Committee (Mauritius), 104
export processing zones (EPZs), xviii; in Madagascar, xviii, 59, 69–70; in Mauritius, xxi, 106, 118, 120, 123–24, 125, 126, 129; in Seychelles, xxv
exports (*see also under individual products*): from Comoros, xxiii, 147–48, 161, 184; earnings from, 161; from Madagascar, 65, 68, 71, 72; from Maldives, 259; from Mauritius, xxi, 122, 123, 125; from Seychelles, 207, 208, 237

families: in Maldives, 267

family planning: in Comoros, 172, 177; in Madagascar, 59; in Maldives, 264, 265; in Mauritius, 106, 112–13; in Seychelles, 217
FAO. *See* United Nations Food and Agriculture Organization
farms: size of, in Madagascar, 65
Faradofay. *See* Tôlanaro
Fayences Mountain (Mauritius), 110
FD. *See* Democratic Front
Federal Assembly (Comoros): under constitution of 1992, xxii, 191
Federal Republic of Germany. *See* Germany, Federal Republic of
Fenerive (Madagascar), 34
Fianarantsoa (Madagascar): investment in, 61
finance: in Seychelles, xxv
First Republic (Madagascar) (1960–72), 16–18; language policy of, 41
First Republic (Maldives) (1953–54), 259
fishing: in Comoros, 153, 187; employment in, 212, 233; exports, 68, 207, 259, 237; in Madagascar, xviii, 64–65; in Maldives, xxvi, 267, 273–74, 278; in Mauritius, 123; in Seychelles, 207, 211, 212, 214, 224–25, 226, 232–33
Fishing Development Company (Seychelles), 226
Flacq District (Mauritius), 110
flora and fauna: in Comoros, 170, 214; conservation of, 214–16; in Madagascar, 29–30, 71; in Mahoré, 170; in Maldives, 263; unique species of, 29, 30, 214
FNDR. *See* National Front for the Defense of the Revolution
FNUK-Unikom. *See* United National Front of Comorans-Union of Comorans
*fokonolona* (village council) (Madagascar), 10–11, 20, 77–79; role of, 78–79
Fomboni (Comoros), 169; harbor at, 190
food: import of, xxii, 66, 145, 162, 181, 184, 185–87, 209, 231, 279; production, 100, 145, 149, 185, 224, 231; self-sufficiency in, 58; shortages, 14, 21, 146, 153, 259; subsidies for, 120, 123
Forces Armée Populaires. *See* armed forces of Madagascar
Force de Police Nationale. *See* National Police Force

Force Républicaine de Sécurité. *See* Republican Security Force

Forces Armées Populaires. *See* People's Armed Forces

Forces Vives. *See* Comité des Forces Vives

foreign assistance (Comoros): from African Development Bank, 161, 178; from Arab Bank for Economic Development in Africa, 161, 186; from Arab states, 156, 161, 323; dependence on, 145–46, 182; for education, 178; from European Community, 156, 161, 323; from European Development Fund, 162, 184, 186; for family planning, 177; from France, 145, 161, 180, 182, 184, 186; for health, 180; from International Fund for Agricultural Development, 162, 186; from Iraq, 323; from Kuwait, 323; from Organization of the Petroleum Exporting Countries, 178; from Saudi Arabia, 323; from South Africa, 161; from United Nations Development Programme, 184, 186; from United States, 184, 186; from World Bank, 161; from World Food Program, 186

foreign assistance (Madagascar), 84; from China, 82; from Cuba, 82; from European Common Market, 84; from France, xx, 83, 84; from Germany, 84; from International Monetary Fund, 84; from Japan, 84; reforms demanded for, 21; from the United States, 84

foreign assistance (Mahoré): from France, 145

foreign assistance (Maldives), 279; from Arab states, 279; from Asian Development Bank, 279; from Brunei, 268; from India, 279; from Japan, 270–71, 279; from Kuwait, 279; from Malaysia, 268; from Pakistan, 268, 279; from Persian Gulf states, 268; from Saudi Arabia, 279; from United Arab Emirates, 279; from United Nations, 279; from United States, 279; from World Bank, 279

foreign assistance (Mauritius): from France, 132–33

foreign assistance (Seychelles): from Britain, 211, 246; for education, 222–23; from France, 246; from Soviet Union, 246; from Tanzania, 212; from United States, 246; from World Bank, 229

foreign debt: of Comoros, xxiii, 146, 182; of Madagascar, 56, 61–62

foreign exchange: earnings, 234; problems, 236

foreign investment: in Mauritius, xxii, 124; in Seychelles, 211

foreign policy: of Madagascar, 20, 85–86

foreign relations (Comoros), 195–96; with Arab states, 196; with China, 156, 196; with France, xxiii, 195, 322, 323; with Israel, xxiii; with Japan, 196; with Kuwait, 196; with Libya, 156; with Madagascar, 154; with Nigeria, 156; with Persian Gulf states, 156; with Saudi Arabia, 196; with South Africa, 195–96; with Tanzania, 156

foreign relations (Madagascar), 79–86; with Australia, xx; with Comoros, 154; with France, 12, 79; with India, xx; with South Africa, xx, 294; with United States, 80, 83, 306

foreign relations (Maldives), 282; with Britain, xxvi, 282

foreign relations (Mauritius), 132–35; with Britain, xxi, 132; with France, xxi, 132–33; with India, 132, 134; with South Africa, 132, 134; with United States, xxi, 134

foreign relations (Seychelles), 245–47

forests: exploitation of, 29, 111–12, 187, 208; fuelwood from, 30, 170; rain, 29–30, 169

Forum for National Recovery (Forum pour le Redressement National—FRN) (Comoros), 194

Forum pour le Redressement National. *See* Forum for National Recovery

France, Anatole, 13

France, 288–89; aid to Comoros from, 145, 160, 161, 180, 182,187; aid to Madagascar from, xx, 62, 83, 84; aid to Mahoré from, 145; aid to Mauritius from, 132–33; aid to Seychelles from, 246; and attempted coups in Seychelles, 314; Comorans in, 172; dependence of Comoros on, xxiii; education in, 116, 222; exploration by, 9, 287, 288; influences of, 79; investment by, 124; matériel from, 298, 312;

military assistance from, 302, 321, 326; military exercises of, 302; military interests of, 287, 294, 325; military intervention by, in Comoros, 195, 324, 325, 326, 327; military relations of, with Comoros, 195, 325–27; military relations of, with Madagascar, 79, 303; military relations of, with Mauritius, 133; military training by, 298, 301, 303, 304, 312, 325, 326; occupation of Diégo Suarez by, 297; occupation of Madagascar by, 297; occupation of Mahoré by, 149; relations of, with Comoros, xxiii, 152, 154, 156, 195, 322, 323; relations of, with Madagascar, 12, 16–17, 79, 83, 303–4; relations of, with Mahoré, 145; relations of, with Mauritius, xxi, 132–33; relations of, with Seychelles, xxiv, 213; study in, 79; tourists from, 125, 235; trade of, with Comoros, 160, 184; trade of, with Madagascar, xx, 71, 72; trade of, with Mauritius, 125; trade of, with Seychelles, 237

Franco-Mauritians, 102; social status of, 102

Franc Zone, 79

French: investment by, 70; in Comoros, 181; in Madagascar, 39, 55–56; in Mauritius, 114, 115; occupations of, 115; in Seychelles, xxiv

French Aid and Cooperation Fund, 184

French East India Company, 99

French Foreign Legion: in Mahoré, 165

French language: broadcasts in, 73, 115, 117, 118, 181, 218; in Comoros, 173, 181; as language of instruction, 79, 117, 222; in Madagascar, 41, 52, 79; in Mauritius, 97, 100, 115, 132; popular view of, 115; publications in, 79, 117; in Seychelles, 217, 218

French League for Madagascar, 13

French Military Academy at St. Cyr, 302

French rule (Comoros), 145, 147, 148–52

French rule (Madagascar), 12–16, 149; declared, 12, 13, 297; education under, 50; Merina under, 36; opposition to, 13, 15

French rule (Mauritius), 97, 148; origins of, 99

French rule (Seychelles), 148, 207, 208;

declared, 208

French settlements: in Madagascar, 9, 148

French Union: Madagascar as overseas territory of, 14

FRN. *See* Forum for National Recovery

Front National pour la Défense de la Révolution. *See* National Front for the Defense of the Revolution

Front Démocratique. *See* Democratic Front

Front National Uni des Komoriens-Union des Komoriens. *See* United National Front of Comorans-Union of Comorans

FRS. *See* Republican Security Force

Fua Mulaku Island (Maldives), 263

fuel: bagasse, 71, 127; wood, 30, 170

Galawa Beach (Comoros), 188

Gallieni, Joseph, 297

Gan Island (Maldives): airport on, 277; British air base on, 257, 260, 261, 277, 282, 329

Gandhi, Mohandas K., 103

Gandhi, Rajiv, 261

Garde Présidentielle. *See* Presidential Guard

GATT. *See* General Agreement on Tariffs and Trade

Gayoom, Maumoon Abdul, xxvi; cabinet of, 281; in elections of 1983, 261; in elections of 1988, 261; in elections of 1993, 261; as president, xxvi, 261, 328–29, 281; reform under, 281

GDP. *See* gross domestic product

General Agreement on Tariffs and Trade (GATT), 121

General Directorate of Information and Documentation, Internal and External (Direction Générale de l'Information et de la Documentation, Intérieure et Extérieure) (Madagascar), 301

geostrategic situation, 288–90; of Comoros, 146; of Madagascar, 9; of Maldives, 257, 258, 330

German Democratic Republic (East Germany): military training by, 301, 302; relations of, with Seychelles, 245

Germany: aid from, 62, 84; colonies of,

289; investment by, 124; military assistance from, 304; relations of, with Madagascar, 80; tourists from, 235, 274; trade with, 71, 72, 125, 184

Germany, Federal Republic of (West Germany): military assistance from, 303

Giraavaru people (Maldives), 265

Global Environment Trust Fund of the World Bank, 214

GMP. *See* Mobile Police Group

GNP. *See* gross national product

gold: in Madagascar, 70

Gooyer, Cornelius Simonsz, 98

Governing Council (Comoros), 150

government (Comoros): structure of, 190–92

government (Madagascar): participation in, xviii; structure of, 74–77

government (Maldives): factions in, 280–81; structure of, 279–80

government (Mauritius): control of media, xxii; structure of, 129–31; and women's rights, 119–20

government (Seychelles): role of, in economy, 225–28; structure of, 238–40

government, local (Madagascar), 77–78

government, local (Mauritius), 130–31; under British rule, 102–3

government budget (Comoros): deficit, 184; freeze on, xxiii

government budget (Madagascar): for agriculture, 61; austerity, xix; for defense, 61, 298–99; deficit, 58, 59; for education, 51, 61; for health care, 54, 61

government budget (Maldives): deficit, 276; for education, 269; revenues, 276

government budget (Mauritius), 127–29; for debt service, 128; deficits, 128; for education, 116, 128; goals in, 129; for health, 128; revenues, 128; for social security, 128

government budget (Seychelles), 228–29; austerity, 229; for defense, 228; deficit, 228, 229; for education, xxv; for 1995, xxv; revenues, 228

governor general (Mauritius), 130

GP. *See* Presidential Guard

Grand Comore. *See* Njazidja

Grand Friday Mosque (Maldives), 268

Grand Police Military Training Center (Seychelles), 319

Grand Port District (Mauritius), 110

Grand Port Range (Mauritius), 110

Green Party. *See* Parti Vert

gross domestic product (GDP): of Comoros, 182; of Madagascar, 60; of Maldives, 272–73; of Mauritius, 121; of Seychelles, xxiv, 224

gross domestic product fractions (Madagascar): agriculture, 65; budget deficit, xix, 59; foreign debt, 62; industry, 69

gross domestic product fractions (Maldives): agriculture, xxvi, 273; fishing, xxvi, 273; tourism, xxvi, 273, 274

gross domestic product fractions (Mauritius): budget deficit, 128; construction, 124

gross domestic product fractions (Seychelles): budget deficit, 229; fishing, 224–25; service sector, 211; tourism, 234

gross national product (GNP): in Comoros, 181–82; in Madagascar, 60; in Maldives, 272; in Mauritius, 128

Groupe Mobile de Police. *See* Mobile Police Group

guestworkers: in Maldives, xxvi; in Mauritius, 126; in Seychelles, 217

Gujarati language (Mauritius), 114

Habib Bank of Pakistan, 276

Hachim, Said, 159

Hahaya airport (Comoros), 190

Hanimadu Island (Maldives): airport on, 277

harbors (*see also* ports): in Madagascar, 24, 27; in Mauritius, 110

*Haveeru* (Maldives), 282

health: and causes of death, 53, 118; in Comoros, 146, 149, 179–80, 184; and disease, 53–54, 55, 112, 118, 179, 223, 271; and immunization, 179; in Madagascar, 53–55; in Maldives, 271–72; in Mauritius, 102, 106, 112, 118, 128; in Seychelles, 207, 223–24

health care: aid for, 180, 184; budget for, 54, 61, 128, 228; in Comoros, 180; in Madagascar, 54; in Maldives, 271–72; in Mauritius, 128; in Seychelles, 212; traditional, 54–55

health care professionals: in Comoros, 180; in Madagascar, 54; in Maldives, 271–72; in Mauritius, 118; in Seychelles, xxv; traditional, 272

health facilities: in Madagascar, 54, 59; in Maldives, 272; in Mauritius, 118; in Seychelles, 223

Henri, Marcel, 165

Heyerdahl, Thor, 258

High State Authority (Madagascar), 22

Hindi language: broadcasts in, 117, 283; in Mauritius, 114, 115

Hindus: ancestors of, 113–14; caste system of, 114; in Mauritius, xx, 103, 104, 113–14, 115, 129; occupations of, 115; as percentage of population in Mauritius, 113, 115; in Seychelles, 220

*Hindustani* (Mauritius), 103

Hoarau, Gérard, 242

Hoare, Michael, 212, 313–14

Hong Kong: investment by, 124; trade of, with Mauritius, 125, 135

housing: construction, 44; low-income, 118, 128; in Madagascar, 44; in Mauritius, 118, 128; in Seychelles, 212, 224, 229

Hulele Island (Maldives): airport on, 265, 277

*Human Development Report* (UNDP), 60–61

human rights, xviii; abuses, 160, 162, 301, 307; in Comoros, xxiii, 160, 162, 190, 327–28; in Madagascar, xx, 301, 307–8; in Maldives, xxvi, 330; in Mauritius, 313; in Seychelles, xxv, 321–22, 244

Hummingbird Helicopters (Maldives), 277–78

Husain ibn Ali, 146

Ibn Battutah, 259

Ibrahim, Ilyas, 281

Ibraham, Said, Prince, 150, 173

IDA. *See* International Development Association

IFB. *See* Independent Forward Block

Ikopa River (Madagascar), 27

Île aux Vaches (Seychelles), 214

Île Denis (Seychelles), 214

Île Pamanzi, 169–70

IMET. *See* International Military Education and Training

IMF. *See* International Monetary Fund

imports: by Comoros, 147, 162, 181, 184, 185–86; of food, xxii, 66, 145, 162, 181, 185–87, 209, 231, 279; by Madagascar, 66, 71–72; by Mauritius, 125; by Mahoré; by Seychelles, 231, 237

income: per capita, in Madagascar, 56; per capita, in Maldives, xxvi, 272; per capita, in Seychelles, 207

income distribution: in Madagascar, 56

indentured workers: in Mauritius, 97, 100–101, 113

independence: of Comoros, 145, 151, 152, 322; of Madagascar, 9, 16–18; of Maldives, 257, 260; of Mauritius, 105, 131; opposition to, 105, 164; of Seychelles, xxv, 207, 211

independence movements: in Africa, 151; in Comoros, 151, 152; in Seychelles, 211

Independent Forward Block (IFB) (Mauritius): in elections of 1959, 104

Independents (Mauritius): in elections of 1959, 104

India, 283, 287; aid to Maldives from, 279; education in, 116; guestworkers from, xxvi; indentured workers from, 97, 100–101; in Indian Ocean conference, xxi; matériel from, 312; military assistance from, 321; military intervention by, in Maldives, 261–62, 329, 282, 329; military training by, 312; military relations of, with Madagascar, 80, 85; relations of, with Maldives, 257; relations of, with Mauritius, 132, 133–34; relations of, with Seychelles, xxiv, 245–46; trade of, with Comoros, xxii; trade of, with Madagascar, 85; trade of, with Maldives, 279; trade of, with Mauritius, 125, 133–34

Indian Cultural Association (Mauritius), 103

Indian Ocean: area of, xvii; balance of power in, xvii; strategic interests in, 326, 330; trade through, xvii, 102

Indian Ocean Commission, xxiii, 134, 196

Indian Ocean conference (1995), xxi

*Indian Ocean Newsletter*, 195, 327

Indian Ocean Rim Association, xxi, xxvii

Indian Ocean Zone of Peace Resolution

(1971): support for, xxi, 133, 245, 282

Indians: in Comoros, 172; in Maldives, 265–66; in Mauritius, 97, 99, 100–101, 102, 309; social status of, 102; tensions of, with Creoles, 97, 309; in Seychelles, 208, 217

Indira Gandhi Memorial Hospital (Maldives), 272

Indonesia, 287; relations of, with Madagascar, 80

Indo-Pakistanis: in Madagascar, 39, 46; religion of, 46

industrial development: in Madagascar, 58, 68–71; output, 69

Industrial Relations Act of 1973 (Mauritius), 126

industry: in Comoros, 187–88; cottage, 277; employment in, 276; in Madagascar, 68–71; in Maldives, 276; in Mauritius, 123–24: in Seychelles, 233–34

inflation: in Comoros, 182; in Madagascar, xix, 59; in Mauritius, xx, 120, 121; in Seychelles, 225

Information against X for Plotting and Attacking State Security (Madagascar), 307–8

infrastructure; in Comoros, 161–62, 188; in Madagascar, xix, 59; in Maldives, 274; in Mauritius, 133; in Seychelles, 216

Institute for Advanced Studies (Madagascar), 51

Institute for Health Sciences (Maldives), 272

International Development Association (IDA), 29, 170, 172; Special Program of Assistance, 182

International Finance Investment and Credit Bank of Bangladesh, 276

International Fund for Agricultural Development: aid to Comoros from, 162, 186

internal security. *See* security, internal

Intelsat. *See* International Telecommunications Satellite Organization

International Capital and Securities Exchange, 70

International Development Association (IDA): loans from, 273

International Finance Corporation, xix, 70

International Military Education and

Training (IMET): in Comoros, 327; in Madagascar, 302; in Mauritius, 312; in Seychelles, 321

International Monetary Fund (IMF): and Comoros, 182, 196; economic reforms under, xxiii; and Madagascar, 21, 56, 58, 60, 84; and Maldives, 261; and Mauritius, 107, 128, 135; and Seychelles, 245; structural adjustment programs, 56, 58, 128, 182

International Telecommunications Satellite Organization (Intelsat), 73, 127, 236

investment: in Madagascar, xix, 69; in Mauritius, 124

Iraq: aid to Comoros from, 323; relations of, with Seychelles, 245

Iron And Stone Ramification (Vy Vato Sakelika—VVS) (Madagascar), 13

irrigation: in Madagascar, 58, 63, 65; in Mauritius, 111; in Seychelles, 231

Isalo Roiniforme Massif, 24

Islam: in Comoros, 171, 177; introduction of, 147, 257; reform of, 153; sharia, 268, 280, 327, 330; as state religion of Comoros, xxii, 154, 190; as state religion of Maldives, xxvi, 257, 267–68, 279; in Seychelles, 220

Islamic Center (Maldives), 268

Islamists: in Maldives, 261, 282

Islands Development Company (Seychelles), 226

Islands Resorts (Seychelles), 226

Israel: relations of, with Comoros, xxiii; relations of, with Madagascar, 82, 85

Italy: aid from, 62; colonies of, 289; relations of, with Madagascar, 80; tourists from, 235, 274

Itasy volcano (Madagascar), 24

Ivakoany Massif (Madagascar), 24

Ivato-Antananarivo airport (Madagascar), 73, 79

Ivondro River (Madagascar), 27

ivory, 288


Jaffar, Said Mohammed, 322

Jaona, Monja, 17, 295

Japan, 289; aid from, 270–71, 62, 274, 279, 84; relations of, with Comoros, 196; relations of, with Madagascar, 80, 83; tourists from, 274; trade with, 71,

72, 125, 135, 184
Japanese Marubeni Corporation, 273
Jeerooburkhan, Jooneed, 106
Jimilime mountains (Comoros), 169
Jones, David, 50
judges: in Maldives, 280; in Mauritius, 312
Judicial and Legal Service Commission (Mauritius), 130
judiciary: in Comoros, 191–92, 327; in Madagascar, 76; in Maldives, 280; in Mauritius, 130; in Seychelles, 243–44
Jugnauth, Anerood, xxi; assassination attempts on, 134, 308–9; as prime minister, 107, 131

Kadu Island (Maldives): airport on, 277
Kalfane and Company, 162, 181
Kartala (Comoros), 169; eruption of, 146, 153
Kemal, Said Ali, 157, 159, 192
Kennedy, Donald Mackenzie, 103–4
Kenya, 293; in Indian Ocean conference, xxi; relations of, with Seychelles, 245
*kibushi* dialect (Comoros), 172
Kim Il Sung, 82
Kodedu Island (Maldives): airport on, 277
Korea, Democratic People's Republic of (North Korea): matériel from, 304; military advisers from, 304, 320; military assistance by, 153, 303; military training by, 300, 302, 320; relations of, with Madagascar, 81, 82; relations of, with Seychelles, 245
Korea, Republic of (South Korea): relations of, with Madagascar, 85
Kreol Institute (Seychelles), 218
Kung Fu conflicts (Madagascar), 296
Kuwait: aid to Comoros from, 323; aid to Maldives from, 279; relations of, with Comoros, 196

Laborde, Jean, 12
labor unions: in Comoros, 185; in Mauritius, 106, 126
Lac Alaotra (Madagascar), 24, 27
La Digue (Seychelles), 213; health facilities in, 223; population of, 217
La Grille (Comoros), 169

Lakandranon' Ampalangalana. *See* Canal des Pangalanes
Lake Ihotry (Madagascar), 27
Lake Itasy (Madagascar), 24
Lake Kinkony (Madagascar), 27
land ownership: in Comoros, 149; in Mauritius, 100, 102
land reform: in Madagascar, 65
land use: in Madagascar, 55
language (*see also under individual languages*): in Comoros, 171; of instruction, 52–53, 115, 116–17, 221, 222, 269, 270; in Madagascar, 32, 39–41, 52–53; in Maldives, 265–66, 269; in Mauritius, xx, 113, 115; in Seychelles, 217–18
*L'Archipel* (Comoros), 181
Latin America: exports to, 72
Laurent, Eugene, 103
League of Arab States: Comoros in, 196
*L'Echo des Îles* (Seychelles) 243
legal system: of Comoros, 190–91, 327; of Maldives, 279–80, 330; of Mauritius, 130; of Seychelles, 243–44
legislature: of Comoros, 191, 322; of Madagascar, 75–76; of Maldives, xxvi, 280; of Mauritius, 129–30; of Seychelles, 238
Legislative Assembly (Mauritius), 104
Legislative Council (Mauritius), 104; members of, 104
*Le Mauricien* (Mauritius), 117
*Le Militant* (Mauritius), 106
*L'Express* (Mauritius), 117
Liberal Action (Action Libérale) (Mauritius), 103; dissolved, 103; formed, 103
Libya: relations of Comoros with, 156; relations of, with Seychelles, 245
literacy rate: in Comoros, 146, 178; in Madagascar, 11, 50, 51; in Maldives, xxvi, 269; in Mauritius, 116, 117; in Seychelles, xxiv, 221
literature: of Antaimoro people, 34, 40; Creole, 218
livestock: in Comoros, 187; in Madagascar, 36, 38, 64, 65, 68; in Mauritius, 123; in Seychelles, 232
living standards: in Madagascar, 18; in Maldives, 266; in Mauritius, 112
Livingstone, David, 170
Lomé Convention, 122
London Club: loans from, 62

London Missionary Society, 40, 50
Luthufi, Abdullah, 262, 329
Luxembourg: trade with, 184

Madagascar: Comorans in, 172; geographical regions of, 23; in Indian Ocean Commission, 134; land area of, xviii; migration to, 149
Madagascar Capital Development Fund, 70; established, xx
Madi, Mohamed Abdou, 194
Mahafaly people (Madagascar), 10, 38; agriculture of, 64; as percentage of Madagascar population, 38; tombs of, 42
Mahajamba River (Madagascar), 27
Mahajanga (Madujascar): harbor at, 27; investment in, 61; port of, 73
Mahatma Gandhi Institute (Mauritius), 116, 133
Mahé (Seychelles): airport on, 210, 211; fishing off, 232; health facilities in, 223; population of, 217; size of, 213
Mahébourg (Mauritius): harbor at, 110
Mahoré, 145, 168; agriculture on, 168; aid to, 145; airport of, 168, 190; anti-Comoran demonstrations on, 168; construction on, 168; as French department, 145, 152, 164; French Foreign Legion in, 165; French military installations, on, 326; French occupation of, 149; as French territorial community, 166; integration issue, 145, 152, 157, 164–68, 195; land area of, 169; population of, 171; population density of, 171; relations of, with France, 145; role of women in, 176–77; tourism on, 168
Majlis. *See* legislature
Makoa people (Madagascar), 36; in Comoros, 173; as percentage of Madagascar population, 36
Malagasy language, 32, 39–41; broadcasts in, 73; literacy in, 50; number of speakers of, 52; as official language of Madagascar, 11; origins of, 40; pronunciation of, 40; publications in, 40, 79; vocabulary of, 40; written, 11, 40–41
Malagasy people (Madagascar): in Comoros, 172; investment by, 70; kin-

ship system of, 32; origins of, 31; *razana* (respect for the dead), 32, 41–44; souls of, 43–44; stratification of, 32; taboos of, 45; traditional religion of, 44–45
Malagasy Radio-Television, 308
Malagasy-Soviet Intergovernmental Commission on Economic and Technical Cooperation and Trade, 81
Malayo-Polynesian language family, 39
Malaysia: aid from, to Maldives, 268
Malaysians, 288; in Comoros, xxii, 147, 173; influence of, on Comoros, 146; in Seychelles, 208
Maldives: etymology of, 258; number of islands in, 262–63; relations of, with Seychelles, 245; size of, 262
Maldives Center for Social Education, 271
Maldives Fisheries Corporation, 273
Maldives Institute of Technical Education, 271
Maldives Monetary Authority, 274
Maldives National Ship Management, Limited, 278
Maldives Nippon Corporation, 273
Male Central Hospital (Maldives), 272
Male International Airport (Maldives), 277
Male Island (Maldives): population on, 264; port of, 278; social structure of, 266–67
Male Port Development projects (Maldives), 278
Male Water Supply and Sewerage Project (Maldives), 271
Maloney, Clarence, 265, 268
Mamoudzou (Comoros): population of, 172
Mananara River (Madagascar), 27
Mananjary River (Madagascar), 27
Mancham, James, 207; background of, 210; as chief minister, 210; opposition by, 213, 239, 240; as president, 211, 242, 314
Mandarin language, 114
Mandrare River (Madagascar), 27
Mangoky River (Madagascar), 27
Mangoro River (Madagascar), 27
Mania River (Madagascar), 27
Maningory River (Madagascar), 27
manufacturing: in Madagascar, 11, 12; in

Mauritius, 97, 126; in Seychelles, 234
Mare aux Vacoas (Mauritius), 110
Maroansetra (Madagascar), 34
marriage (*see also* polygamy): in Comoros, 174; *en ménage*, 219; interethnic, 208–9, 173; intraethnic, 37, 48; in Maldives, 267; in Seychelles, 219
martial law: in Madagascar, 19, 20, 295
Mascarene Islands, xx, 109
Mascarene Plateau, 109
matériel: from Britain, 312; from China, 304; from France, 298, 303, 304, 312; from India, 312; for Madagascar, 81, 298, 299–300, 303, 304; from North Korea, 304; for Seychelles, 316; from the Soviet Union, 81, 304, 320; from United States, 299–300
Maurice of Nassau, 98
Mauritian Militant Movement (MMM), 98; in elections of 1987, 108; in elections of 1991, 108; political base of, 106
Mauritian Party (Parti Mauricien—PM): in elections of 1959, 104; in elections of 1963, 104
Mauritian Police Force. *See* police (Mauritius)
Mauritian Social Democratic (Party (Parti Mauricien Social Démocrate—PMSD), 105; in coalition government, 107
Mauritian Socialist Movement (Mouvement Socialiste Mauricien—MSM), 107; in elections of 1991, 108
Mauritian Socialist Party (Parti Socialiste Mauricien—PSM): formed, 107
Mauritius, 109; central tableland of, 109; coastal plains of, 109–10; districts of, 110; drainage in, 110; etymology of, 98; geography of, 108–11; in Indian Ocean Commission, 134; investment by, 70; land area of, 108; location of, 108; lowland plains of, 110; relations of, with Madagascar, 85; relations of, with Seychelles, 245; rivers of, 110; Seychelles as a dependency of, 207, 208; trade of, with Madagascar, 85; trade of, with Seychelles, 237
Mauritius Broadcasting Corporation, 117
Mauritius College of the Air, 116
Mauritius Commercial Bank, 124

Mauritius Housing Corporation, 118, 124
Mauritius Institute of Education, 116
Mauritius Labor Party (MLP), 98; in coalition government, 107; in elections of 1959, 104; in elections of 1963, 104; founded, 103
Mauritius Sugar Industry Research Institute, 122
Mauritius Sugar Syndicate, 122
Mauritius Tea Factories Company, 123
Mayotte. *See* Mahoré
Mayotte Popular Movement (Mouvement Populaire Mahorais—MPM), 165
M'Dere, Zeina, 165
MDRM. *See* Democratic Movement for the Malagasy Restoration
media: in Comoros, 161, 180–81, 184; in Maldives, 282–83; in Mauritius, xxii, 117–18; in Seychelles, xxv, 212, 243
Menabe kingdom (Madagascar), 10
Menalamba groups (Madagascar), 297
mercenaries: attempted coup in Maldives by, 261, 262, 282, 329; in Comoran coups, 146, 154, 159, 322, 324; in Presidential Guard, 159, 325; rule by, in Comoros, 146; in Seychelles armed forces, 318–19; in Seychelles coups, 212, 313–14
merchant marine (Maldives), 278
Merina kingdom (Madagascar), 10–12; *fokonolona* of, 10–11; legacy of, 10; military campaigns of, 12, 35, 36–37, 148, 296–97; political system of, 10–11
Merina people (Madagascar), 10, 32, 34; attitudes of, toward dead, 43; agriculture of, 63–64; conflict of, with *côtiers*, 15, 19, 32, 75; culture of, 37; descent among, 48; education of, 52; in elite class, 36; etymology of, 36; kin groups of, 48; marriage of, 37, 48; in officer corps, 302; as percentage of Madagascar population, 36; physical characteristics of, 37; religion of, 45; slave descendants among, 49; social classes of, 47; social structure of, 47, 48–49; souls of, 43–44; tomb groups of, 49; tombs of, 42; women, 48
M'Hadjou, Said Mustapha. *See* Denard, Bob
Michel, James, 319

middle class: in Comoros, 148; education of, 53; in Mauritius, 103

Middle East: exports to, 72; imports from, 72

Mid-Indian Ridge, 109

migration: to Madagascar, 149; from Seychelles, 216

Militant Movement for Malagasy Socialism (Mouvement Militant pour le Socialisme Malgache—MMSM), 22

Militant Socialist Movement (Mouvement Socialiste Militant) (Mauritius), 107

Military Academy (Académie Militaire) at Antsirabe, 302; foreign students at, 302

military assistance: to Comoros, 153, 195, 326–27; to Madagascar, 81, 302–6; to Mauritius, 312; to Seychelles, 319–21

military assistance sources: Britain, 312; France, 302, 303, 321, 326; Germany, 304; India, 312, 319, 321; North Korea, 153, 319, 320; Saudi Arabia, 153; South Africa, 321, 326, 327; Soviet Union, 81, 312, 319, 320; Tanzania, 315, 319–20, 326; United States, 312, 319, 320–21, 326, 327

military bases: on Diego Garcia, xxi

military officers: in Madagascar, 298, 302; training of, 153

military rule: in Madagascar, 18–19

military training: by Britain, 312; by China, 306; in Comoros, 153, 325; by Cuba, 302, 304; by East Germany, 301, 302; by France, 298, 302, 303, 304, 325, 326; by Germany, 304; by India, 312; in Madagascar, 301–2, 304; by North Korea, 302, 320; by Romania, 304; in Seychelles, 319, 320; by Soviet Union, 302, 306; by Tanzania, 153, 322; by United States, 302, 306, 312, 325, 327

minerals and mining: in Madagascar, 55, 70–71

Ministry of Agricultural Production (Madagascar), 65

Ministry of Agriculture and Marine Resources (Seychelles), 231

Ministry of Defense (Madagascar), 300

Ministry of Economic Planning and Development (Mauritius), 117

Ministry of Education and Cultural Affairs (Mauritius), 116

Ministry of Employment and Social Affairs (Seychelles), 230–31

Ministry of Finance (Seychelles), 225–26

Ministry of Health (Madagascar), 53

Ministry of Health (Maldives), 271

Ministry of Health (Mauritius), 113; Maternal and Child Health Care Division, 113

Ministry of Health (Seychelles), 223

Ministry of Home Affairs (Maldives), 270

Ministry of Interior (Madagascar), 301

Ministry of Planning and Development (Seychelles), 225

Ministry of Population and Women's Affairs (Comoros), 177

Ministry of Social and Women's Affairs (Comoros), 177

Ministry of the Environment (Mauritius), 112

Ministry of Women's Rights and Family Welfare (Mauritius), 119

missions, Christian: expelled from Madagascar, 46; schools of, 11

Mitterrand, François, 133, 304

MLP. *See* Mauritius Labor Party

MMM. *See* Mauritian Militant Movement

MMSM. *See* Militant Movement for Malagasy Socialism

Mobile Police Group (Groupe Mobile de Police—GMP) (Madagascar), 295

Mohamed, Said, 324

Mohamed, Situ, 177

Mohéli. *See* Mwali

Moka District (Mauritius), 110

Moka-Long Mountain Range (Mauritius), 110

Monetary Authority (Seychelles), 226

Molinaco. *See* National Liberation Movement of Comoros

Monima. *See* National Movement for the Independence of Madagascar

Montagne d'Ambre (Ambohitra) (Madagascar), 24

Mont Blanche (Mauritius), 110

Mont Piton (Mauritius), 110

Moroni (Comoros), 169; harbor of, 190; population of, 172; port of, 184

Movement for Resistance (Mouvement pour la Résistance) (Seychelles), 240, 315

mountains: in Comoros, 169; in Madagascar, 24; in Mauritius, 109, 110; in Seychelles, 213

Mouvement de la Libération Nationale des Comores. *See* National Liberation Movement of Comoros

Mouvement Démocratique de la Rénovation Malgache. *See* Democratic Movement for the Malagasy Restoration

Mouvement National pour l'Indépendance de Madagascar. *See* National Movement for the Independence of Madagascar

Mouvement Populaire Mahorais. *See* Mayotte Popular Movement

Mouvement pour la Résistance. *See* Movement for Resistance

Mouvement Socialiste Mauricien. *See* Mauritian Socialist Movement

Mouvement Socialiste Militant. *See* Militant Socialist Movement

MPM. *See* Mayotte Popular Movement

Mroudjae, Ali, 157

MSM. *See* Mauritian Socialist Movement

Mtingui Mountain (Comoros), 169

Muhammed ibn Idris ash Shafii, 147, 177–78

municipal councils (Mauritius), 102–3

Muslims (*see also* Islam): ancestors of, 113–14; languages of, 115; in Madagascar, 39, 45; in Mauritius, xx, 103, 113–14, 115, 129; occupations of, 115; as percentage of population in Mauritius, 113, 115

Muslims, Shia: in Madagascar, 46; in Maldives, 266, 267; in Mauritius, 114

Muslims, Sunni: in Comoros, xxii, 147, 177; in Madagascar, 46; in Maldives, xxvi, 267; in Mauritius, 114

Mutsamudu (Comoros), 169; harbor of, 190; population of, 172; port of, 169, 184

M'Vouni School for Higher Education (Comoros), 178

Mwali (Comoros), 145, 168, 169; land area of, 169; population density of, 171; treaty of, with France, 149

Nababsing, Prem, 108, 132

Naseem, Ahmed, 329

Nasir, Ibrahim, 260; attempted coup by, 329; flight of, 261, 281; as president, 260, 280

National Army of Madagascar. *See* army of Madagascar

National Assembly (Comoros), 322; elections for, 157, 325

National Assembly (Madagascar), 75–76; elections for, xix, 22, 76

National Assembly (Mauritius): members of, 129; terms in, 130

National Assembly (Seychelles), 240, 321–22

National Bank for Rural Development (Madagascar), 60

National Bank for Trade Development (Madagascar), 60

National Bank of Paris-International (Banque Nationale de Paris-Internationale), 185

National Coast Guard (NCG) (Mauritius), 311

National Committee for Public Safety (Comité National de Salut Public) (Comoros), 157

National Day (Maldives), 259

National Development Plan (1990–94) (Seychelles), 216

National Electoral Commission (Comoros), 194

National Executive Council (Comoros), 322

National Front for the Defense of the Revolution (Front National pour la Défense de la Révolution—FNDR) (Madagascar), 20; members of, 20

National Gendarmerie (Madagascar), 300

National Investigative Unit (Mauritius), 311

nationalist movement, 289; in Madagascar, 13, 15

nationalization: in Comoros, 182; in Madagascar, 56, 80; in Maldives, 259

National Liberation Movement of Comoros (Mouvement de la Libération Nationale des Comores—Molinaco), 151; platform of, 151

National Medical Service (Seychelles), 223

National Military Directorate (Madagascar), 19, 296

National Military Office for Strategic

Industries (Office Militaire National pour les Industries Stratégiques) (Madagascar), 70

National Movement for the Independence of Madagascar (Mouvement National pour l'Indépendance de Madagascar—Monima), 17; dissolved, 18; peasant uprising under, 17–18, 295

National Police Force (Force de Police Nationale) (Comoros). *See* police (Comoros)

National Police Force (Mauritius). *See* police (Mauritius)

National Remuneration Board (Mauritius), 126

National Representative Assembly (Madagascar), 14

National Security Service (Maldives), 329

National Union for Comoran Democracy (Union Nationale pour la Démocratie Comorienne—UNDC), 193

National Workers' Union (Seychelles), 230

National Youth Service, 222

Nature Conservancy Commission, 214

NCG. *See* National Coast Guard (Mauritius)

Netherlands: colony of, on Mauritius, 98; exploration by, 9, 147, 287, 288; influence of, on Maldives, 257; occupation of Maldives by, 259

New Democratic Party (Seychelles), 239

newspapers (*see also* media; press): Chinese, 117; in Comoros, 180–81; Dhivehi, 282; English, 282; French, 79, 117; in Malagasy, 79; in Maldives, 282; in Mauritius, 103, 106, 117; in Seychelles, 243

Nioumakele mountains (Comoros), 169

Njazidja (Comoros), 145, 39, 168, 323; land area of, 169; population density of, 171; treaty of, with France, 149

Non-Aligned Movement: Madagascar in, 82; Mauritius in, 135; Seychelles in, 245

nonalignment: in Madagascar, 20, 80; in Maldives, xxvi; in Seychelles, 245

North Korea. *See* Korea, Democratic People's Republic of

North Mahavavy River (Madagascar), 27

Nosy-Be Island (Madagascar), 24; French occupation of, 148

Nosy-Lava Island (Madagascar): deportations to, 13, 18

Nzwani (Comoros), 145, 168, 323; archaeological research on, 146; French occupation of, 149; land area of, 169; population density of, 171; port for, 184; treaty of, with France, 149

OAU. *See* Organization of African Unity

Office Militaire National pour les Industries Stratégiques. *See* National Military Office for Strategic Industries

Ogaden War, 82

oil: exploration for, 233; imports, 71, 184, 233, 237; in Madagascar, 71; in Seychelles, 233–34, 237

Oimatsaha people, 173

Oman, 287–88, 293; in Indian Ocean conference, xxi

Onilahy River, 27

OPEC. *See* Organization of the Petroleum Exporting Countries

Organization of African Unity (OAU), 151; Comoros in, 154, 196; and Mahoré issue, 166; Mauritius in, 135; Seychelles in, 245, 247

Organization of the Petroleum Exporting Countries (OPEC): aid to Comoros from, 178; aid to Seychelles from, 222–23, 247

Pakistan: aid from, to Maldives, 268, 279; trade with, 237

Palestine Liberation Organization: relations of, with Madagascar, 82

Pamplemousse District (Mauritius), 110

parastatal companies: in Madagascar, 57, 66; in Seychelles, 225, 226, 228, 234

Paris Club: loans to Madagascar, 62

Parti Blanc (White Party) (Comoros), 150, 173; platform of, 150

Parti des Déshérités Malagaches. *See* Party of the Malagasy Disinherited

Parti Mauricien. *See* Mauritian Party

Parti Mauricien Social Démocrate. *See* Mauritian Social Democratic Party

Parti pour l'Évolution des Comores. *See*

Party for the Evolution of Comoros
Parti Seselwa (Seychelles), 242
Parti Social Démocrate de Madagascar. *See* Social Democratic Party of Madagascar
Parti Socialiste des Comores. *See* Socialist Party of Comoros
Parti Socialiste Mauricien. *See* Mauritian Socialist Party
Parti Vert (Green Party) (Comoros), 150, 173; platform of, 150
Party for the Evolution of Comoros (Parti pour l'Évolution des Comores), 151
Party of the Malagasy Disinherited (Parti des Déshérités Malgaches), 14; members of, 14
Pasoco. *See* Socialist Party of Comoros
peasants: uprising by, in Madagascar, 17-18
penal code: of Madagascar, 306; of Seychelles, 244
penal system: of Comoros, 327; of Madagascar, 306-7; of Maldives, 330; of Mauritius, 312; of Seychelles, 321
Pentecostal church: in Seychelles, 220
People's Armed Forces (Forces Armées Populaires). *See* armed forces of Madagascar
People's Assembly (Seychelles), xxv, 238
People's Militia (Seychelles), 316, 318, 320
Persia, 287
Persian Gulf states: aid from, to Maldives, 268; relations of Comoros with, 156
Petite Rivière Noire Mountains (Mauritius), 110
Pieter Both Mountain (Mauritius), 110
Plaines Wilhems District (Mauritius), 110
plantations: in Comoros, 181; in Madagascar, 55; in Mauritius, 121
Platte Island (Seychelles), 214
PM. *See* Mauritian Party
PMSD. *See* Mauritian Social Democratic Party
police (Comoros), 326; French control of, 192, 326
police (Madagascar), 300, 301
police (Mauritius), xxii, 309, 310-11; equipment of, 310; number of personnel in, 309, 310; training of, 310

police (Seychelles), 315, 318
Police Service Commission (Mauritius), 130
political demonstrations: banned, 18; casualties in, xxiii, 159; in Comoros, xxiii, 159; in Madagascar, 21, 304, 308; on Mahoré, 168
political opposition, xviii; in Comoros, 156-57, 158-59, 160, 324-25; in Madagascar, 296; in Maldives, 261; in Seychelles, 207, 213, 240-43
political parties (*see also under individual parties*): banned, 19, 156, 295; in Comoros, 156, 157, 194; in Madagascar, 14, 19, 295; in Maldives, xxvi; in Mauritius, 131-32; in Seychelles, 239
political unrest: anti-Denard, 164; anti-French, 13, 15; in Comoros, 152, 324-25; in Madagascar, 13, 15, 146; in Maldives, 259; in Mauritius, 103, 104
pollution: in Seychelles, 214; in Mauritius, 112
polygamy (*see also* marriage): in Comoros, 176; in Madagascar, 12; in Maldives, 267; outlawed, 12
Pope-Hennessy, John, 102
population (Comoros): age distribution in, 171; density, 145, 171; of 1991, 171; of slaves, 148; urban, 172
population (Madagascar), xviii, 30-39; age distribution in, xx, 30, 31; of Chinese, 31, 39; of Comorans, 31, 39; density, 31; foreign, 31; of French, 31, 39; of Indians, 31, 39; in 1900, 30; in 1975, 30; in 1993, 30; projected, 30; rural, 65; urban, 31
population (Maldives), 264-65; density, 171, 264, 265; in 1977, 265; in 1985, 265; in 1990, 264, 265
population (Mauritius), 112-13; age distribution in, 112; density, 112; in 1993, 112; in 1993, 112; rural, 112; of slaves, 99; urban, 112
population (Seychelles), 216-17; density, 171; distribution of, 207, 214, 217
population fractions (Madagascar): Antaifasy, 35; Antaimoro, 34; Antaisaka, 35; Antakarana, 38; Antalaotra, 34; Antambahoaka, 34; Antandroy, 38; Antanosy, 35; Bara, 37; Betsileo, 37; Betsimisaraka, 33; Bezanozano, 35; Mahafaly, 38; Makoa, 36;

Merina, 36; Sakalava, 35; Sihanaka, 35; Tanala, 35; Tsimihety, 38

population fractions (Mauritius): Catholics, 115; Chinese, 101–2, 113; Creoles, 101; Hindus, 113, 115; Indians, 101; Muslims, 113, 115; Protestants, 115

population statistics (Comoros): birthrate, 179; death rate, 179; fertility rate, 177; growth rate, 146, 149, 171–72; infant mortality rate, 179; life expectancy, 179

population statistics (Madagascar): growth rate, 30, 31; infant mortality rate, 30–31, 55; life expectancy, 53; mortality rate, 53

population statistics (Maldives): birthrate, 264, 271; death rate, 271; growth rate, 264; infant mortality rate, 271; life expectancy, 271

population statistics (Mauritius): birthrate, 113; death rate, 113; growth rate, 106, 112; infant mortality rate, 118; life expectancy, 106, 118

population statistics (Seychelles): birthrate, 216, 217; death rate, 216, 217; growth rate, 216; infant mortality rate, 216, 223; life expectancy, 217, 223

Port Louis (Mauritius), 97, 110; government of, 130; population of, 112; port of, 127, 133; schools in, 116; stock exchange, 121; transportation in, 127

Port Louis District (Mauritius), 110

ports (*see also* harbors): in Comoros, 156, 169, 184; of France, 148–49; in Madagascar, 24, 73; in Maldives, 278; in Mauritius, 97, 148, 127, 133; in Seychelles, xxiv, 148

Portugal: colonies of, 289; exploration by, 9, 9, 98, 147, 208, 287, 288; influence of, on Maldives, 257; occupation by, of Maldives, 257, 259

poverty: in Madagascar, 56; in Seychelles, xxv, 208

*Poverty in Paradise* (World Bank), xxv

Praslin (Seychelles), 213; health facilities in, 223; population of, 217

Preferential Trade Area for Eastern and Southern Africa, 133, 237

president (Comoros): under constitution of 1992, xxii, 190; succession to, 158, 191; term of, 190–91

president (Maldives): under constitution

of 1968, xxvi, 280; term of, xxvi, 280

Presidential Guard (Garde Présidentielle—GP) (Comoros), 158, 324, 325; corruption in, 160; in coup of 1989, 164; French control of, 192, 326; mercenaries in, 159, 325; missions of, 159, 325; mutiny in, 160; number of personnel in, 159, 326; and South Africa, 160–61, 327; torture by, 160

Presidential Guard (Madagascar), 300–301, 304, 308; training of, 300, 301

Presidential Guard (Seychelles), 316, 318, 320

Presidential Security Regiment (Régiment de Sécurité Présidentielle—Reser). *See* Presidential Guard

press (*see also* media; newspapers): censored, 20, 308, 328; in Comoros, 328; in Madagascar, 20, 76, 308; in Maldives, xxvi, xxvii, 330; in Mauritius, 117; in Seychelles, xxv

Press Council (Maldives), xxvii

prime minister (Comoros): abolished, 158; under constitution of 1992, xxii

prisoners, political: in Comoros, 328; in Maldives, 330

prison system: of Madagascar, 307; of Mauritius, 312; of Seychelles, 244–45, 321

privatization: in Comoros, xxiii; in Madagascar, 57, 59; in Seychelles, xxiv, 228

Protestant London Missionary Society, 11

Protestants: conflict of, with Catholics, 15; in Madagascar, 12, 45–46; in Mauritius, 115; in Seychelles, 220

PSD. *See* Social Democratic Party of Madagascar

PSM. *See* Mauritian Socialist Party

publications: in French, 79; in Malagasy, 11, 79

Public Gathering Act (1991) (Mauritius), 313

Public Investment Program (Madagascar), 61

Public Order Act (1971) (Mauritius), 98, 106

public sector: in Madagascar, 58

Public Security Act (Seychelles), 244, 321

Public Services Commission (Mauritius), 130

Quatre Bornes (Mauritius), 112; government of, 130

Rabemananjara, Jacques, 14
racial distinctions: in Merina culture, 37
Radama I (r. 1816–28): education under, 50; language under, 40, 50; unification of Madagascar under, 11
Radama II (r. 1861–63), 12; assassination of, 12; modernization under, 12
radio: broadcast languages, 73; in Comoros, xxiii, 180, 181, 195; in Madagascar, 73; in Maldives, 278, 283, 283; in Mauritius, 117; in Seychelles, 236, 240, 243
Radio Australia, 283
Radio Beijing, 283
Radio Comoros, 180
Radio Nederlands, 73
Radio Tropique (Comoros), 181
railroads: in Madagascar, xix, 55, 72; in Mauritius, 127
Rainilaiarivony, 12
Ramanantsoa, Gabriel, 18–19, 56, 295
Ramanantsoa government (Madagascar), 295; foreign relations under, 80, 303–4; local government under, 77–78
Ramgoolam, Navin, 132
Ramgoolam, Sir Seewoosagur, 98, 103; death of, 108; in elections of 1963, 104; opposition to, 131–32
Ramgoolam government (Mauritius), 98
Raminia, 34
Ramkalanan, Wavel, 239, 242
Ranavalona I (r. 1828–62), 12, 46, 50
Ranavalona III, 12, 297; deported, 13
Raseta, Joseph, 14
Rassemblement Démocratique du Peuple Comorien. *See* Democratic Assembly of the Comoran People
Rassemblement des Travaillistes Mauriciens. *See* Assembly of Mauritian Workers
Ratsimandrava, Richard, 19, 295; assassinated, 295
Ratsimilaho, 34
Ratsiraka, Didier, xviii, 9; in elections of 1993, 22; language policy of, 41; opposition to, 296; as president, 19, 296; refusal to vacate President's Palace, 22
Ratsiraka government (Madagascar):

economy under, 56; foreign relations under, 80; local government under, 78; revolution from above, 56
Ravare people (Maldives), 265
Ravelojoana, Pastor, 13
Ravelomanana, Raoul, 60
Ravoahangy, Joseph, 14
Ravony, Francisque: ethnicity of, 75; as prime minister, xix, 22, 85
*razana* (respect for the dead) (Madagascar), 32, 41–44; tombs in, 42; turning of the dead, 42–44
RDPC. *See* Democratic Assembly of the Comoran People
Reagan, Ronald, 83
Redin people (Maldives), 258
refugees: from Comoros, 153; from Madagascar, 153; to Mahoré, 153
Régiment de Sécurité Présidentielle. *See* Presidential Guard
religion (*see also under individual denominations*): in Comoros, xxii, 177–78; in Madagascar, 41–46; in Maldives, xxvi, 267–68; in Mauritius, 113–15; in Seychelles, 220–21
religion, indigenous (Seychelles), 220–21, 268
religious leaders: in Madagascar, 44–45
René, France Albert, xxv, 207, 237; background of, 210; in elections of 1979, 212; in elections of 1993, 240; as opposition leader, 210; as vice president, 211
René government (Seychelles), 207, 314, national security under, 313; opposition to, 207; reform program of, 212
Republican Security Force (Force Républicaine de Sécurité) (Madagascar), 18, 295, 300
Reser. *See* Presidential Guard
Reunion Island, 109; French occupation of, 148, 133; French military installations on, 326; in Indian Ocean Commission, 134; tourists from, 125; trade of, with Seychelles, 237
Revolt of 1947 (Madagascar), 15, 36, 297
rice: in Madagascar, 62–64, 65–67
Ringadoo, Veerasamy, 131
Rivière du Rempart District (Mauritius), 110
Rivière Noire Mountains (Mauritius), 110

roads: in Comoros, 156, 190; construction of, 156; in Madagascar, 72; in Maldives, 278; in Mauritius, 126; in Seychelles, 216, 235

Roberos, Diogo, 147

Rodrigues Fracture Zone, 109

Rodrigues Island (Mauritius), 109; British occupation of, 148; formation of, 111; French occupation of, 148; land area of, 108; location of, 108; population of, 112

Roman Catholic Church. *See* Catholic Church, Roman

Romania: military training by, 304

Rondon, Fernando E., 83

Royal Dutch Shell, 70

Royal Mauritius Regiment, 309

Royal Military Academy at Sandhurst, 310–11

RTM. *See* Assembly of Mauritian Workers

rural areas: education in, 116; population in, 65, 112

Rural Youth Vocational Training Program (Maldives), 270

Russia (*see also* Soviet Union): strategic interests, 289; trade with, 72

SAARC. *See* South Asian Association for Regional Cooperation

Sadeco. *See* Seychelles Agricultural Development Company

St. Brandon Rocks, 108

Sakalava people (Madagascar), 10, 11, 35–36; in Comoros, 173; culture of, 35–36; French treaties with, 12; livestock of, 64; Merina conquest of, 35, 148; occupations of, 36; as percentage of Madagascar population, 35; social classes of, 47; social structure of, 47; tombs of, 42

Sambirano River (Madagascar), 27

*Sangu* (Maldives), 281

Saudi Arabia: aid to Comoros from, 323; aid to Maldives from, 279; military assistance by, 153; relations of, with Comoros, 196

Savanne District (Mauritius), 110

Savanne Mountains (Mauritius), 110

schools: in Comoros, 178; distribution of, 52; English, 269; enrollment in, 116, 178, 270; French, 50, 178; in

Madagascar, 11, 50, 51–52, 53; in Maldives, xxvi, 269, 270; mission, 11, 50, 221; preschool, 116; primary, 50, 51–52, 116, 269; private, 53; public, 53; Quranic, xxvi, 178, 269, 269–70; secondary, 50, 269; in Seychelles, 207, 221; vocational, 50–51, 116, 178, 270, 271

Science Education Center (Maldives), 270

Seagull Airways, 277–78

Second Republic (Madagascar) (1975–92), 19–22; foreign relations under, 85

Second Republic (Maldives): inaugurated, 260

security, internal: in Comoros, 322–25; in Madagascar, 294–96, 300–301; in Maldives, 328–29; in Mauritius, 311; in Seychelles, 313–15; threats to, 294, 308

security, national: in Comoros, 322; in Madagascar, 294; in Mauritius, 308, in Seychelles, 313–15

Senate (Comoros), 191

service sector: employment in, 211; as percentage of gross domestic product, 211; in Seychelles, 211

Seventh-Day Adventist church: in Seychelles, 220

Seychelles: as crown colony, 209; as dependency of Mauritius, 207, 208; etymology of, 208; in Indian Ocean Commission, 134; land area of, 213; topography of, 213–14

Seychelles Agricultural Development Company (Sadeco), 231

Seychelles Archipelago, 207–8; number of islands in, 213

Seychelles Broadcasting Corporation, 236, 243

Seychelles Defence Academy, 319

Seychelles Democratic Party, 242

Seychelles Development Bank, 246

Seychelles Fishing Authority, 233

Seychelles Liberation Committee, 240, 315

Seychelles Marketing Board, 226

Seychelles-Mauritius Joint Cooperation Commission, xxi

*Seychelles Nation*, 243

Seychelles National Environment Commission, 214

Seychelles National Investment Corporation, 226
Seychelles National Movement, 242, 315
Seychelles People's Defence Forces. *See* armed forces of Seychelles
Seychelles People's Liberation Army. *See* armed forces of Seychelles
Seychelles People's Progressive Front (SPPF), xxv, 207, 212; dominance of, xxv
Seychelles People's United Party (SPUP), 207; platform of, 210, 211
Seychelles Polytechnic, 219, 222
Seychelles Popular Anti-Marxist Front (SPAMF), 240, 315
Seychelles Savings Bank, 226
Seychelles Shipping Line, 236
Seychelles Taxpayers' and Producers' Association (STPA), 209–10
Seychelles Timber Company, 226
Seychellois Party (Parti Seselwa), 239
shipping, 214, 290
Sihanaka people. as percentage of Madagascar population, 35
Sima Mountains (Comoros), 169
Singapore: trade of, with Maldives, 279; trade of, with Seychelles, 237
Sinhalese people (Maldives), xxvi, 265
Sino-Mauritians, xx
SINPA. *See* Association for the National Interest in Agricultural Products
Sir Seewoosagur Ramgoolam International Airport (Mauritius), 127, 128
slave class. in Comoros, 148
slave descendants: in Comoros, 174–76; in Merina culture, 49; religion of, 45
slavery: abolished, 97, 99, 100, 149, 208, 297; in Comoros, 148; conditions of, 208; in Madagascar, 10; in Mauritius, 97, 99
slaves: in Comoros, 148; Comoros as source of, 147–48; Madagascar as source of, 10, 12; in Mauritius, 98, 99, 113; raids for, 148; in Seychelles, 208, 209
slave trade, 288; in Madagascar, 10, 12, 31, 36; outlawed, 12
smuggling: in Madagascar, 70; in Maldives, 330; in Mauritius, 310
social classes: of Merina, 47; of Sakalava, 47; in Seychelles, 218–19
Social Democratic Party of Madagascar

(Parti Social Démocrate de Madagascar—PSD), 15; platform of, 15; political base of, 17
Socialist Party of Comoros (Parti Socialiste des Comores—Pasoco), 151; formed, 151; political base of, 151
socialist revolution (Madagascar): goals of, 19–20
social security. *See* welfare
social structure (Comoros): clans in, 173; *grand mariage* in, 174
social structure (Madagascar), 46–49; kinship in, 46–47; ranking in, 46–47
social structure (Maldives), 266–67; caste system in, 266
social structure (Mauritius): caste system in, 114
social structure (Seychelles), 218–19; marriage in, 219; matriarchal, 219; race in, 218, 219
Société Bambao (French), 181, 182
Société Comorienne de Navigation. *See* Comoran Navigation Company
Société Comorienne des Viandes. *See* Comoran Meat Company
Société de Développement de la Pêche Artisanale des Comores. *See* Development Company for Small-Scale Fisheries of Comoros
Société d'Intérêt National des Produits Agricoles. *See* Association for the National Interest in Agricultural Products
Socovia. *See* Comoran Meat Company
Sogecom, 160
Soilih, Ali: assassination attempts on, 153; as head of state, 152, 322; killed, 154, 322
Soilih government (Comoros), 152–54, 322; armed forces under, 153; overthrown, 146; reform program of, 152–53, 322; retribution on, 156
soils: erosion of, 187; of Madagascar, 27–28
Somalia, 293
Souli, Andrian, 148
South Africa, 287; aid to Comoros from, 161; in Comoran economy, 159, 188; in Indian Ocean conference, xxi; investment by, 70; military assistance from, 321, 327; and Presidential Guard, 161, 325; relations of, with

Comoros, 145, 160–61, 195–96, 324, 326, 327; relations of, with Madagascar, xx, 82, 85, 294; relations of, with Mauritius, 132, 134, 135; relations of, with Seychelles, xxiv, 247, 313, 314; in Seychelles coups, 212; tourists from, 125, 235; trade with, 125; trade of, with Madagascar, 85; trade of, with Seychelles, 237

South Africans: in Comoros, 172

South Asian Association for Regional Cooperation (SAARC), 282

South Korea. *See* Korea, Republic of

South Mahavavy River (Madagascar), 27

southwest region of Madagascar, 23, 27, 33; agriculture in, 64; climate in, 28; peoples of, 38

Soviet Indian Ocean Squadron, 294

Soviet Union (*see also* Russia): aid from, to Seychelles, 246; invasion of Afghanistan by, 293; matériel from, 81, 304, 320; military advisers from, 81, 320; military assistance from, 320; military interests of, 287, 290, 293; military training by, 302, 306; relations of, with Madagascar, 81–82; relations of, with Seychelles, 245; study abroad in, 81

Spain: aid from, 62

SPAMF. *See* Seychelles Popular Anti-Marxist Front

Special Mobile Force (Mauritius), 309

SPPF. *See* Seychelles People's Progressive Front

SPUP. *See* Seychelles People's United Party

Sri Lanka: guestworkers from, xxvi, 266; relations of, with Maldives, 257; trade of, with Maldives, 273, 279

Stabex (Stabilization of Export Earnings), 186

Stabilization of Export Earnings. *See* Stabex

State Bank of India, 276

state of emergency: in Comoros, 328; in Madagascar, 18, 295; in Mauritius, 98, 105–6; in Seychelles, 239

State Finance Corporation (Mauritius), 124

state security: in Comoros, 326; in Madagascar, 300–301; in Seychelles, 318–19

State Service (Mauritius), 311

Stationery, Printing, and Computer

Equipment (Seychelles), 228

Stein, Peter, 115

stock exchange: in Mauritius, 121

STPA. *See* Seychelles Taxpayers' and Producers' Association

strikes: in Comoros, 185, 195; general, 18, 295; in Madagascar, 18, 22, 295; in Mauritius, 103, 106; in Seychelles, 230

structural adjustment program: of Comoros, 182, 193; of Madagascar, 56, 58–60, 66

student demonstrations: in Comoros, 151, 179; in Madagascar, 18, 21, 52, 295, 302

subsidies: in Madagascar, 66; in Mauritius, 120, 123; in Seychelles, 228

Suez Canal, 288

suffrage: in Comoros, 153, 190; in Madagascar, 15, 75, 77; in Mauritius, 102, 104, 107; in Seychelles, 209, 238

sugar, xxi; export of, 97, 125; introduction of, 99; plantations, 97, 148; production of, 55, 97, 100, 110, 112, 121; refining, 99

sultanate (Maldives), 280; elective, 259; restored, 260; suspended, 259, 260

Supreme Court: of Comoros, 158, 191–92, 193, 327; of Madagascar, 76, 307; of Mauritius, 130, 132, 312; of Seychelles, 321, 243

Supreme Revolutionary Council (Madagascar), 19, 296; members of, 20

Swahili: broadcasts in, 181

Switzerland: relations of, with Madagascar, 80

Taiwan. *See* China, Republic of

Taki, Mohamed, 158, 192

Tamil language: in Mauritius, 115

Tamou, Omar, 328

Tanala people (Madagascar), 35

Tanjon' i Bobaomby. *See* Cap d'Ambre

Tanora Tonga Saina (Madagascar), 296

Tanzania: aid from, to Seychelles, 212; Comorans in, 172; military assistance from, 315, 326; military training in Comoros by, 322, 326; relations of, with Comoros, 156; relations of, with Seychelles, 245, 246

taxes: in Madagascar, xix, 59; in Maldives, 276; in Mauritius, 128; in

Seychelles, xxv, 228

teachers: training of, 51, 116, 178, 221

Tea Development Authority (Mauritius), 122

telecommunications: in Comoros, 156, 184, 190; in Madagascar, 73; in Maldives, 274, 276, 278; in Mauritius, 127; in Seychelles, xxiv, 235

telephones: in Comoros, 161, 190; in Madagascar, 73; in Maldives, 278; in Mauritius, 128, 133, 134; in Seychelles, 236

television: in Comoros, 181; languages of broadcast, 117, 118, 218; in Madagascar, 73; in Maldives, 283; in Mauritius, 117; in Seychelles, 218, 236, 240, 243

Television Maldives, 283

Texaco Corporation, 234

Thakurufaan, Muhammad, 259

Third Republic (Madagascar) (1993– ), 22–23; foreign relations under, 85

Toamasina (Madagascar), 34; investment in, 61; port of, 73

Tôlanaro (Madagascar), 9

Toliara (Madagascar): investment in, 61; rainfall in, 28

topography: of Comoros, xxii; of Madagascar, 23–28; of Maldives, xxvi; of Seychelles, xxiii

tortoises: in Seychelles, 208, 214

tourism: in Comoros, 162, 188; in Madagascar, xx, 71; on Mahoré, 168; in Maldives, xxvi, 261, 266, 273, 274, 276; in Mauritius, xxi, 97, 120, 125, 129, in Seychelles, xxiv, 207, 211, 216, 224, 228, 229, 234–35, 246, 247

trade (*see also* exports; imports): balance, 125; by Comoros, 147; deficit, 61, 145, 125, 184, 225, 278; with Europeans, 10, 147; with France, xx, 71; with Germany, 71; with India, xxii; through Indian Ocean, xvii; with Japan, 71; by Madagascar, 10, 61, 71–72; by Maldives, 278–79; by Mauritius, 125, 133–34, 135; by Seychelles, 225, 236–37; with United Arab Emirates, xxii; with United States, xxii, 71

Trade Union Industrial Act (1993) (Seychelles), 230

transportation: airports, 73, 127, 168, 188–90, 210, 211, 216, 235, 236, 277; in Comoros, 188–90; in Madagascar,

24, 72–73; in Maldives, 274, 277–78; in Mauritius, 126–27; ports, xxiv, 24, 73, 97, 127, 133, 148–49, 156, 169; railroads, xix, 55, 72–73, 127; roads, 72, 126, 156, 190, 216, 235, 278; in Seychelles, 228, 235–36; vehicles, 126, 235, 278; water, 24, 235

Travail pour Tous. *See* Work for All

treaties: between France and Comoro Islands, 149; between France and Sakalava people, 12

Treaty of Paris (1814), 100, 208

Tromelin Island (Mauritius), 108 , 133

Tsaratanana Massif (Madagascar), 23, 24, 33; peoples of, 38

Tsimihety people (Madagascar), 36, 38; as percentage of Madagascar population, 38; social structure of, 49

Tsiranana, Philibert, 9, 15; consolidation of power by, 17; opposition to, 16–17; as president, 16, 303

Tsiranana government (Madagascar): dissolved, 18, 56, 295; economy under, 18

Tuna Fishing Association, 233


UCP. *See* Comoran Union for Progress

UDC. *See* Comoros Democratic Union

Udzima. *See* Comoran Union for Progress

Ultramar Canada, Inc., 234

UNDC. *See* National Union for Comoran Democracy

underemployment: in Madagascar, xx

UNDP. *See* United Nations Development Programme

unemployment: in Comoros, xxiv; in Madagascar, xx; in Maldives, 276; in Mauritius, 106, 126

UNESCO. *See* United Nations Educational, Scientific, and Cultural Organization

Union Comorienne pour le Progrès. *See* Comoran Union for Progress

Union Démocratique des Comores. *See* Comoros Democratic Union

Union des Travailleurs des Comores. *See* Union of Comoran Workers

Union for a Democratic Republic in Comoros (Union pour une République Démocratique aux Comores—

URDC), 159
Union Nationale pour la Démocratie Comorienne. *See* National Union for Comoran Democracy
Union of Comoran Workers (Union des Travailleurs des Comores), 185
Union pour une République Démocratique aux Comores. *See* Union for a Democratic Republic in Comoros
United Arab Emirates: aid to Maldives from, 279; trade of, with Comoros, xxii
United National Front (Comoros), 152
United National Front of Comorans-Union of Comorans (Front National Uni des Komoriens-Union des Komoriens—FNUK-Unikom), 156
United Nations: Comoros in, 154, 196; and Mahoré issue, 166; Maldives in, 282; Seychelles in, 245
United Nations Development Programme (UNDP), 60, 184
United Nations Educational, Scientific, and Cultural Organization (UNESCO): aid from, 181
United Nations Food and Agriculture Organization (FAO), 118, 186
United Nations World Food Program (WFP), 67
United Opposition Party (Seychelles), 240, 242
United States: aid from, 80, 84, 184, 187, 279, 246; and attempted coups in Seychelles, 314; education in, 222; military assistance from, 303, 306, 312, 320–21, 327; military base on Diego Garcia, xxi, 80, 107, 134–35, 245, 290, 293–94; military interests of, 287, 290, 293; military relations of, with Madagascar, 306; military training by, 302, 306, 312, 325, 326, 327; relations of, with Madagascar, 80, 83, 306; relations of, with Mauritius, xxi, 134; relations of, with Seychelles, 246–47; satellite tracking stations, 20, 80, 247, 320; strategic interests of, 289; trade of, with Comoros, xxii, 184; trade of, with Madagascar, 71, 72; trade of, with Maldives, 279; trade of, with Mauritius, 99, 125, 134
United States Army Command and General Staff College, 306

United States Central Command, 293
United States Commander in Chief Pacific, 293
United States Naval War College, 306
United States Peace Corps, 246
United States Rapid Deployment Joint Task Force, 293
United Suvadivan Republic, 260
University of Madagascar, 51
University of Mauritius, 116
urban areas: in Comoros, 172; education in, 116; population in, 31, 112, 172; in Madagascar, 31; in Mauritius, 112
URDC. *See* Union for a Democratic Republic in Comoros
Urdu language, 114
Uteem, Cassam, 131

Vacoas-Phoenix (Mauritius), 112; government of, 130
Vanguard of the Malagasy Revolution (Atokin'ny Revolisiona Malagasy—Arema), 20
vanilla, xxii, 55, 58, 67, 68, 145, 149, 161, 162, 168, 181, 184, 185, 186, 187–88, 209, 232
Veillard, Max, 328
Very Important Persons Security Unit (Mauritius), 311
Victoria (Seychelles), 213; port of, xxiv
Victoria Hospital (Seychelles), 223
Virahsawmy, Dev, 106; assassination attempt on, 106
Vital Forces Committee. *See* Comité des Forces Vives
Voice of the Islands. *See* Voix des Îles
Voix des Îles (Voice of the Islands) (Comoros), 195
volcanoes: in Comoros, 169; in Madagascar, 24; in Mauritius, 109
VVS. *See* Iron And Stone Ramification
Vy Vato Sakelika. *See* Iron And Stone Ramification

wages: in Mauritius, 126; in Seychelles, 230
water: in Comoros, 170, 180; in Madagascar, 28; in Maldives, 263, 271, 274; in Mauritius, 127; in Seychelles, 214, 216, 229

welfare (Mauritius), 106, 118
welfare (Seychelles), 207, 212, 224
west coast of Madagascar, 23, 27, 33; agriculture in, 64; climate in, 28; peoples of, 35–36
West Germany. *See* Germany, Federal Republic of
Western Indian Ocean Tuna Organization, xxiv
Western Sahara: relations of, with Madagascar, 82
West Germany. *See* Germany, Federal Republic of
White Party. *See* Parti Blanc
women: in Comoros, 176–77, 328; education of, 176, 219; employment of, 116, 118–19, 120, 126, 176, 277; in legislature, xxvi, 219–20; in Mahoré, 176–77; in Maldives, 267, 276, 330; in Mauritius, 118–20; Merina, 48; rights of, xviii, xxii, xxiv, xxvi, 219, 259, 328, 330; in Seychelles, 219–20; single, status of, 176, 219–20, 267; suffrage of, 176; violence against, 119–20
Women's Federation (Comoros), 177
workers: conditions for, 103; in Madagascar, 18; in Mauritius, 103, 120, 126; rights of, xviii, xxii, xxiv, xxvi–xxvii, 231, 328, 330; in Seychelles, xxv, 231

Work for All (Travail pour Tous) (Mauritius), 106
work force: in Seychelles, 229
World Bank: and Comoros, 182, 196; economic reforms under, xxiii; education aid from, 117; and Madagascar, 56, 58; and Maldives, 261, 274, 279, 282; and Mauritius, 107, 128, 135; and Seychelles, 229; structural adjustment programs, 56, 58, 128, 182
World Food Program, 186
World Health Organization (WHO), 54; aid from, 180, 271; family planning program, 265
World War I, 289, 297
World War II, 289, 297, 309

ylang-ylang, xxii, 145, 149, 161, 168, 170, 181, 184, 185, 186, 187–88

Zafi-Raminia people (Madagascar), 34
Zafy, Albert, 9; in elections of 1993, xviii–xix, 296; ethnicity of, 75; as president, 22, 75
Zafy government (Madagascar): agriculture under, 58; economy under, 57, 59, 61; foreign relations under, 304
Zaki, Ahmed: as prime minister, 260

# Contributors

**Vincent Ercolano** has edited and written works on various geographic areas.

**Helen Chapin Metz** is Supervisor, Middle East/Africa/Latin America Unit, Federal Research Division, Library of Congress.

**Thomas P. Ofcansky** is a Senior African Analyst with the Department of Defense.

**Karl E. Ryavec**, formerly an analyst at the Defense Mapping Agency, is a doctoral candidate, Department of Geography, University of Hawaii, Honolulu.

**Peter J. Schraeder**, Assistant Professor, Department of Political Science, Loyola University, Chicago, is the author of numerous published works on Africa.

**Jean R. Tartter**, a retired Foreign Service Officer, has written extensively on Africa for the Country Studies series.

**Anthony Toth** has written for various publications on the Middle East and Africa.

# Published Country Studies

## (Area Handbook Series)

| | | | | |
|---|---|---|---|---|
| 550–65 | Afghanistan | | 550–36 | Dominican Republic |
| 550–98 | Albania | | | and Haiti |
| 550–44 | Algeria | | 550–52 | Ecuador |
| 550–59 | Angola | | 550–43 | Egypt |
| 550–73 | Argentina | | 550–150 | El Salvador |
| | | | | |
| 550–111 | Armenia, Azerbaijan, | | 550–28 | Ethiopia |
| | and Georgia | | 550–167 | Finland |
| 550–169 | Australia | | 550–173 | Germany, East |
| 550–176 | Austria | | 550–155 | Germany, Fed. Rep. of |
| 550–175 | Bangladesh | | 550–153 | Ghana |
| | | | | |
| 550–112 | Belarus and Moldova | | 550–87 | Greece |
| 550–170 | Belgium | | 550–78 | Guatemala |
| 550–66 | Bolivia | | 550–174 | Guinea |
| 550–20 | Brazil | | 550–82 | Guyana and Belize |
| 550–168 | Bulgaria | | 550–151 | Honduras |
| | | | | |
| 550–61 | Burma | | 550–165 | Hungary |
| 550–50 | Cambodia | | 550–21 | India |
| 550–166 | Cameroon | | 550–154 | Indian Ocean |
| 550–159 | Chad | | 550–39 | Indonesia |
| 550–77 | Chile | | 550–68 | Iran |
| | | | | |
| 550–60 | China | | 550–31 | Iraq |
| 550–26 | Colombia | | 550–25 | Israel |
| 550–33 | Commonwealth Carib- | | 550–182 | Italy |
| | bean, Islands of the | | 550–30 | Japan |
| 550–91 | Congo | | 550–34 | Jordan |
| | | | | |
| 550–90 | Costa Rica | | 550–56 | Kenya |
| 550–69 | Côte d'Ivoire (Ivory | | 550–81 | Korea, North |
| | Coast) | | 550–41 | Korea, South |
| 550–152 | Cuba | | 550–58 | Laos |
| 550–22 | Cyprus | | 550–24 | Lebanon |
| | | | | |
| 550–158 | Czechoslovakia | | 550–38 | Liberia |

| | | | | |
|---|---|---|---|---|
| 550–85 | Libya | 550–184 | Singapore |
| 550–172 | Malawi | 550–86 | Somalia |
| 550–45 | Malaysia | 550–93 | South Africa |
| 550–161 | Mauritania | 550–95 | Soviet Union |
| 550–79 | Mexico | 550–179 | Spain |
| | | | |
| 550–76 | Mongolia | 550–96 | Sri Lanka |
| 550–49 | Morocco | 550–27 | Sudan |
| 550–64 | Mozambique | 550–47 | Syria |
| 550–35 | Nepal and Bhutan | 550–62 | Tanzania |
| 550–88 | Nicaragua | 550–53 | Thailand |
| | | | |
| 550–157 | Nigeria | 550–89 | Tunisia |
| 550–94 | Oceania | 550–80 | Turkey |
| 550–48 | Pakistan | 550–74 | Uganda |
| 550–46 | Panama | 550–97 | Uruguay |
| 550–156 | Paraguay | 550–71 | Venezuela |
| | | | |
| 550–185 | Persian Gulf States | 550–32 | Vietnam |
| 550–42 | Peru | 550–183 | Yemens, The |
| 550–72 | Philippines | 550–99 | Yugoslavia |
| 550–162 | Poland | 550–67 | Zaire |
| 550–181 | Portugal | 550–75 | Zambia |
| | | | |
| 550–160 | Romania | 550–171 | Zimbabwe |
| 550–37 | Rwanda and Burundi | | |
| 550–51 | Saudi Arabia | | |
| 550–70 | Senegal | | |
| 550–180 | Sierra Leone | | |

# Jordan
## a country study

Federal Research Division
Library of Congress
Edited by
Helen Chapin Metz
Research Completed
December 1989

On the cover: Mosaic of a man with a bird, from a Byzantine church in Madaba, ca. 500–700

Fourth Edition, First Printing, 1991.

**Library of Congress Cataloging-in-Publication Data**

Jordan : a country study / Federal Research Division, Library of
    Congress ; edited by Helen Chapin Metz. — 4th ed.
        p.   cm. — (Area handbook series) (DA pam ; 550-34)
    "Research completed December 1989."
    Includes bibliographical references (pp. 293–305) and index.
    1. Jordan.  I. Metz, Helen Chapin, 1928-   . II. Library of
Congress. Federal Research Division. III. Series. IV. Series: DA
pam ; 550-34.
DS153.J677     1991                                      91-6858
956.9504—dc20                                            CIP

Headquarters, Department of the Army
DA Pam 550-34

For sale by the Superintendent of Documents, U.S. Government Printing Office
Washington, D.C. 20402

# Foreword

This volume is one in a continuing series of books now being prepared by the Federal Research Division of the Library of Congress under the Country Studies—Area Handbook Program. The last page of this book lists the other published studies.

Most books in the series deal with a particular foreign country, describing and analyzing its political, economic, social, and national security systems and institutions, and examining the interrelationships of those systems and the ways they are shaped by cultural factors. Each study is written by a multidisciplinary team of social scientists. The authors seek to provide a basic understanding of the observed society, striving for a dynamic rather than a static portrayal. Particular attention is devoted to the people who make up the society, their origins, dominant beliefs and values, their common interests and the issues on which they are divided, the nature and extent of their involvement with national institutions, and their attitudes toward each other and toward their social system and political order.

The books represent the analysis of the authors and should not be construed as an expression of an official United States government position, policy, or decision. The authors have sought to adhere to accepted standards of scholarly objectivity. Corrections, additions, and suggestions for changes from readers will be welcomed for use in future editions.

Louis R. Mortimer
Acting Chief
Federal Research Division
Library of Congress
Washington, D.C. 20540

# Acknowledgments

The authors wish to acknowledge the contributions of the following individuals who wrote the 1980 edition of *Jordan: A Country Study:* Robert Rinehart, Irving Kaplan, Darrel R. Eglin, Rinn S. Shinn, and Harold D. Nelson. Their work provided the organization of the present volume, as well as substantial portions of the text.

The authors are grateful to individuals in various government agencies and private institutions who gave their time, research materials, and expertise to the production of this book. Special thanks are owed to the Jordan Information Bureau, which provided numerous photographs not otherwise credited, as well as photographs that served as the basis for the art work in this volume. Thanks go also to Dr. Helen Khal for her assistance in obtaining both the photographs and some data on Jordanian social welfare legislation.

The authors also wish to thank members of the Federal Research Division who contributed directly to the preparation of the manuscript. These people include Thomas Collelo, who reviewed all drafts and graphic material; Richard F. Nyrop, who reviewed all drafts and who served as liaison with the sponsoring agency; and Marilyn Majeska, who managed editing and production. Also involved in preparing the text were editorial assistants Barbara Edgerton and Izella Watson.

Individual chapters were edited by Sharon Costello. Catherine Schwartzstein performed the final prepublication editorial review, and Shirley Kessel compiled the index. Malinda B. Neale and Linda Peterson of the Library of Congress Composing Unit prepared the camera-ready copy, under the supervision of Peggy Pixley.

Invaluable graphics support was provided by David P. Cabitto, Sandra K. Ferrell, and Kimberly A. Lord. Harriett R. Blood assisted in preparing the final maps.

The authors would like to thank several individuals who provided research and operational support. Arvies J. Staton supplied information on ranks and insignia, and Ly H. Burnham assisted in obtaining demographic data.

# Contents

|  | Page |
|---|---|
| **Foreword** | iii |
| **Acknowledgments** | v |
| **Preface** | xiii |
| **Country Profile** | xv |
| **Introduction** | xxi |
| **Chapter 1. Historical Setting** | 1 |
| *Mark Lewis* | |
| THE JORDAN REGION IN ANTIQUITY | 5 |
| ISLAM AND ARAB RULE | 10 |
| OTTOMAN RULE | 13 |
| CONFLICTING NATIONALISMS: ARAB NATIONALISM AND ZIONISM | 17 |
| WORLD WAR I: DIPLOMACY AND INTRIGUE | 20 |
| TRANSJORDAN | 26 |
| HASHEMITE KINGDOM OF JORDAN | 29 |
| Hussein's Early Reign | 30 |
| Crisis and Realignment | 34 |
| Development and Disaster | 36 |
| The Guerrilla Crisis | 38 |
| WAR AND DIPLOMACY | 44 |
| THE RABAT SUMMIT CONFERENCE AND AFTER | 46 |
| Relations with the Palestine Liberation Organization | 50 |
| Jordanian-Syrian Relations | 50 |
| The Camp David Accords and Inter-Arab Politics | 52 |
| JORDAN IN THE 1980s | 55 |
| The Islamic Revolution and a New Arab Alignment | 55 |
| In Search of a Solution to the Palestinian Problem | 57 |
| Economic Austerity | 58 |
| The Israeli Invasion of Lebanon | 59 |
| **Chapter 2. The Society and Its Environment** | 63 |
| *Julie M. Peteet* | |
| GEOGRAPHY | 66 |
| Boundaries | 66 |

Topography ................................. 67
Climate ................................... 71
POPULATION ................................ 72
THE ORGANIZATION OF SOCIETY: COHESION
AND CONFLICT .............................. 76
Ethnicity and Language ..................... 77
Tribes and Tribalism ....................... 81
Villages ................................... 86
Palestinians ............................... 90
Urban Areas and Urbanization ............... 92
Migration ................................. 93
KINSHIP, FAMILY, AND THE INDIVIDUAL ........ 95
Family and Household ....................... 95
Family Relationships ....................... 97
Changing Social Relations and Values ....... 100
Women and Work ............................ 101
RELIGIOUS LIFE ............................. 103
Early Development of Islam ................. 104
Tenets of Sunni Islam ...................... 106
Islam in Social Life ....................... 109
Islamic Revival ........................... 110
Religious Minorities ....................... 112
EDUCATION ................................. 114
HEALTH AND WELFARE ........................ 117

**Chapter 3.** The Economy ..................... 125
*Robert Scott Mason*

STRUCTURE AND DYNAMICS OF THE ECONOMY ... 128
GDP by Sector ............................. 129
The Late 1980s ............................ 133
THE ROLE OF THE GOVERNMENT ................ 137
A Mixed Economy ........................... 138
The Budget ................................ 141
Development Planning ...................... 142
LABOR FORCE ............................... 145
Labor Emigration .......................... 145
Remittance Income ......................... 145
Labor Force and Unemployment .............. 146
INDUSTRY .................................. 147
Manufacturing ............................. 149
Industrial Policy ......................... 149
Electricity Generation .................... 153
TRANSPORTATION AND COMMUNICATIONS ........ 154
Transportation ............................ 154

Telecommunications ........................... 158
NATURAL RESOURCES ........................... 160
    Phosphates ............................... 160
    Potash ................................... 161
    Oil and Gas .............................. 161
    Water .................................... 164
AGRICULTURE ................................. 166
    Agricultural Development ................... 167
    Cropping and Production ................... 168
    Livestock ................................. 170
INTERNATIONAL TRADE ....................... 170
    Trade Balance ............................. 170
    Composition of Exports and Imports ............. 170
    Direction of Trade ......................... 173
BANKING AND FINANCE ......................... 174

**Chapter 4.** Government and Politics ........... 179
                   *Eric Hooglund*

THE CONSTITUTION ........................... 182
THE GOVERNMENT ............................. 183
    The King ................................. 185
    The Council of Ministers ................... 187
    The Legislature ........................... 188
    The Judiciary ............................. 191
    Local Administration ....................... 192
THE POLITICAL SETTING ....................... 193
    The Political Elite ......................... 193
    Political Dissent and Political Repression ......... 197
    The Palestinians and the Palestine Liberation
      Organization ........................... 198
FOREIGN POLICY ............................. 209
    Relations with Israel ....................... 209
    Relations with Arab States ................... 212
    Relations with the United States ............... 215
    Relations with Other Countries ............... 218
    Membership in International Organizations ........ 219
MEDIA ...................................... 219

**Chapter 5.** National Security ................... 221
                   *Jean R. Tartter*

SECURITY: A PERENNIAL CONCERN ............... 224
    Dimensions of the Military Threat ............... 225
    Internal Security ........................... 229
    The Palestinian Factor ....................... 232

THE MILITARY HERITAGE ....................... 233
   Historical Role .............................. 234
   World War II to 1967 ........................ 235
   June 1967 War and Aftermath ................. 236
THE MILITARY IN NATIONAL LIFE ............. 238
THE ARMED FORCES ......................... 241
   Command Structure ......................... 241
   Army ...................................... 243
   Air Force .................................. 247
   Defense Spending ........................... 250
PERSONNEL: COMPOSITION, RECRUITMENT,
  AND TRAINING ............................. 251
   Conscription ............................... 254
   Women in the Armed Forces .................. 255
   Conditions of Service ........................ 255
   Ranks and Insignia ......................... 256
   Training and Education ...................... 256
   People's Army and Reserves .................. 257
MILITARY RELATIONS WITH OTHER COUNTRIES .. 259
   Meeting Jordan's Equipment Needs in the 1980s .... 260
   Military Cooperation with the United States ....... 261
   Military Cooperation with Other Arab States ....... 263
THE INTERNAL SECURITY SYSTEM ............... 265
   Police Forces .............................. 265
   General Intelligence Department ............... 269
CRIMINAL JUSTICE .......................... 270
   Criminal Code ............................. 272
   Incidence of Crime ......................... 273
   Procedures in Criminal Law .................. 274
   Martial Law Courts ......................... 276
   Penal System .............................. 276

**Appendix. Tables** ........................... 279

**Bibliography** ................................ 293

**Glossary** ................................... 307

**Index** ..................................... 311

## List of Figures

1 Administrative Divisions of Jordan, 1989 ............... xx
2 The Jordan Valley in Biblical Times ................. 8
3 Mandate Allocations at the San Remo Conference,
  April 1920 ........................................ 24
4 Topography and Drainage .......................... 70
5 Population of the East Bank by Age and Sex, 1987 ....... 74

6 United Nations Relief and Works Agency Camps in Jordan,
    1989 .......................................... 78
7 Gross Domestic Product (GDP) by Sector of Origin,
    1978 and 1987 ................................. 132
8 Land Use and Other Economic Activities, 1989 .......... 148
9 Transportation System, 1989 ....................... 156
10 Government Organization, 1989 ..................... 184
11 Abbreviated Genealogy of the Hashimite Family, 1989 .... 186
12 Structure of the Palestine Liberation Organization
    (PLO), 1989 ..................................... 204
13 Comparison of Force Strengths in the Middle East, 1988 .. 228
14 Organization of National Defense, 1989 ............... 244
15 Major Military Installations, 1988 ................... 246
16 Military Ranks and Insignia, 1989 ................... 258

# Preface

Like its predecessor, this study is an attempt to treat in a concise and objective manner the dominant social, political, economic, and military aspects of contemporary Jordanian society. Sources of information included scholarly journals and monographs, official reports of governments and international organizations, newspapers, and numerous periodicals. Chapter bibliographies appear at the end of the book; brief comments on some of the more valuable sources suggested as possible further reading appear at the end of each chapter. Measurements are given in the metric system; a conversion table is provided to assist those readers who are unfamiliar with metric measurements (see table 1, Appendix). A glossary is also included.

The transliteration of Arabic words and phrases follows a modified version of the system adopted by the United States Board on Geographic Names and the Permanent Committee on Geographic Names for British Official Use, known as the BGN/PCGN system. The modification is a significant one, however, in that diacritical markings and hyphens have been omitted. Moreover, some personal and place names, such as King Hussein, Jordan River, and Petra, are so well known by these conventional names that their formal names—Husayn, Nahr al Urdun, and Batra, respectively, are not used.

# Country Profile

## Country

**Formal Name:** Hashemite Kingdom of Jordan.

**Short Form:** Jordan.

**Term for Citizens:** Jordanian(s).

**Capital:** Amman.

**Date of Independence:** May 25, 1946 (as Transjordan).

## Geography

**Size:** About 91,880 square kilometers.

**Topography:** Most of East Bank (see Glossary) consists of arid desert. Dead Sea lowest point on surface of earth (more than 400 meters below sea level). Jabal Ramm (1,754 meters) is Jordan's highest point. Except for short coastline on Gulf of Aqaba, country landlocked.

## Society

**Population:** In 1987 East Bank population—about 70 percent urban—2.9 million with annual growth rate variously given as between 3.6 and 4 percent.

**Languages:** Almost all Jordanians speak a dialect of Arabic as mother tongue; increasing numbers speak or understand Modern Standard Arabic. Most of those people who have another native language (e.g., Circassians, Armenians) also speak Arabic.

**Ethnic Groups:** Significant distinction between Palestinians (see Glossary)—estimated 55 to 60 percent of population—and Transjordanians (see Glossary). Small numbers of non-Arabs originating elsewhere include Circassians, Shishans (Chechens), Armenians, and Kurds.

**Religion:** Most Jordanians Sunni (see Glossary) Muslims; about 2,000 Shia (see Glossary) Muslims. Christians (Eastern Orthodox, Greek Orthodox, Greek Catholics, Roman Catholics, a few Protestants) constitute between 5 and 8 percent of population. Also other small religious groups, such as Druzes and Bahais.

**Education:** First six years (primary) and next three years (preparatory) compulsory and free; grades ten through twelve (secondary) also free. In 1987 more than 900,000 students enrolled in 3,366 schools with approximately 39,600 teachers. Nearly 68 percent of adult population literate; nearly 100 percent of ten-to-fifteen age-group literate.

**Health:** Water shortage and concomitant sanitary problems contribute to health problems. Steady increase in health facilities and medical personnel in major urban areas. Following adoption of primary health care concept, facilities and personnel better distributed in rural areas than in past. In 1986 life expectancy at birth was sixty-five years.

## Economy

**Gross Domestic Product (GDP):** In 1987 estimated at slightly more than US$5 billion; in 1988 about US$2,000 per capita; GDP real growth rate in 1989 estimated at 2 to 3 percent.

**Currency and Exchange Rates:** 1 Jordanian dinar (JD) = 1,000 fils. Average exchange rates 1989 US$1 = 571 fils; 1 JD = $1.75 (see Glossary).

**Government Budget:** Forecast in 1989 at JD1.035 billion, including a JD122 million deficit.

**Fiscal Year:** Calendar year.

**Industry:** Contributed about 14.6 percent of GDP in late 1980s; 90 percent of small and large industries concentrated in north between Amman and Az Zarqa. Industry consisted mainly of small establishments with few large companies accounting for much of employment and value added. In 1989 largest industries phosphate mining, fertilizers, potash, cement, oil refining, and electric power generation; most such firms partially government owned. Jordan turning in late 1980s to light-manufactured goods and technical industries, such as pharmaceuticals.

**Agriculture:** Main crops cereals, vegetables, fruit. Self-sufficient in poultry and eggs. Dependent on imports for substantial part of food supply.

**Imports:** In 1987 JD915.5 million. Major commodities: oil, foodstuffs, machinery, and transportation equipment, mostly from Western Europe, United States, Iraq, and Saudi Arabia.

**Exports:** In 1987 JD248.8 million. Major commodities: phosphates, potash, fertilizers, fruits, and vegetables to member countries of Arab Cooperation Council, Asian countries, and European countries.

## Transportation and Communications

**Roads:** In 1989 more than 7,500 kilometers, of which 5,500 kilometers asphalted; remainder gravel and crushed stone. Two major roads: north-south Desert Highway from Amman to Al Aqabah; east-west highway from Al Mafraq to Iraqi border.

**Railroads:** In 1989 619 kilometers of 1-meter narrow gauge, single track; newer spur lines to connect old Hijaz Railway with phosphate mines and port of Al Aqabah.

**Port:** Al Aqabah on Gulf of Aqaba contains sections for general cargo, phosphates in bulk, and potash and fertilizers.

**Airports:** In 1989 nineteen usable airports, of which fourteen had permanent surface runways. Two major airports: Queen Alia International Airport, thirty kilometers south of Amman, and old international airport at Marka, King Abdullah Airport, used primarily by Royal Jordanian Air Force.

**Pipelines:** In 1989 total of 209 kilometers, consisting mainly of segment of Trans-Arabian Pipeline (Tapline) and connecting link to refinery at Az Zarqa.

**Telecommunications:** In 1989 government-owned communications system included telephones, telex, telegraph, fax, and television. Telephone service being improved, with more than 200,000 telephones in service and 85,000 customers awaiting phones; one Atlantic Ocean Intelsat station; one Indian Ocean Intelsat station; one Arabsat station.

## Government and Politics

**Government:** Constitution of 1952 grants king both executive and legislative powers. Between 1967 and 1989, King Hussein has ruled as almost absolute monarch. Bicameral legislature, National Assembly, consists of Senate appointed by king and popularly elected House of Representatives. In late 1989 first national election since 1967 held. National Assembly met in December 1989. In July 1988, government renounced claims to reassert sovereignty over West Bank, under Israeli military occupation since June 1967 War, and turned over responsibility for links with West Bank to Palestine Liberation Organization (PLO). Subsequently, Jordan recognized PLO's declaration of independent Palestinian state in West Bank and Gaza Strip.

**Politics:** Political parties banned from 1957 to 1990; political groupings, in addition to existent Muslim Brotherhood, began to form for 1989 elections. Latent pressures for political participation, especially among Palestinians, who were underrepresented in top layers of narrowly based, Transjordanian-dominated power structure.

**Justice:** Court system consisted of civil, religious, and special courts. Tribal law abolished in 1976. No jury system; judges decide matters of law and fact.

**Administrative Divisions:** Jordan divided into eight governorates or provinces. Governorates further subdivided into districts, subdistricts, municipalities, towns, and villages.

**Foreign Affairs:** Jordan traditionally maintained close relations with United States, Britain, and other Western countries. During 1980s, however, Jordan expanded relations with Soviet Union, while remaining strongly committed to pan-Arabism and closely aligned with countries such as Egypt, Iraq, and Saudi Arabia.

## National Security

**Armed Forces:** In 1988 armed forces totaled about 85,300; components were army, 74,000; navy, 300; and air force, 11,000. National Service Law of 1976 required two years' service by males at age eighteen or when education completed; liberal exemptions granted for medical or compassionate reasons.

**Major Tactical Military Units:** Army had two armored divisions, two mechanized divisions (each division had three brigades), a Royal Guards Brigade, a Special Forces airborne brigade, and independent artillery and air defense battalions. Air force had four fighter ground-attack squadrons, two fighter squadrons, one advanced training squadron with backup combat potential, one transport squadron, and four helicopter squadrons. Navy, an integral part of army with coast guard mission, operated five coastal patrol boats in Gulf of Aqaba; three larger armed craft ordered in 1987.

**Major Equipment:** Bulk of armored vehicles, artillery, and antitank missiles provided by United States; additional tanks from Britain; tactical air defense missiles from Soviet Union; fixed Hawk air defense missiles from United States. Combat aircraft consisted of newer French-manufactured Mirages and older United States F–5s.

**National Security Costs:** Defense budget of JD256 million (US$763 million) in 1988, although not all assistance from Arab states—mainly Saudi Arabia—recorded in budget. Defense budget constituted 22 percent of total government spending in 1987.

**Internal Security Forces:** National police, known as Public Security Force, estimated to total 4,000 in 1988, under Ministry of Interior in peacetime but subordinated to Ministry of Defense in event of war. Internal and external security responsibility of General Intelligence Directorate, civilian agency headed by senior army officer reporting directly to prime minister and King Hussein.

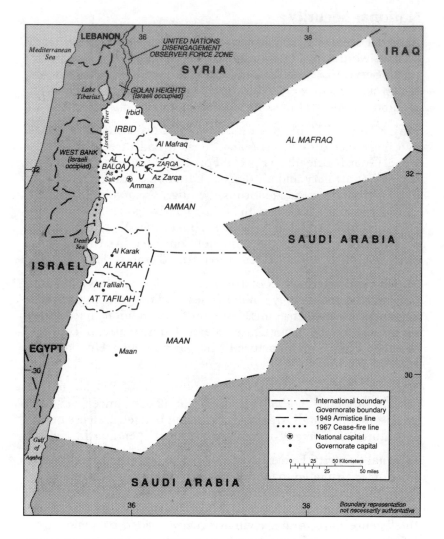

*Figure 1. Administrative Divisions of Jordan, 1989*

# Introduction

THE PRESENT KINGDOM of Jordan has had a separate existence for almost seventy years, from the time of the creation in 1921 of the Amirate of Transjordan under Abdullah of the Hashimite (also seen as Hashemite) family, the grandfather of King Hussein. To form Transjordan, the Palestine Mandate was subdivided along the Jordan River-Gulf of Aqaba line. At its creation, Jordan was an artificial entity because inhabitants of northern Jordan have traditionally associated with Syria, those of southern Jordan have associated with the Arabian Peninsula, and those of western Jordan have identified with Palestinians in the West Bank (see Glossary). Moreover, the area that constituted Jordan in 1990 has served historically as a buffer zone between tribes living to the west of the Jordan River as far as the Mediterranean Sea and those roaming the desert to the east of the Jordan River. Over the centuries, the area has formed part of various empires; among these are the Assyrian, Achaemenid, Macedonian, Nabataean, Ptolemaic, Roman, Ghassanid, Muslim, Crusader, and Ottoman empires.

Transjordan's creation reflected in large measure a compromise settlement by the Allied Powers after World War I that attempted to reconcile Zionist and Arab aspirations in the area. Britain assumed a mandate over Palestine and Iraq, while France became the mandatory power for Syria and Lebanon. In a British government memorandum of 1922, approved by the League of Nations Council, Jewish settlement in Transjordan was specifically excluded.

As Transjordan moved toward nationhood, Britain gradually relinquished control, limiting its oversight to financial and foreign policy matters. In March 1946, under the Treaty of London, Transjordan became a kingdom and a new constitution replaced the 1928 Organic Law. Britain continued to subsidize the Arab Legion, a military force established in 1923. In the Arab-Israeli War of 1948, the Arab Legion gained control for Transjordan of the West Bank, including East Jerusalem. The war added about 450,000 Palestinian Arab refugees as well as approximately 450,000 West Bank Arabs to the roughly 340,000 East Bank (see Glossary) Arabs in Jordan. In December 1948, Abdullah took the title King of Jordan, and he officially changed the country's name to the Hashemite Kingdom of Jordan in April 1949. The following year he annexed the West Bank.

Abdullah was assassinated in Jerusalem in July 1951. Abdullah's son, Talal, who was in ill health, briefly succeeded to the throne before being obliged to abdicate in favor of his son, Hussein, in 1952. Hussein, who had been studying in Britain, could not legally be crowned until he was eighteen; in the interim he attended the British Royal Military Academy at Sandhurst and returned to Jordan in 1953 to become king.

The survival of Hussein as king of Jordan represents one of the longest rules in the Arab world, thirty-seven years. Hussein's survival has entailed a keen sense of what is politically possible; moving cautiously and seeking to build consensus, he has exercised skillful diplomacy, both domestically and regionally. For Hussein survival has involved achieving a balance between more liberal Palestinians and more traditionally oriented Transjordanians, particularly the loyal beduin tribes of the East Bank, as well as negotiating a place for Jordan among the Baathist regimes of Syria and Iraq, the Arab nationalism of Gamal Abdul Nasser and Egypt's successor governments, and the conservative rulers of Saudi Arabia and the Persian Gulf states. Moreover, Jordan has the longest border with Israel of any Arab state. Although Jordan has never signed a peace treaty with Israel, having lost the West Bank and East Jerusalem to Israel in the June 1967 War, Hussein nevertheless achieved an unofficial working relationship with Israel concerning the West Bank.

Despite Hussein's preference for cautious consensus, he is capable of decisive action when the maintenance of Hashimite rule is threatened. He took such action in connection with the Palestine Liberation Organization (PLO) guerrilla groups (fedayeen) in Jordan, based in the refugee camps, who became almost a state within a state. Intermittent fighting occurred from 1967 onward, with Israel engaging in reprisal raids against Jordan for fedayeen operations launched from Jordan, and the fedayeen increasingly directing their efforts against the Jordanian government rather than against Israel. Ultimately, in September 1970 a civil war broke out, martial law was reaffirmed, and as many as 3,500 persons are thought to have died. Despite various cease-fire agreements, sporadic fighting continued through July 1971, when the Jordanian government ordered the fedayeen either to leave Jordan or to assume civilian status. Isolated by the other Arab states because of its repression of the fedayeen, Jordan gradually had to repair relations with those countries because they constituted the major source of its financial aid.

In the process of maintaining Jordan's tenuous position in the region, Hussein's basic orientation has been pro-Western; he has sought economic and military assistance from the United States and Britain in particular. When arms purchases were blocked by the United States Congress, however, he did not hesitate to buy weapons from the Soviet Union. Regionally, following the Arab world's boycott of Egypt as a result of Anwar as Sadat's signing the Camp David Accords with Israel in 1978, Hussein sought a more significant leadership role. Fearful of Syria, which had intervened in Jordan in 1970, and apprehensive over the 1979 Iranian Islamic Revolution's destabilizing influence on the area, Hussein strongly supported Iraq in the 1980–88 Iran-Iraq War and established friendly relations with Iraqi president Saddam Husayn.

Hussein's precarious balancing act has resulted, to a significant degree, from Jordan's disparate population. According to unofficial estimates (the government does not provide a breakdown of statistics on East Bank and West Bank inhabitants), from 55 to 60 percent of Jordan's population is Palestinian. Moreover, in contrast to the strong rural element in Jordan's early history, according to the World Bank (see Glossary) in the late 1980s about 70 percent of the population was urban, one-third of the total residing in the capital of Amman (see fig. 1). Tribal relations characterized pre-1948 Transjordan, extending to village dwellers and many in the cities as well as rural areas. Such relations hindered the assimilation of West Bank Palestinians, who by the 1980s had established substantial economic and cultural influence in Jordan and who tended to be more liberal regarding the role of women. The government sought to minimize distinctions between people from the East Bank and those from the West Bank in large part by upgrading education; in 1989 Jordan had the highest number of students per capita of any country except the United States. A societal problem Jordan faced, however, was the disrespect for technical education and manual labor as opposed to academic education. Despite this difficulty, Jordan regarded its educated work force as its major economic asset. Having such a work force enabled Jordan to provide skilled and professional workers to other Arab states, particularly those in the Persian Gulf, and worker remittances were a leading source of gross national product (GNP—see Glossary). In 1988 such remittances exceeded US$1 billion.

Jordan's relatively small population of fewer than 3 million persons in 1987 resulted in a limited domestic market unable to achieve economies of scale; thus, Jordan needed to develop export markets. Apart from its labor force, which the government actively encouraged to seek work abroad in view of scanty domestic employment opportunities, Jordan's principal natural resource consisted of phosphates—it was the world's third largest phosphates producer—and potash. It also was actively engaged in a search for oil and gas; small amounts of both had been discovered. These extractive industries, however, required large capital investments beyond the capability of Jordan's private sector. In consequence, the government not only played the key role in development planning but also became a major economic participant, ultimately sharing in forty semipublic companies, contrary to its avowed advocacy of free enterprise. In addition, Jordan benefited from the Civil War in Lebanon that began in 1975 and the war's troubled aftermath, which heightened Jordan's role as a provider of banking, insurance, and professional services formerly supplied by Lebanon.

Jordan's long-term plans called for economic self-sufficiency, and the king's brother, Crown Prince Hasan, and the Jordan Technology Group that he founded in 1988 were key elements in Jordan's economic endeavors. The surface prosperity of the early 1980s, however, was ended by the downturn of oil prices in the late 1980s, the resulting return home from the Persian Gulf of thousands of Jordanian workers, the decrease in Arab subsidies to Jordan (from more than US$1 billion in 1981 to about US$400 million in 1990), and Jordan's increasing debt (estimated in early 1990 at between US$6 and US$8 billion). Austerity was reflected in the 1988–89 devaluation of the dinar (for value of the dinar—see Glossary) by more than 40 percent to counter the black market, the freezing of the exchange rate, and increased import duties on luxury goods. These measures, combined with the reduction of subsidies on many basic commodities to comply with International Monetary Fund (IMF—see Glossary) requirements led to riots by East Bankers and beduins in several towns in late 1989. Jordan had been obliged to reduce subsidies as part of an economic stabilization program so as to qualify for a US$79.3 million IMF credit. IMF loan endorsement was a precondition for Jordan's rescheduling payment on many of its outstanding loans and obtaining new loans of more than US$300 million from the World Bank, Japan, and the Federal Republic of Germany (West Germany). Furthermore, Jordan was sharply affected by the end of the Iran-Iraq War in 1988; during the war, because of its good transportation facilities, especially between the port of Al Aqabah and Amman, Jordan served as the primary transshipment point for goods destined for Iraq.

The development of service industries, of industries involving import substitution, and of export industries, such as industrial chemicals and pharmaceuticals that required technical expertise, was an economic necessity for Jordan because its agricultural potential was very limited—the greater part of the country is desert. Moreover, Jordan was facing a water shortage in the near future. With a population estimated to be growing by at least 3.6 percent per year, plus expanded industrial use of water, some experts estimated that the demand for water could outstrip supply by the early 1990s. Jordan's attempt to stimulate exports was a major factor in its formation in early 1989 of the Arab Cooperation Council, consisting of Jordan, Egypt, Iraq, and the Yemen Arab Republic (North Yemen), with headquarters in Amman. This regional arrangement, however, promised relatively little economic advantage because the participants tended to produce similar goods. In spite of all of its efforts, Jordan continued to rely heavily on foreign aid, which in the 1980s constituted between 30 and 40 percent annually of government revenue before borrowing.

Economic reasons thus shaped not only Jordan's domestic development and employment policies—the government was the largest single employer, accounting for more than 40 percent of the work force—but also its foreign policy because of Jordan's dependence on foreign aid. Although Jordan is a constitutional monarchy, the king has extensive legal powers that allow him to shape policy by appointing the prime minister, other cabinet ministers, and the thirty-member Senate, as well as by dismissing the National Assembly (composed of the Senate and the eighty-member House of Representatives) and ruling by decree if he sees fit. Traditionally, prime ministers have come from East Bank families loyal to the Hashimites. The House of Representatives originally had equal representation from both the East Bank and the West Bank; prior to the elections of November 1989, no general election had been held for more than twenty-two years (since the June 1967 War) in view of the impossibility of elections in the Israeli-occupied West Bank. Experts believe that a major reason for holding the 1989 elections was to defuse discontent, reflected in the 1989 riots, among beduins and East Bankers traditionally loyal to the crown.

Although martial law remained in effect, the 1989 elections were free, the king having released all political prisoners in a general amnesty in the first half of 1989. Elections were preceded by considerable press criticism of government policies and active campaigning by 647 candidates. Among the criticisms was that of disproportionate representation: electoral districts were so drawn as to give greater weight to rural areas at the expense of cities. Political parties had been banned since 1957 so candidates ran with only informal affiliations. To the government's chagrin, twenty Muslim Brotherhood adherents, fourteen Islamists with other affiliations, and ten secular antigovernment candidates were elected, leaving progovernment representatives in the minority. The success of the Muslim Brotherhood was not surprising because it was the only organized quasi-political organ participating in the elections and because the PLO intentionally remained on the sidelines.

The Muslim Brotherhood appealed to the poor particularly and advocated jihad, or holy war, against Israel to liberate the West Bank. Many observers believed that the Muslim Brotherhood garnered protest votes primarily and that genuine Brotherhood sympathizers were relatively few. It should be noted, however, that Jordan is an overwhelmingly Muslim country. More than 90 percent of the population are Sunni (see Glossary) Muslims; there are some Shishans who are Shia (see Glossary) Muslims; and the remainder of the population is made up of a small number of Christians of various sects, Druzes, and Bahais.

In November 1989, the king named as prime minister Mudar Badran, considered to have better Islamic links than his predecessor, Zaid ibn Shakir. Badran succeeded in forming a cabinet that included two independent Islamists and two leftist nationalists from the Democratic Bloc, a new informal political group, but he was obliged to make some concessions to the Muslim Brotherhood, such as bringing Jordanian law closer to Islamic sharia law. A major task facing the new government is the drawing up of the National Charter (Mithaq al Watani), a statement of principles to guide the country's political system. This charter is to be devised by sixty representatives of various political persuasions appointed by the king in May 1990. The charter is expected to stress popular loyalty to the monarchy and to limit the existence of political parties controlled by external influences, such as the Communist Party of Jordan.

Because of Jordan's large Palestinian population, a major aspect of its external relations concerns its dealings with the PLO. Following the 1970–71 civil war, relations between Jordan and the PLO were strained, but in 1975 Hussein and PLO chief Yasser Arafat agreed to end recriminations. The king, however, refused to allow the PLO to reestablish a military or political presence in Jordan. Jordan was formally linked to the peace process as a result of the signature of the 1978 Camp David Accords, and a number of meetings occurred between Hussein and Arafat. When the PLO was expelled from Lebanon in 1982, Hussein relaxed his restrictions and allowed some PLO presence in Jordan. The Palestine National Council met in Amman in November 1984, strengthening Arafat's position with the more moderate PLO elements.

Cooperation between Hussein and Arafat continued with the signing in February 1985 of a joint Jordanian-Palestinian agreement on a peace framework. By terms of the agreement, the PLO would represent Palestinians but be part of a joint Jordanian-Palestinian delegation at an international peace conference. Hussein, who has long supported United Nations (UN) Security Council

Resolution 242 setting forth terms for a Middle East settlement, sought to persuade Arafat to endorse publicly both UN resolutions 242 and 338, which implicitly recognize Israel's right to exist. Arafat's failure to do so eroded their relationship, and Hussein ended the Jordanian-PLO agreement in February 1986. Both Hussein and Arafat vied for influence in the West Bank in 1986 and 1987, but the *intifadah,* or Palestinian uprising, which began in December 1987, showed the tenuous nature of West Bank support for Hussein. As a result of this weak support and the resolutions of the June 1988 Arab summit conference in Algiers that provided funds to support West Bank Palestinians through the PLO, in July 1988 Hussein formally abandoned Jordan's claim to the West Bank.

Jordan has stressed its support of the Arab cause in general, and its relations with most of the Arab states have been cordial, particularly relations with Egypt, Iraq, Kuwait, and Saudi Arabia. Hussein had advocated Egypt's reintegration into the Arab family of nations as early as 1981—Egypt was expelled from the League of Arab States (Arab League) in 1978, following the Camp David Accords. Jordan was one of the first Arab states to reestablish diplomatic relations with Egypt, doing so in 1984; after this date, relations between Hussein and Egyptian president Husni Mubarak became close. A friendly relationship with Iraq had arisen out of Jordan's support for Iraq in the Iran-Iraq War. Saudi Arabia and Kuwait, also having hereditary royal families, were the major contributors of financial aid to Jordan, in accordance with resolutions reached at Arab summit conferences. (At the Arab summit conference held in Baghdad in late May 1990, Hussein obtained renewed commitments of financial support for Jordan from various participants.) Jordan's relations with Syria were correct but distant. Despite the restoration of diplomatic relations with Libya in June 1990, relations remained somewhat tense because of Libyan support of anti-Hussein Palestinian guerrilla groups since 1970.

Potential threats to Jordan's external and internal security led to Jordan's devoting approximately 30 percent of government spending to national security. In view of his military training and qualification as a jet pilot, Hussein took a keen personal interest in Jordan's armed forces, both as regards top military appointments and matériel purchases. Because of Jordan's military tradition, dating back to the establishment of the Arab Legion in 1923, in 1990 the Jordan Arab Army was a well-trained and disciplined force with impressive firepower although it had not seen battle since 1971. Historically, Israel has been seen as Jordan's primary threat. Since the latter half of 1989, Hussein has stressed repeatedly the danger to the stability of the area, particularly to the West Bank and to Jordan, of the influx of thousands of Soviet Jewish immigrants to Israel.

In principle, two-year military service was compulsory for Jordanian males, but the number called up annually was limited by economic considerations and potential inductees could postpone service to complete higher education. Jordan also provided qualified military personnel to a number of other Arab states, especially those of the Arabian Peninsula, and trained their nationals in Jordanian military institutions.

Jordan's internal security forces, which like the military dated back to the Arab Legion, operated under constitutional legal restraints. The Public Security Force, the national police, came under the Ministry of Interior and was traditionally commanded by a senior army general. Other than maintaining law and order, the police and the General Intelligence Department monitored potentially disruptive elements in the population, such as left-wing factions and right-wing Muslim extremists.

The Iraqi invasion of Kuwait on August 2, 1990 found Jordan itself in a difficult situation, hard pressed both economically and politically. The enforcement of austerity measures in accordance with IMF loan requirements had improved Jordan's balance of payments position, but because of the decrease in the transit trade across Jordan to Iraq after the Iran-Iraq War ended and the return of Jordanian workers from the Persian Gulf states resulting from the downturn of oil prices, Jordanian unemployment had increased to between 15 and 20 percent. Economic austerity measures had widened the gap between the "haves" and the "have nots" and had caused discontent among elements of the population traditionally loyal to the monarchy: the beduins and the East Bankers.

To some extent, the discontent had been countered by the opportunity for political expression reflected in the November 1989 elections and by the king's ability to devote more time to East Bank problems following his giving up claim to the West Bank. The latter action minimized to some degree the competing nationalisms of Jordanians and Palestinians. The election results, however, indicated a marked degree of dissatisfaction with the government. This dissatisfaction was seen in the growing criticism of corruption among government officials and the demand for trials of those involved. There was also resentment that martial law as well as limitations to press freedom remained in force. Members of the middle class particularly seemed to have gained an awareness that the liberties they enjoyed were based primarily on the king's benevolence rather than on acknowledged democratic rights and a system of checks and balances on what appeared to be increasingly centralized authority. The urban majority of the population considered themselves underrepresented in the National Assembly, and the conservative religious elements felt that little had been done to make existing legislation conform with Islam. The victories of the left in elections of professional associations and trade unions in late 1989 and early 1990 indicated the growing public role of the left.

Organized political parties began to come into existence after the November 1989 elections. One of the first political entities to be formed, in July 1990, was a leftist grouping, the Arab Jordanian Nationalist Democratic Bloc (AJNDB), composed of Marxists, pan-Arab nationalists, and independent leftists. In August the Democratic Unity and Justice Party was formed, advocating the "liberation of occupied Palestinian Arab territory" by force and a strong role for government in a free economy. In contrast to these leftist inclined groups, in October the Muslim Brotherhood and other Islamists announced the formation of the Arab Islamic Coalition. The Jordanian Democratic Unity Party, an offshoot of the leftist Popular Front for the Liberation of Palestine, a member of the overall PLO organization, came into being in November. Thus, it was not surprising that in early January 1991, responding to these political realities, Prime Minister Badran announced that five Muslim Brotherhood members and two AJNDB members were being incorporated into the cabinet. The king also announced his approval in early January of the National Charter that endorsed constitutional rule, political pluralism, and the legalization of political parties.

Regionally, Jordan found itself between Scylla and Charybdis. Iraq's invasion of Kuwait in August 1990 and the United States response in sending forces to Saudi Arabia and the Persian Gulf and encouraging UN economic sanctions against Iraq put Jordan in a quandary. In accordance with the UN resolution, it closed the port of Al Aqabah to Iraq, and Hussein announced that Jordan refused to recognize Iraq's annexation of Kuwait. But Jordan expressed reservations concerning the Arab League resolution to endorse the sending of an Arab force to Saudi Arabia.

Hussein saw his role as that of an active mediator between Saddam Husayn and both the other Arab states and the West. Between August 1990 and late January 1991, the king held countless meetings with Western and Arab world leaders, including President Bush in mid-August. Initially, Hussein sought to promote an "Arab solution" to the Gulf crisis. Disappointed at the failure of this effort, he pursued an "Islamic solution" involving Islamic states outside the Arab world, and after the war began on January 16 he strove to end the conflict. This policy resulted from a number of factors. The king shared the view of the majority Palestinian element of Jordan's population that the West, led by the United States, was using a double standard in denouncing Iraq's invasion of Kuwait to the point that it was willing to go to war, while ignoring Palestinian grievances over Israel's occupation policies in the West Bank. This stance made the king popular with Palestinians, as did permission for the September holding of a pro-Iraqi conference by Jordanians and representatives of several major PLO groups, sponsored by the AJNDB. Yasser Arafat's August endorsement of Saddam Husayn had, however, created a rift in the PLO as well as cut off Saudi financial assistance to the PLO. Hussein also had a longstanding fear that Israel planned to make Jordan the substitute Palestinian state—this aim had been stated on numerous occasions by prominent members of Prime Minister Yitzhak Shamir's Likud Bloc—thus leading to the downfall of the Hashimite monarchy. The Gulf crisis was seen as a focus that would divert attention from the Israeli-Palestinian question and allow Israel greater latitude to pursue such a course of action. Both of these elements were reflected in the king's request to Jordanian parliamentarians in August to refer to him as ''sharif'' Hussein, demonstrating the king's view that the Gulf crisis represented a conflict between the Arab sovereignty and foreign domination similar to the situation that his greatgrandfather, Sharif Hussein of Mecca, faced at British hands in 1925.

Perhaps the most important reason for the king's seeking to reconcile the conflict was the economic consequence to Jordan of the crisis and the subsequent war. The Iraqi invasion of Kuwait created a stream of refugees, primarily Arab and Asian expatriate workers and their dependents, who had been living in Iraq and Kuwait. These persons entered Jordan at the rate of more than 10,000 per day, a total of more than 500,000 as of late September; they required food and shelter before most could be repatriated. This influx further strained Jordan's economy, in part because promised Western financial contributions to help defer costs of the humanitarian enterprise were slow in arriving. For example, Jordan was obliged to ration subsidized foods such as rice, sugar, and powdered milk at the beginning of September. Meanwhile, the boycott of Iraq had a major impact on Jordan because Iraq had been Jordan's principal export market and its major source of cheap oil (providing almost 90 percent of Jordan's oil), whereas Kuwait had been Jordan's second largest market.

Furthermore, Saudi Arabia, which had provided substantial economic support to Jordan in the past, was so angered over Jordan's failure to back it in its dispute with Iraq that it cut off oil exports to Jordan on September 20 and shortly afterward expelled twenty Jordanian diplomats. In turn, in early October Jordan closed its borders to trucks bound for Saudi Arabia and instituted fuel austerity conservation measures. The crisis also resulted in a dramatic drop in tourism income, a major component of Jordan's GDP. The situation caused Minister of Finance Basil Jardanah in the latter half of September to estimate that Jordan would lose US$2.1 billion the first year of the boycott and would need US$1.5 billion (by January this figure had been revised to US$2 billion) in aid to avoid economic collapse. He made a strong plea for financial aid to the UN and the West in general; various Western nations and Japan promised loans.

In early January, reflecting Jordan's concern over being caught between Iraq and Israel and the tension prevailing, Jordan mobilized its armed forces and transferred a number of troops from the east to the Jordan Valley, indicating that it considered the threat from Israel to be the more serious. As the deadline for Iraqi withdrawal from Kuwait came on January 15, Jordan announced that it would protect its land and air borders against external aggression.

Whatever the final outcome of the crisis resulting from Iraq's annexation of Kuwait, Middle East alignments have changed appreciably, and the fiction of Arab unity has been destroyed. Jordan's position in the midst of this regional dilemma has been rendered more precarious than it has been for many years.

January 29, 1991                          Helen Chapin Metz

# Chapter 1. Historical Setting

*Mosaic of a man in a boat, from the Byzantine Church of Saint Lots and Saint Prokopius at Khirbat al Muhayyat, ca. 550*

JORDAN'S LOCATION as a buffer zone between the settled region of the Mediterranean littoral west of the Jordan River and the major part of the desert to the east contributed significantly to the country's experience in ancient and more recent times. Until 1921, however, Jordan had a history as a vaguely defined territory without a separate political identity. Its earlier history, closely associated with the religions of Judaism, Christianity, and Islam, therefore comes under the histories of the contending empires of which it often formed a part.

By the time the area was conquered by the Ottoman Empire in the sixteenth century, the inhabitants of three general geographic regions had developed distinct loyalties. The villagers and town dwellers of Palestine, west of the Jordan River, were oriented to the major cities and ports of the coast. In the north of present-day Jordan, scattered villagers and tribesmen associated themselves with Syria while the tribesmen of southern Jordan were oriented toward the Arabian Peninsula. Although most of the populace were Arab Muslims, the integration of peoples with such differing backgrounds and regional characteristics hampered the creation of a cohesive society and state.

In 1921 the Amirate of Transjordan was established under British patronage on the East Bank by the Hashimite (also seen as Hashemite) prince Abdullah ibn Hussein Al Hashimi, who had been one of the principal figures of the Arab Revolt against the Ottoman Empire during World War I. Direct British administration was established in Palestine, where Britain (in the Balfour Declaration of 1917) had pledged to implement the founding of a Jewish homeland.

In 1947 Britain turned the problem of its Palestine Mandate over to the United Nations (UN). The UN passed a resolution that provided for the partition of the mandate into an Arab state, a Jewish state, and an international zone. When on May 14, 1948, the British relinquished control of the area, the establishment of the State of Israel was proclaimed. Transjordan's Arab Legion then joined the forces of other Arab states that had launched attacks on the new state. The end of the 1948–49 hostilities—the first of five Arab-Israeli wars—left Transjordan in control of the West Bank (see Glossary) and the Old City of Jerusalem. Abdullah changed the name of the country to Jordan, proclaimed himself king, and in 1950 annexed the West Bank. In the June 1967 War (known to Israelis as the Six-Day War), Israel seized the West Bank and reunited Jerusalem. In late 1989, the area remained under Israeli occupation (see fig. 1).

The dominant characteristic of the Hashimite regime has been its ability to survive under severe political and economic stress. Major factors contributing to the regime's survival have included British and United States economic and military aid and the personal qualities first of King Abdullah and then of his grandson, Hussein ibn Talal ibn Abdullah ibn Hussein Al Hashimi. King Hussein has been a skillful politician who has dealt adroitly with foreign and domestic crises by using caution and by seeking consensus. One exception to this style of policy making occurred during the 1970–71 battle against Palestinian resistance fighters, when the king ordered his mostly beduin-manned army to remove completely the Palestinian guerrillas, even after neighboring Arab states had called for a cease-fire.

During the late 1970s and early 1980s, regional events severely tested Jordan's stability. The election of the more hawkish Likud government in Israel and the expansion of Israeli settlements in the West Bank lent urgency to Hussein's quest for an Arab-Israeli territorial settlement. Arab ostracism of Egypt following the 1978 signing of the Camp David Accords and the 1979 Treaty of Peace Between Egypt and Israel ended Jordan's alliance with the Arab world's most politically influential and militarily powerful state. Jordan's vulnerability increased significantly in February 1979, when Shia radicals overthrew Mohammad Reza Shah Pahlavi of Iran. The Iranian revolutionaries threatened to expunge Western influences from the region and to overthrow non-Islamic Arab governments such as that of Jordan. Less than two years later, Iran and Iraq were embroiled in a costly war that caused a further shifting of Arab alliances; Jordan and the Arab states of the Persian Gulf sided with Iraq, while Syria supported Iran. Syrian-Jordanian relations deteriorated and nearly erupted in military conflict during the 1981 Arab summit conference in Amman, when Syrian president Hafiz al Assad accused Hussein of aiding the antigovernment Muslim Brotherhood in Syria. Finally, the downward slide of world oil prices that began in 1981 drained Jordan's economy of the large quantities of Arab petrodollars that had stirred economic development throughout the 1970s.

The turmoil besetting the Arab states in the 1980s presented Jordan with both risks and opportunities. With the traditional Arab powers either devitalized or, in the case of Egypt, isolated, Jordan was able to assume a more prominent role in Arab politics.

Moreover, as the influence of Jordan's Arab neighbors waned, Hussein pursued a more flexible regional policy.

The weakness of the Arab states, however, enabled the Begin government in Israel to pursue a more aggressive foreign policy and to accelerate the pace of settlements in the occupied territories. Thus, between 1981 and 1982, the Arab states reacted apathetically to Israel's attack on the Iraqi nuclear reactor, its annexation of the Golan Heights, and its June 1982 invasion of Lebanon. Israeli aggressiveness and Arab passivity combined to raise fears in Jordan that Israel might annex the occupied territories and drive the Palestinians into Jordan. These fears were fueled by frequent references by Israel's hawkish Minister of Agriculture Ariel Sharon to Jordan as a Palestinian state.

## The Jordan Region in Antiquity

The Jordan Valley provides abundant archaeological evidence of occupation by paleolithic and mesolithic hunters and gatherers. A people of neolithic culture, similar to that found around the Mediterranean littoral, introduced agriculture in the region. By the eighth millennium B.C., this neolithic culture had developed into a sedentary way of life. Settlements at Bayda on the East Bank and Jericho on the West Bank date from this period and may have been history's first "cities." Bronze Age towns produced a high order of civilization and carried on a brisk trade with Egypt, which exercised a dominant influence in the Jordan valley in the third millennium. This thriving urban culture ended after 2000 B.C., when large numbers of Semitic nomads, identified collectively as the Amorites, entered the region, which became known as Canaan. Over a period of 500 years, the nomads encroached on the settled areas, gradually assimilated their inhabitants, and—by the middle of the second millennium—settled in the Jordan Valley, which became a Semitic language area. At about this time, Abraham (known to the Arabs as Ibrahim) and his household entered the area from the direction of Mesopotamia. The Canaanites and others referred to this nomadic group of western Semites as the *habiru*, meaning wanderers or outsiders. The name *Hebrew* probably derived from this term. More abrupt was the incursion of the Hyksos from the north, who passed through Canaan on their way to Egypt.

After recovering from the Hyksos invasion, Egypt attempted to regain control of Syria, but its claim to hegemony there was contested by the empire-building Hittites from Anatolia (the central region of modern Turkey). The prolonged conflict between these two great powers during the fifteenth to thirteenth centuries B.C.

5

bypassed the East Bank of the Jordan, allowing for the development of a string of small tribal kingdoms with names familiar from the Old Testament: Edom, Moab, Bashan, Gilead, and Ammon, whose capital was the biblical Rabbath Ammon (modern Amman). Although the economy of the countryside was essentially pastoral, its inhabitants adapted well to agriculture and were skilled in metallurgy. The Edomites worked the substantial deposits of iron and copper found in their country, while the land to the north was famous for its oak wood, livestock, resins, and medicinal balms. The towns profited from the trade routes crisscrossing the region that connected Egypt and the Mediterranean ports with the southern reaches of the Arabian Peninsula and the Persian Gulf.

Midway through the thirteenth century B.C., Moses is believed to have led the Exodus of the Israelites from Egypt and to have governed them during their forty-year sojourn in the Sinai Peninsula. When they were barred by the Edomites from entering Canaan from the south, the Israelites marched north toward Moab. Under Joshua, they crossed west over the Jordan River. The conquest of Canaan by the Israelite tribes was completed between 1220 and 1190 B.C. The tribes of Gad and Reuben and half of the tribe of Manasseh were allocated conquered land on the East Bank. At about this time the Philistines, sea peoples who originated from Mycenae and who ravaged the eastern Mediterranean, invaded the coast of Canaan and confronted the Israelites in the interior. It was from the Philistines that Palestine derived its name, preserved intact in the modern Arabic word *falastin*.

Late in the eleventh century B.C., the Israelite tribes submitted to the rule of the warrior-king Saul. Under his successor David (ca. 1000–965 or 961 B.C.), Israel consolidated its holdings west of the Jordan River, contained the Philistines on the coast, and expanded beyond the old tribal lands on the East Bank. Ancient Israel reached the peak of its political influence under David's son, Solomon (965–928 B.C. or 961–922 B.C.), who extended the borders of his realm from the upper Euphrates in Syria to the Gulf of Aqaba in the south. Solomon, the first biblical figure for whom historical records exist outside the Bible, exploited the mineral wealth of Edom, controlled the desert caravan routes, and built the port at Elat to receive spice shipments from southern Arabia. With Solomon's passing, however, his much reduced realm divided into two rival Jewish kingdoms: Israel in the north and Judah (Judea), with its capital at Jerusalem, in the south. The history of the Jordan region over the next two centuries was one of constant conflict between the Jewish kingdoms and the kingdoms on the East Bank (see fig. 2).

In 722 B.C. Israel fell to the Assyrian king, Shalmaneser, ruler of a mighty military empire centered on the upper Tigris River. As a result, the Israelites were deported from their country. Judah preserved its political independence as a tributary of Assyria, while the rest of the Jordan region was divided into Assyrian-controlled provinces that served as a buffer to contain the desert tribes—a function that would be assigned to the area by a succession of foreign rulers.

Assyria was conquered in 612 B.C., and its empire was absorbed by the Neo-Babylonian Empire in Mesopotamia. Judah was taken by Nebuchadnezzar, who destroyed Jerusalem in 586 B.C. and carried off most of the Jewish population to Babylon. Within fifty years, however, Babylon was conquered by the Persian Cyrus II. The Jews were allowed to return to their homeland, which, with the rest of the Jordan region, became part of the Achaemenid Empire.

The Achaemenids dominated the whole of the Middle East for two centuries until the rise of Macedonian power under Alexander the Great. With a small but well-trained army, Alexander crossed into Asia in 334 B.C., defeated Persia's forces, and within a few years had built an empire that stretched from the Nile River to the Indus River in contemporary Pakistan. After his death in 323 B.C., Alexander's conquests were divided among his Macedonian generals. The Ptolemaic Dynasty of pharaohs in Egypt and the line of Seleucid kings in Syria were descended from two of these generals.

Between the third century B.C. and the first century A.D., the history of Jordan was decisively affected by three peoples: Jews, Greeks, and Nabataeans. The Jews, many of whom were returning from exile in Babylonia, settled in southern Gilead. Along with Jews from the western side of the Jordan and Jews who had remained in the area, they founded closely settled communities in what later became known in Greek as the Peraea. The Greeks were mainly veterans of Alexander's military campaigns who fought one another for regional hegemony. The Nabataeans were Arabs who had wandered from the desert into Edom in the seventh century B.C. Shrewd merchants, they monopolized the spice trade between Arabia and the Mediterranean. By necessity experts at water conservation, they also proved to be accomplished potters, metalworkers, stone masons, and architects. They adopted the use of Aramaic, the Semitic lingua franca in Syria and Palestine, and belonged entirely to the cultural world of the Mediterranean.

In 301 B.C. the Jordan region came under the control of the Ptolemies. Greek settlers founded new cities and revived old ones as centers of Hellenistic culture. Amman was renamed Philadelphia

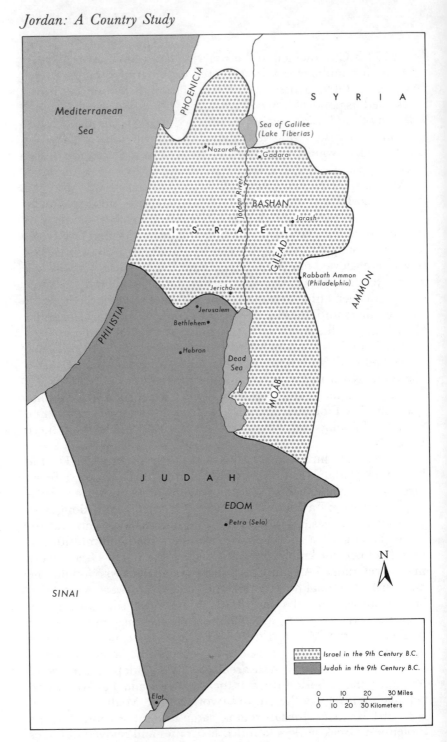

*Figure 2. The Jordan Valley in Biblical Times*

in honor of the pharaoh Ptolemy Philadelphus. Urban centers assumed a distinctly Greek character, easily identified in their architecture, and prospered from their trade links with Egypt.

The East Bank was also a frontier against the rival dynasty of the Seleucids, who in 198 B.C. displaced the Ptolemies throughout Palestine. Hostilities between the Ptolemies and Seleucids enabled the Nabataeans to extend their kingdom northward from their capital at Petra (biblical Sela) and to increase their prosperity based on the caravan trade with Syria and Arabia.

The new Greek rulers from Syria instituted an aggressive policy of Hellenization among their subject peoples. Efforts to suppress Judaism sparked a revolt in 166 B.C. led by Judas (Judah) Maccabaeus, whose kinsmen in the next generation reestablished an independent Jewish kingdom under the rule of the Hasmonean Dynasty. The East Bank remained a battleground in the continuing struggle between the Jews and the Seleucids.

By the first century B.C., Roman legions under Pompey methodically removed the last remnants of the Seleucids from Syria, converting the area into a full Roman province. The new hegemony of Rome caused upheaval and eventual revolt among the Jews while it enabled the Nabataeans to prosper. Rival claimants to the Hasmonean throne appealed to Rome in 64 B.C. for aid in settling the civil war that divided the Jewish kingdom. The next year Pompey, fresh from implanting Roman rule in Syria, seized Jerusalem and installed the contender most favorable to Rome as a client king. On the same campaign, Pompey organized the Decapolis, a league of ten self-governing Greek cities also dependent on Rome that included Amman, Jarash, and Gadara (modern Umm Qays), on the East Bank. Roman policy there was to protect Greek interests against the encroachment of the Jewish kingdom.

When the last member of the Hasmonean Dynasty died in 37 B.C., Rome made Herod king of Judah. With Roman backing, Herod (37–4 B.C.) ruled on both sides of the Jordan River. After his death the Jewish kingdom was divided among his heirs and gradually absorbed into the Roman Empire.

In A.D. 106 Emperor Trajan formally annexed the satellite Nabataean kingdom, organizing its territory within the new Roman province of Arabia that included most of the East Bank of the Jordan River. For a time, Petra served as the provincial capital. The Nabataeans continued to prosper under direct Roman rule, and their culture, now thoroughly Hellenized, flourished in the second and third centuries A.D. Citizens of the province shared a legal system and identity in common with Roman subjects throughout the empire. Roman ruins seen in present-day Jordan attest to the civic vitality of the region, whose cities were linked to commercial centers throughout the empire by the Roman road system and whose security was guaranteed by the Roman army.

After the administrative partition of the Roman Empire in 395, the Jordan region was assigned to the eastern or Byzantine Empire, whose emperors ruled from Constantinople. Christianity, which had become the recognized state religion in the fourth century, was widely accepted in the cities and towns but never developed deep roots in the countryside, where it coexisted with traditional religious practices.

In the sixth century direct control over the Jordan region and much of Syria was transferred to the Ghassanids, Christian Arabs loyal to the Byzantine Empire. The mission of these warrior-nomads was to defend the desert frontier against the Iranian Sassanian Empire to the east as well as against Arab tribes to the south; in practice, they were seldom able to maintain their claim south of Amman. The confrontations between Syrian, or northern, Arabs— represented by the Ghassanids—and the fresh waves of nomads moving north out of the Arabian Peninsula was not new to the history of the Jordan region and continued to manifest itself into the modern era. Contact with the Christian Ghassanids was an important source of the impulse to monotheism that flowed back into Arabia with the nomads, preparing the ground there for the introduction of Islam.

## Islam and Arab Rule

By the time of his death in A.D. 632, the Prophet Muhammad and his followers had brought most of the tribes and towns of the Arabian Peninsula under the banner of the new monotheistic religion of Islam (literally, submission), which was conceived of as uniting the individual believer, the state, and the society under the omnipotent will of God. Islamic rulers therefore exercised both temporal and religious authority. Adherents of Islam, called Muslims (those who submit to the will of God), collectively formed the House of Islam, or Dar al Islam (see Early Development of Islam, ch. 2).

Arab armies carried Islam north and east from Arabia in the wake of their rapid conquest, and also westward across North Africa. In 633, the year after Muhammad's death, they entered the Jordan region, and in 636, under Khalid ibn al Walid, they crushed the Byzantine army at the Battle of Uhud at the Yarmuk River. Jerusalem was occupied in 638, and by 640 all Syria was in Arab Muslim hands. Conversion to Islam was nearly complete among Arabs on the East Bank, although the small Jewish community in

*The Monastery, or Dir, at Petra,*
*a 2,000-year-old Nabataean city*

*The Treasury,*
*or Khaznah, at Petra*

Palestine and groups of Greek and Arab Christians were allowed to preserve their religious identities. Arabic soon supplanted Greek and Aramaic as the primary language of the region's inhabitants in both town and countryside.

Muhammad was succeeded as spiritual and temporal leader of all Muslims by his father-in-law, Abu Bakr, who bore the title caliph (successor or deputy) for two years. Under Umar (A.D. 634–44), the caliphate began efforts to organize a government in areas newly conquered by the Muslims. The Quran, Islam's sacred scripture, was compiled during the caliphate of Uthman (644–56), whose reign was brought to an end by an assassin. Uthman was succeeded by Muhammad's cousin and son-in-law Ali, the last of the four so-called orthodox caliphs, who was also assassinated in 661.

A dispute over the caliphal succession led to a permanent schism that split Islam into two major branches—the Sunni (see Glossary) and the Shia (see Glossary). The Shias supported the hereditary claim of Ali and his direct descendants, whereas the Sunnis favored the principle of consensual election of the fittest from the ranks of the *ashraf* (or *shurfa*—nobles; sing., sharif—see Glossary). Muslims in the Jordan region are predominantly Sunni.

After Ali's murder, Muawiyah—the governor of Syria and leader of a branch of Muhammad's tribe, the Quraysh of Mecca—proclaimed himself caliph and founded a dynasty—the Umayyad—that made its capital in Damascus. The Umayyad caliphs governed their vast territories in a personal and authoritarian manner. The caliph, assisted by a few ministers, held absolute and final authority but delegated extensive executive powers to provincial governors. Religious judges (qadis) administered Islamic law (sharia) to which all other considerations, including tribal loyalties, were theoretically subordinated.

The Umayyad Dynasty was overthrown in 750 by a rival Sunni faction, the Abbasids, who moved the capital of the caliphate to Baghdad. The Jordan region became even more of a backwater, remote from the center of power. Its economy declined as trade shifted from traditional caravan routes to seaborne commerce, although the pilgrim caravans to Mecca became an important source of income. Depopulation of the towns and the decay of sedentary agricultural communities, already discernible in the late Byzantine period, accelerated in districts where pastoral Arab beduins, constantly moving into the area from the south, pursued their nomadic way of life. Late in the tenth century A.D. the Jordan region was wrested from the Abbasids by the Shia Fatimid caliphs in Egypt. The Fatimids were in turn displaced after 1071 by the Seljuk Turks, who had gained control of the Abbasid caliphate in Baghdad.

The Seljuk threat to the Byzantine Empire and a desire to seize the holy places in Palestine from the Muslims spurred the Christian West to organize the First Crusade, which culminated in the capture of Jerusalem in 1099. The crusaders subsequently established the Latin Kingdom of Jerusalem, a feudal state that extended its hold to the East Bank. The crusaders used the term *Outre Jourdain* (Beyond Jordan) to describe the area across the river from Palestine—an area that was defended by a line of formidable castles like that at Al Karak.

In 1174 Salah ad Din Yusuf ibn Ayyub—better known in the West as Saladin—deposed the last Fatimid caliph, whom he had served as grand vizier, and seized power as sultan of Egypt. A Sunni scholar and experienced soldier of Kurdish origin, Saladin soon directed his energies against the crusader states in Palestine and Syria. At the decisive Battle of Hattin on the west shore of Lake Tiberias (Sea of Galilee), Saladin annihilated the crusaders' army in 1187 and soon afterward retook Jerusalem.

Saladin's successors in the Ayyubid Sultanate quarreled among themselves, and Saladin's conquests broke up into squabbling petty principalities. The Ayyubid Dynasty was overthrown in 1260 by the Mamluks (a caste of slave-soldiers, mostly of Kurdish and Circassian origin), whose warrior-sultans repelled the Mongol incursions and by the late fourteenth century held sway from the Nile to the Euphrates. Their power, weakened by factionalism within their ranks, contracted during the next century in the face of a dynamic new power in the Middle East—the Ottoman Turks.

## Ottoman Rule

Mamluk Egypt and its possessions fell to the Ottoman sultan, Selim I, in 1517. The Jordan region, however, stagnated under Ottoman rule. Although the pilgrim caravans to Mecca continued to be an important source of income, the East Bank was largely forgotten by the outside world for more than 300 years until European travelers "rediscovered" it in the nineteenth century.

For administrative purposes Ottoman domains were divided into provinces (*vilayets*) that were presided over by governors (pashas). The governors ruled with absolute authority, but at the pleasure of the sultan in Constantinople. Palestine was part of the *vilayet* of Beirut, and Jerusalem was administered as a separate district (*sanjak*) that reported directly to the sultan. The East Bank comprised parts of the *vilayets* of Beirut and Damascus. The latter was subdivided into four *sanjaks*: Hama, Damascus, Hawran, and Al Karak. Hawran included Ajlun and As Salt and Al Karak comprised the area mostly south of Amman. The territory south of the

*Columns and temple ruins at Jarash, second century A.D.*
*Greco-Roman city north of Amman*

Az Zarqa River down to Wadi al Mawjib was under the control of the pasha of Nabulus, who was under the *vilayet* of Beirut.

From 1831 until 1839, Ottoman rule was displaced by that of Muhammad Ali—pasha of Egypt and nominally subject to the sultan—when his troops occupied the region during a revolt against the Sublime Porte, as the Ottoman government came to be known. Britain and Russia compelled Muhammad Ali to withdraw and they restored the Ottoman governors.

The Ottomans enforced sharia in the towns and settled countryside, but in the desert customary tribal law also was recognized. Because of the unitary nature of Islamic law—encompassing religious, social, civil, and economic life—it was inconceivable that it could be applied to non-Muslims. The Ottoman regime used the millet system, which accorded non-Muslim communities the right to manage their personal affairs according to their own religious laws. The European powers also concluded separate treaties (capitulations) with the Porte whereby their consuls received extraterritorial legal jurisdiction over their citizens and clients in the Ottoman Empire. In addition, France claimed the special right to protect the sultan's Roman Catholic subjects, and Russia to protect the sultan's more numerous Orthodox subjects.

At every level of the Ottoman system, administration was essentially military in character. On the East Bank, however, Ottoman rule was lax and garrisons were small. Ottoman officials were satisfied as long as order was preserved, military levies were provided when called for, and taxes were paid. These goals, however, were not easily achieved. To stabilize the population, in the late 1800s the Ottomans established several small colonies of Circassians—Sunni Muslims who had fled from the Caucasus region of Russia in the 1860s and 1870s (see Ethnicity and Language, ch. 2). Although the Ottoman sultan in Constantinople was the caliph, Ottoman officials and soldiers were despised by the Arabs, who viewed them as foreign oppressors. Truculent shaykhs regularly disrupted the peace, and the fiercely independent beduins revolted frequently. In 1905 and again in 1910, serious uprisings were suppressed only with considerable difficulty.

In 1900 the Porte, with German assistance, began construction of the Hijaz Railway. By 1908 the railroad linked Damascus with the holy city of Medina. Its purpose was to transport Muslim pilgrims to Mecca and to facilitate military control of the strategic Arabian Peninsula. To protect the railroad, the Porte increased its Ottoman military presence along the route and, as it had done earlier to safeguard caravan traffic, subsidized rival Arab tribal shaykhs in the region.

## Conflicting Nationalisms: Arab Nationalism and Zionism

In the last two decades of the nineteenth century, two separate movements developed that were to have continuing effects for all of the Middle East—the Arab revival and Zionism. Both movements aimed at uniting their peoples in a national homeland. They were to converge and confront each other in Palestine where, it was initially thought by some, they could each achieve their aspirations in an atmosphere of mutual accommodation. The two movements would, in fact, prove incompatible.

By 1875 a small group of Western-oriented Muslim and Christian Arab intellectuals in Beirut were urging the study of Arab history, literature, and language to revive Arab identity. By means of secretly printed and circulated publications they attempted to expose the harsh nature of Ottoman rule and to arouse an Arab consciousness in order to achieve greater autonomy or even independence. The idea of independence always was expressed in the context of a unified entity—"the Arab nation" as a whole. After only a few years, however, Ottoman security operations had stifled the group's activities.

At about the same time, a Jewish revival that called for the return of the Jews in the Diaspora to their historic homeland was finding expression in Europe. The impulse and development of Zionism were almost exclusively the work of European Jews. In 1897 Theodor Herzl convened the First Zionist Congress at Basel, Switzerland, where the Zionist Organization was founded with the stated aim of creating "for the Jewish people a home in Palestine secured by public law." As a result of Zionist efforts, the number of Jews in Palestine rose dramatically to about 85,000, or 12 percent of the total population, by the start of World War I.

The increased Jewish presence and the different customs of the new settlers aroused Arab hostility. The rising tension between Jewish settler and Arab peasant did not, however, lead to the establishment of Arab nationalist organizations. In the Ottoman-controlled Arab lands the Arab masses were bound by family, tribal, and Islamic ties; the concepts of nationalism and nation-state were viewed as alien Western categories. Thus, a political imbalance evolved between the highly organized and nationalistic Jewish settlers and the relatively unorganized indigenous Arab population.

A few Western-educated Arab intellectuals and military officers did form small nationalist organizations demanding greater local autonomy. The major impetus for the coming together of these

17

educated Arabs was their discontent with the rule of Sultan Abdul Hamid II (reigned 1876–1909).

In 1908 a group of reform-minded nationalist army officers in Constantinople, known as the Young Turks, forced Sultan Abdul Hamid II to restore the 1876 Ottoman constitution. The next year the Young Turks deposed Hamid in favor of his malleable brother, Mehmed V. Under the constitution, Ottoman provinces were represented by delegates elected to an imperial parliament. The restoration of the constitution and installation of Mehmed V initially generated a wave of good feeling among the empire's non-Turkish subjects and stimulated expectations of greater self-government.

It soon became clear, however, that the Young Turks, led by Enver Pasha, were bent instead on further centralizing the Ottoman administration and intensifying the "Turkification" of the Ottoman domains. Arab opposition to the Turkish nationalist policies asserted itself in two separate arenas: among urban intellectuals and in the countryside. One source of opposition developed among Arab intellectuals in Cairo, Beirut, and Damascus, who formulated the ideas of a new Arab nationalism. The primary moving force behind this nascent Arab nationalist movement was opposition to the policies of Sultan Abdul Hamid. The removal of Sultan Abdul Hamid by the Committee of Union and Progress (the umbrella organization of which the Young Turks was the major element) was widely supported by Arab nationalists. The committee's program of institutional reform and promised autonomy raised Arab nationalist hopes.

After 1908, however, it quickly became clear that the nationalism of Abdul Hamid's successors was Turkish nationalism bent on Turkification of the Ottoman domain rather than on granting local autonomy. In response, Arab urban intellectuals formed clandestine political societies such as the Ottoman Decentralization Party, based in Cairo; Al Ahd (The Covenant Society), formed primarily by army officers in 1914; and Jamiat al Arabiyah al Fatat (The Young Arab Society), known as Al Fatat (The Young Arabs), formed by students in 1911. The Arab nationalism espoused by these groups, however, lacked support among the Arab masses.

A more traditional form of opposition emerged among the remote desert tribes of Jordan and the Arabian Peninsula, which were politically inarticulate but resentful of foreign control. The link between the urban political committees and the desert tribesmen was Hussein ibn Ali Al Hashimi, the grand sharif and amir of Mecca and hereditary custodian of the Muslim holy places. Hussein, head of the Hashimite branch of the Quraysh tribe, claimed descent from the Prophet. Hussein and his sons Abdullah and Faisal (who had

*The street of columns at Jarash*

been educated as members of the Ottoman elite as well as trained for their roles as Arab chieftains) had spent the years 1893 to 1908 under enforced restraint in Constantinople. In 1908 Abdul Hamid II appointed Hussein amir of Mecca and allowed him and his sons to return to the Hijaz, the western part of present-day Saudi Arabia. Some sources contend that Hussein's nomination was suggested by the Young Turks, who believed that he would be a stabilizing influence there, particularly if he were indebted to them for his position. In his memoirs, however, Abdullah stated that Abdul Hamid II named his father in preference to a candidate proposed by the Young Turks. Hussein reportedly asked for the appointment on the grounds that he had an hereditary right to it. From the outset, Abdullah wrote, his father was at odds with the attempts of the Young Turk regime to bring the Hijaz under the centralized and increasingly secularized administration in Constantinople. Once in office, Hussein proved less tractable than either the sultan or the Turkish nationalists had expected.

Abdullah and Faisal established contact with the Arab nationalists in Syria. Faisal delivered to his father the so-called Damascus Protocol in which the nationalists, who appealed to Hussein as "Father of the Arabs" to deliver them from the Turks, set out the demands for Arab independence that were used by Faisal in his subsequent negotiations with the British. In return, the nationalists accepted the Hashimites as spokesmen for the Arab cause.

## World War I: Diplomacy and Intrigue

On the eve of World War I, the anticipated break-up of the enfeebled Ottoman Empire raised hopes among Arab nationalists. The Arab nationalists wanted an independent Arab state covering all the Ottoman Arab domains. The nationalist ideal, however, was not very unified; even among articulate Arabs, competing visions of Arab nationalism—Islamic, pan-Arab, and statist—inhibited coordinated efforts at independence.

Britain, in possession of the Suez Canal and playing a dominant role in India and Egypt, attached great strategic importance to the region. British Middle East policy, however, espoused conflicting objectives; as a result, London became involved in three distinct and contradictory negotiations concerning the fate of the region.

In February 1914, Abdullah visited Cairo, where he held talks with Lord Kitchener, the senior British official in Egypt. Abdullah inquired about the possibility of British support should his father raise a revolt against the Turks. Kitchener's reply was necessarily noncommittal because Britain then considered the Ottoman Empire a friendly power. War broke out in August, however, and by November the Ottoman Empire had aligned with Germany against Britain and its allies. Kitchener was by then British secretary of state for war and, in the changed circumstances, sought Arab support against the Turks. In Cairo, Sir Henry McMahon, British high commissioner and Kitchener's successor in Egypt, carried on an extensive correspondence with Hussein.

In a letter to McMahon in July 1915, Hussein specified that the area under his independent "Sharifian Arab Government" should consist of the Arabian Peninsula (except Aden, a British colony), Palestine, Lebanon, Syria (including present-day Jordan), and Iraq. In October McMahon replied on behalf of the British government. McMahon declared British support for postwar Arab independence, subject to certain reservations, and "exclusions of territory not entirely Arab or concerning which Britain was not free to act without detriment to the interests of her ally France." The territories assessed by the British as not purely Arab included "the districts of Mersin and Alexandretta, and portions of Syria lying to the west of the districts of Damascus, Homs, Hama, and Aleppo."

As with the later Balfour Declaration, the exact meaning of the McMahon pledge was unclear, although Arab spokesmen have maintained that Palestine was within the area guaranteed independence as an Arab state. In June 1916, Hussein launched the Arab Revolt against the Ottoman Empire and in October proclaimed himself "king of the Arabs," although the Allies recognized him only as king of the Hijaz, a title rejected by most peninsular Arabs. Britain provided supplies and money for the Arab forces led by Abdullah and Faisal. British military advisers also were detailed from Cairo to assist the Arab army that the brothers were organizing. Of these advisers, T.E. Lawrence (Lawrence of Arabia) was to become the best known.

While Hussein and McMahon corresponded over the fate of the Middle East, the British were conducting secret negotiations with the French and the Russians over the same territory. Following the British military defeat at the Dardanelles in 1915, the Foreign Office sought a new offensive in the Middle East, which it thought could only be carried out by reassuring the French of Britain's intentions in the region. In February 1916, the Sykes-Picot Agreement (officially the "Asia Minor Agreement") was signed, which, contrary to the contents of the Hussein-McMahon correspondence, proposed to partition the Middle East into French and British zones of control and interest. Under the Sykes-Picot Agreement, Palestine was to be administered by an international "condominium" of the British, French, and Russians, whereas Transjordan would come under British influence.

The final British pledge, and the one that formally committed Britain to the Zionist cause, was the Balfour Declaration of November 1917. The Balfour Declaration stated that Britain viewed with favor "the establishment in Palestine of a National Home for the Jewish People." After the Sykes-Picot Agreement, Palestine had taken on increased strategic importance because of its proximity to the Suez Canal, where the British garrison had reached 300,000 men, and because of the planned British attack from Egypt on Ottoman Syria. As early as March 1917, Lloyd George was determined that Palestine should become British and he thought that its conquest by British troops would abrogate the Sykes-Picot Agreement. The new British strategic thinking viewed the Zionists as a potential ally capable of safeguarding British imperial interests in the region.

The British pledge transformed Zionism from a quixotic dream into a legitimate and achievable undertaking. For these reasons the Balfour Declaration was widely criticized throughout the Arab world, and especially in Palestine, as contrary to the British pledges contained in the Hussein-McMahon correspondence. The wording of the document itself, although painstakingly devised, was interpreted differently by different people. Ultimately, it was found to contain two incompatible undertakings: establishment in Palestine of a national home for the Jews and preservation of the rights of existing non-Jewish communities. The incompatibility of these two goals sharpened over the succeeding years and became irreconcilable.

In November 1917, the contents of the Sykes-Picot Agreement were revealed by the Bolshevik government in Russia. Arab consternation at the agreement was palliated by British and French reassurances that their commitments to the Arabs would be honored and by the fact that Allied military operations were progressing favorably. Hussein had driven the Turkish garrison out of Mecca in the opening weeks of the Arab Revolt. Faisal's forces captured Al Aqabah in July 1917, and the British expeditionary force under General Sir (later Field Marshal Viscount) Edmund Allenby entered Jerusalem in December. Faisal accepted the military subordination of his army to overall British command, but for him the fighting was essentially a war of liberation in which Britain was actively cooperating with the Arabs. The British command, however, considered the Arab army an adjunct to the Allied offensive in Palestine, intended primarily to draw Turkish attention to the East Bank while Allenby mopped up resistance in

Galilee and prepared for a strike at Damascus. In September 1918, the British army decisively defeated the Turks at Megiddo (in contemporary Israel), and an Arab force under Lawrence captured Daraa, thus opening the way for the advance into Syria. Faisal entered Damascus on October 2, and the Ottoman government consented to an armistice on October 31, bringing the war in that theater to a close.

Between January 1919 and January 1920, the Allied Powers met in Paris to negotiate peace treaties with the Central Powers. At the conference, Amir Faisal (representing the Arabs) and Chaim Weizmann (representing the Zionists) set forth their cases. Weizmann and Faisal reached a separate agreement on January 3, 1919, pledging the two parties to cordial cooperation; however, Faisal wrote a proviso on the document in Arabic that his signature depended upon Allied war pledges regarding Arab independence. Since these pledges were not fulfilled to Arab satisfaction after the war, most Arab leaders and spokesmen have not considered the Faisal-Weizmann agreement as binding.

President Woodrow Wilson appointed an American panel, the King-Crane Commission, to investigate the disposition of Ottoman territories and the assigning of mandates. After extensive surveys in Palestine and Syria, the commission reported intense opposition to the Balfour Declaration among the Arab majority in Palestine and advised against permitting unlimited Jewish immigration or the creation of a separate Jewish state. The commission's report in August 1919 was not officially considered by the conference, however, and was not made public until 1922.

Mandate allocations making Britain the mandatory power for Palestine (including the East Bank and all of present-day Jordan) and Iraq, and making France the mandatory power for the area of Syria and Lebanon, were confirmed in April 1920 at a meeting of the Supreme Allied Council at San Remo, Italy (see fig. 3). The terms of the Palestine Mandate reaffirmed the Balfour Declaration, called on the mandatory power to "secure establishment of the Jewish national home," and recognized "an appropriate Jewish agency" to advise and cooperate with British authorities toward that end. The Zionist Organization was specifically recognized as that agency. Hussein and his sons opposed the mandate's terms on the grounds that Article 22 of the League of Nations Covenant adopted at Versailles had endorsed the Wilsonian principle of self-determination of peoples and thereby, they maintained, logically and necessarily supported the cause of the Arab majority in Palestine.

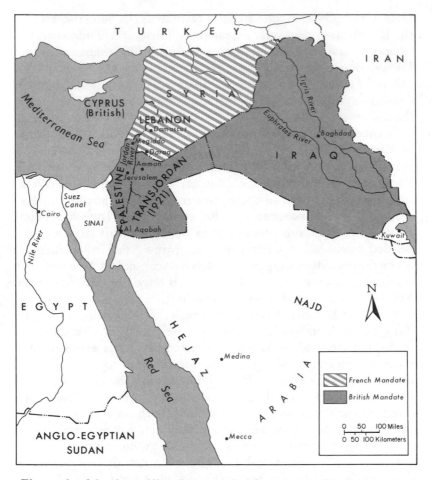

*Figure 3. Mandate Allocations at the San Remo Conference, April 1920*

For the British government, pressed with heavy responsibilities and commitments after World War I, the objective of mandate administration was the peaceful development of Palestine by Arabs and Jews under British control. To Hussein, cooperation with the Zionists had meant no more than providing a refuge for Jews within his intended Arab kingdom. To Zionist leaders, the recognition in the mandate was simply a welcome step on the way to attainment of a separate Jewish national state. A conflict of interests between Arabs and Jews and between both sides and the British developed early in Palestine and continued thereafter at a rising tempo throughout the mandate period.

After the armistice, the Allies organized the Occupied Enemy

Territory Administration to provide an interim government for Palestine, Syria, and Iraq. In July 1919, the General Syrian Congress convened in Damascus and called for Allied recognition of an independent Syria, including Palestine, with Faisal as its king. When no action was taken on the proposal, the congress in March 1920 unilaterally proclaimed Syria independent and confirmed Faisal as king. Iraqi representatives similarly announced their country's independence as a monarchy under Abdullah. The League of Nations Council rejected both pronouncements, and in April the San Remo Conference decided on enforcing the Allied mandates in the Middle East. French troops occupied Damascus in July, and Faisal was served with a French ultimatum to withdraw from Syria. He went into exile, but the next year was installed by the British as king of Iraq.

At the same time, Abdullah was organizing resistance against the French in Syria, arousing both French ire and British consternation. Assembling a motley force of about 2,000 tribesmen, he moved north from Mecca, halting in Amman in March 1920. In October the British high commissioner for Palestine called a meeting of East Bank shaykhs at As Salt to discuss the future of the region, whose security was threatened by the incursion of Wahhabi sectarians (adherents of a puritanical Muslim sect who stressed the unity of God) from Najd in the Arabian Peninsula. It became clear to the British that Abdullah, who remained in Amman, could be accepted as a ruler by the beduin tribes and in that way be dissuaded from involving himself in Syria.

In March 1921, Winston Churchill, then British colonial secretary, convened a high-level conference in Cairo to consider Middle East policy. As a result of these deliberations, Britain subdivided the Palestine Mandate along the Jordan River-Gulf of Aqaba line. The eastern portion—called Transjordan—was to have a separate Arab administration operating under the general supervision of the commissioner for Palestine, with Abdullah appointed as amir. At a follow-up meeting in Jerusalem with Churchill, High Commissioner Herbert Samuel, and Lawrence, Abdullah agreed to abandon his Syrian project in return for the amirate and a substantial British subsidy.

A British government memorandum in September 1922, approved by the League of Nations Council, specifically excluded Jewish settlement from the Transjordan area of the Palestine Mandate. The whole process was aimed at satisfying wartime pledges made to the Arabs and at carrying out British responsibilities under the mandate.

## Transjordan

At its inception in 1921, the Amirate of Transjordan had fewer than 400,000 inhabitants. Of this number, about 20 percent lived in four towns each having populations of from 10,000 to 30,000. The balance were farmers in village communities and pastoral nomadic and seminomadic tribespeople. The amirate's treasury operated on British financial aid established on the basis of an annual subsidy. A native civil service was gradually trained with British assistance, but government was simple, and Abdullah ruled directly with a small executive council, much in the manner of a tribal shaykh. British officials handled the problems of defense, finance, and foreign policy, leaving internal political affairs to Abdullah. To supplement the rudimentary police, in 1921 a reserve Arab force was organized by F. G. Peake, a British officer known to the Arabs as Peake Pasha. This Arab force soon was actively engaged in suppressing brigandage and repelling raids by the Wahhabis. In 1923 the police and reserve force were combined into the Arab Legion as a regular army under Peake's command (see The Military Heritage, ch. 5).

In 1923 Britain recognized Transjordan as a national state preparing for independence. Under British sponsorship, Transjordan made measured progress along the path to modernization. Roads, communications, education, and other public services slowly but steadily developed, although not as rapidly as in Palestine, which was under direct British administration. Tribal unrest remained a persistent problem, reaching serious proportions in 1926 in the Wadi Musa-Petra area. In the same year, Britain attached senior judicial advisers to Abdullah's government, and formed the Transjordan Frontier Force. This body was a locally recruited unit of the British Army assigned to guard the frontier and was distinct from the Arab Legion (see The Military Heritage, ch. 5).

Britain and Transjordan took a further step in the direction of self-government in 1928, when they agreed to a new treaty that relaxed British controls while still providing for Britain to oversee financial matters and foreign policy. The two countries agreed to promulgate a constitution—the Organic Law—later the same year and in 1929 to install the Legislative Council in place of the old executive council. In 1934 a new agreement with Britain allowed Abdullah to set up consular representation in Arab countries, and in 1939 the Legislative Council formally became the amir's cabinet, or council of ministers.

In 1930, with British help, Jordan launched a campaign to stamp out tribal raiding among the beduins. A British officer, John Bagot

Glubb (better known as Glubb Pasha), came from Iraq to be second in command of the Arab Legion under Peake. Glubb organized a highly effective beduin desert patrol consisting of mobile detachments based at strategic desert forts and equipped with good communications facilities. When Peake retired in 1939, Glubb succeeded to full command of the Arab Legion.

Abdullah was a faithful ally to Britain during World War II. Units of the Arab Legion served with distinction alongside British forces in 1941 overthrowing the pro-Nazi Rashid Ali regime that had seized power in Iraq and defeating the Vichy French in Syria. Later, elements of the Arab Legion were used in guarding British installations in Egypt.

During the war years, Abdullah—who never surrendered his dream of a Greater Syria under a Hashimite monarchy—took part in the inter-Arab preliminary discussions that resulted in the formation of the League of Arab States (Arab League) in Cairo in March 1945. The original members of the League of Arab States were Transjordan, Egypt, Syria, Lebanon, Saudi Arabia, Iraq, and Yemen.

In March 1946, Transjordan and Britain concluded the Treaty of London, under which another major step was taken toward full sovereignty for the Arab state. Transjordan was proclaimed a kingdom, and a new constitution replaced the obsolete 1928 Organic Law. Abdullah's application for membership in the UN was disapproved by a Soviet Union veto, which asserted that the country was not fully independent of British control. A further treaty with Britain was executed in March 1948, under which all restrictions on sovereignty were removed, although limited British base and transit rights in Transjordan continued, as did the British subsidy that paid for the Arab Legion.

By 1947 Palestine was one of the major trouble spots in the British Empire, requiring a presence of 100,000 troops to maintain peace and a huge maintenance budget. On February 18, 1947, Foreign Minister Ernest Bevin informed the House of Commons of the government's decision to present the Palestine problem to the UN. On May 15, 1947, a special session of the UN General Assembly established the United Nations Special Committee on Palestine (UNSCOP), consisting of eleven members. UNSCOP reported on August 31 that a majority of its members supported a geographically complex system of partition into separate Arab and Jewish states, a special international status for Jerusalem, and an economic union linking the three members. Supported by both the United States and the Soviet Union, this plan was adopted by the UN General Assembly in November 1947. Although it considered the plan defective in terms of expectations from the mandate agreed to by the League of Nations twenty-five years earlier, the Zionist General Council stated its willingness in principle to accept partition. The Arab League Council, meeting in December 1947, said it would take whatever measures were required to prevent implementation of the resolution. Abdullah was the only Arab ruler willing to consider acceptance of the UN partition plan.

Amid the increasing conflict, the UN Implementation Commission was unable to function. Britain thereupon announced its intention to relinquish the mandate and withdrew from Palestine on May 14, 1948. On the same day, the Declaration of the Establishment of the State of Israel was proclaimed in Jerusalem. Palestinian Arabs refused to set up a state in the Arab zone.

In quick succession, Arab forces from Egypt, Transjordan, Iraq, Syria, Lebanon, and Saudi Arabia advanced into Israel. Except for the British-trained Arab Legion, they were composed of inexperienced and poorly led troops. Abdullah, the sole surviving leader of the Arab Revolt of World War I, accepted the empty title of commander in chief of Arab forces extended to him by the Arab League. His motive for ordering the Arab Legion into action was expressly to secure the portion of Palestine allocated to the Arabs by the 1947 UN resolution. The Arab Legion, concentrated on the East Bank opposite Jericho, crossed the Jordan on May 15 and quickly captured positions in East Jerusalem and its environs. The Legion also created a salient at Latrun northwest of Jerusalem to pinch the Israeli supply line into the city. Abdullah had been particularly insistent that his troops must take and hold the Old City of Jerusalem, which contained both Jerusalem's principal Muslim holy places and the traditional Jewish Quarter. Other Arab Legion units occupied Hebron to the south and fanned out through Samaria to the north (Samaria equates to the northern part of the West Bank—see Glossary). By the end of 1948, the areas held by the Arab Legion and the Gaza Strip, held by the Egyptians, were the only parts of the former Mandate of Palestine remaining in Arab hands.

Early in the conflict, on May 29, 1948, the UN Security Council established the Truce Commission headed by a UN mediator, Swedish diplomat Folke Bernadotte, who was assassinated in Jerusalem on September 17, 1948. He was succeeded by Ralph Bunche, an American, as acting mediator. The commission, which later evolved into the United Nations Truce Supervision Organization-Palestine (UNTSOP), attempted to devise new settlement plans and arranged truces. Armistice talks were initiated with Egypt in January 1949, and an armistice agreement was established with

Egypt on February 24, with Lebanon on March 23, with Transjordan on April 3, and with Syria on July 20. Iraq did not enter into an armistice agreement but withdrew its forces after turning over its positions to Transjordanian units.

## Hashemite Kingdom of Jordan

The population of Transjordan before the war was about 340,000. As a result of the war, about 500,000 Palestinian Arabs took refuge in Transjordan or in the West Bank. Most of these people had to be accommodated in refugee camps, which were administered under the auspices of the United Nations Relief and Works Agency (UNRWA) for Palestine Refugees in the Near East, set up in 1949. In addition there were about 500,000 indigenous residents of the West Bank.

In December 1948, Abdullah took the title of King of Jordan, and in April 1949 he directed that the official name of the country— East Bank and West Bank—be changed to the Hashemite Kingdom of Jordan, a name found in the 1946 constitution but not until then in common use. In April 1950, elections were held in both the East Bank and the West Bank. Abdullah considered the results favorable, and he formally annexed the West Bank to Jordan, an important step that was recognized by only two governments: Britain and Pakistan. Within the Arab League, the annexation was not generally approved, and traditionalists and modernists alike condemned the move as a furtherance of Hashimite dynastic ambitions.

Abdullah continued to search for a long-term, peaceful solution with Israel, although for religious and security reasons he did not favor the immediate internationalization of Jerusalem. He found support for this position only from Hashimite kinsmen in Iraq. Nationalist propaganda, especially in Egypt and Syria, denounced him as a reactionary monarch and a tool of British imperialism.

The Arab League debates following the Jordanian annexation of the West Bank were inconclusive, and Abdullah continued to set his own course. The residual special relationship with Britain continued, helping to keep the East Bank relatively free from disturbance. Although not yet a member of the UN, Jordan supported the UN action in Korea and entered into an economic developmental aid agreement with the United States in March 1951, under President Harry S Truman's Point Four program.

On July 20, 1951, Abdullah was assassinated as he entered the Al Aqsa Mosque in Jerusalem for Friday prayers. His grandson, fifteen-year-old Prince Hussein, was at his side. Before the assassin was killed by the king's guard, he also fired at Hussein. The assassin was a Palestinian reportedly hired by relatives of Hajj Amin al Husayni, a former mufti of Jerusalem and a bitter enemy of Abdullah, who had spent World War II in Germany as a pro-Nazi Arab spokesman. Although many radical Palestinians blamed Abdullah for the reverses of 1948, there was no organized political disruption after his murder. The main political question confronting the country's leaders was the succession to the throne.

Abdullah's second son, Prince Naif, acted temporarily as regent, and some support existed for his accession to the throne. Naif's older brother, Prince Talal, was in Switzerland receiving treatment for a mental illness diagnosed as schizophrenia. It was widely believed that Abdullah would have favored Talal so that the succession might then pass more easily to Talal's son, Hussein. Accordingly, the government invited Talal to return and assume the duties of king. During his short reign, Talal promulgated a new Constitution in January 1952. Talal showed an inclination to improve relations with other Arab states, and Jordan joined the Arab League's Collective Security Pact, which Abdullah had rejected. Talal was popular among the people of the East Bank, who were not aware of his periodic seizures of mental illness. But the king's condition steadily worsened, and in August the prime minister recommended to a secret session of the Jordanian legislature that Talal be asked to abdicate in favor of Hussein. Talal acceded to the abdication order with dignity and retired to a villa near Istanbul, where he lived quietly until his death in 1972.

Hussein, who was a student at Harrow in Britain, returned immediately to Jordan. Under the Constitution he could not be crowned because he was under eighteen years of age, and a regency council was formed to act on his behalf. Before he came to the throne, he attended the British Royal Military Academy at Sandhurst. When he was eighteen years old by the Muslim calendar, he returned to Jordan and in May 1953 formally took the constitutional oath as king.

## Hussein's Early Reign

The chief influences that guided the young Hussein were the example and teachings of his grandfather and his own education in conservative English schools. Although Jordan was a constitutional monarchy, as king Hussein had extensive legal powers. For example, the Constitution allowed him to dismiss the National Assembly and to appoint the prime minister and other ministers. In addition, he enjoyed the traditional support of the East Bank beduin tribes. Considered the backbone of the Hashimite monarchy, the Arab Legion was composed of intensely loyal beduins, whose equipment and salaries were paid for by Britain.

The majority of Jordan's population, however, did not consist of beduins. Between one-half and two-thirds of Hussein's subjects were Palestinians, whereas the government elite was mostly from the East Bank. This elite was more conservative and traditional in its political attitudes than the Palestinians, whose spokespersons often reflected a radical brand of Arab nationalism. In Cairo the successful coup d'état carried out by the Egyptian Free Officers movement (headed by Gamal Abdul Nasser) had overthrown the monarchy in July 1952 and established a republic. Palestinians, who generally blamed Britain, the United States, and the Hashimites for their misfortunes, regarded Nasser as a champion of Arab nationalism.

As border incidents with Israel escalated into a succession of reprisals and counterreprisals between Palestinian infiltrators and Israeli security forces, Hussein's problems grew. The Arab Legion tried to secure the armistice line and prevent infiltration, but its numbers were inadequate to provide complete and continuous coverage of the border. In response to the terrorist attacks, Israel adopted the technique of massive retaliation that often went deep into Jordanian territory (see The Guerrilla Crisis, this ch.).

In 1953 and early 1954, Israel tentatively accepted a United States plan (the Eric Johnston Plan) for distribution of the water taken from the Jordan River. Although the plan was recognized as technically sound from an engineering standpoint, ultimately it was rejected by Jordan and the other Arab states concerned because it involved cooperation with—and the implied recognition of—Israel. Given the stress of inter-Arab political relationships, it was impracticable for Jordan to initiate a settlement with Israel, even though there were strong incentives to do so.

Britain agreed to a new financial aid arrangement with Jordan in 1954 in which London evinced an interest in coordinating military and economic aid to Amman, with Jordanian participation, in the context of an overall Middle Eastern defense system. In February 1955, Turkey, Iraq, Iran, and Pakistan joined Britain in signing the Baghdad Pact, which ultimately became the Central Treaty Organization (CENTO). A high-ranking British military delegation visited Amman to discuss conditions under which Jordan might also become a participant. The purpose of the visit was generally known, and Arab nationalist propaganda, especially from Palestinians and Radio Cairo, raised a storm of protest denouncing the pact and the monarchy as "tools of Western imperialism" and a "sellout to the Jews." In December Hussein asked Hazza al Majali to form a government. Majali came from a distinguished family of tribal shaykhs and was known to be pro-Western. Shortly after forming his cabinet, he stated unequivocally that he intended to take Jordan into the Baghdad Pact. Three days of demonstrations and rioting in Amman began after the announcement, and the Arab Legion was called in to restore order. The Majali government resigned after only a week in power, and it became clear that Jordan would not become a signatory of the Baghdad Pact.

In March 1956, Hussein, responding to the public reaction against joining the British-sponsored Baghdad Pact, attempted to show his independence from Britain by dismissing Glubb as commander of the Arab Legion. Glubb's dismissal precipitated a diplomatic crisis that threatened to isolate Hussein from his principal benefactor, Britain. Relations were strained for many years although the British subsidy was not withdrawn.

Hussein designated Ali Abu Nuwar, an officer known for his nationalist sympathies, as Glubb's successor in the Arab Legion. The name of the force was officially changed to the Jordan Arab Army, and British officers were phased out of the service (see World War II to 1967, ch. 5).

Border incidents with Israel were a continuing source of anxiety in 1956. In October an Israeli task force, supported by aircraft and artillery, attacked the West Bank village of Qalqilyah, killing forty-eight persons in reprisal for a guerrilla attack in Israel. Palestinians clamored for war, and in this crisis atmosphere Jordanian politics ventured into anti-Western nationalism.

In the parliamentary elections of October 21, 1956, the National Socialist Party received a plurality of votes, and Hussein designated its leader, Sulayman Nabulsi, as prime minister. Several National Front Party (Communist Party of Jordan) members and members of the Baath Party (Arab Socialist Resurrection Party) also gained seats in the National Assembly, although independents and the older, conservative parties were represented about equally with the leftists and nationalists. Nabulsi was an ardent admirer of Nasser and shaped the policies of his government accordingly. Nonetheless, when Israel attacked Egyptian forces in the Sinai Peninsula on October 29 and after British and French forces landed at Port Said on November 5, Nabulsi suddenly proved indecisive. Hussein proposed that Jordan attack Israel at once but Nasser discouraged him from wasting Jordan's forces in a war that by then was already lost. British participation in the attack on Egypt made it politically imperative that Jordan end its special relationship with Britain.

Under the Arab Solidarity Agreement that resulted from the Arab summit meeting in Cairo in January 1957, Saudi Arabia, Egypt, and Syria undertook to pay Jordan the equivalent of US$35.8

*A fresco from the palace of an eighth century Umayyad caliph at Qasr Amrah, east of Amman*

million annually for ten years, with Saudi Arabia paying an amount equivalent to that paid by Egypt and Syria together. The money would effectively free Jordan from the British subsidy. Saudi Arabia, however, made only one quarterly payment; Egypt and Syria made no payments. The Anglo-Jordanian Agreement of March 1957 abrogated the basic Anglo-Jordanian Treaty of 1948, terminated the British subsidy, and initiated the turnover of British installations and the withdrawal of all British troops still in Jordan.

In early 1957, Jordan's internal political scene shaped up as a power struggle between the monarchy and the Nasserist Nabulsi government. Hussein and the conservatives suspected that Nabulsi was maneuvering to abolish the monarchy. Nabulsi began negotiations to open diplomatic relations with the Soviet Union and obtain Soviet arms aid. In April, as political tension increased, Hussein, exercising his constitutional prerogative, demanded the resignation of the Nabulsi government.

The situation was further confused when Ali Abu Nuwar, the commander of the Jordan Arab Army (then still popularly known in English as the Arab Legion), made a statement to Said al Mufti, who was then attempting to form a caretaker government. Said al Mufti misinterpreted the statement to be an ultimatum that any new cabinet be approved by the army. A sequence of dramatic events followed that became known as the "Az Zarqa affair." The public in Amman, sensing the explosive political atmosphere, became restive. Rumors that the king was dead spread at the main army base at Az Zarqa. Taking Abu Nuwar with him to demonstrate that he, the king, was very much alive and that he, not Abu Nuwar, was in control Hussein set off for Az Zarqa. En route he met several truckloads of troops, who were overjoyed at seeing the king alive but who demanded the execution of Abu Nuwar. At Abu Nuwar's request, Hussein allowed him to retreat to the safety of the royal palace. Continuing to Az Zarqa, Hussein spent several hours amid wildly enthusiastic troops anxious to demonstrate their loyalty to him and to the throne; he returned to Amman after reassuring and quieting the troops. On the next day, Abu Nuwar fled the country. During the balance of April, several cabinet crises occurred, as the remnants of the Nabulsi faction fought a rearguard action against Hussein. Ibrahim Hashim, a Hussein loyalist, eventually succeeded in forming a government and outlawed all political party activity.

Hussein had won a remarkable political victory. What had mattered most was the loyalty of the combat units of the army, and that loyalty clearly belonged to the king. But Jordan was beleaguered—Nasserites were arrayed against the king, the British subsidy was gone, the Arab Solidarity Agreement had evaporated, and the rift was wider than ever between the East Bank and the West Bank. To counteract these disabilities, Hussein unequivocally placed his country in the Western camp and sought a new source of aid—the United States.

## Crisis and Realignment

The United States replaced Britain as Jordan's principal source of foreign aid, but it did so without a bilateral treaty or other formal alliance mechanisms. In April 1957, the White House officially noted that President Dwight D. Eisenhower and Secretary of State John Foster Dulles regarded "the independence and integrity of Jordan as vital." Although Hussein did not specifically request aid under the Eisenhower Doctrine—by which the United States pledged military and economic aid to any country asking for help in resisting communist influence—he did state publicly that Jordan's security was threatened by communism. Within twenty-four hours of Hussein's request for economic assistance, Jordan received an emergency financial aid grant of US$10 million from the United States—the first of a long series of United

States grants. Washington expanded existing development aid programs and initiated military aid.

In seeking a viable, long-term arrangement for political stability in the face of the hostile, Nasser-style revolutionary nationalism then prevalent in the Middle East, Jordan turned to neighboring Iraq. Iraq, far larger and more populous than Jordan, was also far wealthier because of its oil and other resources. Iraq had usually supported Jordan in Arab councils, although without deep involvement, since the 1948 war. Its conservative government had taken Iraq into the Bagdad Pact in 1955 to ensure continued Western support against the Soviet Union or, more particularly, against radical movements.

On February 1, 1958, Egypt and Syria announced the integration of their two countries to form the United Arab Republic (UAR). This development was greeted with great enthusiam by the new nationalist advocates of Arab unity, but it made the position of conservative or moderate regimes more perilous. The initial phase of Jordanian-Iraqi negotiation was quickly concluded, and on February 14, 1958, Hussein and his cousin, King Faisal II, issued a proclamation joining the Hashimite kingdoms of Iraq and Jordan in a federation called the Arab Union. Faisal was to be head of state and Hussein deputy head of state.

The Arab Union, however, was short-lived. The Hashimite monarchy in Iraq was overthrown on July 14, 1958, in a swift, predawn coup executed by officers of the Nineteenth Brigade under the leadership of Brigadier Abd al Karim Qasim and Colonel Abd as Salaam Arif. The coup was triggered when King Hussein, fearing that an anti-Western revolt in Lebanon might spread to Jordan, requested Iraqi assistance. Instead of moving toward Jordan, Colonel Arif led a battalion into Baghdad and immediately proclaimed a new republic and the end of the old regime. An Iraqi motorized brigade under the command of Brigadier Qasim seized control of Baghdad. King Faisal and other members of the Iraqi royal family were murdered. Hussein, enraged and overcome by shock and grief, threatened to send the Jordanian army into Iraq to avenge Faisal's murder and restore the Arab Union. His civilian ministers, however, advised against taking this course. In Iraq the army and police supported the coup, and Qasim became president-dictator, taking Iraq out of the Arab Union and the Baghdad Pact.

Jordan was isolated as never before. Hussein appealed both to the United States and to Britain for help. The United States instituted an airlift of petroleum, and Britain flew troops into Amman to stabilize the regime. Ironically, these aircraft overflew Israel, because clearances for alternate routes over Arab countries could not be obtained in time. These events in Iraq and Jordan coincided with the landing of United States troops in Lebanon to bolster the regime there.

For some weeks, the political atmosphere in Jordan was explosive, but the government kept order through limited martial law. The army continued its unquestioning loyalty to the king, and the Israeli frontier remained quiet.

The ensuing two-year period of relative tranquility was broken in August 1960 when the pro-Western prime minister, Hazza al Majali who had been reappointed in May 1959, was killed by the explosion of a time bomb concealed in his desk. Analysts speculated that the conspirators expected the killing to generate a public uprising. It had precisely the opposite effect; beduin troops who moved into Amman maintained order, and Hussein appointed a new conservative prime minister, Bahjat at Talhuni. The plot was traced to Syria and further identified with Cairo. Four suspects were caught, convicted, and hanged, and the army made a show of force. In June 1961, Talhuni was replaced by Wasfi at Tal to improve relations with Egypt, after Cairo implicated Amman for influencing Damascus's decision to secede from the United Arab Republic.

## Development and Disaster

By early 1964, Arab governments and Palestinian spokesmen had become alarmed by an Israeli project to draw water from Lake Tiberias to irrigate the Negev Desert. Nasser invited the Arab heads of state to attend a summit conference in Cairo in January 1964 at which the principal issue was the Jordan water question. Despite Syria's militant rhetoric, the conference rejected the idea of provoking a war because—it was argued—the Arab states lacked a unified military command. Instead, three alternative courses of action were approved: the diversion of the tributary sources of the Jordan River north of Lake Tiberias in Lebanon and Syria; the establishment of the United Arab Command under an Egyptian commander; and the recognition of the new Palestine Liberation Organization (PLO), headed by a former Jerusalem lawyer, Ahmad Shuqayri (also cited as Shukairi), as the representative of Palestinian resistance against Israel. The Cairo Conference of January 1964 ended in an euphoric atmosphere of goodwill and brotherhood.

Talhuni became prime minister for the second time in July 1964, pledging his government to implement the spirit of the Cairo Conference "according to the king's instructions." Jordan cultivated friendship with Egypt. In May 1965, Jordan joined nine other Arab states in breaking relations with the Federal Republic of Germany

(West Germany) because of its recognition of Israel. Jordan and Saudi Arabia signed an agreement in August defining for the first time the boundary between the two countries. Under this agreement, Jordan gave up some territory in the southeast but was able to gain an extension of about eighteen kilometers down the gulf from the crowded port of Al Aqabah.

Almost from the start, trouble developed between the PLO and Hussein's government. Shuqayri, famous for his often hysterical political rhetoric, had organized the PLO in Jerusalem in 1964 with the objective of liberating Palestine in cooperation with all Arab states but without interfering in their internal affairs or claiming sovereignty in the West Bank. Conflict arose because the PLO attempted to assume quasi-governmental functions, such as taxing Palestinians and distributing arms to villagers in the West Bank and among the refugees, acts that infringed on Jordanian sovereignty. The guerrilla organization, Al Fatah, was formed in Damascus with Syrian assistance in December 1957, under the leadership of Yasir Arafat.

Jordanian policy since 1949 had been to avoid border incidents and terrorism that would generate Israeli reprisals. Al Fatah and the PLO, however, carried out raids and sabotage against Israel without clearance from either the United Arab Command or Jordan. These attacks, although planned in Syria, most often were launched into Israel by infiltration through Lebanon or Jordan. Israeli reprisals against selected West Bank targets became harsher and more frequent from May 1965 onward. Meanwhile, Syrian propaganda against Hussein became increasingly strident. In July 1966, when Hussein severed official endorsement and support for the PLO, both that organization and the Syrian government turned against him. In reprisal for the terrorist attacks by the fedayeen (Palestinian guerrillas), in November Israel assaulted the West Bank village of As Samu. Israel was censured by the UN, but public rioting against the Jordanian government broke out among the inhabitants of the West Bank. The levels of rioting exceeded any previous experience. As in the past, Hussein used the army to restore public order. Political pressure against Hussein mounted, however, along with armed clashes on the Syrian-Jordanian border.

Tension also mounted on the Syria-Israel border, where a land and air engagement took place on April 7, 1967. Syria and Jordan severely criticized Egypt for failing to send support. In mid-May Egypt commenced an extensive military build-up in Sinai in response to Syrian allegations that Syria was in imminent danger of invasion by Israel. Nasser declared a state of emergency on

May 16 and two days later demanded removal of the United Nations Emergency Force (UNEF) from Sinai, where it had served as a peacekeeping force since 1957. The UN secretary general acceded to Nasser's demand.

On May 23–24, Nasser announced the closure to Israeli shipping of the Strait of Tiran at the entrance to the Gulf of Aqaba, a measure that Israel immediately declared to be an act of war. Hussein quickly decided that this time it would be impossible for Jordan to stay out of the impending conflict. He hurriedly proceeded to Cairo and on May 30 signed a military alliance with Egypt. Hussein's move represented a response to political pressures at home and the fulfillment of basic pan-Arab commitments. The alliance put the Jordanian army under the field command of an Egyptian general officer.

On June 5, Israel launched a preemptive attack against Egyptian forces deployed in Sinai. The Israeli prime minister, Levi Eshkol, attempted in vain to contact Hussein through UN channels to keep him out of the war. The Egyptian field marshal in overall command of Arab forces ordered Jordanian artillery to open fire on Israeli positions, and Jordan's small air force conducted a bombing raid in the Tel Aviv area. Within hours, however, Israeli warplanes had effectively eliminated the Arab air forces on the ground. After only two days of combat, Jordan's main armored unit had been defeated. Hard fighting continued, as Hussein was determined to hold as much ground as possible in the event that a cease-fire was arranged. By the time he agreed to a truce on June 7, Israeli forces had seized the West Bank and the Old City of Jerusalem.

Of all the Arab belligerents, Jordan, which could least afford it, lost most in the war. Government figures listed over 6,000 troops killed or missing. During the short war, about 224,000 refugees—many of whom had first been refugees from the 1948–49 war—fled from the West Bank to the East Bank. One-third to one-half of the country's best agricultural land and its main tourist attractions were lost to Israel. On June 27, the Israeli parliament (Knesset) formally annexed the Old City of Jerusalem, an act that the United States and many other nations refused to recognize.

## The Guerrilla Crisis

In the wake of the June 1967 War, Hussein's government faced the critical problems of repairing a shattered economy, providing for the welfare of the refugees, obtaining external aid, readjusting foreign policy, and rebuilding the armed forces. Internally, however, the major problem was the continuing confrontation with the several Palestinian guerrilla organizations.

The Arab League heads of state met in Khartoum at the end of August 1967. The conference reached four major decisions generally considered to represent the views of Arab moderates: resumption of oil production, which some oil-producing states had suspended during the war; continued nonrecognition of and nonnegotiation with Israel, individually and collectively; continued closure of the Suez Canal and the elimination of all foreign military bases in Arab territory; and provision of financial subsidies to Egypt and Jordan by Saudi Arabia, Libya, and Kuwait. The total annual subsidy promised for the indefinite future amounted to the equivalent of US$378 million, of which Jordan was to receive about US$112 million. Donor states at first regularly paid their shares in quarterly installments, but Libya and Kuwait withdrew their support to Jordan during the 1970–71 war between the Jordanian government and the fedayeen.

In addition to the Khartoum subsidies, Jordan also received grants from Qatar, and the shaykhdom of Abu Dhabi, and a special grant of US$42 million from Saudi Arabia for arms purchases. Aid also came from Britain and West Germany, with whom Jordan had resumed relations. Although direct United States aid had been terminated, substantial long-term government loans were extended to Jordan for emergency relief, development, and military assistance. In February 1968, the United States resumed arms shipments to Jordan. Jordan narrowly averted financial disaster.

After months of diplomatic wrangling, on November 22, 1967, the UN Security Council adopted Resolution 242 as a guideline for a Middle East settlement. The principal provisions of the resolution proclaimed the inadmissability of territorial acquisition by war; withdrawal of Israeli forces from areas occupied in the June 1967 war; termination of all states of belligerency; acknowledgment of the sovereignty of all states in the area—including Israel—within secure and recognized boundaries; freedom of navigation on all international waterways in the area; and a just settlement of the refugee problem. Jordan, Egypt, and Israel all accepted this resolution in principle but each country interpreted it differently (see Relations with Arab States, ch. 4).

King Hussein has been the most consistent advocate of UN Resolution 242. He viewed it as the most viable means by which the Palestinian problem could be resolved while also preserving an important Jordanian role in the West Bank.

The intractability of the Palestinian problem has been due in large part to the widely differing perspectives that evolved after the June 1967 War. For the Israelis, in the midst of the nationalist euphoria that followed the war, talk of exchanging newly captured

territories for peace had little public appeal. The government of
Levi Eshkol followed a two-track policy with respect to the territories that would continue under future Labor Party governments:
on the one hand, it stated a willingness to negotiate, while on the
other, it laid plans to create Jewish settlements in the disputed territories. Thus, immediately following the war, Eshkol stated that
he was willing to negotiate "everything" for a full peace, which
would include free passage through the Suez Canal and the Strait
of Tiran and a solution to the refugee problem in the context of
regional cooperation. This was followed in November 1967 with
his acceptance of UN Security Council Resolution 242. At the same
time, Eshkol's government announced plans for the resettlement
of the Old City of Jerusalem and of the Etzion Bloc (kibbutzim
on the Bethlehem-Hebron road wiped out by Palestinians in the
1948–49 War), and for establishing kibbutzim in the northern sector
of the Golan Heights. Plans also were unveiled for new neighborhoods around Jerusalem, near the old buildings of Hebrew University and near the Hadassah Hospital on Mount Scopus.

The 1967 defeat radicalized the Palestinians, who had looked
to the Arab countries to defeat first the Yishuv (the Jewish community of Palestine before 1948) and after 1948 the State of Israel, so that they could regain their homeland. The PLO had no
role in the June 1967 War. After the succession of Arab failures
in conventional warfare against Israel, however, the Palestinians
decided to adopt guerrilla warfare tactics as the most effective
method of attacking and defeating Israel. In February 1969, Arafat
(who remained the leader of Al Fatah) became head of the PLO.
By early 1970, at least seven guerrilla organizations were identified in Jordan. One of the most important organizations was the
Popular Front for the Liberation of Palestine (PFLP) led by
George Habash. Although the PLO sought to integrate these various groups and announced from time to time that this process had
occurred, they were never effectively united (see The Palestinians
and the PLO, ch. 4).

At first by conviction and then by political necessity, Hussein sought
accommodation with the fedayeen and provided training sites and
assistance. In Jordan's internal politics, however, the main issue
between 1967 and 1971 was the struggle between the government
and the guerrilla organizations for political control of the country.
Based in the refugee camps, the fedayeen virtually developed a state
within a state, easily obtaining funds and arms from both the Arab
states and Eastern Europe and openly flouting Jordanian law.

As the guerrilla effort mounted, Israel retaliated quickly and with
increasing effectiveness. In March 1968, an Israeli brigade attacked

the Jordanian village of Al Karamah, said to be the guerrilla capital. Although the brigade inflicted damage, it was driven back and in the process suffered substantial losses. The incident boosted Palestinian morale and gave the PLO instant prestige within the Arab community. In reprisal, Israel launched heavy attacks on Irbid in June 1968 and on As Salt in August. It soon became obvious to the PLO that the generally open terrain of the West Bank did not provide the kind of cover needed for classic guerrilla operations. Moreover, the Palestinian population residing in the territories had not formed any significant armed resistance against the Israeli occupation. By late 1968, the main fedayeen activities in Jordan seemed to shift from fighting Israel to attempts to overthrow Hussein.

A major guerrilla-government confrontation occurred in November 1968 when the government sought to disarm the refugee camps, but civil war was averted by a compromise that favored the Palestinians. The threat to Hussein's authority and the heavy Israeli reprisals that followed each guerrilla attack became a matter of grave concern to the King. His loyal beduin army attempted to suppress guerrila activity, which led to sporadic outbursts of fighting between the fedayeen and the army during the first half of 1970. In June 1970, an Arab mediation committee intervened to halt two weeks of serious fighting between the two sides.

In June Hussein designated Abd al Munim Rifai to head a "reconciliation" cabinet that included more opposition elements than any other government since that of Nabulsi in 1957. Although the composition of the cabinet maintained a traditional balance between the East Bank and the West Bank, it included a majority of guerrilla sympathizers, particularly in the key portfolios of defense, foreign affairs, and interior. But the king's action did not reflect a new domestic policy; rather, it indicated Hussein's hope that a nationalist cabinet would support peace negotiations generated by a proposed UN peace mission to be conducted by Gunnar Jarring. On June 9, 1970, Rifai and Arafat signed an agreement conciliatory to the fedayeen. According to its provisions, the government allowed the commandos freedom of movement within Jordan, agreed to refrain from antiguerrilla action, and expressed its support for the fedayeen in the battle against Israel. In return, the commandos pledged to remove their bases from Amman and other major cities, to withdraw armed personnel from the Jordanian capital, and to show respect for law and order.

Small-scale clashes continued throughout the summer of 1970, however; and by early September, the guerrilla groups controlled several strategic positions in Jordan, including the oil refinery near

Az Zarqa. Meanwhile, the fedayeen were also calling for a general strike of the Jordanian population and were organizing a civil disobedience campaign. The situation became explosive when, as part of a guerrilla campaign to undermine the Jarring peace talks to which Egypt, Israel, and Jordan had agreed, the PFLP launched an airplane hijacking campaign.

Within the space of two hours on September 6, PFLP gangs hijacked a TWA jet, a Swissair jet, and made an unsuccessful attempt to seize control of an El Al airplane. About two hours later, another PFLP group hijacked a Pan Am jet and forced the crew to fly to Beirut airport, where the airplane landed almost out of fuel. The next day the airliner was flown to the Cairo airport, where it was blown up only seconds after the 176 passengers and crew had completed their three-minute forced evacuation.

King Hussein viewed the hijackings as a direct threat to his authority in Jordan. In response, on September 16 he reaffirmed martial law and named Brigadier Muhammad Daud to head a cabinet composed of army officers. At the same time, the king appointed Field Marshal Habis al Majali, a fiercely proroyalist beduin, commander in chief of the armed forces and military governor of Jordan. Hussein gave Majali full powers to implement the martial law regulations and to quell the fedayeen. The new government immediately ordered the fedayeen to lay down their arms and to evacuate the cities. On the same day, Arafat became supreme commander of the Palestine Liberation Army (PLA), the regular military force of the PLO.

During a bitterly fought ten-day civil war, primarily between the PLA and Jordan Arab Army, Syria sent about 200 tanks to aid the fedayeen. On September 17, however, Iraq began a rapid withdrawal of its 12,000-man force stationed near Az Zarqa. The United States Navy dispatched the Sixth Fleet to the eastern Mediterranean, and Israel undertook "precautionary military deployments" to aid Hussein, if necessary, against the guerrilla forces. Under attack from the Jordanian army and in response to outside pressures, the Syrian forces began to withdraw from Jordan on September 24, having lost more than half their armor in fighting with the Jordanians. The fedayeen found themselves on the defensive throughout Jordan and agreed on September 25 to a cease-fire. At the urging of the Arab heads of state, Hussein and Arafat signed the cease-fire agreement in Cairo on September 27. The agreement called for rapid withdrawal of the guerrilla forces from Jordanian cities and towns to positions "appropriate" for continuing the battle with Israel and for the release of prisoners by both sides. A supreme supervisory committee was to implement the provisions of the agreement. On September 26, Hussein appointed a new cabinet; however, army officers continued to head the key defense and interior ministries.

On October 13, Hussein and Arafat signed a further agreement in Amman, under which the fedayeen were to recognize Jordanian sovereignty and the king's authority, to withdraw their armed forces from towns and villages, and to refrain from carrying arms outside their camps. In return the government agreed to grant amnesty to the fedayeen for incidents that had occurred during the civil war.

The civil war caused great material destruction in Jordan, and the number of fighters killed on all sides was estimated as high as 3,500. In spite of the September and October agreements, fighting continued, particularly in Amman, Irbid, and Jarash, where guerrilla forces had their main bases. Hussein appointed Wasfi at Tal as his new prime minister and minister of defense to head a cabinet of fifteen civilian and two military members. The cabinet also included seven Palestinians. Tal, known to be a staunch opponent of the guerrilla movement, was directed by Hussein to comply with the cease-fire agreements; furthermore, according to Hussein's written directive, the government's policy was to be based on "the restoration of confidence between the Jordanian authorities and the Palestinian resistance movement, cooperation with the Arab states, the strengthening of national unity, striking with an iron hand at all persons spreading destructive rumors, paying special attention to the armed forces and the freeing of the Arab lands occupied by Israel in the war of June 1967." The closing months of 1970 and the first six months of 1971 were marked by a series of broken agreements and by continued battles between the guerrilla forces and the Jordanian army, which continued its drive to oust the fedayeen from the populated areas.

Persistent pressure by the army compelled the fedayeen to withdraw from Amman in April 1971. Feeling its existence threatened, Al Fatah abandoned its earlier posture of noninvolvement in the internal affairs of an Arab state and issued a statement demanding the overthrow of the Jordanian "puppet separatist authority." In a subsequent early May statement, it called for "national rule" in Jordan. Against this background of threats to his authority, Hussein struck at the remaining guerrilla forces in Jordan.

In response to rumors that the PLO was planning to form a government-in-exile, Hussein in early June directed Tal to "deal conclusively and without hesitation with the plotters who want to establish a separate Palestinian state and destroy the unity of the Jordanian and Palestinian people." On July 13, the Jordanian army undertook an offensive against fedayeen bases about fifty kilometers northwest of Amman in the Ajlun area—the fedayeen's last stronghold. Tal announced that the Cairo and Amman agreements, which had regulated relations between the fedayeen and the Jordanian governments, were no longer operative. On July 19, the government announced that the remainder of the bases in northern Jordan had been destroyed and that 2,300 of the 2,500 fedayeen had been arrested. A few days later, many of the captured Palestinians were released either to leave for other Arab countries or to return to a peaceful life in Jordan. Hussein became virtually isolated from the rest of the Arab world, which accused him of harsh treatment of the fedayeen and denounced him as being responsible for the deaths of so many of his fellow Arabs.

In November members of the Black September terrorist group—who took their name from the civil war of September 1970—avenged the deaths of fellow fedayeen by assassinating Prime Minister Tal in Cairo. In December the group again struck out against Hussein in an unsuccessful attempt on the life of the Jordanian ambassador to Britain. Hussein alleged that Libya's Colonel Muammar al Qadhafi was involved in a plot to overthrow the monarchy.

In March 1973, Jordanian courts convicted seventeen Black September fedayeen charged with plotting to kidnap the prime minister and other cabinet ministers and to hold them hostage in exchange for the release of a few hundred fedayeen captured during the civil war. Hussein subsequently commuted the death sentences to life imprisonment ''for humanitarian reasons'' and, in response to outside Arab pressures, in September released the prisoners—including their leader Muhammad Daud Auda (also known as Abu Daud)—under a general amnesty.

## War and Diplomacy

After his victory over the fedayeen, Hussein sought to reestablish his authority in the country and his image in the Arab world through the implementation of dynamic domestic and foreign policies. In September 1971, he announced the formation of the Jordanian National Union to serve as the nation's sole authorized political organization, representing—at least in theory—both banks of the Jordan. The union was not a political party in the traditional sense but, according to the king, would be used ''as a melting pot for the Jordanian people.'' With the exception of communists, Marxists, and ''other advocates of foreign ideologies,'' all citizens were eligible for membership within the union, which would ''provide constructive opposition from within its own ranks.''

Hussein also introduced a plan for the creation of a federation to be called the United Arab Kingdom. Under the plan, the West Bank and the East Bank would become autonomous provinces within the sovereign Hashimite kingdom. Seats in the National Assembly would continue to be divided equally among representatives of the two regions. The PLO repudiated the United Arab Kingdom and the Jordanian National Union, and neither plan was ever implemented.

Hussein paid a state visit to the United States in February 1973 during which President Richard M. Nixon assured him of his "firm . . . support for Jordan" and promised increased economic and military aid. During interviews Hussein, who earlier had called for United States intervention to bring about a comprehensive Middle East settlement, reaffirmed that he contemplated no partial or separate agreements with Israel that would be prejudicial to Arab unity, but he left the door open for bilateral talks and condemned the PLO for its divisive influence. On his return to Amman, Hussein reemphasized that all of East Jerusalem must be returned but offered to put the holy places there under international supervision.

At the Arab summit in Cairo in September 1973, a reconciliation mediated by King Faisal of Saudi Arabia took place among Egypt, Syria, and Jordan, the "front-line" or confrontation states against Israel. On October 6, less than a month after the meeting, Egyptian and Syrian armies launched simultaneous attacks across the Suez Canal and the Golan Heights that caught the Israelis by surprise. After initially threatening to break through Israel's inner defenses, the Syrians were checked and then thrown back by an Israeli counteroffensive that drove to within thirty kilometers of the strong defense emplacements surrounding Damascus. By October 10, Jordan had mobilized nearly 70,000 men, forcing Israeli troops to deploy in the West Bank. Hussein did not open a third front against Israel, but he sent 3,000 Jordanian troops in two armored brigades to the Golan front on October 13, and they saw limited action under Syrian command in fighting near Lake Tiberias. More than 25,000 regular Palestinian troops also were engaged under separate command.

With the Arab armies in retreat, the Soviet Union called a special session of the UN Security Council on October 21 to impose an immediate cease-fire. Although accepted by Israel and Egypt, the cease-fire did not become effective for another three days. On the northern front, Israeli troops retained control of the Golan Heights, and in the southwest they had opened bridgeheads across the Suez Canal and occupied more than 1,500 square kilometers of territory in Egypt. UN Security Council Resolution 338, submitted on October 22, reiterated the Security Council's position on Israeli-occupied territory, first expressed in Resolution 242 in 1967.

At a postmortem on the fourth Arab-Israeli war held in November in Algiers, the Jordanian representative stressed that the cease-fire did not mean peace and called again for Israel to evacuate the occupied territories that combined Arab forces had failed to win back in battle. Over Jordanian protests, the summit conference voted to recognize the PLO as the legitimate representative of the Palestinian people. Hussein, who conceded in Amman that he did not claim to speak for the Palestinians, supported their right to self-determination—"but," he added, "only after the occupied territories are liberated."

Hussein stated on more than one occasion his willingness to leave the liberation of the West Bank to the PLO, but he pointedly boycotted a meeting with PLO officials in Cairo at which Egypt and Syria were expected to deal with the PLO as the "only legitimate representatives" of the Palestinian people—a position that Hussein admitted he had no alternative but to accept in practice. President Anwar as Sadat of Egypt, however, warned the PLO that its refusal to cooperate with Hussein could lead to an Arab civil war on a broader scale than that of 1970–71. When the Palestinians refused to compromise their claim to total sovereignty in the West Bank, Hussein requested a postponement of the Arab summit scheduled for Rabat in October 1974. The purpose of the summit was to give formal recognition to the PLO's role. In an abrupt turnabout in policy, Egyptian foreign minister Ismail Fahmi responded by declaring that Egypt now opposed the return of the West Bank to Jordan and accepted without reservation the PLO claim to represent the Palestinian people.

## The Rabat Summit Conference and After

The Rabat Summit conference in October 1974 brought together the leaders of twenty Arab states, including Hussein, and representatives of the PLO. PLO leaders threatened a walkout if their demands for unconditional recognition were not met. The PLO required a statement from the conference that any Palestinian territory liberated by Arab forces would be turned over to the "Palestinian people" as represented by their organization. Jordan protested, pointing out that recognition on these terms would give the PLO sovereignty over half of the population in the East Bank and that in fact the annexation of the West Bank had been approved by popular vote.

A compromise solution was adopted that nonetheless favored PLO interests. The conference formally acknowledged the right of the Palestinian people to a separate homeland but without specifying that its territory was restricted to the West Bank. Most important, the PLO was for the first time officially recognized by all the Arab states as the "sole legitimate representative of the Palestinian people." The Arab heads of state also called for close cooperation between the front-line states and the PLO but prohibited interference by other Arab states in Palestinian affairs.

The Rabat Summit declaration conferred a mantle of legitimacy on the PLO that was previously absent. It gave official Arab recognition to PLO territorial claims to the West Bank and unambiguously put the fate of the Palestinian people solely in the hands of the PLO. Hussein opposed the declaration, although he eventually signed it under intense Arab pressure and after the Arab oil-producing states promised to provide Jordan with an annual subsidy of $US300 million. Despite his acquiescence to the Rabat declaration and subsequent statements in support of the PLO, Hussein persisted in viewing the declaration as an ambiguous document that was open to differing interpretations. The PLO, along with the rest of the Arab world, viewed Hussein's consent at Rabat as a renunciation of Jordanian claims to the West Bank. Hussein nonetheless continued to have aspirations concerning Jordanian control of the occupied territories. The wide gulf separating the two views was the major source of tension between the PLO and Jordan throughout the late 1970s and early 1980s.

Following the Rabat Summit, the PLO scored an impressive political victory in the international arena. In late November 1974, the UN recognized PLO representation of the Palestinian people, and PLO Chairman Yasir Arafat addressed the General Assembly in Arabic, his pistol at his side. In addition, in a joint communiqué issued the same month, President Gerald R. Ford of the United States and General Secretary of the Communist Party of the Soviet Union Leonid Brezhnev acknowledged the "legitimate interests" of the Palestinians in accordance with the UN resolutions. Nonetheless, a UN draft resolution in 1976 proposing to reaffirm the right of the Palestinians to self-determination—and including the right to establish an independent state—was vetoed in the Security Council by the United States, which called instead for a "reasonable and acceptable definition of Palestinian interests."

After the Rabat Summit, Hussein stressed the need for Jordanian political self-sufficiency. He told his subjects, "A new reality exists and Jordan must adjust to it. The West Bank is no longer Jordanian." But having surrendered title to half his kingdom at the behest of the Arab states, Hussein confessed concern that the East Bank might become a "substitute Palestine," swallowed up as the balance of political power there shifted to its Palestinian majority.

The tone of Hussein's approach to the Palestinians in the East Bank changed markedly following the Rabat Summit. He advised that the resident Palestinians—estimated at 900,000 or more—must choose between Jordanian citizenship or Palestinian identity. No attempt would be made to oust those who chose the latter, he said, and they would be permitted to remain in Jordan as "guests." He also insisted that any Palestinian choosing to keep his Jordanian citizenship must be allowed to do so without endangering his rights in the West Bank; he further promised that any Palestinian living in the East Bank who chose to identify his interests with those of the "Palestinian people" could do so without jeopardizing his rights as a Jordanian citizen.

In response to the new political situation following the Rabat Summit, Hussein reorganized Jordan's political and administrative institutions. On November 9, he amended the Constitution to give the king authority to dissolve the House of Representatives (also called the Chamber of Deputies—see The Legislature, ch. 4) and to delay elections as he saw fit. Using this constitutional prerogative, Hussein dissolved the lower house of the National Assembly—the elected House of Representatives—when it had completed its work on November 23. The House of Representatives, half of whose sixty members represented West Bank constituencies, could no longer function without undermining the newly recognized representative status of the PLO. The Constitution was amended to provide for the indefinite postponement of elections for a new House of Representatives so as to avoid elections in the East Bank alone, which if held would have symbolized the final separation of the West Bank from Jordan. In addition to dissolving the House of Representatives, Hussein directed Prime Minister Zaid ar Rifai to form a new government that did not include Palestinians from the West Bank. No move was made, however, to relieve Palestinians in the Jordanian army, where they composed one-third of the officer corps, albeit mostly in noncombatant functions (see Personnel: Composition, Recruitment, and Training, ch. 5). The government also continued to pay the salaries of 6,000 civil servants and teachers in the West Bank, which amounted to about US$40 million a year.

As a result of Hussein's partial reversal from the commitments made at Rabat, Jordanian-PLO relations deteriorated throughout much of 1975. At the year's end, however, the Palestine National

*The Timna arches in the Wadi al Jayb, southern Jordan*

Council, meeting in Damascus, backed an effort to reconcile its differences with Hussein. The broadcast of antiregime propaganda was temporarily suspended and, although PLA units remained stationed in Jordan in military camps, the PLO accepted restrictions on its political and military presence there. At the Arab summit conference held at Cairo in January 1976, Jordan and the PLO once again were embroiled in a dispute over Jordan's role in negotiating an Israeli withdrawal from the West Bank. Jordan declared that it had no responsibility for negotiating such a withdrawal. In response, the PLO resumed its hostile propaganda shortly after the meeting.

In February 1976, Hussein summoned an extraordinary session of the National Assembly—attended by about half of the representatives elected from the West Bank—to enact legislation enabling the king to postpone indefinitely the general elections scheduled for later in the month. The king's spokespersons explained that the action was necessary because of ''compelling circumstances'' that prevailed in the country. That same month, Hussein abolished the Jordanian National Union.

In July Zaid ar Rifai, who had led the government since 1973, stepped down as prime minister. Hussein replaced him with Mudar Badran, chief of the royal court. The Badran government set up the Bureau of Occupied Homeland Affairs, headed by former members of parliament from West Bank constituencies, ostensibly to coordinate and advise on relations with Palestinians in Israeli-occupied territory. The government also conducted discussions on the renewed possibility of some form of federation between the West Bank and the East Bank. The PLO charged that the newly created Bureau of Occupied Homeland Affairs had been formed to channel support to pro-Jordanian candidates in municipal elections to be held in the West Bank in April 1977. Badran denied these allegations and reaffirmed Jordan's commitment to the concept that the Palestinians themselves must decide the future of the West Bank. PLO-backed candidates won an overwhelming victory in the April elections.

## Relations with the Palestine Liberation Organization

The recrudescent tension between Jordan and the PLO was symptomatic of their differing visions of an Arab-Israeli settlement. Jordan accepted UN Security Council resolutions 242 and 338 as the basis for any settlement, including the question of Palestinian national rights. Within this framework, Jordan demanded total Israeli withdrawal from all territories occupied in 1967; a solution to the refugee problem either by repatriation or compensation; the right of Palestinians to self-determination; and mutual guarantees for peace. The PLO consistently rejected both 242 and 338 on the grounds that the Palestinian people are only mentioned in the resolutions as refugees and not as a people deserving a national homeland.

On the issue of self-determination, Hussein agreed with the PLO that the Palestinians had the right to establish "a national and political entity," but he refrained from giving his support to a fully independent Palestinian state, which he saw as a direct threat, particularly if headed by the PLO. Moreover, he believed that if he could neutralize the PLO, the West Bank and Gaza Strip populations would accept an arrangement based on his own federation plan.

Despite his desire to be the primary Arab negotiator over the territories, Hussein also realized that his role in any future negotiations required a clear mandate from the Arab states. He could not deviate too far from the Arab consensus concerning the occupied territories for fear of losing badly needed economic aid or instigating military attacks from Iraq and Syria. As a result, Hussein chose to participate in the proposed October 1, 1977, Geneva Conference on the Middle East as a "confrontation state" but not as the representative of the Palestinians.

## Jordanian-Syrian Relations

Despite a long history of hostility, between 1975 and 1977 Jordan's major regional ally was Syria. During 1975 Jordan and

Syria agreed to coordinate their defense, foreign policy, economic, information, education, and cultural activities. They established a joint military command to provide a single defensive line against Israel. Syria halted anti-Hussein propaganda and imposed restrictions on Syrian-based Palestinian activities that might be considered prejudicial to Jordan's sovereignty.

The marked improvement in relations between Hussein and Syrian president Hafiz al Assad primarily reflected a shared desire to minimize the role of the PLO in any future Middle East peace negotiations. Despite the commitments made at Rabat, neither Jordan nor Syria wanted the PLO to emerge from Middle East peace talks as leader of a proposed Palestinian national entity in the occupied territories. Their opposition to the PLO, however, stemmed from very different sources. Jordan opposed the PLO because of conflicting territorial objectives; Hussein wanted to reintegrate the West Bank as a part of a pre-1967 Jordan. Assad opposed a PLO-led ministate because he feared that such an entity would reduce Syria's regional role and would significantly lessen the chances of Syria regaining the Golan Heights. At the same time, Damascus rejected Hussein's claims to the West Bank and vehemently opposed any Jordanian attempts to reach a separate peace agreement with Israel. This position severely limited the flexibility of Jordanian diplomacy and ultimately divided Jordan and Syria.

In 1975 Lebanon became engulfed in a bloody civil war that had major ramifications for the regional political balance. Like the Black September incident of 1970, the Lebanese Civil War pitted a rapidly expanding Palestinian political infrastructure against a sovereign Arab state. Between September 1970 and 1975, the Palestinians created in Lebanon a "state within a state." They had their own military establishment, an autonomous political structure, and separate collection of taxes. Unlike Jordan in 1970, however, Lebanon had a weak and badly divided political structure. As a result, in the spring of 1975, after a number of skirmishes with Lebanese Christian militias, the Palestinians allied with an array of leftist Lebanese forces and began an offensive. In the spring of 1976, it appeared that the Palestinians and their leftist allies would win the fighting. President Assad, fearing a radical Palestinian force on Syria's southern border, entered the fray on the side of the Christians and tilted the military balance in their favor. Jordan supported the Syrian intervention, fearing that a Palestinian victory would give the PLO a base of operations from which to destabilize the region.

Jordan's relationship with Syria also improved as Jordan became increasingly disenchanted with its relationship with the United

States. Since the early 1970s, Jordan had negotiated for the purchase of a US$540 million air defense system from the United States to be financed by Saudi Arabia. When the United States Congress objected to the arms sale, Hussein commented that relations with his one-time sponsor had reached "a sad crossroads." In 1976, with Syrian encouragement, he traveled to Moscow to sound out the Soviet Union on its willingness to provide a similar system. In the face of persuasive American and Saudi lobbying, Hussein eventually opted to purchase the American Improved Hawk air defense system (see Military Cooperation with the United States, ch. 5). His trip to Moscow, however, marked a significant improvement in Jordanian-Soviet relations and was a factor in his decision to support the concept of a Middle East peace conference attended by both the Soviet Union and the United States.

## The Camp David Accords and Inter-Arab Politics

During the spring of 1977, the international climate strongly supported some type of superpower-sanctioned settlement to the Arab-Israeli dispute. Newly elected United States president Jimmy Carter and Soviet leader Brezhnev advocated a comprehensive Arab-Israeli settlement that would include autonomy for the Palestinians. On October 1, 1977, in preparation for a reconvened Geneva Conference, the United States and the Soviet Union issued a joint statement committing themselves to a comprehensive settlement incorporating all parties concerned and all questions. The proposed summit, however, was preempted by events in Egypt.

Jordan, like the rest of the Arab states, was taken by surprise by President Sadat's decision to travel to Jerusalem in November 1977. Hussein, however, muted his criticism of the Egyptian president's historic trip and called on the Arab states to reserve judgment. The king feared that an outright rejection of the Egyptian initative might provoke an alienated Sadat to seek a separate agreement with Israel. He also saw many positive elements in Sadat's opening statement to the Knesset, such as his rejection of a separate settlement to the Palestinian problem, his emphasis on the need to find a solution to the Palestinian problem, the recognition of Jordan's special relationship with the West Bank, and the proposal to incorporate Jordan, rather than the PLO, into the peace process.

Despite his enthusiasm for Sadat's speech, Hussein was reluctant to join the Egyptian-Israeli peace process. He feared that by joining the negotiations he would isolate Jordan in the Arab world, incur Syria's wrath, and potentially destabilize Palestinians on the East Bank with little possibility for Jordanian gains. Moreover,

Hussein did not want to represent Palestinian interests at such negotiations unless he had a clear Arab and Palestinian mandate to do so.

The final version of the Camp David Accords signed by Egyptian president Sadat, Israeli prime minister Menachem Begin, and United States president Carter separated the issues of the future of the West Bank and the return of Sinai. Whereas the sections dealing with the return of Sinai were very explicit, the sections on the West Bank were vague and open to various interpretations. They called for Egypt, Israel, and "the representatives of the Palestinian people to negotiate about the future of the West Bank and Gaza." A five-year period of "transitional autonomy" was called for "to ensure a peaceful and orderly transfer of authority." The agreement also called for peace talks between Israel and its other Arab neighbors, particularly Syria.

The Camp David Accords fell far short of meeting even Jordan's minimal demands. Hussein expressed anger that Jordan was included in the Camp David framework without his prior knowledge or approval. He viewed the division of the accords into two agreements with no linkage between Israel's withdrawal from Sinai and progress on the Palestinian issue as a sign that Sadat was more interested in regaining Sinai than in brokering a viable peace settlement on the West Bank and the Gaza Strip. Hussein was further alienated from the Camp David peace process because Israel refused to negotiate over East Jerusalem, insisted on its rights to establish settlements in the occupied territories, and reserved the right to demand sovereignty over those areas at the end of the transition period.

Following the signing of the Camp David Accords, Jordan accepted an Iraqi invitation—accompanied by a US$30 million Iraqi grant—to attend the Baghdad Conference. The summit conference's decision to allot to Jordan the relatively large sum of US$1.25 billion per year helped keep Jordan in the Arab fold. At the Baghdad Conference held in November 1978, the Arab states unequivocally rejected the Camp David Accords and officially ostracized Egypt from the Arab League.

Jordanian-Egyptian relations deteriorated even further after the signing of the Treaty of Peace Between Egypt and Israel in March 1979. The Israeli government's limited view of Palestinian autonomy became apparent shortly after the peace treaty was signed. In April the Begin government approved two new settlements between Ram Allah and Nabulus, established civilian regional councils for the Jewish settlements in the territories, and prepared autonomy plans in which Israel would keep exclusive control over the West

Bank's water, communications, roads, public order, and immigration into the territories. The acceleration of settlements, the growth of an increasingly militaristic Jewish settler movement, and Israel's stated desire to retain complete control over resources in the territories precluded the participation in the peace process of either moderate Palestinians, such as the newly formed National Guidance Committee composed of West Bank mayors, or of Hussein. The PLO refused from the beginning to participate in the peace process.

In response, the Jordanian government recalled its ambassador from Cairo on March 28 and on April 1 it severed diplomatic relations with Egypt. Not all ties were broken, however; the Jordanian and Egyptian airlines still flew about ten flights a week between their respective cities and, most important, Egyptian workers in Jordan continued to enjoy the same status as before. The Jordanian media and public officials intensified anti-Israel rhetoric, showing particular hostility toward the United States for supporting the accords. Hussein's greatest fear was that, with Egypt removed from the Arab-Israeli military balance, Israel might be tempted to transform the East Bank into an "alternative homeland" for the Palestinians. Jordanian fears were fueled when, at the end of March 1979, Israeli minister of agriculture Ariel Sharon issued a statement to the effect that the Palestinians ought to take over Jordan and establish a government there.

Hussein, although fully backing the Baghdad accords, sought a very different objective than the more hard-line Arab states such as Syria and Iraq. His goal was not to punish Egypt or overthrow Sadat, but rather to set up an alternative strategy to the Camp David framework supported by an Arab consensus that would provide a more equitable and viable solution to the Middle East conflict. The essence of the Jordanian alternative was to return the Palestinian problem either to the UN Security Council or to the Geneva Conference where all the relevant parties—including the United States, the Soviet Union, and the European Economic Community—could work together in reaching a comprehensive Middle East peace plan.

Hussein's attempt to develop a united Arab stand did not succeed. At the Tunis Summit of November 1979, in the face of strong Syrian objections, Hussein was unable to mobilize an Arab consensus behind an alternative to the Camp David Accords. Syrian president Assad's strong objections to Hussein's proposal marked the beginning of rapid deterioration in Syrian-Jordanian relations. Hussein was further rebuffed when Assad revived the Steadfastness and Confrontation Front consisting of Syria, Libya, Algeria, the People's Democratic Republic of Yemen (South Yemen), and the PLO. The Syrian leader accused Jordan of supporting Syrian elements of the Muslim Brotherhood, which had been involved in a series of attacks against his regime. Although Syria continued to be a major Soviet ally in the Middle East, Jordan joined nearly the entire Arab world in condemning the Soviet invasion of Afghanistan. Finally, Syria, unlike Jordan, was unwilling to participate in any alternative to the Camp David Accords.

## Jordan in the 1980s

The overthrow of the shah of Iran in February 1979 and the emergence of Ayatollah Sayyid Ruhollah Musavi Khomeini caused grave concern in Amman. The vehement anti-Western, antimonarchical, Islamic revolutionary fervor sweeping Iran throughout 1979 cast a threatening shadow over Jordan. Not only was Hussein a monarch allied with the West, but also he had been a close ally of the shah for many years.

### The Islamic Revolution and a New Arab Alignment

Hussein followed a two-track policy to counteract the looming Iranian threat. One track was domestic; the other, foreign. Domestically, he made a more concerted effort to appear religiously observant in public and to emphasize Islam in the day-to-day life of Jordan. He also increased financial support for mosques and Islamic charities and encouraged the payment of *zakat* (the Muslim religious tax) by exempting those who paid it during the month of Ramadan from 25 percent of their income tax. In addition, during the month of Ramadan some of the provincial governors closed down bars and night clubs on some religious holidays and banned films described as obscene.

For most of his reign, Hussein had appeased the Muslim Brotherhood and other Islamic groups in Jordan as a way of counterbalancing the more radical and, in his view, more destabilizing groups such as the communists, Baathists, and Nasserists. Although the Muslim Brotherhood came out in support of the Islamic Revolution in Iran, the organization in Jordan was not prepared to challenge openly the authority of the Hashimite regime that opposed the Iranian Revolution.

Hussein altered Jordan's Arab alignments in response to the new regional balance of power caused by the Islamic Revolution in Iran, the Egyptian-Israeli peace treaty, and the growing rift with Syria. The focus of Jordan's new regional outlook was improved relations with Iraq. Both countries saw ominous implications in the developments in Iran. Moreover, with Egypt no longer in the Arab fold, Jordan sought an Arab military alliance capable of deterring a more militaristic regime in Israel from meddling in Jordanian affairs. Hussein also needed Iraqi support to stave off the Syrian threat, which had grown significantly during 1980. Finally, Baghdad and Amman feared the Soviet invasion of Afghanistan and its implications for the regional balance of power.

After a series of high-level meetings in the early 1980s, a wide range of exchanges took place. Iraq greatly increased economic assistance to Jordan and discussed a possible project for supplying Jordan with water from the Euphrates. The outbreak of the Iran-Iraq War in September 1980 further tightened relations. From the beginning of the war, Jordan was the most outspoken of the Arab states supporting Iraq. The Iraqi connection became increasingly important as tensions mounted between Jordan and Syria. Between September 1980 and late 1981, Jordan reportedly received US$400 million in economic aid from Iraq. In October 1981, an Iraqi-Jordanian Joint Committee for Economic and Technical Cooperation was set up. Jordan's most demonstrative act of support for the Iraqi war effort occurred in January 1982 when Hussein announced the formation of the Yarmuk Brigade, a Jordanian force of volunteers that pledged to fight for Iraq.

Throughout 1982, as Iran scored significant victories in the Iran-Iraq War, Jordan substantially increased its support to Iraq. Al Aqabah replaced the besieged Iraqi port of Basra as Iraq's major marine transportation point. During 1981 and 1982, the turmoil besetting the Arab states both benefited and threatened Jordan. Egypt, the most populous and militarily strongest Arab country, was ostracized; Syria faced serious domestic unrest and a growing rebellion in Lebanon; Iraq seemed to be losing its war with Iran and was in danger of losing strategically important territory in the south; Syria and Iraq were hostile to each other; and the Persian Gulf states were suffering from the downturn in world oil prices. The weakness of the other Arab states enabled Jordan to play a more important role in Arab politics and allowed Hussein to pursue a more flexible regional diplomacy.

Jordan's improved status in the Arab world resulted in Amman hosting its first Arab summit in November 1981. Hussein reportedly hoped to obtain a breakthrough on the Palestinian question and to mobilize support for the Iraqi war effort. The summit, however, was boycotted by members of the Steadfastness and Confrontation Front led by Syria. In addition, Syria had massed troops on the Jordanian border. Hussein countered by mobilizing a force of equal strength on the Syrian border. Although the situation was eventually defused through Saudi mediation efforts, the potential for future Syrian-Jordanian conflict remained.

### In Search of a Solution to the Palestinian Problem

Jordan's relations with the PLO have reflected the conflicting territorial claims of the Palestinians and Jordan. Since the June 1967 War, both the PLO and Jordan have staked claims to the West Bank and East Jerusalem. Although Hussein and the PLO, like the rest of the Arab world, have rejected Israeli suzerainty over the territories, they differed widely on how the occupied territories should be administered and by whom.

Throughout the late 1970s and early 1980s, Jordan asserted its role in the lives of West Bank Palestinians in various ways. Jordan distributed financial assistance, oversaw the freedom of movement of people and merchandise across the bridges of the Jordan River, assumed the role of protector of the rights of the population under Israeli occupation, and sought the condemnation of Israel in the international community for alleged acts of injustice against the people of the West Bank. Beginning in 1979, individuals from the West Bank, like other Jordanian citizens, were required to obtain new identity cards to benefit from Jordanian government services and to obtain Jordanian passports. Mutual mistrust, however, had prevented agreement between Jordan and the PLO on any form of long-term political cooperation beyond the joint distribution of funds to the occupied territories.

Jordanians, however, remained adamantly opposed to the fedayeen reestablishing bases in Jordan from which to launch guerrilla operations against Israel. Hussein feared that Israel, maintaining a distinct military advantage over the badly divided Arab states, would launch punishing reprisal raids against Jordan if guerrilla operations were to resume. This appraisal was strongly reinforced by the Israeli air raid on the Iraqi nuclear reactor in June 1981.

During the second half of 1980, talk of the so-called "Jordanian option" revived because of the approaching elections in Israel, President Ronald Reagan's election victory in the United States, and talk of a new European initiative in the Middle East. On the surface, the Jordanian option resembled Hussein's version of a settlement with Israel; it envisioned Jordan acting as the major Arab interlocutor in a peace settlement with Israel. Jordan, however, could not outwardly appear as if it were breaking away from the Arab fold and usurping Palestinian prerogatives, unless it were likely that concessions made by Jordan would be reciprocated by Israel. Given the right-wing Likud government in power in Israel, Hussein surmised that such Israeli territorial concessions would not be forthcoming.

As a result, Jordan's public posture on the Palestinian question was ambiguous. In public statements acknowledging PLO representation of the Palestinian people Hussein frequently emphasized the important role Jordan had played in the Palestinian struggle against Israel. Moreover, he rarely identified the PLO as the "sole" legitimate representative of the Palestinians.

## Economic Austerity

Since the creation of Transjordan in 1921, the nation had depended on external economic aid. This dependence rendered it economically vulnerable. For many years the economy was underwritten by Britain. By the early 1950s, after Jordan had officially annexed the West Bank, foreign aid accounted for 60 percent of government revenues. The crucial event for the Jordanian economy, as it was for the Arab world as a whole, was the quadrupling of world oil prices that followed the October 1973 War. Possessing little oil of its own, Jordan nonetheless became inexorably linked to the volatile world oil market. Between 1973 and 1981, direct Arab budget support rose more than sixteen-fold, from US$71.8 million to US$1.179 billion. In the same period, the value of Jordanian exports jumped almost thirteen-fold, from US$57.6 million to US$734.9 million. In addition, Jordan sent to the Persian Gulf states an estimated 350,000 doctors, engineers, teachers, and construction workers who by 1981 had sent back home more than US$1 billion. Even after deducting the outward flow of dinars from the 125,000 foreign workers inside Jordan holding agricultural and unskilled jobs, net worker remittances rose from US$15 million in 1970 to US$900 million in 1981 (see Structure and Dynamics of the Economy, ch. 3).

The accelerated pace of economic growth fueled by the oil price increases of the 1970s also caused inflation and growing import bills. Most important for Jordan, the economic boom years of the 1970s raised popular expectations of continued economic prosperity. As a result, when world oil prices began spiraling downward in the early 1980s, the government halted many large-scale construction projects, slashed food and other subsidies, and significantly reduced public employment. These actions stirred public dissatisfaction.

Hussein's response to the rise in public discontent was to ease restrictions on the political process. First, in 1981 he increased membership of the National Consultative Council (NCC) from sixty to seventy-five. The NCC had been created in April 1978 to fulfill the legislative functions of the dissolved House of Representatives. The NCC, however, was empowered only to debate and discuss bills and had no authority to make laws. As a result, the enlargement of the NCC's membership did not appease the opposition seeking democratic reforms. In addition, in March 1982 a new weekly publication, *Al Ufuq* (Horizons), campaigned for greater democratic freedom and for the reestablishment of political parties banned since 1957 (see Political Dissent and Political Repression, ch. 4). Two political groups were formed: the Arab Constitutional Alignment and the Arab National group. Both groups called for greater public participation in the affairs of state.

## The Israeli Invasion of Lebanon

The June 1982 Israeli invasion of Lebanon significantly altered Jordan's geostrategic position. Israel's willingness to remove PLO bases from Lebanon by force, despite widespread international criticism, raised apprehensions that Israel might launch an offensive against Jordan. The Arab states, weakened by internal rivalries, the Iran-Iraq War, and Egypt's isolation, did not respond forcefully to the Israeli actions. Hussein viewed the Lebanon invasion as part of a pattern of more aggressive Israeli policies that included the 1981 bombing of the Iraqi nuclear reactor, confrontations with Syria, and an ambitious settlement policy in the occupied territories. The government of Menachem Begin, unlike its predecessors, was willing to use force to attain its territorial objectives. This led to concerns that Israel might have designs on Jordan, or that the PLO, after having its major base of operations in Lebanon destroyed, might attempt to reestablish itself in Jordan. Hussein also feared that Israeli settlement activity in the West Bank was rapidly reducing the chances of an acceptable settlement there.

To many Middle East experts, the increase in settlements, their strategic location, the militancy of many of the Israeli settlers, the rise of religious nationalism inside the political mainstream in Israel, and the expansionary views of the Likud leadership lent urgency to the need to reach a negotiated settlement. Jordan hoped to convince the Reagan administration to push policy makers in Jerusalem toward an acceptable peace settlement.

On September 1, 1982, President Reagan launched the Reagan Plan. Hussein applauded the new American proposal, seeing in it a clear break from the Camp David framework. In announcing the new plan, Reagan stated that "it was the firm view of the United States that self-government by the Palestinians of the West Bank and Gaza in association with Jordan offers the best chance for a durable and lasting peace," specifying that the United States would not support the establishment of a Palestinian state. The

Reagan Plan also stressed UN Resolution 242, stating that the resolution applied to all fronts, including the West Bank and the Gaza Strip, and that the final status of Jerusalem should be decided through negotiation.

The war in Lebanon and the publication of the Reagan Plan ushered in a new symbiosis in Jordanian-PLO relations. Hussein needed PLO acceptance of Jordan's participation in the peace process in the framework of the Reagan Plan; PLO chairman Yasir Arafat, considerably weakened by the PLO's devastating defeat in the war in Lebanon, needed Jordanian support to gain access to the political process. In October 1982, Hussein and Arafat began a series of meetings designed to formulate a joint response to the Reagan Plan. These negotiations centered around the formation of a Jordanian-Palestinian delegation to future peace talks, and--because neither Israel nor the United States recognized the PLO-ón the extent to which the PLO would be directly associated with this delegation. Jordan proposed that the PLO appoint West Bank residents who were not members of the PLO to represent the Palestinians. In November 1982, agreement was reached on the formation of a Higher Jordanian-Palestinian Committee headed by Prime Minister Mudar Badran and Arafat.

Because of conflicting objectives sought by Arafat and Hussein, the joint Palestinian-Jordanian committee never materialized. Whereas Hussein saw the proposed confederation as a means to reestablish Jordanian control over the West Bank, Arafat viewed the negotiations as a means to gain PLO sovereignty over the occupied territories. In addition, Hussein and Arafat required evidence that Washington was willing to pressure Israel to make significant territorial concessions. Meanwhile, Israeli troops still occupied part of southern Lebanon, and the Israeli government had not made any commitments on the settlement issue. Moreover, given Iran's recent victories in its war with Iraq, tensions with Syria, and a depressed world oil market, Hussein could not isolate Jordan by unilaterally participating in the Reagan Plan without some show of Israeli flexibility.

Following Hussein's decision in April 1983 not to join the Reagan Plan, Jordan increasingly criticized Washington's inability to apply pressure on Israel to halt settlements in the West Bank. United States-Jordanian relations were further strained in May 1983 when the Reagan administration lifted a ban on the sale of F-16 aircraft to Israel. The ban had been imposed to pressure Israel to withdraw its forces from Lebanon. The United States opposed a Jordanian draft resolution submitted to the UN Security Council in July 1983 asserting the illegality of Israeli settlement activity in the

West Bank, and relations between the two countries were further soured by the signing in November 1983 of a new agreement on strategic cooperation between Israel and the United States.

Syria emerged from the war in Lebanon as a pivotal regional power, able and willing to play a role in the affairs of neighboring Arab states. Whereas Syrian power was on the rise, Jordan's most powerful Arab ally, Iraq, seemed to be losing its costly war with Iran. Hussein tried to counterbalance the Syrian threat by making overtures to President Husni Mubarak of Egypt, but did not yet reestablish diplomatic relations. Hussein hoped that Mubarak, who had replaced Sadat after the latter's assassination in September 1981, would bring Egypt back into the Arab fold after Sinai was returned to Egypt in September 1982.

High-level talks between Egypt and Jordan occurred regularly throughout 1983 and 1984. In addition, Egyptian newspapers, banned in Jordan after the Egyptian-Israeli peace treaty, were allowed into the country in October 1983. Also, Jordan and Egypt signed a trade protocol in December 1983 and discussed the expansion of scientific and agricultural cooperation. Finally, in September 1984, Jordan officially announced the resumption of diplomatic relations with Egypt.

\* \* \*

Philip K. Hitti's *History of the Arabs from the Earliest Times to the Present* is a classic survey of the subject by an eminent historian. Much material on the origin and development of the Transjordanian amirate is found in J.C. Hurewitz's *The Struggle for Palestine* and Christopher Sykes's *Crossroads to Israel, 1917–1948*. For a scholarly analysis of the growth of Arab nationalism, see Zeine N. Zeine's *The Emergence of Arab Nationalism* and *The Struggle for Arab Independence*, which may be used to supplement George Antonius's more familiar *The Arab Awakening*. *Glubb's Legion*, by Godfrey Lias, is a sympathetic, popular treatment of the activities of the Arab Legion. Sir John Bagot Glubb's memoir, *A Soldier with the Arabs*, is both entertaining and informative. Another firsthand British account of Jordan's historical development is Charles Johnston's *The Brink of Jordan*. Both King Abdullah and his grandson, Hussein, have provided readable memoirs that can be studied profitably in conjunction with more objective scholarly works. Peter Snow, a British journalist, has written the most accessible biography of Hussein.

Two excellent scholarly books focusing on Britain's role in the development of Jordan were published in the late 1980s. These are

Mary C. Wilson's *King Abdullah, Britain, and the Making of Jordan* and Avi Shlaim's highly controversial *Collusion Across the Jordan*, which depicts secret Zionist-Hashimite collaboration over the final settlement of Palestine. Another useful work covering the early history of Jordan is Uriel Dann's *Studies in the History of Transjordan, 1920–1949*. Avi Plascov's *The Palestinian Refugees in Jordan, 1948–1957* offers an interesting analysis of the Palestinian refugee problem.

A solid general survey of Jordan is Peter Gubser's *Jordan*. The Jordan sections in the *Middle East Contemporary Survey* provide fairly detailed coverage of political and economic events. Robert B. Satloff's *Troubles on the East Bank: Challenges to the Domestic Stability of Jordan* focuses on the more recent history of Jordan. Bernard Avishai's articles on Jordan in the *New York Review of Books* during the early 1980s provide keen insights into contemporary Jordanian history. (For further information and complete citations, see Bibliography.)

# Chapter 2. The Society and Its Environment

*Mosaic of a gazelle from a Byzantine church in Amman, ca. 500–700*

WHEN THE AMIRATE of Transjordan was created by the British in 1921, the vast majority of the people consisted of an assortment of tribally organized and tribally oriented groups, some of whom were sedentary cultivators and some nomadic or seminomadic. The total population was fewer than 400,000 people. By 1988 nearly 3,000,000 people, more than half of whom were Palestinians, inhabited the region east of the Jordan River-Dead Sea-Gulf of Aqaba line, referred to as the East Bank (see Glossary). The term *Palestinians* refers narrowly to citizens of the British mandated territory of Palestine (1922–48). In general usage, however, the term has come to refer to Muslims or Christians indigenous to the region between the Egyptian Sinai and Lebanon and west of the Jordan River-Dead Sea-Gulf of Aqaba line who identify themselves primarily as Palestinians. Narrowly defined, the term *Transjordanian* referred to a citizen of the Amirate of Transjordan (1921–46). Generally speaking, however, a Transjordanian was considered a Muslim or Christian indigenous to the East Bank region, which was within the approximate boundaries of the contemporary state of Jordan. The formerly rural society of Jordan had been transformed since independence into an increasingly urban one; by 1985 nearly 70 percent of the population resided in urban centers that were growing at an annual rate of between 4 and 5 percent.

In the late 1980s, class polarization was increasingly evident. Nonetheless, a variety of social forces (such as national identity and regional or tribal affiliation) continued to cut across class lines. The uprooting of so many East Bank citizens from their places of origin contributed to social fragmentation. In addition to the Palestinians, who retained a strong sense of national identity and outrage at the loss of their homeland, many Transjordanians had migrated from their rural and/or desert villages to urban centers in search of work for themselves and education for their children. Many Transjordanians thus shared a sense of loss and rootlessness.

Probably the most important force supporting cohesion and integration was the Arab-Islamic cultural tradition common to all but a few members of the society. Arabic, a potent force for unity throughout the Middle East, was the mother tongue of the overwhelming majority of residents. Also, more than 90 percent of the population adhered to Sunni (see Glossary) Islam. These commonalities, although important, have been insufficient to forge an integrated society.

Every year since the late 1950s, increasing numbers of Jordan's youth have received formal training in the country's rapidly expanding education system. By the late 1980s, all children aged six years to twelve years were attending free and compulsory primary schools. Nearly 80 percent of children between the ages of thirteen and fifteen attended three-year preparatory schools, also free and compulsory. But possession of an education, once a near certain vehicle for upward mobility, no longer guaranteed employment. Unemployment was probably one of the most critical issues facing Jordan in the late 1980s. It was accompanied by growing political frustration and radicalization over the Palestinian uprising (*intifadah*) in the Israeli-occupied West Bank (see Glossary).

## Geography

The territory of Jordan covers about 91,880 square kilometers. Until 1988, when King Hussein relinquished Jordan's claim to the West Bank, that area was considered part of Jordan, although only officially recognized as such by Britain and Pakistan. At that time the West Bank—which encompasses about 5,880 square kilometers—had been under Israeli occupation since the June 1967 War between Israel and the states of Egypt, Jordan, and Syria.

Jordan is landlocked except at its southern extremity, where nearly twenty-six kilometers of shoreline along the Gulf of Aqaba provide access to the Red Sea. A great north-south geological rift, forming the depression of Lake Tiberias (Sea of Galilee), the Jordan Valley, and the Dead Sea, is the dominant topographical feature.

### Boundaries

Except for small sections of the borders with Israel and Syria, Jordan's international boundaries do not follow well-defined natural features of the terrain. The country's boundaries were established by various international agreements, and, with the obvious exception of the border with Israel, none was in dispute in early 1989.

The de jure border with Israel is based on the Armistice line agreed on in April 1949 by Israel and what was then Transjordan, following negotiations held under the auspices of a United Nations (UN) mediator. In general, the border represents the battle positions held by Transjordanian and Israeli forces when a cease-fire went into effect and has no relation to economic or administrative factors. Until the Israeli occupation of the West Bank that occurred during the June 1967 War (also known as the Six-Day War), the demarcation line divided the city of Jerusalem, with Jordan holding the Old City and most of the holy places.

Jordan's boundaries with Syria, Iraq, and Saudi Arabia do not have the special significance that the border with Israel does; these borders have not always hampered tribal nomads in their movements, yet for a few groups borders did separate them from traditional grazing areas and water sources. By the time political boundaries were drawn across the deserts around Transjordan after World War I, most of the nomadic tribes in that region had long-established areas lying within the confines of the new state. To accommodate the few cases where tribal peoples traditionally had moved back and forth across the country's borders, agreements with neighboring countries recognized the principle of freedom of grazing and provided for a continuation of migratory practices, subject to certain regulations.

The border between Jordan and Saudi Arabia (only partially delimited by a series of agreements between Britain and the government of what eventually became Saudi Arabia) was first formally defined in the Hadda Agreement of 1925. In 1965 Jordan and Saudi Arabia concluded a bilateral agreement that realigned and delimited the boundary. The realignment resulted in some exchange of territory, and Jordan's coastline on the Gulf of Aqaba was lengthened by about eighteen kilometers. The new boundary enabled Jordan to expand its port facilities and established a zone in which the two parties agreed to share petroleum revenues equally if oil were discovered. The agreement also protected the pasturage and watering rights of nomadic tribes inside the exchanged territories.

## Topography

The country consists mainly of a plateau between 700 and 1,000 meters high, divided into ridges by valleys and gorges, and a few mountainous areas. Fractures of the earth's surface are evident in the great geological rift that extends southward from the Jordan Valley through the Gulf of Aqaba and the Red Sea, gradually disappearing south of the lake country of East Africa. Although an earthquake-prone region, as of early 1989 no severe shocks had been recorded for several centuries.

By far the greatest part of the East Bank is desert, displaying the land forms and other features associated with great aridity. Most of this land is part of the great Syrian (or North Arabian) Desert (see fig. 4). There are broad expanses of sand and dunes, particularly in the south and southeast, together with salt flats. Occasional jumbles of sandstone hills or low mountains support only meager and stunted vegetation that thrives for a short period after the scanty winter rains. These areas support little life and are the least populated regions of Jordan.

The drainage network is coarse and incised. In many areas the relief provides no eventual outlet to the sea, so that sedimentary deposits accumulate in basins where moisture evaporates or is absorbed in the ground. Toward the depression in the western part of the East Bank, the desert rises gradually into the Jordanian Highlands—a steppe country of high, deeply cut limestone plateaus with an average elevation of about 900 meters. Occasional summits in this region reach 1,200 meters in the northern part and exceed 1,700 meters in the southern part; the highest peak is Jabal Ramm at 1,754 meters. These highlands are an area of long-settled villages. Until about the 1940s, persons living in these villages depended upon rain-fed agriculture for their livelihood.

The western edge of this plateau country forms an escarpment along the eastern side of the Jordan River-Dead Sea depression and its continuation south of the Dead Sea. Most of the wadis that provide drainage from the plateau country into the depression carry water only during the short season of winter rains. Sharply incised with deep, canyonlike walls, the wadis, whether wet or dry, can be formidable obstacles to travel.

The Jordan River is short, but from its mountain headwaters (approximately 160 kilometers north of the river's mouth at the Dead Sea) the riverbed drops from an elevation of about 3,000 meters above sea level to more than 400 meters below sea level. Before reaching Jordanian territory the river forms Lake Tiberias, the surface of which is 212 meters below sea level. The Jordan River's principal tributary is the Yarmuk River. Near the junction of the two rivers, the Yarmuk forms the boundary between Israel on the northwest, Syria on the northeast, and Jordan on the south. The Az Zarqa River, the second main tributary of the Jordan River, rises and empties entirely within the East Bank.

A 380-kilometer-long rift valley runs from the Yarmuk River in the north to Al Aqabah in the south. The northern part, from the Yarmuk River to the Dead Sea, is commonly known as the Jordan Valley. It is divided into eastern and western parts by the Jordan River. Bordered by a steep escarpment on both the eastern and the western side, the valley reaches a maximum width of twenty-two kilometers at some points. The valley is properly known as the Al Ghawr (the depression, or valley, also seen as Al Ghor; see Water, ch. 3).

The rift valley on the southern side of the Dead Sea is known as the Southern Ghawr and the Wadi al Jayb (popularly known as the Wadi al Arabah). The Southern Ghawr runs from Wadi al Hammah, on the south side of the Dead Sea, to Ghawr Faya, about twenty-five kilometers south of the Dead Sea. Wadi al Jayb

is 180 kilometers long, from the southern shore of the Dead Sea to Al Aqabah in the south. The valley floor varies in level. In the south, it reaches its lowest level at the Dead Sea (more than 400 meters below sea level), rising in the north to just above sea level. Evaporation from the sea is extreme because of year-round high temperatures. The water contains about 250 grams of dissolved salts per liter at the surface and reaches the saturation point at 110 meters.

The Dead Sea occupies the deepest depression on the land surface of the earth. The depth of the depression is accentuated by the surrounding mountains and highlands that rise to elevations of 800 to 1,200 meters above sea level. The sea's greatest depth is about 430 meters, and it thus reaches a point more than 825 meters below sea level. A drop in the level of the sea has caused the former Lisan Peninsula to become a land bridge dividing the sea into separate northern and southern basins.

## Climate

The major characteristic of the climate is the contrast between a relatively rainy season from November to April and very dry weather for the rest of the year. With hot, dry, uniform summers and cool, variable winters during which practically all of the precipitation occurs, the country has a Mediterranean-style climate. In general, the farther inland from the Mediterranean Sea a given part of the country lies, the greater are the seasonal contrasts in temperature and the less rainfall. Atmospheric pressures during the summer months are relatively uniform, whereas the winter months bring a succession of marked low pressure areas and accompanying cold fronts. These cyclonic disturbances generally move eastward from over the Mediterranean Sea several times a month and result in sporadic precipitation.

Most of the East Bank receives less than twelve centimeters of rain a year and may be classified as a dry desert or steppe region. Where the ground rises to form the highlands east of the Jordan Valley, precipitation increases to around thirty centimeters in the south and fifty or more centimeters in the north. The Jordan Valley, lying in the lee of high ground on the West Bank, forms a narrow climatic zone that annually receives up to thirty centimeters of rain in the northern reaches; rain dwindles to less than twelve centimeters at the head of the Dead Sea.

The country's long summer reaches a peak during August. January is usually the coolest month. The fairly wide ranges of temperature during a twenty-four-hour period are greatest during the summer months and have a tendency to increase with higher elevation and distance from the Mediterranean seacoast. Daytime temperatures during the summer months frequently exceed 36°C and average about 32°C. In contrast, the winter months— November to April—bring moderately cool and sometimes cold weather, averaging about 13°C. Except in the rift depression, frost is fairly common during the winter, and it occasionally snows in Amman.

For a month or so before and after the summer dry season, hot, dry air from the desert, drawn by low pressure, produces strong winds from the south or southeast that sometimes reach gale force. Known in the Middle East by various names, including the khamsin, this dry, sirocco-style wind is usually accompanied by great dust clouds. Its onset is heralded by a hazy sky, a falling barometer, and a drop in relative humidity to about 10 percent. Within a few hours there may be a 10°C to 15°C rise in temperature. These windstorms ordinarily last a day or so, cause much discomfort, and destroy crops by desiccating them.

The *shammal,* another wind of some significance, comes from the north or northwest, generally at intervals between June and September. Remarkably steady during daytime hours but becoming a breeze at night, the *shammal* may blow for as long as nine days out of ten and then repeat the process. It originates as a dry continental mass of polar air that is warmed as it passes over the Eurasian landmass. The dryness allows intense heating of the earth's surface by the sun, resulting in high daytime temperatures that moderate after sunset.

## Population

Official Jordanian statistics gave a 1987 population figure of 2,896,800 for the East Bank. A 1982 population of 2,399,300 thus indicated an annual growth rate of between 3.6 and 4 percent. United Nations statistics projected a peak in the annual growth rate at 4.11 percent in the period from 1990 to 1995, followed by a steady decline to 2.88 percent in 2020.

Rapid development in the provision of health care services during the 1970s and 1980s led to a decline in the crude death rate from 17 per 1,000 population in 1965 to 7 per 1,000 population by 1986 (see Health and Welfare, this ch.). During the same period, the infant mortality rate, a major indicator of a country's development and health status, dropped from 115 to 46 per 1,000 live births. In 1986 life expectancy at birth was sixty-five years (sixty-three for males and sixty-seven for females). The lowered death rate, a high birth rate, and lowered infant mortality rate combined to generate a major demographic problem in the late 1980s. At the end of the decade, more than half Jordan's population was below fifteen years of age (see fig. 5). This situation strained the country's already limited resources, and employment for the burgeoning group of young people became increasingly difficult to provide.

Accurate demographic figures were difficult to compile because of the substantial number of Jordanians residing and working abroad and the continuous flow of West Bank Palestinians with Jordanian passports back and forth between the East and West banks. According to the United Nations Relief and Works Agency (UNRWA) for Palestine Refugees in the Near East, about 224,000 people were admitted to UNRWA refugee camps in the East Bank immediately after the June 1967 War. In 1986 UNRWA cited 826,128 registered refugees living on the East Bank, of whom about 205,000 were living in refugee camps.

The exact number of Palestinians living on the East Bank was unknown. Estimates usually ranged from 60 to 70 percent of the total population. Official government statistics did not distinguish between East Bank and West Bank Jordanians (see Palestinians, this ch.).

The government did not have an officially articulated population policy or birth control program. Rather, in 1979 it adopted a ''child spacing program'' that was designed to improve the health of mother and child but not specifically to lower the fertility rate. This noninterventionist approach considered family planning to be one component of an integrated maternal-child health and primary health care program. Government clinics and private medical services delivered family planning services upon request, and contraceptives were widely available at low cost. In 1987 there were 116 maternal-child health care centers—up from 93 in 1983—providing prenatal and postnatal care and a wide range of birth control information.

Jordan's high population growth can be attributed primarily to high fertility rates. In 1986 the World Bank (see Glossary) calculated this rate as 6.0 births for each woman over the span of her reproductive years, one of the highest fertility rates in the region. This rate was projected to decline to 4.2 births by the year 2000. The fertility rate varied, however, between women residing in rural and urban areas and according to educational attainment. Educated women tended to marry at a slightly older age than uneducated women, and this delay contributed to a lower fertility rate. Urban women achieved lower fertility rates through modern methods of contraception, particularly the pill. Fertility rates were lowest in Amman, higher in smaller urban areas such as Irbid

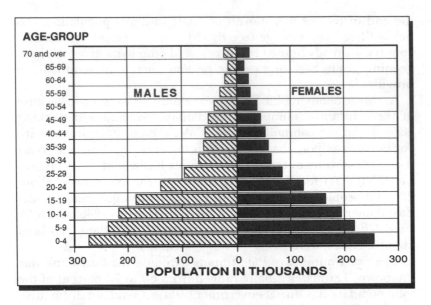

Source: Based on information from Jordan, Department of Statistics, *Statistical Yearbook, 1987,* Amman, 1988, 18.

*Figure 5. Population of the East Bank by Age and Sex, 1987*

and Az Zarqa, and highest in rural areas. In rural areas modern contraceptive usage was lower, although breast-feeding, which serves to delay the return of fertility, was extended for a longer period than in the cities. World Bank data indicated that 27 percent of married women of child-bearing age were using contraception in the 1980s.

A woman was expected to have to bear five children, including at least two sons, in fairly rapid succession. Women gained status and security in their marital household by bearing children. According to a study conducted in the early 1980s by Jordanian anthropologists Seteney Shami and Lucine Taminian in a poor, squatter area in Amman, reproductive behavior was subject to several factors. If a woman had given birth to two or more sons, she might begin to space her pregnancies or stop bearing children for a while. Household structure—nuclear, extended, or multiple family—also appeared to be a crucial factor in determining fertility. The presence of other women in a household encouraged women to bear more children to improve their relative position in the household.

The overall population density for the East Bank in 1987 was established at about thirty persons per square kilometer. There was wide regional variation and the rate of urbanization was high. East of Al Mafraq, in an area encompassing almost two-thirds of the country, no towns had a population of more than 10,000. The bulk of Jordan's population was centered in the governorate of Amman and the smaller urban areas of Irbid, As Salt, and Az Zarqa. The 1987 population totals of the eight governorates ranged from 1,203,000 in Amman to 101,000 in the Maan Governorate. According to World Bank figures, about 70 percent of the population lived in urban areas. The nation's capital, Amman, accounted for more than one-third of the total population. Rapid urbanization appeared to be the result of a high fertility rate and rural-urban migration. If urbanization continued at the high annual rate of 4 to 5 percent, it was estimated that by the year 2000, nearly three-fourths of the population could be living in Amman, Az Zarqa, Irbid, As Salt, and Ar Ramtha.

The remainder of the population resided in villages scattered in an uneven pattern throughout Jordan. The nomadic and seminomadic population was very small, at most 2 to 3 percent of the population. The clearest concentrations of villages were in the fertile northwest corner and the Jordan Valley. Village size varied markedly from region to region. At one time, size related to the productive capacity of the surrounding farmland. Larger villages were located in the more fertile, generally irrigated regions where family members could reach their fields with relative ease. While village populations continued to grow, rural-urban migration drained off a steady stream of young men and sometimes whole families. Villages provided little employment for their residents, and agriculture as a way of life had declined precipitously since the 1950s.

Camps of nomadic and seminomadic beduins still existed in the late 1980s. Nomadic tribes were found mainly in the desert area east of a line from Al Mafraq to Maan. The area, about 400 kilometers long and 250 kilometers wide, is known as the *badiya* (pl., *bawaadi*, meaning desert or semidesert). Seminomadic beduins were located in the Al Ghawr and near Irbid. These seminomads descended to the Jordan Valley in the winter because of its warm climate and grazing ground for their herds. Traditionally, many of these seminomads also farmed plots of land in the valley. In the summer, they moved their herds up into the hills to avoid the intense heat.

The native inhabitants of the Jordan Valley are known as Al Ghawarna, or people of Al Ghawr. Prior to the June 1967 War, the valley was home to about 60,000 people engaged in agriculture and pastoralism. In 1971 the population had declined to 5,000 as a result of the June 1967 War and the 1970–71 conflict between the Palestinian guerrillas and the Jordanian armed forces (see The

Guerrilla Crisis, ch. 1). By 1979, however, the population had reached 85,000 as a result of government development efforts designed to attract people to settle in this area.

Refugee camps emerged in the wake of the Arab-Israeli War of 1948. The original refugee settlements were tent camps, but in most places tents were replaced by rows of galvanized steel, aluminum, and asbestos shelters. There were initially five refugee camps—Irbid, Az Zarqa, Amman New (Al Wahdat), Al Karamah (later dismantled), and Jabal al Hussein— but six additional emergency camps were established for refugees from the June 1967 War—Al Hisn, Suf, Jarash, Baqah, Talbiyah, and Marka. Most of the camps were located near major cities in the northwest (see fig. 6).

## The Organization of Society: Cohesion and Conflict

In the pre-1948 East Bank, the dominant sociopolitical order was tribalism. Tribalism was characteristic not only of the beduin nomads and seminomads upon whom the Hashimite (also seen as Hashemite) rulers relied for support, but also of many of the village people and even those who were technically urban. After 1948 this sociocultural system was inundated by masses of Palestinians, largely sedentary village and town dwellers, many of them literate and well educated. The sheer numbers of Palestinians who came to the East Bank after 1948 and the comparatively simple economy and society of the indigenous Transjordanians made the assimilation of the Palestinians to the local patterns improbable. Indeed, some analysts have argued that by the early 1970s Palestinians had established a cultural dominance in the East Bank. In any case, by the late 1980s, Palestinians had considerable economic and cultural influence.

Jordanians responded in part to the development of Palestinian economic and cultural elites by upgrading education. By the late 1980s, the gap between Transjordanian and Palestinian educational achievements had narrowed considerably. Jordan's position also was changing in the global political economy. Agriculture and nomadism had gradually given way to more viable livelihoods based on skilled labor, secular education, and increasing levels of literacy. Labor migration, particularly of the skilled and educated, was a key factor in social mobility in the 1970s and 1980s. A concomitant shift in values was apparent: prestige was increasingly associated with modern occupations, and education came to be seen as the key to social mobility.

Aside from the fundamental distinction between Jordanians of East Bank origin and those of Palestinian origin, other sociocultural distinctions or affiliations were evident in Jordanian society, including ethnic and regional origins, gender, class, tribe, religion, and life-style (e.g., nomadic, village, or urban). These various patterns of affiliations structured the ways in which Jordanians related to one another and gave rise to different sorts of individual identity. For example, most Christian Jordanians were Arabs and shared many cultural habits and values with Muslim Jordanians. Their sense of identity, however, was based less on Islamic influences than that of Muslim Jordanians. Christians interacted daily with Muslims, working, studying, and socializing together. But intermarriage between Muslims and Christians remained infrequent in the late 1980s. Little information was available on the extent to which these social interactions contributed to conflict or tension. The most that observers could conclude was that religious differences carried a potential for conflict.

Class structure in Jordan was exceedingly difficult to assess. Many social divisions, such as East Bank or Palestinian origins and identity, tribal affiliation, ethnicity, and rural or urban lifestyle, cut across class divisions. The forces of the political economy in the late 1970s and 1980s were forging embryonic classes; however, it was debatable to what extent they were self-conscious and cohesive.

Class structure in Jordan resembled a pyramid. At the top was a small, wealthy group comprising large landowners, industrialists, leading financial figures, and members of their families. The oil boom of the 1970s and early 1980s also had created a new class of wealthy Jordanians who made large amounts of money abroad, which was displayed by conspicuous consumption at home in Jordan. Just below this group were professionals, army officers, and government officials who lived a somewhat less grand but still comfortable life. White-collar workers, schoolteachers, and returning migrants struggled to retain a style of life that separated them socially from the small shopkeepers and artisans below them. At the bottom of the pyramid, a large lower class included increasing numbers of the unemployed. The system of family support tended to cushion unemployed university graduates and professionals from falling into the ranks of the poor.

## Ethnicity and Language

In the late 1980s, several ethnic and religious groups coexisted on the East Bank. Roughly 5 to 8 percent of the total population were Christians (see Religious Minorities, this ch.). Of these, most were Arabs, including a small number—unique among Christians in the Middle East—who recently had been pastoral nomads.

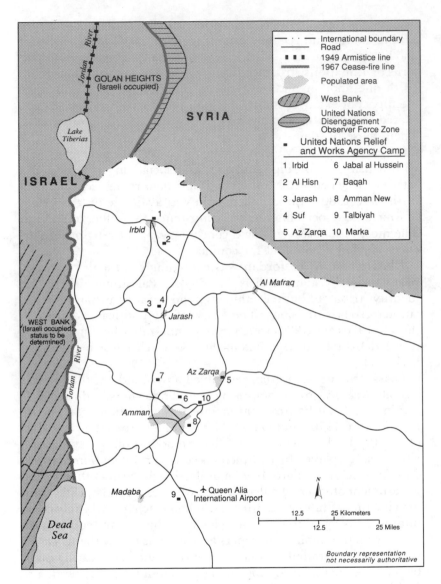

Source: Based on information from United Nations Relief and Works Agency for Palestine Refugees in the Near East.

*Figure 6. United Nations Relief and Works Agency Camps in Jordan, 1989*

The largest group of non-Arab Christians were the Armenians,
perhaps 1 percent of the population, who resided primarily in Irbid and Amman.

The Circassians, a Sunni Muslim community of approximately

25,000 people, were descendants of families brought from the region of the Caucasus Mountains when Caucasian territory was ceded to Russia in the 1880s. By encouraging the Circassians to settle in northern Jordan, the Ottomans sought to provide an element loyal to the sultan that could counterbalance the beduins. Circassians originally settled in Amman and the then-abandoned city of Jarash. Despite their small numbers, they have long been important in government, business, and the military and security forces. In 1938, for example, Circassians constituted 7.3 percent of the non-British government officials in Transjordan. Twenty-six of the thirty-three cabinets between 1947 and 1965 included one or more Circassians. Circassian families included prominent landowners and leaders in commerce and industry. Peter Gubser, a United States authority on Jordan, contended in 1983 that the Circassians were not "politically assertive as a group," although they were known for "their loyalty to the Hashemites." It is likely, however, that their relative cultural and economic importance diminished with the increasing predominance of the Palestinians, on the one hand, and the improved education level of the Jordanians, on the other. The Circassians remained heavily represented in senior military ranks, however, which caused some resentment among other Jordanians. All Circassians spoke Arabic, and the rate of intermarriage between Arab Jordanians and Circassians was high.

Another, much smaller group originating in the Caucasus was the Shishans (also seen as Chechens), whose roughly 2,000 members were Shia (see Glossary) Muslims, the only representatives of this branch of Islam in Jordan. Another religious minority were small numbers of Arabic-speaking Druze villagers. A few Arabic-speaking Kurds lived in several northern villages.

A category of immigrants different from the Palestinian refugees may be noted. Between the early 1920s and the late 1940s, some hundreds of families, perhaps more, settled in Transjordan, having left Palestine, Syria, and the Hijaz region in Saudi Arabia. Arabs, and usually Sunni Muslims, they were nevertheless only partially integrated into the local communities in which they lived. This incomplete assimilation occurred in part because they were foreigners in the context of the tribal structure of such communities, and in part because, as merchants, most were looked at askance by tribally oriented groups. Generally, they tended to marry among themselves or with persons of similar origin. In the 1980s, however, most of these families had lived in the East Bank for nearly three generations, and the tribal system that had excluded them had become less significant within the society.

All Jordanians, regardless of ethnicity or religion, speak Arabic, the official language of Jordan. Throughout the Arab world, the language exists in three forms: the classical Arabic of the Quran, the literary language developed from the classical and known as Modern Standard Arabic, and the local form of the spoken language. Modern Standard Arabic has virtually the same structure wherever it is used, although its pronunciation and lexicon may vary locally. Educated Arabs tend to know two forms of Arabic—Modern Standard Arabic and their own dialect of spoken Arabic. Even uneducated Arabic speakers usually can comprehend the general meaning of something said in Modern Standard Arabic although they cannot speak it themselves and often have difficulty understanding specific expressions. Classical Arabic is known chiefly to scholars; many people have memorized Quranic phrases by rote but cannot speak the classic form.

Dialects of spoken Arabic vary greatly throughout the Arab world. Most Jordanians speak a dialect common to Syria, Lebanon, Jordan, and parts of Iraq and, like people speaking other dialects, they proudly regard theirs as the best. (Small numbers of nomads traversing Jordan from Saudi Arabia may speak a dialect akin to one used in that country.) Few people believe that their dialect is actually good Arabic in the sense of conforming to the ideal. Although they converse in colloquial Arabic, they generally agree that the written form of Modern Standard Arabic is superior to the spoken form because it is closer to the perfection of the Quranic language. Arabs generally believe that the speech of the beduins resembles the purer classical form most closely and that the local dialects used by the settled villagers and townspeople are unfortunate corruptions.

Within a given region, slight differences in speech distinguish a city dweller from a villager and more significant ones distinguish either of these from a nomad. Even within the villages, various quarters often display unique pronunciations, idioms, and vocabulary specialized to particular lifestyles. Grammatical structure may differ as well.

Arabic is a Semitic language related to Aramaic, Hebrew, various Ethiopic languages, and others. Rich in synonyms, rhythmic, highly expressive and poetic, Arabic can have a strong emotional effect on its speakers and listeners. As the language of the Quran, believed by Muslims to be the literal word of God, it has been the vehicle for recounting the historic glories of Islamic civilization. Arabic speakers are more emotionally attached to their language than are most peoples to their native tongues. Poetic eloquence was one of the most admired cultural attainments and signs of cultivation in the Arab world, among rural people, sedentary and nomadic, as well as among literate city dwellers. Arabic speakers long have striven to display an extensive command of traditional phrases and locutions. Beauty of expression was highly valued, and the speaker and writer traditionally sought an elaboration and circumlocution in both spoken and written forms that Westerners might find flowery or verbose.

## Tribes and Tribalism

Before the events of the post-World War II period thrust it onto the center stage of international affairs, the territory that is now the East Bank was first a provincial backwater of the Ottoman Empire and later a small and weak desert amirate. Straddling the transitional area between the "desert and the sown," it participated only marginally in the social and intellectual changes that began sweeping the Arab world during the nineteenth century (see Ottoman Rule, ch. 1). Although ringed by the hinterlands of such major cities as Jerusalem and Damascus, Jordan lacked a significant urban center of its own until the late 1940s; consequently, it did not display artistically, intellectually, commercially, or governmentally the sophisticated form of Arab culture characteristic of urban life. The basic form of social organization in Transjordan was tribal, and the social relations among the various nomadic and seminomadic tribes and between them and villagers (many of whom were also tribally organized) were based on trade and the exchange of tribute for protection.

In 1983 Gubser classified Jordanians along a continuum: nomadic, seminomadic, semisedentary, and sedentary. Nomads, or beduins, were a fully nomadic group whose livelihood was based on camel herding. Tribes and animals existed in a symbiotic relationship; the camels supplied much of the food and other needs of the beduins, while the tribespeople assured the animals' survival by locating and guiding them to adequate pasturage. This fine adaptation to an extremely demanding ecological niche required a versatile, portable technology that was, in its way, extremely sophisticated. It also required a high degree of specialized knowledge and a flexible social structure that could be expanded and contracted according to need. The beduins, however, were also dependent upon settled communities—villages, towns, and cities—for trading animals and their products for goods they did not produce.

Tribal social structure, as described by tribal members, was based on the ramification of patrilineal ties among men. In reality, matrilineal ties also were significant in providing access to material and social resources. The ideological dimension to patrilineality became more apparent when endogamy, or marriage within the group, was considered. The preference for endogamy—historically prevalent in the Middle East, especially for paternal cousin marriage in the first instance and then in descending levels of relatedness—gives rise to a network of kin relations that are both maternal and paternal at the same time. Ultimately, the kinship system takes on many characteristics of a bilateral system. Descent and inheritance, however, are traced in a patrilineal fashion.

Tribes in Jordan were groups of related families claiming descent from a supposed founding ancestor. Within this overall loyalty, however, descent from intermediate ancestors defined several levels of smaller groups within each tribe. Tribespeople described their system as segmentary; that is, the tribe resembled a pyramid composed of ascending segments, or levels, each of which was both a political and a social group. At some point, each unit automatically contained within it all units of the lower level. Ideally, in the event of conflict, segments would unite in an orderly fashion from the lowest level to the highest as conflict escalated. In reality, the system was not so orderly; tribal segments underwent fission, and in the event of conflict, fusion did not necessarily follow the ideal pattern. The pattern of unity was much more varied and complex.

Beduins traditionally have placed great importance on the concept of honor (*ird*). Slight or injury to a member of a tribal group was an injury to all members of that group; likewise, all members were responsible for the actions of a fellow tribal member. Honor inhered in the family or tribe and in the individual as the representative of the family or tribe. Slights were to be erased by appropriate revenge or through mediation to reach reconciliation based on adequate recompense.

Beduins had specific areas for winter and summer camping that were known to be the territory of a specific tribe. Seminomadic groups raised sheep and goats and moved much shorter, well-defined distances; they also practiced some agriculture. But the semisedentary groups were more involved in agriculture than either nomads or seminomadic peoples. Parts of a semisedentary group moved during different seasons, while others in the group remained in permanent abodes.

By the 1980s, these differences among beduin groups were minimal. Substantial numbers of nomads and seminomads had increasingly adopted a sedentary way of life. In his 1981 study of one section of the Bani Sakhar tribe, Joseph Hiatt noted that settlement began in the post-World War I period and expanded rapidly after the mid-1950s. In this case and many others, sedentarization

*King Talal Dam, Jordan River Valley*

was neither completely voluntary nor a result of an official settlement policy. Rather, it appeared to be a natural response to changing political and economic circumstances, particularly the formation and consolidation of the state. In some cases, the administrative policies of the state disrupted the nomads' traditional pastoral economy. For example, national borders separated the nomads from grazing lands and permanent wells. The creation of a standing army that recruited nomads diluted labor once available for herding. Education had a similar effect. As the nomads took up agriculture and as private titles to land were granted, the nomads' traditional relationship to tribal territory decreased. Faced with these obstacles to a pastoral way of life, nomads increasingly chose alternative occupations, particularly in the military, and the sedentarization process accelerated.

Government policies encouraged settlement by providing schooling, medical services, and the development of water resources. The decrease in the number of nomads continued despite the influx of pastoralists from the Negev Desert after the founding of Israel. By the early 1970s, the beduin tribes constituted no more than 5 percent of Jordan's population. That proportion had dwindled to less than 3 percent by the late 1970s. Their small numbers, however, did not correspond to their cultural and political importance in Jordan.

Despite the near-disappearance of the nomadic way of life, tribal social structure and organization have not necessarily been transformed as drastically. Hiatt contended that tribal organization actually was reinforced during the initial process of sedentarization because the tribe itself was the basis for allocation of land. Leadership patterns have changed significantly, however, as government-appointed officials have assumed many of the tasks formerly associated with the position of shaykh (see Glossary). In the end, tribal social structure was weakened; individual titles to land, which can be rented or sold to outsiders, and individual employment diluted lineage solidarity and cohesiveness.

Some indication of the recent status and aspirations of beduin groups, both settled and nomadic, was provided by a 1978 survey by a team from the University of Jordan. Among the beduins studied, males increasingly were engaged in more or less sedentary occupations. Many were in the government or the army. The researchers found that most beduin parents wanted a different way of life for their children. Willingness to settle was contingent upon settlement being more advantageous than the nomadic way of life. For the beduins, settlement often meant a continued association with livestock raising and its attendant requirements of access to food and water. These hopes and wishes seemed to be consistent with the government's strategy for a revitalized livestock (sheep and goat) industry.

The beduin attitude toward education was two-sided and reflected the difficulty of adapting to a new way of life. Early observers noted that an army career tended to motivate beduins to acquire an education. Some, such as the French ethnographer Joseph Chelhod, argued that "an educated beduin means an abandoned tent." Implied was abandonment of the entire beduin way of life. Many beduin parents interviewed in the 1978 survey were concerned that the education of their children beyond a certain level would threaten the survival of the family. They feared that "an educated child would naturally emigrate to work or pursue further studies in Amman or even outside the country." At the same time, these parents acknowledged that "the best future of their children lay in education and in living and working in a settled society close to the country's urban centers." It is not altogether clear whether the beduins who have acquired enough education for an ordinary career in the army have abandoned their allegiance to their families and tribes or whether they have permanently rejected the beduin style of life.

Jordan was unique among primarily sedentary Middle Eastern countries in that, at least until the mid-1970s, the Hashimite government gained its most significant political support from the beduin tribes. Mindful of the intensely personal nature of his ties with the beduins, Hussein visited them often, socializing in their tents and playing the role of paramount tribal shaykh. People of beduin origin constituted a disproportionate share of the army; that disproportion continued to prevail at the higher command levels in the mid-1980s (see The Military in National Life, ch. 5). The opportunity for a lucrative, secure career that also carried high prestige and conformed to traditional martial tribal attitudes has for over half a century drawn recruits from the desert, first into the Arab Legion under the British and later into its successor force, the Jordan Arab Army. Army service was an important influence for social change among nomadic tribes because it fostered desire for education and often provided the wherewithal for adaptations to factors affecting the pastoral economy. For example, army pay could permit a beduin family to buy a truck as a substitute for or in addition to camels, or to invest in the economically more significant sheep.

Observers in the 1980s noted that a process of detribalization was taking place in Jordan, whereby the impact of tribal affiliation on the individual's sense of identity was declining. Sedentarization and education were prime forces in this process. Smaller groups, such as the extended family and clan, were gradually replacing tribes as primary reference groups. The weakening of tribal affiliation and identity led to the questioning of support for the Hashimite regime. Tribal shaykhs no longer could guarantee the support of tribal members, particularly the younger ones. This process was uneven, however, with some tribes displaying more cohesiveness than others.

The term *tribalism* was much in use in the 1980s. The intelligentsia proposed that meritocracy rather than tribalism be the basis of selection in the 1984 parliamentary by-elections. Anthropologist Linda Layne compared the intelligentsia's views of tribalism with the electoral behavior of the beduins. Layne defined the intelligentsia's interpretation of tribalism as "the placing of family ties before all other political allegiances" and concluded that tribalism "is therefore understood to be antithetical to loyalty to the State." Layne recognized the prominent role of tribalism in the 1984 election but stated that this was not at odds with a modern political system. Rather, in reconstructing their identity in a modern Jordanian state, Layne held that the beduins were maintaining a tribalism suffused with new elements such as a narrower role for tribal shaykhs in national politics and new sources of political legitimacy. Beduin electoral behavior was not homogeneous along tribal lines, evidence that tribal shaykhs could no longer automatically deliver the votes of their fellow tribesmen and women. In this sense,

Layne found no tension between the beduin's identity as tribesman or tribeswoman and as citizen; rather, these were complementary forms of identity.

Tribalism and tradition also lent legitimacy to Hashimite rule. The legitimacy of tradition, considered almost synonymous with beduin or tribal culture, has been defended as part of the near sacrosanct foundations of the state and as central to cultural heritage. In the 1985 public exchange between King Hussein and Minister of Information Layla Sharaf, Hussein responded to Sharaf's calls for liberalizing the law, particularly lifting censorship and diluting the influence of tribalism in society. In the 1980s, a debate raged among Jordanians and observers of Jordanian society over the appropriate role tribal influence and tradition should play in a modern state. In early 1985, in the midst of this debate, King Hussein publicly supported the role of the tribe and tradition in Jordan's past and future by stating, "Whatever harms tribes is considered harmful to us. Law will remain closely connected to norms, customs, and traditions. . . . Our traditions should be made to preserve the fabric of society. Disintegration of tribes is very painful, negative and subversive."

Thus, the role of tribes and tribalism, although transformed, remained a fundamental pillar of both society and political culture in the late 1980s. Although numerically few Jordanians lived the traditional life of the nomadic beduin, the cultural traditions based on this life-style were hardly diminished. Indeed, conceptions of modern Jordanian cultural and national identity were deeply intertwined with the country's beduin heritage.

## Villages

The principles of organization in settled communities resembled those of the beduins in that villages were organized around kin groups. The resemblance to nomadic groups was closest in the villages of central and southern Jordan. There villagers retained, in somewhat loose form, a tribal form of organization. Most villagers lived in the much more densely settled north, where tribal organization in the late 1980s remained significant only among the recently settled.

In most northern villages, the descendants of a common, relatively distant ancestor formed a *hamula* (pl., *hamail,* meaning a clan). The *hamula* ordinarily had a corporate identity; it often maintained a guesthouse, its members usually resided in a distinguishable quarter or neighborhood, and it acted in concert in village, and often regional, political affairs. The *hamula* was the repository of family honor and tended to be endogamous. Some villages in the north were dominated by one *hamula;* that is, everyone in a village belonged to the same descent group. Sometimes several smaller *hamail* also resided in a village dominated by one large *hamula.* Other villages were characterized by the presence of several *hamail* of nearly equal numerical size and importance in village political affairs and landholdings. In some northern regions, a large *hamula* might have sections in several villages.

Intermediate kin groups existed below the level of the *hamula* and above that of the household. In many cases, a group of closely related households, descendants of a relative closer than the founder of the *hamula,* formed entities called lineages (or branches). A still smaller unit was the *luzum,* a close consultation group, usually composed of several brothers and their families. A father's brothers' sons and their families could be included in or even constitute the *luzum.* This group had the most significance for everyday life in the village. Members of a *hamula,* especially those spread over several villages, sometimes saw each other only on occasions such as weddings, births, deaths, religious holidays, or a conflict involving a *hamula* member. Anthropologist Richard Antoun found the *luzum* to be the significant unit in a variety of matters in the community he studied; its members were responsible for paying truce money in cases where honor had been violated. This was the group that acted as a support system for the individual in the event of need, providing access to resources such as land, bridewealth, or financial aid in the event of illness or to pay for schooling.

Lineages and *luzums* varied in size and sometimes overlapped in functions. For example, a large *luzum* sometimes carried the weight of a smaller lineage in village politics, and it could be difficult to distinguish them. Kin groups, even at the level of lineages, were not homogenous in terms of class; some members could be quite well off and others rather poor. This internal differentiation increased as some members migrated to urban areas or abroad in search of work, entered the army, or sought higher education (see Migration, this ch.).

Social control and politics in the village traditionally grew out of the interactions of kin groups at various levels. Social control over individual behavior was achieved through the process of socialization and a system that imposed sanctions for unacceptable behavior. Such sanctions could range from gossip damaging to one's reputation and that of one's kin, to censure by one's kin group, to penalties imposed by the state for infractions of its criminal codes.

Respected elder males from the various *hamail* (or lineages if the village were populated predominantly by members of one *hamula*) provided leadership in villages. They often made decisions by consensus. With the formation and consolidation of the state, traditional leaders lost some power, but they continued in the late 1980s to mediate conflicts, and state officials often turned to them when dealing with village affairs. In cases of conflict in the village, leaders of the appropriate kin sections of groups attempted to mediate the problem through kinship ties. Such leaders were usually elderly men respected for their traditional wisdom and knowledge of customs, or slightly younger, secularly educated men, or persons in intermediate positions between the two. If the conflict escalated or involved violence, the state, through the police and the court system, tended to become involved. The state encouraged recourse to traditional forms of mediation sometimes as an alternative and sometimes as an accompaniment to processing the case through the court system.

The *mukhtar,* or headman, of a small village linked the villagers with the state bureaucracy, especially if there were no village or municipal council. The *mukhtar*'s duties included the registering of births and deaths, notarizing official papers for villagers, and assisting the police with their investigations in the village. Where there were municipal or village councils, generally in villages with a population of 3,000 or more, the *mukhtar* had little influence. Instead, the councils—bodies elected by the villagers—allocated government authority and village resources. Young, educated men from influential families, whose fathers may have been traditional leaders in the village, often ran the councils.

As villages increasingly became integrated into the state economic and political system, social stratification grew. Traditionally, large landowners were able to command labor, surplus, and services as well as social deference from less wealthy villagers. However, a variety of village and religious customs eased this apparent class differentiation. Religious teachings and practices, such as the giving of alms and the distribution of gifts at the festival marking the end of Ramadan and at other festival seasons, emphasized the responsibility of the prosperous for the less fortunate (see Religious Life, this ch.). Wealth also implied an obligation to provide a place for men to gather and for visitors to come, in order to maintain the standing of the village as a whole. Events such as weddings were occasions for the wealthy to provide feasts for the whole village.

In the late 1980s, social change had strained village structure and values. The older generation's uncontested control of the economic resources necessary for contracting marriage, participating in politics, and even earning a livelihood had guaranteed their authority. The decline in significance of agriculture as a way of life and the appearance of other opportunities led many younger

*Women cleaning wool at Samar,*
*northwest of Amman*
*Courtesy Julie Peteet*

*A village scene with a mosque*
*in the background*
*Courtesy Julie Peteet*

people into other pursuits. As a result, some ''agricultural'' villages eventually contained a majority of men engaged in other kinds of work. Earning an income independent of their elders' control and often considerably larger than the older generation could command, such young people were in a position to challenge their elders' authority. Nevertheless, in the late 1980s, the individual still remained enmeshed in a network of family relations and obligations. The young deferred less frequently to their elders in decisions about life choices than had been the custom, but respect for parents and elders remained evident.

## Palestinians

Jordanians tended to refer to Palestinians as persons who fled or were driven from Palestine during the Arab-Israeli War of 1948 and the June 1967 War. Some immigrants from Palestine who had entered Jordan in preceding centuries, however, were so thoroughly integrated into the local society as to be indistinguishable from their neighbors. The Majalis, for more than a century the leading tribe in Al Karak area, came originally from Hebron. For political and social purposes, they and others like them were considered Jordanians. Other Palestinians from Hebron, who came to Al Karak as merchants well before 1948, remained to a considerable degree outsiders, for the most part taking their spouses from the Hebron area and maintaining economic and other ties there.

Al Karak is not representative of the impact of Palestinians on East Bank society and culture. In 1948 the population of the East Bank was about 340,000. The 1950 annexation of the West Bank increased the population by about 900,000. This increase included the West Bank population itself (around 400,000 to 450,000) and about 450,000 refugees from those areas of Palestine that became Israel in 1948. In addition, many thousands of Palestinians not classified as refugees entered Jordan after 1948. As a result of the June 1967 War, in 1967 an additional 250,000 to 300,000 West Bank Palestinians entered Jordan as refugees.

Most of the refugees, inside and outside refugee camps, continued to live in Amman and areas to the north. In 1986 UNRWA reported that 826,128 Palestinians were registered as refugees in the East Bank; of these, nearly one-fourth resided in camps. Many other refugees lived on the fringes of the economy in urban areas.

A substantial number of Palestinians had the kind of education and entrepreneurial capacity that enabled them to achieve substantial economic status. A few brought some of their wealth from Palestine. Some became large landowners or businessmen, whereas others became professionals or technicians. A number worked for the government, often in posts requiring prior training. Many Palestinians were merchants on a small or medium scale, craftsmen or skilled workers, or peasants.

Whatever the social or economic status of Palestinians in the East Bank, their sense of national identity had aroused much debate. Such identity depended on international and regional political developments with respect to the Palestine question, the interests of Palestinians themselves on the East Bank, and the balancing act of the government between East Bank Jordanians and those of Palestinian origin. One observer indicated that the regime had an interest in perpetuating the idea of a Palestinian majority so that East Bank Jordanians would continue to perceive Hussein as ensuring their interests and that of the East Bank.

An autonomous Palestinian political identity did not begin to assert itself until the mid-1960s. In the 1950s, no political organization existed around which a specifically Palestinian identity could be articulated. Pan-Arabism was a dominant mode of political expression, and the Hashimite regime strongly promoted Jordanian sovereignty over Palestinian affairs and identity. Nevertheless, and in spite of a security apparatus that kept a close watch on political affairs, Palestinian national identity emerged and grew. The loss of the West Bank in 1967 and the repressive Israeli occupation contributed to nationalist sentiments, as did the Jordanian government's repression of opposition political movements. The rise in the mid-1960s of the Palestine Liberation Organization (PLO) and its international recognition furthered this nationalist climate. The PLO offered an organizational format to Palestinian political identity separate from a Jordanian identity. The 1970–71 war between the fedayeen (Arab guerrillas) and the Jordanian government and the 1974 Rabat Summit further enhanced Palestinian nationalist sentiment (see The Palestinians and the PLO, ch. 4).

Wide divergences in political identity and sentiment existed among the Palestinians in the East Bank. Factors influencing a person's identity included the date of arrival in the East Bank, whether the person was a refugee or lived in a camp, and the degree of the person's economic success. The merchants and professionals who came prior to 1948 generally identified closely with the East Bank. Refugees who came in 1948 but who did not reside in the camps and were government employees or successful professionals or businesspeople tended to be tacit supporters of the regime and to invest heavily in homes and businesses. More militant were the refugees who arrived in the wake of the June 1967 War, including those refugees who were not living in camps. Persons residing in the camps tended to be the most militant. They were the poorest and had the least stake in the survival of the Hashimite regime.

Socioeconomic and political events in the late 1980s converged to fuel growing frustration with East Bank political policies. The reduced flow of remittances to Jordan from expatriate workers in the oil-producing states was a source of anxiety for the regime. For refugees living in the camps and for urban squatters, the economic downturn led to greater poverty, compounded by the high unemployment rate in the East Bank.

The Palestinian uprising (*intifadah*) in the occupied territories caused the Hashimite regime concern. The continuation of the uprising and the occupation seemed likely to radicalize less prosperous Palestinians in the East Bank.

## Urban Areas and Urbanization

From ancient times, Middle Eastern society has been characterized by the interaction of nomads and peasants with the urban centers. The region's highest achievements in cultural, political, economic, and intellectual life took place in the vibrant cosmopolitan centers. Arab-Islamic claims to be one of the world's major civilizations rest largely on the products of city populations.

No major urban center existed in what is now Jordanian territory until the late 1940s. East Bank towns served as local markets and administrative centers rather than as centers of high culture. Truncated by external political considerations rather than by internal social or cultural realities, the East Bank consequently lacked the kind of long-established metropolis that for centuries had dominated other parts of the Middle East.

Amman, the major city of the East Bank, had ancient roots, but in the 1980s it was scarcely more than a generation old as a modern city. The Circassians were the first permanent inhabitants of Amman, settling there in 1878. In 1921 Amir Abdullah ibn Hussein Al Hashimi established his capital in Amman. It passed its first decades as a provincial trading center and garrison on the margin of the desert. In 1943 Amman had only 30,000 inhabitants. As capital of the new kingdom of Jordan, Amman grew over the next three decades into a booming, overcrowded metropolitan center. Population growth was largely a function of the influx of Palestinians since 1948. A high birth rate and internal migration, however, have also been prominent features of the urbanization process (see Population, this ch.).

In 1989 Amman lacked both the old quarters characteristic of most Middle Eastern cities and an established urban population with a unified cultural outlook and an organic bond to the indigenous society of the area. Its people were a mixture of all the elements of the country. Circassians and Christians, rather than Muslim Transjordanians, set the tone before the arrival of the Palestinians, who in the late 1980s probably constituted 60 to 80 percent of its population. The smaller towns of the East Bank retained a good deal of the traditional kin- and quarter-based social organization characteristic of Middle Eastern towns.

In rapidly urbanizing areas such as Amman, the quasi-paternal relationship of the rich to the poor had begun to break down, and the old egalitarian values had given way to class distinctions based on income and style of life. Increasingly evident, class polarization was fueled by remittances from those working abroad. Remittances were invested in residential property, thus driving up the cost of land and housing. New urban areas, dotted with lavish stone villas and supermarkets and boutiques supplied with expensive imported items, coexisted with overcrowded areas where a jumble of buildings housed the multitudes of the lower-middle class and the poor. Furthermore, Western culture had introduced foreign ideas among the educated that gradually estranged them from the culture of the masses. Cultural and recreational facilities, for example, were limited to the well-to-do because of the high membership fees in the clubs that provided them.

## Migration

In the late 1980s, Jordan experienced more than one form of migration. Large segments of the labor force worked abroad, and rural-urban migration continued unabated. In rural areas, substantial numbers of men were employed outside the village or were engaged in military service.

Jordan often has been referred to by economists as a laborexporting country. With the oil boom of the 1970s in the Persian Gulf countries and Saudi Arabia, substantial numbers of the welleducated and skilled labor force, from both rural and urban areas, temporarily emigrated for employment. Government figures for 1987 stated that nearly 350,000 Jordanians were working abroad, a remarkably high number for such a small domestic population. Approximately 160,900 Jordanians resided in Saudi Arabia alone. Most of the Jordanians working abroad were of Palestinian origin.

The typical Jordanian migrant was a married male between twenty and thirty-nine years of age. His education level was higher than that of the average person on the East Bank. More than 30 percent of those working abroad were university graduates, and 40 percent were in professional positions. The average stay abroad ranged from 4.5 years to 8 years, and the attraction of work abroad was the higher salary. Unlike most male migrants in the Middle East, Jordanian migrants had a greater tendency to take their families with them to their place of employment.

Migration from Jordan was not a recent phenomenon. As early as the late nineteenth century, Jordanian villagers were migrating abroad. Migration abroad since the 1960s has generally been to Saudi Arabia and other oil-producing Gulf states. Although most of those migrant workers came from urban areas, more data is available on the rural migrants.

The authors of a 1985 study of the effects of migration on a village in the northwest noted that more than 10 percent of families had at least one member working abroad and 32 percent of male heads of household were serving in the armed forces. Many others held jobs in nearby urban centers and commuted between the village and their place of employment. Of village migrants to the oil-producing states, more than half were employed in the public sector, particularly in teaching and in the military security forces. As of the late 1980s, both of these areas faced a decline in employment if the oil-producing states continued to reduce their foreign labor force.

Labor migration in the 1970s and 1980s did not necessarily indicate a migrant's alienation from the village or a weakening of his ties with fellow villagers. Nearly 75 percent of rural migrants had a relative or village friend in the place of employment abroad. In fact, migrants tended to facilitate the process for others, acting as points of contact for individuals who migrated later. Migration did not radically alter the authority of absent males in their households, whether rural or urban. Wives made many daily household decisions, but, in most cases, major decisions awaited consultation with the husband. The flow of remittances to the village was also a strong indication of the continuing ties between a migrant and his family.

Remittances were used overwhelmingly by both rural and urban migrants to pay off debts and then to invest in residential property. The many new villa-style houses built in and around Amman and Irbid and in the villages reflected the large numbers of men working abroad and the presence of "oil money." In the northwest highlands, the purchase of property and the subsequent building of housing reduced the area of cultivable land. In contrast, in the Jordan Valley remittances figured prominently in investments in agricultural technologies. Returning rural migrants resided for the most part in the village and worked in Irbid, casting doubt on projections that international labor migration would contribute significantly to further urbanization in the Amman area.

Since the 1970s, increasing numbers of villagers had migrated to Amman. Most of them had remained poor and had shallow roots in the city. A significant land shortage, lack of job opportunities in rural areas, and the availability of education and health resources in Amman had sent a steady stream of villagers toward the city, overcrowding its housing and overtaxing its resources. Urban housing for the city's poor was neither readily available nor affordable. Rural migrants, however, maintained close ties with their natal villages. On Fridays (the official day off in Jordan) and during holidays, the villages were witness to family reunions of men who worked in the cities during the week and returned home at week's end.

## Kinship, Family, and the Individual

In the late 1980s, social life and identity in Jordan centered around the family. The household was composed of people related to one another by kinship, either through descent or marriage, and family ties extended into the structure of clans and tribes. Individual loyalty and the sense of identity arising from family membership coexisted with new sources of identity and affiliation. The development of a national identity and a professional identity did not necessarily conflict with existing family affiliations. Although rapid social mobility strained kin group membership, kinship units were sometimes able to adapt to social change.

Gender and age were important determinants of social status. Although the systematic separation of women from men was not generally practiced, all groups secluded women to some extent. The character of gender-based separation varied widely among different sectors of society; it was strictest among the traditional urban middle class and most flexible among the beduins, where the exigencies of nomadic life precluded segregation. However, the worlds of men and women intersected in the home. Age greatly influenced an individual man or woman's standing in society; generally, attaining an advanced age resulted in enhanced respect and social stature.

The formation of an educated middle class that included increasing numbers of educated and working women led in the late 1980s to some strains in the traditional pattern. Men and women now interacted in public—at school and in the universities, in the workplace, on public transportation, in voluntary associations, and at social events.

### Family and Household

The extended family continued to be a viable form of household in the late 1980s. More families had begun to live in nuclear households, but Jordanians continued to rely on extended kin relations for a variety of purposes, which can be described as exchanges. Exchanges might include financial support; job information; social connections; access to strategic resources; marital partners; arrangements, protection, and support in the event of conflict; child care and domestic services; and emotional sustenance. In turn, an individual's social identity and loyalty continued to be oriented largely to the family.

Formally, kinship was reckoned patrilineally, and the household usually was based on blood ties between men. There was no one form of family; and household structure changed because of births, deaths, marriages, and migration. A household could consist of a married couple, their unmarried children, and possibly other relatives such as parents, or a widowed parent or an unmarried sister. Alternatively, a household could consist of parents and their married sons, their wives, and their children. At the death of the father, each married son ideally established his own household to begin the cycle again. Although the kinship system was considered patrilineal, maternal kin also were significant.

Because the family was central to social life, all children were expected to marry at the appropriate age, and eligible divorced or widowed persons were expected to remarry. Marriage conferred adult status on both men and women. The birth of children further enhanced this status, especially for women, who then felt more secure in their marital households. Polygyny was practiced in only a minority of cases and was socially frowned upon.

Traditionally, the individual subordinated his or her personal interests to those of the family. The importance of the group outweighed that of the individual. In the late 1980s, it was still uncommon for a man to live apart from a family group unless he were a migrant worker or a student. Grown children ordinarily lived with parents or relatives until marriage. Children were expected to defer to the wishes of their parents.

Marriage was a family affair rather than a personal choice. Because the sexes ordinarily did not mix much socially, young men and women had few acquaintances among the opposite sex, although among beduins a limited courtship was permitted. Parents traditionally arranged marriages for their children, finding a mate either through the family or their social contacts. In the late 1980s, this pattern had changed substantially (see Changing Social Relations and Values, this ch.).

Among village and tribal populations, the preferred marriage partner was the child of the father's brother. In most areas, a man had a customary right to forbid his father's brother's daughter from marrying an outsider if he wished to exercise his right to her hand. If the ideal cousin marriage was not possible, marriage within the patrilineal kin group was the next best choice. Such endogamous marriages had several advantages for the parties: the bridewealth payments demanded of the groom's kin tended to be smaller; the family resources were conserved; the dangers of an unsuitable match were minimized; and the bride was not a stranger to her husband's house.

A University of Jordan medical department study in the late 1980s pointed to a 50 percent rate of family intermarriage: 33 percent of marriages were between first-degree relatives, 7 percent between second-degree relatives, and 10 percent were within the extended family. Nonetheless, in the 1980s, endogamous marriages had declined in frequency; previous rates of intermarriage may have been as high as 95 percent. Increasing female education and employment allowed young people more opportunities to meet and marry outside family arrangements. Also, there was growing awareness that genetic problems could arise in the offspring of endogamous marriages.

In Islam, marriage is a civil contract rather than a sacrament. Representatives of the bride's interests negotiate a marriage agreement with the groom's representatives. The future husband and wife must give their consent. Young men often suggest to their parents whom they would like to marry; women usually do not do so but have the right to refuse a marriage partner of their parents' choice. The contract establishes the terms of the union, and, if they are broken, outlines appropriate recourse. Special provisions inserted into the contract become binding on both parties.

Islam gives to the husband far greater leeway than to the wife in terms of polygyny and in matters of divorce. For example, a man may legally take up to four wives at one time provided he can treat them equally; a woman can have only one husband at a time. A man may divorce his wife by repeating "I divorce thee" three times before witnesses and registering the divorce in court; a woman can instigate divorce only under very specific circumstances. Few women seek divorce because of the difficulty of taking a case to court, the stigma attached to a divorced woman, and the possibility of a woman's losing custody of her children. In theory and as a matter of public appearance, men exercise authority over women. That authority, however, is not as absolute as once thought. Women wield considerable power within the home and decision making often is a joint affair between husband and wife.

## Family Relationships

The social milieu in which a Jordanian family lived significantly affected the position of the wife and her degree of autonomy.

In rural agricultural areas and among the urban poor, women fulfilled important economic functions. Traditionally, some women of poor urban families worked outside the home, and rural women performed a wide variety of tasks in the household and in the fields. Such women occupied a position of relative importance and enjoyed a modicum of freedom in their comings and goings within the village or neighborhood. Although casual social contact between the sexes of the kind common in the West was infrequent, segregation of the sexes was less pronounced than in traditional towns. Among the traditional urban bourgeoisie, women fulfilled fewer and less important economic functions. Artisan and merchant families earned their living from the skills of the men. Women's responsibilities were more confined to the home. Among the new urban middle class, women occupied a variety of positions, some of them contradictory. Some women of this class were educated and employed, and enjoyed a fair measure of mobility within society; others, also educated and skilled, lived a more sheltered life, with minimal mobility. Both groups of women frequently were seen in the streets wearing Islamic dress (see Women and Work, this ch.).

The allocation of space within the home was often gender-specific. The houses of prosperous urban and rural families traditionally contained distinct men's and women's areas: the reception room where the men of the family entertained male guests and the women's quarters from which adult males other than relatives and servants were excluded. Less wealthy urban or rural families were unable to conform as easily to the standards of segregation. They could not afford the extra room for male gatherings. In poorer rural areas, men and women often socialized together in the house.

Status within the household varied considerably depending on sex, age, and type of household. In principle, men had greater autonomy than women. Their movements in public were freer, and their personal decisions were more their own. Within the household, however, younger males were subject to the authority of senior males, their grandfathers, fathers, and uncles. Decisions about education, marriage, and work remained family affairs. Older women exerted substantial authority and control over children and adolescents, the most powerless sector within a household.

Household structure, whether nuclear or extended, also determined the extent to which women wielded power in a household. In a household with multiple married women, senior women held more power and could exert more control over younger wives. Younger women often preferred to live in a nuclear household where they had more autonomy in running the household and in child rearing. They were then more subject, however, to the direct control of the husband and had to manage the household alone without the help of other women.

Children were given much affection and attention. Although not spared spanking and occasional harsh scolding, children were indulged and given much physical affection by household members and neighbors alike. Their behavior was tolerated with amusement until close to the ages of four and five. Children then were expected to assume some responsibilities in the household. Little girls at this age began to help their mothers with household chores and to care for younger children.

Segregation by gender was tied closely to the concept of honor (*ird*). In most Arab communities, honor inhered in the descent group— the family and, to a varying extent, the lineage or clan. Honor could be lost through the failure of sisters, wives, and daughters to behave properly (modestly) and through the failure of men to exert self-restraint over their emotions toward women. For women, the constraints of modesty were not confined to sexual matters. Also, women could be held accountable for a loss of honor although they might not have had any obvious responsibility in the matter. Loud speech, a woman's bearing or dress, or her appearing in public places could lead to a loss of honor. For men, overt expressions of emotions (such as romantic love) that revealed vulnerability to women could cause a man's strength to be questioned, leading to a loss of honor. Men were expected to be above such matters of the heart. A wife's failure to behave properly reflected on the honor of her husband and his kin, but even more on her father and brothers and others of the group from which she came. A man's failure to conform to the norms of self-control and invulnerability to women shamed his immediate and extended kin group.

Above all, honor was a matter of reputation. Perceptions were as important as actions or events. An offense against honor could be very lightly punished if it appeared that only the person's family knew of it. Harsher steps were required if persons outside the family knew of the offense or believed it to have occurred.

The penalties for violation of the honor code differed for men and women. Custom granted the males of a family the right to kill female kin known to have engaged in illicit sexual relations. A more common practice, however, was for the families involved to arrange a hasty marriage. Men who lost honor through their actions were ostracized and lost face and standing in the community.

On the one hand, the segregation of women worked to minimize the chances that a family's honor would be lost or diminished. On the other hand, the education of women and their participation in a modern work force tended to erode the traditional concept of honor by promoting the mingling of the sexes in public life.

## Changing Social Relations and Values

Relations between men and women, along with all other aspects of Jordanian society, had begun to change as people adopted values, attitudes, and customs much different from those traditional in the country. As new ideas reached all sectors of society, new perceptions and practices began to appear.

Increased social and physical mobility have undermined the familial ties and the values that subordinated the individual to the kin group. A growing individualism has appeared, especially among the educated young. Many young people prefer to set up their own household at marriage rather than live with their parents. Labor migration has had a considerable impact on family structure and relations. In some cases, where men migrate without their families, their wives and children see the husband only once or twice a year when he visits. If the wife and children live alone, this arrangement leads to increased responsibility and autonomy for women. Also, the children in such families grow up without knowing their fathers well. When the wife and children live with the migrant's extended family, they are usually under the authority of her husband's family.

Some of the most marked social changes have affected women's roles. In urban areas, young women have begun to demand greater freedom and equality than in the past, although traditional practices still broadly govern their lives. Since the 1960s, women have become more active outside the home. In the 1980s, girls' school enrollment was nearly parallel to that of boys, and female graduates entered the work force in increasing numbers (see Education, this ch.). Girls who attended school were not as closely chaperoned as they formerly were, although they rarely went out with friends in the evening. Educated women also tended to marry later, often after working for several years. The average age of marriage for women had risen from the mid-teens to the early twenties; the average age for males was between twenty-six and twenty-eight years. The narrowing of the gap in age between marriage partners signified a changing conception of the conjugal unit and its relation to the larger family group. Companionship and notions of romantic love were playing a greater role in marital arrangements than heretofore. Marriages were still a family affair, but the relationship between man and wife was assuming increasing significance. This change reflected a dilution in the strength of families as social units with corporate interests that subordinated those of the individual.

By the late 1980s, some observers had noted that couples tended to want fewer children. This trend appeared to parallel the changes in women's position in society and shifts in the political economy, which had implications for family structure, relations, and values. Women's education and employment patterns meant that child rearing was no longer the only role open to women. The need for dual-income households pointed to a decrease in the amount of time women could devote to child rearing. In the transition from an agricultural and pastoral society to one based on services, where literacy was a must, children required longer periods of education and thus were dependent for extended periods upon their families. Large families were no longer as economically feasible or desirable as in the past.

The spread of the nuclear household encouraged the detachment of the individual from the demands of the extended family. At the same time, social security lessened the dependence of the aged on their children and other relatives. The functions of the extended family, however, were not necessarily diminished; given economic upheavals and a weak infrastructure for state social services, Jordanians continued to rely upon the extended family, even if many of its members resided in nuclear units.

Generational conflicts, which observers believed to be increasing, strained family relations when young people attempted to adopt standards and behavior different from those of their parents. Modern, secular education, with its greater emphasis on utility and efficiency, tended to undermine respect for the wisdom of age and the rightness of tradition. Male wage earners also were less dependent on older males for access to resources such as land and bridewealth.

## Women and Work

Despite a seemingly conservative milieu, the number of women working outside the home increased in the 1980s. Women formed a little over 12 percent of the labor force in 1985. Many poor and lower-class women worked out of economic necessity, but a substantial number of working women came from financially secure families. According to the Ministry of Planning, the proportion of women working in professional and technical jobs was high. In 1985 women constituted 35.4 percent of technical workers and 36.1 percent of clerical staff. Women were least represented in agriculture and production. Women's increased access to education had led them to greater aspirations to work outside the home. Moreover, inflation had made the dual-income family a necessity in many cases.

Jordanian women served as a reserve labor force and were encouraged to work during the years of labor shortages when economic expansion and development plans were high on the government's priority list. In a 1988 study of women and work in Jordan, journalist Nadia Hijab argued that cultural attitudes were not the major constraint on women's employment; rather, need and opportunity were more significant factors.

Most employed women were single. Unmarried women, in particular, were initially considered a source of untapped labor. Yet cultural constraints clearly militated against women working in agriculture, industry, and construction—areas of low prestige, but also the sections with the most critical labor shortages. Development programs for women focused on technical training. Hijab mentions that a typical project was "to train women on the maintenance and repair of household appliances."

To make work more attractive to women with children, the government discussed amending the labor laws to improve conditions. Such proposed amendments included granting more maternity leave and providing day-care facilities at the workplace. In addition, the media encouraged a more liberal attitude to women's working. Women's employment gained further legitimacy through national ceremonies sponsored by the government and the royal family honoring women's work.

The critical years of labor shortages were 1973 to 1981. By the mid-1980s, the situation had changed as unemployment surged. With the onset of high unemployment, women were asked to return to their homes. Publicly and privately, Jordanians hotly debated whether women should work. Letters to the editors of daily newspapers argued for and against women's working. Some government leaders had decided that women should return to their homes. Discussion about amending labor laws was shelved, and Hijab observed that by 1985 there was "almost an official policy" to encourage married women to stay at home. Then Prime Minister Zaid ar Rifai bluntly suggested in 1985 that working women who paid half or more of their salary to foreign maids who sent the currency abroad should stop working.

Differences in attitude towards women's employment frequently were based on the conditions of work. In a study of attitudes toward women and work, Jordanian sociologist Mohammad Barhoum found that resistance was least to women working in traditionally female occupations such as teaching, nursing, and secretarial work. He believed the change in attitude resulted from increased educational opportunities for girls and their parents' realization

*Women weaving a carpet*

that education was as important for girls as for boys, especially in the event of widowhood or divorce. The erosion of male wages, no longer adequate to support a family, had also been a prominent factor in legitimizing female employment.

The impact of women's employment on relations within the family remained difficult to assess in 1989. Employment and contribution to family income accorded women a greater voice in family matters. The traditional division of labor between men and women within the family often remained relatively untouched when women worked. Women's work at home was often taken up by other women rather than shared between men and women. Women earning lower incomes relied on their extended network of female relatives to help with child care and housework, while upper and middle income women hired maids (usually foreigners from the Philippines, Sri Lanka, or Egypt) to tend to their homes and children.

## Religious Life

More than 90 percent of Jordanians adhered to Sunni Islam in the late 1980s. Although observance was not always orthodox, devotion to and identification with the faith was high. Islam was the established religion, and as such its institutions received government support. The 1952 Constitution stipulates that the king and his successors must be Muslims and sons of Muslim parents.

103

Religious minorities included Christians of various denominations, a few Shia Muslims, and even fewer adherents of other faiths.

## Early Development of Islam

In A.D. 610, Muhammad, a merchant belonging to the Hashimite branch of the ruling Quraysh tribe in the Arabian town of Mecca, began to preach the first of a series of revelations granted him by God through the angel Gabriel and to denounce the polytheism of his fellow Meccans. Because the town's economy was based in part on a thriving pilgrimage business to the Kaaba, the sacred structure around a black meteorite, and the numerous pagan shrines located there, Muhammad's vigorous and continuing censure eventually earned him the bitter enmity of the town's leaders. In 622 he was invited to the town of Yathrib, which came to be known as Medina (the city) because it was the center of his activities. The move, or hijra (known in the West as the hegira), marks the beginning of the Islamic era. The Muslim calendar, based on the lunar year, begins in 622. In Medina, Muhammad—by this time known as the Prophet—continued to preach, eventually defeated his detractors in battle, and consolidated both the temporal and spiritual leadership of all Arabia in his person before his death in 632.

After Muhammad's death, his followers compiled those of his words regarded as coming directly from God into the Quran, the holy scripture of Islam. Others of his sayings and teachings as recalled by those who had known Muhammad (a group known as the Companions) became the hadith. The precedent of his personal behavior was set forth in the sunna. Together the Quran, the hadith, and the sunna form a comprehensive guide to the spiritual, ethical, and social life of an orthodox Sunni Muslim.

During his lifetime, Muhammad was both spiritual and temporal leader of the Muslim community; he established Islam as a total and all-encompassing way of life for human beings and society. Muslims believe that Allah revealed to Muhammad the rules governing proper behavior and that it therefore behooves them to live in the manner prescribed by the law, and it is incumbent upon the community to strive to perfect human society according to holy injunctions. Islam traditionally recognizes no distinction between religion and state, and no distinction between religious and secular life or religious and secular law. A comprehensive system of religious law (sharia—see Glossary) developed gradually during the first four centuries of Islam, primarily through the accretion of precedent and interpretation by various judges and scholars. During the tenth century, however, legal opinion began to harden into authoritative doctrine, and the figurative *bab al ijtihad* (gate of interpretation) gradually closed, thenceforth eventually excluding flexibility in Islamic law. Within the Jordanian legal system, sharia remains in effect in matters concerning personal status (see The Judiciary, ch. 4).

After Muhammad's death, the leaders of the Muslim community consensually chose Abu Bakr, the Prophet's father-in-law and one of his earliest followers, as caliph, or successor. At that time, some persons favored Ali, the Prophet's cousin and husband of his daughter Fatima, but Ali and his supporters (the so-called Shiat Ali or Party of Ali) eventually recognized the community's choice. The next two caliphs—Umar, who succeeded in 634, and Uthman, who took power in 644—enjoyed recognition of the entire community. When Ali finally succeeded to the caliphate in 656, Muawiyah, governor of Syria, rebelled in the name of his murdered kinsman Uthman. After the ensuing civil war, Ali moved his capital to Mesopotamia, where a short time later he, too, was murdered.

Ali's death ended the period in which the entire community of Islam recognized a single caliph. Upon Ali's death, Muawiyah proclaimed himself caliph from Damascus. The Shiat Ali, however, refused to recognize Muawiyah or his line, the Umayyad caliphs; in support of claims by Ali's line to a presumptive right to the caliphate based on descent from the Prophet, they withdrew and established a dissident sect known as the Shia.

Originally political in nature, the differences between the Sunni and Shia interpretations rapidly took on theological and metaphysical overtones. Ali's two sons, Hasan and Husayn, became martyred heroes to the Shias and repositories of the claims of Ali's line to mystical preeminence among Muslims. The Sunnis retained the doctrine of the selection of leaders by consensus, although Arabs and members of the Quraysh, Muhammad's tribe, predominated in the early years. Reputed descent from the Prophet, which King Hussein claims, continued to carry social and religious prestige throughout the Muslim world in the 1980s. Meanwhile, the Shia doctrine of rule by divine right became more and more firmly established, and disagreements over which of several pretenders had a truer claim to the mystical powers of Ali precipitated further schisms. Some Shia groups developed doctrines of divine leadership far removed from the strict monotheism of early Islam, including beliefs in hidden but divinely chosen leaders with spiritual powers that equaled or surpassed those of the Prophet himself.

The early Islamic polity was intensely expansionist, fueled both by fervor for the new religion and by economic and social factors.

Conquering armies and migrating tribes swept out of Arabia, spreading Islam. By the end of Islam's first century, Islamic armies had reached far into North Africa and eastward and northward into Asia. The territory of modern Jordan, among the first to come under the sway of Islam, was penetrated by Muslim armies by A.D. 633 (see Islam and Arab Rule, ch. 1).

Although Muhammad had enjoined the Muslim community to convert the infidel, he had also recognized the special status of the "people of the book," Jews and Christians, whose own revealed scriptures he considered revelations of God's word and which contributed in some measure to Islam. Jews and Christians in Muslim territories could live according to their own religious law, in their own communities, and were exempted from military service if they accepted the position of *dhimmis,* or tolerated subject peoples. This status entailed recognition of Muslim authority, additional taxes, prohibition on proselytism among Muslims, and certain restrictions on political rights.

Social life in the Ottoman Empire, which included Jordan for 400 years, revolved around a system of millets, or religious communities (see Ottoman Rule, ch. 1). Each organized religious minority lived according to its own personal status laws under the leadership of recognized religious authorities and community leaders. These recognized leaders also represented the community to the rest of society and the polity. This form of organization preserved and nourished cultural differences that, quite apart from theological considerations, distinguished these communities.

## Tenets of Sunni Islam

The *shahada* (testimony) succinctly states the central belief of Islam: "There is no god but God (Allah), and Muhammad is his Prophet." This simple profession of faith is repeated on many ritual occasions, and recital in full and unquestioning sincerity designates one a Muslim. The God preached by Muhammad was not a new deity; *Allah* is the Arabic term for God rather than a particular name. Muhammad denied the existence of the many minor gods and spirits worshiped before his prophecy, and he declared the omnipotence of the unique creator, God. Islam means submission to God, and one who submits is a Muslim. Being a Muslim also involves a commitment to realize the will of God on earth and to obey God's law.

Muhammad is the "seal of the Prophets"; his revelation is said to complete for all time the series of biblical revelations received by Jews and Christians. Muslims believe God to have remained one and the same throughout time, but that men strayed from his true teaching until set right by Muhammad. Prophets and sages of the biblical tradition, such as Abraham (Ibrahim), Moses (Musa), and Jesus (Isa), are recognized as inspired vehicles of God's will. Islam, however, reveres as sacred only the message, rejecting Christianity's deification of the messenger. It accepts the concepts of guardian angels, the Day of Judgment, general resurrection, heaven and hell, and eternal life of the soul.

The duties of the Muslim—corporate acts of worship—form the five pillars of Islamic faith. These are *shahada,* affirmation of the faith; *salat,* daily prayer; *zakat,* almsgiving; *sawm,* fasting during the month of Ramadan; and hajj, pilgrimage to Mecca. These acts of worship must be performed with a conscious intent and not out of habit. *Shahada* is uttered daily by practicing Muslims, affirming their membership in the faith and expressing an acceptance of the monotheism of Islam and the divinity of Muhammad's message.

The believer is to pray in a prescribed manner after purification through ritual ablutions at dawn, midday, midafternoon, sunset, and nightfall. Prescribed genuflections and prostrations accompany the prayers, which the worshiper recites facing toward Mecca. Prayers imbue daily life with worship, and structure the day around an Islamic conception of time. Whenever possible, men pray in congregation at the mosque under a prayer leader and on Fridays they are obliged to do so. Women also may attend public worship at the mosque, where they are segregated from the men, although most frequently women pray at home. A special functionary, the muezzin, intones a call to prayer to the entire community at the appropriate hours; those out of earshot determine the proper time from the position of the sun.

In the early days of Islam, the authorities imposed a tax on personal property proportionate to one's wealth; this was distributed to the mosques and to the needy. In addition, free-will gifts were made. While still a duty of the believer, almsgiving in the twentieth century has become a more private matter. Properties contributed by pious individuals to support religious activities are usually administered as religious foundations, or waqfs.

The ninth month of the Muslim calendar is Ramadan, a period of obligatory fasting that commemorates Muhammad's receipt of God's revelation, the Quran. Fasting is an act of self-discipline that leads to piety and expresses submission and commitment to God. Fasting underscores the equality of all Muslims, strengthening sentiments of community. During this month all but the sick, weak, pregnant or nursing women, soldiers on duty, travelers on necessary journeys, and young children are enjoined from eating, drinking, smoking, or sexual intercourse during the daylight hours. Official work hours often are shortened during this period, and some businesses close for all or part of the day. Since the months of the lunar calendar revolve through the solar years, Ramadan falls at various seasons in different years. A fast in summertime imposes considerable hardship on those who must do physical work. Each day's fast ends with a signal that light is insufficient to distinguish a black thread from a white one. Id al Fitr, a three-day feast and holiday, ends the month of Ramadan and is the occasion of much visiting.

Finally, Muslims at least once in their lifetime should, if possible, make the hajj to the holy city of Mecca to participate in special rites held during the twelfth month of the lunar calendar. The Prophet instituted this requirement, modifying pre-Islamic custom to emphasize sites associated with Allah and Abraham, father of the Arabs through his son Ishmael (Ismail). The pilgrim, dressed in a white, seamless garment (*ihram*), abstains from sexual relations, shaving, haircutting, and nail paring. Highlights of the pilgrimage include kissing the sacred black stone; circumambulation of the Kaaba, the sacred structure reputedly built by Abraham that houses the stone; running seven times between the mountains Safa and Marwa in imitation of Hagar, Ishmael's mother, during her travail in the desert; and standing in prayer on Mount Arafat. These rites affirm the Muslim's obedience to God and express intent to renounce the past and begin a new righteous life in the path of God. The returning male pilgrim is entitled to the honorific ''hajj'' before his name and a woman the honorific ''hajji.'' Id al Adha marks the end of the hajj month.

The permanent struggle for the triumph of the word of God on earth, jihad, represents an additional general duty of all Muslims. This concept is often taken to mean holy war, but most Muslims see it in a broader context of civil and personal action. Besides regulating relations between the human being and God, Islam regulates the relations of one human being to another. Aside from specific duties, Islam imposes a code of ethical conduct encouraging generosity, fairness, honesty, and respect and explicitly propounds guidance as to what constitutes proper family relations. In addition, it forbids adultery, gambling, usury, and the consumption of carrion, blood, pork, and alcohol.

A Muslim stands in a personal relationship to God; there is neither intermediary nor clergy in orthodox Islam. Those men who lead prayers, preach sermons, and interpret the law do so by virtue of their superior knowledge and scholarship rather than because of any special powers or prerogatives conferred by ordination.

Any adult male versed in prayer form is entitled to lead prayers—a role referred to as imam (see Glossary).

## Islam in Social Life

Despite a strong identification with and loyalty to Islam, religious practices varied among segments of Jordan's population. This unevenness in practice did not necessarily correlate with a rural-urban division or differing levels of education. The religious observance of some Jordanians was marked by beliefs and practices that were sometimes antithetical to the teachings of Islam. Authorities attributed at least some of these elements to pre-Islamic beliefs and customs common to the area.

In daily life, neither rural dwellers nor urbanites were overly fatalistic. They did not directly hold God responsible for all occurrences; rather, they placed events in a religious context that imbued them with meaning. The expression *inshallah* (God willing) often accompanied statements of intention, and the term *bismallah* (in the name of God) accompanied the performance of most important actions. Such pronouncements did not indicate a ceding of control over one's life or events. Jordanian Muslims generally believed that in matters that they could control, God expected them to work diligently.

Muslims have other ways of invoking God's presence in daily life. Despite Islam's unequivocal teaching that God is one and that no being resembles him in sanctity, some people accepted the notion that certain persons (saints) have *baraka,* a special quality of personal holiness and affinity to God. The intercession of these beings was believed to help in all manner of trouble, and shrines to such people could be found in some localities. Devotees often visited the shrine of their patron, especially seeking relief from illness or inability to have children.

Numerous spiritual creatures were believed to inhabit the world. Evil spirits known as jinn—fiery, intelligent beings that are capable of appearing in human and other forms—could cause all sorts of malicious mischief. For protection, villagers carried in their clothing bits of paper inscribed with Quranic verses (amulets), and they frequently pronounced the name of God. A copy of the Quran was said to keep a house safe from jinn. The "evil eye" also could be foiled by the same means. Although any literate Muslim was able to prepare amulets, some persons gained reputations as being particularly skilled in prescribing and preparing them. To underscore the difficulty in drawing a fine distinction between orthodox and popular Islam, one only need note that some religious shaykhs were

109

sought for their ability to prepare successful amulets. For example, in the 1980s in a village in northern Jordan, two elderly shaykhs (who also were brothers) were famous for their abilities in specific areas: one was skilled in warding off illness among children; the other was sought for his skills in curing infertility (see Health and Welfare, this ch.).

Their reverence for Islam notwithstanding, Muslims did not always practice strict adherence to the five pillars. Although most people tried to give the impression that they fulfilled their religious duties, many people did not fast during Ramadan. They generally avoided breaking the fast in public, however. In addition, most people did not contribute the required proportion of alms to support religious institutions, nor was pilgrimage to Mecca common. Attendance at public prayers and prayer in general increased during the 1980s as part of a regional concern with strengthening Islamic values and beliefs.

Traditionally, social segregation of the sexes prevented women from participating in much of the formal religious life of the community. The 1980s brought several changes in women's religious practices. Younger women, particularly university students, were seen more often praying in the mosques and could be said to have carved a place for themselves in the public domain of Islam.

Although some women in the late 1980s resorted to unorthodox practices and beliefs, women generally were considered more religiously observant than men. They fasted more than men and prayed more regularly in the home. Education, particularly of women, diminished the folk-religious component of belief and practice, and probably enhanced observance of the more orthodox aspects of Islam.

## Islamic Revival

The 1980s witnessed a stronger and more visible adherence to Islamic customs and beliefs among significant segments of the population. The increased interest in incorporating Islam more fully into daily life was expressed in a variety of ways. Women wearing conservative Islamic dress and the head scarf were seen with greater frequency in the streets of urban as well as rural areas; men with beards also were more often seen. Attendance at Friday prayers rose, as did the number of people observing Ramadan. Ramadan also was observed in a much stricter fashion; all public eating establishments were closed and no alcohol was sold or served. Police responded quickly to infractions of the rules of Ramadan. Those caught smoking, eating, or drinking in public were reprimanded and often arrested for a brief period.

Women in the 1980s, particularly university students, were actively involved in expressions of Islamic revival. Women wearing Islamic garb were a common sight at the country's universities. For example, the mosque at Yarmuk University had a large women's section. The section was usually full, and women there formed groups to study Islam. By and large, women and girls who adopted Islamic dress apparently did so of their own volition, although it was not unusual for men to insist that their sisters, wives, and daughters cover their hair in public.

The adoption of the Islamic form of dress did not signify a return to segregation of the sexes or female seclusion. Indeed, women who adopted Islamic clothing often were working women and students who interacted daily with men. They cited a lag in cultural attitudes as part of the reason for donning such dress. In other words, when dressed in Islamic garb they felt that they received more respect from and were taken more seriously by their fellow students and colleagues. Women also could move more readily in public if they were modestly attired. Increased religious observance also accounted for women's new style of dress. In the 1980s, Islamic dress did not indicate social status, particularly wealth, as it had in the past; Islamic dress was being worn by women of all classes, especially the lower and middle classes.

Several factors gave rise to increased adherence to Islamic practices. During the 1970s and 1980s, the Middle East region saw a rise of Islamic observance in response to economic recession and to the failure of nationalist politics to solve regional problems. In this context, Islam was an idiom for expressing social discontent. In Jordan, opposition politics had long been forbidden, and since the 1950s the Muslim Brotherhood had been the only legal political group. These factors were exacerbated by King Hussein's public support for the shah of Iran in his confrontation with Ayatollah Sayyid Ruhollah Musavi Khomeini and the forces of opposition, by continued relations with Egypt in the wake of the 1979 Treaty of Peace Between Egypt and Israel, and by the king's support for Iraq in the Iran-Iraq War.

Although Islamic opposition politics never became as widespread in Jordan as in Iran and Egypt, they were pervasive enough for the regime to act swiftly to bring them under its aegis. By the close of the 1970s and throughout the 1980s, government-controlled television regularly showed the king and his brother Hasan attending Friday prayers. The media granted more time to religious programs and broadcasts. Aware that the Islamic movement might become a vehicle for expressing opposition to the regime and its policies, and in a move to repair relations with Syria, in the mid-1980s the government began to promote a moderate form of Islam, denouncing fanatical and intolerant forms.

## Religious Minorities

Jordan's Constitution guarantees freedom of religious beliefs. Christians formed the largest non-Muslim minority. Observers estimated in the late 1970s that the Christian community—comprising groups of several denominations—constituted roughly 5 to 8 percent of the population. The principal points of concentration of the East Bank's indigenous Christians were a number of small towns in the "sown," such as Al Karak, Madaba, As Salt, and Ajlun (see fig. 1). Christians also lived in Amman and other major cities.

Overwhelmingly Arabic in language and culture, many Christians belonged to churches whose liturgical languages were, until recently, other than Arabic. With some exceptions, the lower clergy were Arabs, but the higher clergy were rarely so. In the past, Christians were disproportionately represented among the educated and prosperous. With increased access to education for all of the East Bank's peoples, this disproportion was less significant in the 1980s.

As of 1989, religious conflict had not been a problem in Jordan. The influence of Islamic observance that made itself felt in Jordan in the late 1970s and 1980s had not given rise to religious tensions. As a minority in a largely Muslim society, however, Christians were affected by Islamic practices. With the stricter observance of Ramadan in the 1980s, hotels and restaurants were prohibited by the government from serving liquor to local Christians or foreigners. Restaurants that formerly had remained open during the day to serve such persons were closed. The press and television also gave a greater emphasis to religion.

The largest of the Christian sects in the late 1980s, accounting for roughly half of all Jordanian Christians, was that part of the Eastern Orthodox complex of churches that falls under the patriarch of Jerusalem. With an elaborately organized clerical hierarchy, the patriarchate administered most of the Christian shrines in Jerusalem and the West Bank. The parent church of Eastern Orthodoxy was the Greek Orthodox Church, and the liturgical language of the church in the patriarchate of Jerusalem included both Greek and Arabic. The higher clergy, including the patriarch, were predominantly of Greek descent, but the priests were native speakers of Arabic. Because of the typically national organization of orthodox churches, the relatively small numbers of Syrians and Armenians adhering to orthodoxy had their own churches.

*Training in catering at a community college in Amman*

The Greek Catholic Church (Melchite, also seen as Melkite; Catholics of the Byzantine rite) in Jordan was headed by the patriarch of Antioch, Jerusalem, and Alexandria, who in turn was subject to the authority of the pope in Rome. The clergy generally were Arabs, and Arabic was used in most of the liturgy. Most Greek Catholics lived in the West Bank, but one diocese—that of Petra-Philadelphia, the latter an old Greek name for Amman—had its seat in Amman.

The Roman Catholic Church had its own patriarch, who was also subject to papal authority. Several other Catholic groups, each headed by a patriarch who was in turn subordinate to Rome, were represented. These included several hundred Syrian Catholics and Armenian Catholics.

The approximately 11,000 members of various Protestant denominations had been converted primarily from the Orthodox and Catholic churches. Muslims rarely converted to another faith. In the rural areas, conversions from one Christian group to another usually involved an entire kin-based group of some size. Such conversions often caused stress between the converting group and another group of which it was part or with which it was allied. Individual conversions in such areas were rare. The effect of urbanization on this pattern has not been examined.

Protestant communities, generally established by North American and European missionary activities, also were represented by the

113

personnel of various international organizations. Some Protestant groups established schools and hospitals and constructed a few churches. The Christian churches also had their own ecclesiastical courts that decided matters of alimony, divorce, annulment, and inheritance.

Non-Christian religious minorities in the late 1980s included a small community of Druzes who lived in an area near the Syrian border. They were members of a sect that originally had derived from the Ismaili branch of Shia Islam. Ismailis were Shias who believed that Imam Muhammad ibn Ismail (died ca. A.D. 765), the Seventh Imam, was the last Imam, as opposed to others who recognized Twelve Imams. The Druzes, primarily located in the mountains of Lebanon and in southwestern Syria, have many secret beliefs and maintain that Hakim, the sixth Fatimid caliph, was divine in nature and is still alive in hiding. A small settlement of Bahais inhabited the village of Al Adasiyah in the northern Jordan Valley. The Shishans, a group whose origins lie in the Caucasus Mountains, were Shias. Estimates in the early 1980s placed the number of Shishans at 2,000.

## Education

The government's good intentions in the area of education contended with straitened financial circumstances, a rapidly changing labor force, and the demographic problem of a youthful population (53 percent of the population was below the age of fifteen in 1988). Nevertheless, significant progress had been made in various spheres. Education has been a stated priority of the government for a number of years. In 1986 government expenditures on education were 12.2 percent of the national budget. Education has become widely available, although some observers have questioned both the quality of the instruction and the appropriateness of the curriculum to the economy's requirements. Recognizing the need to supply training more suited to realistic employment prospects and to improve the level of teacher training, the government was continuing to strengthen vocational and technical education and to provide in-service training for its teachers.

In 1921, when the Amirate of Transjordan was created, educational facilities consisted of twenty-five religious schools that provided a rather limited education. By 1987 there were 3,366 schools, with more than 39,600 teachers and an enrollment of 919,645 students. Nearly one-third of the population in 1987 was involved in education as a teacher or a student at home or abroad (see table 2, Appendix). In 1985 nearly 99 percent of the nation's six- to twelve-year-olds were in the primary cycle, nearly 79 percent of the twelve- to fifteen-year-olds were in the preparatory cycle, and 37 percent of the fifteen- to eighteen-year-olds were in the secondary cycle (see table 3, Appendix). Progress in literacy was impressive. The *Encyclopedia of the Third World,* edited by George T. Kurian, reported that in the mid-1980s Jordan had a 67.6 percent literacy rate, 81 percent for males and 59.3 percent for females. The gap between rural and urban areas in terms of literacy was closing, but rural levels remained below those of the urban areas; Maan Governorate lagged behind other rural areas.

Education was free and compulsory for children between the ages of six and fifteen. The educational ladder consisted of four parts: primary (grades one through six); preparatory (grades seven through nine); secondary (grades ten through twelve); and postsecondary (all higher education). Promotion from the compulsory cycle to the more specialized secondary schools was controlled by a standardized written examination, as was passage from secondary to the postsecondary programs. The Ministry of Education, which controlled all aspects of education (except community colleges), administered the examinations. For grades one through twelve, nearly 75 percent of the students attended the free government schools in the late 1980s; about 15 percent attended the UNRWA schools, also free; and about 10 percent attended private schools. In 1987 the Department of Statistics reported that there were 194 UNRWA schools and 682 private schools.

The primary curriculum stressed basic literacy skills. Subjects taught included reading and writing in Arabic; religion (Islam for Muslims and the appropriate religion for non-Muslims); arithmetic; civics and history, with emphasis on the history of the Arabs and the concept of the Arab nation; geography, with emphasis on the Arab countries; science; music; physical education; and drawing for male students and embroidery for females. In the fifth grade, English was added to the official curriculum (although many private schools taught it earlier) and some schools offered French. Within the primary cycle, promotion from grade to grade was required by law and was essentially automatic. Children could be held back only twice in six years, after which they proceeded to higher grades regardless of the quality of their work.

In the preparatory cycle, work on academic subjects continued, both to improve the skills of terminal students and to prepare those going on to secondary studies. In addition, vocational education began on a limited basis. Each school was required to provide at least one course in a vocational subject for each grade. In general, each school offered only one vocational option, and all students had to take that subject for three periods a week for three years.

The preparatory curriculum added geometry, algebra, and social studies to the academic courses offered in the primary grades.

On completion of the ninth grade, students could sit for the public preparatory examination for promotion to the secondary level. Secondary education was somewhat selective in enrollment and quite specialized in purpose. This level had both academic (general) and vocational divisions; the former was designed to prepare students for university-level studies and the latter to train middle-level technical personnel for the work force. Within the academic curriculum, students further specialized in scientific or literary studies. Because of the specialized nature and relatively limited number of secondary facilities, male and female students did not necessarily attend separate schools. The secondary program culminated in the public secondary education examination, which qualified students for postsecondary study.

In 1987 around 69,000 students were enrolled in higher education. Nearly half of these were women. Jordan had four universities with a combined enrollment of nearly 29,000; more than one-third of the students were women (11,000). The University of Jordan in Amman had a 1986–87 enrollment of nearly 13,000 students; Yarmuk University in Irbid had nearly 12,000 students; Jordan University of Science and Technology in Ar Ramtha had nearly 3,000 students; and Mutah University near Al Karak had an enrollment of about 1,300.

In the 1980s, Jordan strove to implement an education system that would address serious structural problems in its labor force. The country faced high rates of unemployment among educated young people, particularly in the professions of medicine, engineering, and teaching, and also had a need for skilled technical labor. In the 1970s and 1980s, the government began to expand its vocational and technical training programs to counteract the skilled labor shortage brought about by the large-scale migration of workers to high-paying jobs in the oil-producing countries of the Persian Gulf and Saudi Arabia. In spite of the recession and high unemployment among professionals, skilled technical labor remained in short supply in the late 1980s. Cultural factors also played a prominent role; great prestige attached to academic higher education as opposed to vocational training.

In response to the need for education reform, the king called for a reorientation of education policy to meet the needs of the country and the people. Community colleges played an essential role in this reorientation. They were consonant with the cultural value placed on higher education and also helped provide a skilled technical labor force. In the early 1980s, the government's teacher training institutes and all other private and public training institutes were transformed into community colleges. These education institutions offered a variety of vocational, technical, and teacher training programs and granted associates degrees based on two years of study. Upon graduation students were eligible to apply for transfer to the university system if they wished. In the late 1980s, more than fifty-three community colleges operated under the Ministry of Higher Education, which was created in 1985 to regulate the operations of all community colleges, although individual colleges were administered by a variety of agencies. Scattered throughout the country, the community colleges had an enrollment of about 31,000 students, slightly more than half of all students in higher education. More than half their students, about 17,000, were women.

Nearly 100 areas of specialization were offered in nine categories of professional study: education, commerce, computers, communications and transportation, engineering, paramedical technologies, agriculture, hotel management, and social service professions. According to observers, graduates were able to find employment in industry, business, and government. The government sought to confront the issue of unemployment among university graduates by encouraging more students to join community colleges. In 1987 the government introduced a career guidance program in the secondary schools that explained the country's problems with unemployment.

Most Jordanian students in Eastern Europe and the Soviet Union were studying medicine and engineering. Some observers have suggested that many of the students in Eastern Europe and the Soviet Union were Palestinians whose education costs were being borne by the host government. Observers believed that most of the students in Western Europe and the United States were being financed by their families and the rest by the government of Jordan. Perhaps because of these connections, students from West European and American schools tended to obtain the more desirable and prestigious positions on their return home. The perceived higher quality of education in the West also was a factor in making these graduates more competitive in the job market.

## Health and Welfare

Factors affecting the standard of living for the average citizen were difficult to assess in early 1989. Information was scanty. Living conditions varied considerably according to region, kind of settlement, social position, and fortune of war. At the high end of the spectrum, well-to-do city dwellers appeared to enjoy all the amenities of modern life. In cities, basic public services such as water, sewage, and electricity were sufficient to meet the needs of most residents. Nevertheless, mounting pressure on these services, particularly the demand for water, rose steeply during the 1980s and was bound to increase as the urban population continued its high rate of growth. World Health Organization (WHO) figures indicated that, in the mid-1980s, the urban population had a 100-percent rate of access to safe water within the home or within 15 minutes walking distance; in rural areas the figure was 95 percent. Adequate sanitary facilities were available to 100 percent of the urban population and to 95 percent of the rural population. The rural poor, however, generally lived in substandard conditions. Homes in some villages still lacked piped water. At the bottom were the poorest of the refugees, many living in camps with minimal services. Open sewage ran through dusty, unpaved streets. During the late 1970s and the 1980s, electricity was gradually extended to nearly all rural areas.

Diet was generally adequate to support life and activity. Average daily caloric intake for adults in the 1980s was 2,968 (117 percent of the requirement), and protein intake was 52.5 grams, 115 percent of the daily requirement. Nonetheless, nutritional deficiencies of various kinds reportedly were common.

The number of health care personnel increased so that by the mid-1980s Jordan had a surplus of physicians. The "brain drain," or emigration from Jordan of skilled professionals, apparently peaked in 1983, after which the number of physicians started a gradual climb. According to the WHO, in 1983 Jordan had 2,662 physicians. In 1987 the Jordan Medical Association reported a figure of 3,703, of whom 300 were unemployed. In the early 1980s, the medical college of the University of Jordan started to graduate students, further increasing the numbers. Fewer opportunities for physicians became available in the Gulf states and Saudi Arabia because of the recession in these countries.

In 1987 the Ministry of Health and the Jordan Medical Association, concerned about high unemployment among physicians, put forth various suggestions. These included opening more clinics in rural areas and assigning physicians to schools, colleges, and large industrial concerns.

Other health care professions showed moderate increases; the number of government-employed dentists, for example, increased from 75 to 110. Pharmacists, a profession increasingly entered by women, nearly tripled in number from thirty-eight in 1983 to

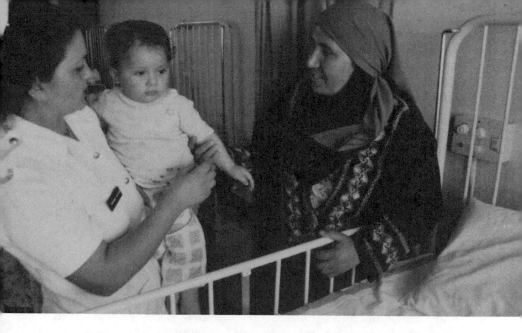

*A child patient at King Hussein Medical Center, Amman*

ninety-six in 1987. Government-employed nurses increased from 292 to 434 over the same period (see table 4, Appendix).

In the early 1980s, Jordan had thirty-five hospitals, of which about 40 percent were state run. A number of other health facilities scattered throughout the country included health centers, village clinics, maternal and child care centers, tuberculosis centers, and school health services. In 1986 government health expenditures represented 3.8 percent of the national budget.

Medical care services were distributed more evenly than in the past. Previously most health professionals, hospitals, and technologically advanced medical equipment were located in major urban areas, such as Amman, Irbid, Ar Ramtha, Az Zarqa, and As Salt. People in smaller villages and remote rural areas had limited access to professional medical care. With the focus on primary health care in the 1980s, the WHO commented that treatment for common diseases was available within an hour's walk or travel for about 80 percent of the population. The expense and inconvenience of traveling to major urban areas did, however, hinder rural people from seeking more technologically sophisticated medical care.

The WHO reported a general decrease in the incidence of diseases related to inadequate sanitary and hygienic conditions. A reduction in the incidence of meningitis, scarlet fever, typhoid,

119

and paratyphoid was noted, while an increase was registered in infectious hepatitis, rubella, mumps, measles, and schistosomiasis. In the mid-1980s, only one reported case of polio and none of diphtheria occurred. Childhood immunizations had increased sharply, but remained inadequate. In 1984 an estimated 44 percent of children were fully immunized against diphtheria, pertussis, and tetanus (DPT); 41 percent had received polio vaccine; and 30 percent had been vaccinated against measles. Cholera had been absent since 1981. Jordan reported its first three cases of acquired immunodeficiency syndrome (AIDS) to the WHO in 1987.

The most frequently cited causes of morbidity in government hospitals, in descending frequency, were gastroenteritis, accidents, respiratory diseases, complications of birth and the puerperium, and urogenital and cardiovascular diseases. Among hospitalized patients, the most frequent causes of mortality were heart diseases, tumors, accidents, and gastrointestinal and respiratory diseases.

Traditional health beliefs and practices were prevalent in urban and rural areas alike. These practices were the domain of women, some of whom were known in their communities for possessing skills in treating injuries and curing ailments. Within the family, women assumed responsibility for the nutrition of the family and the treatment of illness.

Local health beliefs and practices were important not only for their implications in a family's general state of health but also in determining when, and if, people would seek modern medical care. Local beliefs in the efficacy of healers and their treatments prevented or delayed the seeking of medical care. For example, healers often treated illness in children by massages with warm olive oil, a harmless procedure but one that often delayed or prevented the seeking of medical care.

Modern medicine had made tremendous inroads, however, into popular knowledge and courses of action. People combined traditional and modern medical approaches. They sought modern medical facilities and treatments while simultaneously having recourse to traditional health practitioners and religious beliefs. Infertility, for example, was often dealt with by seeking the advice of a physician and also visiting a shaykh for an amulet. In addition, traditional cures such as "closing the back" were used. In this cure, a woman healer rubbed a woman's pelvis with olive oil and placed suction cups on her back. This acted to "close the back"; an "opened back" was believed to be a cause of infertility.

The acceptance of modern health practices and child care

techniques was closely related to household structure. A study by two anthropologists noted that younger, educated women encountered difficulties in practicing modern techniques of child health care when they resided in extended family households with older women present. The authority in the household of older women often accorded them a greater voice than the mother in setting patterns of child care and nutrition and in making decisions on health expenditures.

Discrimination on the basis of gender in terms of nutrition and access to health care resources was documented. In a study conducted in the mid-1980s, the infant mortality rate for girls was found to be significantly higher than for boys. It was also noted that male children received more immunizations and were taken to see physicians more frequently and at an earlier stage of illness than girls. Girls were more apt to die of diarrhea and dehydration than males. Malnutrition also was more common among female children; boys were given larger quantities and better quality food. In addition, more boys (71 percent) were breastfed than girls (54 percent).

In the 1980s, government efforts to improve health were often directed at women. In the summer, when outbreaks of diarrhea among infants and children were common, commercial breaks on television included short health spots. These programs advised mothers how to feed and care for children with diarrhea and advertised the advantages of oral rehydration therapy (ORT) to prevent and treat the accompanying dehydration. The WHO noted that the use of ORT helped lower the fatality rate among those children hospitalized for diarrhea from 20 percent in 1977 to 5 percent in 1983.

During the 1980s, the Ministry of Health launched an antismoking campaign. Posters warning of the dangers to health could be seen in physicians' offices and in government offices and buildings. Success was slow and gradual; for example, cigarettes were less frequently offered as part of the tradition of hospitality.

Social welfare, especially care of the elderly and financial or other support of the sick, traditionally was provided by the extended family. Nursing homes for the elderly were virtually unknown and were considered an aberration from family and social values and evidence of lack of respect for the elderly. Social welfare in the form of family assistance and rehabilitation facilities for the handicapped were a service of the Department of Social Affairs and more than 400 charitable organizations. Some of these were religiously affiliated, and the overwhelming majority provided multiple services.

UNRWA provided an array of social services, such as education, medical care, vocational training and literacy classes, and nutrition centers to registered refugees.

Government expenditures on social security, housing, and welfare amounted to 8.6 percent of the budget in 1986. Social security was governed by the Social Security Law of 1978, which was being applied in stages to the private sector. As of 1986, all establishments employing ten persons or more came under the law's provisions. Ultimately the law will apply to all establishments employing five or more persons. The employer contributed 10 percent of salary and the employee contributed 5 percent, and the contribution covered retirement benefits, termination pay, occupational diseases, and work injuries. The plan was for medical insurance to be included eventually under the social security contribution. In April 1988, the Social Security Corporation covered 465,000 workers employed by approximately 7,000 public and private establishments.

* * *

Adequate published research in East Bank society and culture remained limited as of the late 1980s. Richard T. Antoun's books, *Arab Village: A Social Structural Study of a Transjordanian Peasant Community* and *Low Key Politics: Local Level Leadership and Change in the Middle East,* describe a village and its surroundings in the northwest corner of the East Bank. Peter Gubser's book, *Politics and Change in Al-Karak, Jordan: A Study of a Small Arab Town and Its District,* describes a town and its environs in west-central Jordan in which tribal organization was still significant. Gubser also has published a very general book, *Jordan: Crossroads of Middle Eastern Events,* on Jordanian history, politics, society, and economy. More recent research studies are Linda Layne's "Women in Jordan's Workplace" and "Tribesmen as Citizens: 'Primordial Ties' and Democracy in Rural Jordan"; Seteney Shami and Lucine Taminian's *Reproductive Behavior and Child Care in a Squatter Area of Amman;* Nadia Hijab's *Womenpower: The Arab Debate on Women at Work;* Ian J. Seccombe's "Labour Migration and the Transformation of a Village Economy: A Case Study from North-West Jordan"; Lars Wahlin's "Diffusion and Acceptance of Modern Schooling in Rural Jordan"; and Laurie Brand's *Palestinians in the Arab World: Institution Building and the Search for State.* These works provide background on a variety of social issues in Jordan such as tribalism, health behavior, women and work, labor migration, education, and the

Palestinians in Jordan. No recent work, however, deals in a comprehensive fashion with the social changes and emerging social forms in Jordan in the 1980s. (For further information and complete citations, see Bibliography).

# Chapter 3. The Economy

*Mosaic of a man carrying a basket of grapes from the Byzantine Church of Saint Lots and Saint Prokopius, Khirbat al Muhayyat, ca. 550*

JORDAN, A SMALL NATION with a small population and sparse natural resources, has long been known by its Arab neighbors as their "poor cousin." In the late 1980s, Jordan was compelled to import not only many capital and consumer goods but also such vital commodities as fuel and food. Officials even discussed the possibility of importing water. Nevertheless, the Jordanian economy flourished in the 1970s as the gross domestic product (GDP—see Glossary) enjoyed double-digit growth. The economy continued to fare well in the early 1980s, despite a recessionary regional environment. Indeed, by the late 1980s, Jordanians had become measurably more affluent than many of their Arab neighbors. The 1988 per capita GDP of approximately US$2,000 placed Jordan's citizens well within the world's upper-middle income bracket.

Economic prosperity rested on three primary bases. Jordan's status as the world's third largest producer of phosphates ensured a steady—if relatively modest—flow of export income that offset some of its high import bills. More important, Jordan received billions of dollars of invisible or unearned income in the form of inflows of foreign aid and remittances from expatriates. These financial inflows permitted domestic consumption to outpace production and caused the gross national product (GNP—see Glossary) to exceed the GDP. In the late 1970s and early 1980s, GNP exceeded GDP by 10 percent to 25 percent. High financial inflows from the mid-1970s to the mid-1980s allowed Jordan to maintain a low current account deficit; in some years it registered a current account surplus, without much external borrowing and despite trade and budget deficits. Jordan's economy, therefore, demonstrated many of the characteristics of wealthier and more technologically advanced rentier economies. Jordan also capitalized on its strategic geographic location, its educated work force, and its free enterprise economy to become a regional entrepôt and transit point for exports and imports between Western Europe and the Middle East. Because of these factors, it also became a magnet for foreign direct investment, and a purveyor of banking, insurance, and consulting services to foreign clients. Jordan's heritage as a merchant middleman was centuries-old, dating back to the Nabatean kingdom of Petra. Because the economy depended so heavily on the professional service sector and remittance income from expatriates, the government sometimes called Jordan's manpower the nation's most valuable resource.

Jordan's economic strategy succeeded during the Middle East oil boom of the 1970s. In the late 1980s, however, as the worldwide plunge in oil prices persisted, economic problems emerged. Foreign aid was cut, remittances declined, and regional trade and transit activity was suppressed by lack of demand, leading to a deterioration in the current account. The government was deeply concerned about the economy's vulnerability to external forces. Jordan's economy depended heavily on imported commodities and foreign aid, trade, investment, and income. But because plans to increase self-sufficiency were only in the early stages of implementation, a short-term decline in the national standard of living and increased indebtedness loomed as the 1990s approached; observers forecast that austerity would replace prosperity.

## Structure and Dynamics of the Economy

In the late 1980s, despite recent economic setbacks, Jordan remained more prosperous than many developing countries, and its citizens were more affluent than their neighbors from other nonpetroleum-exporting countries. Jordan's persistent economic viability was surprising in several respects. Measured both in terms of population and production, the Jordanian economy was one of the smallest in West Asia, according to the United Nations (UN). Its population—not including the West Bank (see Glossary)—numbered only about 3 million in 1989. Jordan's 1987 gross domestic product was estimated at less than US$5.5 billion. Furthermore, Jordan's natural resources were not nearly as abundant as those of other Middle Eastern nations.

Added to these disadvantages was the incalculable cost to economic development of the regional political and military environment. The economy was dismembered by the 1967 Israeli occupation of the West Bank (see The Military Heritage, ch. 5). Jordanians regarded the loss of this territory not only as a military and political defeat, but also as an enduring economic catastrophe that cost them a large part of their infrastructure, resources, and manpower. Jordan's defense burden, although only average by Middle Eastern standards, was very large by world standards (see Defense Spending, ch. 5). The country's 1987 defense expenditure of US$635 million constituted 22 percent of total government spending.

Despite such handicaps, the economy grew rapidly in the 1970s and continued to grow in the early 1980s. According to UN data, the annual real (inflation-adjusted) growth rate of GDP averaged almost 16.5 percent between 1972 and 1975. The average annual growth rate fell to 8.5 percent between 1976 and 1979, then peaked at almost 18 percent in 1980. Jordan's economic growth appeared more spectacular in percentage terms than in absolute terms because it started from low base figures; nonetheless, the pace of economic development was one of the highest in the world during this period. Jordan was not a petroleum exporter, a fact that made this growth rate all the more phenomenal.

Jordan dealt relatively well with the recession in the Middle East triggered by plummeting petroleum prices. Between 1980 and 1985, the average growth rate decelerated to about 4 percent a year, but Jordan's economy was able to sustain this growth rate at a time when other regional economies, such as those of the oil-producers on the Arabian Peninsula, were actually contracting. The boom in transit trade to and from Iraq after the start of the Iran-Iraq War in 1980 accounted for much of the growth. The immunity of the large service sector to demand slowdown also postponed the effects of the regional recession. The government, however, constituted a large component of the service sector. In its role as a major customer and employer, the government sustained an artificial level of growth through continued deficit spending and a relaxed fiscal policy. Despite the extra money and demand that the government injected into the economy, GDP growth eventually stagnated in the late 1980s. GDP growth in 1989 was estimated at only 2 or 3 percent.

## GDP by Sector

The large contribution of the service sector to GDP, versus the small contribution of the industrial and agricultural sectors, has long been a source of concern to economic planners. In the late 1980s, Jordan's aggregate private and public service sector continued to contribute about 60 to 65 percent of total GDP. This figure was exceeded only in some of the world's most industrially advanced market economies. Figures nearly as high were reached by several of the world's poorest economies, however, where unproductive surplus labor was absorbed into the service sector. Some segments of the service sector, such as banking and engineering, relied on advanced and sophisticated skills. Nonetheless, the sector's overall contribution to GDP remained roughly constant in the 1970s and 1980s, even though its share of total employment increased significantly. The relative lack of growth called into question the overall efficiency and productivity of the service sector.

In 1987 the government, which employed more than 40 percent of the labor force and more than 67 percent of service sector employees, contributed about 18 percent to GDP. Retail and wholesale trade—which included well-developed hotel and restaurant subsectors—was the second largest contributor to GDP. This sector generated 17 percent of GDP in 1987, a share that had declined about 2 percent over the preceding decade. Finance, banking, real estate transactions, insurance, and business services made up 8 percent of GDP. Transportation and communications contributed about 11 percent of GDP (see fig. 7).

Manufacturing, mining, agriculture, and construction—the sectors that produced consumer or capital goods or inputs—together accounted for only about 32 percent or less of GDP. The steady growth of manufacturing, which climbed from about 4 percent of GDP in 1970 to almost 15 percent in 1987, was regarded as a promising sign. Agriculture—including animal husbandry, forestry, and fishing—constituted almost 40 percent of GDP in the 1950s and about 15 percent of GDP in the early 1970s. By 1987, however, its share had declined to 7 percent, which caused the government considerable concern. Construction's contribution doubled between 1970 and 1975, reaching about 8 percent of GDP as spending on both public works and private housing increased, and then stabilized. By 1987 construction had declined to 6 percent. Utilities such as electricity and water supply accounted for 3 percent of GDP, and mining contributed 4 percent in 1987.

Jordan's demand structure in terms of GDP consumption was distorted. In 1986 the government consumed more than 26 percent of GDP, a figure that was the fourth highest in the noncommunist world. Private consumption was about 87 percent of GDP, also among the highest in the world. Consumption exceeded GDP by 13 percent, the highest margin in the world except for the Yemen Arab Republic (North Yemen). Jordan's exports of goods and nonfactor services (i.e., freight, insurance, and travel) amounted to 49 percent of GDP, and its negative resource gap—the excess of imports over exports as a proportion of GDP—was minus 44 percent, by far the highest in the world. Inflows of capital from external sources financed all gross domestic investment (31 percent of GDP) and part of domestic consumption.

Insofar as consumption exceeded GDP and the difference was made up partially by aid and remittances, Jordan did not fully earn the growth it experienced in the 1970s and early 1980s. Jordan's GDP, which rose from about US$2 billion to US$4 billion during the period, was only between 75 percent and 90 percent of its GNP. At the same time, annual inflows of unrequited—or, as the Jordanian government sometimes called them, ''unrequested'' transfer payments—were in some years more than US$1 billion. These unearned transfers, in the form of foreign aid and expatriate worker remittances, permitted Jordan to register only a relatively small current account deficit. In several years, Jordan actually registered current account surpluses despite outspending its GDP by the highest margin in the world. In 1980, for example, Jordan had a current account surplus of almost US$375 million. As foreign aid declined and remittance income tapered off, Jordan suffered a current account deficit of US$390 million in 1983. By 1987 the current account deficit had shrunk considerably, because a reduced trade deficit more than compensated for declining aid and remittance inflows (see table 5, Appendix).

The total amount of foreign aid that Jordan received was difficult to pinpoint. Jordan never received all the aid it was promised, and some aid was in the form of loans at concessionary interest rates or in the form of commodities and services. Although the amount of aid varied from year to year, it was always substantial. In 1980, for example, foreign aid constituted 46 percent of government revenue before borrowing; in 1985, it constituted 30 percent of pre-borrowing revenue.

Financial aid was received mostly from the Arab Organization of Petroleum Exporting Countries (AOPEC). At the Baghdad Conference in November 1978, seven countries promised to donate US$1.25 billion annually to Jordan for ten years as a "war chest" to fund its ongoing confrontation with Israel. Libya and Algeria reneged on their commitments from the outset, and Iraq stopped paying after the Iran-Iraq War started in 1980. In 1984 Qatar and the United Arab Emirates stopped paying except on an ad hoc basis, and in 1985 Kuwait suspended its payments. Only Saudi Arabia consistently met its payment obligations, which amounted to US$360 million per year disbursed in six equal bimonthly installments. Total Arab aid to Jordan stood at about US$750 million in 1980, with aid from non-Arab countries boosting total aid to about US$1.3 billion. Arab aid fell to about US$670 million in 1983 and to about US$320 million in 1984. In 1988, according to Jordanian government figures, financial aid totaled about US$474 million and development aid and soft loans (bearing no interest or interest below the cost of the capital loaned) totaled about US$260 million, yielding a total of US$734 million in outside assistance. This figure included a United States aid package that authorized US$28 million of military training, US$20 million in budget support, and up to US$80 million in commodity credits. The figure also included United Nations Relief and Works Agency (UNRWA) for Palestine Refugees in the Near East aid of about US$10 million, World Bank soft loans in excess of US$100 million,

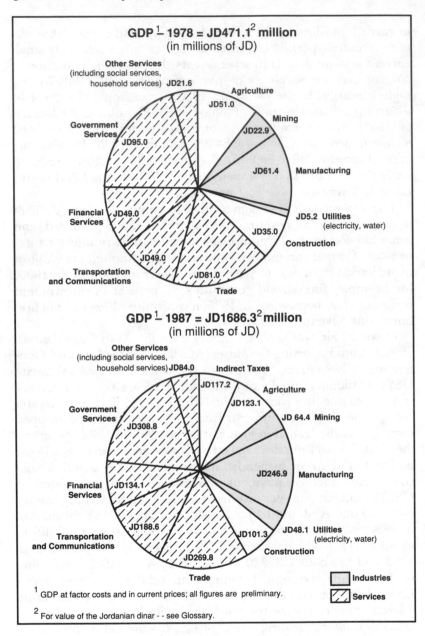

GDP [1] 1978 = JD471.1[2] million
(in millions of JD)

Other Services
(including social services,
household services) JD21.6

Agriculture
JD51.0

Mining
JD22.9

Government
Services
JD95.0

Manufacturing
JD61.4

Financial
Services JD49.0

JD5.2 Utilities
(electricity, water)

JD35.0

Construction

Transportation
and Communications JD49.0

JD81.0

Trade

GDP [1] 1987 = JD1686.3[2] million
(in millions of JD)

Other Services
(including social services,
household services) JD84.0

Indirect Taxes
JD117.2

Agriculture
JD123.1

Government
Services
JD308.8

JD 64.4 Mining

Manufacturing
JD246.9

Financial
Services JD134.1

JD48.1 Utilities
(electricity, water)

JD188.6

JD101.3

Construction

Transportation
and Communications

JD269.8

Trade

Industries

Services

[1] GDP at factor costs and in current prices; all figures are preliminary.

[2] For value of the Jordanian dinar - - see Glossary.

Source: Based on information from Jordan, Central Bank of Jordan, *Monthly Statistical Bulletin,*
Amman, April 1979, Table 40; and Jordan, Department of Statistics, *Statistical
Yearbook, 1987,* 383.

*Figure 7. Gross Domestic Product (GDP) by Sector of Origin, 1978 and 1987*

and Arab aid of at least US$350 million. The European Economic Community authorized US$112.5 million in aid to Jordan to be paid in installments between 1987 and 1991. Worker remittances, the other main source of external income, could not be estimated precisely in 1988, but exceeded US$1 billion (see Remittance Income, this ch.).

Foreign direct investment and reexports, particularly of goods destined for Iraq, also contributed to GDP growth. The government of Jordan was one of only a few Arab governments that chose to stake its future on an economic system that, if not laissez-faire, was by regional standards free, open, and market oriented. In the 1980s, however, Jordan began to compete for foreign investment with Egypt, which was pursuing its own open-door policy. On the one hand, Jordan's open-door policy posed risks insofar as the country had to compete and cooperate with Arab governments that had protectionist and subsidized state-controlled economies. On the other hand, the policy was particularly effective because it was so rare in the Middle East. Furthermore, with the devastation of Beirut after the start of Lebanon's Civil War in 1975, Jordan was at least partially successful in replacing that city as a prime regional commercial center. In this role of merchant middleman, Jordan became an entrepôt and conduit for trade and investment between the West and the rest of the Arab world. It encouraged transit trade through duty-free zones. Its open-door policy acted as a magnet for inflows of foreign direct investment. It provided tax concessions to both domestic and foreign businesses. Until 1988 it maintained a sound and freely convertible currency backed by substantial gold reserves. A sound currency, combined with relative political stability, made Jordan a safe haven for Arab bank deposits. Jordan also established a strong professional service sector, including well-developed banking and insurance industries that catered to international business. Total net foreign direct and portfolio investment in Jordan could not be estimated, however, because foreign investment was offset by capital flight abroad. Estimates of Jordanian capital invested abroad ranged from US$4 billion to US$40 billion. Net direct investment in Jordan was estimated at US$23 million in 1985.

## The Late 1980s

Superficial economic prosperity masked deep underlying structural problems; in the late 1980s, a number of intractable long-term economic problems and a host of short-term potential crises loomed. In the long range, if Jordan's domestic market could not grow sufficiently to permit the economies of scale necessary to sustain large manufacturing industries, capital investment and manufacturing value added would continue to be low; however, this difficulty might be offset if export markets were obtained. Gross barter terms of trade would decline further if the volume and value of manufactured imports rose faster than the volume and value of raw material exports. The merchandise trade deficit would continue because imports of certain commodities would continue to be necessary far into the future. The standard of living as measured by per capita GNP could eventually decrease as modest real economic growth was offset by a rapidly growing population. Domestic unemployment could increase to more than 9 percent as the young population matured and the domestic work force grew. Although a price increase for oil could restimulate the Jordanian economy by reopening Arabian Peninsula markets for goods and services, the resultant increased oil import bill would offset some of the gains. In the late 1980s, however, short-term financial problems including deflation, debt, and devaluation of the dinar (see Glossary), which lost 42.5 percent of its value between October 1988 and May 1989, commanded the government's attention more than did long-term problems.

### Deflation

The problem of deflation, a sustained fall in overall prices, was complex and not readily apparent to the average consumer. Prices were stable in 1986, and in 1987 the cost of living index actually dropped, albeit by less than 0.5 percent. The greatest drops were in housing, food, fuel, and utility costs. Although consumers preferred deflation to the double-digit inflation of the early 1980s, deflation had ominous implications for an economic downturn. Because import costs rose during 1987, average domestic prices fell significantly, as much as 10 percent for some goods and services. Total prices declined by 0.5 percent. Insofar as growth in domestic demand had contributed some 60 percent of manufacturing growth, business and industry began to suffer. Companies that had incurred dinar-denominated debts at high interest rates, expecting to repay their loans with inflated currency, were expected to suffer even more. The low interest rates that disinflation, a reduction in inflation, implied could spark even greater capital flight and lower remittances. Increased government spending would revive aggregate demand but would entail more external borrowing.

### External Debt

As foreign aid and remittances declined in the 1980s, Jordan started to draw down its foreign reserves. In 1980 Jordan's international

*Al Aqabah Port, Jordan's only seaport*

reserves, including gold and hard currency, totaled US$1.74 billion. By 1983 international reserves had shrunk to US$1.24 billion—US$824 million in currency and US$416 million in gold. By 1986 international reserves had been reduced to US$854 million; currency reserves were down to US$438 million, but gold reserves remained at previous levels. The Central Bank of Jordan (hereafter Central Bank) held about US$130 million, and the rest was held by Jordan's private commercial banks. Whereas total international reserves were sufficient to cover six months' worth of imports in 1980, by 1986 they equaled only three months' worth of imports.

In the late 1980s, the government resorted to borrowing to cushion the economy from the shortfall of outside income. In 1970 external debt stood at US$120 million. By 1980, however, external debt had risen to about US$1 billion, and in 1986 it stood at US$4.13 billion. Total debt outstanding, including undisbursed debt (obligations contracted but not yet received as loans), was US$4.31 billion. Whereas lower figures were reported by various sources, such figures presumably did not count as debt some soft loans for development or trade credits that could be construed as debt or aid.

Earlier loans had been contracted at concessional interest rates through foreign export credit agencies, other Arab governments, and multilateral agencies. Debt to such official creditors rose from

US$2.3 billion in 1982 to US$2.8 billion by 1986. Beginning in 1983, however, Jordan started to supplement soft loans from governments with commercial credit. In 1982 debt to private creditors stood at US$512 million, but by 1986 that amount had tripled to US$1.5 billion. Funds raised on the Eurodollar market (dollars held and loaned by European banks) included four commercial loans obtained between 1983 and 1987. But 1987 Eurodollar borrowing totaled US$640 million.

In part because it had previously borrowed so little, Jordan was regarded as a good credit risk. But as the country borrowed more and as it turned to private sector creditors, terms tended to stiffen. For example, although the average interest rate that Jordan paid in 1986 (7.3 percent) was the same as in the early 1980s, the amount of debt subject to variable interest rates had doubled to 20 percent of total debt; thus, Jordan was more vulnerable to a possible increase in world interest rates. At the same time, however, almost 50 percent of all debt remained at concessional interest rates. In 1986 Jordan paid an estimated US$610.5 million in debt service, of which nearly US$431.8 million was for principal and nearly US$178.8 million was for interest. These short-term interest and principal payments as a percentage of export earnings—the debt service ratio—rose from less than 8 percent in 1980 to almost 29 percent in 1986.

### Devaluation

Growing external debt, declining remittance income and foreign aid, and shrinking foreign currency reserves made Jordanian citizens wary of keeping their savings in dinars. King Hussein's severance of Jordan's official ties to the West Bank in July 1988 added to the worries of both foreign investors and citizens about the long-term viability of the economy. These concerns culminated in a financial crisis in 1988 as Jordanians—especially those of Palestinian origin—tried to exchange dinars for foreign currencies and to move their savings outside the country, circumventing a Central Bank restriction that limited individual Jordanians to sending no more than JD5,000 worth of foreign currency out of the country per year for personal use.

This capital flight brought pressure on the value of the dinar. The dinar, pegged to the special drawing right (SDR—see Glossary), had long been one of the most stable and realistically valued currencies in the Middle East. From 1982 to 1987, the dinar varied only slightly in value, from about US$2.55 to US$3.04, reflecting fluctuations in the value of both the dollar and the dinar. During this period, no significant black market for dollars existed. But in a one-year period ending in January 1989, the dinar depreciated by more than 30 percent, from an official exchange rate of US$2.90 per dinar to US$1.96. The Central Bank attempted to freeze the exchange rate at the latter level, but money changers ignored the official rate and opened a black market for United States dollars and other foreign currencies. Although the Central Bank eased restrictions on the amount of foreign currency Jordanians could keep or bring into the country, it nevertheless was forced to cut the official rate repeatedly, chasing down the value of the dinar. By February 1989, the official rate had been cut another 10 percent to US$1.76, at which point it appeared to stabilize.

### Austerity Measures

To contain its financial crisis, the Jordanian government embraced several austerity measures in the late 1980s. It froze the currency exchange rate and halted the operation of money changers, who had facilitated the dinar's drop by ignoring official exchange rates and acting as an open black market. In November 1988, the government also imposed new import duties of 20 to 30 percent on most consumer goods and banned a wide array of so-called luxury imports, including automobiles, refrigerators, cameras, televisions, telephones, cosmetics, and cigarettes. The ban on luxury imports was to last for at least one year, but statements by Jordanian officials indicated that it might last considerably longer. Taxes and service charges at airports and hotels were increased, as were work permit fees for guest workers. The government also adopted an austerity budget that cut both current expenditure and development investment (see The Budget, this ch.). Prime Minister Zaid ar Rifai sought to reassure Jordanians that the problems were temporary. In a February 1989 interview, he stated that "the Jordanian economy is active and suffers no troubles at all. Its troubles are financial, not economic." To the extent that this was true, however, observers noted that Jordan's successful growth in the 1970s and early 1980s was likewise more financial than economic.

## The Role of the Government

In the late 1980s, the government of Jordan remained a staunch advocate of free enterprise. Unlike many of its Arab neighbors, and for both pragmatic and ideological reasons, Jordan had never nationalized businesses, seized private assets without compensation, or implemented socialism. But although the economic system was as liberal and market oriented as those of many fully developed nations, the government continued to play a large economic role, both in development planning and as a financier.

## A Mixed Economy

Government encroachment on the economy in the form of ownership or equity participation in corporations was inevitable and, to some extent, inadvertent. The government's role as financier derived from several interrelated factors. Most important, the government was the only channel through which foreign aid, loans, and most expatriate worker remittances were funneled into the country. Acting as an intermediary in the distribution of these funds, the government acquired a reputation in the private sector for its "deep pockets" and fostered in the business world a feeling of entitlement to government support in the capitalization of certain enterprises. Inadequate private capital investment, resulting in part from an entrenched "merchant mentality," has been a weak point in the economy for which the government has had to compensate. Moreover, the large amount of capital investment required by some extractive industries was beyond the reach of willing private sector investors. In some industries, such as telecommunications, government ownership was viewed simply as a prerogative. In numerous other cases, the government felt compelled to bolster private investor confidence and so stepped in to rescue insolvent private sector companies and banks with an infusion of capital, to buy the receivables of exporting companies unable to collect payment from foreign customers, and, when publicly held companies went bankrupt, to compensate shareholders for the lost value of their stocks. In this manner, the government essentially adopted companies that were abandoned by the private sector.

Eventually, the government came to preside over a large mixed economy of some forty semipublic corporations. The government's share of the combined nominal equity of these companies was about 18 percent, but its share of their combined paid-up capital—a more realistic measure of ownership—was over 40 percent. The government had contributed 100 percent of the paid-up capital of eleven of the companies, although its share of their nominal capital was much lower. These firms included Arab International Hotels, the Arab Company for Maritime Transport, the Jordan Cement Factories Company, the Arab Investment Company, and a number of joint ventures with Iraq and Syria. In six of the companies, the government was a minor investor, holding less than 10 percent of the equity. The largest company in this group was the Jordan Refinery Company, in which the government held only a 3 percent share. This group also included the Arab Pharmaceutical Manufacturing Company and the Jordan Ceramic Company. Public investment tended to be highest in those companies with strong

*Women workers in a shoe factory*

domestic and export markets. In 1988 the government was pursuing plans to offer the government-owned telecommunications industry and the national air carrier, Royal Jordanian Airlines, for sale to a combination of Jordanian and other Arab private sector investors.

Clearly, the government assumed responsibility for some aspects of the economy by default because of lack of investment activity and initiative in the private sector. Although total gross fixed capital formation was targeted by the 1980–85 Five-Year Plan for Economic and Social Development (known as the 1980–85 Five-Year Plan) to grow at about 12 percent annually, it grew at less than 1 percent per year. Public sector capital investment during the period totaled almost JD60 million, 40 percent more than stipulated in the plan, but private and mixed sector capital investment, at JD540 million, was only 75 percent of the planned target. The declining value of share prices on the Amman Financial Market since the early 1980s also indicated low private participation in equity markets.

Government officials have, on occasion, criticized the private sector for its unwillingness to make capital investments and its general preference for trade and consumption rather than production and investment. Revitalization and expansion of the private sector has been a long-standing official development priority. Perhaps the government's most important policy tool has been

Central Bank regulation of bank interest rates on both loans and deposits. By setting ceilings on the interest rates that banks can charge certain borrowers, the government has tried to channel loans to capital-starved enterprises. The government also has encouraged foreign direct investment in the hope of stimulating growth of the domestic private sector through partnerships and joint ventures with foreign companies.

The incentives that the government has had to provide foreign and domestic businesses to invest in the economy have, however, run somewhat contrary to the free market philosophy. Under the 1984 Encouragement of Investment Law, foreign investors were permitted to own up to 49 percent of a Jordanian company. In certain cases (for example, export-oriented manufacturing enterprises), foreign investors could own all of a Jordanian company. To encourage investment, companies received customs exemptions, almost complete tax exemption for up to nine years, and unlimited profit repatriation. In some cases, they were given free land and facilities. Free zones granting similar concessions were established near Al Aqabah and near the Syrian border to encourage wholly owned Jordanian companies to engage in manufacture for export. Five industrial estates throughout the country offered the use of government-built infrastructure and extensive government-run services to Jordanian companies.

Although government economic support was weighted toward fostering investment, the government also provided subsidies that were deemed necessary to guarantee citizens' welfare and political stability. The main government agent for subsidizing and setting prices was the Ministry of Supply, which was established in 1974 after merchants hoarded sugar to force up prices. The hoarding sparked discontent in the country at large and particularly in the armed forces. In the late 1980s, the Ministry of Supply imported wheat, meat, and other basic foodstuffs and distributed them at subsidized prices and bought crops from Jordanian farmers at higher-than-market prices. In the 1989 budget, JD33.2 million was allocated to food subsidies alone. The government also subsidized fuel, water, and electricity.

The government repeatedly has stated that it intends to phase out subsidies. The import restrictions imposed in 1988, however, had almost immediate unintended price effects that necessitated further subsidies and price setting. Although the government intended to ban only luxury imports, merchants began to hoard their inventory of imported goods in expectation of future restrictions. Hoarding led to sharp and sudden price inflation of such vital items as medicines and food. Domestic producers of goods that could substitute for imports also raised prices. In 1988 the Ministry of Supply announced that for the first time it would set or subsidize prices for tea, matches, electrical appliances, construction materi-. als, and numerous other goods. For similar welfare reasons, un- employment was mitigated by public sector hiring, and the public payroll swelled to account for more than 40 percent of the work force in 1987.

In 1989 it was difficult to assess whether the government's role in the economy was increasing or decreasing. The government's forceful intervention with specific restrictions to stabilize the econ- omy during the 1988 financial crisis was uncharacteristic. In gen- eral, the government appeared uncomfortable with the size of the role it was forced to play in the economy.

## The Budget

The government of Jordan consistently has run budget deficits. Domestic revenues were 67 percent of current expenditure in 1980, but this figure had improved to 80 percent in 1985. Budgets tended to be only approximations of actual expenditure and revenue. The government did not present a consolidated budget; that is, the cen- tral government budget did not encompass the separate budgets of the municipalities and some public institutions. Moreover, central government income depended on unpredictable disbursements of aid from foreign donors, while spending usually was increased by supplemental budgets submitted throughout the year.

### Expenditures

The discrepancy between income and expenditures appeared each year as the difference between the planned and actual budget deficit, with disclosure of the latter figure often delayed considerably. For example, the 1988 budget called for a JD67 million deficit, but the 1989 budget planned for a JD122 million deficit. Although the actual 1988 deficit had not been announced by early 1989, the Ministry of Finance disclosed that the planned 1989 deficit represented a 45 percent reduction from the 1988 level. The minister of finance claimed that the government's 1989 assessment of income and spending was more realistic than in previous years, and that the government was committed to adhering strictly to the budget (see table 6, Appendix).

Years of deficit spending effectively precluded the option of pur- suing a relaxed fiscal policy, which Jordan's price deflation might have warranted in 1989. The 1989 budget called instead for austerity to achieve cuts in spending from 1988 levels. The 1989 budget fore- cast an expenditure of JD1 billion, as compared to JD1.1 billion in the 1988 budget. Of the 1989 planned expenditure, capital investment and development spending were budgeted at JD346.5 million, a cut of JD105 million from the previous year. This cut apparently reflected the government's inability to spend the full capital budget in 1988 because of the economy's limited absorptive capacity. Recurrent expenditure was budgeted at JD688.9 million, an increase of about JD65 million over 1988. Insofar as the defense component of recurrent expenditure was cut JD4.5 million from 1988, it appeared that other recurrent spending, for example on government salaries and services, was set to increase (see table 7, Appendix).

### *Revenue and Taxation*

Customs revenues from tariffs and a 15-percent across-the-board import surcharge traditionally have been the largest sources of domestically generated revenue, accounting for almost 40 percent of government income before foreign aid receipts in 1985. Because of a narrow tax base and the granting of numerous exemptions, direct taxes on income have made only a small contribution to government revenue. In 1985 direct taxes accounted for 13 percent of government revenue, or 4 percent of GDP. Various indirect taxes, however, were relatively high, so that indirect and direct taxes combined represented 14 percent of GDP. Jordan's revenue policy dovetailed with its investment policy. High customs charges and indirect taxes were designed to stifle consumer spending, while low personal income taxes and even lower business taxes were meant to channel the resulting savings to investments. For similar reasons, domestic borrowing was limited. In 1986 outstanding internal public debt was only JD419 million (see table 8, Appendix).

Total 1989 revenue was projected at JD913 million. Customs revenues were expected to contribute JD155 million, but it was possible that the government import ban on luxury goods would slash this figure. Other local revenue generated through direct and indirect taxes was expected to contribute JD392 million. Foreign aid was expected to contribute JD225 million, the same level as projected for 1988, although actual aid disbursed to Jordan in 1988 amounted to JD164 million. Development loans were expected to contribute another JD103 million to 1989 revenues.

## Development Planning

To the extent that achieving development planning goals depended on unpredictable inflows of transfer payments, the five-year plans were more useful as guides to intentions rather than capabilities; 37 percent of the total financing requirements for the

*Solar energy plant near Al Aqabah*

1986–90 Five-Year Plan for Economic and Social Development (known as the 1986–90 Five-Year Plan) were to be provided by aid and remittances. Moreover, even when full funding was available, the economy's limited absorptive capacity prevented the government from spending the full annual development budget.

### The 1986–90 Five-Year Plan

In early 1989, it was not feasible to make a comprehensive assessment of Jordan's progress toward accomplishing the goals of its 1986–90 Five-Year Plan. In the past, development goals had been ambitious but progress was modest. For example, several important goals of the 1980–85 plan were not met: planned GDP growth was 11 percent per year, but actual growth was about 4 percent; planned investment growth was about 12 percent per year, but actual investment growth was less than 1 percent; and planned growth in export of goods and services was 21 percent per year, but actual growth was 3.4 percent.

Total investment spending under the 1986–90 Five-Year Plan was targeted at JD3.2 billion, of which the government was to contribute JD1.8 billion and the private and mixed sectors JD1.4 billion. National savings were to provide about 36 percent of the plan's financing, transfer payments such as aid and remittances were to finance about 37 percent, and external borrowing was to finance about 26 percent. The plan listed seven broad goals in order of priority assigned by the government. The foremost goal was to attain and sustain a 5-percent rate of GDP growth and to increase real per capita GDP by 1.3 percent per year. The second goal was to cap unemployment through the creation of more than 200,000 new jobs, of which almost 100,000 would be created through investment-led economic growth. The remainder were to be created

143

through the eviction of foreign guest workers and the emigration of Jordanian labor. The third goal was to keep growth in public and private consumption below GDP growth so that by 1990 consumption would equal production. The fourth goal was to increase domestically generated government revenue to eliminate deficit spending. The fifth goal was to reduce, but not eliminate, the goods and services trade deficit. The sixth goal was to strengthen inter-Arab economic cooperation through the establishment of international joint ventures and the reduction of trade barriers. Finally, the plan called for more equitable distribution throughout the country of the benefits of development.

The plan also listed growth targets for the various economic sectors, including 46-percent real increases in agricultural income and mining income and a 40-percent real increase in manufacturing income over the five-year period. The plan envisioned a 23-percent real increase in service sector income over the same period. Because the goods-producing sectors were to grow faster than the service sector, the latter's contribution to GDP would be reduced to about 61 percent.

### Long-Range Planning

The 1986–90 Five-Year Plan listed several longer range economic goals to be attained by the year 2000. The most important was to keep Jordan's economy growing at a rate faster than the projected rate of population growth so that gains in the standard of living would not be diluted. Assuming a drop in the birthrate over the decade beginning in 1990, this objective would entail maintaining an annual real (inflation-adjusted) growth rate in GNP of 2 percent. Another goal was to foster 6-percent annual growth of the consumer and capital goods producing sector of the economy through the year 2000, so that it would eventually account for more than 40 percent of GDP. Manufacturing value added was to be increased by substituting domestic materials for imported industrial and raw material inputs. A related goal was to reduce imported goods and services to 56 percent of GDP by the year 2000, down from 90 percent in 1985. Technical training was to continue to ensure that the labor force remained among the most skilled and professional in the Arab world. Finally, domestic savings were to finance an increasing share of investment. The plan also listed several socioeconomic priorities for the year 2000: to continue to distribute development more equitably throughout the country; to make the country's arid desert regions a focus of future development; and to ensure that all citizens had access to health, education, communications services, housing, and utilities.

# Labor Force

In the late 1980s, Jordan both exported and imported labor. The total domestic active labor force in 1987 was about 659,000 workers. Of this number, approximately 150,000 (23 percent) were foreign guest workers, and approximately 509,000 were Jordanian citizens. Concurrently, an estimated 350,000 Jordanians worked abroad. In 1988 the number of Jordanians living abroad, including dependents, was estimated at up to 1 million (see table 9, Appendix).

## Labor Emigration

The oil price increases of 1973 and 1974 stimulated tremendous labor demand in the Arab petroleum-exporting nations, which tended to have small populations. Jordan, suffering from unemployment and having an educated and skilled work force, was prepared to fill this vacuum; over the following decade, several hundred thousand Jordanians left their country to work in neighboring Arab nations (see Migration, ch. 2). About 60 percent of Jordanian emigrants worked in Saudi Arabia, about 30 percent worked in Kuwait, and most of the remainder found employment in other Persian Gulf states.

## Remittance Income

Remittances to Jordan traditionally have been the largest source of foreign currency earnings and a pillar of economic prosperity. In 1980 remittance income was US$666 million, but by 1986, according to official statistics published by the Central Bank, remittance income had increased to an estimated US$1.5 billion at the then-prevailing exchange rate. According to a UN estimate, however, Jordan's 1986 remittance income was about US$1.25 billion and subsequently declined slightly. Actual remittance income was probably higher because much of the money was funneled back to Jordan through unofficial channels. Economist Ian J. Seccombe, who has produced authoritative studies of the Jordanian economy, estimated that real remittance inflows were perhaps 60 percent higher than the official receipts. Another expert, Philip Robins, estimated that real remittances could be twice the official receipts. Official figures did not include remittances in kind, such as automobiles brought back to Jordan and then sold by returning expatriates, nor remittance income exchanged at money changers rather than at banks.

Throughout the late 1970s and early 1980s, official statistics reported that remittance income exceeded export income, in some years by over 200 percent. Remittance income accounted for between 25 percent and 33 percent of the liquid money supply, about 20 percent of the GNP, and exceeded the figures for total government development spending, or total foreign aid receipts.

As early as the mid-1970s, however, remittance income and labor export created economic and demographic distortions. The problems were so pronounced that in the 1970s Crown Prince Hasan called for the creation of an international fund to compensate Jordan and other labor-exporting nations for the negative effects of emigration.

The billions of dollars that Jordanian emigrants pumped back into their home economy fueled prolonged double-digit inflation, especially of housing prices. To rein in inflation and to attract and capture remittances, the government tried to tighten the money supply by maintaining high interest rates for bank deposits. As a consequence, loan costs rose, hampering the investment activity of businesses and farms that needed finance. Also, and because remittances tended to be spent on imported luxury goods, the merchandise trade deficit expanded.

Jordanian labor export also had an unanticipated impact on the domestic labor force. Over time, foreign demand grew disproportionately for Jordan's most highly educated and skilled technocrats and professionals, such as engineers. This "brain drain" caused a serious domestic scarcity of certain skills. At the same time, wages for unskilled labor were bid up as Jordanian employers competed for manual workers. Progress on major infrastructure development projects was hampered. For example, according to a United States government study, the labor shortage idled heavy equipment on the East Ghor (also seen as Ghawr) Canal project for up to 70 percent of the work day. Ironically, Jordan was obliged eventually to import "replacement labor"—usually low-skilled workers from Egypt and South Asia—who transferred their wages out of Jordan. The number of foreign guest workers in Jordan grew compared to the number of Jordanians working abroad. The foreign guest workers also sent home a greater proportion of their wages than did the Jordanians working abroad. In the 1970s, such wage outflows constituted less than 10 percent of Jordan's remittance inflows, but by the late 1980s they offset nearly 25 percent of inflows, neutralizing much of the benefit of labor export.

## Labor Force and Unemployment

In the late 1980s, after years of internal labor shortages, Jordan faced a looming unemployment problem. Throughout the 1970s and 1980s, Jordan sustained a high average annual population growth rate of between 3.6 and 4 percent. This growth rate was augmented by about 0.5 percent per year because of immigration into Jordan from the Israeli-occupied West Bank. In 1985 the government calculated that the work force would grow 50 percent to 750,000 by 1990. In the late 1980s, this prediction was proving accurate; about 40,000 people were joining the domestic labor pool every year. A combination of GNP growth, increased worker efficiency, emigration, and attrition created jobs for most new workers, and unemployment was kept to about 9 percent.

Experts believed, however, that unemployment and underemployment would probably increase rapidly in the 1990s as the labor pool continued to grow more quickly than labor demand. In 1986 only about 20 percent of Jordanian citizens worked or sought work, a figure expected to grow dramatically as the youthful population aged. In addition, because of the recession in Saudi Arabia and the Gulf states caused by slumping oil prices, Jordanians who had been working abroad were repatriating and seeking work at home. The Ministry of Labor estimated that about 2,500 Jordanians returned from abroad in 1986. Another source, however, estimated the number of returning workers and their dependents at 35,000 in 1986. Moreover, women—who in 1986 made up only a little more than 12 percent of the working population but almost 50 percent of secondary school and college enrollment—were expected to attempt to join the labor force in growing numbers (see Women and Work, ch. 2). The work force had some elasticity in that approximately 150,000 foreign guest workers could be sent home and their jobs given to Jordanian citizens; but even if all guest workers were repatriated, unemployment would persist. By one estimate that did not include repatriating Jordanian workers, unemployment could grow to 30 percent of the work force in the 1990s in the absence of extraordinary government action.

Therefore, although aware of the problems caused by labor emigration, the government remained far more concerned about unemployment—and declining remittances—than about the problem of emigration. As of 1989, the government had stated explicitly that it would continue to permit unrestricted worker emigration.

## Industry

Manufacturing contributed about 14 percent of GDP in the late 1980s. Much manufacturing activity related to exploitation of natural resources and to the mining sector. Although extractive industries

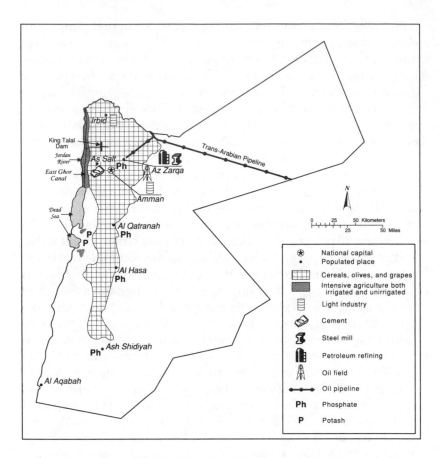

*Figure 8. Land Use and Other Economic Activities, 1989*

were distributed throughout the country, about 90 percent of both small and large manufacturing entities were concentrated in the north, in an industrial belt between Amman and Az Zarqa (see fig. 8). Between 1975 and 1985, total manufacturing value added grew at roughly the same rate as GNP, at an annual average rate of 13 percent through 1980, then decelerating to about 5 percent. Employment in manufacturing grew slowly, and in the late 1980s was estimated at slightly more than 50,000, less than 10 percent of the working population. For decades the government had emphasized industrial manufacturing development over other economic sectors, but growing excess industrial capacity prompted a greater priority to agriculture and water resource development in the 1986–90 Five-Year Plan.

## Manufacturing

The manufacturing sector had two tiers. On one level were the large-scale, wholly or partially state-owned industrial establishments that produced chemicals, petrochemicals, fertilizers, and mineral products. These manufacturing entities included the "big five" companies that constituted the pillars of the industrial base: the Jordan Phosphate Mines Company, the Jordan Fertilizer Industries Company, the Arab Potash Company, Intermediate Petrochemical Industries, the Jordan Cement Factories Company, and also a recently enlarged oil refinery at Az Zarqa that employed about 3,000 persons. The chemical products sector employed about 4,000 workers at about seventy facilities. Because these industries were established to process the products of Jordan's mining and extractive sector, it was difficult to distinguish between the industrial and natural resource sectors of the economy (see Natural Resources, this ch.).

Petroleum refining contributed 39 percent to gross output manufacturing; fertilizers, potash, and other nonmetallic minerals, 13 percent; industrial chemicals, about 8 percent; and iron, steel, and fabricated metal products, about 10 percent. Thus, about 70 percent of total manufacturing output was closely linked to the mining and extractive sector. The high contribution of these industries to the total value of manufacturing output resulted in part from the high underlying value of the natural resource inputs on which they were based. The same industries accounted for about 57 percent of total value added in manufacturing (see table 10, Appendix).

On the other level were small or medium-sized light manufacturing entities, many privately owned, that produced a wide array of consumer products. Many of these entities were cottage industries or small bazaar workshops. By one estimate, in 1984 more than 75 percent of the approximately 8,500 manufacturing companies employed fewer than five persons each. The most important, in order of contribution to gross output value, were food processing, tobacco and cigarettes, paper and packaging, beverages, furniture, textiles, and plastics. These companies and other smaller industries such as publishing, glass and rubber products, electrical equipment, and machinery—each of which contributed less than 1 percent of total manufacturing output value—together contributed about 30 percent of gross manufacturing output and 43 percent of manufacturing value added.

## Industrial Policy

Like most nations with ambitious development plans, Jordan pinned its hopes on growth, particularly in the export of manufactured goods. Although high tariff and nontariff barriers sheltered selected industries from competition from lower cost imports, both nominal and effective rates of protection generally were low by the standards of developing economies. On the one hand, effective protection was high for paper and wood products, furniture, and apparel. On the other hand, imports of machinery, electrical equipment, and transport equipment were effectively subsidized. In view of its sustained high level of import of manufactured goods, observers viewed Jordan's pursuit of import-substitution industrialization as moderate.

Jordan's import policy theoretically was designed to promote domestic manufacturing industries by ensuring their access to cheaper imported capital goods, raw materials, and other intermediate inputs rather than by granting them monopoly markets. The government believed that development of a domestic manufacturing base had to be led by exports because Jordan's small population could not generate enough consumer demand for manufacturing plants to achieve economies of scale or scope. In some cases, consumer demand was too low to justify building even the smallest possible facility. Domestic consumer demand alone was insufficient to support some manufacturing industries despite the relatively high wages paid to Jordanian workers; the high wages resulted in increased product costs and diminished export sales of manufactured goods. In the late 1980s, according to a Jordanian economist, the country continued to experience constant returns to scale despite its significant exports. Essentially, Jordan was still in the first stage of industrial production, in which the per unit costs were high because of limited output.

The relative contributions to manufacturing expansion made by domestic demand growth, export growth, and import substitution were difficult to assess accurately. Growth in domestic demand stimulated almost 60 percent of manufacturing expansion, export growth contributed a moderate 12 percent, and import substitution contributed nearly 30 percent. But exports accounted for about 33 percent of the growth of intermediate goods (fertilizers and other inputs) industries and about 25 percent of the growth of consumer goods industries. In contrast, external demand contributed virtually nothing to growth in the metal products, iron and steel, rubber, and glass industries; import substitution, domestic demand growth, or a combination of the two accounted for all domestic manufacturing growth, resulting in self-sufficiency. In the case of the furniture, apparel, textile, and industrial chemical industries, however, either increased domestic demand, increased foreign demand, or a combination of both led to simultaneous domestic manufacturing growth and increased imports.

150

In the 1970s and early 1980s, the government concentrated on developing the first tier of the manufacturing sector—the production of chemicals and fertilizers—because, unlike consumer goods, these commodities appeared to have guaranteed export markets. The government followed this policy although the second tier of the manufacturing sector—the production of consumer goods— had significantly higher value added. The government strategy was to increase value added in exported commodities by producing and exporting processed commodities, such as fertilizers from raw phosphates and metal pipes from ore and ingots. Because some other Middle Eastern and West Asian nations had adopted the same strategy, competition for markets increased at the same time that demand slumped. Jordan suffered from declining terms of trade as the value of its processed commodity exports fell relative to the value of its consumer and capital goods imports.

In the late 1980s, therefore, Jordan was reassessing its industrial strategy and searching for potential areas of comparative advantage in exporting light-manufactured goods and consumer and capital goods that had higher value added. Consumer goods were protected in many foreign markets, and Jordanian exports as a percentage of output in the consumer goods sector ranged only between 2 percent and 9 percent, as opposed to a range of 12 percent to 35 percent in the extractive industry based manufacturing sector. Accordingly, Jordan hoped to take advantage of its educated work force and increase the manufacture of capital goods that were either technical in nature or required engineering and technical expertise to manufacture. Those types of products had more appeal in foreign markets. To promote such development, the government established the Higher Council for Science and Technology, which in turn founded the private-sector Jordan Technology Group as an umbrella organization for new high-technology companies.

Throughout the 1970s and 1980s, the profitability of some capital goods industries, measured as a ratio of both gross output value and of value added, fell steeply compared to profit ratios in the commodities and consumer goods sectors. During the same period, profitability of the natural resources sector declined minimally, while profitability of the consumer goods sector rose. The capital goods sector had been much more profitable than the natural resources sector; but by the late 1980s, the two sectors were equally profitable. The main cause of the plunge in profitability among capital goods apparently was price inflation of imported intermediate inputs. Especially affected, for example, were the electrical equipment and plastics industries—precisely the type of technical industries that Jordan envisaged as important to its economic future.

The drop in profitability was not irremediable, however, and government officials continued to be optimistic about prospects in technical industries, particularly those that were skill intensive and labor intensive rather than capital intensive.

The pharmaceuticals and veterinary medicines industries were examples of the new direction of industrial development policy. The government-established Arab Pharmaceutical Manufacturing Company exported more than 70 percent of its production in 1987. A half-dozen other drug and medical equipment companies were garnering a large share of the Middle Eastern market in the late 1980s. Engineering industries also were a development target. In 1985 this manufacturing sector accounted for about 9 percent of manufacturing value added, 14 percent of total manufacturing employment, and about US$5 million in export sales. About 95 percent of the sector was devoted to basic fabrication of metal sheets, pipes, and parts. Jordan also exported in limited quantities more sophisticated products, such as domestic appliances, commercial vehicles, electrical equipment, and machinery; eventually it wanted to produce and export scientific equipment and consumer electronics. Another developing industry was plastic containers and packaging, of which about one-quarter of output was exported.

The strategy to boost manufactured exports ultimately had to take into account the low manufacturing productivity growth of the 1980s. Average annual productivity growth was estimated at 2 percent to 3 percent, and in 1986 it was a mere 1.4 percent. In several specific sectors, productivity was actually falling. Because this low or negative growth occurred at a time when labor productivity was increasing rapidly, it was attributable to some combination of insufficient investment and stagnant domestic and foreign demand. Jordan's average industrial capacity utilization, according to a UN report, was about 57 percent, but varied widely according to industry. Pent up consumer demand for some products was great enough so that any increase in capacity could be translated automatically into increased production and sales. Capacity utilization was almost 100 percent for certain chemical and consumer goods factories, indicating that more investment might be warranted, whereas capacity utilization in the production of certain household furnishings and building products was very low, suggesting suppressed or little demand. Spare production capacity meant that manufacturers would be able to meet sudden demand surges. In 1987, following a period of declining production, Egypt agreed to import construction materials, and output of cement and metal pipes jumped 32 percent and 48 percent, respectively. Production of paper and cardboard also increased about 36

*Fertilizer plant, Al Aqabah*

percent as the packaging industry developed, but production of detergent dropped 8 percent and production of textiles dropped 13 percent, leaving spare capacity. The variability of capacity utilization indicated the problems that the government had to confront in forecasting domestic and foreign demand for manufactured goods.

## Electricity Generation

Between 1980 and 1985, per capita consumption of electricity doubled from 500 kilowatt hours per year to 1,000 kilowatt-hours per year. The demand increase reflected the doubling in the number of households supplied with electricity as rural villages were electrified. By 1985 about 400,000 households, or 97 percent of the population, had access to electricity. Electricity generation increased to a 712-megawatt capacity in 1987 and production of 3.2 million megawatt-hours. After rural electrification was completed, growth in capacity outpaced growth in consumption, which was limited by conservation measures to about 3 percent to 4 percent per year. Roughly 40 percent of the electric power generated was used by industry, 30 percent was used by private citizens, 13 percent was used by commercial businesses, and the remainder was used by water pumping stations. The Hussein Thermal Power Station at Az Zarqa historically had produced more than 70 percent of the country's electricity, but at the end of 1987, the opening of the Al Aqabah Thermal Power Station added 260 megawatts, boosting Jordan's generating capacity to 972 megawatts and ensuring self-sufficiency into the early 1990s. A 400-kilovolt transmission line connected Al Aqabah and Amman. The Al Aqabah plant was to be expanded to a total capacity of 520 megawatts by the mid-1990s, and was planned eventually to supply 1,540 megawatts.

Although Jordan depended entirely on imported oil to fire its generating plants in 1988, the government planned to reduce this dependency. The 1988 discovery of natural gas at Rishah, near the Iraqi border, led to feasibility studies of retrofitting the Az Zarqa plant with gas turbine generators. A 20-megawatt hydroelectric station was to be included as part of the planned Al Wahdah Dam on the Yarmuk River. Discoveries of shale oil in the southern Wadi as Sultani region kindled hopes of a 100-megawatt shale-fired electric plant in that area. In 1989 Jordan also was prospecting for underground geothermal sources.

## Transportation and Communications

An underdeveloped system of transportation and communications for many years impeded Jordanian economic development, hampering in particular efforts to attract foreign direct investment and to conduct transit trade. The government lavished spending on transportation and communication facilities in the late 1970s and early 1980s. By 1989 in many respects Jordan had surpassed its Arab neighbors in such facilities. Most such development, however, has been confined to a narrow north-south corridor between Amman and Al Aqabah.

### Transportation

The transportation system in Jordan comprised roads, railroads, airports, and one port. Road quality varied widely, and newer railroad lines were used primarily for transporting phosphates. One national airline and two smaller airline companies served the public.

#### Roads

In 1989 the Jordanian road network, administered by the Ministry of Transportation, was more than 7,500 kilometers long. Of the total system, 5,500 kilometers were asphalted and the remainder were composed of gravel and crushed stone. The backbone of the road system was the 320-kilometer-long Desert Highway running from Amman to Al Aqabah (see fig. 9). A second major highway ran east to west from Al Mafraq to the Iraqi border. Because these two highways were also the two main parts of the transit trade route between the port of Al Aqabah and Iraq, they often were congested by truck traffic. Jordan's road construction plans focused on building ring roads, bypasses, and overpasses in the vicinity of Amman, Al Aqabah, and other major cities to divert this truck traffic and eliminate bottlenecks.

The quality of the major traffic arteries varied greatly. Only about 50 percent of the Desert Highway was more than two lanes wide. A four-lane highway ran south from the Syrian border near Ar Ramtha to Jarash, but the road between Jarash and Amman was winding and narrow. Moreover, the common practice among freight companies of grossly overloading their trucks had resulted in severe damage to many stretches of road. This practice led in 1988 to increased government enforcement of load limits and the imposition of penalties that could effectively put companies that violated the limits out of business.

The freight and trucking sector was overdeveloped in the 1980s. Competition among many private freight companies and several large government-owned entities led to price-cutting and excess capacity. The Iraqi-Jordanian Land Transport Company (IJLTC) was the largest of the government-owned freight companies. Established in 1980, in 1987 it carried 1.3 million tons of goods and almost 70,000 passengers between Al Aqabah and Iraq. In 1988 the IJLTC had a fleet of about 900 trucks, 1,400 employees, and profits of over JD3 million. The Jordanian-Syrian Land Transport Company, established in 1976, was smaller but organized along similar lines. In 1988 trucks made more than 13,000 trips between Al Aqabah and Baghdad, of which Jordanian trucks made 7,500 trips.

In 1987 about 250,000 vehicles were registered in Jordan, an increase from 60,000 vehicles ten years previously. This figure included about 131,000 passenger cars, 13,000 taxis, 4,000 buses, and 8,500 heavy trucks of various types.

## Railroads

Jordan had 619 kilometers of single-track narrow gauge (1.05 meters) railroad tracks. The main system was the Hedjaz-Jordan Railway, part of the old Ottoman-era Hijaz Railway that had once connected Istanbul and the Arabian Peninsula. It ran north-south through the length of the country and lay thirty kilometers east of the Desert Highway. Newer spur and branch lines constituted the Al Aqabah Railway Corporation, and connected Al Aqabah's port and mines to the main north-south axis. Both railroad entities came under the jurisdiction of the Ministry of Transportation. The newer system was used almost exclusively for transport of phosphates from the mines at Al Hasa and Wadi al Abyad to Al Aqabah.

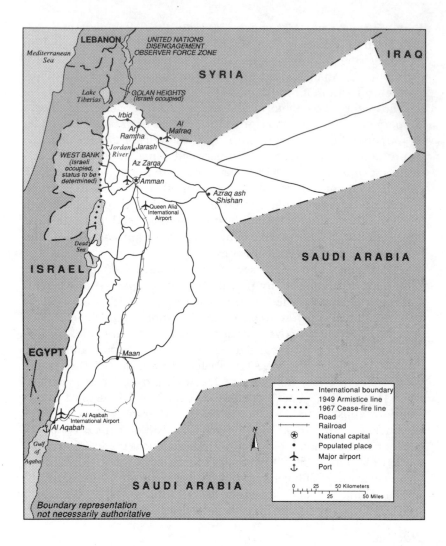

*Figure 9. Transportation System, 1989*

In 1987, about 2.6 million tons of freight and 20,000 passengers were conveyed by rail. Rolling stock included 26 locomotives and 600 freight, passenger, and tanker cars. The government envisioned in the late 1980s upgrading capacity to 4.5 million tons a year.

## Ports

Located on the Gulf of Aqaba, which leads to the Red Sea, Al Aqabah was Jordan's only port. The modern port, established in the 1950s, was under the authority of the Al Aqabah Ports Corporation, part of the Ministry of Transportation. The port grew tremendously in the 1970s and especially in the early 1980s as transit trade through Al Aqabah became one of Iraq's few lifelines to the outside world during its war with Iran. In 1985, according to the government, 55 percent to 60 percent of Al Aqabah's total cargo capacity was devoted to transit trade with Iraq. Another estimate placed this figure at 70 percent. Port facilities included seventeen berths, two of them floating, that were specially equipped for loading or unloading general cargo, crude oil, and phosphates. One of the newest berths, completed in 1985, was 580 meters long and configured for handling roll on/roll off cargo and container cargo. Associated facilities and services included warehouses and railheads. Five new tugboats were ordered in 1988 to escort cargo ships in the Gulf of Aqaba, which would bring to twelve the total number of tugs. In 1987, more than 2,600 vessels called at Al Aqabah, loading 8.7 million tons of freight and unloading about 11.3 million tons. The combined total tonnage represented a 19-percent increase over the previous year.

Jordan has also established a small merchant marine. The National Maritime Company had four merchant vessels with a combined freight capacity of 71,400 tons. Also, the Syrian-Jordanian Marine Transport Company operated two freighters with a combined capacity of 6,000 tons that transported about 70,000 tons of freight annually between the Middle East and Western Europe. Since 1985 Jordan and Egypt have jointly operated an intermittent bridge and ferry service capable of carrying trucks and cars from Al Aqabah to the Sinai port of Nuwaybi. The service has cut transit time between Al Aqabah and Cairo in half, to about nine hours.

### Civil Aviation and Airports

Royal Jordanian Airlines—known until 1987 as Alia—was the national carrier. Wholly owned by the government and operating since 1946, Royal Jordanian by 1988 had become one of the major Middle Eastern air carriers. From the mid-1970s to the early 1980s, passenger and freight traffic and reported profits grew almost 25 percent annually (although fuel and other hidden subsidies made calculation of actual profitability impossible). Annual traffic growth tapered off to single-digit figures after 1983 and the airline experienced a US$30 million loss in 1984. A budget cut of almost 10 percent in 1986 resulted in staff and other overhead cuts that apparently made the carrier more efficient, and in that year it reported a profit of US$5.6 million. In 1986 Royal Jordanian carried more than 1 million passengers and 42,500 tons of cargo. Load factors averaged over 48 percent. Jordan also had established some of the most advanced flight crew training and maintenance and repair facilities in the Middle East, and it sold these services to African and other Arab airlines.

In the late 1980s, Royal Jordanian was in the midst of a major program of long-term expansion and financial restructuring. The program included the low-cost lease and purchase of new Airbus Industrie airliners. Royal Jordanian also was negotiating an agreement to sell and lease back some of its Boeing and Lockheed aircraft to cut corporate debt. After restructuring the balance sheet, the government planned to offer Royal Jordanian for sale to its 4,600 employees and to private sector investors, retaining only a 15-percent stake.

In 1988 the Royal Jordanian fleet consisted of two Boeing 747–200s, eight Lockheed L–1011 Tristars, three Boeing 727–200As, and three Boeing 707–320Cs. In 1987 Royal Jordanian acquired the first two of six Airbus Industrie A–310–300s, which were to replace its Boeing 707s. Royal Jordanian also had an option to purchase six Airbus Industrie A–320s to replace its Boeing 727s over the decade from 1990 to 2000, and planned eventually to phase out use of its Lockheeds in favor of new Airbus Industrie A–340s.

In 1987 Royal Jordanian added Moscow and Calcutta to the more than forty worldwide destinations it already served. New scheduled flights were planned to East Asia, including Seoul, Tokyo, Manila, and Sydney, as well as to Rio de Janeiro via Abidjan.

Jordan had two other minor airlines: Arab Air Cargo and Arab Wings. Arab Air Cargo was owned in equal shares by Royal Jordanian and Iraqi Airways. Arab Wings, a passenger charter service, was owned by Royal Jordanian (88 percent) and the Sultanate of Oman (12 percent). The latter company also included a flying ambulance service. There were nineteen usable airfields in Jordan in 1988, of which fourteen had permanent surface runways. Of these, two near Amman were major airfields: the Queen Alia International Airport, opened in 1983 and located at Al Jizah, thirty kilometers south of Amman, and the old international airport at Marka, King Abdullah Airport, used primarily by the Royal Jordanian Air Force.

## Telecommunications

The Jordan Telecommunications Corporation (TCC), a wholly government-owned semi-autonomous entity under the Ministry of Communications, was in charge of providing domestic and international telecommunications services in 1988. Since 1971 the TCC

*Queen Alia International Airport at Al Jizah, south of Amman,
showing Royal Jordanian Airlines airplanes*

had exercised a monopoly over all forms of public telecommunications, including telephone, telex, telegraph, facsimile, and television transmissions. The TCC was profitable and a net contributor to the budget. In 1988 the government was moving forward cautiously with plans to privatize the company in stages—using as its model the privatization of British Telecom—and planned eventually to sell all or part of the equity to public stockholders.

In the 1980s, TCC increased the number of connected telephone lines by almost 20 percent per year while introducing technological improvements such as digital switching and microwave links. International direct dialing was introduced in 1982; in 1989, Jordan had one Atlantic Ocean International Telecommunications Satellite Organization (Intelsat) station, one Indian Ocean Intelsat station, and one Arab Satellite Organization (Arabsat) station. In 1988, more than 200,000 direct lines were in service, with about 85,000 applicants on a waiting list, so that only about 70 percent of demand was satisfied. A private citizen waited about five years for a line, but most businesses could obtain a line quickly by paying a surcharge to avoid the waiting list. Line density in 1988 was 7 percent of the population, better than in most countries with similar per capita GNP. Telephone service was concentrated in Amman, where more than 60 percent of all lines were installed. Altogether, about 75 percent of Jordanian villages and cities had access to telephone service. Despite 12-percent forecast annual demand growth, line density was expected to grow to 12 percent of the population by the early 1990s because of a planned US$340 million investment in new equipment and services. Local calls in Amman were free and were subsidized by exorbitant international rates. In 1987, however, because of protests by businesses and private citizens, international rates were cut drastically (up to 50 percent, depending on the country called).

## Natural Resources

Jordan's mineral wealth and extractive industries constituted a major source of its gross output manufacturing as well as of its total value added in manufacturing (see Manufacturing, this ch.). Such natural resources also represented a significant element in Jordan's exports.

### Phosphates

Phosphate deposits were Jordan's primary natural resource and a major source of export income. Estimates of Jordan's proven, indicated, and probable reserves ranged from 1.5 billion to 2.5 billion tons. Even if the more conservative figure were the most accurate, Jordan could produce at its present rate for hundreds of years. Total 1987 production was 6.7 million tons, of which 5.7 million tons were exported as raw rock. The remainder was upgraded into fertilizer at several facilities and either retained for domestic use or exported. Jordan was the third ranked phosphate exporter in the world, after Morocco and the United States, and it had the capacity to produce well over 8 million tons annually. In 1986 phosphate sales generated US$185 million in income, which made up 25 percent of export earnings and gave Jordan a 10-percent share of the world market. Sales by volume in 1986 increased approximately 14 percent over the previous year, but profits rose only 4 percent, an indication of the depressed price for phosphates on the world market. In 1986 long-term agreements were concluded with Thailand and Yugoslavia that assured the added export of almost 1 million tons per year.

In 1985 the Jordan Phosphate Mines Company closed the country's original phosphate mine at Ar Rusayfah near Amman because it produced low-grade rock; this left major phosphate mines in operation at Al Hasa and Wadi Abu Ubaydah near Al Qatranah in central Jordan, and a new high-grade mine at Ash Shidiyah, forty kilometers south of Maan, where according to one estimate, reserves were more than 1 billion tons.

Among Jordan's major development projects was the construction of a US$450-million processing facility near Al Aqabah, completed in 1982, to produce monoammonium phosphate and diammonium phosphate fertilizer, and other chemicals such as phosphoric acid from raw phosphate rock. The project was envisioned as a boon to the extractive industry because it would increase value added in its major export commodity. Instead, it became an encumbrance as the prices of sulfur and ammonia (which Jordan had to import to produce the diammonium phosphate) rose while the price of diammonium phosphate on the world market slumped. Production costs of diammonium phosphate at various times between 1985 and 1987 ranged from 110 percent to 160 percent of world market price for the product. Nevertheless, Jordan remained cautiously optimistic about the long-term prospects for the fertilizer industry because of its geographic proximity to the large Asian markets. In 1985 Jordan exported more than 500,000 tons of fertilizer, primarily to India and China.

## Potash

Potash was the other major component of Jordan's mining sector. A US$480-million potash extraction facility at Al Aghwar al Janubiyah (also known as Ghor as Safi) on the Dead Sea, which was operated by the Arab Potash Company, produced 1.2 million tons of potash in 1987 and yielded earnings of almost US$100 million. The facility processed the potash into potassium chloride. Future plans included the production of other industrial chemicals such as potassium sulfate, bromine, magnesium oxide, and soda ash. As in the case of phosphates, India was a major customer, buying almost 33 percent of output. Jordan was the world's lowest cost producer, in part because it used solar evaporation. There was lingering concern that possible Israeli construction of a Mediterranean-Dead Sea canal would dilute the Dead Sea, making extraction far more expensive.

## Oil and Gas

By the late 1980s, a twenty-year-long period of exploration had resulted in the discovery and exploitation of three oil wells in the Hamzah field in the Wadi al Azraq region west of Amman that yielded only a small fraction of domestic energy requirements. Jordan also had just discovered gas from what appeared to be a field in the eastern panhandle near the Iraqi-Saudi Arabian border. Jordan remained almost entirely dependent on oil imported from Saudi Arabia and Iraq to meet its energy needs. Jordan refined the imported crude petroleum at its Az Zarqa refinery. In 1985 the Az Zarqa refinery processed about 2.6 million tons of petroleum. Of this total, about 1.8 million tons came from Saudi Arabia, 700,000 tons from Iraq, and 2,800 tons from Jordan's Hamzah field. An additional 400,000 tons of fuel were imported from Iraq. The Saudi Arabian oil was transported to Jordan via the Trans-Arabian Pipeline (Tapline). Oil from Iraq was transported by tanker truck. About 40 percent of oil imports were used by the transport sector, 25 percent to generate electricity, 16 percent by industry, and the remainder for domestic use.

Jordan's oil bill was difficult to calculate and was subject to fluctuation as the Organization of Petroleum Exporting Countries (OPEC) changed its posted price for crude. Since 1985, barter agreements with Iraq to trade goods for crude oil have removed some of Jordan's oil bill from the balance sheet. Jordan also varied its imports of crude oil and other, more expensive fuels, depending on its immediate fuel demand and its refinery capacity, and cut consumption through conservation measures and price increases.

The oil bill remained very large, however. A major irony of Jordan's energy dependence was that despite—or because of—its proximity to its main oil suppliers, it was sometimes obliged to pay extremely inflated prices for its oil. In mid-1986, for example, Saudi Arabia charged Jordan the official OPEC price of US$28 per barrel at a time when oil was selling on the international spot market for US$10 per barrel. Saudi Arabia's motives were perhaps as much political as economic, in that it wanted to maintain the integrity of the OPEC floor price for oil. Dependent on Saudi financial aid, Jordan could not alienate its patron by shopping on the world market. In 1985 estimates of Jordan's oil import bill ranged between US$500 million and US$650 million. At that time, imported oil constituted approximately 20 percent of total imports and offset 80 percent of the value of commodity exports. In 1986 and 1987, Jordan's estimated fuel bill declined considerably, to less than US$300 million. The drop resulted from barter with Iraq, decreased fuel imports, and OPEC's reduction of its official price of crude oil to bring it into line with world market prices. As prices dropped, the Jordanian government—which had subsidized domestic fuel prices—was able to cut the subsidy from US$70 million to US$14 million instead of passing on savings to consumers.

Since 1984 Saudi Arabia has forced Jordan to underwrite the entire cost of operating the Tapline. This has added more than US$25 million per year to Jordan's oil bill. During the Iran-Iraq War, therefore, Jordan tried to persuade Iraq to obtain an alternative oil outlet by building a pipeline across Jordan to Al Aqabah.

*Phosphate mine, southern Jordan*
*Unloading phosphates, Al Aqabah Port*

The project foundered because of Iraqi concern that the line was vulnerable to Israeli attack and embarrassment over disclosure of Jordanian attempts to obtain a secret Israeli pledge not to attack the line.

The 1980 discovery of from 10 billion to 40 billion tons of shale oil deposits in the Wadi as Sultani area raised Jordanian hopes of greater self-sufficiency, but there were doubts that large-scale exploitation of the deposits would be commercially viable in the near future. Since 1985 Jordan has attempted to interest Western oil companies in exploring for oil. Amoco, Hunt Petroleum, Petro-Canada, Petrofina of Belgium, and the Japanese National Oil Company were conducting survey work in Jordan in the late 1980s. Jordanian planners hoped that potentially extensive natural gas reserves discovered at Rishah in eastern Jordan could eventually replace oil for electricity generation, cutting imports by one-quarter.

## Water

The government was concerned that scarcity of water could ultimately place a cap on both agricultural and industrial development. Although no comprehensive hydrological survey had been conducted by the late 1980s, some experts believed that demand for water could outstrip supply by the early 1990s. Average annual rainfall was about 8 billion cubic meters, most of which evaporated; the remainder flowed into rivers and other catchments or seeped into the ground to replenish large underground aquifers of fossil water that could be tapped by wells. Annual renewable surface and subterranean water supply was placed at 1.2 billion cubic meters. Total demand was more difficult to project. In 1985 Jordan consumed about 520 million cubic meters of water, of which 111 million cubic meters went for industrial and domestic use, and 409 million cubic meters went for agricultural use. By 1995 it was estimated that domestic and industrial consumption would almost double and agricultural demand would increase by 50 percent, so that total demand would be about 820 million cubic meters. By the year 2000, projected demand was estimated at 934 million cubic meters. Jordan, therefore, would need to harness almost all of its annual renewable water resources of 1.2 billion cubic meters to meet future demand, a process that would inevitably be marked by diminishing marginal returns as ever more expensive and remotely situated projects yielded less and less added water. The process also could spark regional disputes—especially with Israel—over riparian rights.

The government had completed several major infrastructure projects in an effort to make maximum use of limited water supplies, and was considering numerous other projects in the late 1980s. The King Talal Dam, built in 1978 on the Az Zarqa River, formed Jordan's major reservoir. In the late 1980s, a project to raise the height of the dam by ten meters so as to increase the reservoir's capacity from 56 million cubic meters to 90 million cubic meters was almost complete. A second major construction project underway in 1989 was the Wadi al Arabah Dam to capture flood waters of the Yarmuk River and the Wadi al Jayb (also known as Wadi al Arabah) in a 17-million cubic meter reservoir. These two dams and innumerable other catchments and tunnels collected water from tributaries that flowed toward the Jordan River and fed the 50-kilometer-long East Ghor Canal (see fig. 4). Plans called for the eventual extension of the East Ghor Canal to the Dead Sea region, which would almost double its length. In 1989 about fifteen dams were in various stages of design or construction, at a total projected cost of JD64 million.

By far the largest of these projects was a joint Jordanian-Syrian endeavor to build a 100-meter-high dam on the Yarmuk River. The project, which had been contemplated since the 1950s but had foundered repeatedly because of political disputes, was revived in 1988 after the thaw in Jordanian-Syrian relations and appeared to be progressing in early 1989. Called the Maqarin Dam in previous development plans, it was renamed the Al Wahdah Dam to reflect the political rapprochement that made construction feasible (Al Wahdah means unity). The dam was to create a reservoir of 250 million cubic meters. The Jordanian estimate of the cost, which Jordan was to bear alone, was US$397 million. Independent estimates placed the figure at more than US$500 million. Building time was estimated at two years after the planned 1989 starting date, but new political problems threatened to stall construction. In 1988 the United States attempted to mediate between Jordan and Israel, which feared the dam would limit its own potential water supply; Syria, however, refused to join any tripartite negotiations.

In 1989 serious consideration was being given to two proposals to construct major pipelines to import water. Completion of either project could be a partial solution to Jordan's water scarcity. Because of cost, however, neither project was likely to be constructed in the near future. One project was to construct a multibillion dollar 650-kilometer-long pipeline from the Euphrates River in Iraq. The pipeline would supply Jordan with about 160 million cubic meters of water per year. The other project, on which feasibility studies had been conducted, was to construct a 2,700-kilometer-long pipeline from rivers in Turkey, through Syria and Jordan, to Saudi Arabia. Jordan could draw an allotment of about 220 million cubic meters per year from this second pipeline. The estimated US$20 billion cost of the latter project was thought to be prohibitive.

## Agriculture

Agriculture contributed substantially to the economy at the time of Jordan's independence, but it subsequently suffered a decades-long steady decline. In the early 1950s, agriculture constituted almost 40 percent of GNP; on the eve of the June 1967 War, it was 17 percent. By the mid-1980s, agriculture's share of GNP was only about 6 percent. In contrast, in Syria and Egypt agriculture constituted more than 20 percent of GNP in the 1980s. Several factors contributed to this downward trend. With the Israeli occupation of the West Bank, Jordan lost prime farmland. Starting in the mid-1970s, Jordanian labor emigration also hastened the decline of agriculture. Many Jordanian peasants abandoned farming to take more lucrative jobs abroad, sometimes as soldiers in the armies of Saudi Arabia and the Persian Gulf states or in service industries in those countries. Others migrated to cities where labor shortages had led to higher wages for manual workers. Deserted farms were built over as urban areas expanded. As the Jordanian government drove up interest rates to attract remittance income, farm credit tightened, which made it difficult for farmers to buy seed and fertilizer.

In striking contrast to Egypt and Iraq, where redistribution of land irrigated by the Nile and Euphrates rivers was a pivotal political, social, and economic issue, land tenure was never an important concern in Jordan. More than 150,000 foreign laborers—mainly Egyptians—worked in Jordan in 1988, most on farms. Moreover, since the early 1960s, the government has continuously created irrigated farmland from what was previously arid desert, further reducing competition for arable land. Ownership of rain-fed land was not subject to special restrictions. Limited land reform occurred in the early 1960s when, as the government irrigated the Jordan River valley, it bought plots larger than twenty hectares, subdivided them, and resold them to former tenants in three-hectare to five-hectare plots. Because the land had not been very valuable before the government irrigated it, this process was accomplished with little controversy. In general, the government has aimed to keep land in larger plots to encourage efficiency and mechanized farming. The government made permanently indivisible the irrigated land that it granted or sold so as to nullify traditional Islamic inheritance laws that tended to fragment land.

*Grain silos, Al Aqabah*

## Agricultural Development

Although the agricultural sector's share of GNP declined in comparison with other sectors of the economy, farming remained economically important and production grew in absolute terms. Between 1975 and 1985, total production of cereals and beans rose by almost 150 percent, and production of vegetables rose by more than 200 percent, almost all of the increase occurring between 1975 and 1980. Production of certain cash export crops, such as olives, tobacco, and fruit, more than quadrupled. Because farming had remained labor intensive, by one estimate about 20 percent to 30 percent of the male work force continued to depend on farming for its livelihood.

Even with increased production, the failure of agriculture to keep pace with the growth of the rest of the economy, however, resulted in an insufficient domestic food supply. Jordan thus needed to import such staples as cereals, grains, and meat. Wheat imports averaged about 350,000 tons per year, ten to twenty times the amount produced domestically. Red meat imports cost more than JD30 million per year, and onion and potato imports cost between JD3 million and JD4 million per year. Between 1982 and 1985, the total food import bill averaged about JD180 million per year, accounting for more than 15 percent of total imports during the period. At the same time, cash crop exports—for example, the export of

167

7,000 tons of food to Western Europe in 1988—generated about JD40 million per year, yielding a net food deficit of JD140 million. One emerging problem in the late 1980s was the erosion of Jordan's traditional agricultural export market. The wealthy oil-exporting states of the Arabian Peninsula, concerned about their "food security," were starting to replace imports from Jordan with food produced domestically at costs far higher than world market prices, using expensive desalinated water.

## Cropping and Production

Observers expected food imports to remain necessary into the indefinite future. Much of Jordan's soil was not arable even if water were available; by several estimates, between 6 percent and 7 percent of Jordan's territory was arable, a figure that was being revised slowly upward as dry-land farming techniques became more sophisticated. In 1989 the scarcity of water, the lack of irrigation, and economic problems—rather than the lack of arable land—set a ceiling on agricultural potential (see Water, this ch.). Only about 20 percent of Jordan's geographic area received more than 200 millimeters of rainfall per year, the minimum required for rain-fed agriculture. Much of this land was otherwise unsuitable for agriculture. Moreover, rainfall varied greatly from year to year, so crops were prone to be ruined by periodic drought.

In 1986 only about 5.5 percent (about 500,000 hectares), of the East Bank's (see Glossary) 9.2 million hectares were under cultivation. Fewer than 40,000 hectares were irrigated, almost all in the Jordan River valley. Because arable, rain-fed land was exploited extensively, future growth of agricultural production depended on increased irrigation. Estimates of the additional area that could be irrigated were Jordan to maximize its water resources ranged between 65,000 and 100,000 hectares.

Most agricultural activity was concentrated in two areas. In rain-fed northern and central areas of higher elevation, wheat, barley, and other field crops such as tobacco, lentils, barley, and chick-peas were cultivated; olives also were produced in these regions. Because of periodic drought and limited area, the rain-fed uplands did not support sufficient output of cereal crops to meet domestic demand (see table 11, Appendix).

In the more fertile Jordan River valley, fruits and vegetables including cucumbers, tomatoes, eggplants, melons, bananas, and citrus crops often were produced in surplus amounts. The Jordan River valley received little rain, and the main source of irrigation water was the East Ghor Canal, which was built in 1963 with United States aid.

Although the country's ultimate agricultural potential was small, economic factors apparently limited production more than environmental constraints, as reflected by up to 100,000 hectares of potentially arable land that lay fallow in the late 1980s. The government has expressed considerable concern about its "food security" and its high food import bill, and it was implementing plans to increase crop production in the 1990s. Growth in agricultural output was only about 4 percent during the 1980–85 Five-Year Plan, despite investment of approximately JD80 million during the period, indicating the slow pace of progress.

In the late 1980s, Jordan was implementing a two-pronged agricultural development policy. The long-term strategy was to increase the total area under cultivation by better harnessing water resources to increase irrigation of arid desert areas for the cultivation of cereal crops, the country's most pressing need. In the short term, the government was attempting to maximize the efficiency of agricultural production in the Jordan River valley through rationalization or use of resources to produce those items in which the country had a relative advantage.

Rationalization started with a controversial 1985 government decision to regulate cropping and production, primarily in the Jordan River valley. Farmers there had repeatedly produced surpluses of tomatoes, cucumbers, eggplants, and squashes because they were reliable and traditional crops. At the same time, underproduction of crops such as potatoes, onions, broccoli, celery, garlic, and spices led to unnecessary imports. The government offered incentives to farmers to experiment with new crops and cut subsidy payments to those who continued to produce surplus crops. In 1986 cucumber production dropped by 25 percent to about 50,000 tons and tomato harvests dropped by more than 33 percent to 160,000 tons, while self-sufficiency was achieved in potatoes and onions.

Production of wheat and other cereals fluctuated greatly from year to year, but never came close to meeting demand. In 1986, a drought year, Jordan produced about 22,000 tons of wheat, down from 63,000 tons in 1985. In 1987 Jordan harvested about 130,000 tons, a record amount. Because even a bumper crop did not meet domestic demand, expansion of dry-land cereal farming in the southeast of the country was a major agricultural development goal of the 1990s. One plan called for the irrigation of a 7,500-hectare area east of Khawr Ramm (known as Wadi Rum) using 100 million cubic meters per year of water pumped from a large underground aquifer. Another plan envisioned a 7,500-hectare cultivated area in the Wadi al Arabah region south of the Jordan River valley using desalinated water from the Red Sea for irrigation.

## Livestock

Livestock production was limited in the late 1980s. Jordan had about 35,000 head of cattle but more than 1 million sheep and 500,000 goats, and the government planned to increase their numbers. In the late 1980s, annual production of red meat ranged between 10,000 and 15,000 tons, less than 33 percent of domestic consumption. A major impediment to increased livestock production was the high cost of imported feed. Jordan imported cereals at high cost for human consumption, but imported animal feed was a much lower priority. Likewise, the arid, rain-fed land that could have been used for grazing or for fodder production was set aside for wheat production. Jordan was self-sufficient, however, in poultry meat production (about 35,000 tons) and egg production (about 400,000 eggs), and exported these products to neighboring countries.

# International Trade

Since independence, Jordan has imported far more than it has exported. Throughout the 1970s, the gap widened as imports grew faster than exports.

## Trade Balance

Jordan did not seek to achieve a trade balance with any major trading partner. In the mid-1980s, the United States and Western Europe supplied almost 50 percent of Jordan's imports, while Arab nations purchased nearly half of the country's exports.

Although Jordan's merchandise trade deficit was always high, the total volume of external trade—defined as imports plus exports—was much higher, indicating that exports were significant enough to offset part of the large import bill. Between 1982 and 1985, as economic growth slowed, import volume contracted by about 4 percent per year. Exports grew by about 5 percent per year during the same period, shrinking the annual trade deficit from more than JD800 million in the early 1980s to JD623 million in 1985. In 1987 the total value of imports was about JD916 million while total exports were valued at about JD249 million, leaving a trade deficit of JD667 million.

## Composition of Exports and Imports

When it became apparent that Jordan could not shift the trade balance in the short term by dramatically reducing imports and increasing exports, government economic planners attempted to alter the composition and direction of external trade by slowly

*Government agricultural project using underground water
in Khawr Ramm Desert, southern Jordan
Hothouse in the Jordan River valley*

171

pursuing a two-pronged policy. Jordan tried to improve its gross barter terms by exporting products with higher value added; for example, prices of consumer goods tended to be higher and more stable than those of raw materials. Likewise, Jordan tried to increase the efficiency of its imports by increasing imports of capital goods and raw materials while lowering imports of consumer goods. The concept was that Jordan should import relatively more and export relatively less of goods that contributed directly toward economic growth.

The changes in the relative composition of exports were more pronounced than changes in the relative composition of imports between 1974 and 1986, according to figures compiled by the Central Bank. Nonetheless, changes were not dramatic in either category. Consumer goods declined from 45 percent to about 37 percent of total imports, but capital goods also declined from 26 percent to 23 percent of total imports. Raw materials increased from 19 percent to 34 percent of total imports, but this rise primarily reflected a growing oil bill, as Jordan could no longer obtain oil at discount prices. Raw material exports declined from 53 percent to 38 percent of total exports, capital goods exports were cut in half from 12 percent to 6 percent, and consumer goods exports were boosted from 35 percent to 56 percent of total exports. Phosphates continued to generate 20 percent of export earnings.

Although the shift in external trade composition appeared to coincide with government policy, economist Rodney Wilson has pointed out that part of the shift was illusory. Customs classifications may have been misleading and also may have changed over time. Many consumer imports were listed as capital imports, and raw material or capital goods exports often were listed as consumer goods exports. For example, fertilizers, a major export, were listed as consumer goods.

Because the categorization of imports and exports according to their value added or ultimate economic disposition was ambiguous, a more specific breakdown of exports and imports by product was warranted. In 1987 energy imports made up approximately 13 percent of the import bill; food imports constituted about 11 percent of the import bill. Basic manufactures, such as textiles, iron, and steel together represented 9 percent of import cost; machinery and transportation equipment constituted 20 percent, and imports of miscellaneous manufactured articles constituted 10 percent of imports (see table 12, Appendix). In 1987 28 percent of Jordanian export earnings were of chemical products, including fertilizers. Raw phosphate exports generated about 25 percent of export earnings, and potash exports accounted for about 11 percent of export earnings. Food and food products constituted about 8 percent and basic manufactures, such as cement, about 4 percent (see table 13, Appendix).

At least some of the shift in import composition appeared to contribute to economic growth insofar as it was correlated with GNP growth. In the early 1980s, the average value of consumer goods imports as a percentage of GNP dropped marginally, from 23 percent to 21 percent, while capital goods imports increased from 15 percent to 23 percent of GNP. The value of total imports as a percentage of GNP climbed almost 40 percent between 1973 and 1983, reaching about 87 percent; however, the rate of this growth slowed during the period and was outpaced by GNP growth.

## Direction of Trade

Whereas almost 50 percent of Jordan's imports came from the United States and Western Europe, these same countries bought less than 10 percent of Jordanian exports. The direction of external trade generally followed Jordan's self-perceived economic identity as an indirect intermediary between the West and the developed world on the one hand, and the Arab countries and the Third World on the other. But because other Arab nations remained the most important customers—buying almost 50 percent of the 1987 export total of almost JD249 million—Jordanian markets were insufficiently diversified to benefit fully from this strategy. In early 1989, the Arab Cooperation Council, composed of Jordan, Egypt, Iraq, and the Yemen Arab Republic (North Yemen), was established to promote trade. This development, as well as the creation of the Joint Syrian-Jordanian Economic Committee, could reinforce Jordan's concentration on nearby markets. In the late 1980s, Jordan nevertheless sought to expand its export markets and had targeted Asia, Eastern Europe, and Africa as potential prospects.

In 1987 Iraq continued to be Jordan's largest export customer. Jordan exported nearly JD60 million worth of goods to Iraq, but most of this figure resulted from transit and reexport rather than from bilateral trade. Saudi Arabia was Jordan's second largest export customer. Jordanian exports to Egypt had grown more than fourfold since 1985, demonstrating that Egypt was an important new outlet. Other major Arab export markets included Kuwait, Syria, and the United Arab Emirates (see table 14, Appendix).

South Asian and East Asian nations were regarded as promising markets, particularly for the sale of fertilizer and industrial chemicals. In 1987 India was Jordan's third largest export customer. Exports to China, Pakistan, Indonesia, and Japan also were growing. Furthermore, trade protocols signed in 1987 with both Thailand

and Turkey may have opened the door to greater exports to both the Asian and the European markets.

Italy was Jordan's only major West European customer. Jordanian officials envisioned improved prospects in Eastern Europe, particularly in Poland, Romania, and Yugoslavia. Jordan regarded Africa as a potentially vast market that could constitute one of the first experiments with the ''South-South'' relationship advocated in Third-World circles. Whereas exports to Africa remained minimal in 1987, Jordan's apparent willingness to consider countertrade and barter remained attractive to such markets.

Jordan imported about JD916 million worth of goods in 1987. Iraq was the largest source of imports, but much of the JD99 million worth of products it sent to Jordan were intended for reexport. Imports from Saudi Arabia, Jordan's third largest import source in 1987, consisted mainly of oil. Almost 40 percent of Jordan's total import bill in 1987 came from eight West European nations, headed by the Federal Republic of Germany (West Germany), Britain, and Italy. The United States was Jordan's second largest source of imports and Japan was another significant import source.

## Banking and Finance

The dominant financial institutions in Jordan were the Central Bank and the Amman Financial Market. Jordan's largest commercial bank was the Arab Bank. Until 1989 many small money-changing offices were operated by small proprietors. Jordan also had three Islamic banks.

The Central Bank, established in 1964, was responsible for note issue, management of exchange reserves, and regulation of credit. It acted as the fiscal agent for the government, regulated the commercial banking sector, and sponsored the creation of certain new financial institutions. In 1985, for example, the Central Bank acted jointly with the Egyptian government to establish a new bank to finance bilateral trade. The government's presence in the financial sector was augmented by several specialized institutions that filled voids in commercial lending activity: the Agricultural Credit Corporation, the Housing Bank (which provided mortgages), and the Industrial Development Bank (which channeled capital to small start-up manufacturing businesses). The government also channeled equity capital to the private sector through large government pension and social security funds.

The banking sector more than doubled loans and deposits between the mid-1970s and the early 1980s. During the same period, the number of financial institutions tripled. The government encouraged the expansion of banking services as a key to its economic development policy. Deposits were attracted from other Arab nations, and the savings and remittances of the many Jordanians who traditionally had never used banks were captured. These deposits were in turn funneled as loans to growing companies that needed capital. Monetization—the use of legal tender as a medium of exchange rather than barter—was very successful. By the mid-1980s, Jordan was the only Arab country in which the value of bank assets exceeded GDP. Total commercial bank assets rose from JD1.1 billion in 1980 to JD2.3 billion in 1985. During the same period, total deposits increased from about JD800 million to JD1.7 billion. Demand deposits decreased from about 35 percent to 20 percent of total deposits, while savings deposits grew. Strict Central Bank consumer credit controls and government success in encouraging savings also were indicated by the growth of the liquid money supply at about 7 percent per year from 1980 to 1987. The liquid money supply reached about JD900 million during this period, with no significant inflation.

In the mid-1980s, however, the government became apprehensive that the banking sector was expanding too rapidly. One concern was that the proliferation of banks could engender excessive competition for assets and risky lending activity; as a result, in 1984 the Central Bank imposed a moratorium on the establishment of new commercial banks. The government also was worried that Jordanian banks preferred making loans to foreign companies rather than to Jordanian companies, that the banks avoided long-term lending, and that loans often financed trade rather than capital investment. In 1985 more than 27 percent of commercial bank credit financed trade, whereas less than 10 percent financed corporate investment.

Another concern was that banks had been so successful in attracting deposits that they were diverting public investment from Jordan's stock exchange, the Amman Financial Market. As a result, companies were unable to obtain equity finance and had no choice but to finance themselves through bank loans. The value of traded shares—less than JD70 million in 1984—had always been dwarfed by banking activity. The total value of share prices on the stock market grew an average of 20 percent annually from 1978 to 1982. From 1983 to 1986, however, share prices dropped an average of 13 percent annually. Companies in the service and manufacturing sectors were especially hard hit, and in 1986 their total share value was less than it had been in 1978. In 1987 and 1988, the stock market recovered as investors tried to hedge against the shaky dinar. Trading volume reached a record high of JD149 million in 1987.

To counterbalance fluctuating stock values and the rapid expansion of banking, the government initiated greater regulation of bank activity. Banks were required to invest 8 percent of their deposits in government bills and bonds. Investment of at least 15 percent of capital in public and mixed sector corporate equity also was mandated, and the minimum capital requirement was increased to JD5 million. Binding interest rate ceilings were set on both loans and deposits, and the dinar exchange rate was fixed by the Central Bank.

In the late 1980s, thirty major banks and financial institutions operated in Jordan, including eight major locally based conventional commercial banks with numerous branch offices, six foreign banks, two major Islamic banks, and a host of smaller or more specialized foreign and domestic financial institutions, some of which conducted merchant banking, investment banking, and trade or agricultural finance. By far the largest locally based commercial bank was the Arab Bank, a Palestinian institution that moved to Amman from Jerusalem in 1948. Because the Arab Bank catered mainly to Palestinians throughout the world, it was not a dominant force in the local market. In terms of total assets (primarily loans) the Jordan National Bank, the Cairo-Amman Bank, the Jordan-Kuwait Bank, and the Petra Bank were perhaps more important local institutions. Foreign banks included Citibank, Grindlays Bank, the Hong Kong-based British Bank of the Middle East, as well as Iraq's Rafidayn Bank and Egypt's Arab Land Bank. Chase Manhattan Bank left Jordan following the 1984 government-imposed financial regulations.

The Central Bank had permitted the virtually unsupervised operation of hundreds of small money-changing offices by individual proprietors. The system had worked well when the dinar was valued realistically compared to foreign currencies. But throughout 1988, as the government attempted to prop up the value of the dinar by freezing the official exchange rate, money changers became an open black market that facilitated the slide of the dinar. In February 1989, the government abruptly canceled the licenses of all money changers, closed their offices, froze their bank accounts, and seized their records.

Jordan also had permitted the establishment of three Islamic banks that adhered to Islamic legal tenets proscribing interest rate (*riba*) transactions. The Islamic banks paid no interest on deposits, and collected no interest on loans. Instead, they made equity investments in companies and then shared in the venture's profit or loss, some of which would then be passed on to depositors. The Islamic banks also were active in financing rural or low-cost housing as well as capital investment by manufacturing companies.

Typically, Islamic banks built or bought a housing development or a piece of equipment and then leased it to a client or company on terms that approximated loan repayments. Jordan's Islamic banks attracted the savings of pious Muslims from Jordan and other Arab countries who would not use conventional, interest-charging banks. The Islamic banks also financed socially desirable projects that conventional banks regarded as too risky or unprofitable.

Islamic banks have had mixed success in Jordan. The Jordan Islamic Bank for Finance and Investment was created in 1978 as a member of the Saudi Arabian-based Al Baraka network of Islamic banks, but 90 percent of its capital was Jordanian owned. By 1986 it had become the sixth largest of Jordan's banks in assets and had financed numerous projects. The Islamic Investment House, which was established with Kuwaiti backing in 1981, was shut down for an indefinite period by the government in 1984 because the projects it had financed were losing money and were putting deposits at risk.

\*    \*    \*

The reader interested in more information on the Jordanian economy can consult primary as well as secondary sources. The economic reports and statistics published and disseminated by the government of Jordan are probably more comprehensive, reliable, and up-to-date than those produced by any other Arab country. Of particular value is the *Five-Year Plan For Economic and Social Development: 1986–1990,* published by the Ministry of Planning, which contains in-depth information on all aspects of the economy, from macroeconomic national income accounting to infrastructure development.

One of the recognized experts on the Jordanian economy is Ian J. Seccombe, who has produced numerous authoritative articles discussing Jordanian labor emigration and remittance income. Another expert is Rodney Wilson, who has produced excellent work on Jordan's banking and financial system. In 1987 Seccombe and Wilson together produced *Trade and Finance in Jordan.* Both authors contributed to *The Economic Development of Jordan,* an anthology edited by Bichara Khader and Adnan Badran, which is arguably the best book on the Jordanian economy. Of the many good articles appearing in the book, those by Michel Chatelus and François Rivier are noteworthy for their penetrating and original analysis. Another valuable source of information on the Jordanian economy is *Jordan to 1990: Coping with Change* by Philip Robins, a special report published in 1986 by the Economist Intelligence Unit. It concentrates on information that businesses would want to know about

Jordan. Pamela Dougherty, a journalist who covers Jordan for the *Middle East Economic Digest,* has produced high quality, informative, and timely articles. (For further information and more complete citations, see Bibliography.)

# Chapter 4. Government and Politics

*Mosaic of the city of Amman, or Philadelphia, from the*
*Umm ar Rasas pavement in a Byzantine church, ca. 780*

IN LATE 1989, KING HUSSEIN ibn Talal ibn Abdullah ibn Hussein Al Hashimi remained in firm control of Jordan's political system as the central policymaker and legislative and executive authority. He maintained tight control over key government functions, such as national defense, internal security, justice, and foreign affairs. Crown Prince Hasan, the king's younger brother and heir apparent, complemented the small, Hussein-centered circle of power in his role as the king's right-hand man, especially in the areas of economy and administration.

Hussein's main power base continued to rest on the beduin-dominated army, which had been loyal to the Hashimite (also seen as Hashemite) family for seven decades. Another source of strength was his astute ability to balance sociopolitical interests at home. Equally important, Hussein was Jordan's most accomplished diplomat-negotiator. During the 1980s, Hussein's autocracy also was substantially bolstered by his rapprochement with the Palestine Liberation Organization (PLO). This significant development greatly reduced the threat to Hussein's rule posed since 1970 by various Palestinian guerrilla groups. Some groups, however, notably the Black September and Abu Nidal factions, continued to seek the overthrow of the entire monarchical structure.

The Transjordanians (see Glossary) occupied a dominant place in the existing power structure. Hussein's palace staff and his top civil, judicial, and military officials were mostly Transjordanians. Although there was a Palestinian (see Glossary) presence on the periphery of power, the Palestinians' continued exclusion from substantive decision-making positions tended to alienate the Palestinian community and served as a potential source of political instability. Hussein's decision in July 1988 to renounce Jordan's claim to sovereignty over the West Bank (see Glossary) and his subsequent recognition of the PLO's declaration of an independent Palestine may further affect the systemic integrity of Jordan because the Palestinians living on the East Bank (see Glossary) must choose whether they want Jordanian or Palestinian nationality.

Another source of political instability for Hussein's regime at the close of the 1980s was the continued severe recession that had plagued the economy since the mid-1980s. This economic retrenchment was in sharp contrast to the economic growth experienced during the late 1970s and early 1980s. The combination of high inflation and high unemployment rates contributed to the pervasive sense of dissatisfaction that erupted in major antigovernment riots in several cities and towns in April 1989. Although all Jordanians were adversely affected by rising prices and falling income, the Palestinians living in refugee camps—most of whom were poor before the recession—bore the brunt of the economic decline. Their economic frustrations helped reinforce their political alienation.

## The Constitution

The Constitution that was promulgated in 1952 and amended in 1974, 1976, and 1984 remained in force in 1989. It declares Jordan a hereditary monarchy with a parliamentary form of government and defines the people as "the source of all powers." The people are officially stated as being part of "the Arab nation." Islam is the official religion of the state and Arabic the official language. In nearly forty years of experience with the Constitution, adherence to the fundamental law of the land has varied in spirit as well as in practice from time to time, depending upon domestic and external circumstances.

Articles 5 through 23 of the Constitution stipulate the rights and duties of citizens and guarantee a long list of personal freedoms. Citizens are assured freedom from compulsory labor or forced loans, and no one may be discriminated against for reasons of race, religion, or language. Arrest, imprisonment, exile, forced residence, and the expropriation of property without due process of law are forbidden. Freedom of worship, opinion, and the press and the right of peaceful assembly are ensured within the limits of the law. Censorship is allowed in time of martial law or when a state of national emergency exists. The right of petition is guaranteed, and citizens are free to form political parties, trade unions, and associations— provided their objectives are lawful. Political refugees may not be extradited. For grades one through nine, education is compulsory and free in public schools. Every citizen is eligible for appointment to public posts, subject only to the candidate's merit and qualification. The Constitution also outlines various principles of labor legislation and directs the government to promote work and to protect labor.

Martial law was declared in 1967 and remained in force in 1989. The emergency regulations under martial law effectively abridged certain constitutionally guaranteed freedoms. These regulations permitted the martial law authorities and the secret police—popularly referred to as the Mukhabarat rather than by its formal name of Dairat al Mukhabarat or General Intelligence Department (GID)— to arrest persons suspected of security offenses and to detain them without trial or access to legal counsel for indefinite periods (see General Intelligence Department, ch. 5). The emergency regulations also authorized the government to censor the press and other publications, banned political parties, and restricted the rights of citizens to assemble for political meetings and peaceful demonstrations.

The powers and functions of the state organs are elaborated in articles 41 through 110. The Constitution includes sections on finance, enforcement of laws, interpretation of the Constitution, and emergency powers and constitutional amendments. An amendment requires the affirmative vote of two-thirds of the members of each legislative house, deliberating separately. When an amendment bill is twice rejected by either house, however, the bill must be deliberated in a joint session of the legislature; in this instance, a two-thirds vote is required for adoption. An amendment bill takes effect only on royal consent. In a move to ensure dynastic stability, the Constitution forbids any amendment concerning the rights of the king and his heirs during a period of regency.

The five amendments to the Constitution that have been approved since 1952 all pertain to the National Assembly. Two amendments were adopted in November 1974. The first permitted the king to dissolve the Senate and to dismiss any individual senator for behavior unbecoming of the office. The second amendment permitted the king to postpone elections for the House of Representatives for one year. In February 1976, a third amendment permitted the king to postpone parliamentary elections indefinitely. The two amendments adopted in 1984 authorized the government to hold parliamentary elections in any part of the country where it was feasible, thus, only in the East Bank. Until late 1988, when Jordan renounced claims to political sovereignty over the West Bank, the House of Representatives was empowered to select deputies to fill vacant seats from the West Bank.

## The Government

The Constitution divides the powers and functions of the government into executive, legislative, and judicial categories (see fig. 10). The Constitution assigns the legislative power to both the bicameral National Assembly and the king, who is also vested with executive power. The king exercises his executive authority with the aid of his cabinet ministers, collectively known as the Council of Ministers. Judicial power is vested in independent courts. The authority and services of the central government are extended to all corners of the kingdom through the eight governorates or provinces.

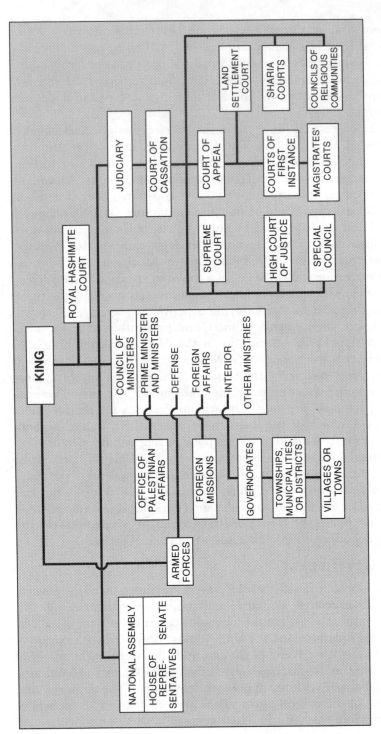

*Figure 10. Government Organization, 1989*

## The King

Under the Constitution, the monarchy is the most important political institution in the country. Articles 28 through 40 of the Constitution enumerate the king's powers. He appoints the prime minister, the president and members of the Senate, judges, and other senior government and military functionaries. He commands the armed forces, approves and promulgates laws, declares war, concludes peace, and signs treaties (which in theory must be approved by the National Assembly). The king convenes, opens, adjourns, suspends, or dissolves the legislature; he also orders, and may postpone, the holding of elections. He has veto power that can be overridden only by a two-thirds vote of each house. The Constitution states that the king exercises his jurisdiction by *iradah* (sing.; pl., *iradat*—royal decrees), which must be signed by the prime minister and the minister or ministers concerned. As head of state, the king is accountable to no one.

Royal succession devolves by male descent in the Hashimite dynasty (see fig. 11). The royal mandate is passed to the eldest son of the reigning king, to the eldest son of the successor king, and by similar process thereafter. Should the king die without a direct heir, the deceased monarch's eldest brother has first claim, followed by the eldest son of the other brothers according to their seniority in age. Should there be no suitable direct heir, the National Assembly selects a successor from among "the descendants of the founder of the Arab Revolt, the late King Hussein ibn Ali" (see World War I: Diplomacy and Intrigue, ch. 1).

The heir apparent to the throne must be sane, a male Muslim, the son of Muslim parents, and born of a lawful wife. In addition, he must not have been excluded by a royal decree from the succession "on the ground of unsuitability." In 1965 Hussein (b. 1935) used this rule to exclude from the line of succession his two sons by his Muslim but British second wife Princess Muna. He also issued a royal decree that excluded his next younger brother Muhammad (b. 1945) and designated a second brother, Hasan (b. 1948), as crown prince. In June 1978, Hussein designated Prince Ali (b. 1975), his son from his third wife (Queen Alia, who was killed in a helicopter crash in February 1977) to succeed Hasan as heir apparent on the latter's succession to the throne.

When the throne is inherited by a minor, the powers of the king are exercised by a regent or by a council of regency, both of which may be appointed by a decree of the (previous) reigning king; if the king dies without having made such an appointment, the appointment is made by the Council of Ministers. The king attains

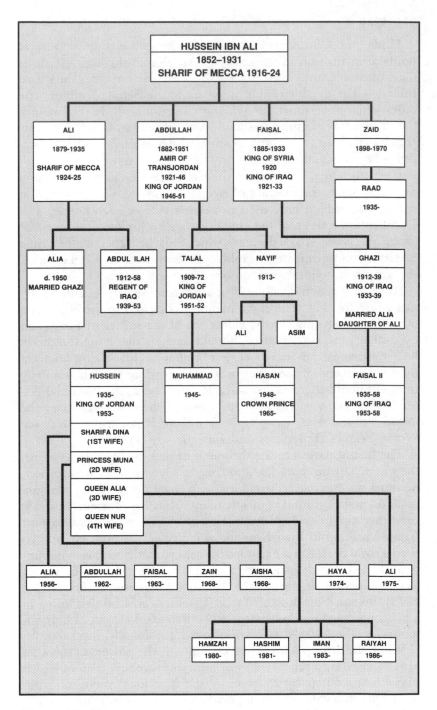

*Figure 11. Abbreviated Genealogy of the Hashimite Family, 1989*

majority on his eighteenth birthday based on the Muslim lunar calendar. Should the king be disabled by illness, his powers are exercised by a deputy, by a council of the throne appointed by the king, or by the Council of Ministers if the king is incapable of such appointment. The deputy or the council of the throne may also perform royal duties during the absence of the king from the country. If the absence extends to more than four months, the House of Representatives is empowered to "review" the matter.

The king has full responsibility for all matters pertaining to the royal household. He appoints the chief of the royal court, an official who can play an influential political role through his control of access to the monarch. Although the rank of the chief of the royal court is equivalent to that of a cabinet minister, his office is not part of the executive branch.

## The Council of Ministers

The cabinet, consisting of the prime minister and the other ministers, is the top executive arm of the state. Its members serve at the pleasure of the king, but the Constitution requires every new cabinet to present its statement of programs and policies to the House of Representatives for approval by a two-thirds vote of the members of that house. If the house passes a vote of no confidence, the cabinet must resign.

Traditionally, prime ministers have been recruited from families that have loyally served the Hashimites for many years. Zaid ar Rifai, who was prime minister from 1985 to 1989, is the son of a prominent Transjordanian politician who had served as prime minister to Hussein's grandfather. His successors, Ash Sharif Zaid ibn Shakir (April–November 1989) and Mudar Badran (designated prime minister in November 1989), have each worked with the king in a variety of political capacities. Significantly, both men served as chief minister of the royal court prior to becoming prime minister.

In September 1989, the cabinet included ministers responsible for the following portfolios: agriculture; communications; culture and information; defense; education; energy and mineral resources; finance and customs; foreign affairs; health; higher education; tourism and antiquities; interior; justice; labor and social development; municipal, rural, and environmental affairs; planning; religious affairs and holy places; supply; trade and industry; transportation; and youth. In 1989 the government also was served by a minister of state for prime ministerial affairs.

In 1986 the bureaucracy employed 109,523 Jordanians, making the government the principal employer in society. Selection generally was based upon merit, although patronage and nepotism remained fairly widespread. The government trained civil servants at a school of public administration in Amman, Jordan's capital. A majority of them were Palestinians who had opted for Jordanian citizenship; at the higher levels of the administrative hierarchy, however, Transjordanians probably outnumbered Palestinians. Allegiance to the monarchy and the Constitution remained an important factor in government service. In the aftermath of the Az Zarka affair in 1957 and the civil war of 1970 and 1971, numerous Palestinian civil servants were dismissed because of suspected disloyalty to the throne.

From the beginning of the Israeli occupation of the West Bank in June 1967 until Hussein relinquished Jordan's claim to sovereignty of the territory in July 1988, Amman continued to pay salaries and pensions to serving and retired West Bank municipal government employees. During this period, the West Bank came under the jurisdiction initially of the Bureau of Occupied Homeland Affairs, attached to the prime minister's office and headed by a cabinet-level minister; later this office became the Ministry of Occupied Territories. In addition to paying salaries, it was responsible for channeling Jordan's loans and development funds to Palestinian concerns in the West Bank. Following the decision at the Baghdad Summit meeting in November 1978 to set up a special fund for development and other projects in the Israeli-occupied territories, this ministry worked jointly with the PLO in administering aid funds for Palestinians in both the West Bank and the Gaza Strip. By 1988, when Jordan terminated payments, more than 20,000 West Bank Palestinians were estimated to be receiving salaries from the Jordanian government. All of these employees were granted retirement benefits or severance pay according to the number of years they had been municipal employees.

## The Legislature

Under the Constitution, the bicameral legislature is called the National Assembly and consists of the thirty-member appointed Senate (sometimes called the House of Notables) and the popularly elected House of Representatives (also called the Chamber of Deputies). Prior to July 1988, both houses had an equal number of representatives from each bank of the Jordan River. The Constitution stipulates that the size of the Senate cannot be more than half that of the lower house. Of the two chambers, the Senate is regarded as the more elite; but like the lower chamber, it has had little real influence in the legislative process. Although the House of Representatives was vested with more legislative power than the upper house, both chambers have been overshadowed by the executive side of government.

The senators are appointed by the king for four-year terms, with half the membership retiring every two years at the end of a senate session. A senator may be reappointed. Qualifications for a senator include a minimum age of forty years and prior government or military service in relatively senior positions. Senators have included present and past prime ministers, former members of the House of Representatives who had been elected at least twice, former senior judges and diplomats, and retired officers who have attained the rank of general.

Members of the House of Representatives are elected to four-year terms by secret ballot. Candidates must be Jordanian citizens more than thirty years of age. Individuals representing foreign interests or having material interests in any government contract are disqualified. Also excluded are persons who have been debarred from public office or who have blood ties to the king within a prescribed degree of relationship. Ten of the eighty seats are reserved for minorities, including Christians, beduins, and Circassians (see Ethnicity and Language, ch. 2).

Voters must be at least nineteen years of age. Suffrage has been universal since 1973, when women were enfranchised. All Palestinian refugees who have adopted Jordanian citizenship enjoy equal voting privileges with Transjordanians.

Prior to the November 1989 elections, the last national elections for the House of Representatives had been held in April 1967. In 1970 Hussein cited the Israeli occupation of the West Bank as reason for postponing elections, but he decreed that serving members would continue in office until circumstances permitted the holding of new elections. The 1974 decision by Arab heads of state at a summit meeting in Rabat, Morocco, that the PLO was the sole representative of the Palestinian people raised questions about the political relationship of the West Bank to Jordan. In response to this decision, in November 1974 Hussein dissolved the House of Representatives, half of whose members represented the West Bank. Nevertheless, Hussein was reluctant to sever ties to the Israeli-occupied territory, and subsequently he decreed that elections for a new house would be held in March 1976. Whether the elections would include or exclude the West Bank had serious consequences for Jordan's relations with the PLO. Moreover, some Arab states interpreted the Rabat decision to mean that Jordan should renounce its claims to the West Bank—an interpretation to which Hussein did not then subscribe. As the time for the elections drew near, Hussein decided that postponing the elections would be the prudent course to avoid foreclosing future political options. Consequently, in February 1976, he recalled the old house, with its West Bank members. It convened briefly to approve the indefinite suspension of elections for a new House of Representatives, then it adjourned.

In 1978, Hussein issued a royal decree that granted some legislative functions to a newly created sixty-member appointive body, the National Consultative Council (NCC). The NCC, which did not include any members from the West Bank, had a limited mandate to study, debate, and render advice on bills drafted by the Council of Ministers. The NCC possessed no authority, however, to make policy or to approve, amend, or reject any bill. The NCC provided advisory opinions to the Council of Ministers on general state policy when requested by the prime minister. The decree establishing it stated that the NCC would be "lawfully dissolved when the House of Representatives is elected and convened."

In January 1984, Hussein dismissed the NCC and reconvened the suspended National Assembly. He appointed new members to the Senate but called back those members of the House of Representatives who were serving when the lower house last met in 1976. By-elections were held in the East Bank in March to fill eight vacancies in the house that had resulted from the deaths of members since the 1967 elections. In accordance with a January 1984 constitutional amendment, the house also voted to fill seven vacant West Bank seats. In March 1986, the house approved a new electoral law that would increase its membership from 60 to 142; 71 members would be elected from the East Bank, 60 from the West Bank, and 11 from Palestinian refugee camps on the East Bank; this law was never implemented. In 1987 the government began registering Jordanians on the East Bank so that they could vote in parliamentary elections scheduled for 1988; these would have been the first national elections in more than twenty-one years. At the end of 1987, however, registration was halted, and the king issued a royal decree that postponed elections for two years.

In July 1988, Hussein renounced Jordan's claims to the West Bank. In light of the new political situation, the king dissolved the House of Representatives. A royal decree issued in October postponed indefinitely elections for a reorganized legislature. A subsequent decree in December abolished the ministerial-level Office of Parliamentary Affairs. Following antigovernment riots in April 1989, however, outgoing Prime Minister Rifai promised that the interim government would concentrate on carrying out the long delayed parliamentary elections. In July Prime Minister Shakir scheduled the elections for November. They were the first national elections for the House of Representatives in more than twenty-two years.

## The Judiciary

The legal system of Jordan is based on sharia (Islamic law) and laws of European origin. During the nineteenth century, when Jordan was part of the Ottoman Empire, some aspects of European law, especially French commercial law and civil and criminal procedures, were adopted. English common law was introduced in the West Bank between 1917 and 1948, during most of which time the area was incorporated into the British-administered Mandate of Palestine, and introduced in the East Bank during the years 1921 to 1946, when the East Bank comprised the British Mandate of Transjordan. Under the Court Establishment Law of 1951 and the Constitution, the judiciary is independent. There are three kinds of courts: civil courts, religious courts, and special courts. The civil courts adjudicate all civil and criminal cases not expressly reserved to the religious or special courts.

The civil jurisdiction is exercised at four levels: the magistrates' courts, the courts of first instance, the Court of Appeal, and the Court of Cassation (the supreme court of the land). There are fourteen magistrates' courts throughout the country. They exercise jurisdiction in civil cases involving small claims of no more than JD250 (JD or Jordanian dinar; for value of the dinar—see Glossary) and in criminal cases involving maximum fines of JD100 or maximum prison terms of one year. The seven courts of first instance exercise general jurisdiction in all matters civil and criminal. A panel of three judges sits for all felony trials; two judges sit for misdemeanor and civil cases. The courts of first instance also exercise limited appellate jurisdiction in cases involving judgments or fines under JD20 and JD10 respectively.

There is a three-judge panel Court of Appeal that sits in Amman. Its appellate review extends to judgments of the courts of first instance, the magistrates' courts, and the religious courts. The highest court is the Court of Cassation in Amman; its president, who is appointed by the king, serves as the country's chief justice. All seven judges of the court sit in full panel when important cases are being argued. For most appeals, however, only five judges hear and rule on the cases.

The religious courts are divided into sharia courts for Muslims and ecclesiastical courts for the minority Christian communities. These courts are responsible for disputes over personal status (marriage, divorce, child custody, and inheritance) and communal endowment among their respective communities. One judge, called a qadi, sits in each sharia court and decides cases on the basis of Islamic law. Three judges, usually members of the clergy, sit in each ecclesiastical court and render judgments based on various aspects of canon law as interpreted by the Greek Orthodox, Melchite, Roman Catholic, and Anglican traditions (see Religious Minorities, ch. 2). Appeals from the judgments of the religious courts are referred to the Court of Appeal sitting in Amman. If any dispute involves members of different religious communities, the civil courts have jurisdiction unless the parties mutually agree to submit to the jurisdiction of one of the religious courts. In case of jurisdictional conflicts between any two religious courts or between a religious court and a civil court, the president of the Court of Cassation appoints a three-judge special tribunal to decide jurisdiction or to hear the case.

Special courts include the High Tribunal (or High Council or Supreme Council), which interprets the Constitution at the request of the prime minister or of either chamber of the National Assembly; the Special Council, which may be called on by the prime minister to interpret any law that has not been interpreted by the courts of law; and the High Court of Justice, which is to be constituted when necessary by the Court of Cassation. The High Court of Justice hears habeas corpus and mandamus petitions and may issue injunctions involving public servants charged with irregularities; it is also empowered to try cabinet ministers charged with offenses. There is also a special court known as the Land Settlement Court. After 1976 when tribal law was abolished, tribal matters came under the formal jurisdiction of the regular courts, but adjudication apparently was still handled informally in traditional ways by local intermediaries or tribal authorities.

## Local Administration

In 1989 local government authorities were essentially an extension of the central government seated in Amman. Under the general supervision and control of the Ministry of Interior, the local units operated at the governorate (sing., *liwaa*; pl., *alwiyah*), municipality, township and village (or town) levels. The East Bank was divided into the eight governorates of Amman, Al Balqa, Irbid, Az Zarqa, Al Mafraq, Al Karak, At Tafilah, and Maan (see fig. 1). Each governorate was subdivided into districts (sing., *qada*) and subdistricts (sing., *nahiya*). The subdistricts comprised towns, villages, and rural areas. Each of the eight governorates was headed by an appointed commissioner. These commissioners were the principal agents of the king and supervised and coordinated the activities of various central government functions within their respective administrative divisions.

The basic administrative unit was the village or town. The towns and larger villages had municipal councils elected by popular vote. The normal practice was for the minister of municipal, rural, and environmental affairs to confirm as mayor the council member who received the highest number of votes in each municipal election. Smaller villages continued to be governed by traditional headmen known as *mukhtars*. The village and town authorities had limited responsibilities for administration of markets, law and order, sanitation, and other community activities.

The central government provided for local-level social services such as education, health, welfare, and public works. The multiplication and extension of government services during the 1970s and 1980s increased the influence of central authorities throughout the country. The elimination of tribal law in 1976 attested to the all-pervasiveness of central government penetration even in rural areas where tribal leaders traditionally had provided security and limited welfare services.

## The Political Setting

In 1989 the Jordanian political system continued to revolve around Hussein, who ruled firmly and tolerated no opposition. He had acceded to the throne in 1953, and the longevity of his tenure has been almost unparalleled in the contemporary Middle East. His reign, however, has been marked by numerous political crises: abortive coups, assassination attempts, and the disastrous consequences of the June 1967 Arab-Israeli war. Undoubtedly the most serious threat to his rule was the civil war with the PLO guerrillas in 1970 and 1971 (see The Guerrilla Crisis, ch. 1; The Palestinian Factor, ch. 5). Hussein's ability to remain in power for nearly four decades can be attributed to his own political acumen and a fortuitous combination of domestic and external situations. Nevertheless, the continued absence of institutions through which citizens could participate in the political process raised questions about the ultimate stability of his regime.

### The Political Elite

In 1989 Hussein remained the single most important person in Jordan's politics. His political preeminence derived in part from his skill in dealing with various domestic and external problems. He has traveled frequently to keep in touch with cross sections of the population and to establish rapport with his troops, with university students, and with members of tribes. Hussein's personalized approach has tended to counterbalance the virtual lack of independent, institutionalized channels that could serve as barometers of popular sentiments and attitudes toward the government. Also, Hussein's frequent visits to foreign capitals have enabled him to keep abreast of external developments and to obtain needed financial and technical assistance for his kingdom. His ability to maintain generally cordial relations with foreign states has been a critical asset for Jordan, in view of the country's heavy dependence on external aid.

Hussein has relied upon various political options to consolidate his power. He has used his constitutional authority to appoint principal government officials as a critical lever with which to reward loyalty and performance, neutralize detractors, and weed out incompetent elements. The Hussein-centered power structure comprised the cabinet ministers, members of the royal family, the palace staff, senior army officers, tribal shaykhs, and ranking civil servants. King Hussein has filled most of the sensitive government posts with loyal Transjordanians. Since the early 1950s, he also has appointed to responsible positions Palestinians supportive of the Hashimites. Beginning in the 1970s, he permitted an increasing number of Palestinians from families not traditionally aligned with the Hashimites to be co-opted into government service.

The Hashimites, the royal family headed by Hussein, form an extended kinship group related through marriage to several prominent Transjordanian families. The Hashimite family traces its ancestry back to the family of the Prophet, and for centuries it had been politically prominent in what is now Saudi Arabia. Abdullah ibn Hussein Al Hashimi (1882–1951), a son of Sharif Hussein of Mecca (1851–1931), established the Jordanian branch of the family in 1921 after Britain had created the Mandate of Transjordan and confirmed him as amir. London also permitted Abdullah's younger brother, Faisal (1885–1933), to assume the kingship of Iraq, another future state set up after World War I as a British-administered mandate. Abdullah changed his title from amir to king in 1946, when Transjordan was granted independence. Following his assassination in 1951, Abdullah's son Talal (1909–1972) ruled briefly.

Hussein was Talal's oldest son. Before succeeding his father as king in 1953, Hussein was educated at Victoria College in Alexandria, Egypt and at Harrow School and the Royal Military Academy, Sandhurst, both in Britain. In 1955, Hussein married his first wife, Dina Abdul Hamid al Aun, an Egyptian of Hashimite ancestry. They had one daughter before their marriage ended in divorce. His second wife, Antoinette Gardiner of Britain, converted to Islam and took the name Muna al Hussein. She and Hussein had four children, two sons and twin daughters. Hussein divorced

*King Hussein*
*Crown Prince Hasan*
*Queen Nur*

Princess Muna in 1973 and married his third wife, Palestinian Alia Tukan. Hussein and Queen Alia had one daughter and one son before her February 1977 death in a helicopter crash. In June 1978 Hussein married his fourth wife, Elizabeth Halaby, an American of Arab and Swiss descent. He proclaimed her Queen Nur al Hussein (light of Hussein). Hussein and Queen Nur have four children, two sons and two daughters. Throughout the 1980s, Queen Nur had a visible and active role promoting educational, cultural, social welfare, architectural, and urban planning projects in Jordan.

Hussein has two younger brothers and one sister. His brothers Muhammad and Hasan had significant political roles in 1989. The most important Hashimite after Hussein was Hasan, whom the king had designated as crown prince through royal decree in 1965. Muhammad was a businessman and was active politically behind the scenes. Families that were related to the Hashimites included the politically prominent Sharaf and Shakir families. Hussein's cousin, Sharif Abdul Hamid Sharaf, was a close political adviser throughout the 1970s and served briefly as prime minister before his death in 1980. Another member of the family, Layla Sharaf, was Jordan's first woman cabinet officer, serving as minister of culture and information in 1984–85. A third cousin, Field Marshal Ash Sharif Zaid ibn Shakir, was a longtime political confidant who served the king in many sensitive positions. In December 1988, Hussein appointed Shakir chief of the royal court and director of the secret police (Mukhabarat); beginning in late April 1989 he served for seven months as prime minister (see Political Dissent and Political Repression, this ch.).

Hussein has been supported throughout his reign by the original Transjordanian population, particularly the beduin tribes who revered him as a descendant of the family of the Prophet Muhammad and as a ruler imbued with those qualities of leadership they valued most—courage, self-reliance, valor, and honesty. The beduin have formed a prominent segment within the army, especially among the senior ranks of the officer corps. Their loyalty helped Hussein survive a number of crises and thereby served as a stabilizing force within the country. Nevertheless, since the mid-1980s there has been evidence of erosion of beduin and Transjordanian support for Hussein's regime. Significantly, it was primarily East Bankers, rather than Palestinians, who participated in widespread antigovernment riots that swept several towns of Jordan in 1989.

Other politically influential individuals were affiliated with the old East Bank families. For example, Zaid ar Rifai, appointed prime minister in 1985, was the son of Samir ar Rifai, a politician who had served several terms as prime minister under the rule of

Abdullah during the 1930s and 1940s and subsequently was a prime minister for Hussein. Many members of the Abdul Huda, Majali, Badran, Hashim, Tal, and Qassim families also served the Hashimites loyally.

Another element of the political elite were the non-Arab Circassians, the descendants of Muslim immigrants who came from the Caucasus Mountains in the late nineteenth century and settled in Amman and its environs. The Circassians allied with the Hashimites in the 1920s, and since that time leading Circassian politicians have held important and sensitive positions in the government and military. The Al Mufti family has been one of the most politically prominent Circassian families, and one of its members, Said al Mufti, served as prime minister.

In the 1980s, the influential scions of traditional and aristocratic Palestinian families known for their Hashimite sympathies were outnumbered by Transjordanians in almost all top government posts. The distinction between Transjordanians and Palestinians tended to be played down, however, because officially the Palestinians of the East Bank have been accepted as Jordanian citizens. Palestinians continued to hold an important place in society as leading merchants, financiers, professionals, educators, and technocrats.

## Political Dissent and Political Repression

All political parties were banned in 1957 and have been illegal since the establishment of martial law in 1967. In addition, Marxist-oriented parties were forbidden under the Anti-Communist Law of 1953. Evidence of illegal political activity is monitored by the Mukhabarat, or secret police. Persons suspected of engaging in political activities are arrested by the Mukhabarat and may be detained without charges for prolonged periods. In 1989 several Jordanian political parties existed in exile and were believed to have many secret sympathizers and underground cells operating in Jordan. These parties included the Arab Constitutionalist Party, the Communist Party of Jordan, the Palestine Communist Party, the Islamic Liberation Party, the National Jordanian Movement, the Muslim Brotherhood, and the Unionist Democratic Association. In addition, the various Palestinian guerrilla organizations clandestinely recruited in the refugee camps.

Up to mid-1989, observers concluded that the Mukhabarat continued to be generally effective in discouraging the expression of political dissent or political activities within Jordan. It remained unclear how extensive the political liberalization inaugurated in the summer of 1989 would become and what role the Mukhabarat would have. It was also uncertain how greater tolerance of dissident

197

views would affect political groups outside the country. As late as 1988, several Jordanian and Palestinian political groups engaged in terrorism directed against Jordanian officials and government offices. The Black September group, formed by Palestinians to avenge the Jordanian army attack on Palestinian guerrilla bases in Jordan in September 1970, remained committed to the overthrow of the Hashimite monarchy. Throughout the 1980s, it claimed responsibility for assassinations of Jordanian diplomats in various cities of Asia and Western Europe; in 1988 it claimed responsibility for several bombings that took place in Amman.

Although the government did not officially permit the banned political parties to participate in the fall campaign for the November 1989 House of Representatives elections, it ignored the claims of many candidates that they actually represented such parties. The campaign for the eighty contested seats was relatively free of voter intimidation, with the Mukhabarat keeping an uncharacteristically low profile. A total of 647 candidates took part, including several former political prisoners who were released from detention in the summer. The Muslim Brotherhood supported twenty-six candidates, of whom twenty actually won seats. Candidates affiliated with other Islamist groups won an additional fourteen seats. Thus, Islamists emerged as the largest bloc in Parliament, controlling more than 42 percent of the seats. Candidates representing various secular groups opposed to the government won a total of ten seats. As a result, the House of Representatives convened with a majority of forty-four members upon whom the government could not count for support, thirty-three government supporters, and three seats to be determined.

## The Palestinians and the Palestine Liberation Organization

Palestinians have been a complicating factor in the Jordanian political process since the annexation of the West Bank in 1950. Transjordanians tended to fear that the numerically preponderant Palestinians could emerge as a dominant force if competitive politics were permitted to resume. For years many Palestinians openly opposed Hussein's monarchical absolutism and demanded equality and proportional participation in the political process. Their frustrations under Hussein's rule, at least through the 1960s and early 1970s, provided a fertile ground for their empathy and support for the PLO. Since 1971, when the PLO guerrilla forces were crushed and driven out of Jordan, Palestinians generally have been politically dormant. Given the authorities' effective discouragement of political expression critical of the regime, it was difficult in

1989 to ascertain what the political aspirations or preferences of the Palestinians in Jordan might be.

The Palestinian equation became further complicated after October 1974 as external pressures were brought to bear on Jordan. The catalyst was the unanimous decision of the Arab states meeting in Rabat to recognize the PLO as the sole authorized representative of the Palestinian people. Strongly prodded by Egypt, Syria, and other Arab states, Hussein was obliged to assent to the Rabat decision although he still claimed the West Bank as Jordanian territory until 1988. This development has portended uncertain implications for Jordan's domestic politics and its relationship with the West Bank.

Following the Rabat Summit, Hussein and PLO leader Yasir Arafat met to reconcile relations, strained since the 1970–71 civil war. Their discussions resulted in the decision in early 1975 for Jordan and the PLO to cease mutual recriminations. Hussein rejected, however, a PLO demand that it be permitted to reestablish its military and political presence in the East Bank. After 1974 there was a noticeable resurgence of Palestinian empathy for and identification with the PLO in many parts of the world. This sentiment was nowhere more evident than in the West Bank. There, in the municipal elections that Israel permitted to be held in April 1976, candidates supporting the PLO defeated most of the candidates identified with Hussein. The outcome was a reversal of the municipal elections held in 1972, when pro-Hussein candidates handily won over pro-PLO candidates.

The process of reconciliation also was complicated by the linkage of the Jordanian-PLO equation to the broader configuration of Middle East problems. In March 1977, Hussein and Arafat met in Cairo as part of the Egyptian-Syrian efforts to prepare for an upcoming Geneva peace conference on the Middle East. The two leaders addressed, inter alia, the question of future relations between Jordan and a proposed Palestinian state on the West Bank. Their discussions focused on whether the PLO should be represented as an independent delegation at the conference in Geneva or as part of Jordan's delegation. The latter course was preferred by Hussein.

The Hussein-Arafat contact became more frequent in the wake of Egyptian president Anwar as Sadat's visit to Jerusalem in November 1977 and his signing of the United States-mediated Camp David Accords in 1978 and the Treaty of Peace Between Egypt and Israel in 1979. Nevertheless, Arafat and other PLO leaders were suspicious of Hussein's ultimate intentions vis-à-vis the Camp David Accords. Although Jordan had no part in the

Egyptian-Israeli negotiations, it was directly linked to the process for settling the future of the West Bank. The first agreement, called "A Framework for Peace in the Middle East," stipulated that Egypt and Israel would negotiate with Jordan and Palestinian representatives for a transitional self-governing authority to administer the West Bank and the Gaza Strip, a noncontiguous Palestinian enclave on the Mediterranean Sea that also was occupied by Israel. Jordan declared it was neither legally nor morally obligated to this agreement and refused to participate in the negotiations, which consequently made no progress. Hussein's decision to maintain a dialogue with the United States, however, fueled the fears of some Palestinians that the monarch tacitly supported the Camp David Accords and was seeking ways to preclude the PLO from gaining control of the West Bank.

The expulsion of the PLO from Lebanon in the wake of Israel's 1982 invasion of that country brought the contradictory Jordanian and PLO objectives into open conflict. Initially, relations improved because Hussein agreed to accept a small contingent of expelled fighters and to permit the reopening of PLO political offices for the first time since the 1970–71 civil war. In several face-to-face meetings held between September 1982 and April 1983, Hussein and Arafat discussed Jordan's role in future negotiations over the fate of the West Bank. Because neither the United States nor Israel was willing to talk with the PLO at this time, Hussein tried to obtain Arafat's endorsement for Jordan to serve as spokesman for the Palestinians. More extreme Palestinian guerrilla leaders—often called "rejectionists" because they rejected any compromises that would circumscribe their goal of an independent Palestinian state that included all of pre-1948 Palestine—distrusted Hussein and would not be assuaged by Arafat's reassurances. Without a broad-based consensus within the PLO, Arafat apparently felt he could not agree to a common negotiating strategy with Hussein. Consequently, Hussein broke off the talks in April 1983; for the remainder of the year, Jordan's relations with the PLO were strained.

Violent factional feuding engulfed the PLO beginning in May 1983, inducing the moderate elements (who generally coalesced around Arafat) to revive contacts with Hussein. By this time, Jordan had decided to assert its influence in the West Bank more aggressively, albeit within the limits tolerated by the Israeli occupation authorities. The National Assembly, dissolved following the Rabat decision in 1974, was recalled in January 1984 and deputies were appointed to fill vacant West Bank seats in the House of Representatives. Nevertheless, Hussein seemed to welcome the rapprochement with the moderate faction of the PLO and gave his blessing to the holding of a Palestine National Council (PNC) meeting in Amman in November 1984. The PNC meeting was an historic event that was broadcast on Jordanian television and picked up by viewers in the West Bank. The meeting strengthened Arafat's authority as leader of the PLO and enabled him to negotiate with Hussein without fear of the inevitable recriminations from extremist factions who had boycotted the Amman meeting.

Hussein and Arafat continued to cooperate after the PNC meeting, both leaders speaking of the need for Jordan and a Palestinian state to maintain a special relationship. In February 1985, they announced a joint Jordanian-Palestinian agreement on a peace framework. This agreement called for the convening of an international peace conference whose participants would include the five permanent members of the United Nations (UN) Security Council and all parties to the Arab-Israeli conflict. Although the PLO would represent Palestinians, its PLO delegates would not attend the conference separately but rather as part of a joint Jordanian-Palestinian contingent. The agreement stipulated that the Palestinian people would have the right to exercise national self-determination within the context of a proposed confederated state of Jordanians and Palestinians.

Following his agreement with Arafat, Hussein pursued two policies simultaneously. While trying to serve as a spokesman for the Palestinians in talks with the United States, and eventually even with Israeli politicians, Hussein also tried to persuade Arafat to make a public declaration of PLO support for UN Security Council resolutions 242 and 338, both of which implicitly recognized Israel's right to exist. Arafat, who still felt he had to be wary of the influence of the more extreme factions in the PLO, was unwilling to be pushed as far toward moderation as Hussein had hoped. The extremist guerrilla groups criticized Arafat for the agreement, claiming that it would deny Palestinians the right to establish a sovereign state within the pre-1948 boundaries of Palestine. Some of the extremists demonstrated their potential for undermining any possible compromise solutions by carrying out sensational terrorist acts in September and October of 1985. The international response to these incidents, especially the Israeli aerial bombing of PLO headquarters in Tunisia, increased Arafat's reluctance to make the political concessions that Hussein believed were required to obtain United States support for an international conference.

Hussein's disappointment in Arafat contributed to an erosion of their political relationship. In February 1986, Hussein announced that he was terminating the year-old Jordan-PLO agreement. Tensions with the PLO were exacerbated in May by the student demonstrations at Yarmuk University in the northern Jordanian city of Irbid. In July Hussein ordered the offices of Arafat's Al Fatah organization closed following criticisms of the harsh manner in which Jordanian security forces had put down the Yarmuk demonstrations.

During 1986 both Hussein and Arafat intensified their competition for influence in the West Bank. The king appeared to have the upper hand in this contest because Jordan's banking system controlled the disbursement of pan-Arab funds earmarked for West Bank (and also Gaza Strip) development projects. However, the Palestinian uprising, the *intifadah,* which began in December 1987, exposed the fragility of Hussein's influence in the occupied territories. It became obvious during the first half of 1988 that, compared with the PLO, pro-Hashimite sympathizers had little support. Hussein decided that political circumstances required a bold move that would preserve Jordan's interests. Thus, in July he renounced all claims to sovereignty over the West Bank. By doing so, Hussein apparently hoped to enhance the Jordanian position in a post-*intifadah* era. If the PLO succeeded in consolidating its influence in the occupied territories and in winning international support for its claim to rule the West Bank and the Gaza Strip, then Hussein's abdication of responsibility would stand Jordan in good stead. It would enable Jordan to forge political and economic links with a new state, which, because of its small area and lack of natural resources, would be dependent in various ways on its only neighbor to the east. If the PLO failed to deliver on the political aspirations being expressed by the *intifadah,* then Hussein would be ready to offer Jordan's services as negotiator in terminating the Israeli occupation.

The PLO accepted Hussein's challenge. Arafat met with the king during the late summer and early fall to discuss strategy. Among the practical measures agreed to was a scheme for the PLO to assume responsibility for payment of the salaries of West Bank and Gaza Strip municipal employees through Jordanian financial institutions. Subsequently, at an historic PNC meeting in Algiers in November 1988 at which all major factions were represented, the PNC declared the West Bank and the Gaza Strip to be the independent state of Palestine. The PNC also renounced the use of terrorism, accepted UN Security Council resolutions 242 and 338 (both of which recognized the existence of Israel), and declared its willingness to negotiate the end of the occupation. Jordan was one of the first nations to recognize the new state and announced its readiness to discuss how the two countries could maintain a special relationship.

In 1989 the PLO remained essentially an umbrella organization of numerous civilian and military groups (see fig. 12). It was originally founded in 1964 as a political organization to represent the interests of Palestinians. The various Palestinian guerrilla groups were formed independently of the PLO, and they initially were critical of the PLO's objectives and policies. In 1968–69, however, most of the guerrilla groups joined the PLO, and their leaders assumed dominant roles in the organization. Although the PLO has greatly expanded its various service functions in the cultural, diplomatic, economic, educational, health, humanitarian, political, social, and welfare fields since 1969, for most Western observers these functions have been overshadowed by the military and terrorist activities associated with the guerrilla groups.

The PLO guerrilla groups recruited most of their fighters from the Palestinian refugee camps in Jordan, Lebanon, and Syria. Although some of these camps were established as early as 1948 and all have long since been transformed into permanent villages or urban neighborhoods, high levels of poverty and unemployment remain dominant characteristics. Many young men raised in these camps found the guerrillas' idealization of Palestinian nationalism and politico-military organization appealing alternatives to the despair fostered by routine idleness and lack of opportunity. Joining one of the guerrilla groups enabled such men to assert their identity and channel their energies. Although the various guerrilla organizations differed in temperament, ideology, and tactics, they all shared the objective of establishing an independent Palestinian state.

The oldest, largest, and best equipped of the PLO guerrilla groups was Al Fatah—the Palestine National Liberation Movement as the group was officially known. Arafat (also called Abu Ammar) has led Al Fatah since its formation in 1957. Since 1969, Arafat has also been chairman of the PNC's fifteen-member Executive Committee—and hence the dominant figure of the PLO leadership. For more than thirty years, Al Fatah has been a coalition of moderate, conservative, and radical nationalists who accepted the tactical necessity of cooperating with Arab governments, including those they regarded as reactionary, to help achieve their goals. Predominantly Muslim in membership, Al Fatah generally has eschewed commitment to radical ideologies such as Islamic revolution or Marxism and refrained from interference in the internal affairs of Arab states.

The progressive moderation of Al Fatah's goals after 1973 led to major splits within the organization. The original objective to liberate all of pre-1948 Palestine was replaced in 1974 with the aim

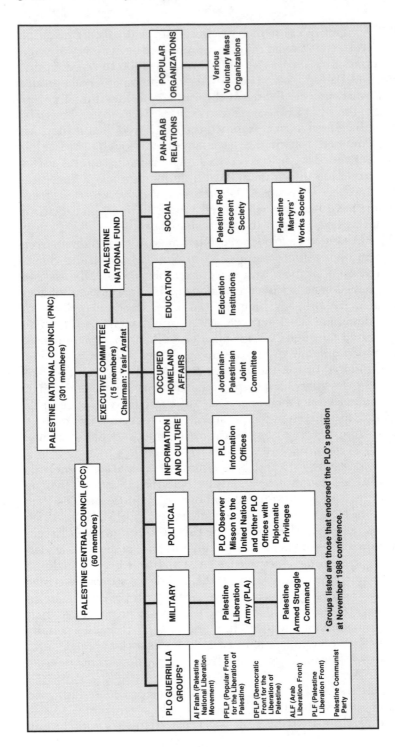

*Figure 12. Structure of the Palestine Liberation Organization (PLO), 1989*

of establishing a transitional state on the West Bank and the Gaza Strip. Sabri Khalil al Banna, known by his code name of Abu Nidal, vehemently opposed this change. Abu Nidal and a small group of his supporters defected from Al Fatah and formed the Al Fatah Revolutionary Council. A more serious split occurred in 1983 when Said Musa Muragha (also known as Abu Musa) organized Al Fatah fighters in Lebanon who feared Arafat's reconciliation with Egypt would lead eventually to recognition of Israel. The supporters of Arafat and Abu Musa fought each other for control of Palestinian refugee camps in Lebanon during 1983 and 1984, with heavy casualties on both sides. The anti-Arafat forces received support from Syria that helped them expel Arafat loyalists from camps in areas occupied by the Syrian army. Abu Musa and the Al Fatah dissidents eventually formed a new group called Al Fatah Uprising.

From a tactical and ideological standpoint, the Popular Front for the Liberation of Palestine (PFLP) was the principal counterpoint to Al Fatah. George Habash and Ahmad Jibril founded the PFLP after the June 1967 War. The PFLP was a consciously Marxist-Leninist organization. It defined as enemies not just Israel and Zionism, but also imperialism and the Arab regimes that cooperated with the United States, the country it proclaimed to be the main imperialist power. It called such Arab regimes reactionary, advocated their overthrow and the establishment of progressive, democratic, and secular governments in all Arab states, including Palestine. Habash and the other PFLP leaders soon were divided, however, on the issue of whether armed struggle or political considerations should take precedence in achieving their objectives. Jibril broke with Habash in 1968 and formed a rival organization, the Popular Front for the Liberation of Palestine-General Command (PFLP-GC), which placed primary emphasis on armed struggle. The following year Nayif Hawatmah, who was an East Bank Jordanian, also split from the PFLP and organized the Democratic Front for the Liberation of Palestine (DFLP). Hawatmah's DFLP tended to stress exploring political options before resorting to armed struggle.

The PFLP, PFLP-GC, and DFLP held attitudes toward reactionary Arab regimes that precluded cooperation with Hussein, whose government they regarded as a prime candidate for revolutionary overthrow. Their openly professed ideology and maintenance of armed bases within Jordan's Palestinian refugee camps were major factors in precipitating the 1970 conflict between the guerrillas and the Jordanian army. After the guerrillas were suppressed, Habash, Hawatmah, and Jibril remained hostile and unforgiving toward Hussein. When Arafat began the process of reconciliation with Hussein in 1973, they opposed any PLO ties or even dialogue with Jordan and publicly called for Hussein's overthrow. Habash and Jibril were the principal organizers in 1974 of the rejectionist front of guerrilla groups, which refused to accept the PLO decision to establish a Palestinian state on the West Bank and the Gaza Strip. The rejectionists were those groups that rejected any negotiations or compromises with Israel and insisted on using armed struggle to liberate all of historic Palestine. In 1983 Jibril supported Abu Musa and the Al Fatah dissidents, joining with them to form the National Alliance, which opposed any diplomatic initiatives or cooperation with Hussein.

In addition to Al Fatah and the Marxist groups, several smaller guerrilla organizations were active in 1989. The most important of these were As Saiqa, the Arab Liberation Front (ALF), the Popular Struggle Front (PSF), and the Palestine Liberation Front (PLF). As Saiqa was formed in 1968 in Damascus and has continued to be politically and financially dependent upon Syria. Palestinians who lived outside of Syria generally perceived As Saiqa as a tool of the Syrian government. As Saiqa's counterpart was the ALF, formed in Baghdad in 1969. In the 1970s, the ALF supported the rejectionist front, as did Iraq. In the 1980s, however, the ALF aligned itself with Arafat's Al Fatah, a position consistent with that of Iraq. The PSF has consistently advocated armed struggle since it was founded in 1967. Prior to 1980, the PSF was supported by Iraq, but since 1980 Syria has been its principal backer. The PLF was formed in 1977 as a result of a split within the PFLP–GC. Originally part of the rejectionist front, since 1983 it has been one of the groups trying to effect a reconciliation between Arafat and Abu Musa.

The PLO's organizational equivalent to a parliament was the Palestine National Council (PNC), in 1989 based in Algiers. The PNC's 301 deputies represented the Palestinian diaspora. Included among them were representatives of the Palestinian parties (the political wings of the various guerrilla groups); the six guerrilla groups that accepted the policies of the PLO (Al Fatah, PFLP, DFLP, ALF, PLF, and the Palestine Communist Party); student and educational groups; youth and women's groups; professional associations; labor unions; and the Palestine Red Crescent Society. In addition, the Palestinian communities in various Arab and non-Arab countries were represented.

The PNC was supposed to meet once a year, but political complications often forced the postponement of annual gatherings. The factional strife that plagued the PLO following the sixteenth PNC conclave in February 1983 prevented convening a full session for four years. Although a PNC meeting was held in Amman in November 1984, its legitimacy was questioned because several of the guerrilla leaders, including Habash of the PFLP and Hawatmah of the DFLP, refused to attend. The eighteenth PNC, which met in Algiers in April 1987, represented the first effort to heal the rift in the PLO and achieve a consensus on policy. Although the PFLP-GC, As Saiqa, the PSF, and the Abu Musa faction did not participate, the PFLP, DFLP, and the Palestine Communist Party—the three guerrilla groups that, like Al Fatah, had a reputation for independence of Arab governments—did attend and agreed to accept PNC decisions. Abu Nidal also attended the eighteenth PNC. However, the other leaders voted not to grant his group representation on the PNC because they believed his reputation as a notorious terrorist would tarnish the PLO's image at a time when the organization was seeking diplomatic support for an international peace conference.

The 1987 PNC meeting adopted several significant resolutions pertaining to the PLO's conflict with Israel. It voted to endorse an international peace conference on the basis of UN General Assembly resolutions that recognized the PLO and the right of the Palestinians to self-determination; it called for PLO participation in such a conference as a full partner, and not as part of a Jordanian delegation; it abrogated the PLO-Jordan accord of 1985, but also advocated maintaining "special" ties between Jordanians and Palestinians; and it authorized the PLO to develop relations with groups in Israel that supported Palestinian self-determination. These decisions were a prelude to the even more significant resolutions that were passed at the historic nineteenth PNC meeting in Algiers in November 1988.

Between PNC congresses, the Palestine Central Committee (PCC), created in 1973, set policies and carried out specific programs and actions undertaken by the PLO's cabinet, the fifteen-member Executive Committee. The PCC's actual function, however, was limited to a consultative role; its sixty members, appointed by the PNC based on the recommendation of the Executive Committee, included representatives from the Executive Committee and the major guerrilla groups. The PNC's speaker or chairman presided over PCC meetings. The legislative and executive functions of these top PLO bodies were in accordance with the principles and policies contained in three key documents: the Palestinian National Charter; the Fifteen-Point Political Program; and the National Unity Program.

Although the PNC was officially described as the highest policymaking body and supreme organ of the PLO, the real center of power was the fifteen-member Executive Committee. The committee's members were elected by and collectively responsible to the PNC. The manner of their election ensured representation of the major guerrilla and political groups on the committee. Arafat was re-elected chairman of the Executive Committee in 1988, a position he has held since 1969. Al Fatah had three seats on the committee; in addition, Arafat generally obtained the support of the seven "independents," the committee members who were not affiliated with any of the guerrilla groups.

The administration of the PLO was grouped under nine main functions that were carried out in different countries depending on local Palestinian needs. These were supported by funds collected and distributed by the PLO's treasury and financial arm, the Palestine National Fund. The fund obtained its revenues from payments made by Arab governments in accordance with agreements made at the summit level (i.e., the Baghdad Summit of 1978); from voluntary contributions by Palestinians; from the 3 to 6 percent income tax levied by some Arab states on the salaries of resident Palestinian workers; and from loans and grants by Arab as well as non-Arab countries. Iraq and Syria provided financial aid directly to particular guerrilla groups despite persistent efforts by the PLO to terminate this practice and to centralize fund-raising and fund-distributing procedures.

In 1989 the PLO maintained "diplomatic" missions in more than 120 countries that recognized it as the legitimate representative of the Palestinian people. Although the PLO had not proclaimed a government-in-exile for the West Bank and the Gaza Strip, more than twenty-five countries recognized it as the de jure government of the independent state of Palestine, declared at the 1988 PNC meeting in Algiers. The PLO has maintained a mission at UN headquarters in New York since being granted observer status in 1974. The PLO also operated numerous "information offices" in the major cities of the world. In 1988 the United States government ordered the closure of PLO's information office in Washington.

The PLO's nearest equivalent to a Red Cross Society was called the Palestine Red Crescent Society (PRCS). The PRCS supported hospitals and clinics for Palestinians in Arab countries as well as in the West Bank and the Gaza Strip. Prior to the Israeli invasion of Lebanon in 1982, the PRCS operated ten major hospitals and eleven clinics in that country. These facilities provided a broad range of medical services to Palestinian refugees at no cost or for nominal fees. The hospitals and clinics were severely damaged during the occupation of south Lebanon and the siege of Beirut. Since 1983, the periodic fighting in Lebanon has seriously impeded the

PRCS's efforts to reconstruct medical centers and provide health services.

The PLO also sponsored numerous educational and cultural projects and operated an economic enterprise called the Palestine Martyrs' Works Society, better known by its Arab acronym SAMED, which ran small factories. SAMED's workshops produced such items as blankets, tents, uniforms, civilian clothes, shoes, handicrafts, furniture, and toys. SAMED was originally established in 1970 to provide vocational training for the children of Palestinian men and women killed in service to the Palestinian national cause. After 1976 SAMED decided to accept any Palestinian needing employment if work were available. Most SAMED workshops were in the refugee camps in northern Lebanon and thus were not affected by the Israeli invasion of south Lebanon in 1982. SAMED workshops and activities were disrupted, however, during the 1983–84 fighting between Arafat loyalists and dissidents in Palestinian camps in northern Lebanon.

The military function of the PLO was under the supreme command of the chairman of the Executive Committee. The PLO's regular military arm was called the Palestine Liberation Army (PLA). Its units were stationed in various Arab countries where they coordinated their activities with those of Arab armies. The coordination was centrally handled by the Palestinian Armed Struggle Command, which also was responsible for law and order in Palestinian refugee camps in Jordan, Lebanon, and Syria.

## Foreign Policy

Jordan's foreign policy has been a function mainly of its response to developments in the Arab-Israeli conflict. Its generally moderate and carefully measured response has been based on its appraisal that effective Arab unity is a precondition for substantive peace negotiations with Israel. The persistence of intra-Arab differences over the form and substance of pan-Arab cooperation has constrained Jordan to steer a flexible and prudent course. In addition, the scarcity of domestic resources and the consequent heavy dependence on outside powers for economic and military support have contributed to Jordan's caution in foreign policy. Moreover, the PLO's enhanced stature since the mid-1970s as a key factor in the processes of Middle East reconciliation and peace has been a further compelling reason for Jordan's generally pragmatic responses to an uncertain foreign policy milieu.

### Relations with Israel

In 1989 Jordan still refrained from establishing diplomatic relations with Israel. The absence of formal relations notwithstanding, the two countries had cooperated directly or indirectly since 1967 in a multiplicity of matters pertaining to the West Bank, the Israeli-occupied territory whose Palestinian population retained Jordanian citizenship until 1988. Hussein's aim was to maintain influence and eventually regain control of the West Bank, a goal that had not been realized by 1988, when he renounced Jordan's claim to sovereignty of the area. Hussein's ambitions were frustrated by Israel's unwillingness to negotiate seriously any withdrawal from the West Bank and by the increasing popularity of the PLO. As early as 1974, Israel's refusal to consider a United States-mediated disengagement agreement with Jordan, similar to the ones that had then been concluded with Egypt and Syria, weakened Hussein's image as a leader who could recover occupied Arab land. Israel's refusal also helped to strengthen pan-Arab support for the PLO's claim to represent West Bank Palestinians. Later that year, Arab heads of state meeting in a summit conference in Rabat, Morocco, agreed to recognize the PLO's right to establish an independent state in the West Bank once the latter was liberated from Israel.

Although Hussein paid lip service to the 1974 Rabat decision, he continued to hope Jordan would recover the West Bank. His hopes were nurtured by Israel's refusal to deal with the PLO. To maximize Jordan's political leverage from the new situation, Hussein pursued simultaneously a highly visible policy of reconciliation with the PLO and a less perceptible policy of cultivating pro-Hashimite politicians in the West Bank. The measures intended to preserve Jordan's traditional links to the West Bank actually were undertaken with the tacit approval of Israel. These measures included authorizing the continuation of the long-standing economic and family ties between the East and West banks under the "open bridges" policy; continuing payment (until 1988) of salaries to Palestinian officials on the government payroll before and since 1967; strengthening economic links by increased imports from the West Bank and by continued extension of development grants and loans to Palestinian firms in the West Bank; and providing government guarantees for private Jordanian loans to West Bank municipalities.

After 1977, when Egypt's President Anwar as Sadat initiated direct negotiations with Israel that led to a separate peace agreement (and Egypt's temporary ostracism from the Arab world), Hussein was unwilling to follow Sadat's lead without prior pan-Arab acquiescence. Hussein apparently believed that in the absence of broad Arab support to legitimize any political talks with Israel, his own rule in the East Bank could be threatened. Consequently, he refused to participate in the Camp David process and was skeptical

*View of Amman, Jordan's capital*

of President Reagan's 1982 proposal for a West Bank "entity" in association with Jordan. Israel's rejection of the Reagan Plan provided Hussein the boon of not needing to respond to an initiative that the Palestinians claimed would deny them genuine self-determination. Two years later, when Shimon Peres became prime minister of Israel, in September 1984, he offered to negotiate directly with Jordan without the participation of the PLO. Hussein decided the state of pan-Arab politics precluded his consideration of a "Jordanian option" at that time. Instead, he called for an international peace conference that would include a joint Jordan-PLO delegation. Hussein perceived an international forum that brought together both the United States and the Soviet Union as well as the principal Arab states and Israel as a protective umbrella under which he could enter into negotiations with the Israelis.

Peres, whose Labor Party was willing to consider Israeli withdrawal from at least part of the West Bank, endorsed Hussein's idea of an international peace conference in an October 1985 speech before the United Nations. Subsequently, he initiated secret meetings with Hussein to discuss procedures for convening such a conference and ways to finesse the issue of PLO participation. Peres opposed the presence of the PLO at a possible conference, but did not object to non-PLO representatives of Palestinians attending. Hussein was not able to obtain firm Israeli commitments, however, because Peres's coalition partner, Likud Bloc leader Yitzhak Shamir, opposed the convening of an international conference and prevented the government from achieving consensus on the issue. After Shamir became prime minister in late 1986, Peres, as foreign minister, continued his diplomatic efforts on behalf of an international conference. Peres had at least one publicized meeting with Hussein in London, but he lacked support from his own government. Hussein, who believed that Peres was interested in substantive negotiations over the West Bank while Shamir was not, took the unprecedented step during the Israeli elections of 1988 of announcing that a Labor Party victory would be better for the peace process.

## Relations with Arab States

In 1989 Jordan maintained relatively cordial relations with most other Arab states. Jordan's closest ties were with Egypt, Iraq, Kuwait, and Saudi Arabia. King Hussein made frequent trips to these countries to confer with their leaders on regional and international strategy. Kuwait, Saudi Arabia and other Arab oil-producers provided Jordan with financial aid in accordance with guidelines originally agreed on at the November 1978 Baghdad

Summit. The total amount of these grants had declined dramatically by 1984 because of the budgetary problems that depressed oil prices caused in petroleum-producing countries. Nonetheless, they remained an important source of total government revenue for Jordan (see GDP by Sector, ch. 3).

Jordan's close relations with Iraq developed as a result of Hussein's strong support for President Saddam Husayn during the latter's eight-year war with Iran (1980–88). The monarch's ardent backing of Saddam was attributable at least in part to his fears that a collapse of the Iraqi regime could result in Jordan's eastern neighbor being ruled by a radicalized Shia religious government allied to Iran. The relationship also benefited Jordan in various ways. For example, Jordan's only port, Al Aqabah, served throughout the war as a major transshipment center for Iraqi imports. Goods off-loaded at Al Aqabah were trucked overland to Iraq by Jordanian transportation companies, in the process generating local employment, handling fees, and profitable business. Jordan also exported a variety of light consumer goods to Iraq, although the value and volume of this trade fluctuated in accordance with Iraqi foreign exchange problems. Both during and after the war, Iraq, whose army used primarily Soviet-made equipment, periodically gave to Jordan United States- and British-made military hardware captured from Iran, including at least sixty United States-manufactured M–47 tanks (see Military Cooperation with Other Arab States, ch. 5).

In 1984 Jordan became the first Arab state to reestablish diplomatic relations with Egypt. Hussein had begun advocating Egypt's reintegration into the Arab community of nations as early as 1981. The king perceived Egypt as an effective bulwark against the spread of radical Islamic political movements that he believed were being engendered by the Iran-Iraq War. Following the 1982 Israeli invasion of Lebanon and the expulsion of the PLO from that country, unofficial consultations with Egypt on regional security issues became routine. PLO chief Arafat's trip to Egypt in December 1983—the first by an Arab leader since the Baghdad Summit of November 1978—paved the way for Jordan's resumption of official relations without fear of being branded a traitor to Arab nationalism.

Following the reestablishment of diplomatic relations, Jordan and Egypt became extremely close allies. Hussein frequently praised Egyptian president Husni Mubarak as one of the Arab world's great leaders. Mubarak supported Hussein's pro-Iraq policy, his efforts to involve moderate Palestinians in the peace process, and his call for an international peace conference. Hussein and Arafat met several times on "neutral" Egyptian territory; when their personal relations were tense, such as in 1986–87, Mubarak mediated and kept them on civil terms. Hussein reciprocated Mubarak's diplomatic support by trying to persuade other Arab heads of state that Egypt should be readmitted to the League of Arab States (Arab League). In February 1989, Egypt and Jordan joined with Iraq and the Yemen Arab Republic (North Yemen) to form a new Arab Cooperation Council, a regional organization modeled after the Gulf Cooperation Council.

Jordan's relations with Syria were correct in 1989, although there had been considerable strain between them during most of the previous two decades. In September 1970, a Syrian military unit had crossed into Jordan to aid the Palestinian guerrillas who were fighting the Jordanian army. The Syrian force was repulsed, but relations remained tense and were severed in July 1971. Relations with Syria improved briefly following the October 1973 War, but deteriorated again by the late 1970s. Syria apparently feared Hussein's close ties with Washington would involve Jordan in the Camp David process. When religiously inspired disturbances broke out in Aleppo and other Syrian cities during the winter of 1979–80, the government immediately suspected—and accused—Jordan of complicity. In addition, Syria had a bitter rivalry with Iraq. Damascus perceived Amman's support of Iraq in that country's war with Iran (initiated by an Iraqi invasion of Iran in September 1980) as confirmation of conspiracy theories about Baghdad trying to encircle Syria. By the end of 1980, relations between Jordan and Syria had deteriorated to such an extent that military clashes appeared possible along the common border where both countries had massed troops. The escalating tension eventually was defused by Saudi Arabian diplomatic intervention, although relations remained strained.

Jordan broke diplomatic relations with Syria in 1981, charging Damascus with plotting to assassinate its prime minister and kidnapping its ambassador to Lebanon. For the next five years, the two neighbors were estranged. Amman accused Syria of assisting radical Palestinian groups who carried out several political killings of Jordanian diplomats in Europe and the Middle East. Tentative efforts to improve relations in 1983–84 were aborted by Syrian denunciation of Jordan's resumption of relations with Egypt. Finally, in the fall and winter of 1985–86, Saudi Arabia mediated reconciliation talks that led to a restoration of diplomatic ties. In May 1986, the Jordanian prime minister became the first high-ranking official from Amman to visit Syria since 1977. Relations between Jordan and Syria gradually improved since then.

Jordan maintained cordial relations with the Arab states of the Persian Gulf in 1989. These countries—Bahrain, Kuwait, Oman, Qatar, Saudi Arabia, and the United Arab Emirates—were collectively Jordan's most important source of foreign financial aid. The level of their assistance, especially that from Kuwait, has fallen, however, since 1981. Thousands of Jordanians and Palestinians holding Jordanian passports continued to work in the Persian Gulf in business, government, education, and engineering. The remittances they sent to their families in Jordan, especially those living in the refugee camps, represented a significant proportion of Jordan's foreign exchange earnings. The Persian Gulf countries also were markets for Jordanian agricultural and consumer exports.

Jordan's relations with the other Arab states—excepting Libya—were generally good in 1989. Tensions existed over economic policy between Jordan and Morocco, however, as both countries exported phosphates. The amount of Jordan's reserves of these minerals and the value of its exports were significantly less than those of Morocco, a major international producer. Jordan, which traditionally exported its phosphates to Southeast Asia, complained that Morocco had stolen its Asian markets between 1985 and 1987 by deliberately selling its phosphates at prices lower than it cost Jordan to mine and transport the minerals.

Jordan had a history of tense relations with Libya, deriving from Libyan support since 1970 for Palestinian guerrilla groups opposed to Hussein. The most serious incident between the two countries occurred in February 1984, when the Jordanian embassy in Tripoli was destroyed during demonstrations organized by the Libyan government to protest Hussein's support of Arafat and his call for reconciliation with Egypt. Jordan broke diplomatic relations following this episode. In 1988 Jordan received a Libyan delegation sent to Amman to discuss normalizing relations between the two countries.

## Relations with the United States

Although Amman established diplomatic relations with Washington in 1949, the United States did not become actively involved in Jordan until 1957, when it replaced Britain as the Hashimite Kingdom's principal Western source of foreign aid and political support. Jordan and the United States never entered into treaty commitments, but Washington's policy was to ensure Jordan's continued independence and stability. Thus, the United States assisted Jordan in equipping and training its military forces. During the civil war of 1970–71, the United States firmly supported Hussein, although it did not become directly involved in the conflict. After

Jordan's army had defeated the PLO guerrillas, Washington extended substantial budgetary and military aid to the Hashimite Kingdom. This aid contributed significantly toward Jordanian recovery from the damages suffered not only in the civil war but also in the June 1967 War and during the intensive Israeli shelling of the Jordan Valley between 1968 and 1970. Hussein's close alignment with the United States before and after the civil war predictably aroused strong anti-American sentiment among Palestinians in Jordan and elsewhere.

The October 1973 War, in which Jordan was not a direct participant, brought Jordan and the United States much closer in the peace process that began after the conflict. Jordan joined with the United States in support of UN Security Council Resolution 338. This resolution called on the parties involved in the October 1973 War to cease their hostilities and to implement UN Security Council Resolution 242 of 1967 providing for a peace based on Israeli withdrawal from occupied territories. Hussein hoped to obtain American backing for a return of the West Bank to Jordanian control. His expectations were buoyed by Washington's success in negotiating disengagement and limited withdrawal of forces agreements between Egypt and Israel and Syria and Israel.

The failure of the United States during 1974 to persuade Israel to pull back its forces from part of the West Bank as an initial step toward a peace agreement with Jordan disillusioned Hussein with respect to the ability of the Americans to pressure Israel on the issue of withdrawal from the occupied Palestinian territories. Although he continued to value Washington's reaffirmations of support for Jordan's security and economic progress, Hussein became increasingly skeptical of American assurances that the West Bank would be reunited with the East Bank. Consequently, he refrained from participation in the Camp David process, which he was convinced would be used by Israel to perpetuate its control of the West Bank. After Egyptian and Israeli negotiations on the autonomy plan had stalled, Hussein tried to rekindle United States interest in an international conference to deal with territory for the Palestinians.

Throughout the 1980s, the United States continued to assign Jordan a key role in a resolution of the status of the West Bank. Hussein believed, however, that Washington did not understand how essential it was for the stability of his regime to regain full control over all of the West Bank and how politically dangerous it would be for him to agree to any partial measures. For example, Hussein did not publicly criticize President Reagan's September 1982 proposal for Middle East peace; but since this plan restricted self-determination for Palestinians on the West Bank to an "autonomous authority" in association with Jordan, he regarded American expectation of his endorsement as unrealistic. Hussein accepted that political developments since 1974 made it impossible to ignore the PLO in any peace negotiations. Thus, one of his policy aims vis-à-vis the United States became to convince Washington to deal—at least unofficially—with the PLO. From the end of 1982 until the end of 1988, Hussein served as an intermediary between the United States and the PLO, attempting to get both parties to make the kind of political concessions that were necessary before a dialogue could be initiated.

During the early 1980s, Hussein seriously considered expanding Jordan's military relations with the United States. He gave tentative approval for the creation of an unpublicized 8,000-strong Jordanian strike force that would respond to requests for assistance from Arab countries within a 2,400-kilometer radius of Jordan. The intended target of this special force was to be the Persian Gulf, where the traditional allies of both Jordan and the United States feared the potentially destabilizing consequences of the Iran-Iraq War. The United States agreed to provide the special Jordanian unit with weapons and other military equipment. In an apparent effort to obtain approval of the United States Congress for the extra funding needed to arm the strike force, in early 1984 the Reagan administration disclosed its formation. This unexpected disclosure caused consternation in Amman, and news of the Jordanian strike force provoked harsh criticism from Syria and from Palestinian guerrilla groups opposed to Hussein. In order to minimize negative repercussions, Hussein tried to distance his country from the strike force by portraying it as a United States initiative in which Jordan had no real interest or substantive involvement. Congress did not approve the requested funds, and the plan was subsequently abandoned.

Hussein's disappointment with American policy increased when Congress later refused to authorize selling weapons to Jordan and voted to reduce the amount of aid the administration requested as punishment for its perception that Amman had failed to cooperate with Israel. Hussein resented these measures because he believed he had exerted great efforts in persuading Palestinian and other Arab leaders to adopt more moderate and flexible positions and had himself agreed to several private meetings with Peres. In 1989 Jordan's relations with the United States remained friendly and cooperative in economic and military matters but were clouded by Hussein's lack of confidence in Washington's policy toward Israel and the occupied territories.

## Relations with Other Countries

In the years after independence, Jordan followed a generally pro-Western foreign policy as a result of its special relationship with Britain, to which the Hashimite Kingdom owed its existence and which became the principal supplier of financial and other aid. Jordan's special relationship with Britain ended, for all practical purposes, in 1957, when the Anglo-Jordanian Treaty of 1948 was terminated by mutual agreement. Thereafter, the United States became actively involved in Jordan, replacing Britain as the principal Western source of foreign aid and political support but without treaty commitments. Nevertheless, Britain and Jordan continued to maintain cordial relations. Hussein made annual official visits to London to discuss Middle East policy. In 1984, Queen Elizabeth II made the first trip ever by a British monarch to Jordan. Prime Minister Margaret Thatcher subsequently visited Amman in 1985. During the 1980s, Britain again became a major weapons supplier for Jordan. As of 1989, the most recent sale (in September 1988) was an agreement to provide Jordan with the advanced Tornado aircraft.

In 1989 Jordan maintained friendly relations with the Soviet Union. Amman first established relations with Moscow in 1963. Two years later, Jordan signed its first cultural and technical cooperation agreement with the Soviet Union. Hussein made his first state visit to Moscow in the wake of the June 1967 War. Since then there have been numerous exchanges of high-level visits, including several official trips by Hussein. Jordan has purchased military equipment from the Soviet Union periodically since 1980 as part of a policy to diversify military supply sources. In 1985 Jordan bought a major Soviet air defense system after the United States Congress canceled a planned sale of Stinger antiaircraft missiles to the country. Jordan and the Soviet Union have signed several accords pertaining to cultural, economic, and scientific cooperation. In his advocacy of an international peace conference to deal with the occupied Palestinian territories, Hussein has insisted that the Soviet Union be included.

In 1989 Jordan had friendly relations with most other countries, including those in both Eastern Europe and Western Europe. The major exception was Iran, with which Jordan had severed diplomatic relations in 1981 as a demonstration of solidarity with Iraq. The countries of the European Economic Community and Japan were major sources of Jordan's imports. France also sold weapons to Jordan, including twenty Mirage-2000 aircraft in 1988.

## Membership in International Organizations

In 1989 Jordan was a member of the League of Arab States and the Arab Cooperation Council, a regional economic pact that included Egypt, Iraq, and North Yemen. Jordan was a member of the International Committee of the Red Cross and had been a member of the UN since 1955. The United Nations Relief and Works Agency (UNRWA) for Palestine Refugees in the Near East maintained ten refugee camps in Jordan (see fig. 6). UNRWA's biggest task was the provision of primary, secondary, and vocational schools for Palestinian refugee children living in the camps. UNRWA also operated health clinics and provided food for indigent refugees.

# Media

In 1989 Jordan had four daily newspapers, all published in Amman. One, *The Jordan Times,* was printed in English. The three Arabic dailies were *Sawt ash Shaab* (Voice of the People), *Ar Rai* (Opinion), and *Ad Dustur* (The Constitution). The press was mostly privately owned and subject to censorship. The Arabic-language papers had been suspended at various times throughout the 1980s for publishing articles that the government considered objectiona ble. In 1988 the government ordered the dissolution of the board of directors of all three Arabic papers. The Ministry of Culture and Information was responsible for most press censorship on a daily basis and frequently provided editors with guidance on how to report on sensitive foreign policy and security matters. In practice, editors generally exercised self-censorship to minimize conflicts with the authorities.

The government also tried to control individual journalists by rewarding those deemed cooperative and by punishing those whose stories it considered critical. The most common punishment was the withdrawal of government-issued press credentials, which all writers were required to have in order to work for a newspaper or news agency. This procedure was used to prevent several journalists (including a principal writer for *The Jordan Times*) from publishing during 1987 and 1988. Journalists also have been subjected to house arrest. In June 1987, the government dissolved the Writers' Association, a professional organization of journalists, charging that it had become a political group and had contacts with illegal parties. The Ministry of Culture and Information subsequently sponsored an official union, the Journalists' Association, and required all writers to join it.

The government attempted to discourage the Arabic press of East Jerusalem from publishing critical stories, especially about Hussein's

219

relations with the PLO, by such means as banning single issues of papers and magazines, refusing to renew the passports of West Bank journalists, and sending messages through discreet channels that certain writers or editors would be arrested if they entered Jordan. Foreign publications and journalists also were banned when their articles criticized Jordan. In 1986 Western correspondents expressed concern about the government's interference with press freedom during and after the disturbances at Yarmuk University. In 1988 the government expelled an American correspondent for National Broadcasting Company (NBC) because he had reported on political repression in Jordan.

The government operated an official news agency known as PETRA. Several international news services maintained offices in Amman, including Agence France-Presse, Associated Press, Reuters, and TASS. Radio and television broadcasting were controlled by the government. Jordan Radio and Television had twenty hours of Arabic radio programs daily, and fifteen hours in English. There were an estimated 700,000 privately owned radio receivers in 1989; also, radio reception in village cafés was popular. Jordan Radio and Television also broadcast ninety hours weekly of television programs in Arabic and English. In 1989 there were an estimated 250,000 television sets in the country. Both radio and television accepted advertisements.

\* \* \*

The literature on Jordanian government and politics since the early 1970s is relatively scarce. Among the readily available studies in English that merit reading are Peter Gubser's *Jordan: Crossroads of Middle Eastern Events* and Clinton Bailey's *Jordan's Palestinian Challenge, 1948–1983: A Political Challenge.* Both books were written in the early 1980s and thus do not cover events from 1983 on. *Middle East Insight, Middle East International* [London], and *Middle East Report* are magazines that regularly feature articles about Jordan's politics, relations with the PLO, and foreign policy. Lamis Andoni, Naseer H. Aruri, Rashid Khalidi, and Robin Wright are the principal writers who specialize on Jordanian affairs. Articles by these authors also may be found in various other journals that deal with international relations and Middle East politics. (For further information and complete citations, see Bibliography.)

# Chapter 5. National Security

*Mosaic of a walled city, called Castron Mephaon,*
*from the Umm ar Rasas pavement in a Byzantine church, ca. 780*

IN ASSESSING THE DIMENSIONS of national security in Jordan, it is essential to recall that for centuries conflicts and rivalries of differing political and religious ideologies have generated tension and crisis in this region. Since achieving sovereignty in 1946, Jordan has experienced such destabilizing traumas as the assassination of the country's first king and subsequently of two prime ministers, five Arab-Israeli wars, a vicious civil war with Palestinian (see Glossary) guerrillas, and repeated assassination attempts targeting King Hussein ibn Talal ibn Abdullah ibn Hussein Al Hashimi.

Jordan not only has survived in this volatile climate but also, as of 1989, the thirty-sixth year of Hussein's reign, had achieved a degree of stability in its domestic situation and in its relations with its neighbors. The king's position has been strongly reinforced by the allegiance of the Jordan Arab Army, the former Arab Legion. A highly motivated, disciplined force with impressive firepower and mobility despite its compact scale, the Jordan Arab Army has been regarded as the most competent of any Arab army in the Middle East. In contrast to the Syrian, Iraqi, or Israeli armies, however, Jordanian troops have not been tested by exposure to major conflict for many years.

Jordan's international security situation in 1989 seemed less precarious than it had been at almost any time in the past. Relations with surrounding states were on a relatively solid footing. The border facing Israeli-held territories was peaceful. Jordan had succeeded in suppressing attacks from its land that might bring Israeli retaliation, except for isolated incursions into Israeli-held territory by extremist elements of the Palestine Liberation Organization (PLO). Although differences remained between Jordan and various Palestinian leaders over the approaches to Arab-Israeli peace negotiations, Jordan's relations with the dominant Yasir Arafat wing of the PLO were less strained than with Syrian-supported extremists such as the Popular Front for the Liberation of Palestine-General Command. Disruptive actions by Palestinian militants in Jordan were curbed quickly by the security forces. Worries that the uprising (*intifadah*) among Palestinians under Israeli occupation might spill over to the Palestinian population of Jordan had not materialized. Unrest arising from the deteriorating economic situation in 1989 had been directed against the prime minister rather than the institutions of the monarchy.

Jordan's military posture was based primarily on the possibility of conflict with Israel, although on its own Jordan would be unable to counter a full-scale Israeli attack. The country's borders also were exposed to a long-term threat from a potentially hostile Syria. Jordan retained sufficient capability to give an aggressively inclined neighbor pause, but it did not have the resources to keep pace with the buildup of modern arms by nearby countries of the Middle East. As of 1989, however, most observers considered the prospect of armed conflict between Jordan and Israel, Syria, or other states in the region as remote.

Jordan has had a tradition of military cooperation with Britain and the United States, and its organizational pattern, the outlook of its military leaders, training concepts, and weapons arsenal have reflected these links. The United States Congress had prevented the executive branch from providing Jordan with certain advanced ground and air weapons in the late 1980s. Forced to shift to other sources of equipment, Jordan turned to France as the principal supplier of combat aircraft and to the Soviet Union for an array of air defense missile systems. Even with heavy reliance on financial backing from other Arab countries, notably Saudi Arabia, defense imposed a heavy burden on the nation's frail economy. By the late 1980s, Jordan's deepening domestic economic plight had combined with the tapering off of Arab aid to place severe pressure on the military budget.

Backed by a traditionally loyal military and the efficient forces of public order, Hussein's throne appeared to be secure. Nonetheless, in an era of rapidly evolving weapons technology, a constant effort would be necessary to maintain the credibility of national security institutions as the guarantors of Jordan's domestic stability, its territorial integrity, and its role as a moderating factor in Middle East peace efforts.

## Security: A Perennial Concern

From the beginning of Hussein's reign in 1953, the king's position as a pro-Western moderate in the continuing struggle between Middle East Arab states and Israel has kept him in the forefront of political uncertainty. He has had to deal with the preeminent strategic drawback of sharing a longer common border with Israel than any other Arab country. To compound the unease generated by this 345-kilometer frontier, repeated Arab-Israeli wars demonstrated that Israeli forces always fielded vastly superior military capability. As a consequence, the king for many years has avoided engaging Israel in battle and has prevented provocations launched from Jordanian territory by PLO militants that could spark Israeli retaliation. Domestically, the danger posed to Hussein's rule by armed Palestinian groups during the 1960s had by the late 1980s given way to new sources of potential instability—the increasing militancy of the Islamic revival movement and the frustration of lowered economic expectations, together with civilian impatience over the limits on political expression. For the immediate future, however, the security forces seemed sufficiently well equipped to suppress agitation and organized attempts to subvert the monarchy.

## Dimensions of the Military Threat

As of mid-1989, the Jordan River valley, forming the boundary zone with Israel and the Israeli-occupied West Bank (see Glossary), had been quiet for nearly two decades. In 1970 Hussein's army had begun its drive against the PLO militia that was using Jordan as a base for attacks on Israeli positions in the West Bank (see The Palestinian Factor, this ch.). The Israeli leadership has acknowledged that pacification of this border has been the result of Jordanian measures taken to prevent PLO terrorism. Jordan was not a declared belligerent in 1973 when Egypt and Syria simultaneously attacked Israel; however, Jordan did commit armored units to support Syrian defenders on the Golan Heights during the last stages of the war in actions confined to Syrian territory (see The Military Heritage, this ch.). Jordan did not join Syria and the PLO in contesting Israel's invasion of Lebanon in 1982.

Although Israel throughout the 1980s exercised restraint in its military conduct with respect to Jordan, the destructive potential of the Israel Defense Forces (IDF) continued to preoccupy the Jordanian command. Despite the long period intervening since raids and bombardments by Israel in retaliation for attacks by PLO guerrillas, the ferocity of Israel's earlier punitive actions—most of the victims being Jordanians with no links to the PLO—had left a permanent impression of Israeli belligerence and hostility. Jordan was also conscious of the sentiment in Israel that favored solving the West Bank Palestinian problem by ejecting all Arabs from the area and sending them to Jordan. Any attempt to execute such a plan would inevitably require military intimidation or the direct application of Israel's military superiority.

In the event of renewed hostilities between Israel and Syria, it was also possible that Israel would try to outflank Syrian positions in the Golan Heights area by swinging south into Jordan. Such an action would present its own problems, including a difficult river crossing. During the 1973 conflict, neither Israel nor Syria violated Jordanian territorial integrity in spite of Jordan's efforts to reinforce the Syrian defenses.

Jordan was also obliged to take account of Syrian military power. The aggressive Damascus regime had frequently been at odds politically with Hussein until an easing of bilateral relations began in late 1985. Syrian tank units had crossed into Jordan in 1970 to aid the Palestinian militia defying the government. The Syrians had massed three divisions and more than 800 tanks on the Jordanian border in 1980 in a dispute over military training camps in Jordan for opponents of the Syrian regime. Only pressure from the United States and Saudi Arabia, together with Hussein's promise to limit anti-Syrian activity inside the kingdom, caused Damascus to back down. Syrian-sponsored terrorist activity beginning in 1983 was intended to intimidate Hussein in his efforts to get the peace process under way between the PLO and Israel.

Like Israel's, Syria's military establishment vastly outmatched that at Hussein's command. Syria had a quantitative personnel advantage over Jordan by a ratio of four to one, its tank and artillery inventory exceeded Jordan's by a ratio of four to one, and it had four times as many combat aircraft, most of them of more advanced design. A corresponding disparity of scale existed between the Jordanian and Israeli armed forces. The normal personnel strength of the IDF was about 60 percent larger than that of Jordan's armed forces, but Israel could rapidly expand its personnel by mobilizing well-trained reserve units (see fig. 13).

Jordan also had common borders with Saudi Arabia and Iraq and was separated from Egypt only by a narrow strip of Israeli territory in the Negev Desert. The 1988 cease-fire in the Iran-Iraq War left Iraq with a large number of experienced fighting units. As a revolutionary Arab state opposed to settlement with Israel, Iraq had in the past been perceived as a potential threat by the Amman government. Relations between Jordan and Iraq had been good, however, throughout the 1980s. Jordan viewed Iraq as a buffer against the strict Islamic interpretations expounded by Iran's leaders and provided tangible support to the Iraqi war effort. Saudi Arabia, with an armed establishment about the size of Jordan's but with no combat experience, was not regarded as a military rival. To the contrary, the Saudi government had been the primary financial source for equipment acquisitions by the Jordanian forces. During the 1960s, Egypt's militant Arab nationalist leader Gamal Abdul Nasser had tried to destabilize Hussein's rule. Since that time, however, Egypt had not been a source of concern militarily to Jordan. Under the political conditions prevailing in the late 1980s, Egypt was perceived as a peaceful neighbor against which no special security precautions were required. Rather, the

Jordanian-Egyptian rapprochement had progressed so far that joint military exercises were held by the two countries in 1985.

Further evidence of Jordan's intention to increase its cooperation with other Arab states were the meetings in Amman on February 12, 1989, and in Baghdad on February 16, 1989, that resulted in the founding of an Arab economic association. King Hussein took the lead in creating this organization, to be known as the Arab Cooperation Council, consisting of Egypt, Iraq, Jordan, and the Yemen Arab Republic (North Yemen). The permanent secretariat of the body, which is patterned on the European Economic Community and the Gulf Cooperation Council, will probably be located in Amman.

Except for the Jordan River valley separating Jordan from the West Bank, no major terrain features present a barrier to an invading army. Jordan shares a 375-kilometer border with Syria, and the Syrian frontier is only 60 kilometers from Amman. The Yarmuk River, which forms the western part of the boundary between the two countries, falls into a deep gorge to Lake Tiberias (Sea of Galilee), but farther east a number of major roads link the two countries across undulating terrain with no natural obstacles. The city of Irbid and the air base at Al Mafraq are fewer than twenty kilometers from the border, vulnerable to surprise attack or artillery bombardment. The 742-kilometer border with Saudi Arabia and the 134-kilometer border with Iraq are in open desert areas to the south and east.

The bulk of Jordan's population and its most productive agriculture have concentrated in the northwestern corner of the country, an area only about 60 kilometers wide and 160 kilometers long. In the event of conflict, Amman and other cities would have only a few minutes' warning against air attack from either Syrian or Israeli planes based nearby. Israeli ground forces advancing from the West Bank would face a major terrain obstacle in the form of the escarpment about 800 to 1,200 meters above the floor of the Jordan River valley. Although a number of surfaced roads lead to the top of it, a well-entrenched defending force could make the operation very costly. In the end, however, Israel's superior air power, possibly combined with a helicopter assault on key high points, would almost certainly succeed in dislodging the Jordanians blocking an advance up the main routes to the central plateau. Israel also would have the option of seizing Jordan's sole port of Al Aqabah in the south, although its army would face long and exposed supply lines in a subsequent drive north toward Amman.

In the event of aggression by one of Jordan's stronger neighbors, the modest forces at Hussein's command might be obliged

227

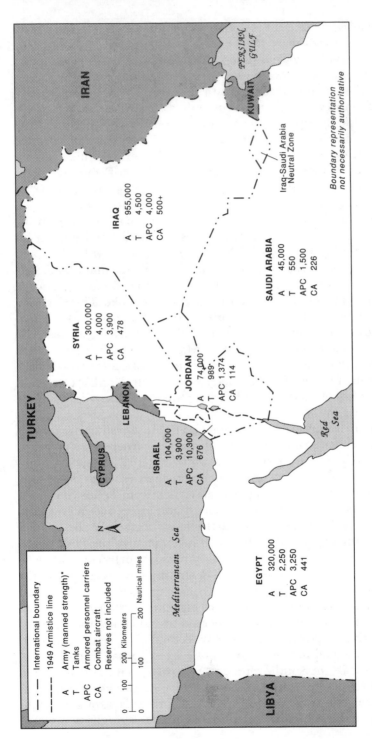

Source: Based on information from *The Military Balance, 1988–1989*, London, 1988, 98–116.

*Figure 13. Comparison of Force Strengths in the Middle East, 1988*

to confine resistance to the vital northern upland region, holding the heights above the East Bank (see Glossary) or defending the likely invasion routes from Syria. The army combat units and most of the air bases were concentrated in the northwest. Jordan's vulnerability, particularly its limited defense against sustained air strikes, would make it difficult for even a well-trained and highly motivated army to prevail for long against a strong invading force.

The overall national defense strategy was to maintain forces that could give a good account of themselves, even when faced by superior attackers. A potential aggressor might thereby be deterred, realizing that a move against Jordan would be a costly venture. Moreover, a strong defensive posture by Jordan would oblige any aggressor to precede its attack by a mobilization in expectation of major conflict, thus obviating the danger of a surprise takeover. If an invasion nevertheless occurred, the Jordanian strategy would be to conduct a stubborn delaying action to allow time for pressure to be brought to bear by Jordan's friends and the international community for abandonment of the aggression.

## Internal Security

Violence and political murder were hallmarks of the early years of the Hashimite (also seen as Hashemite) Kingdom. Hussein was present and was himself a target when his grandfather, King Abdullah ibn Hussein Al Hashimi, was shot to death in Jerusalem in 1951. Two prime ministers were murdered, one in 1960 and the other in 1971. As of 1989, Hussein had survived at least nine attempted assassinations that could be documented; numerous other plots had been rumored but denied by the Jordanian authorities. The monarchy was beset by attempts at subversion, conspiracy, and assassination and by smoldering tensions in many parts of the society. The principal sources of these threats to overthrow or discredit Hashimite rule were Arab militants openly hostile to the king's position as a pro-Western moderate in the Arab-Israeli conflict. Hussein's pragmatic change of attitude in the late 1970s, when he joined other Arab states in rejecting the Egyptian-Israeli peace treaty, ended his estrangement and diminished Arab hostility to his regime. Since that time, the internal security risk has assumed two forms—leftist, anti-Hashimite factions of the PLO and extremist groups associated with the Islamic revival. Most of these movements were small and scattered and, as of 1989, appeared to be effectively controlled and contained by the efficient Jordanian security apparatus (see General Intelligence Department, this ch.).

Military support was so integral to the monarchy that the stability of the regime was assumed to be in no danger unless the armed forces themselves were to be subverted. Although episodes of discontent over conditions of service had occurred from time to time, the beduin-dominated army as a whole was one of the most stable institutions in the kingdom. The only open insurrection in the army occurred early in Hussein's reign, in 1957, when a group calling itself the Free Officers (possibly in imitation of the Egyptian 1952 movement by that name) attempted to wrest the throne from the king. The loyalty of most officers and enlisted personnel, together with Hussein's own decisive action, defeated the plot and ushered in much stricter security precautions (see Hussein's Early Reign, ch. 1). The last known conspiracy to involve military personnel occurred in 1972 when 300 army and civilian personnel were arrested after Palestinian militants bribed the acting commander of an armored car unit to stage a coup d'état.

The Islamic revival was growing in strength in Jordan as in other Arab countries but, as a security problem, appeared to be under control as of 1989. The Muslim Brotherhood, the most important of the politico-religious movements, had appeared in Jordan as early as 1946. It was officially recognized by the government and had rights of expression denied to other groups. It was believed to have many thousands of members as of 1988, enjoying the support of perhaps 10 percent of the population. The Muslim Brotherhood had gained a foothold in certain government ministries and was also believed to have insinuated itself into the police and intelligence organizations. Proselytizing had occurred in the armed forces. Although hitherto not a source of antigovernment protests and disturbances (as in Egypt and elsewhere), the Muslim Brotherhood had adopted an increasingly activist and critical tone in its pronouncements by the mid-1980s. Other, more militant, Islamic groups remained small and fragmented. Jordanians were uncertain of the potential danger of the Islamic movement to the stability of the monarchy and whether its adherents might make a bid for power should the regime falter.

In late 1985, the government cracked down on the Muslim Brotherhood as a warning against its growing stridency and political involvement. The action was also linked to Hussein's efforts to normalize relations with Syria. Syrian members of the Muslim Brotherhood who had been forced to flee to camps in Jordan were accused by the king of subversion aimed against the Damascus government. They were rounded up and extradited to Syria. A new law enacted in the same year prohibited political incitement and accusations by imams and speakers in the mosques. The Ministry of Religious Endowments and Islamic Affairs was designated to review Friday sermons and religious education in the mosques.

Since Jordan's population adhered overwhelmingly to the mainstream Sunni (see Glossary) form of Islam, the militancy of the Shia (see Glossary) branch emanating from Iran had made no inroads. Unlike most neighboring Arab countries, Jordan had no significant minority groups that were perceived as problems for the security forces. The 25,000 Circassians, whose forebears had migrated from the Caucasus region of southern Russia, were Sunni Muslims and traditionally loyal supporters of the monarchy (see Ethnicity and Language, ch. 2). Many Circassians served in the higher ranks of the military or were engaged in security work.

Student activism was carefully controlled through restrictions on political organizations, demonstrations, and meetings. At the two major institutions of higher learning, the University of Jordan in Amman and Yarmuk University in Irbid, the student groups were segmented into small organizations, generally associated with some form of Islamic activism. Student protest rallies occurred at Yarmuk University in 1986, a few days after the United States bombing of installations in Libya. The students rallied against rising tuition costs, dismissals for low grades, and King Hussein's relationship with the United States. The protests were put down violently by government forces, with a number of student deaths and many injuries.

Concerned over the possible ideological indoctrination of the several thousand Jordanian students attending universities in Eastern Europe, the Soviet Union, and the People's Democratic Republic of Yemen (South Yemen), the government followed a policy of strict passport controls and withdrawal of passports from students believed to have questionable contacts abroad.

In April 1989, young people in several southern towns rioted for five days over the sharp price rises on gasoline, cigarettes, and other consumer goods attendant upon certain economic measures agreed to between Jordan and the International Monetary Fund (see Glossary). The demonstrations were aimed at the prime minister and the cabinet, but there was apprehension that the resulting political disequilibrium could escalate into attacks on the monarchy itself. The Palestinian population did not join the protesters, who consisted primarily of beduins (normally considered the base of the king's support). Observers claimed that Islamic activists exerted some influence over the young demonstrators.

Various small underground groups that formed the core of leftist opposition to the Hashimite regime were carefully watched by the security services. They included the Soviet-oriented Communist Party of Jordan (Al Hizb ash Shuyui al Urduni) and the Jordanian Baath Party (Arab Socialist Resurrection Party), linked to the socialist movement of Syria. These movements in turn backed other groups that opposed Jordan's association with the West and with the United States, and called for closer relations with Syria and other Arab leftist elements. In addition to supporting some of these groups, Syria had been linked to a number of assassination attempts on Jordanian diplomats abroad, rocket attacks on Jordanian airliners, and grenade and bomb attacks within Jordan between 1983 and 1985. The attacks by Black September, Abu Nidal, or other terrorist groups under Syrian control apparently were calculated to intimidate Jordan into abandoning its Middle East peace initiatives, which ran contrary to Syria's policies. Although the attacks ceased as relations with Syria improved in 1985, the government remained alert to the danger of renewed destabilizing attempts by radical Arab groups.

The Communist Party of Jordan, led by General Secretary Yaqub Zayadin, had been illegal since 1957, although the organization enjoyed periods of toleration by the regime, interspersed with periods of repression. A tightly organized network of small cells, its membership was believed to be about 500, but through the party's organ it published steady attacks on the government's Middle East policies and restrictions on civil rights. In an effort to fix blame for the 1986 riots at Yarmuk University, the government arrested the entire seventeen-member politburo. They were released several months later, but the party remained banned. During the April 1989 protests against the government's price increases for many consumer goods, 120 members of the Communist Party were detained after circulating leaflets calling for general strikes.

## The Palestinian Factor

Over a long period, the most serious threat to Hussein's continuance in power had been posed by the militant and rejectionist elements of the PLO that were supported by Syria and Libya. Although the PLO's avowed goal was to regain the traditional Palestinian homeland for millions of Palestinians scattered throughout the Middle East, the PLO's actions at times had given the impression that the initial phase of its program was to gain control over Jordan. In the aftermath of the June 1967 War, Hussein was persuaded by fellow Arab leaders to permit the PLO to station some of its military forces in the East Bank. By 1970 the fedayeen (Palestinian guerrillas) had acquired a powerful presence in the country and had become openly defiant of Hussein's government. They threatened to topple the monarchy and replace it with a regime that would not interfere with guerrilla operations against Israel. After a series of crises during which Palestinian behavior became increasingly disruptive, a fierce civil war broke out in September 1970. By the summer of 1971, after suffering heavy losses, the organized PLO militia was forced to withdraw to new bases primarily in Lebanon (see The Guerrilla Crisis, ch. 1).

Having ended the Palestinian military threat, Hussein was determined not to permit its reappearance. The departure of the PLO meant relief from Israeli retaliatory shelling and incursions in reprisal for PLO raids and rocket attacks on the West Bank. Hostility between Hussein and the PLO gradually abated after the October 1973 War. The king reluctantly assented to a decision taken at a conference of Arab leaders in 1974 to designate the PLO as the sole authorized representative of the Palestinian people, in effect relinquishing his traditional role as representative of Palestinians residing on the West Bank. In 1988 the king formally renounced Jordanian claims to sovereignty over the West Bank. At the same time, Hussein intensified his efforts to promote national unity in the East Bank by encouraging the integration of Palestinians into the indigenous political and social structure. Many Palestinian residents had by 1989 become well absorbed into Jordanian society, achieving prominence in government, business, finance, and industry, with an investment in the stability of the Hashimite regime. But there was still widespread discrimination against Palestinians in favor of Transjordanians, and thousands of Palestinians remained in Jordan as impoverished refugees.

As of 1989, the remaining potential for political subversion among the Palestinians appeared to be confined to scattered and poorly organized extremist groups operating mostly out of refugee camps. These groups included radical factions of the Syrian-supported anti-Arafat wing of the PLO, such as the Popular Front for the Liberation of Palestine-General Command (PFLP–GC) and the Democratic Front for the Liberation of Palestine (DFLP). In late 1987 and early 1988, the government detained without charge or expelled more than 100 Palestinians to prevent them from agitating in support of the *intifadah* (the Palestinian uprising in the West Bank) and against Hussein's inaction. The Black September terrorist group claimed responsibility for bomb explosions in Amman later in 1988 and charged the king with "conspiring against the Palestinian revolution."

## The Military Heritage

When the Amirate of Transjordan was formed in 1921, the small scattered police elements left over from Ottoman days were inadequate to maintain order and establish central government control. The police units were expanded, and a small mobile force of balanced elements of infantry, cavalry, and artillery was created. Two years later the police, numbering about 300, and the military force of about 1,000 were combined under the command of British Captain F.G. Peake. The establishment was originally known as the Arab Army (Al Jaysh al Arabi)—a perpetuation of the military force led by the Hashimites in World War I against the Turks—and this Arabic title has been retained. In English, however, the name became the Arab Legion, a designation that lasted until 1956 (see Transjordan, ch. 1).

## Historical Role

From the Arab Legion's inception, its primary mission was the establishment of the central government's authority through the maintenance of public order and the preservation of internal security. It was originally composed of Arabs from the defeated Ottoman armies and others from outside the amirate. Under the early agreements between Transjordan and Britain, defense of the borders against external attack remained a British responsibility. To this end, a British Royal Air Force (RAF) squadron and British army armored car unit were stationed in the country. In 1924 they joined with the Arab Legion to beat back a Wahhabi invasion from the area to the south that within a few years became Saudi Arabia. The ability of the legion to protect the amirate from outside raids helped to cement the legitimacy of Hashimite rule.

By 1926 the Arab Legion had established an image as the protective arm of the central government, functioning as an agency for tax collection as well as for security. The beduins remained wary and hostile, however, convinced that the legion strengthened the hand of the regime, whose purposes they mistrusted. Initially the beduins refused to join the legion, thus forcing reliance on villagers and townspeople to replenish its personnel.

In early 1926 the British high commissioner for Palestine created the Transjordan Frontier Force (TJFF) to defend Transjordan's northern and southern borders. The legion immediately incurred a loss of more than half of its forces when they were transferred as cadre for the new border security force. In addition to the drop in personnel, the legion also was stripped of its machine guns, artillery, and communications troops. The much reduced force reverted to a role of policing the towns and villages. The TJFF (roughly 1,000 officers and men) never was part of the legion and was responsible to the British high commissioner in Jerusalem rather than to Amir Abdullah of Transjordan. All officers above the rank of major were British. Officers of lesser rank were Arabs, Circassians, and

Jews, but the promotion system precluded the advancement of any Middle Easterners to a position of command over British troops.

With its effectiveness reduced by creation of the TJFF, the Arab Legion was unable to cope with raids by tribal groups in the vast desert regions of Transjordan during the late 1920s and early 1930s. To counter these disturbances, a British captain was transferred to the legion as second in command to Peake. This officer—later to become known as Lieutenant General Sir John Bagot Glubb, or Glubb Pasha, the strongman of Jordan—had previously faced similar pacification problems while serving in the Iraqi government. Glubb understood the beduins and had acquired a knowledge of strategy and tactics required for long-range desert operations. Under his command a camel-mounted Desert Mobile Force was organized in 1930, reflecting its leader's concepts of a military unit functioning in a desert environment. The Desert Mobile Force, which eventually merged with the Arab Legion, attracted principally beduins to its ranks, establishing the identification of the beduins with the monarchy that has persisted through Hussein's reign.

## World War II to 1967

The Arab rebellion that occurred in Palestine from 1936 to 1939 led to additional measures to strengthen the legion, which on the eve of World War II consisted of about 1,350 officers and men. One thousand of these troops were organized for police duties and the remaining 350 made up the Desert Mobile Force, which then comprised two mechanized cavalry companies, having as its mission the prevention of Arab rebel incursions from Palestine.

Although the Arab Legion saw little action in the war, the mobile force became part of the tiny British columns that marched against Iraq and the Vichy French in Syria and Lebanon in 1941. It established an excellent record that prompted its expansion to a mechanized infantry brigade but, by the time this unit was ready for action, the war in the desert was over. The Arab Legion was subsequently detailed to strategic guard duties as individual companies throughout the Middle East. These operations provided experience that was to prove valuable when Arab-Israeli difficulties erupted in the postwar era. By the end of the war, the legion had expanded to a force of about 8,000, but postwar economy measures reduced its size to 6,000 by May 1948, when the British gave up their Palestine Mandate. At the same time, the TJFF was disbanded, and many members of the unit were absorbed into the legion.

About 4,500 legionnaires were combat troops at the time the Arab-Israeli War began in 1948. Moving across the Jordan River, the legion occupied most of the West Bank and assumed control of the strategic Jerusalem-Tel Aviv highway. Commanded by Glubb and about forty British officers, the legion fought better than any other Arab force and held its positions longer when Israel took the offensive in January 1949. The fighting left the legion in occupation of the Old City of Jerusalem and much of the Arab areas of Palestine that made up the West Bank.

During the 1948 war, the legion's strength was expanded hurriedly to approximately 8,000. As a consequence of the British withdrawal, for the first time the legion had to develop its own technical support services. A small air force unit was created for logistics, reconnaissance, and liaison purposes, then enlarged in 1955 to include a modest combat element (see Air Force, this ch.). By early 1956, when Hussein dismissed Glubb as commander of the military establishment, the legion had grown to about 23,000 officers and men. After Glubb's departure it was redesignated the Jordan Arab Army, and the national police element of about 6,000 was shifted from the military to be brought under the supervision of the minister of interior.

Between 1951 and 1956 an entirely new National Guard was formed, originally consisting merely of armed Palestinians in villages of the West Bank vulnerable to Israeli raids. It was later built up within Jordan proper by a conscription system, forming a territorial reserve army. Guardsmen, predominantly Palestinians, were unpaid except for a small wage during their annual training period under officers and noncommissioned officers (NCOs) of the legion. In 1965 the National Guard, by then a force of 30,000, was disbanded because of its unreliability and susceptibility to PLO influence. About 40 percent of these troops, after passing careful screening for loyalty to the monarchy, were allowed to join the Jordan Arab Army.

Although Jordan had signed a tripartite military treaty with Egypt and Syria in October 1956, a few days before Israel's attack on Egypt in the Sinai Peninsula, the conflict was confined to the Egyptian front. Israeli troops were positioned along the borders with Syria and Jordan in the event that these countries joined the fighting, but the alliance was not invoked.

## June 1967 War and Aftermath

At the onset of the June 1967 War, Jordan had four infantry brigades and one armored brigade in the Jerusalem-Ram Allah-Hebron sector, two infantry brigades reinforced by armor and artillery in the Nabulus area, and one infantry brigade and one armored brigade in the Jordan River valley as reserve for the Nabulus forces. After fighting from June 5 to June 7, the overwhelmed Jordanians were forced to abandon Jerusalem and the entire West Bank, withdrawing across the Jordan River to prevent the annihilation of their army. The Jordanians fought tenaciously, but the Arab air forces were destroyed on the first day of battle by continual Israeli air attacks, leaving the Jordanian army without air cover. Mauled by Israeli jets, those reserve armored units from the Jordan River valley that were able to reach the battle zone were in poor condition to support the infantry. In the Old City of Jerusalem, where Israeli air power could not be brought to bear, Jordan's defense caused almost half the Israeli casualties in the war. Confusion and discord resulted from the Jordanian army's placement under an Egyptian commander and from false reports received from President Nasser claiming Egyptian successes in air and land fighting. Expected reinforcements from Syria, Iraq, and Saudi Arabia failed to reach the battle area in time, leaving the Jordanian army to fight almost entirely alone. Jordan suffered 7,000 killed and wounded and the destruction of its entire air force and 80 percent of its armor.

Since the June 1967 War, the Jordanian armed forces have not been involved in major hostilities, except for the bloody internal battles in 1970 and 1971 that ended with the withdrawal of the PLO's fedayeen from Jordan. The Palestinians were armed with light modern weapons and were entrenched in central Amman and in refugee camps surrounding the city. During three days of stiff fighting in September 1970, one Jordanian infantry division and one armored division gradually gained control of the core of the city. But the course of the conflict shifted when a Syrian division reinforced with armor and a brigade of the Palestine Liberation Army crossed the border at Ar Ramtha. Dug-in Jordanian tanks battered about 200 advancing Syrian tanks before retiring to new positions. The next day Hawker Hunters of the Royal Jordanian Air Force decisively blunted the Syrian attack against a new Jordanian defensive line. The failure of the Syrians to commit their air force enabled the Jordanians to turn back the invasion, taking a severe toll in destroyed Syrian armor. Iraq had deployed a 12,000-man force near Az Zarka but began to withdraw it when the fighting broke out.

Returning its attention to the entrenched PLO militias, the Jordanian army was able to clear Amman and the city of Irbid, which the PLO had also occupied, within a week. A fragile cease-fire was negotiated with the help of surrounding Arab states but intermittent fighting continued in early 1971. The remaining fedayeen were gradually pushed back into a mountain defensive complex in the north. A four-day attack launched in July 1971 resulted in the dispersal of the last PLO holdouts.

Jordan was not a formal belligerent in the October 1973 War when Syria and Egypt joined in attacking Israel. Hussein was asked to open a third front but merely placed his army on alert, defending his action by claiming that Jordan had few combat aircraft and no antiaircraft missile protection. By the fifth day of fighting, the Syrian drive had been broken and Syrian troops, abandoning their tanks and artillery, had fallen back to their Golan Heights defensive line. Jordanian armor was moved into position at the southern end of the line and, along with Iraqi forces, took part in one limited attack before a United Nations (UN) cease-fire commenced. Jordanian losses were twenty-eight soldiers killed and eighteen tanks destroyed. The Jordanian forces fought well but again lacked air cover, and their actions were poorly coordinated with the Syrians and Iraqis.

## The Military in National Life

Among the various social, economic, and political institutions affecting Jordanian national life, none—with the exceptions of the monarchy itself and the Muslim religion—has been more pervasive than the presence and power of the armed forces. This condition has persisted since the formation of the first military units early in the country's political evolution. Soon after becoming king in 1953, Hussein remarked that "everywhere I go in Jordan I find the Arab Legion doing everything." Throughout Hussein's reign, the armed forces have been an indispensable instrument for the protection of the monarchy. The government has periodically turned to the army to prevent internal disruption and to maintain law and order. The loyalty of the army during periods of stress has permitted the king latitude in the conduct of foreign policy by offsetting domestic constraints on his actions.

The king spent eight months at the British Royal Military Academy at Sandhurst at age sixteen, soon after ascending the throne. He continued to take a close interest in military affairs, cultivating the armed forces and identifying himself with the performance of their national security mission. A number of foreign observers and knowledgeable Jordanians have testified that Hussein was seldom as relaxed or as filled with confidence as when he visited his military units, attired in suitable uniform. Hussein made frequent visits to army units where he knew many of the officers by name. Even privates felt they might approach the king directly, often tugging at his sleeve for attention. The empathy that existed between him and his troops was enhanced by his fascination for modern

*Soldier firing a mortar*
*Cobra attack helicopter armed with*
*TOW antitank missiles of the Royal Jordanian Air Force*

weapons, such as jet aircraft, tanks, self-propelled artillery, and missiles. The king was a qualified pilot who often personally tested new planes. He made the final decision on equipment acquisitions and other matters affecting the modernization of the military establishment.

Since the 1957 coup attempt, the armed forces have conducted themselves in a professional manner, accepting their subordination to civil legal authority. No officer caste has developed with ambitions to interfere with or dominate the government, although the king has called upon trusted individual officers to serve in important civilian posts. The continued acceptance by the military of Hussein's political and religious legitimacy has been a foundation stone of national stability. Authorities on Jordanian politics believed that, in the event of the king's death, the army would act to guarantee the legitimate Hashimite succession (see The King, ch. 4).

The consensual relationship between the state and the army was cemented by the privileges and economic benefits accruing to the career military. This situation was particularly true for the beduin constituency, which felt a special affinity to the throne. Its powers and privileges were unlikely to survive if the monarchy were replaced by a Palestinian-controlled government. Even soldiers of Palestinian origin perceived a greater certainty of their status under Hussein than under any regime that might replace his. During the civil war in 1970 and 1971, units staffed exclusively with Palestinians showed no hesitancy in mounting assaults on the Palestinian guerrillas.

Key officers and senior NCOs continued to be disproportionately of beduin background in the mid- to late 1980s. A considerable number of Palestinian officers had always been present, although they were more heavily represented in the technical units such as signals and engineering, and they did not often rise above battalion-level command in the main combat units. The social composition was changing, however, as a higher proportion of recruits originated from nontribal sectors. Younger personnel, although better educated and more cosmopolitan, were less imbued with the zealous loyalty of the past. As the army modernized and became more professional, the tribal basis of support for the king was a diminishing factor. Nevertheless, the army had become a valuable adjunct to Hussein's efforts to foster a sense of national character and patriotism. As changes in structure took place both within the military and in civilian society, it was difficult to foresee how these would ultimately affect the intimate relationship between the king and his soldiers. Observers predicted, however, that the political reliability of the Jordan Arab Army would remain intact through the 1990s.

In addition to their basic security role, the armed forces have participated in a variety of civic action programs designed to benefit the country's development efforts—projects that at the same time have enhanced the public image of the military. Public services by the armed forces have included such major items as bridge and road construction and disaster relief, organized campaigns against locust infestation, and such lesser actions as repair of wells and rescue of people lost or stranded in the country's vast desert region.

Technical skills learned in the service eased the transition to civilian life. Persons with army or air force training in mechanics, electronics, or engineering were looked upon as technically proficient, disciplined additions to the civilian work force. The military was, moreover, a channel for upward mobility. It was one of the few institutions in the country that provided a means for those from the lower strata of society to embark on a respected career and earn a measure of personal prestige.

## The Armed Forces

Composed of both regular or career personnel and conscripts, the armed forces in 1988 had an active-duty strength estimated at 85,300 officers and enlisted personnel. Included in this total were an army of 74,000, an air force of 11,000, and a naval element of 300. The naval force, with a coast guard-type mission, was organizationally part of the army. The air force, which enjoyed high prestige arising in part from Hussein's avid personal interest in aviation, had semi-autonomous status.

### Command Structure

Article 32 of the Constitution states that "the king is the Supreme Commander of the Army, Naval, and Air Forces." The words here have a connotation similar to commander in chief as applied to the president of the United States. King Hussein has, however, generally exercised close control over the armed forces and has even assumed direct command of the army on many occasions. The king has the constitutional right to declare war, conclude peace, and sign treaties. The declaration of a state of emergency may be made by decision of the Council of Ministers and is promulgated by royal decree when required to "ensure the defense of the realm." In such situations, the country's ordinary laws are suspended. As of mid-1989, Jordan had been formally in a state of martial law since 1967, enabling the king to legislate by the issuance of decrees.

Broad policy issues relating to security were decided by the king, advised by a small circle of officials and personal associates. These included his brother, Crown Prince Hasan, senior palace officials, and the prime minister. The post of minister of defense customarily had been held by the prime minister. The Ministry of Defense had mainly administrative functions, including logistics, mobilization, conscription, and preparation of the defense budget. The operational commander of the armed forces was theoretically responsible to the minister of defense, but in reality the minister did not issue directives of an operational nature unless they had the king's approval. The commanding officer of the armed forces had invariably been a confidant of the king and was generally a leading member of a prominent beduin clan. Until he was appointed a ranking palace official—chief of the royal court—in late 1988, Field Marshal General of the Army Ash Sharif Zaid ibn Shakir, a cousin of the king, had been commander in chief for more than twelve years. Zaid ibn Shakir's family had always been close to the royal family, and Zaid ibn Shakir himself had been personally linked with Hussein throughout his military career. In addition to his high palace position, he also filled a newly created post of adviser to the king on national security. The new position implied that Shakir would retain considerable influence over military policies.

Operational command of the armed forces was assumed by the chief of staff, Lieutenant General Fathi Abu Talib, after the departure of Zaid ibn Shakir. It was expected that the title of commander in chief of the armed forces would be eliminated. Accordingly, the senior military commander under the king would henceforward bear the title of chief of staff of the armed forces.

The chief of staff presided over a headquarters in Amman known as the Armed Forces General Command. Subordinate to him were the air force commander and chiefs of staff for personnel, intelligence, operations, and administration, corresponding roughly to the G–1, G–2, G–3, and G–4 functional sections of the general staff under the United States system. These positions were normally held by officers of major general rank (see fig. 14). By legislation enacted in 1983, Jordan was divided into eight military regions corresponding to the eight governorates, although it was not clear how these regions fitted into the overall military command structure.

The commander of the semi-autonomous Royal Jordanian Air Force—subordinated to the chief of staff—derived some logistical support from the army and carried out a degree of policy coordination with the principal officers of the Armed Forces General

Command staff. The air force, however, had a separate headquarters at King Abdullah Air Base near Amman. The headquarters had its own staff for the specialized operations, training, logistic, and other requirements of the air force.

## Army

The 74,000 troops of the Jordan Arab Army were organized into two armored divisions, two mechanized divisions, two independent brigades, and sixteen independent artillery battalions. After the June 1967 War, Hussein and his government undertook a major rebuilding and modernization program for the army. As of 1989, it was still considered to be the best trained of all the Arab armies and was larger and better equipped than at any time in its existence. Nevertheless, it had long been outstripped in equipment by the nearby Israeli and Syrian armies, which had been expanded and re-equipped with modern armor and missile systems after the October 1973 War.

The basic organization was pyramidal, with three brigades to a division and three battalions in each brigade. Each of the two armored divisions consisted of two tank brigades and one mechanized infantry brigade. The two mechanized divisions were made up of two mechanized infantry brigades and one tank brigade. The independent brigades consisted of a Royal Guards Brigade and a Special Forces Brigade, the latter made up of three airborne battalions. Some significant units were missing from each division, and the weapons inventory of each division was closer to that of a reinforced brigade. For economy, the divisions did not have fully integrated organic logistics and support units but depended on main bases for supplies. Although the ratio of combat to support strength was favorable, the capability of independent brigades to operate at a distance from these bases was seriously impaired.

The bulk of the ground forces were concentrated in the north, at base complexes at Amman and Az Zarqa and at other installations in the vicinity of Irbid and Al Mafraq. Smaller bases were at Maan and Al Aqabah to the south (see fig. 15). No Jordanian forces were deployed in the Jordan River valley, where they would have been exposed to Israeli air power and artillery. They were instead emplaced on the heights above the valley where they could obstruct enemy movement up the routes to the central plateau leading to the main cities. The most forward troop dispositions were at Umm Qays overlooking the Jordan River in the northwest corner of the country to counter any potential Israeli flanking movement around the strong Syrian defenses concentrated in the Golan Heights.

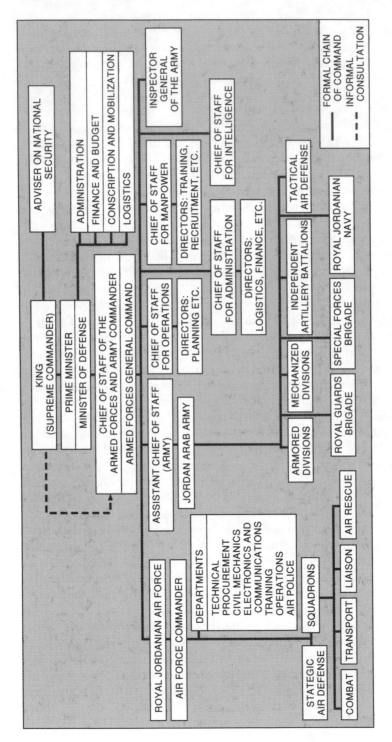

*Figure 14. Organization of National Defense, 1989*

In spite of years of American training, British military concepts continued to influence individual units. British forms of organization were particularly evident in administration, maintenance, and many technical units. The weapons inventory was predominantly of United States and British origin. Jordan's tank force consisted of the United States M-60 model, together with its own conversion of the obsolete British Centurion, known as the Tarik, and an improved version of the British Chieftain called the Khalid. Armored personnel carriers were the familiar United States M-113 model. In 1988 Jordan benefited from a substantial gift of Chieftain and Scorpion tanks and M-113s captured by Iraq from Iran, but it was not known whether the equipment could be introduced into the armored inventory without extensive repair or reconditioning. The artillery battalions were equipped by the United States with guns ranging from 105mm to 203mm, both towed and self-propelled (see table 15, Appendix).

The ground forces were considered to be insufficiently protected from attack from the air, although efforts were being made to overcome the problem by the introduction of Soviet air defense systems. When the United States refused to replace obsolete forward air defense weapons, Jordan turned to the Soviet Union for help in 1981. Initial Soviet deliveries consisted of the SA-8 truck-mounted surface-to-air missile (SAM) with a range of between ten and fourteen kilometers and the ZSU-23 radar-controlled gun mounted on a lightly armored carriage. Both weapons had proved vulnerable to suppression measures by Israel in fighting against Syria. In spite of this, additional SA-8s were acquired in 1984, together with infantry SAMs, the shoulder-fired SA-7, and the SA-9. In 1985 the SA-13 and SA-14 were purchased as successors to the SA-9 and SA-7, respectively. Separate air defense brigades (actually, battalion size) were being equipped with the larger Soviet SAMs to be attached as needed to ground formations to provide close, mobile tactical air defense.

Antitank defense was based on the TOW (tube-launched, optically-sighted, wire-guided) antitank missile and the man-portable Dragon system, both from the United States, together with more recent acquisition of the Apilas rocket launcher from France. The LAW-80 antitank missile was acquired from Britain in 1987 to replace the Dragon. In 1985 the air force began taking delivery of twenty-four Cobra AH-1S helicopters equipped with TOW missiles; these were eventually to be transferred to the army.

The naval element of the armed forces, although designated the Royal Jordanian Navy, remained an integral part of the army. Performing essentially a coast guard mission, it had 300 officers and

*Figure 15. Major Military Installations, 1988*

men based at Al Aqabah, the country's only port, with access to the Red Sea. The navy operated five coastal patrol boats of United States manufacture armed with light machine guns. The navy assisted in the maintenance of harbor security, operating in conjunction with customs and immigration personnel to ensure the enforcement of the country's laws and regulations. In late 1987, three larger craft of ninety-five tons each were ordered from Brittain. When introduced, each would have a crew of sixteen and would be armed with 20mm and 30mm guns. Israeli units at the adjacent Israeli naval facility at Elat similarly consisted of small, lightly-armed patrol boats.

## Air Force

The Royal Jordanian Air Force was charged with the missions of air defense of territorial integrity, close support of the army, tactical bombing, and airlift of troops and supplies. The air force began operations in 1949 as a component of the Arab Legion. Designated initially as the Arab Legion Air Force, the service depended in large part on pilots and other technical personnel seconded to the legion from the RAF. Eventually, selected volunteers from the legion were trained at the unit's airfield near Amman, and some were sent to flight and technical schools operated by the RAF in Britain. Growing unrest in the Middle East soon convinced the Jordanian government of the need to expand the air force's mission to include combat capability, which was achieved in 1955 with a British gift of nine Vampire MK 9 fighter-bombers.

Since its inception, the air force has struggled to develop and maintain a level of combat capability that would be viable against potential enemies in the region. The primary perceived threat has been the superior air power of Israel. The constant modernization of aircraft and associated weaponry essential to afford Jordanian pilots some chance of success has posed a severe challenge.

From the late 1950s through the mid-1960s, the primary combat airplanes of the air force inventory consisted of Hawker Hunter fighter-bombers that were transferred from the RAF but paid for by the United States. During the first few hours of the June 1967 War, Israeli pilots destroyed all but one of Jordan's serviceable combat airplanes as well as three Hunters on loan from Iraq. To assist Jordan in its recovery from the loss of virtually its entire air arm, additional Hunter aircraft were supplied by Britain and Saudi Arabia. In mid-1969, the United States provided twenty F-104 Starfighters to form the first Jordanian fighter-interceptor squadron. To preclude a future recurrence of the 1967 disaster, Jordan installed surveillance radars to cover most of the country, constructed hardened shelters to protect all combat aircraft, and implemented plans for the emergency dispersal of the air force.

When the October 1973 War broke out, Israel refrained from attacking the Jordanian bases and Hussein's air force did not play an active role in the war. In 1974 the United States began deliveries of F-5s. The F-5 was well regarded as a light fighter plane but lacked modern avionics, thus limiting it to daylight, fair-weather combat. Unable to obtain an American replacement for the obsolete

Starfighters because of United States congressional opposition, Hussein turned to France, acquiring between 1981 and 1983 more than thirty Mirage F–1s, with Saudi Arabian financial assistance. Armed with Matra and Magic air-to-air missiles, the Mirage aircraft were an improvement in terms of range and avionics but were considerably inferior to the American F–15s and F–16s in the Israeli inventory and to the more advanced MiG-25 and MiG-29 Soviet fighters in the Syrian inventory.

During the 1980s, repeated efforts were made to include an air defense version of the F–16 or the F–20 in United States military assistance packages, but these were vetoed by Congress because of Israeli objections (see Military Cooperation with the United States, this ch.). In early 1988, it was announced that an order had been placed with France for the purchase of twenty Mirage 2000 fighters and for the modernization of fifteen of the Mirage F–1s. The transaction included an option for the acquisition of a further twenty Mirage 2000s. The cost, estimated at US$1.3 billion, was to be repaid under generous credit terms offered by the French and may have involved partial funding by Saudi Arabia. It was also announced that Jordan had contracted to buy eight Tornado strike aircraft from Britain but, according to a subsequent report, Jordan canceled the transaction for cost reasons.

In 1988 the air force was organized tactically into four fighter-ground-attack squadrons of F–5Es and F–5Fs, two fighter squadrons of Mirage F–1s, an advanced training squadron of F–5As and F–5Bs, a transport squadron, and four helicopter squadrons (see table 16, Appendix). The main air bases were King Abdullah Air Base at Marka near Amman, King Hussein Air Base at Al Mafraq, and Prince Hasan Air Base at pumping station H5 in the desert east of Amman. These bases were all in the north within a few minutes' flight time of either Israel or Syria. Other bases were at Azraq ash Shishan, also in the eastern desert, and dispersal bases at King Faisal Air Base, Al Jafr and at Al Aqabah in the south. The tactical fighter squadrons operated from the bases at Azraq ash Shishan, Al Mafraq, and pumping station H5. In addition to serving as home for the air force headquarters, King Abdullah Air Base near Amman accommodated the service's transport squadron and its liaison and air rescue units.

Training of flight personnel, formerly accomplished in the United States and Britain, in the later 1980s was conducted in Jordan. The Royal Jordanian Air Academy at King Abdullah Air Base provided cadets with both military instruction and an academic education over a twenty-seven-month period preparatory to being commissioned as second lieutenants. Initial flight training consisted

*Flight simulator used in pilot training
at Royal Jordanian Air Force Academy*

of 250 flying hours in British Bulldogs, followed by training on Spanish C–101 Aviojets that could be fitted as light fighters and reconnaissance aircraft. Pilots who qualified for jets progressed to F–5As and F–5Bs at Al Mafraq in a five-month course in tactics and weapons employment before being assigned to combat squadrons.

The new Mirage 2000s on order and the upgrading planned for the Mirage F–1s and the F–5s helped to compensate in some degree for Jordan's weaknesses in comparison to the air power of its Israeli and Syrian neighbors. As of 1989, however, both potential adversaries maintained a decisive advantage, rendering Jordan extremely vulnerable to air attack. The main Jordanian base at Al Mafraq was only fifty-five kilometers from Israel and only twelve kilometers from the Syrian frontier. Even pumping station H5 in the eastern desert was only 120 kilometers from Israel and 30 kilometers from Syria. Although the aircraft were sheltered against surprise attack, bombardment of the runways could make the bases inoperative. Radar coverage was being improved but, because of the rough terrain features, gaps remained that experienced Israeli pilots could exploit as attack corridors.

Ground-based strategic air defense was the responsibility of the air force rather than the army. The air force operated fourteen

Improved Hawk SAM batteries (126 launchers) that were sited to afford protection to key military and civil targets. The Hawk was a high-quality, all-weather system with reliable target detection and resistance to electronic countermeasures. Being immobile and at well-known sites, however, the Hawks were considered vulnerable to low-level Israeli air attack. Plans by the United States to provide upgrading and mobility packages for these batteries and to sell additional Hawk systems to Jordan had been frustrated by congressional opposition, and as of 1989 no comparable air defense system was being considered as an alternative.

## Defense Spending

Jordan's defense outlays have been burdensome for a small country without major resources or a highly developed industrial base. Offsetting this burden to some degree has been the positive impact of defense spending on the national economy. Soldiers' pay, the employment created by the military and security forces, and the contracts and support services generated in the name of national security provided important stimulation for what generally has been regarded as a sluggish economy. The financial and military subsidies that Jordan traditionally has received from other Arab states have represented a net benefit to the economy while reducing the actual burden of the military effort to somewhat less than it appeared to be in statistical terms. Nevertheless, the Jordanian defense effort was facing acute budgetary and financial difficulties in the late 1980s, as a consequence of decreased financial aid from the oil-producing Persian Gulf states and reduced remittance levels from Jordanian workers in other Middle Eastern countries. Together, these sources had brought in as much as US$2.5 billion annually in earlier years. Although other Arab states had pledged at the Baghdad Summit in 1978 to provide Jordan with more than US$1.2 billion annually for ten years, only Saudi Arabia had fulfilled its commitment (see GDP by Sector, ch. 3; Military Relations with Other Countries, this ch.).

The 1988 defense budget of JD256 million (US$763 million) was about 60 percent higher than the allocation of a decade earlier. When inflation was taken into account, however, officially acknowledged defense costs appeared to have remained fairly steady until 1986, when an upward trend became evident. Possible explanations for this rise included moderate increases in the number of men under arms, pay raises, some domestically absorbed equipment outlays, sharp increases in the international price of armaments, and a higher amortization level of foreign military debt. Published government figures were incomplete since they did not include important elements of defense spending and were therefore understated. The United States Department of State estimated that a little more than half of the subsidies from other Arab states was reflected in the budget, with the remainder applied to off-budget defense expenditures.

The military debt had become a serious problem by early 1989, as the difficulties of meeting the kingdom's overall debt-servicing obligations continued to mount, placing additional strains on the balance of payments. It was reported that Jordan was running about eleven months behind on its military debt payments, with more than US$95 million overdue.

In 1988 the officially acknowledged defense budget constituted 15.4 percent of gross national product (GNP—see Glossary). In a comparative analysis by the United States Arms Control and Disarmament Agency (ACDA) covering 1987 defense outlays, the proportion of Jordan's GNP absorbed by defense in that year (13.9 percent) was near the average for the Middle East, which was 11 percent, and among the highest in the world, although below that of Israel (16.6 percent of GNP). Nevertheless, defense expenditures as a ratio of GNP have followed a declining trend from 35 percent in the early 1970s to 20 percent in the early 1980s. According to the same ACDA study, Jordan's defense expenditures in 1987 were 22 percent of total government expenditures, well below the Middle East average of 32 percent. The portion of Jordan's government spending devoted to the military also reflected a steady decline during the 1970s and 1980s. Military expenditures of US$285 per capita in 1987 were also lower than the average of US$396 per capita for the Middle East as a whole. Jordan had one of the highest proportions in the world of men under arms, with 36.4 uniformed personnel per 1,000 of population. Its ratio of armed forces to population was exceeded only by such countries as Iraq, Israel, Syria, and North Korea.

## Personnel: Composition, Recruitment, and Training

Because such heavy reliance was placed on the military to safeguard the monarchy, the composition and attitudes of armed forces personnel have been of vital importance to Hussein. Recruitment policies and promotion of senior personnel were subject to the approval of the king. During the early years of the Hashimite regime, a traditional system of recruitment was followed that grew out of British practices associated with the formation and maintenance of the Arab Legion. The legion was officered, trained, and financed by Britain. The enlisted personnel were all locally recruited villagers and tribesmen. Most British officers detached to serve with

251

the legion were contract employees of the Transjordanian government; others were simply seconded from the British army.

Initial public reaction to the Arab Legion was indifferent or at times even hostile, and recruiting was difficult. The military establishment, however, soon developed high standards of organization, discipline, and training. Tribal uprisings and raiding practices were suppressed, and criminal activity by restive tribal elements diminished. Civic assistance activities enhanced the legion's public image, and it evolved into a proud and respected professional force. Its well-trained regulars gained a reputation for firm and effective action, as well as for discipline and justice in dealing with the civilian population. As a result, recruiting became easy, with the further incentive of generous pay scales in the enlisted ranks in relation to other Middle Eastern armies.

The flow of volunteers made it possible to impose a system of selection that strengthened confidence in the army as a stabilizing factor in defense of the monarchy. As Glubb later wrote, ''The character and antecedents of every recruit were checked by the police before his acceptance. Then again, in the Arab Legion, a confidential report was submitted on every officer and man every year.'' This careful screening to exclude potential subversives and those of doubtful loyalty was expensive and time-consuming. But support of a monarchy was at stake, and the background investigation of even the lowest recruit was an important detail in the process. The long-term success of the effort was evident in the devotion the armed forces demonstrated to Hussein through three decades of conflict with Israel, internecine Arab strife, and repeated assassination attempts.

The system produced good soldiers, as the legion's record of performance amply demonstrated, and this tradition has persisted. Jordanian troops have proved to be tough and resilient fighters. Men of beduin origin, long accustomed to living in a harsh physical environment and enduring Spartan conditions, showed a particular affinity for and pride in military service. For many years, the system of carefully selected volunteers resulted in an army in which the beduin element constituted the vast majority, particularly in infantry and armored units. According to Glubb's account, nearly all of the legion's troops before and during World War II were recruited from the beduins of southern Transjordan. After the war, enlistment of beduins of northern Transjordan as well as residents of the West Bank was also encouraged.

Following the dissolution of the National Guard in 1965, many of its Palestinian members were accepted into the Jordan Arab

*Women military personnel receiving instruction*

Army after careful security screening. Palestinians formed about 40 percent of the armed forces. The Palestinian component fell to 15 percent during the 1970s, when the country was wracked by internal turbulence (highlighted by the assassination of the prime minister in 1971 and the coup attempt financed by Palestinian bribes in 1972). As many as 5,000 Palestinians were estimated to have succumbed to PLO pressure to defect during the 1970–71 civil war, but approximately 20,000 remained loyal to the king and the armed forces. Although no official statistics were available, observers believed that the proportion of Palestinians in the armed forces had risen to between 30 percent and 40 percent by 1986. Observers expected this percentage would probably continue to rise as a result of conscription and as doubts over Palestinian loyalty further subsided. Although education standards among the beduins had risen sharply, there continued to be a premium in the late 1980s on the educational and technical attainments that Palestinian recruits could more readily offer.

Families of traditional background still dominated among senior military officers. The principal tribes were well represented, but a balance was deliberately maintained so that no one group enjoyed a prevailing influence. A significant portion of lower echelon officer positions, excluding first-line combat units, were held by Palestinians. In the upper reaches of the officer corps, however, Palestinians still constituted well under 10 percent.

253

## Conscription

After an Israeli raid on a West Bank border village in 1966, the government passed an emergency conscription act under which physically fit males would be drafted for training and service with regular military units for periods of up to two years. The same law, however, provided the loophole of a fixed fee payable in lieu of service, as well as other exemption provisions. In practice, military units kept their original character, recruiting continued for a time to be more than adequate, and the law became inoperative.

On January 1, 1976, a new National Service Law was issued by royal decree, establishing a service commitment of two years for men called to active duty by the General Directorate of Conscription and Mobilization of the Ministry of Defense. The new law coincided with government plans to modernize the army, which was to be completely mechanized within eighteen months. Moreover, the projected acquisition of sophisticated aircraft and missiles for the air force had brought into sharp focus the need to upgrade the skills and technical abilities of active-duty personnel. The new military service law was an effort to reduce reliance on the less educated beduin servicemen by incorporating the better educated and skilled city dwellers—most of them Palestinians—to meet personnel needs in an era of modern weaponry.

The new law provided for conscription at the age of eighteen but encouraged students to continue their schooling through university level by a complex system of service postponements. Once an academic degree was received or the student reached the age of twenty-eight, the two-year service commitment had to be fulfilled. Jordanians working abroad also could postpone their military obligation. Exemptions were limited to those who could not pass the required medical examination because of permanent disability, those who were only sons, and the brothers of men who had died while in service in the armed forces. Any male of conscription age was prohibited from being employed unless he had been exempted from service or unless his call-up had been deferred because the armed forces had a temporary sufficiency. The law established an extensive system of veterans' rights, including job seniority, for men who had fulfilled their service commitment.

Of approximately 30,000 Jordanians who reached military age annually, about 20,000 were available for compulsory service, although the actual number called up was limited by the prevailing budgetary situation. The conscription system also assisted in filling gaps that had developed as a result of insufficient recruitment by inducing a greater number of young men to join the regular army. Volunteers for an initial five-year enlistment were paid on an adequate scale instead of the very low wage of conscripts and could aspire to higher positions and training opportunities.

## Women in the Armed Forces

Although they were not subject to compulsory service and did not serve in combat-related positions, women had been recruited at both officer and enlisted levels. Most of the female service personnel occupied administrative or secretarial positions or served in communications units. Women also were employed as doctors and nurses in military hospitals. In 1989 the highest ranking woman, a colonel, was in the Medical Corps. The facilities formerly occupied by the Jordanian Military Academy near Az Zarqa had been converted to a training school for women soldiers.

## Conditions of Service

Because of their critical role in safeguarding the monarchy, members of the armed forces have always enjoyed privileged status. The few occasions of discord have almost invariably been caused by dissatisfaction with the failure of pay increases to keep up with inflation or the perception that rising living standards in the private sector were outdistancing military compensation. With the more heterogeneous ethnic composition of the armed forces rendering traditional loyalty to the Hashimites less reliable, the king has been personally concerned to ensure adequate, if not generous, financial provision for service personnel. As a consequence, maintaining income levels of existing personnel has remained a priority even if this meant restrictions on the size of the armed forces and a delay in improving the reserve system.

As of 1989, remuneration of the career military was extremely modest by the standards of the United States armed forces. Pay scales were low, although the total compensation and benefits for an enlisted soldier were calculated to be worth three times the basic wage. Conscript pay was far lower than that of career personnel, amounting to only about JD20 (for value of the Jordanian dinar—see Glossary) per month—barely sufficient to cover personal expenses. In addition to salary, military personnel were entitled to family allowances and access to subsidized post exchanges. Full medical services were provided to soldiers, their immediate family, and their parents. Free transportation was available; the military had its own fleet of buses to convey soldiers between their posts and their home communities. Family housing normally was not provided on post, but a system of thirty-year loans on generous terms enabled many officers and NCOs to purchase or build their own homes.

Most officers of the rank of major and above were provided with automobiles for both official and private use, including free fuel and maintenance. Successful completion of training and education courses also resulted in a significant supplement to income. In the case of a senior officer receiving a master's degree after completion of the War College course, the increase could amount to as much as 60 percent of base pay. The minimum period of pensionable service was twenty years. Taking into account all forms of compensation, it was estimated that military personnel enjoyed a standard of living superior to that of civilian government officials in equivalent positions.

## Ranks and Insignia

The rank structure of the Jordanian army and air force was identical to that of the United States and British armies. There were, however, fewer enlisted grades (see fig. 16). Insignia of rank were worn on shoulder straps by officers; chevrons with points down were worn by enlisted men on upper right and left sleeves. Designation of officer ranks was based on combinations of seven-pointed stars (sometimes called pips), the Hashimite crown, crossed sabers, and wreaths. The system was similar to that of the British army with minor differences in design. In the army the basic color of the metal of insignia and buttons was gold; in the air force, silver.

Many units were authorized to wear identifying shoulder patches or flashes, but these were not worn during periods of combat or civil disturbance. In the field, branch and service were indicated by the color of the beret: chocolate brown for infantry, black for armor, navy blue for artillery, light blue for engineers, dark green for the Royal Guards, maroon for the Special Forces, and red for military police.

## Training and Education

Army basic training in primary military skills and discipline was conducted over a fourteen-week period for both volunteers and conscripts. More advanced training in individual weapons, as well as in artillery, engineering, communications, and other specialties, was provided after recruits were assigned to their permanent units. Soldiers qualifying for promotion attended a general NCO school providing instruction in leadership techniques. Additional courses for NCOs were offered at training centers specializing in armor, artillery, engineering, and logistics. A branch of the infantry school trained Special Forces personnel in techniques of night patrol, demolition, map reading, and hand-to-hand combat.

With the exception of a very limited number of officers commissioned from NCO ranks, officer candidates were selected from applicants who were graduates of the country's secondary schools. Until the early 1980s, the cadets attended a two-year course of instruction at the Jordanian Military Academy, where they pursued a program modeled on that of Sandhurst. In 1987, however, the first graduates of the four-year program at Mutah Military University in the town of Mutah (also seen as Moata) south of Amman, were commissioned as second lieutenants. The curriculum at Mutah has been described as similar to that of the Citadel in Charleston, South Carolina, a military college offering bachelor of arts and bachelor of science degrees in a number of fields.

Two general courses of advanced officer training were available, one at the Jordanian Staff College and the other at the War College, both located near Amman. Both programs were one year in length. The Staff College course was offered to senior captains, majors, and lieutenant colonels. The War College course was offered to senior lieutenant colonels, colonels, and brigadier generals. Virtually all officers attended the Staff College or its equivalent abroad. Both institutions were affiliated with Mutah. Graduates of the Staff College were awarded bachelor of arts degrees in military science from Mutah, and graduates of the War College earned masters degrees.

Many Jordanian officers also attended the United States Army Command and General Staff College or the British Army Staff College. Both officers and NCOs also could attend more specialized technical schools in the United States and Britain. Some training positions continued to be available at Sandhurst for selected army cadets.

The training offered at Jordan's military schools was considered to be of high quality. The schools attracted several hundred military officers and enlisted personnel annually from nearby Arab countries (see Military Cooperation with Other Arab States, this ch.). The armed forces also administered a high school in Amman and a number of schools in other areas of the country, particularly at the more remote posts in the south, to educate children of military personnel. The schools were conducted on semimilitary lines and provided some introductory training, but the curriculum was comparable to that used in civilian schools and was coordinated with the Ministry of Education.

## People's Army and Reserves

In 1983 the Jordanian parliament approved a People's Army Law requiring male and female students in high schools and colleges

## COMMISSIONED OFFICERS

| JORDANIAN RANK | MULAZIM | MULAZIM AWWAL | NAQIB | RAID | MUQADDAM | AQID | AMID | LIWA | FARIQ | FARIQ AWWAL | MUSHIR |
|---|---|---|---|---|---|---|---|---|---|---|---|
| ARMY |  | | | | | | | | | | |
| U.S. RANK TITLES | 2D LIEUTENANT | 1ST LIEUTENANT | CAPTAIN | MAJOR | LIEUTENANT COLONEL | COLONEL | BRIGADIER GENERAL | MAJOR GENERAL | LIEUTENANT GENERAL | GENERAL | GENERAL OF THE ARMY |
| AIR FORCE |  | | | | | | | | | | |
| U.S. RANK TITLES | 2D LIEUTENANT | 1ST LIEUTENANT | CAPTAIN | MAJOR | LIEUTENANT COLONEL | COLONEL | BRIGADIER GENERAL | MAJOR GENERAL | LIEUTENANT GENERAL | GENERAL | GENERAL OF THE AIR FORCE |

## ENLISTED PERSONNEL

| JORDANIAN RANK | JUNDI | WAKIL ARIF | | ARIF | RAQIB | RAQIB AWWAL | | WAKIL | |
|---|---|---|---|---|---|---|---|---|---|
| ARMY AND AIR FORCE | NO INSIGNIA | 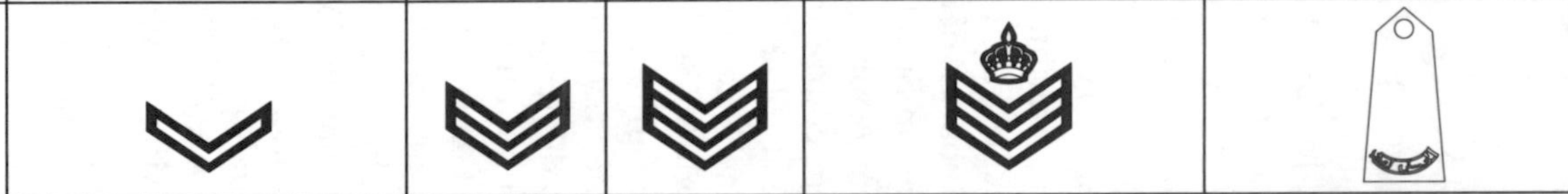 | | | | | | 1 | |
| U.S. ARMY RANK TITLES | BASIC PRIVATE | PRIVATE | PRIVATE 1ST CLASS | CORPORAL | SERGEANT | STAFF SERGEANT | SERGEANT 1ST CLASS | MASTER SERGEANT | COMMAND SERGEANT MAJOR |
| U.S. AIR FORCE RANK TITLES | AIRMAN BASIC | AIRMAN | AIRMAN 1ST CLASS | SERGEANT | STAFF SERGEANT | TECHNICAL SERGEANT | MASTER SERGEANT | SENIOR MASTER SERGEANT | CHIEF MASTER SERGEANT |

NOTE -- Because the navy is an integral part of the army, their ranks and insignia are the same. [1] Insignia in the Royal Jordanian Air Force not known.

*Figure 16. Military Ranks and Insignia, 1989*

and males between the ages of sixteen and fifty-five who had not undergone military service (including government employees and farm workers) to become members of an auxiliary force called the People's Army. Women between the ages of sixteen and forty-five who were not students could volunteer for the program. Special uniforms and insignia were worn. Training included weapons handling and indoctrination in patriotism, although some emphasis was placed on civil defense and rescue work and first aid in the event of natural disasters. Persons employed in vital areas of production were exempt. Instruction for members of the People's Army was administered at secondary schools and colleges by visiting teams of regular uniformed personnel, although annual refresher training was given at military camps. Exercises were carried out jointly with regular military units. Women's training occurred in schoolyards under the supervision of female teachers. Islamic activists in parliament had opposed compulsory service for women and any mixing of the sexes in training. The prime minister rejected the criticism, however, noting that women had participated in the Prophet Muhammad's conquests.

The original intention was to raise a people's militia of about 200,000 people comprising students and persons deferred from military service. By the close of 1986, however, the program had been introduced in only one governorate, and no more than 10,000 individuals had been enrolled. *The Military Balance, 1989–90*, published by the London-based International Institute for Strategic Studies, estimated enrollment in the People's Army to be more than 15,000 as of 1989. The People's Army was equipped with light weapons obtained from the Soviet Union and Eastern Europe, including the Soviet AK–47 assault rifle (the regular army continued to use the United States M–16 as its basic infantry weapon).

A separate reserve program was maintained but was reported to enjoy lower priority after the formation of the People's Army. The estimated 30,000 army and 5,000 air force reservists were conscripts who, having completed their two years of service, remained on call for another five years. Reservists had assignments to fill in existing regular units if called up during a crisis. Mobilization plans based on the development of separate reserve elements were reportedly in abeyance because of the lack of funds for regular training and equipment.

## Military Relations with Other Countries

Given Jordan's limited resources and state of development, the maintenance of its modern armed establishment has been possible only with extensive reliance on foreign aid. The sources of military assistance have shifted somewhat during the different periods of the country's existence; however, until the 1980s, Jordan had looked primarily to Britain and the United States for military matériel. During the 1980s, France emerged as an increasingly important supplier of combat aircraft, and the Soviet Union increasingly supplied air defense systems. To a great extent, major acquisitions have been purchased on generous credit terms, with financing of the military debt made possible by grants from other Arab countries.

From the time the amirate was created in 1921, British aid took the form of direct annual subsidies in conformance with a special treaty relationship. Britain continued to underwrite the entire cost of the Arab Legion until early 1957, when the defense treaty was dissolved by mutual consent. During the last years of the subsidy, the annual payment for the legion was the equivalent of about US$33.6 million. After 1957 a British-reinforced army brigade and an RAF squadron remained in Jordan for a short period and contributed significantly to the preservation of political stability and internal security. British aid, no longer part of a treaty commitment, eventually tapered off to a moderate level of military sales.

American military aid began on a small scale in 1950, but in 1957 the United States became the kingdom's principal source of assistance in meeting its national security needs. In the mid-1970s, however, conditions imposed by the United States during lengthy negotiations leading to the sale of Hawk SAMs initiated a period of increasing strain in the relations between the two countries.

Hussein's growing independence in purchasing military matériel was facilitated in part by his strengthened ties to other Arab countries after Jordan joined them in opposing the United States-sponsored 1978 Camp David Accords between Israel and Egypt. During the Baghdad Summit of Arab leaders in that year, oil-producing Arab states of the Persian Gulf area, plus Libya and Algeria, pledged to compensate Jordan in the form of US$1.25 billion annually for ten years for its rejection of the accords. Following the precipitous drop in oil prices, however, most countries reneged on their commitments or made only partial payments. By 1984, it was estimated that Jordan was receiving only US$550 million annually, and only Saudi Arabia was current on its pledge. When the Baghdad Summit commitments expired in 1988, Jordan continued to look to Saudi Arabia, which in that year supplied an estimated US$350 million in assistance.

## Meeting Jordan's Equipment Needs in the 1980s

When problems were encountered with supply from the United States, Jordan's preferred alternative source for weaponry has been

Western Europe. Increasingly, however, Hussein has purchased weapons from the Soviet Union, which has been willing to provide weapons at low prices and on attractive credit terms. According to ACDA, the Soviet Union was the largest single source of Jordanian weapons imports between 1982 and 1986, supplying weaponry valued at US$1.1 billion. France was second, with US$825 million. The United States was third, with US$725 million, followed by Britain with US$575 million. The initial Soviet arms agreement, concluded in 1981, was for US$360 million—partially underwritten by Iraq—and covering SA-8 vehicle-mounted SAMs and air defense artillery systems. This agreement was followed in 1984 by a further purchase of US$300 million worth of SAMs and in 1985 by additional contracts for unspecified quantities of equipment, including the SA-13 low-altitude SAM and the SA-14 shoulder-fired SAM (regarded as a substitute for the Stinger, which Hussein had been unable to obtain from the United States).

France has actively promoted sales of military equipment to Jordan since the 1970s. In addition to the Mirage F-1, it has supplied Alouette helicopters and air-to-air missiles. Since 1980, France has sold considerable quantities of munitions and artillery to Jordan and in 1988 won a major aircraft contract to supply the Mirage 2000 and to upgrade Mirage F-1s in Jordan's existing inventory.

Significant purchases from Britain included the Chieftain and Centurion tanks, plus Bulldog trainer aircraft. In 1985 a government-subsidized credit of US$350 million was extended by a consortium of British banks for Jordanian purchases of ammunition, light transport, communications, avionics, and other equipment. In 1987 Spain for the first time became a substantial supplier, receiving a Jordanian contract estimated at about US$90 million for twenty aircraft, including transports and jet trainers.

## Military Cooperation with the United States

United States military assistance to Jordan began on a small scale in 1950, but in 1957 the United States became Jordan's principal source of equipment following the termination of the British subsidy. A large-scale purchase of ground force equipment in 1965 was followed in 1967 by orders for F-104 Starfighter aircraft and support gear. After the disastrous losses of military equipment during the June 1967 War, United States military aid, most of which had been supplied on a credit basis, was shifted to grant form. Additional purchases of American hardware were made possible by massive postwar financing from friendly Arab states.

Although Jordanian forces played only a token role in the October 1973 War with Israel, Arab losses renewed Hussein's determination to expand and modernize Jordan's military capabilities. An improved air defense system had the highest priority. After a study of Jordan's air defense needs, the United States Department of Defense recommended supplying Jordan a mixture of American weapons, including the Improved Hawk SAM, the Vulcan 20mm radar-guided antiaircraft gun, and the Redeye shoulder-fired missile. The proposal resulted in protracted negotiations in Washington between the United States Congress and the executive branch. The Israeli Embassy in Washington and American Jewish organizations applied strong pressure on Congress to reject the sale, arguing that the twenty-one Hawk batteries Jordan wanted would reinforce the Soviet-supplied SAM capability of Syria, making all of Israel vulnerable to the combined weapons coverage. Hussein threatened publicly to withdraw the request and accept an offer of comparable missiles from the Soviet Union. Inasmuch as the weapons were to be paid for by strongly anticommunist Saudi Arabia, however, Hussein was obliged to reject Moscow's offer. Ultimately a compromise was reached under which the United States would provide fourteen Improved Hawk batteries to be permanently emplaced as defensive weapons in the Amman-Az Zarqa area and at airfields and radar installations east and south of Amman. Final agreement was reached on the US$540 million arrangement in September 1976.

Not only did the negotiations over the Hawk system prove humiliating to Hussein, but also the system as finally negotiated did not fully meet Jordan's need because of the limited coverage afforded by the missiles and their extreme vulnerability at fixed sites. Disagreement persisted over the scope and cost of other United States weapons systems that Jordan could buy with funds underwritten by other Arab countries. In 1979 Jordan sought to acquire moderate numbers of F-16 fighter aircraft and approximately 300 M-60 tanks. The United States delayed in responding because of a new policy designed to reduce the amount of weapons transfers to Third World countries. A much reduced shipment of 100 M-60 tanks was eventually made available to Jordan but without important modern features such as night sights and advanced fire control. Hussein accordingly turned to Britain for Chieftain tanks and modernization kits for Jordan's existing Centurion tanks, and to France for Mirage aircraft as substitutes for the F-16s.

In early 1984, President Ronald Reagan proposed selling 315 Stinger launchers and 1,600 missiles to Jordan but was forced to withdraw the proposal because of continued congressional opposition. Hussein's biting criticisms of American policy contributed to the negative attitude in Congress. In 1985 the administration put before Congress a new package valued at US$1.9 billion, which would have included 40 F–16s or F–20 aircraft, 300 advanced air-to-air missiles, 72 Stingers, and 32 Bradley infantry fighting vehicles. The most controversial feature of the package was a proposal to upgrade the existing fixed Hawk batteries by converting them to mobile units and adding six new mobile Hawk batteries.

Congress effectively blocked this transaction as well by setting conditions on the Jordanian-Israeli peace process that Hussein was unprepared to meet. In early 1986, the administration suspended indefinitely its efforts to supply major systems to Jordan. Military assistance has since been carried on at a pace adequate to sustain existing readiness levels by providing selective upgrading of equipment, together with training, spare parts, and service, and help in building up ammunition stocks. Close relationships continued to be maintained with the Jordanian military in spite of differences over new equipment items. The United States and Jordan expanded senior officer exchanges. The United States has supplied technical assistance teams and instructor training programs, and has developed specialized training courses tailored to Jordanian needs. Joint military exercises also have been held annually on Jordanian territory.

From 1950 through 1988, the United States furnished a total of about US$1.5 billion in military aid, US$878 million in loans and US$631 million in grants. The grant program amounted to US$26.5 million in FY 1988. For FY 1989, the administration proposed US$48 million in military sales credits but Congress approved only US$10 million. For FY 1990, the administration again requested US$48 million. The United States also planned to provide funds for military training and education amounting to US$1.0 million in fiscal year 1989. This money would enable a total of 452 Jordanian military personnel to receive training or professional education in military colleges in the United States during FY 1989.

## Military Cooperation with Other Arab States

Jordan traditionally has considered that it shared responsibility for the security of the Middle East, particularly that of Saudi Arabia and the Persian Gulf states. For many years, Jordan has supplied these countries with advisers, mostly personnel in reserve status who had completed their active duty. A total of 565 army officers and 1,420 NCOs served in other Arab countries between 1970 and 1984. The loan of military personnel was regarded as a form of compensation to the Persian Gulf states that have provided Jordan with subsidies over the years. Jordan also has acted as a consultant to these countries in matters such as weapons selection and organization of military forces.

As of 1988, Jordanian personnel were serving in a training or operational capacity in Kuwait, North Yemen, Qatar, Oman, the United Arab Emirates, and Saudi Arabia. Many officers from these countries, the majority Saudi Arabs, were undergoing training in Jordan at Mutah Military University and the Jordanian Staff College. Between 1970 and 1984, more than 4,000 officers and 7,000 enlisted personnel from Arab states had attended military institutions in Jordan.

Jordan has supplied combat troops to assist Persian Gulf states confronting security threats. In 1975 Jordan deployed two squadrons of fighter aircraft and a Special Forces battalion to Oman at that country's request to help defeat an uprising supported by South Yemen. Hussein offered to send a division to assist Saudi Arabia when the main mosque in Mecca was seized by Islamic activists in 1979. Although the division was never sent, the incident alerted Jordanian commanders to the problems of rapidly transporting a large body of troops in a Middle East emergency. Jordan turned to the United States for assistance in providing transport airplanes, missiles, and special equipment to move and maintain a Jordanian rapid deployment force of two brigades (8,000 men) in the event of a threat to the stability of the Persian Gulf area. When the proposal became public in early 1983, it faced so many objections in Congress—where it was seen as a means to circumvent curbs on military aid to Jordan—that it had to be abandoned. The Israelis pointed out that there was no assurance that the new equipment would not be used against them. Finally, the Gulf states resented the public airing of their own security needs, and particularly the involvement of one of the superpowers in such planning.

During the Iran-Iraq War of 1980 to 1988, Jordan sided with Iraq because of Hussein's desire to contain Iran's revolutionary Islamic movement. The Jordanian port of Al Aqabah became an important transshipment point for military supplies essential to the Baghdad government's conduct of the war. In early 1982, Hussein announced that the Yarmuk Brigade, a force of 3,000, would be raised to fight alongside Iraqi forces in the conflict against Iran. A number of recruiting offices were opened to seek volunteers. No definite information was subsequently made available on the role this force played in the fighting. As a reciprocal gesture, the Iraqis transferred to Jordan on at least two occasions quantities of American and British armored equipment captured from Iran.

Although Jordan had no significant defense industry, it was reported in 1983 that components of the Chinese J–6 fighter aircraft, a variant of the Soviet MiG-19, were shipped to the King Faisal Air Base at Al Jafr for assembly and subsequent delivery to Iraq. The United States had assisted in the construction of an armor rebuild facility suitable for work on the M-60, Chieftain, and Centurion tanks, and on armored personnel carriers and self-propelled artillery. The capacity of the rebuild plant exceeded Jordan's own needs with the expectation that orders for the rehabilitation of armored equipment might be obtained from other Arab nations.

## The Internal Security System

The concept of public order founded on the supremacy of law has been stressed by Hussein throughout his reign as a prerequisite to internal stability and the achievement of national development goals. In accordance with the provisions of the Constitution, public order has been successfully maintained through legally established instruments: comprehensive codes of law enforced by a professional police force and an independent judiciary. The police and the General Intelligence Department (GID), generally known as the Mukhabarat from the Arabic name Dairat al Mukhabarat, a civilian agency, exercised broad powers to monitor disruptive segments of the population. The scope of police and GID powers at times have become a source of contention from a human rights standpoint, although in nonsecurity cases legal norms had been generally observed by police and judicial authorities.

### Police Forces

In 1989 primary responsibility for the routine maintenance of law and order was exercised by the Public Security Force, the country's national police establishment. Centralized in time of peace within the Public Security Directorate of the Ministry of Interior, the police were subordinated to the Ministry of Defense and under the control of the army commander in the event of war. Traditionally, the police have been commanded by an officer with the title of director general of public security, usually a senior army general, who reported to the minister of interior. Officers assigned to this important position were personally selected by Hussein on the basis of their military record, leadership qualifications, and loyalty to the crown. As of early 1989, the head of the police organization was Lieutenant General Abdul Hadi al Majali, formerly chief of the general staff.

An outgrowth of the Arab Legion, the Public Security Force was created by law in July 1956, when the legion was separated into distinct police and army elements. During the twenty months of martial law instituted by Hussein from April 1957 to November

1958, the police were again subordinated to army control. As domestic and external threats to Hashimite rule were brought under better control, a new law in July 1958 reestablished the separation of the two security forces.

The strength of the Public Security Force was estimated to be about 4,000 personnel in the late 1980s. A considerable augmentation of the Desert Police Force was reported to be planned in 1988. The relatively large size of the force, combined with the army support, testified to the importance of the internal security function.

The police were classified broadly according to areas of geographic responsibility. The three major divisions were the metropolitan (Amman), rural (small towns and villages), and desert contingents. Police headquarters in Amman provided both an administrative control point for the countrywide system and an array of centralized technical functions that supported police activities throughout the kingdom. A reorganization of the Public Security Directorate announced in 1987 reduced the previous five-tiered structure to only three tiers. Below the central headquarters, with its overall responsibility for police, security, and law enforcement activities, were ten regional directorates. Eight of the directorates corresponded to the governorates, and one covered the city of Amman and its suburbs. The desert region was a separate directorate and was patrolled by the Desert Police Force. Under the 1987 plan, the ten regions were to be subdivided into fifty-nine security centers, each of which typically would be responsible for an area of five to ten square kilometers and serve 50,000 people.

Public Security Force missions included the usual tasks of maintenance of public order, protection of life and property, investigation of criminal activity, and apprehension of suspected offenders. In addition to these basic functions, special elements of the force performed such duties as traffic control, licensing of vehicles and certain business activities, enforcement of trade prohibitions and zoning ordinances, locating missing persons, guarding shrines and other public places, assisting customs and immigration officials in the performance of their duties, and operating the country's penal institutions. In announcing the 1987 reorganization, the director general of public security emphasized an increased social role for the police and strengthened police relations with the local community. He described the police as the conduit through which the public could seek assistance from various government authorities in resolving social problems.

Functionally, the responsibilities assigned to the police were carried out according to a tripartite division of responsibilities at the headquarters level—administrative, judicial, and support operations.

*Traffic policeman, Amman*

Administrative police were charged with prevention of crime and routine maintenance of security and public order. Criminal offenses were under the jurisdiction of judicial police, who conducted criminal investigations, apprehended suspects, and assisted the public prosecutor's office in prosecuting accused offenders. Support police performed budget, planning, training, public affairs, communications, and logistic functions. Insofar as was possible, regional police activities throughout the country conformed to this division of responsibilities. Modern communications facilities connecting regional directorates with the headquarters in Amman provided a direct link to specialized elements such as the Criminal Investigation Department's modern police laboratory, which also assisted regional and local police in their investigations.

The Special Police Force within the Public Security Directorate had principal responsibility for countering terrorism. As part of its antiterrorism program, the Jordanian government cooperated with various international bodies in sharing information and resources. A multimillion dollar project to improve police communications, announced in 1988, was another element of the antiterrorist campaign. In connection with this project, the Special Police Force had participated in bomb detection programs for dogs and their handlers offered by the United States. The Desert Police Force, which had responsibility for detecting and stopping drug and gun smuggling, had also been greatly expanded.

Depending on their location, the police were armed with pistols, rifles, nightsticks, or light automatic weapons. In Amman and the larger towns, special crowd and riot control equipment and armored vehicles were available. The police force was fully motorized, had good communications facilities, and operated much on the pattern of European law enforcement agencies. Police units in rural areas were assigned less modern equipment, and in the desert areas the traditional system of camel-mounted desert patrols survived, supplemented by improved communications gear and four-wheel-drive vehicles.

Police personnel have been recruited throughout the service's existence through voluntary enlistments. The National Service Law of 1976 ensured that most younger members of the force would have had some military training before entering police work. Training for both officers and enlisted ranks was provided primarily by the staff of the Royal Police Academy in Amman, but some recruits received their instruction at the separate Police Training School in Az Zarqa. The school at Az Zarqa also welcomed large numbers of police trainees from friendly Arab countries. In addition to courses in general and administrative police work, cadets at the academy studied the country's legal system, underwent physical training, and were instructed in the use of firearms and other police equipment. Judicial training included courses in criminal investigation procedures, court operations, and the criminal code. As part of efforts to improve the general education level of the Public Security Force, the government announced in 1987 that officer recruits would be required to have university degrees and NCO recruits would be required to be graduates of high schools or vocational schools.

The first Arab country to admit women to its police establishment, Jordan opened a women's police academy in Amman in 1972. Before being assigned to positions in law enforcement, the women recruits completed a four-month classroom course followed by one month of practical training in the field. Assignment opportunities expanded steadily after the program began. Women served primarily in the police laboratory, in budgeting and accounting, public relations, licensing, and in prison operations. Some served in street patrols and traffic control in Amman and in border security.

Ranks and insignia of the Public Security Force were identical with those of the army, although job titles were necessarily different. Police uniforms in the Amman metropolitan area were dark blue in winter and light tan in summer, resembling in style those of the Royal Jordanian Air Force. Rural police wore an olive drab uniform lighter in shade than that of the army but otherwise similar.

*Desert policeman on a camel*  *Desert policemen making coffee,*
*Khawr Ramm*

The Desert Police Force retained their traditional Arab garb. Police pay scales were about the same as those of the army but differed somewhat in the special allowances authorized. The conditions of service were sufficiently favorable to attract and retain enough personnel to staff the force fully.

## General Intelligence Department

Internal security, intelligence, and counterintelligence matters were the concern of the police, the armed forces, and the GID, a civilian organization with principal responsibility for dealing with perceived domestic and foreign threats to security. The GID customarily was headed by a high-ranking army officer answerable directly to the prime minister and concurrently a close personal adviser of Hussein.

The GID was a large organization, although its personnel strength was not a matter of public knowledge. Its members were almost invariably persons of proven loyalty to the monarchy and of East Bank origin. It was generally regarded as an effective internal security agency, alert to any evidence of activity that might

269

have subversive implications. Although Jordan had been the target of clandestine operations by other countries, the GID was not known to have a covert branch that engaged in clandestine activity against its Arab neighbors or Israel. The GID was particularly occupied with rooting out Palestinian militant groups and illegal or underground political organizations. It scrutinized activities in the mosques and among student groups. A GID office was located in each refugee camp. The GID's methods and oppressive tactics frequently have been the subject of criticism among Jordanians, although some of its measures, such as checkpoints to monitor domestic travelers, were less obtrusive during the 1980s than they had been in the tense period following the 1970–71 conflict with the PLO.

The widely employed system of identity documents facilitated GID control over the population. A passport was needed both for travel and to obtain employment. Passports could only be obtained by producing other identity documents issued by the Ministry of Interior and had to be authorized by the GID. In addition, a certificate of good conduct from the GID was required for public sector jobs, for many private sector jobs, and for study abroad. A young person studying in a communist country might, on returning for a visit to Jordan, find his or her passport confiscated if the GID harbored suspicions concerning the student's conduct abroad. Furthermore, GID approval was required for public gatherings or activities sponsored by private organizations.

The GID had authority under martial law to detain persons without trial for indeterminate periods, often lasting from several weeks to many months. Such security detainees normally were held incommunicado for interrogation at GID headquarters in Amman. According to the 1988 annual report of the human rights organization Amnesty International, various forms of torture or ill treatment were believed to have been inflicted at GID headquarters on detainees or arrested persons later transferred to ordinary prisons for trial by martial law courts.

## Criminal Justice

Until the nineteenth century, the only source of law considered to be valid in controlling criminal activity in the region that was to become Jordan was Islamic religious law, or sharia. This law and its application had remained static for centuries, subject only to interpretation by the ulama (pl.; sing. *alim,* religious scholars) and enforcement by Muslim judges (qadis) in sharia courts. Temporal rulers could not, in theory, legislate rules to govern social behavior; they could only hand down edicts to implement the immutable divine law.

In the mid-1800s, reforms of the system were instituted to enhance Ottoman control of the area. Comprehensive codes of law based on European models became the basis of a new legal system, and in 1858 a criminal code was adopted to support the reform movement. The new code was based on French law, but in effect it complemented sharia inasmuch as the French code was modified to accommodate Muslim customs. For example, the Ottoman criminal code imposed the payment of blood money in addition to imprisonment for acts of homicide or bodily injury, and the death penalty for apostasy was retained.

When the Ottoman Empire ceased to exist after World War I and Britain became the mandatory power for Palestine and Transjordan, the Ottoman laws in force were supplemented by British statutes. In Palestine the 1858 criminal code was replaced by a new penal code and a code of criminal procedure patterned on those used in British colonies. The Palestinian courts, staffed by British and British-trained judges, used their power to apply English common law, and decisions could be appealed to the judicial committee of the Privy Council in London. The influence of English law was weaker in Transjordan, however, where there were no British judges, and common law was not applied in the courts. Instead, the laws that dealt with criminal behavior retained the European flavor of the Ottoman code of 1858.

When the Hashemite Kingdom of Jordan was proclaimed in 1949, the ancient Ottoman code had been largely modified at the insistence of moderates who believed that the sharia provisions on which it had been based should be supplemented by—and, if necessary, subordinated to—laws that could deal with modern problems. The period of British tutelage did not significantly change the substantive law, but it had the effect of weakening the absolutist traditions of sharia in the field of criminal jurisprudence. In the early 1950s, a committee of leading Muslim scholars and jurists of several Arab countries convened with the purpose of drafting new codes of criminal law and procedure to replace the 1858 Ottoman code, which had been almost entirely amended during the century it had been in force. In 1956 the Jordanian National Assembly adopted a new criminal code and code of criminal procedure. Both were based on the Syrian and Lebanese codes, which in turn were modeled on French counterparts.

Within the realm of criminal jurisprudence, Jordan retained only nominal application of sharia. Although the codified laws were based on Islamic principles and customs, these were largely modified and

extended along European lines in an effort to adapt to the requirements of a changing economy and culture.

## Criminal Code

The criminal code adopted in 1956, which had been amended
many times, contained the bulk of the country's criminal law. In
addition, certain codified civil statutes also prescribed penalties for
acts such as libel, adultery, and publication of material endangering the security of the kingdom. Individuals could not be punished
except for acts made criminal by virtue of penalties prescribed by
law. Other than where specified, a person also could not be punished
for committing a criminal act in the absence of criminal responsibility or intent, both of which were defined by the code. As a
safeguard of personal liberty, the government had the burden of
proving both the defendant's commission of the act and the ad-
missible intent of the defendant before guilt could be established.

The criminal code, in traditional French form, divided criminal offenses into three categories according to the severity of the
applicable punishments. In English common law these categories
equated roughly to felonies, misdemeanors, and minor violations.
Punishments for felonies ranged from death by hanging to imprisonment for periods ranging from three years to life. Punishments for
misdemeanors included imprisonment for periods ranging from
three weeks to three years and a variety of fines. Minor violations
could be punished by imprisonment for less than three weeks, small
fines, or reprimands by the court. In cases involving misdemeanors
or minor violations, a judge also could invoke preventive measures
including detention for psychiatric examination, forfeiture of material goods, or closure of a place of business. The criminal code
provided for minimum penalties for all major infractions rather
than relying on the discretion of the courts.

The death penalty was authorized for murder, arson of an inhabited building, assassination of the king (or attempts on his life),
and a broad range of serious crimes defined as threats to the security of the state. These latter offenses included acts such as treason, espionage on behalf of an unfriendly foreign power, and armed
insurrection. The act of selling land in the West Bank to occupying Israeli authorities was considered high treason and therefore
a capital offense. Some Palestinians had been sentenced in absentia to death under this decree but as of 1989 these sentences had
never been carried out. Executions were rare and politically sensitive in Jordan. Three death sentences for murder were carried out
in 1985, none in 1986, and only one in 1987. In the 1987 case,

the assassin of a PLO Executive Committee member in the West Bank was put to death.

Imprisonment for life was imposed for such felonies as lesser crimes against national security, homicide during commission of a misdemeanor or that resulted from torture, and the more serious forms of theft. Shorter imprisonment was prescribed for these same offenses if mitigating circumstances warranted. Such punishment also was authorized for terrorist activity, membership in subversive organizations, counterfeiting, forgery of official documents, and abduction.

Misdemeanors included such offenses as gambling in public places, bribery, perjury, simple forgery, slander, embezzlement, assault and battery, and disturbing the peace. The influence of sharia was still evident in the imposition of prison sentences for desertion of a child, abortion, marrying a girl under the age of sixteen, openly ridiculing the Prophet Muhammad, and breaking the fast of Ramadan. Sharia also was important in the criteria for justifiable homicide. No penalty was imposed for the immediate killing of someone who defiled a person's or a family's honor.

Minor violations covered by the code included traffic violations, seeking redress for a crime without recourse to civil authorities, public drunkenness, and violations of administrative regulations such as licensing and safe housing requirements. These infractions were punishable with or without proven intent. Most minor violations resulted in fines being assessed against the offender.

## Incidence of Crime

Detailed criminal statistics were not customarily available but fragmentary data has been released from time to time that provided limited information on the nature and scope of criminal activity in Jordan. According to a Jordanian submission to the International Criminal Police Organization (Interpol), national criminal statistics recorded 16,215 offenses for 1984. Although it was not clear what offenses constituted this total, the number of cases in the following categories was supplied: ordinary theft (3,859 cases reported), aggravated theft (1,208 cases), breaking and entering (1,164 cases), car theft (178 cases), robbery and violent theft (44 cases), other forms of theft (2,473 cases), serious assaults (437), homicide (70), and rape (24). Frauds numbered 276 and currency or counterfeiting violations numbered 31. Only sixty-five drug offenses were reported.

According to Interpol, the total number of criminal offenses reported by Jordanian authorities constituted a rate of 630 crimes per 100,000 people. This rate was far lower than that reported by most countries of Western Europe but was typical of some Middle Eastern countries, and higher than many countries of the Third World. The validity of this index was linked to the reliability of the reports of criminal activity submitted to Interpol.

The Public Security Directorate released similar data for 1986. In that year, 19,618 criminal offenses were reported. Under the category of thefts and robberies, the directorate listed 4,269 violations. According to the directorate, most such crimes were committed by unemployed males and by low-paid laborers between the ages of eighteen and twenty-seven. There were 549 offenses listed as "moral" crimes, including rape, abduction, and various forms of public misbehavior. A total of 348 cases of fraud and embezzlement were recorded, reflecting a rising trend attributed by the police to poor economic conditions and financial difficulties of individuals and companies. The sixty-four murders reported represented a decline from eighty-one in the previous year. Generally, such crimes were the result of personal disputes, family problems, and seeking revenge. Again, the perpetrators of homicides were predominantly in the eighteen to twenty-seven-year-old age-group. The police reported that 71 deaths and 513 injuries had resulted from guns fired in celebration or accidentally.

## Procedures in Criminal Law

When the police believed that a person had committed a crime or when someone was caught committing a criminal act, the suspect was taken to the nearest police station for registration and interrogation. Usually a warrant was required for an arrest; however, in cases where delay would be harmful or when a person was apprehended in a criminal offense, the accused could be detained without a warrant of arrest for as long as forty-eight hours. After forty-eight hours, a court order was required to continue detention of the suspect.

A warrant of arrest could be issued by a magistrate only if there were a presumption that the person had committed the offense for which he or she was charged and if there were reason to believe that the accused intended to escape, destroy traces of the crime, or induce witnesses to make false statements. A warrant also could be issued for offenses against national security or other grave acts specified in the criminal code.

The police magistrate first informed the accused of the charges and questioned the accused and any available witnesses to determine if there were a prima facie case against the detained person, who had the right to counsel at this preliminary investigation. If the magistrate found evidence of guilt, the case was transmitted to the local prosecutor for further investigation. A prosecutor was attached to every magistrate's court and court of first instance (see The Judiciary, ch. 4). The magistrate then could either issue an arrest warrant to bind over the suspect for trial or release the suspect on bail. Release on bail was a matter of right when the maximum penalty prescribed for the offense was imprisonment not exceeding one year and where the accused had an established residence within the country and had not previously been convicted of a felony or sentenced to more than three months in jail.

The right of habeas corpus was provided for under the Constitution, but in practice it had not afforded the same protection as in English common law. The police usually managed to establish the need to detain suspects charged with serious offenses. Persons could be detained pending investigation for fifteen days or longer if the court approved a request by the public prosecutor for an extension. The power of detention had been used effectively by the police to forestall disorder. For example, police occasionally dispersed crowds before a disturbance merely by threatening to arrest those who disobeyed an order to leave the scene.

On deciding that legal action against the accused was necessary, the public prosecutor instituted a trial by issuing an indictment to the appropriate court. The fourteen magistrates' courts handled only those criminal offenses for which the maximum fine was not more than JD100 or the maximum prison sentence was not more than one year. The seven courts of first instance tried cases involving misdemeanors before two judges and major felonies before three judges. Trials were open to the public except in certain cases, such as those involving sexual offenses. The defendant had the right to legal counsel, but defendants often were unaware of this right and failed to exercise it. The court appointed a lawyer for those who could not afford one if the potential sentence was execution or life imprisonment. Defendants had the right of cross-examination and were protected against self-incrimination. There was no jury system in Jordan. The judge, therefore, decided questions of fact, based entirely on the weight of the evidence, as well as questions of the interpretation and application of the criminal law.

Trials began with opening statements by the prosecutor and the defense counsel, followed by an interrogation of the defendant by the presiding judge. After examination of witnesses for the state and for the accused and the submission of documentary evidence, closing arguments by the prosecutor and defense counsel completed the presentation. Decisions were announced in open court and, if the defendant were found guilty, sentence would be pronounced.

Either the public prosecutor or the defendant could appeal the decision to the court of appeal and, ultimately, to the Court of Cassation.

## Martial Law Courts

A state of martial law, in effect since 1967, gave the government authority to detain individuals without charge and to adjudicate specified crimes in the martial law courts. These courts consisted of a panel of three military officers trained in the law. Designated martial law crimes included espionage, bribery of public officials, trafficking in narcotics or weapons, black marketing, and security offenses. Security detainees could be held without charge or brought before the martial law courts for trial. Detainees did not have the right to communicate with their family or legal counsel.

Although the martial law courts were not bound to observe normal rules of evidence or procedures, in practice these military courts observed the law of criminal procedure and defendants were given most of the rights they were entitled to in civilian courts. Trials were held in public; defendants were represented by counsel and could cross-examine witnesses. It was not customary to grant bail, however, and there was no provision for habeas corpus. Normal avenues of appeal were not open from decisions of the military courts, but such court actions were subject to ratification by the prime minister in his capacity as military governor. The prime minister had the authority to increase, reduce, or annul sentences. Before acting, the prime minister received recommendations on the fairness of a sentence by a legal adviser or the minister of justice.

In its annual report for 1988, Amnesty International asserted that some proceedings in the martial law courts failed to meet international standards for fair trials. It noted that in some cases it appeared that confessions allegedly extracted under torture or ill treatment were accepted as evidence. The United States Department of State's *Country Reports on Human Rights Practices for 1986* observed that the very quick trials and subsequent sentencing of the Communist Party of Jordan leadership suggested that there were politically motivated exceptions to the norms of criminal procedures and rights in the martial law courts.

Military courts also adjudicated all crimes committed by military personnel, applying military regulations promulgated by the Ministry of Defense pursuant to relevant laws. In these cases, the commanding officer of the armed forces was required to ratify the sentence.

## Penal System

The penal system, a responsibility of the Ministry of Interior, was administered by the Prisons Department of the Public Security

Directorate. The system was composed of roughly twenty-five prisons and jails. All except Amman Central Prison—the system's major institution—were under the management of regional police chiefs and were sometimes referred to as police jails. In addition to the Amman facility, area prisons were located at Irbid and at Al Jafr, east of Maan in the south-central desert region. The smaller jails were located at or near regional and local police offices. Generally, convicted offenders with more than one year to serve were transferred to the central prison in Amman, those with terms of three months to one year were sent to regional prisons, and those sentenced to three months or less were kept in local jails. Some exceptions were made to this pattern in the case of Palestinian activists or other security prisoners who had been detained for long periods of time in the Al Jafr facility, largely because of its remoteness.

Penal institutions were used to detain persons awaiting trial as well as prisoners serving sentences. Convicted offenders were usually housed separately from those yet to be tried. Major prisons had separate sections for women prisoners, as did a few of the police jails in the larger communities. A juvenile detention center in Amman housed young offenders who had been convicted of criminal offenses. When juveniles reached the age of nineteen, if they had further time to serve, they were transferred to one of the larger prisons for the remainder of their sentences.

All institutions operated in accordance with the provisions of the Prison Law of 1953, as amended. This law provided for decent treatment of prisoners and included comprehensive regulations governing the facilities, care, and administration of the prison system. Jordan was one of the first Arab countries to recognize the theory of rehabilitation, rather than retribution, as the basis for punishment of lawbreakers. This concept emphasized that crime was caused by human weakness resulting from poor social conditions rather than by willfulness and immorality. As such, the approach was in many ways alien to the traditional Muslim custom of personal revenge by the family of the victim, which demanded that the culprit pay for his crime. Although Jordan's penal system was designed to provide punishments suited to bring about the rehabilitation of the wrongdoers, in practice these efforts were hampered by the lack of facilities and professionally trained staff. Some effort was made to provide literacy and limited industrial training classes to prisoners in Amman Central Prison, but few modern techniques of rehabilitation were found in other penal institutions.

According to the annual human rights reports of the United States Department of State, prison conditions were harsh but not intentionally degrading. There appeared to be no discrimination according to religion or social class in treatment of prisoners. Crowded conditions in some prisons were relieved by a royal amnesty in 1985 that resulted in the release of more than 1,000 inmates. In 1986, a new central prison, Juwaidah, was opened in Amman. It replaced the obsolete and cramped Al Mahatta prison, which was scheduled to be closed.

In its 1988 report, Amnesty International cited a number of cases of apparent mistreatment in prisons, notably at Al Mahatta and at the Az Zarqa military prison. The report also questioned the authorities' motives in forcing four students and a writer convicted in the martial law court of membership in illegal leftist organizations to serve their sentences under the harsh conditions found at Al Jafr.

\* \* \*

The general survey of Jordan by Arthur R. Day, *East Bank/West Bank: Jordan and the Prospects for Peace,* includes a chapter appraising the Jordanian military establishment, as well as a number of observations relative to Jordan's internal security. The analysis by Anthony H. Cordesman, *Jordanian Arms and the Middle East Balance,* published in 1983, together with a supplement published in 1985, provides assessments of the military and geostrategic situation of Jordan. The analyses also present arguments for equipping Jordanian forces with advanced weapons to enable the country to resist military pressure from neighboring powers. The problems Jordan encountered with the United States in meeting its desire for these new weapons, especially in the area of air defense, are also reviewed in detail. *The Hashemite Arab Army, 1908–1979,* by S.A. El-Edroos, a Pakistani brigadier who served as adviser to the Jordan Arab Army, is a thorough study of military operations and battles through the October 1973 War. John Bagot Glubb's autobiography, *A Soldier with the Arabs,* provides detail on the evolution of the Arab Legion and the fighting in 1948. *Troubles on the East Bank: Challenges to the Domestic Stability of Jordan* by Robert B. Satloff reviews existing and potential internal security problems, with emphasis on the Muslim Brotherhood.

The discussion of military strengths, formations, and equipment in this chapter is based principally on estimates compiled in *The Military Balance, 1988–89,* by the International Institute for Strategic Studies in London. (For further information and complete citations, see Bibliography.)

# Appendix

Table

1  Metric Conversion Coefficients and Factors
2  Schools, Students, and Teachers in the East Bank, 1986–87
3  Enrollment by Education Level and Sex, 1965 and 1985
4  Medical Care and Medical Personnel, 1987
5  Balance of Payments, 1983–87
6  Summary of Central Government Budget Financing, 1983–87
7  Central Government Expenditures, 1983–87
8  Domestic Revenue of the Central Government, 1983–87
9  Labor Force by Sector, 1987
10  Industrial Production of Selected Commodities, 1984–87
11  Agricultural Production and Cultivated Area, 1987
12  Imports of Selected Commodities, 1983–87
13  Exports of Selected Commodities, 1983–87
14  Principal Trade Partners, 1986–87
15  Major Army Equipment, 1988
16  Major Air Force Equipment, 1988

### Table 1. Metric Conversion Coefficients and Factors

| When you know | Multiply by | To find |
|---|---|---|
| Millimeters ..................... | 0.04 | inches |
| Centimeters ..................... | 0.39 | inches |
| Meters ......................... | 3.3 | feet |
| Kilometers ...................... | 0.62 | miles |
| Hectares (10,000 m²) .............. | 2.47 | acres |
| Square kilometers ............... | 0.39 | square miles |
| Cubic meters ................... | 35.3 | cubic feet |
| Liters ......................... | 0.26 | gallons |
| Kilograms ..................... | 2.2 | pounds |
| Metric tons .................... | 0.98 | long tons |
| .................... | 1.1 | short tons |
| .................... | 2,204 | pounds |
| Degrees Celsius ................. | 9 | degrees Fahrenheit |
| (Centigrade) | divide by 5 and add 32 | |

### Table 2. Schools, Students, and Teachers in the East Bank, 1986–87

| Category | Number |
|---|---|
| Schools | |
| Coeducational ............................................. | 1,372 |
| Male ...................................................... | 1,017 |
| Female ................................................... | 977 |
| Total schools ......................................... | 3,366 |
| Students | |
| Male ...................................................... | 479,682 |
| Female ................................................... | 439,963 |
| Total students ........................................ | 919,645 |
| Teachers | |
| Female ................................................... | 23,612 |
| Male ...................................................... | 15,995 |
| Total teachers ........................................ | 39,607 |

Source: Based on information from Jordan, Department of Statistics, *Statistical Yearbook, 1987,* 38, Amman, 1988, 167.

*Table 3. Enrollment by Education Level and Sex,*
*1965 and 1985*
(in percentages)

| Level | 1965 | 1985 |
|---|---|---|
| Primary | | |
| Male | 100 | 98 |
| Female | 83 | 99 |
| Both sexes | 92 | 99 |
| Preparatory | | |
| Male | 52 | 80 |
| Female | 23 | 78 |
| Both sexes | 38 | 79 |
| Secondary | | |
| Male | n.a. | n.a. |
| Female | n.a. | n.a. |
| Both sexes | 2 | 37 |

n.a.—not available.

Source: Based on information from World Bank, *World Development Report, 1988,* New York,
1988, 281.

Table 4. *Medical Care and Medical Personnel, 1987*

| Category | 1987 |
|---|---|
| **Hospitals** | |
| Government | 14 |
| Private | 21 |
| Total hospitals | 35 * |
| **Hospital beds** | |
| Government | 3,994 |
| Private | 1,563 |
| Total hospital beds | 5,557 |
| **Physicians** | |
| Government | 1,702 |
| Private | n.a. |
| **Nurses** | |
| Government | 434 |
| Private | n.a. |
| **Midwives** | |
| Government | 275 |
| Private | n.a. |
| **Pharmacists** | |
| Government | 96 |
| Private | n.a. |
| **Dentists** | |
| Government | 110 |
| Private | n.a. |

* Figures for 1981.
n.a.—not available.

Source: Based on information from Jordan, Department of Statistics, *Statistical Yearbook, 1987,* 38, Amman, 1988, 213–14; and "Jordan" in George Thomas Kurian (ed.), *Encyclopedia of the Third World,* 2, New York, 1987, 1029.

Table 5. *Balance of Payments, 1983–87*
(in millions of Jordanian dinars) [1]

| | 1983 | 1984 | 1985 | 1986 [2] | 1987 [2] |
|---|---|---|---|---|---|
| Net trade balance in goods and services ..... | – 436.25 | – 382.89 | – 414.91 | – 253.95 | – 317.64 |
| Net unrequited transfers [3] ......... | + 294.93 | + 278.76 | + 315.01 | + 238.00 | + 199.29 |
| Current account balance .......... | – 141.32 | – 104.13 | – 99.90 | – 15.95 | – 118.35 |
| Capital account balance [4] ......... | + 156.76 | + 64.37 | + 137.64 | + 50.95 | + 75.94 |
| Overall balance [5] ...... | + 15.44 | – 39.76 | + 37.74 | + 35.00 | – 42.41 |
| Net errors and omissions .......... | + 34.90 | – 29.54 | – 19.25 | – 16.72 | + 5.86 |
| Net reserves [6] ........ | – 50.34 | + 69.30 | – 18.49 | – 18.28 | + 36.55 |

[1] For value of the Jordanian dinar—see Glossary.
[2] Preliminary figures.
[3] Includes net private and net government unrequited transfers (i.e., worker remittances and foreign aid, respectively). The combination of net trade in goods and services and net unrequited transfers gives the current account balance.
[4] Consists of net government borrowing as well as long- and short-term net private investment.
[5] Consists of the current and capital account balances combined.
[6] Includes reserves held by the Central Bank, commercial banks, and other financial institutions, as well as International Monetary Fund reserves.

Source: Based on information from Jordan, Department of Statistics, *Statistical Yearbook, 1987,* 38, Amman, 1988, 362–63.

*Table 6. Summary of Central Government Budget Financing, 1983-87*
(in millions of Jordanian dinars) [1]

|  | 1983 | 1984 | 1985 | 1986 | 1987 |
|---|---|---|---|---|---|
| **Revenue** | | | | | |
| Domestic revenue ........ | 400.6 | 415.0 | 440.8 | 514.4 | 549.7 |
| Foreign assistance ........ | 197.0 | 106.1 | 187.8 | 143.7 | 134.0 |
| Internal borrowing ........ | 28.8 | 25.5 | 35.3 | 74.8 | 149.3 |
| Foreign borrowing ........ | 76.8 | 122.2 | 162.4 | 159.8 | 89.9 |
| Other revenue [2] .......... | 2.3 | 9.6 | 18.4 | 12.8 | 14.6 |
| Total revenues ......... | 705.5 | 678.4 | 844.8 [3] | 905.4 [3] | 937.5 |
| **Expenditure** | | | | | |
| Current budget .......... | 453.7 | 488.1 | 542.5 | 570.5 | 604.5 |
| Capital budget .......... | 251.6 | 232.7 | 263.2 | 410.8 | 404.2 |
| Total expenditures ...... | 705.3 | 720.8 | 805.7 | 981.3 | 1,008.7 |
| Deficit or surplus .......... | + .2 | − 42.4 | + 39.1 | − 75.9 | − 71.3 [3] |

[1] For value of the Jordanian dinar—see Glossary.
[2] Principal of loans repaid to the central government.
[3] Figures may not add to totals because of rounding.

Source: Based on information from Jordan, Department of Statistics, *Statistical Yearbook,
  1987,* 38, Amman, 1988, 312.

*Table 7. Central Government Expenditures, 1983–87*
(in millions of Jordanian dinars) [1]

|  | 1983 | 1984 | 1985 | 1986 | 1987 [2] |
|---|---|---|---|---|---|
| **Current budget** | | | | | |
| Defense | 168.0 | 168.0 | 190.2 | 209.0 | 209.0 |
| Internal security | 32.6 | 33.5 | 39.3 | 47.0 | 50.4 |
| Financial administration | 128.4 | 154.6 | 171.3 | 158.2 | 174.5 |
| Economic development | 15.3 | 14.3 | 15.2 | 16.7 | 18.1 |
| Social services | 80.0 | 82.7 | 89.7 | 98.6 | 110.2 |
| Transportation and communications | 11.7 | 16.3 | 17.1 | 18.6 | 19.1 |
| Other | 17.7 | 18.7 | 19.8 | 22.5 | 23.4 |
| Total current expenditures | 453.7 | 488.1 | 542.6 | 570.6 | 604.7 |
| **Capital budget** | | | | | |
| Finance | 88.8 | 86.2 | 99.0 | 225.7 | 189.0 |
| Economic development | 130.6 | 122.5 | 144.4 | 162.9 | 178.4 |
| Transportation and communications | 20.2 | 12.7 | 7.1 | 8.1 | 12.0 |
| Social services | 6.9 | 5.1 | 5.5 | 6.5 | 10.1 |
| Defense | 0 | 0 | 0 | 0 | 0 |
| Other | 5.1 | 6.2 | 7.2 | 7.6 | 14.7 |
| Total capital expenditures | 251.6 | 232.7 | 263.2 | 410.8 | 404.2 |
| TOTAL | 705.3 | 720.8 | 805.8 | 981.4 | 1,008.9 |

[1] For value of the Jordanian dinar—see Glossary.
[2] Preliminary estimate.

Source: Based on information from Jordan, Department of Statistics, *Statistical Yearbook, 1987*, 38, Amman, 1988, 315–16.

*Table 8. Domestic Revenue of the Central Government, 1983-87*
(in millions of Jordanian dinars) [1]

| Revenue Source | 1983 | 1984 | 1985 | 1986 | 1987 [2] |
|---|---|---|---|---|---|
| Tax revenues | | | | | |
| Customs duties | 121 | 118 | 118 | 112 | 105 |
| Excise taxes | 35 | 37 | 46 | 52 | 61 |
| Licenses and fees | 68 | 73 | 71 | 71 | 85 |
| Other indirect taxes | 13 | 17 | 15 | 14 | 15 |
| Total indirect taxes | 237 | 245 | 250 | 249 | 266 |
| Income taxes | 46 | 49 | 54 | 48 | 48 |
| Other direct taxes | 10 | 12 | 13 | 12 | 17 |
| Total direct taxes | 56 | 61 | 67 | 60 | 65 |
| Total tax revenues [3] | 294 | 305 | 317 | 309 | 331 |
| Nontax revenues | | | | | |
| Post, telegraph, and telephone | 23 | 33 | 38 | 46 | 48 |
| Interest and profits | 59 | 36 | 44 | 40 | 49 |
| Other | 24 | 40 | 41 | 120 | 123 |
| Total nontax revenues [3] | 107 | 110 | 124 | 205 | 219 |
| Total domestic revenues | 401 | 415 | 441 | 514 | 550 |

[1] For value of the Jordanian dinar—see Glossary.
[2] Preliminary figures.
[3] Figures may not add to totals because of rounding.

Source: Based on information from Jordan, Department of Statistics, *Statistical Yearbook, 1987*, 38, Amman, 1988, 313.

*Table 9. Labor Force by Sector, 1987*
*(in thousands of workers)*

| Sector | Number |
|---|---|
| Agriculture | 37.7 |
| Construction | 53.4 |
| Financial and business services | 16.9 |
| Mining and manufacturing | 53.6 |
| Social services and military personnel | 242.5 |
| Trade | 49.7 |
| Transportation and communications | 47.1 |
| Utilities | 8.5 |
| Total active labor force | 509.3 * |

* Figures may not add to total because of rounding. Total excludes foreign guest workers.

Source: Based on information from Jordan, Department of Statistics, *Statistical Yearbook, 1987*, 38, Amman, 1988, 69.

*Table 10. Industrial Production of Selected Commodities, 1984–87*

| Commodity | Unit | 1984 | 1985 | 1986 | 1987 |
|---|---|---|---|---|---|
| Phosphates (dry) ............. | 1,000 tons | 6,120 | 6,067 | 6,249 | 6,841 |
| Potash ................... | 1,000 tons | 486 | 908 | 1,104 | 1,203 |
| Fertilizers ................. | 1,000 tons | 541 | 511 | 551 | 1,656 |
| Cement ................... | 1,000 tons | 1,994 | 2,022 | 1,837 | 2,472 |
| Petroleum products .......... | 1,000 tons | 2,272 | 2,182 | 2,083 | 2,229 |
| Iron ..................... | 1,000 tons | 112 | 136 | 126 | 219 |
| Alcoholic beverages ......... | 1,000 liters | 7,573 | 5,638 | 5,321 | 4,851 |
| Batteries ................. | 1,000 batteries | 50 | 50 | 55 | 55 |
| Cigarettes ................. | tons | 5,027 | 3,905 | 3,731 | 4,378 |
| Detergents ............... | 1,000 tons | 12 | 8 | 28 | 27 |
| Paper ................... | 1,000 tons | - - - | - - - | 15 | 21 |

- - - means negligible.

Source: Based on information from Jordan, Department of Statistics, *Statistical Yearbook,*
*1987,* 38, Amman, 1988, 123–24.

*Table 11. Agricultural Production and Cultivated Area, 1987*
(in thousands of tons and by thousands of hectares)

| Crop | Harvest | Area |
|---|---|---|
| **Field Crops** | | |
| Wheat ........................................ | 79.8 | 84.3 |
| Barley ........................................ | 33.0 | 51.1 |
| Lentils ........................................ | 5.2 | 5.1 |
| Vetch ......................................... | 1.3 | 1.5 |
| Chick peas .................................... | 1.2 | 1.6 |
| Corn ......................................... | 3.0 | 0.5 |
| Onions ........................................ | 21.6 | 0.8 |
| Garlic ......................................... | 2.0 | 0.4 |
| Tobacco ....................................... | 29.1 | 3.0 |
| Clover ........................................ | 9.1 | 0.6 |
| | | |
| **Vegetables** | | |
| Tomatoes ..................................... | 236.8 | 6.0 |
| Squash ........................................ | 34.3 | 2.2 |
| Eggplants ...................................... | 56.6 | 2.5 |
| Cucumbers .................................... | 64.9 | 1.3 |
| Potatoes ...................................... | 61.7 | 2.4 |
| | | |
| **Fruits** | | |
| Olives ......................................... | 20.4 | 38.1 |
| Grapes ........................................ | 18.6 | 5.4 |
| Citrus fruit .................................... | 118.4 | 5.6 |
| Melons ........................................ | 41.1 | 5.1 |
| Figs .......................................... | 1.3 | 0.6 |
| Almonds ...................................... | 1.1 | 0.5 |
| Peaches ....................................... | 1.4 | 0.7 |

Source: Based on information from Jordan, Department of Statistics, *Statistical Yearbook,*
*1987,* 38, Amman, 1988, 80, 84, 93.

### Table 12. *Imports of Selected Commodities, 1983–87* (in millions of Jordanian dinars) *

| Commodity | 1983 | 1984 | 1985 | 1986 | 1987 |
|---|---|---|---|---|---|
| Live animals .................. | 21.6 | 5.9 | 8.6 | 2.9 | 3.6 |
| Meat ....................... | 24.6 | 23.0 | 33.2 | 24.3 | 27.0 |
| Dairy products ............... | 15.5 | 16.8 | 17.9 | 17.0 | 15.8 |
| Wheat and flour .............. | 32.8 | 39.1 | 28.2 | 15.8 | 28.7 |
| Sugar ...................... | 6.5 | 5.2 | 3.6 | 8.7 | 9.3 |
| Fruits and vegetables .......... | 32.3 | 27.8 | 25.4 | 25.4 | 16.5 |
| Crude oil ................... | 205.5 | 204.0 | 192.6 | 92.8 | 118.6 |
| Other crude materials .......... | 31.4 | 29.9 | 33.1 | 28.6 | 28.5 |
| Chemicals ................... | 57.8 | 79.9 | 67.6 | 74.9 | 91.7 |
| Iron and steel ................ | 40.7 | 37.1 | 41.8 | 41.9 | 51.1 |
| Textile products .............. | 32.0 | 30.1 | 29.2 | 26.1 | 29.5 |
| Machinery ................... | 167.0 | 122.8 | 112.8 | 103.2 | 103.0 |
| Transportation equipment ....... | 95.0 | 93.0 | 94.6 | 73.4 | 83.3 |
| Miscellaneous manufacturing ...... | 92.3 | 95.9 | 105.2 | 79.9 | 87.7 |
| Other ...................... | 218.3 | 260.8 | 280.6 | 235.3 | 221.2 |
| TOTAL .................... | 1,103.3 | 1,071.3 | 1,074.4 | 850.2 | 915.5 |

* For value of the Jordanian dinar—see Glossary.

Source: Based on information from Jordan, Department of Statistics, *Statistical Yearbook, 1987*, 38, Amman, 1988, 349–50.

### Table 13. *Exports of Selected Commodities, 1983–87* (in millions of Jordanian dinars) *

| Commodity | 1983 | 1984 | 1985 | 1986 | 1987 |
|---|---|---|---|---|---|
| Fruits and nuts ............... | 7.6 | 8.4 | 7.5 | 8.5 | 5.2 |
| Vegetables .................. | 17.6 | 18.6 | 16.6 | 13.3 | 14.8 |
| Olive oil .................... | 1.0 | 0.9 | 0.1 | 1.4 | 0.2 |
| Phosphates .................. | 51.6 | 69.6 | 66.1 | 64.8 | 61.0 |
| Potash ..................... | 0.1 | 14.9 | 30.9 | 31.4 | 28.0 |
| Fertilizers ................... | 20.7 | 44.0 | 30.6 | 29.1 | 30.1 |
| Other chemical products ......... | 16.1 | 23.6 | 20.4 | 15.4 | 39.8 |
| Cement ..................... | - - - | 2.9 | 7.1 | 4.0 | 10.5 |
| Machinery and transportation equipment .................. | 2.0 | 2.0 | 2.0 | 1.4 | 2.5 |
| Textile products .............. | 2.1 | 5.1 | 10.0 | 3.31 | 1.2 |
| Miscellaneous manufactures ....... | 9.2 | 23.4 | 18.5 | 7.3 | 9.9 |
| Other ...................... | 32.1 | 47.7 | 45.5 | 45.7 | 35.6 |
| TOTAL .................... | 160.1 | 261.1 | 255.3 | 225.6 | 248.8 |

- - - means negligible.
* For value of the Jordanian dinar—see Glossary.

Source: Based on information from Jordan, Department of Statistics, *Statistical Yearbook, 1987*, 38, Amman, 1988, 347–48.

### Tables 14. Principal Trade Partners, 1986 and 1987
(in thousands of Jordanian dinars) *

| Country | 1986 | 1987 |
|---|---|---|
| Exports | | |
| China | 7,570 | 10,044 |
| Egypt | 3,9791 | 3,448 |
| India | 34,126 | 22,034 |
| Iraq | 42,458 | 59,865 |
| Italy | 7,099 | 9,266 |
| Kuwait | 8,813 | 8,614 |
| Pakistan | 3,456 | 10,253 |
| Saudi Arabia | 27,817 | 26,204 |
| | | |
| Imports | | |
| Britain | 68,786 | 58,303 |
| Iraq | 80,274 | 99,401 |
| Italy | 50,220 | 46,647 |
| Japan | 66,642 | 55,664 |
| Saudi Arabia | 49,670 | 76,761 |
| Turkey | 27,467 | 35,021 |
| United States | 75,529 | 93,389 |
| West Germany | 65,114 | 70,504 |

* For value of the Jordanian dinar—see Glossary.

Source: Based on information from Economist Intelligence Unit, *Country Report: Jordan,* No.
3, 1988, Appendix 2.

## Table 15. *Major Army Equipment, 1988*

| Type and Description | Country of Origin | In Inventory |
|---|---|---|
| **Tanks** | | |
| M–60A1/A3 ..................... | United States | 218 |
| Khalid (Chieftain) ................ | Britain | 270 |
| Tariq (Centurion) ................. | –do– | 291 |
| M–47, M–48A5 .................. | United States | 200 (in storage) |
| **Armored personnel carriers** | | |
| M–113 ......................... | United States | 1,200 |
| Saracen ........................ | Britain | 34 |
| EE–11 Urutu .................... | Brazil | n.a. |
| **Reconnaissance vehicles** | | |
| Ferret scout car ................. | Britain | 140 |
| **Towed artillery** | | |
| 105mm M–101A1 ................ | United States | 36 |
| 155mm M–114 ................... | –do– | 38 |
| M–44 .......................... | –do– | 20 |
| M–59 .......................... | –do– | 17 |
| 203mm M–115 .................. | –do– | 4 (in storage) |
| **Self-propelled artillery** | | |
| 155mm M–109A2 ................ | –do– | 108 |
| 203mm M110 ................... | –do– | 24 |
| **Mortars** | | |
| 107mm and 120mm .............. | –do– | n.a. |
| **Antitank weapons** | | |
| 106mm recoilless rifle ............ | –do– | 330 |
| Apilas 112mm rocket launcher ....... | France | n.a. |
| BGM–71A TOW missile ........... | United States | 330 |
| M–47 Dragon missile ............. | –do– | 310 |
| LAW–80 ....................... | Britain | n.a. |
| **Antiaircraft guns** | | |
| 20mm M–163 Vulcan ............. | United States | 100 |
| 23mm self-propelled ZSU–23–4 ...... | Soviet Union | 36 |
| 40mm self-propelled M–42 ......... | United States | 264 |
| **Surface-to-air missiles** | | |
| SA–7 B2 shoulder-fired ............ | Soviet Union | n.a. |
| SA–8 .......................... | –do– | 20 |
| SA–13 ......................... | –do– | 20 |
| SA–14 shoulder-fired ............. | –do– | n.a. |
| Redeye ........................ | United States | n.a. |
| **Naval vessels** | | |
| Coastal patrol craft, 8 ton .......... | –do– | 5 |
| Vosper coastal patrol craft, 95 ton ..... | Britain | 3 (ordered) |

n.a.—not available.

Source: Based on information from *The Military Balance, 1988–89,* London, 1988, 104; and
*Jane's Fighting Ships, 1988–89,* London, 1988, 332.

*Table 16. Major Air Force Equipment, 1988*

| Type and Description | Country of Origin | In Inventory |
|---|---|---|
| **Fighter-bombers** | | |
| F-5E/F ......................... | United States | 59 |
| **Fighter-Interceptors** | | |
| Mirage F-1 ...................... | France | 35 |
| Mirage 2000 ..................... | -do- | 20 (ordered 1988) |
| **Jet fighter conversion training** | | |
| F-5A/B ......................... | United States | 20 |
| **Transports** | | |
| C-130 Hercules .................. | United States | 6 |
| CASA C-212A .................... | Spain | 3 |
| An-12 Cub ..................... | Soviet Union | 3 |
| **Helicopters** | | |
| Bell AH-1S Cobra, with TOW missiles . | United States | 24 |
| Sikorsky S-76 .................... | -do- | 18 |
| Aérospatiale Alouette III ........... | France | 5 |
| Aérospatiale SA-342L Gazelle ........ | -do- | 8 |
| Hughes 500D ................... | United States | 8 |
| **Training** | | |
| CASA C-101 Aviojet .............. | Spain | 16 |
| CASA C-212 Aviocar ............. | Spain | 1 |
| BAe Bulldog .................... | Britain | 18 |
| Piper (12 Warrior-II and 6 Seneca-II) .. | United States | 18 |
| **Strategic air defense** | | |
| Improved Hawk surface-to-air missile .. | United States | 126 |

Source: Based on information from *The Military Balance, 1988–89,* London, 1988, 105; and
Aviation Advisory Services, *International Air Forces and Military Aircraft Directory,* Essex, United Kingdom, 1988.

# Bibliography

## Chapter 1

Abidi, Aqil. *Jordan: A Political Study, 1948–57.* London: Asia Publishing House, 1965.

Abu Jaber, Kamel S. "The Economy of Jordan: A Current Assessment," *American-Arab Affairs,* 9, Summer 1984, 106–16.

Abu-Lughod, Ibrahim (ed.). *The Transformation of Palestine.* Evanston, Illinois: Northwestern University Press, 1971.

Antonius, George. *The Arab Awakening: The Story of the Arab National Movement.* New York: Capricorn Books, 1965.

Aruri, Naseer H. *Jordan: A Study in Political Development, 1921–1965.* The Hague: Martinus Nijhoff, 1972.

Avishai, Bernard. "Jordan: Looking for an Opening," *New York Review of Books,* 31, September 7, 1984, 46–49.

_____. "Looking over Jordan," *New York Review of Books,* 30, April 8, 1983, 37–42.

_____. *The Tragedy of Zionism: Revolution and Democracy in the Land of Israel.* New York: Farrer Straus Giroux, 1985.

Bailey, Clinton. "Changing Attitudes Toward Jordan in the West Bank," *Middle East Journal,* 32, No. 2, Spring 1978, 155.

_____. *Jordan's Palestinian Challenge, 1948–1983.* Boulder, Colorado: Westview Press, 1984.

Benvenisti, Meron. *The West Bank Data Project.* Washington: American Enterprise Institute, 1984.

Cooley, John K. *Green March, Black September: The Story of the Palestinian Arabs.* London: Frank Cass, 1978.

Dann, Uriel. *Studies in the History of Transjordan, 1920–1949.* Boulder, Colorado: Westview Press, 1984.

Garfinkle, Adam M. "Jordanian Foreign Policy," *Current History,* 83, January 1984, 21–24, 38–39.

Glubb, John Bagot (Glubb Pasha). *Britain and the Arabs.* London: Hodder and Stoughton, 1958.

_____. *A Soldier with the Arabs.* London: Hodder and Stoughton, 1957.

_____. *The Story of the Arab Legion.* London: Hodder and Stoughton, 1948.

Gubser, Peter. *Jordan: Crossroads of Middle Eastern Events.* (Profiles: Nations of the Contemporary Middle East Series.) Boulder, Colorado: Westview Press, 1983.

Halpern, Manfred. *The Politics of Social Change in the Middle East and North Africa.* Princeton: Princeton University Press, 1965.

Hitti, Philip K. *History of Syria.* New York: Macmillan, 1951.
———. *History of the Arabs from the Earliest Time to the Present.* New York: St. Martin's Press, 1956.
Holt, P.M., Ann K.S. Lambton, and Bernard Lewis (eds.). *The Cambridge History of Islam.* Cambridge: Cambridge University Press, 1970.
Hurewitz, J.C. *The Struggle for Palestine.* New York: Schocken Books, 1976.
Johnston, Charles H. *The Brink of Jordan.* London: Hamilton, 1972.
Kedourie, Eli (ed.). *Palestine and Israel.* London: Frank Cass, 1978.
Khuri, Fred J. *The Arab-Israeli Dilemma.* Syracuse, New York: Syracuse University Press, 1976.
Lais, Godrey, *Glubb's Legion.* London: Evans Brothers, 1956.
*Middle East Contemporary Survey, 1976-77,* 1. (Eds. Colin Legum and Haim Shaked.) New York: Holmes and Meir, 1978.
*Middle East Contemporary Survey, 1977-78,* 2. (Eds. Colin Legum and Haim Shaked.) New York: Holmes and Meir, 1979.
*Middle East Contemporary Survey, 1978-79,* 3. (Eds. Colin Legum and Haim Shaked.) New York: Holmes and Meir, 1980.
*Middle East Contemporary Survey, 1979-80,* 4. (Eds. Colin Legum, Haim Shaked, and Daniel Dishon.) New York: Holmes and Meir, 1981.
*Middle East Contemporary Survey, 1980-81,* 5. (Eds. Colin Legum, Haim Shaked, and Daniel Dishon.) New York: Holmes and Meir, 1982.
*Middle East Contemporary Survey, 1981-82,* 6. (Eds. Colin Legum, Haim Shaked, and Daniel Dishon.) New York: Holmes and Meir, 1984.
Miller, Aaron D. "Jordan and the Arab-Israeli Conflict: The Hashemite Predicament," *Orbis,* 29, Winter 1986, 795-820.
———. "Jordan and the Palestinian Issue: The Legacy of the Past," *Middle East Insight,* 4, Nos. 4-5, 1986, 21-29.
Miller, Judith. "King Hussein's Delicate Balance," *New York Times Magazine,* April 1984, 24, 26, 28, 30, 53, 74.
Mishal, Shaul. *West Bank/East Bank: The Palestinians in Jordan, 1949-1967.* New Haven: Yale University Press, 1978.
Mousa, Suleiman. "A Matter of Principle: King Hussein of the Hijaz and the Arabs of Palestine," *International Journal of Middle East Studies,* 9, No. 2, May 1978, 183-94.
Patai, Raphael. *The Kingdom of Jordan.* Princeton: Princeton University Press, 1958.
Peake, Frederick. *A History of Jordan and Its Tribes.* Coral Gables, Florida: University of Miami Press, 1958.
Plascov, Avi. *The Palestinian Refugees in Jordan, 1948-57.* London: Frank Cass, 1981.

Quandt, William B. *Decade of Decisions: American Policy Toward the Arab-Israeli Conflict, 1967-1976.* Berkeley: University of California Press, 1977.

Reed, Stanley. "The Rift with Arafat: Can Hussein Take Over the PLO?" *Nation,* 243, August 30, 1986, 137-38, 140.

Rustow, Dankwart A. *Hussein: A Biography.* London: Barrie and Jenkins, 1972.

Satloff, Robert B. *Troubles on the East Bank: Challenges to the Domestic Stability of Jordan.* (Center for Strategic and International Studies, Georgetown University.) New York: Praeger, 1986.

Segev, Tom. *1949: The First Israelis.* New York: Free Press, 1986.

Shlaim, Avi. *Collusion Across the Jordan.* New York: Columbia University Press, 1988.

Shwadran, Benjamin. *Jordan: A State of Tension.* New York: Council for Middle Eastern Affairs, 1959.

Simon, Reeva S. "The Hashemite Conspiracy: Hashemite Unity Attempts, 1921-1958," *International Journal of Middle East Studies,* 5, No. 3, June 1974, 314-27.

Sinai, Anne, and Allen Pollack (eds.). *The Hashemite Kingdom of Jordan and the West Bank: A Handbook.* New York: American Academic Association for Peace in the Middle East, 1977.

Snow, Peter J. *Hussein: A Biography.* London: Barrie and Jenkins, 1972.

Sykes, Christopher. *Crossroads to Israel, 1917-1948.* Bloomington: Indiana University Press, 1973.

Tehboub, Naser. "Jordan's Role in Middle East Peace: An Analytical Note," *Journal of South Asian and Middle Eastern Studies,* 7, Spring 1984, 58-62.

Vatikiotis, Panayiotios J. *Politics and the Military in Jordan: A Study of the Arab Legion, 1921-57.* New York: Praeger, 1967.

Wilson, Mary C. "Jordan's Malaise," *Current History,* 86, February 1987, 73-76, 84-85.

––––––. *King Abdullah, Britain, and the Making of Jordan.* Cambridge: Cambridge University Press, 1987.

Wolf, John B. "Black September: Militant Palestinianism," *Current History,* 64, No. 377, January 1973, 5-8, 37.

Wren, Christopher S. "Man on the Spot: Sadat's Peace Becomes Hussein's Trial," *New York Times Magazine,* April 8, 1979, 17-19.

Young, Peter. *Bedouin Command with the Arab Legion, 1921-57.* London: Frank Cass, 1967.

Zeine, Zeine N. *The Emergence of Arab Nationalism.* Delmar, New York: Caravan Books, 1973.

––––––. *The Struggle for Arab Independence.* Delmar, New York: Caravan Books, 1977.

## Chapter 2

Abu-Lughod, Lila. *Veiled Sentiments: Honor and Poetry in a Bedouin Society.* Berkeley: University of California Press, 1986.

Antoun, Richard T. *Arab Village: A Social Structural Study of a Transjordanian Peasant Community.* Bloomington: Indiana University Press, 1972.

_____. *Low Key Politics: Local Level Leadership and Change in the Middle East.* Albany: State University of New York Press, 1979.

"The Average Palestine Refugee," *Palestine Refugees Today. UNRWA Newsletter* [Vienna], No. 117, January 1987, 7-8.

Barhoum, Mohammad Issa. "Attitudes of University Students Towards Women's Work: The Case of Jordan," *International Journal of Middle East Studies,* 15, August 1983, 369-76.

Birks, J.S., and C.A. Sinclair. *Arab Manpower: The Crisis of Development.* New York: St. Martin's Press, 1980.

Brand, Laurie. *Palestinians in the Arab World: Institution Building and the Search for State.* New York: Columbia University Press, 1988.

Farid, Samir. "A Review of the Fertility Situation in the Arab Countries of Western Asia and Northern Africa." Pages 340-54 in *Fertility Behavior in the Context of Development: Evidence from the World Fertility Survey.* New York: United Nations, 1987.

Fisher, W.B. "Jordan: Physical and Social Geography." Pages 491-519 in *The Middle East and North Africa, 1988.* (34th ed.) London: Europa, 1987.

Gubser, Peter. *Jordan: Crossroads of Middle Eastern Events.* (Profiles: Nations of the Contemporary Middle East Series.) Boulder, Colorado: Westview Press, 1983.

_____. *Politics and Change in Al-Karak, Jordan: A Study of a Small Arab Town and Its District.* Boulder, Colorado: Westview Press, 1985.

Haddad, Yvonne Y. "Islam: 'The Religion of God'," *Christianity and Crisis,* November 15, 1982, 354-58.

Hiatt, Joseph Merrill. *Between Desert and Town: A Case Study of Encapsulation and Sedentarization Among Jordanian Bedouin.* (Ph.D. dissertation, University of Pennsylvania, 1981.) Ann Arbor, Michigan: University Microfilms International, 1981.

Hijab, Nadia. *Womanpower: The Arab Debate on Women at Work.* (Cambridge Middle East Library Series.) Cambridge: Cambridge University Press, 1988.

Ibrahim, Saad Eddin. *The New Arab Social Order: A Study of the Social Impact of Oil Wealth.* Boulder, Colorado: Westview Press, 1982.

Johnson, Stanley. *World Population and the United Nations: Challenge and Response.* Cambridge: Cambridge University Press, 1987.

"Jordan." Pages 1,018-31 in George Thomas Kurian (ed.), *Encyclopedia of the Third World*, 2. New York: Facts on File, 1987.

"Jordan." Pages 98-103 in World Health Organization (ed.), *Evaluation of the Strategy of Health for All by the Year 2000*. Alexandria, Egypt: World Health Organization Regional Office for the Eastern Mediterranean, 1987.

Jordan. Department of Statistics. *Statistical Yearbook, 1987*, 38. Amman: 1988.

_____. Ministry of Planning. *Jordan: Five-Year Plan for Economic and Social Development, 1986-90*. Amman: 1986.

Jureidini, Paul, and R.D. McLaurin. *Jordan: The Impact of Social Changes on the Role of the Tribes*. (The Washington Papers, No. 108, Center for Strategic and International Studies, Georgetown University.) New York: Praeger, 1984.

Keely, Charles, and Bassem Saket. "Jordanian Migrant Workers in the Arab Region: A Case Study of the Consequences for Labor-Supplying Countries," *Middle East Journal*, 38, No. 4, Autumn 1984, 685-711.

Khouri, Rami G. *The Jordan Valley: Life and Society below Sea Level*. Harlow, Essex, United Kingdom: Longman Group and Jordan Valley Association, 1981.

"King Receives United States Team of University Professors," *Jordan Times* [Amman], June 15, 1987, 3.

Layne, Linda. "Tribesmen as Citizens: 'Primordial Ties' and Democracy in Rural Jordan." Pages 113-51 in Linda Layne (ed.), *Elections in the Middle East*. Boulder, Colorado: Westview Press, 1986.

_____. "Women in Jordan's Workplace," *MERIP Reports*, No. 95, March-April 1981, 19-23.

Lewis, Norman N. *Nomads and Settlers in Syria and Jordan, 1800-1980*. (Cambridge Middle East Library Series.) Cambridge: Cambridge University Press, 1987.

Masri, Salwa. "Sex Discrimination Against Girls in Nutrition and Health Care." Pages 26-27 in *Girls' Adolescence: The Lost Opportunity. The Vital Need for Equality, Development, and Peace*. Amman: United Nations Children's Fund (UNICEF), Information and Community Section, UNICEF Regional Office for the Middle East and North Africa, 1985.

Mdanat, Frida. "Steps to Ease Unemployment," *Jerusalem Star* [Amman], February 1987, 5.

Najjar, Najwa. "Experts Seek to Prevent Defects Caused by Inbreeding," *Jordan Times* [Amman], February 20, 1988, 2.

Sadik, Nafis (ed.). *Population: The UNFPA Experience*. New York: New York University for the United Nations Fund for Population Activities, 1984.

Sahliyeh, Emile. "Jordan and the Palestinians." Pages 279–318 in William Quandt (ed.), *The Middle East: Ten Years after Camp David.* Washington: Brookings Institution, 1988.

Satloff, Robert B. *Troubles on the East Bank: Challenges to the Domestic Stability of Jordan.* (Center for Strategic and International Studies, Georgetown University.) New York: Praeger, 1986.

Seccombe, Ian J. "Labour Migration and the Transformation of a Village Economy: A Case Study from North-West Jordan." Pages 115–44 in Richard Lawless (ed.), *The Middle Eastern Village.* London: Croom Helm, 1987.

Shami, Seteney, and Lucine Taminian. *Reproductive Behavior and Child Care in a Squatter Area of Amman.* (Regional Papers Series.) Dokki, Giza, Egypt: The Population Council, 1985.

Sullivan, Katherine J. "Community Colleges: Serving Jordan's Socioeconomic Needs," *Jordan Times* [Amman], March 2, 1988, 2.

United Nations. Department of International Economics and Social Affairs. *World Population Prospects. Estimates and Projections as Assessed in 1984.* New York: 1986.

United Nations Children's Fund. Regional Office for the Middle East and North Africa. Information and Community Section. *Girls' Adolescence: The Lost Opportunity. The Vital Need for Equality, Development, and Peace.* Amman: 1985.

United Nations Relief and Works Agency for Palestine Refugees in the Near East. *UNRWA Report* [Vienna], 5, No. 3, July 1987.

Wahlin, Lars. "Diffusion and Acceptance of Modern Schooling in Rural Jordan." Pages 145–74 in Richard Lawless (ed.), *The Middle Eastern Village.* London: Croom Helm, 1987.

World Health Organization. "Update: AIDS Cases Reported to Surveillance, Forecasting and Impact Assessment Unit." (Computer print-out, Global Program on AIDS.) Geneva: January 3, 1989, 7.

World Bank. *World Development Report, 1988,* 11. New York: Oxford University Press for the World Bank, 1988.

Yorke, Valerie. *Domestic Politics and Regional Security: Jordan, Syria, and Israel. The End of an Era?* Brookfield, Vermont: Gower Publishing for the International Institute for Strategic Studies, 1988.

## Chapter 3

Abuirmeileh, Naji. "Agricultural Development and Food Security in Jordan." Pages 93–117 in Bichara Khader and Adnan Badran (eds.), *The Economic Development of Jordan.* London: Croom Helm, 1987.

Abu Jaber, Kamel S. "The Economy of Jordan: A Current Assessment," *American-Arab Affairs*, No. 9, Summer 1984, 106-16.

Badran, Adnan, Kapur S. Ahlawat, Elias Baydoun, and Siva Ram Vemuri. "Some Reflections on the Future Issues Concerning Economic Development in Jordan." Pages 221-45 in Bichara Khader and Adnan Badran (eds.), *The Economic Development of Jordan*. London: Croom Helm, 1987.

Burghard, Claus, and Michael Hofmann. "The Development Prospects for the Hashemite Kingdom of Jordan." Pages 32-49 in Claus Burghard and Michael Hofmann (eds.), *The Importance of the Oil Producing Countries of the Gulf Cooperation Council to the Development of the Yemen Arab Republic and the Hashemite Kingdom of Jordan*. Berlin: German Development Institute, September 1984.

Chatelus, Michel. "Rentier or Producer Economy in the Middle East? The Jordanian Response." Pages 204-20 in Bichara Khader and Adnan Badran (eds.), *The Economic Development of Jordan*. London: Croom Helm, 1987.

"Comparisons of Defense Expenditure and Military Manpower." Pages 224-27 in François Heisborg (ed.), *The Middle East Military Balance, 1988-1989*. London: International Institute of Strategic Studies, 1988.

Cooley, John K. "The War Over Water," *Foreign Policy*, No. 54, Spring 1984, 3-26.

Counsell, Anne. "Jordan's New Budget," *Middle East Executive Reports (MEER)*, March 1987, 10-11.

_____. "Jordan Encourages Arab Investors," *Middle East Executive Reports (MEER)*, April 1986, 15.

Dajani, Mazen. "Taxation and Investment in Jordan," *International Journal of Fiscal Documentation Bulletin*, 37, No. 1, January 1983, 31-34.

Dougherty, Pamela. "Jordan Goes Down the Path of Austerity," *Middle East Economic Digest* [London], 32, November 18, 1988, 4-5.

_____. "Jordan-Iraq Link Proves Profitable," *Middle East Economic Digest* [London], 32, October 21, 1988, 14, 17.

_____. "Jordan's Quest for Economic Independence," *Middle East Economic Digest* [London], 32, August 19, 1988, 3-8.

Economist Intelligence Unit. *Country Report: Jordan*. (No. 3, 1988.) London: 1988.

Hammad, Khalil. "An Aggregate Production Function for the Jordanian Economy." Pages 1-11 in Bichara Khader and Adnan Badran (eds.), *The Economic Development of Jordan*. London: Croom Helm, 1987.

_____. "The Role of Foreign Aid in the Jordanian Economy." Pages 11–31 in Bichara Khader and Adnan Badran (eds.), *The Economic Development of Jordan*. London: Croom Helm, 1987.

Hendry, Peter. "The Desert's Challenge and the Human Response: Dimensions and Perceptions," *Ceres*, 19, No. 2, March-April 1986, 17–30.

International Monetary Fund. *World Debt Tables, 1987–88. I: Analysis and Summary Tables, External Debt of Developing Countries.* Washington: 1988.

"Jordan: Economy." Pages 540–48 in *The Middle East and North Africa, 1989*. London: Europa, 1988.

Jordan. Department of Statistics. *Industrial Census of Jordan, 1984.* Amman: December 1986.

_____. Department of Statistics. *Statistical Yearbook, 1987*, 38. Amman: 1988.

_____. Ministry of Planning. *Jordan: Five-Year Plan for Economic and Social Development, 1986–1990*. Amman: 1986.

Khader, Bichara. "Targets and Achievements of Jordan's Last Five-Year Plans, 1976–1980 and 1981–1985." Pages 177–91 in Bichara Khader and Adnan Badran (eds.), *The Economic Development of Jordan*. London: Croom Helm, 1987.

Khouri, Rami. "Respectable Year for Jordanian Banks," *Euromoney* [London], May 1987, 143–45.

Rivier, François. "Jordan: A Disturbing Dependence on a Deteriorating Regional Situation." Pages 192–203 in Bichara Khader and Adnan Badran (eds.), *The Economic Development of Jordan*. London: Croom Helm, 1987.

Robins, Philip. *Jordan to 1990: Coping with Change.* (Economic Prospects Series, Economist Intelligence Unit, Special Report No. 1074.) London: Economist, December 1986.

Sams, Tom. "Jordan: Despite Economic Challenges, Trade Potential is Significant," *Business America*, April 25, 1988, 27.

_____. "Jordan Makes the Most of Limited Resources," *Business America*, May 9, 1988, 34–35.

Schliephake, Konrad. "Jordan, The Economic and Geographic Potential." Pages 62–92 in Bichara Khader and Adnan Badran (eds.), *The Economic Development of Jordan*. London: Croom Helm, 1987.

Seccombe, Ian J. "Economic Recession and International Labour Migration in the Arab Gulf." *Arab Gulf Journal* [London], 6, No. 1, January 1986, 43–52.

_____. *International Labour Migration and Skill Scarcity in the Hashemite Kingdom of Jordan.* Geneva: International Labour Office Press, 1984.

_____. "Labour Emigration Policies and Economic Development in Jordan: From Unemployment to Labour Shortage." Pages 118-32 in Bichara Khader and Adnan Badran (eds.), *The Economic Development of Jordan.* London: Croom Helm, 1987.

Seccombe, Ian J., and Rodney J. Wilson. *Trade and Finance in Jordan.* (Occasional Papers Series, No. 33.) Durham, United Kingdom: University of Durham Press, 1987.

Share, M.A.J. "The Use of Jordanian Workers' Remittances." Pages 32-44 in Bichara Khader and Adnan Badran (eds.), *The Economic Development of Jordan.* London: Croom Helm, 1987.

Sullivan, Michael B. "Industrial Development in Jordan." Pages 133-42 in Bichara Khader and Adnan Badran (eds.), *The Economic Development of Jordan.* London: Croom Helm, 1987.

United Nations. Industrial Development Organization. *Industrial Development Profile of Jordan: Problems and Prospects.* (ICIS 159.) Geneva: 1980.

_____. Industrial Development Organization. Regional and Country Studies Branch. *Jordan: Stimulating Manufacturing Employment and Exports.* Geneva: December 24, 1987.

Vandyk, Anthony. "Royal Jordanian Upholds Its Reputation as a Progressive Carrier," *Air Transport World,* July 1987, 72-73, 76, 80.

Weiss, Dieter. "Development Planning in a Turbulent International Environment: Some Reflections on the Jordanian Case." Pages 143-76 in Bichara Khader and Adnan Badran (eds.), *The Economic Development of Jordan.* London: Croom Helm, 1987.

_____. "Jordan's Trade: Past Performance and Future Prospects," *International Journal of Middle East Studies,* 20, No. 3, August 1988, 325-44.

Wilson, Rodney J. "The Role of Commercial Banking in the Jordanian Economy." Pages 45-61 in Bichara Khader and Adnan Badran (eds.), *The Economic Development of Jordan.* London: Croom Helm, 1987.

(Various issues of the following publications were also used in the preparation of this chapter: *Arab-British Commerce* [London]; Economist Intelligence Unit, *Country Report: Jordan* [London]; Foreign Broadcast Information Service, *Daily Report: Near East and South Asia; Jordan Times* [Amman]; *Middle East Economic Digest* [London]; *Middle East Reporter; Syrie et Monde Arabe* [Damascus]; and *Washington Post.*)

## Chapter 4

Amnesty International. *Amnesty International Report, 1988.* London: 1988.

Andoni, Lamis. "Hussein Throws Out a Multiple Challenge," *Middle East International* [London], No. 331, August 1988, 3–4.

Aruri, Naseer H. "The PLO and the Jordan Option," *Middle East Report,* No. 131, March-April 1985, 3–9.

Bailey, Clinton. *Jordan's Palestinian Challenge, 1948–1983.* Boulder, Colorado: Westview Press, 1984.

Devlin, John. "Syria and Its Neighbors." Pages 321–41 in Robert O. Freedman (ed.), *The Middle East after Irangate.* Baltimore: Baltimore Hebrew University, 1988.

Drysdale, Alasdair. "The Asad Regime and Its Troubles," *MERIP Reports,* No. 110, November-December 1982, 3–11.

Eilts, Hermann. "Reviving the Middle East Peace Process: An International Conference?" *Middle East Insight,* 5, No. 3, August-September 1987, 4–13.

Fernea, Elizabeth, and Robert Fernea. *The Arab World: Personal Encounters.* New York: Anchor Press, 1985.

Garfinkle, Adam M. "The Importance of Being Hussein: Recent Developments in Jordanian Foreign Policy and Their Implications for Peace in the Middle East." Pages 291–320 in Robert O. Freedman (ed.), *The Middle East after Irangate.* Baltimore: Baltimore Hebrew University, 1988.

Gubser, Peter. *Jordan: Crossroads of Middle Eastern Events.* (Profiles: Nations of the Contemporary Middle East Series.) Boulder, Colorado: Westview Press, 1983.

Hirst, David. *The Gun and the Olive Branch: The Roots of Violence in the Middle East.* London: Futura, 1983.

"Jordan." Pages 1523–38 in *The Europa Yearbook, 1986: A World Survey,* 1. London: Europa, 1986.

Khalidi, Rashid. "PNC Strengthens Palestinian Hand," *Middle East Report,* No. 147, July-August 1987, 38–39.

Matusky, Gregory, and John Hayes. *King Hussein.* New York: Chelsea House, 1987.

Peaslee, Amos J. *Constitutions of Nations,* 2. (3d ed.) The Hague: Martinus Nijhoff, 1966.

Peretz, Don. *The Middle East Today.* (2d ed.) Hinsdale, Illinois: Dryden Press, 1971.

*Political Handbook of the World, 1986.* (Ed., Arthur S. Banks.) Binghamton, New York: CSA, 1986.

"Political Rights and Censorship in Jordan," *Middle East Report,* No. 149, November-December 1987, 30–34.

Pollock, David. "Israel's National Unity: Solution or Stalemate?" Pages 231–58 in Robert O. Freedman (ed.), *The Middle East after Irangate*. Baltimore: Baltimore Hebrew University, 1988.

Rubenberg, Cheryl. *The Palestine Liberation Organization: Its Institutional Infrastructure*. (IAS Monograph Series.) Belmont, Massachusetts: Institute of Arab Studies, 1983.

Satloff, Robert B. "Repression in Irbid: Raising the Stakes in Jordan," *Middle East Insight*, 5, No. 1, 1987, 31–37.

Sennitt, Andrew G. (ed.). *World Radio TV Handbook, 1989*. Hvidovre, Denmark: Billboard, 1989.

Tyler, Patrick. "Hussein Shuffles Cabinet, Putting Palace Loyalists in Top Posts," *Washington Post*, December 20, 1988, A20.

United States. Department of State. "Jordan." Pages 1200–1208 in *Country Reports on Human Rights Practices for 1987*. (Report submitted to United States Congress, 100th, 2d Session, House of Representatives, Committee on Foreign Affairs, and Senate, Committee on Foreign Relations.) Washington: GPO, 1988.

Wilson, Rodney J. "Jordan's Trade: Past Performance and Future Prospects," *International Journal of Middle East Studies*, 20, No. 3, August 1988, 325–44.

Wright, Robin. "Three New Dimensions of Palestinian Politics," *Middle East Insight*, No. 6, March-April 1988, 20–29.

(Various issues of the following publications were also used in the preparation of this chapter: *Defense and Foreign Affairs Weekly;* Foreign Broadcast Information Service, *Daily Report: Near East and South Asia; Middle East International* [London]; *New York Times; Wall Street Journal;* and *Washington Post*.)

## Chapter 5

Amnesty International. *Amnesty International Report, 1988*. London: 1988.

Cordesman, Anthony H. *Jordanian Arms and the Middle East Balance*. Washington: Middle East Institute, 1983.

_____. *Jordanian Arms and the Middle East Balance: Update*. Washington: Middle East Institute, 1985.

_____. "The Middle East and the Cost of the Politics of Force," *Middle East Journal*, 40, No. 1, Winter 1986, 5–15.

Day, Arthur R. *East Bank/West Bank: Jordan and the Prospects for Peace*. New York: Council on Foreign Relations, 1986.

Dyer, Gwynne, and John Keegan. "Jordan." Pages 329–34 in John Keegan (ed.), *World Armies*. Detroit: Gale Research, 1983.

El-Edroos, S.A. *The Hashemite Arab Army, 1908–1979: An Appreciation and Analysis of Military Operations.* Washington: Middle East Institute, 1973.

Gabriel, Richard A., and Alan Scott MacDougall. "Jordan." Pages 27–40 in Richard A. Gabriel (ed.), *Fighting Armies: Antagonists in the Middle East: A Combat Assessment.* Westport, Connecticut: Greenwood Press, 1983.

Glubb, John Bagot. *A Soldier with the Arabs.* London: Hodder and Stoughton, 1957.

Haas, Marius. *Husseins Königreich: Jordaniens Stellung im Nahen Osten.* Munich: Tuduv, 1975.

*International Air Forces and Military Aircraft Directory.* Stapleford Airfield, Essex, United Kingdom: Aviation Advisory Services, 1988.

*Jane's Fighting Ships, 1988–89.* London: Jane's, 1988.

"Jordan." *DMS Market Intelligence Report: Middle East/Africa.* Greenwich, Connecticut: Defense Marketing Services, 1988.

"Jordan." Pages 491–519 in *The Middle East and North Africa, 1988.* London: Europa, 1987.

Jureidini, Paul A., and R.D. McLaurin. *Jordan: The Impact of Social Changes on the Role of the Tribes.* (The Washington Papers, No. 108, Center for Strategic and International Studies, Georgetown University.) New York: Praeger, 1984.

Levran, Aharon, and Zeev Eytan. *The Middle East Military Balance, 1986.* Boulder, Colorado: Westview Press, 1987.

*The Middle East: 1986.* (6th ed.) Washington: Congressional Quarterly, 1986.

*Middle East Contemporary Survey, 1983–84, 8.* (Eds., Haim Shaked and Daniel Dishon.) New York: Holmes and Meir, 1986.

*Middle East Contemporary Survey, 1984–85, 9.* (Eds., Itamar Rabinovich and Haim Shaked.) New York: Holmes and Meir, 1987.

*The Military Balance, 1988–89.* London: International Institute for Strategic Studies, 1988.

*The Military Balance, 1989–90.* London: International Institute for Strategic Studies, 1989.

Mutawi, Samir A. *Jordan in the 1967 War.* New York: Cambridge University Press, 1987.

O'Ballance, Edgar. "The Jordanian Wars." Pages 42–50 in Anne Sinai and Allen Pollack (eds.), *The Hashemite Kingdom of Jordan and the West Bank: A Handbook.* New York: American Academic Association for Peace in the Middle East, 1977.

Organisation Internationale de Police Criminelle (Interpol). *Statistiques Criminelles Internationales, 1983–1984.* Paris: n.d.

Robins, Philip. *Jordan to 1990: Coping with Change.* (Economic Prospects Series, Economist Intelligence Unit, Special Report, No. 1074.) London: Economist, 1986.

Satloff, Robert B. *Troubles on the East Bank: Challenges to the Domestic Stability of Jordan.* New York: Praeger, 1986.

Shahar, Uri. "Can Arms Buy Peace? The Strategic Repercussions of the Jordanian Arms Buildup," *IDF Journal* [Tel Aviv], 4, No. 1, 27–33.

*SIPRI Yearbook, 1988: World Armaments and Disarmament.* London: Oxford University Press for Stockholm International Peace Research Institute, 1988.

United States. Arms Control and Disarmament Agency. *World Military Expenditures and Arms Transfers, 1987.* (ACD Publication, No. 128.) Washington: GPO, 1988.

———. Congress. 99th, 1st Session. House of Representatives. Committee on Foreign Affairs. *Proposed Arms Sales to Jordan: Hearing Before the Subcommittee on Europe and the Middle East, October 30, 1985.* Washington: GPO, 1986.

———. Department of Defense. *Congressional Presentation for Security Assistance Programs, Fiscal Year 1989.* Washington: GPO, 1988.

———. Department of State. *Country Reports on Human Rights Practices for 1986.* (Report submitted to United States Congress, 100th, 1st Session, Senate, Committee on Foreign Relations, and House of Representatives, Committee on Foreign Affairs) Washington: GPO, 1987.

———. Department of State. *Country Reports on Human Rights Practices for 1987.* (Report submitted to United States Congress, 100th, 2d Session, Senate, Committee on Foreign Relations and House of Representatives, Committee on Foreign Affairs.) Washington: GPO, 1988.

———. Department of State. Bureau of Public Affairs. *Jordan: Background Notes.* (Department of State Publication, No. 7956.) Washington: GPO, 1988.

Wilson, Mary C. "Jordan's Malaise," *Current History*, 86, No. 517, February 1987, 73–76, 84, 85.

(Various issues of the following publications were also used in the preparation of this chapter: Foreign Broadcast Information Service, *Daily Report: Near East and South Asia;* Keesing's *Contemporary Archives* [London]; *New York Times;* and *Washington Post.*)

# Glossary

dinar—Basic currency unit consisting of 1,000 fils; created in 1950 as replacement for the Palestinian pound. Dinar's value was established at parity with the British pound sterling, or a value of US$2.80 equal to JD1. Jordan, as a member of the sterling area, maintained parity with the British pound until 1967 when the British devalued their currency. Jordan did not follow the pound, retaining the dinar at US$2.80 equal to JD1 through 1972. When United States currency was devalued in 1973, the dinar was unlinked from the dollar, since which time the rate has fluctuated. Beginning in February 1975, the dinar was pegged to the special drawing right (SDR—*q.v.*). According to International Monetary Fund (IMF—*q.v.*) data, the average conversion rate of the dinar for trade and other purposes was US$3.04 in 1987, US$2.10 in 1988, and US$1.54 in 1989.

East Bank—The area east of the Jordan River, the Dead Sea, and the series of wadis from the Dead Sea to the Gulf of Aqaba. Roughly the former Amirate of Transjordan.

GDP (gross domestic product)—A value measure of the flow of domestic goods and services produced by an economy over a period of time, such as a year. Only output values of goods for final consumption and for intermediate production are assumed to be included in final prices. GDP is sometimes aggregated and shown at market prices, meaning that indirect taxes and subsidies are included; when these have been eliminated, the result is GDP at factor cost. The word *gross* indicates that deductions for depreciation of physical assets have not been made.

GNP (gross national product)—GDP (*q.v.*) plus the net income or loss stemming from transactions with foreign countries. GNP is the broadest measurement of the output of goods and services by an economy. It can be calculated at market prices, which include indirect taxes and subsidies. Because indirect taxes and subsidies are only transfer payments, GNP is often calculated at factor cost, removing indirect taxes and subsidies.

imam—A word used in several senses. In general use and lower-cased, it means the leader of congregational prayers; as such it implies no ordination or special spiritual powers beyond sufficient education to carry out this function. It is also used figuratively by many Sunni (*q.v.*) Muslims to mean the leader of the Islamic community. Among Shia (*q.v.*) Muslims, the word is usually upper-cased and takes on many complex and controversial meanings; in general, however, it indicates that particular descendant of the Party of Ali who is believed to have been God's designated repository of the spiritual authority inherent in that line. The identity of this individual and the means of ascertaining his identity have been the major issues causing divisions among Shias.

International Monetary Fund (IMF)—Established along with the World Bank (*q.v.*) in 1945, the IMF is a specialized agency affiliated with the United Nations and is responsible for stabilizing international exchange rates and payments. The main business of the IMF is the provision of loans to its members (including industrialized and developing countries) when they experience balance of payments difficulties. These loans frequently carry conditions that require substantial internal economic adjustments by the recipients, most of which are developing countries.

Palestinian—Narrowly, a citizen of the British mandated territory of Palestine (1922–48). Generally, a Muslim or Christian native or descendant of a native of the region between the Egyptian Sinai and Lebanon and west of the Jordan River-Dead Sea-Gulf of Aqaba line who identifies himself primarily as a Palestinian.

sharia—Body of Islamic law. Courts applying this law are known as sharia courts.

sharif (Arabic pl., *ashraf*)—An individual who claims to be and is accepted as a descendant of the Prophet Muhammad through his daughter Fatima.

shaykh—Leader or chief. Word used to mean either a political leader or a learned religious leader. Also used as an honorific. Frequently spelled sheikh or sheik.

Shia (also Shiite, from Shiat Ali, the Party of Ali)—A member of the smaller of the two great divisions of Islam. Shias supported the claims of Ali and his line to presumptive right to the caliphate and leadership of the Muslim community, and on this issue they divided from the Sunnis (*q.v.*) in the first great schism within Islam. Later schisms have produced further divisions among the Shias over the identity and number of Imams (*q.v.*). Shias revere Twelve Imams, the last of whom is believed to be in hiding.

special drawing right(s) (SDR)—a monetary unit of the International Monetary Fund (IMF—*q.v.*) based on a basket of international currencies consisting of the United States dollar, the German deutschmark, the Japanese yen, the British pound sterling, and the French franc.

Sunni (from *sunna,* orthodox)—A member of the larger of the two great divisions of Islam. Sunnis supported the traditional method of election to the caliphate and accepted the Umayyad line. On this issue they divided from the Shia (*q.v.*) Muslims in the first great schism within Islam.

Transjordanian—Narrowly, a citizen of the Amirate of Transjordan (1921–46). Generally, a Muslim or Christian native of the region east of the Jordan River-Dead Sea-Gulf of Aqaba line and within the approximate boundaries of the contemporary state of Jordan, that is, of the East Bank (*q.v.*).

West Bank—The area west of the Jordan River and the Dead Sea, which was annexed by Jordan in 1950. Area has been under Israeli occupation since the June 1967 War. In July 1988, King Hussein renounced Jordan's claim to the West Bank.

World Bank—Informal name used to designate a group of three affiliated international institutions: the International Bank for Reconstruction and Development (IBRD), the International Development Association (IDA), and the International Finance Corporation (IFC). The IBRD, established in 1945, has the primary purpose of providing loans to developing countries for productive projects. The IDA, a legally separate loan fund but administered by the staff of the IBRD, was set up in 1960 to furnish credits to the poorest developing countries on much easier terms than those of conventional IBRD loans. The IFC, founded in 1956, supplements the activities of the IBRD through loans and assistance specifically designed to encourage the growth of productive private enterprises in the less developed countries. The president and certain senior officers of the IBRD hold the same positions in the IFC. The three institutions are owned by the governments of the countries that subscribe their capital. To participate in the World Bank group, member states must first belong to the International Monetary Fund (IMF—*q.v.*).

# Index

Abbasids, 12
Abdul Hamid II (sultan), 18, 20
Abdul Huda family, 197
Abdullah (king of Jordan), xxi, 3-4, 29,
194; accepts UN partition plan (1947),
28; as amir, 26, 92; becomes king of
Jordan (1948), xxi, 29; early career of,
18, 20, 21, 23, 25; as leader of Arab
forces (1948), 28; role in formation of
Arab League by, 27
Abraham (Ibrahim), 5, 107
Abu Ammar. See Arafat, Yasir
Abu Bakr, 12, 105
Abu Daud. See Daud Auda, Muhammad
Abu Musa: leads Al Fatah Uprising, 205,
207; role in Al Fatah of, 205
Abu Nidal, 205, 207
Abu Nidal faction, 181, 232
Abu Nuwar, Ali, 32, 33, 34
Abu Talib, Fathi, 242
ACDA. See United States
Achaemenid Empire, 7
Afghanistan, 55, 56
Africa, 174
agreements: Arab Solidarity Agreement
(1957), 32-33; armistice (1949), 28-29;
for arms with Soviet Union, 261; be-
tween Britain and Transjordan, 26-27;
cease-fire in Jordanian civil war, 42-43;
Hadda Agreement (1925), 67; between
Jordanian government and PLO, xxvi,
41; Jordanian-Palestinian peace framework (1985), 201; long-term trade, 160;
for Saudi Arabia and Jordan border,
37; Sykes-Picot (1916), 21; trade,
173-74
Agricultural Credit Corporation, 174
agricultural sector: development policy
for, 169; economic performance of,
130, 166; factors limiting potential of,
xxiv, 168-69; foreign guest workers in,
166; incentives and subsidies in, 169;
introduction of, 5; irrigation in, 166;
livestock production in, 170; production in, 167
air bases, 227, 248-49
aircraft assembly industry, 264-65
airfields, 158

air force. See Royal Jordanian Air Force
airline, 157-58
airports, 158
AJNDB. See Arab Jordanian Nationalist
Democratic Bloc (AJNDB)
Al Ahd (The Covenant Society), 18
Al Aqabah (port) (see also entrepôt status;
Iraq), xxiv, xxix, 155, 156-57, 213, 264
Al Aqabah Ports Corporation, 157
Al Aqabah Railway Corporation, 155
Al Aqabah Thermal Power Station, 154
Alexander the Great, 7
ALF. See Arab Liberation Front (ALF)
Al Fatah (Palestine National Liberation
Movement) (see also Palestine Libera-
tion Organization), 37, 40; ALF aligns
with, 206; composition and objectives
of, 203, 205; demands government
overthrow, 43; as guerrilla group, 203;
representation on PNC Executive
Committee of, 208
Al Fatah Revolutionary Council, 205
Al Fatah Uprising, 205
Al Fatat (The Young Arabs), 18
Algeria, 131
Al Ghawr. See Jordan Valley
Al Ghor. See Jordan Valley
Algiers Arab summit (1988), xxvii
Alia (queen of Jordan), 196
Ali (caliph), 12, 105
Allenby, Edmund, 22
Al Mafraq air base, 227, 248-49
Al Mufti family, 197
Al Wahdah Dam, 165
Amirate of Transjordan (see also Abdul-
lah (king of Jordan)): administration of,
26; Arab Army (Al Jaysh al Arabi) of,
234; established (1921), 3, 26; police
units and military force in, 233; popu-
lation composition of, 65
Amman (see also Philadelphia): history of,
92; population composition in, 92-
93
Amman Arab summit (1981), 4, 56
Amman Central Prison, 277-78
Amman Financial Market, 139, 174,
175-76
Ammon, 6

Amnesty International, 270, 276, 278
Amorites, 5
Anatolia, 5
Anglo-Jordanian Agreement (1948), 33, 218
Anti-Communist Law (1957), 197
antiterrorism program, 267
Antoun, Richard, 87
AOPEC. *See* Arab Organization of Petroleum Exporting Countries (AOPEC)
Arab Air Cargo, 158
Arab Army (Al Jaysh al Arabi). *See* Amirate of Transjordan; Arab Legion
Arab Bank, 174, 176
Arab Company for Maritime Transport, 138
Arab Constitutional Alignment, 59
Arab Constitutionalist Party, 197
Arab Cooperation Council (1989), xxv, 173, 214, 219, 227
Arabia as Roman province, 9
Arabian Peninsula, 10
Arabic language, 12, 65, 79; dialects of, 80; of Semitic origin, 80–81; three forms of, 80
Arab International Hotels, 138
Arab Investment Company, 138
Arab Islamic Coalition, xxix
Arab-Israeli wars: in 1948, xxi, 235–36; effect of, 224; June 1967, or Six-Day War, xxii, 3–4, 38, 66, 216, 236–38, 247; October 1973, 45–46, 216, 225, 238, 247, 261–62
Arab Jordanian Nationalist Democratic Bloc (AJNDB), xxix, xxx
Arab Land Bank, 176
Arab League. *See* League of Arab States (Arab League)
Arab Legion (*see also* Jordan Arab Army), 3, 27; air force unit of, 236; in Arab-Israeli war (1948), 235-36; composition and role in Jordan of, 30, 31, 234; development of support for, 252; effect of Transjordan Frontier Force on, 235; invades Israel (1948), 28; Public Security Force as outgrowth of, 265; recruitment for, 252; strengthening of, 235; subsidy from Britain for, xxi, 251-52, 260; Transjordan police and reserve force in, 26
Arab Legion Air Force (*see also* Royal Jordanian Air Force), 247
Arab Liberation Front (ALF), 206

Arab National Party, 59
Arab nations: foreign relations with, 212-15; military cooperation with, 263-65; reject Camp David Accords, 53; trade relations with, 173
Arab Organization of Petroleum Exporting Countries (AOPEC), 131
Arab Pharmaceutical Manufacturing Company, 138, 152
Arab Potash Company, 149, 161
Arab revival, 17
Arab Revolt, 3, 21, 22
Arab Satellite Organization (Arabsat), 159
Arabs in Jordan, 76–77
Arab Solidarity Agreement (1957), 32–33, 34
Arab Union, 35
Arab Wings, 158
Arafat, Yasir: addresses UN General Assembly, 47; as chairman of PNC Executive Committee, 203, 208; as commander of PLA, 42; endorses Saddam Husayn, xxx; as leader of Al Fatah, 37, 203; as leader of PLO, 40; opposition to, 205, 233; relations with King Hussein of, xxvi, 60, 199–201; visits Egypt (1983), 213
Aramaic language, 7
Arif, Abd as Salaam, 35
armed forces (*see also* Jordan Arab Army): compared to Syrian and Israeli, 226; devotion to King Hussein of, 252; Palestinians in, 253, 254; pay scales and benefits of, 255–56; as protection for monarchy, 238; public services by, 241; ranks and insignia of, 256; recruitment policy of, 251; relative size of, 251
Armed Forces General Command staff, 242–43
Armenians in Jordan, 78
armor rebuild facility, 265
army. *See* Arab Legion; Jordan Arab Army
Asia Minor Agreement. *See* Sykes-Picot Agreement
Assad, Hafiz al, 4; objection to Hussein's proposals (1979), 54; relations with Jordan of, 50–51
As Saiqa, 206, 207
assassinations: of Abdullah, king of Jordan, xxi, 29–30, 229; attempted, 229, 232; claims of Black September for,

198; of Faisal (Iraq), 35; of Majali (1958), 36; of Sadat (1981), 61; of Tal, 44
Assyria, 7
austerity program, xxiv, xxviii, 137, 141
Ayatollah Khomeini. *See* Khomeini, Sayyid Ruhollah Musavi
Ayyubid Sultanate, 13
Azraq ash Shishan air base, 248
Az Zarqa affair, 34
Az Zarqa River, 68

Babylon, 7
Badran, Mudar, xxvi, xxix, 49–50, 60, 187
Badran family, 197
Baghdad Conference (summit) (1978), 53, 131, 188, 212–13, 250, 260
Baghdad Pact (*see also* Central Treaty Organization (CENTO)), 31, 32
Baghdad summit (1990), xxvii
Bahai religion, xxvi, 114
Bahrain, 215
balance of payments, xxviii, 127, 131, 251
Balfour Declaration (1917), 3; opposition to, 23; provisions of, 22
banking system, xxiv, 127, 129, 133, 174–76; disbursement of West Bank aid funds, 202
Banna, Sabri Khalil al. *See* Abu Nidal
Barhoum, Mohammad, 102
Bashan, 6
Battle of Hattin (1187), 13
Battle of Uhud (636), 10
beduins (*see also* tribalism)· in army and Arab Legion, 85, 252; effect of changing circumstances on, 82–83; honor (*ird*) among, 82; importance of tribalism among, 76, 81–86; in Jordan, 30; nomadic and seminomadic, 75, 81–82; support for monarchy by, 196, 235, 240, 252
Begin, Menachem, 53, 59
Begin administration (Israel), 5
Bernadotte, Folke, 28
Bevin, Ernest, 27
black market, xxiv, 137
Black September faction, 44, 181, 198, 232, 233
border: with Iraq, Syria, and Saudi Arabia, 67, 226, 227; with Israel (de jure), xxii, 66, 224; between Jordan and Saudi Arabia, 37

border dispute: with Israel, 31, 32, 66; Syria-Israel, 37
Brezhnev, Leonid, 47, 52
Britain: defeats Turks (1918), 23; economic assistance from, 260; mandate for Palestine and Iraq of, 3, 23, 24–25, 235; Middle East policy of (1916), 20–22; military presence (1924), 234; relations of Jordan with, 29–32, 174, 218; role in Palestine Mandate decisions of, 20–25; role in Transjordan of, 26–28; sells military equipment, 260, 262; withdraws all troops from Jordan (1957), 33
British Army Staff College, 257
British Bank of the Middle East, 176
budget deficit, 141
buffer zone, 3
Bunche, Ralph, 28
Bureau of Occupied Homeland Affairs (*see also* Ministry of Occupied Territories), 49–50, 188
Bush, George, xxix
Byzantine Empire, 10, 13

cabinet. *See* Council of Ministers
Cairo-Amman Bank, 176
Cairo Conference (1964), 36
Cairo summit (1973), 45
Cairo summit (1976), 49
camel herding, 81
Camp David Accords (1978), xxii, 4, 53, 199; effect on PLO of, xxvi; Hussein's alternative to, 54; process for, 53, 210, 216
Canaan, 5, 6
canal, 165, 168
capital flows, 127, 130, 133, 136, 175
Carter, Jimmy, 52, 53
Catholic Church: Greek, 113; Roman, 113
censorship, 219
CENTO. *See* Central Treaty Organization (CENTO)
Central Bank of Jordan, 135, 140, 174
Central Treaty Organization (CENTO), 31
charitable organizations, 121–22
Chase Manhattan Bank, 176
Chelhod, Joseph, 84
chemical industry, xxiv, 151
China, People's Republic of, 161, 173

Christianity: in Byzantine Empire, 10; Jordanians practicing, xxvi, 77–78, 104; as religious minority, 112

Christian sects: Catholic, 112–13; Eastern Orthodox, 112; Protestant, 113–14; religious courts for, 191

Churchill, Winston, 25

Circassians: among political elite, 197; in Jordan, 16, 78–79, 92, 231

Citibank, 176

civil courts, 191

civil servants, 187–88

civil war: in Lebanon, 51; with PLO guerrillas (1970–71), xxii, 42, 193, 198–99, 215–16, 233

class structure. *See* social structure

climate, 71–72

colleges, 116–17

commodity distribution, 140

communism, 34, 197, 206, 207, 231–32

Communist Party of Jordan (Al Hizb ash Shuyui al Urduni), 197, 231–32

community colleges, 116–17

conscription system, xxviii, 236; after reform, 254–55; emergency act for (1966), 254

Constantinople, 10, 13

Constitution: Jordan (1952), 30; amendments in 1974, 1976, and 1984, 182–83, 190; electoral system under, 189; legislative powers and responsibilities of, 188–89; powers and functions of government under, 183; powers of king under, 185, 187, 241; provision for instruments for internal security in, 265; provisions related to religion in, 103, 112, 182; right of habeas corpus under, 275

constitution: Transjordan (1928), xxi, 26

constitution: Transjordan (1946), 27, 29

construction sector, 130

consulting services industry, 127

consumption: government, 130; private, 130

contraception, 73–74

corruption, xxviii

Council of Ministers, 183, 241

coups d'état: attempt in Jordan (1957), 240; in Egypt (1952), 31; in Iran (1979), 55; in Iraq (1958), 35

Court of Appeal, 191–92

Court of Cassation (supreme court), 191–92, 276

courts of first instance, 191, 275

court system (*see also* civil courts; courts of first instance; magistrates' courts; religious courts; special courts), 191–92, 275–76

crime, 273–74

criminal code, 271–73

criminal law procedures, 274–76

Crusade, First, 13

crusaders, 13

cultural influence: of Palestinians, 76; of Western countries, 93

cultural tradition, Arab-Islamic, 65

currency, 133; devaluation and depreciation of, 134, 136–37

current account. *See* balance of payments

Cyrus II (king of Persia), 7

dam, 165

Damascus Protocol, 20

Daud, Muhammad, 42

Daud Auda, Muhammad, 44

David (king), 6

Dead Sea, 66, 71, 161

debt: external, xxiv, 128, 135–36; internal, 142; military, 251, 260

Decapolis, 9

defense burden, 128

defense spending. *See* spending, government

defense strategy, 249–50

deflation, 134

Democratic Bloc, xxvi

Democratic Front for the Liberation of Palestine (DFLP), 205, 207, 233

Democratic Unity and Justice Party, xxix

Department of Social Affairs, 121

Desert Highway, 154–55

Desert Mobile Force, 235

Desert Police Force, 266, 267, 269

desert region, xxiv, 67–68, 71, 168–69

DFLP. *See* Democratic Front for the Liberation of Palestine (DFLP)

Dina Abdul Hamid al Aun, 194

disease, 119–20

divorce, 97

drainage network, 68

drought, 168, 169

Druze religion, xxvi, 79, 114

Dulles, John Foster, 34

East Bank, 3; conflict of Jews and Seleucids in, 9; conversion to Islam in, 10, 12; decline in importance of, 13; ethnic groups in, 77; neolithic culture settlements in, 5; under Ottoman rule, 16; population composition, volume, and density of, 65, 72, 74–75; refugees in, 38; rift with West Bank of, 34

Eastern Europe, 117

Eastern Orthodox Church, 112

East Ghor Canal, 165, 168

ecclesiastical courts, 191–92

economic assistance (*see also* military assistance): from Arab League nations, xxiv, 39, 58, 260; from Arab oil-producing countries, xxiv, xxvii, 131, 212–13, 215, 250, 260, 261; from Britain, 31–33, 35, 39, 58, 218; dependence on, 259–60; estimates of requirements for (1991), xxxi; from European Community (EC), 133; foreign, 127, 130–31, 134, 136, 142; from Iraq (1978), 53, 56; from Jordan to Iraq, 56; from multilateral organizations, 131; proportion of revenue from, xxv; from Qatar and Abu Dhabi, 39; from United States, 34–35, 131, 168, 215, 218; used for development planning, 142–43; to West Bank Palestinians, xxvii, 57; from West Germany, 39

economic development, 129

economic performance, 127–29, 181–82, 223–24, 250

economic planning. *See* Five-Year Plans

economic policy (*see also* austerity program; import substitution): austerity measures of, xxiv, xxxviii, 137, 141; for industry and manufacture, 149–53; of self-sufficiency, xxiv, 47–48, 128; for subsidies, 140–41

economy: effect of West Bank loss (1967) on, 128; government role in, xxiv, 137–41, 174; recession in, 181–82

Edom, 6

Edomites, 6

education (*see also* students): for children of military personnel, 257; effect of modern, 101–3, 110; government spending for, 114; students studying abroad, 117, 231

education system (*see also* community colleges; literacy; military training; schools; universities), 66; in Amirate of Transjordan, 114–15; effect of upgraded, xxiii, 76; opportunities for females in, 100, 102–3; universities and community colleges in, 116–17

Egypt: Arab ostracism of (1978–79), xxvii, 4; attacked by Britain (1956), 32; attacks Israel (1948), 28; attacks Israel (1973), 45; conflict with Hittites of, 5–6; forms United Arab Republic with Syria, 35; military alliance with Jordan of (1967), 38; ostracized from Arab League (1978), 53, 56; payments to Jordan (1957), 32–33; relations of Jordan with, xxvii, 53–54, 133, 212–14, 226–27; as republic (1952), 31; trade relations with, 173

Egyptian Free Officers movement, 31

Eisenhower, Dwight D., 34

Eisenhower Doctrine, 34

Elat as ancient port, 6

elections, 1989–90, xxv, xxviii–xxix

electoral system, 189–90

electricity: delivery of, 153–54; demand for, 153; hydroelectric station for, 154

Encouragement of Investment Law (1984), 140

endogamy, 82, 86, 96–97

engineering industries, 129, 152

entrepôt status, xxiv, xxviii, xxx, 127, 133, 264

Enver Pasha, 18

Eshkol, Levi, 38, 40

European Community (EC): economic assistance from, 133; imports from, 218

exchange rate system, xxiv, 137, 176

exports: changes in composition of, 172–73; development of industries for, xxiv; economic performance of, 58, 170; of food supplies, 167–68; incentives for, xxv; to Iraq, 213; to Persian Gulf countries, 215; of phosphates, 127, 160, 215; as proportion of GDP, 130; reexports of entrepôt products, xxiv, xxviii, xxx, 127, 133, 264

Fahmi, Ismail, 46

Faisal I (son of Hussein Ali Al Hashimi), 18, 20–23; as king of Iraq, 25, 194

Faisal II (king of Iraq), 35

Faisal (king of Saudi Arabia), 45

family planning, 73

family structure: allocation of household

space in, 98; honor (*ird*) in, 99; household in, 95–96, 98–99; individual subordinate in, 96
Fatimids, 12, 13
fedayeen. *See* guerrillas
Federal Republic of Germany. *See* Germany, West
fertility rates, 73–75, 92
fertilizer industry, 160–61
Fifteen-Point Political Program. *See* Palestine Liberation Organization (PLO)
financial sector, 174–77
firms: semipublic, xxiv, 138; state-owned, 149
fiscal policy (*see also* budget deficit; revenues; spending, government; tax policy), 129; revenue and taxation of, 142; spending estimates in, 141–42
Five-Year Plans: for 1980–85, 139, 143; for 1986–90, 142–44, 148
Ford, Gerald R., 47
foreign aid. *See* economic assistance
foreign policy, 209–18
France: mandate for Syria and Lebanon of, 23; protection of Catholics by, 16; selling of military aircraft and equipment to Jordan by, 218, 248, 260–62
Free Officers, 230
freight companies, 155

Gardiner, Antoinette, 194
Gaza Strip, 188
GDP. *See* gross domestic product (GDP)
General Intelligence Department (GID), or Dairat al Mukhabarat, xxviii, 182–83, 196, 197–98; methods of control of, 270; responsibilities of, 269–70; secret police (Mukhabarat), 182, 196, 197–98
General Syrian Congress, 25
Geneva Conference on the Middle East (1977), 50, 52
geographic location, 3, 59, 66, 127
Germany, West: broken relations with, 36–37; proposed new loans from, xxiv; trade relations with, 174
Ghassanids, 10
GID. *See* General Intelligence Department (GID), or Dairat al Mukhabarat
Gilead, 6, 7
Glubb, John Bagot (Glubb Pasha), 26–27, 32, 235, 236, 252

GNP. *See* gross national product (GNP)
Golan Heights, 5, 45, 225
government: criticism of (1989), xxv, xxviii–xxix; executive power of, 183–88; judicial power of, 183, 191–93; legislative power of, 183, 188–90
government administration: central, 193; governorates or provinces of, 183, 192; local, 192–93
government intervention: in economic activity, xxiv, 137–41; in financial sector, 174; in media activities, 219–20
governorates. *See* government administration
Greek Catholic Church, 113
Greek Orthodox Church, 112
Greek people, 7
Grindlays Bank, 176
gross domestic product (GDP), 127–30
gross national product (GNP), 127
Gubser, Peter, 79, 81
guerrilla organizations, 37, 40, 198–209
guerrillas (*see also* Black September): Al Fatah as organization of, 37, 40; arms and funds for, 40; fedayeen as another name for, xxii, 37, 40, 232; offensive in Jordan by, 41–42; Palestinian, 4, 38, 197; of PLO, 40, 203; repelling of Israeli attackers (1968) by, 40–41; Syrian assistance during civil war to, 42
Gulf Cooperation Council, 214
Gulf crisis and war (1990–91): effect on Jordan of, xxx–xxxi; role of King Hussein in, xxix–xxx
Gulf of Aqaba, 38, 66, 67

Habash, George, 40, 205–6, 207
Hadda Agreement (1925), 67
hadith, 104
hajj (*see also* Id al Adha), 107–8
Hajj Amin al Husayni, 29–30
Halaby, Elizabeth (*see also* Nur al Hussein (queen of Jordan)), 196
*hamula* or clan, 86–87
Hasan (crown prince), xxiv, 146, 181, 196, 242
Hashim, Ibrahim, 34
Hashim family, 197
Hashimite branch (Quraysh tribe), 3, 4, 18, 20
Hashimite family, 194, 196
Hashimite kingdoms, 35

Hasmonean Dynasty, 9
Hawatmah, Naif, 205, 207
health care program: discrimination in provision of, 121; family planning aspect of, 73; health facilities in, 119; hospitals in, 119; personnel in, 118–19; physicians in, 118
Hedjaz-Jordan Railway (*see also* Hijaz Railway), 155
Hellenistic culture, 7, 9
Herod (king of Judah), 9
Herzl, Theodor, 17
Hiatt, Joseph, 82–83, 84
High Court of Justice, 192
Higher Council for Science and Technology, 151
Higher Jordanian-Palestinian Committee (1982), 60
highlands, 68, 71
High Tribunal (High Council, or Supreme Council), 192
Hijab, Nadia, 102
Hijaz, 20, 21
Hijaz Railway, 16, 155
Hittite people, 5
hoarding, 140
honor (*ird*) concept: among beduins, 82; in family, 99–100
House of Islam (Dar al Islam), 10
Housing Bank, 174
human rights, 277–78
Husayn, Saddam, xxiii, xxix, xxx, 213
Hussein ibn Ali Al Hashimi, 18, 20–24
Hussein ibn Talal ibn Abdullah ibn Hussein Al Hashimi (king of Jordan). *See* Hussein (king of Jordan)
Hussein (king of Jordan), xxii, 4, 29–30; advocacy of UN Resolution 242 by, 39; agreements with PLO of, xxvi, 42–43; assassination attempts against, 223, 229; attitude toward Palestinians of, 57–58; biography of, 194, 196; control by (1989), 181, 193; criticism of, xxviii–xxix; forms military alliance with Egypt, 38; government role after June 1967 War, 38; opposition to, xxvii, 33, 35, 111–12, 229, 231–22, 232–33; plan for Arab federation, 45; plan for Jordanian National Union, 44; political instability of regime of (1980s), 181–82; position on Camp David peace process of, 53, 210, 216; proposes strike force (1980s), 217; pro-Western position of,

xxii; relations with Arafat and PLO of, xxvi–xxvii, 46–48, 50, 60, 186, 199–202, 205–6, 213–14, 232–33; relations with beduins of, 84–86, 181, 240; relations with Egypt of, xxvii, 53–54, 61; relations with PFLP, PFLP-GC, and DFLP of, 205; relations with PLO of, 37; relations with Saddam Husayn of, xxiii, xxix; relations with Syria of, xxvii, 50–56; relations with United States of, 215–17; relinquishes sovereignty over West Bank, xxvii, xxviii, 181, 188, 210, 233; reorganization by, 48; requests assistance from Iraq (1958), 35; role in Arab politics of, 4–5; role in Persian Gulf War (1990–91), xxix–xxx; seeks to disarm refugee camps, 41; stresses self-sufficiency, xxiv, 47–48, 128; supports Iraq in Iran-Iraq War, xxiii, 56, 111, 213, 264; supports shah of Iran, 111
Hussein-McMahon correspondence, 21–22
Hussein Thermal Power Station, 153
Hyksos people, 5

Id al Adha, 108
Id al Fitr, 108
imam, 109
immigrants in Jordan (*see also* refugees), 79, 90, 147
imports, 127; barriers to entry of, xxiv, 149–50; changes in composition of, 172–73; cost of, 134; dependence on, 128, 134; excess over exports of, 130; of food supplies, 167–68; higher duties for, 137, 140; of oil, xxx, 134, 154, 161–62, 174; revenues from, 142; subsidies for, 150; from United States and Western Europe, 170
import substitution, xxiv, 150
India, 161, 173
Indonesia, 173
Industrial Development Bank, 174
industrial policy. *See* economic policy
inflation, 101, 134, 140, 146, 181
infrastructure (*see also* airports; canal; dam; port facilities; railroad system): development in Transjordan of, 26; loss with seizure of West Bank (1967), 128; underdevelopment of, 154
insurance industry, xxiv, 127, 133

interest rate regulation, 140
International Committee of the Red Cross, 219
International Criminal Police Organization (Interpol), 273
International Monetary Fund (IMF), xxiv, xxviii
International Telecommunications Satellite Organization (Intelsat), 159
Interpol. *See* International Criminal Police Organization (Interpol)
*intifadah. See* Palestinian uprising (*intifadah*)
investment: domestic, 130, 139; foreign direct, 127, 133, 140; of Jordanian capital abroad, 133
Iran: overthrow of shah in, 4; relations with, 218; support in Iran-Iraq War for, 4
Iranian Revolution, 55
Iran-Iraq War, 4, 56, 60–61, 129, 157; effect on Jordan of, xxiv; Hussein supports Iraq in, xxiii, xxvii, 56, 111, 213, 264; Iraqi fighting units after, 226
Iraq: British mandate for, 23; coup d'état in, 35–36; economic assistance from, 53, 56, 131; forces invade Israel (1948), 28; gives military equipment to Jordan, 213; invades Kuwait (1990), xxviii, xxix, xxx; military strength after Iran-Iraq War, 226; proclaims independence (1919), 25; relations with, xxvii, 56, 136, 212–14, 226; support in Iran-Iraq War for, 4; trade relations with, 129, 133, 157, 162, 173
Iraqi-Jordanian Joint Committee for Economic and Technical Cooperation (1981), 56
Iraqi-Jordanian Land Transport Company (IJLTC), 155
irrigation system, 166, 168–69
Islam (*see also* Muslims; Shia Islam; Sunni Islam): as established religion, 103; Jordanians practicing, 77; preparation for, 10; in social life, 109; split into two branches, 12; spread of, 10, 106; as way of life, 104
Islamic banks, 176–77
Islamic courts. *See* sharia courts
Islamic Investment House, 177
Islamic law (sharia). *See* sharia (Islamic Law)
Islamic Liberation Party, 197
Islamic revival (*see also* Muslim Brotherhood), 110–12, 225, 226, 230
Israel (*see also* Arab-Israeli wars; Gaza Strip; West Bank): accepts UN Resolution 242, 40; annexes Golan Heights, 5; attacked by Syria and Egypt, 45, 225; bombs PLO Tunisian headquarters (1985), 201; border incidents with Jordan of, 31–32; buys U.S. aircraft, 60; defeats Jordan (1967), 38; establishment of (1948), 3, 28; foreign policy of (1981–82), 5; influence of ancient, 6; invaded by Arab forces (1948), 28; invades and occupies Lebanon (1982), 59–60; Likud government of, 4; military forces of, 224; perspective on Palestinians of, 39–40; PLO and Al Fatah raids against, 37; PNC resolutions related to (1987), 207; recognition by West Germany of, 36–37; relations of Jordan with, 209–10, 212; retaliation against Jordan by, 31, 32, 37, 40–41; seizes West Bank (1967), 4; as threat, xxvii–xxviii, xxxi, 224–25
Israel Defense Forces (IDF), 225
Israeli-occupied territories. *See* Gaza Strip; West Bank
Israelites: conquer Canaan, 66; deportation of, 7
Italy, 174

Jabal Ramm (peak), 68
Jamiat al Arabiyah al Fatat (The Young Arab Society). *See* Al Fatat (The Young Arabs)
Japan, xxiv, 173, 218
Jardanah, Basil, xxxi
Jarring, Gunnar, 41, 42
Jerusalem (*see also* Latin Kingdom of Jerusalem): captured by crusaders, 13; occupation by Arab armies (638), 10; under Ottoman Empire, 13; partition after June 1967 War, 66; reunified (1967), 4; seized by Romans, 9; Transjordan control of, 3
Jerusalem, East, xxii
Jesus (Isa), 107
Jewish kingdoms (*see also* Judah (Judea)), 6
Jewish people, 7
Jibril, Ahmad, 205–6
jihad, 108
Eric Johnston Plan, 31

Joint Syrian-Jordanian Economic Committee, 173

Jordan: annexes West Bank (1950), 3, 29; East and West Bank elections in (1949), 29; official name of, 29; peace agreement with PLO (1985), xxvi; role in 1973 attack on Israel of, 45; Roman ruins in, 9–10

Jordan Arab Army, 32, 33, 42; accepts National Guard members, 252–53; allegiance of, 223, 229–30; beduin-dominated, 85, 181, 240; formation from Arab Legion of, 236; in October 1973 War, 238; organization of, 243; Palestinians in, 240, 253; quality of, xxvii; reform (1976), 254; role in June 1967 Arab-Israeli War of, 236–38; size of, 241

Jordan Cement Factories Company, 138, 149

Jordan Ceramic Company, 138

Jordan Fertilizer Industries Company, 149

Jordanian Baath Party (Arab Socialist Resurrection Party), 32, 231

Jordanian Democratic Unity Party, xxix

Jordanian Highlands, 68

Jordanian Military Academy, 257

Jordanian National Union, 44, 49

Jordanians: Christians among Arab, 77; distinction between Arab and Palestinian, 76–77; as officials of government, 181

Jordanian Staff College, 257, 264

Jordanian-Syrian dam project, 165

Jordanian Syrian Land Transport Company, 155

Jordan Islamic Bank for Finance and Investment, 177

Jordan-Kuwait Bank, 176

Jordan Medical Association, 118

Jordan National Bank, 176

Jordan Phosphate Mines Company, 149, 160

Jordan Radio and Television, 220

Jordan Refinery Company, 138

Jordan region: Muslims in, 12; under Ottoman rule, 13

Jordan River, 31, 36, 68

Jordan River valley, 5, 66, 68, 71, 168–69, 227

Jordan Technology Group, xxiv, 151

Jordan Telecommunications Corporation (TCC), 158

Jordan University of Science and Technology, 116

Joshua, 6

Journalists' Association, 219

Judah (Judea), 6–7, 9

Judaism, 9

Judas (Judah) Maccabaeus, 9

June 1967, or Six-Day War, xxii, 3–4, 38; border with Israel after, 66; damage to Jordan from, 216, 247; economic assistance after, 216; partition of Jerusalem after, 66; role of Jordan Arab Army in, 236–38

jury system, 275

Khalid ibn al Walid, 10

khamsin wind, 72

Khomeini, Ayatollah Sayyid Ruhollah Musavi, 55, 111

King Abdullah Air Base, 248

King Abdullah Airport, 158

King-Crane Commission, 23

King Faisal Air Base, 248

King Hussein Air Base (Al Mafraq), 248

King Talal Dam, 165

kinship (*see also* hamula or clan; family structure), 82, 86–87, 95–97

Kitchener, H. H., 20–21

Kurds in Jordan, 79

Kurian, George T., 115

Kuwait, 131, 173; economic assistance from, xxvii; Iraq invades (1990), xxviii, xxix; relations with, 212, 214

labor force (*see also* labor unions; remittances): demand for skilled and educated, xxiii, 144–46; education of, xxiii, 127; export of, xxiii, xxiv, xxviii, 58, 73, 93–94, 100, 127, 144–47, 166, 215, 250; foreign guest workers in, 58, 144–47, 166; government employment of, xxv, 129–30, 187–88; in manufacturing, 148; motivation for migration in, 76; predicted underemployment in, 147; shortages in, 102, 146–47; unemployment in, xxviii, 66, 102, 134, 145–47, 181; women in, 98, 101–3, 147

labor unions, xxix

Lake Tiberias (Sea of Galilee), 66, 227; formed by Jordan River, 68; Israeli

plan for water from, 36
land ownership: reform for, 166; tenure of, 166
Land Settlement Court, 192
languages: Arabic, 12, 65, 79–81; Aramaic, 7, 12; area of Semitic, 5; Greek, 12
Latin Kingdom of Jerusalem, 13
law. *See* sharia (Islamic law); tribal law
Lawrence, T. E., 21, 23, 25
Layne, Linda, 85–86
League of Arab States (Arab League): Arab League Council of, 28; Collective Security Pact of, 30; formation of (1945), 27; membership in, 219; lack of recognition of West Bank annexation (1950), 29; ostracizes Egypt (1978), xxvii, 53; result of 1967 conference of, 39
League of Nations, 23, 25
Lebanon: effect of civil war in, xxiv, 51; expulsion of PLO from, xxvi, 200; forces invade Israel (1948), 28; French mandate for, 23; invaded by Israel, 5; Israel invades and occupies part of (1982), 59–60; PLO forced to go to, 233; United States troops in (1958), 36
legal system (*see also* criminal code): new, 271; sharia law under, 12, 16, 104–5, 191, 270–71
Libya, xxvii, 131, 215
lineages, 87
Lisan Peninsula, 71
literacy, 115
livestock, 170
Lloyd George, David, 22
loans: from commercial banks, 136; from multilateral organizations, 135–36; from United States, 39
*luzum*, 87

Macedonia, 7
McMahon, Henry, 21
magistrates' courts, 275
Majali, Abdul Hadi al, 265
Majali family, 197
Majali, Habis al, 42
Majali, Hazza al, 31–32, 36
Majali tribe, 90
malnutrition, 121
Mamluks, 13
manufacturing sector: chemical and fertilizer production in, 151; consumer goods in, 151; GDP contributions of, 147; growth of, 130; partially or wholly state-owned firms in, 149
marriage (*see also* divorce; endogamy; polygyny), 82, 96–97, 100
martial law, xxii, xxv, xxviii, 182, 241, 276
martial law courts, 276
Marxism-Leninism, 205
media, 219–20
medical equipment companies, 152
Mediterranean Sea, 71
Mehmed V (sultan), 18
merchant marine, 157
Mesopotamia, 7
Middle East: Arabic language as force for unity in, 65; Geneva Conference on (1977), 50, 52; UN Resolution 242 (1967) for, xxvi–xxvii, 39, 46, 50, 60, 201, 216; UN Resolution 338 for, xxvii, 46, 50, 201, 216
migration, 75, 92–95
military assistance: from Britain, 218, 260; dependence on, 259–60; from United States, 39, 131, 260
military equipment: purchases from France of, 218; purchases from Soviet Union of, 218; purchases from United States of, 224
military power: of Israel, 224–25; of Syria, 226
military regions, 242
military service. *See* conscription system
military training: for air force, 248–49; army basic and advanced, 256–57; of foreign nationals, xxviii; quality of schools for, 257; in United States, 263
militia. *See* People's Army
millet system, 16, 106
mining sector (*see also* phosphate industry; potash industry), 130
Ministry of Communications, 158
Ministry of Culture and Information, 219
Ministry of Defense, 242; General Directorate of Conscription and Mobilization of, 254; Public Security Force under, 265
Ministry of Education, 115, 257
Ministry of Finance, 141
Ministry of Health, 118
Ministry of Higher Education, 117
Ministry of Interior, xxviii, 192, 270;

Public Security Directorate of, 265, 266, 267, 274, 276-77
Ministry of Labor, 147
Ministry of Occupied Territories, 188
Ministry of Planning, 101
Ministry of Religious Endowments and Islamic Affairs, 230
Ministry of Supply, 140-41
Ministry of Transportation, 155, 157
minority groups, 231
Moab, 6
Modern Standard Arabic, 80
monetary policy, 146
monetization, 175
Morocco, 215
mortality rate, 72, 121
Moses (Musa), 6, 107
Muawiyah (caliph), 12, 105
Mubarak, Husni, xxvii, 61, 213-14
muezzin, 107
Mufti, Said al, 33-34, 197
Muhammad Ali (pasha of Egypt), 16
Muhammad (prince of Jordan), 196
Muhammad (prophet) (*see also* hadith; sunna), 10, 12, 104-5, 106-7, 196
Mukhabarat. *See* General Intelligence Department (GID) or Dairat al Mukhabarat
multilateral organizations (*see also* International Monetary Fund (IMF)): economic assistance from, 131; loans from, 135-36
Muna al Hussein (princess), 194
Muragha, Said Musa. *See* Abu Musa
Muslim Brotherhood, xxv-xxvi, xxix, 4, 55, 111, 197-98, 230
Muslims, 10; duties of, 107; religious courts for, 191; Sunni and Shia branches, 12, 105-7
Mutah (Moata) Military University, 257, 264
Mutah University, 116

Nabataean people, 7, 9
Nabulsi, Sulayman, 32-33
Naif (prince in Jordan), 30
Nasser, Gamal Abdul, 31, 32; attempts to destabilize Hussein, 226; leads summit discussing water distribution (1964), 36; role in 1967 War of, 37-38
National Alliance, 206
National Assembly, 188-90, 200

National Charter (Mithaq al Watani), xxvi, xxix
National Consultative Council (NCC), 58-59, 190
National Front Party (Communist Party of Jordan), 32
National Guard, 236, 252
nationalism: of Arab revival, 17-18, 20; of Arabs in Jordan, 31; of Palestinians, 91; of Turks, 18; of Zionism, 17
National Jordanian Movement, 197
National Maritime Company, 157
national police. *See* Public Security Force
national security policy, 223-25, 229
National Service Law (1976), 254, 268
National Socialist Party, 32
National Unity program. *See* Palestine Liberation Organization (PLO)
natural gas, xxiii, 154, 164
natural resources, xxiii, 160-64
naval force, 241
NCC. *See* National Consultative Council (NCC)
Nebuchadnezzar, 7
Negev Desert, 36
Neo-Babylonian Empire, 7
neolithic culture, 5
news agency (PETRA), 220
newspapers, 219
Nixon, Richard M., 45
nomads. *See* beduins
North Yemen. *See* Yemen Arab Republic (North Yemen)
Nur al Hussein (queen of Jordan), 196

Occupied Enemy Territory Administration, 24-25
October 1973 War, 46, 216, 225, 238, 247, 261-62
officer corps, 253, 257
oil industry (*see also* oil refining; shale oil deposits), xxiii, 161-62, 164
oil price downturn, xxiv, xxviii, 4, 58, 93, 128-29, 145, 260
oil refining, 138, 149, 161-62
Oman, 214, 264
Organic Law: 1928 (Transjordan), xxi, 26, 27
Organization of Petroleum Exporting Countries (OPEC) (*see also* Arab Organization of Petroleum Exporting Countries (AOPEC)), 162

Ottoman Decentralization Party, 18
Ottoman Empire (*see also* Sublime Porte), administrative divisions of, 13, 16; conquers area, 3; opposition of Arabs to, 18
Ottoman Turks, 13
*Outre Jourdain* (Beyond Jordan), 13

packaging and container industry, 152–53
Pahlavi, Mohammad Reza Shah. *See* Iran
Pakistan, 173
Palestine, 3; Arab rebellion (1936–39), 235; as British mandate, 23; derivation of name of, 6; under Ottoman Empire, 13; PLO declaration for independent, 181; proposed United Nations partition of, 27–28; strategic geographic location of, 22; under Sykes-Picot Agreement, 21–22
Palestine Central Committee (PCC), 207
Palestine Communist Party, 197, 206, 207
Palestine Liberation Army (PLA), 42, 49, 209
Palestine Liberation Front (PLF), 206
Palestine Liberation Organization (PLO) (*see also* guerrillas; Palestine Central Committee (PCC)), 36, 37; administration of, 208; agreements with Hussein of, 42–43; bombing of Tunisian headquarters of, 201; in civil war (1970–71), 198; declaration of Rabat summit related to, 47; effect on nationalism of, 91; expulsion from Lebanon of (1982), 200; Fifteen-Point Political Program of, 207; guerrilla groups accepting policy of, 206; lack of support from Hussein for (1966), 37; National Unity Program of, 207; opposition of Jordan and Syria to, 51; Palestine Liberation Army of, 42, 209; Palestine Martyrs' Works Society (SAMED), 209; Palestine National Fund of, 208; Palestinian National Charter of, 207; Palestininan Armed Struggle Command of, 209; peace agreement with Jordanian government (1985), xxvi–xxvii; peace agreement with Jordanian government of (1970), 41; recruitment in refugee camps by, 197, 203; relations with Jordan of, 223;

response to endorsement of Saddam Husayn, xxx; role in administering aid funds to occupied territory, 188; role in 1989 elections of, xxv
Palestine Mandate: exclusion of Jews from Transjordan section of, 25; objective of administration of, 24–25; opposition to, 23; partition of, 3; relinquished by British (1948), 235; subdivision of (1921), xxi, 25; terms of, 23
Palestine National Council (PNC) (*see also* Palestine Central Committee (PCC)), 48-49, 201; declares independent state of Palestine, 202; Executive Committee of, 203, 208; meets in Jordan (1984), xxvi; as representative of Palestinian diaspora, 206-7; resolutions related to Israel (1987), 207
Palestine National Fund. *See* Palestine Liberation Organization (PLO)
Palestine National Liberation Movement. *See* Al Fatah (Palestine National Liberation Movement)
Palestine Red Crescent Society (PRCS), 208-9
Palestinian Armed Struggle Command, 209
Palestinian National Charter. *See* Palestine Liberation Organization (PLO)
Palestinians: anti-American sentiment of, 216; in attack against Israel (1973), 45; citizenship in Jordan of, 189, 197; create a state within Lebanon (1970–75), 51; defined, 65; differences in political identity of, 91; differing views of problem of, 39–40; in East Bank, 65; economic assistance from Jordan to, 57; as guerrillas (fedayeen), xxii, 37, 225, 232; human and economic capital of, 90–91, 253, 254; integration of and discrimination against, xxiii, 233; in Jordan (1953), 31; Jordanian alternative for problem of, 54; in Jordanian army, 240; Majali tribe as, 90; National Guidance Committee of, 54; nationalism of, 91; opposition to absolutist monarchy by, 198; place in social structure of, 77; position of King Hussein toward, 48; reasons for lack of assimilation of, 76; in refugee camps, 182; role in government of, 181, 188; role in Jordanian society of, 197; working abroad, 93–94

Palestinian uprising (*intifadah*), xxvii, 66, 92, 223, 233
Pan-Arabism, 91
paper and cardboard production, 152–53
Peake, F. G. (Peake Pasha), 26, 27, 234
penal system, 276–78
People's Army, 257, 259
People's Army Law (1983), 257
Peraea, 7
Peres, Shimon, 212
Persia, 7
Persian Gulf states, 56
Petra Bank, 176
PETRA (news agency), 220
Petra (Sela), 9
PFLP. *See* Popular Front for the Liberation of Palestine (PFLP)
PFLP-GC. *See* Popular Front for the Liberation of Palestine-General Command (PFLP-GC)
pharmaceutical industry, xxiv, 152
Philadelphia, 7, 9
Philistines, 6
phosphate production and export, xxiii, 127, 160, 215
pilgrims, Muslim, 16
pipeline: oil, 162; proposals for water, 165–66
plateau country, 68
PLF. *See* Palestine Liberation Front (PLF)
PLO. *See* Palestine Liberation Organization (PLO)
PNC. *See* Palestine National Council (PNC)
police. *See* Public Security Force
Police Training School, 268
political groups: appearance of, (1989–90), xxix
political organizations, 44, 58; Democratic Bloc as, xxvi; restrictions on activities of, 231
political parties, 59; xxix; banned, xxv; in exile, 197
political structure: Islamic opposition to, 111–12; role of kinship in, 87–88; role of tribalism in, 82–86
political system: elite in, 193–97; National Charter principles for, xxvi; repression and dissent in, 197–98
polygyny, 97
Pompey, 9
Popular Front for the Liberation of Palestine-General Command (PFLP-GC),

205, 207, 223, 233
Popular Front for the Liberation of Palestine (PLFP) (*see also* Jordanian Democratic Unity Party), xxix, 40, 207; airplane high-jacking campaign of, 42
Popular Struggle Front (PSF), 206, 207
population: age distribution in, 72–73; concentration of, xxiii, 227; of East and West Bank combined (1950), 90; of East Bank (1988), 65; effect of size of, xxiii; growth of, xxiv–xxv, 72, 134, 147; of Jordan (1953), 30–31, 128; nomadic and seminomadic, 75; Palestinians in, xxiii; ratio of beduins to total, 83; of Transjordan (1921), 65
port facilities, 67, 155, 156–57
potash industry, xxiii, 161
price system: levels in, 134, 140–41; price setting in, 140–41
Prince Hasan Air Base, 248
Prison Law (1953), 277
Prisons Department. *See* Ministry of Interior, Public Security Directorate
prison system, 276–78
private sector, 138–39
privatization, 159
protectionism, 149–50
Protestant denominations, 113–14
PSF. *See* Popular Struggle Front (PSF)
Ptolemaic Dynasty, 7
Ptolemy Philadelphus, 9
Public Security Force (*see also* Desert Police Force), xxviii; control in peace and war for, 265; duties and responsibilities of, 266–67; geographic organization of, 266–67; judicial, administrative, and support for police of, 266–67; as outgrowth of Arab Legion, 265; ranks and insignia of, 268–69; recruitment for, 268; size of, 266
pumping station H5 air base, 248, 249

qadis (religious judges), 12, 191
Qasim, Abd al Karim, 35
Qassim family, 197
Qatar, 131, 215
Queen Alia International Airport, 158
Quran, 12, 104, 107, 109
Quraysh of Mecca, 12
Quraysh tribe, 18

Rabat Summit (1974), 46–47, 91, 189, 199, 210
radio broadcasting, 220
Rafidayn Bank, 176
railroad system, 16, 155–56
rainfall, 71, 164, 168
Ramadan (*see also* Id al Fitr), 107–8
Reagan, Ronald, 57, 59, 262
Reagan Plan, 59–60, 212, 216–17
recession, 181–82
Red Cross. *See* International Committee of the Red Cross
Red Sea, 66
refugee camps: established after 1948 Arab-Israeli War, 29, 76; established after June 1967 War, 76; GID representation in, 270; guerrilla recruitment in, 203; maintained by UNRWA, 219; militance in, 40, 91–92; political recruitment in, 197; population of East Bank, 90; role of Palestinian Armed Struggle Command in, 209
refugees: impoverished, 233; from Iraq and Kuwait (1990–91), xxx; problem of, 40; from West Bank, 38, 90–92, 147
religion (*see also* Christianity; Druze religion; millet system; Shia Islam; Sunni Islam), 103–9
religious courts, 191
religious minorities, 112–14
religious sects, 114
remittances, 58, 93–94, 127, 130–31, 215, 250; decline in, 134, 136, 147; revenues from, 145–47; used for development planning, 142–43
reserves, international, 134–35, 136
revenues: from economic assistance, xxv; from imports, 142; from remittances, 58, 93–94, 127, 130–31, 215, 250
Rifai, Abd al Munim, 41
Rifai, Samir ar, 196–97
Rifai, Zaid ar, 48, 49, 137, 187, 190, 196
rift valleys, 67–68, 71
riots: in 1986, xxv, 231, 232; in 1989, 182, 190, 196
road system, 154–55
Robins, Philip, 145
Roman Catholic Church, 113
Roman Empire: absorption of Judah into, 9; administrative division of, 10
Royal Jordanian Air Academy, 248–49
Royal Jordanian Air Force: organization of, 248; semi-autonomous nature of,

242–43; size of, 241
Royal Jordanian Airlines, 139, 157–58
Royal Police Academy, 268
Russia, 16

Sadat, Anwar as, 46, 53; signs Camp David Accords, xxiii; visits Jerusalem, 52, 199
Saladin, 13
Salah ad Din Yusuf ibn Ayyub. *See* Saladin
SAMED. *See* Palestine Liberation Organization (PLO)
Samuel, Herbert, 25
San Remo Conference (1920), 23, 25
Sassanian Empire, 10
Saudi Arabia: boundary with, 67; economic assistance from, xxiv, xxvii, 131, 250, 260; forces invade Israel (1948), 28; Jordanians in, 93–94; oil sales by, 162; payments to Jordan (1957), 32–33; relations with, xxx–xxxi, 173–74, 212, 214
Saul (king), 6
schools: for police training, 268; religious, 114–15; of UNRWA, 115
Seccombe, Ian J., 145
security, internal. *See* General Intelligence Department (GID)
Seleucids, 9
Selim I (Ottoman sultan), 13
Seljuk Turks, 12–13
seminomads. *See* beduins
semisedentary groups. *See* beduins
Semitic language, 5, 7
Semitic nomads (*see also* Amorites): Amorites as, 5; *habiru* (Hebrews) as, 5
service sector, xxiv, 127, 129, 133
Shakir, Ash Sharif Zaid ibn, xxvi, 187, 190, 196, 242
Shakir family, 196
shale oil deposits, 154, 164
Shalmaneser (king of Assyria), 7
Shami, Senteny, 74
Shamir, Yitzhak, 212
*shammal* wind, 72
Sharaf, Abdul Hamid, 196
Sharaf, Layla, 86, 196
Sharaf family, 196
sharia courts (*see also* qadis (religious judges)), 191, 270
sharia (Islamic law), 12, 16, 104–5, 191,

270–72, 273; enforcement under Ottoman rule of, 16
Sharon, Ariel, 5, 54
Shia Islam, 12, 105; Ismaili branch of, 114; in minority in Jordan, xxvi, 231
Shia Muslims: Jordanians as, 104; Shishans as, 79, 114
Shia radicals, 4
Shiat Ali (Party of Ali), 105
Shishans (Chechens) in Jordan, xxvi, 79
Shukairi, Ahmad. *See* Shuqayri, Ahmad
Shuqayri, Ahmad, 36–37
Sinai Peninsula: Egyptian military build-up in, 37–38; as home of Israelites, 6
Social Security Corporation, 122
Social Security Law (1978), 122
social services, 122
social structure (*see also* endogamy; *hamula* or clan; kinship; marriage; tribalism; villages): changing relations in, 100; class structure and distinctions in, 77, 93; elite in, 31; fragmentation of, 65; mobility in, 76, 95; status in, 95; in Transjordan, 81; tribalism as element of, 76, 81–86; in villages, 86–90
social welfare, 121–22
Solomon (king), 6
Southern Ghawr, 68
Soviet Union: invades Afghanistan, 55, 56; Jordanians studying in, 117; relations with, 218; sells air defense systems and other equipment, 260, 261; supports proposed UN partition of Palestine (1947), 27
Spain, 261
Special Council, 192
special courts, 191–92
Special Police Force. *See* Ministry of Interior, Public Security Directorate
spending, government: cuts in, 137; for defense (1988), 250–51; for defense and national security, xxvii, 128, 250; for education, 114; for social security, housing, and welfare, 122
standard of living, 117–22, 128, 134
Steadfastness and Confrontation Front, 54–55, 56
stock exchange. *See* Amman Financial Market
Strait of Tiran, 38, 40
students, 231
Sublime Porte, 16
subsidies, 140–41; for imports, 150; requirement to reduce, xxiv
Suez Canal, 20, 22, 40
sunna, 104
Sunni Islam (*see also* hadith; hajj; imam; jihad; Ramadan; sunna), 12, 65, 105; Circassians practicing, 16, 78; as mainstream form in Jordan, xxvi, 231; ratio of those adhering to, 103; tenets of, 106
Sykes-Picot Agreement (1916), 21–22
Syria: after war in Lebanon, 61; as ally, 50–51, 225; attacks Israel (1973), 45; financial support for As Saiqa, 206; forces invade Israel (1948), 28; French mandate for, 23; joint ventures with, 138; Jordanian uneasiness toward, 226; military aid to fedayeen (1970), 42, 226; occupied by Arabs by 640, 10; opposition to Jordanian military training (1980), 226; in and out of United Arab Republic, 35, 36; payments to Jordan (1957), 32–33; proclaims independence (1919), 25; relations with Iraq of, 56; relations with Jordan of, xxvii, 50–56, 173, 214; as Roman province, 9; supports Iran, 4; takes side in Lebanon, 51
Syrian-Jordanian Marine Transport Company, 157
Syrian (or North Arabian) Desert, 67

Tal, Wasfi at, 36, 43–44
Talal (prince (later king) of Jordan), xxi–xxii, 30, 194
Tal family, 197
Talhuni, Bahjat at, 36
Taminian, Lucine, 74
Tapline. *See* Trans-Arabian Pipeline (Tapline)
tax policy, 142
TCC. *See* Jordan Telecommunications Corporation (TCC)
telecommunications system, 158–60
television broadcasting, 220
terrorism: by Black September, 44, 198; of extreme PLO groups, 201; by fedayeen, 37; by Jordanian and Palestinian political groups, 198; Special Police Force role for countering, 267; Syrian-sponsored, 226, 232
Thailand, 160, 173
Thatcher, Margaret, 218
thermal power stations, 153–54

TJFF. *See* Transjordan Frontier Force
topography, 67–68, 71
tourism industry, xxxi
trade policy (*see also* entrepôt status; exports; imports; import substitution; protectionism): to alter composition and direction of, 170, 172; barter agreements with Iraq, 162; entrepôt status in, xxiv, xxviii, xxx, 127, 133, 264; for imports, 137, 149–50; for transit to and from Iraq, 129, 133
trade unions. *See* labor unions
trading partners, 173–74
Trajan (emperor of Rome), 9
Trans-Arabian Pipeline (Tapline), 162
transfer payments. *See* economic assistance; remittances
Transjordan (*see also* Amirate of Transjordan; Jordan): exclusion of Jewish settlement in (1922), 25; forces invade Israel (1948), 28; granted independence (1946), 194; under Palestine Mandate, xxi, 25; Palestinian Arabs in, 29; preparation for independence of, 26; treaties and agreements with Britain of, 26–27
Transjordan Frontier Force (TJFF), 26, 234–35
Transjordanians. *See* Jordanians
transportation system, xxiv, xxviii, 154–58, 162, 213
treaties, 16; between Britain and Transjordan, 26–27; related to religious affiliation, 16
Treaty of London (1946), xxi, 27
Treaty of Peace Between Egypt and Israel (1979), 4, 53, 111, 199
treaty with Egypt and Syria (1957), 236
tribalism, 76, 79; forces related to decline in, 85; foundation for, 82; importance in social and political structure of, xxiii, 83–86; in Transjordan, 81
tribal kingdoms, 6
tribal law, 16, 193
tribesmen, Arab, 18
Truman, Harry, 29
Tunisia, 201
Tunis summit (1979), 54
Turkey, 174

Umar (caliph), 12, 105
Umayyad Dynasty, 12

unemployment, 66, 102, 118, 134, 181
Unionist Democratic Association, 197
United Arab Command, 36, 37
United Arab Emirates, 131, 173, 215
United Arab Kingdom (proposed), 45
United Arab Republic (UAR), 35, 36
United Nations (UN): Emergency Force (UNEF) of, 38; membership in, 219; PLO observer status in, 208; recognizes PLO, 47; Relief and Works Agency (UNRWA) for Palestine Refugees in the Near East, 29, 73, 90, 115, 122, 131, 219; resolution to partition Palestine Mandate, 3; sanctions against Iraq (1990), xxix; Security Council Resolution 242, xxvi–xxvii, 39, 46, 50, 60, 201, 216; Security Council Resolution 338, xxvii, 46, 50, 201, 216; Special Committee on Palestine (UNSCOP), 27; Truce Supervision Organization-Palestine (UNSTOP), 28
United States: Arms Control and Disarmament Agency (ACDA), 251, 261; Congress opposes military sales to Jordan, 247–48, 250, 262–63, 264; Department of State, 277; diminished aid and arms sales of, 217; economic assistance from, 34–35, 131, 168, 215–16; Eric Johnston water distribution plan of, 31; imports from, 170; Jordanians studying in, 117; loans from, 39; military assistance from, 39, 215–16, 217, 261–63; military training and technical assistance from, 263; Point Four program in Jordan of, 29; political support from, 215; relations with, 51–52, 60–61, 215–17; sells military equipment and aircraft to Jordan, 52, 247, 261–63; supports proposed UN partition of Palestine (1947), 27; trade relations with, 174
United States Army Command and General Staff College, 257
universities (*see also* community colleges), 116, 231, 257
University of Jordan, 116, 231
UNRWA. *See* United Nations (UN)
UNSCOP. *See* United Nations (UN)
UNSTOP. *See* United Nations (UN)
urban centers: population concentrations in, 65, 74–75; rise of modern, 92–93
Uthman (caliph), 12, 105
utilities industry, 130

veterans' rights, 254
veterinary medicine industry, 152
villages, 86–90, 193

Wadi al Arabah (Wadi al Jayb), 68
Wadi al Arabah Dam, 165
wages, 146
Wahhabi sectarians, 25, 26, 234
War College, 257
wars: Arab-Israeli, xxi, xxii, 3–4, 38, 46, 66, 216, 224–25, 235–38, 247, 261–62; civil (1970–71), xxii, 42, 193, 198–99, 215–16, 233; civil, Lebanon, 51; Gulf (1991), xxix–xxxi; Iran-Iraq, 4
water demand, xxiv–xxv, 118, 127, 164
water distribution: Israeli plan for, 36; proposal for Lebanon and Syria for, 36; proposed plan by Iraq for, 56; United States plan for, 31
water resources, xxiv–xxv, 164–66, 168–69
Weizmann, Chaim, 23
West Bank: annexed by Jordan (1950), 3, 29, 66; economic assistance to Palestinians in, xxvii; elections (1976), 199; expanding Israeli settlements in, 4, 59; Israel assaults villages in (1966), 37; Israeli plans to retain, 53–54; Jordan relinquishes sovereignty over (1988), xxvii, xxviii, 181, 188, 210, 233; neolithic culture in, 5; Palestinian Arabs in, 29; pan-Arab aid funds for occupied, 188, 202; PLO territorial claims to, 47; seizure by Israel (1967), xxii, 4, 38, 128, 166
Western Europe: imports from, 170; Jordanians studying in, 117

WHO. *See* World Health Organization (WHO)
Wilson, Rodney, 172
Wilson, Woodrow, 23
winds (khamsin; *shammal*), 72
women: in armed forces, 255; effect of social changes on, 100–101; enfranchisement of (1973), 189; honor concept for, 99–100; in labor force, 98, 101–3, 147; Palestinian position on role of, xxiii; in police organization, 268; practicing traditional health remedies, 120; proposals for motivation to work, 102; religious practices of, 110–11; role in family of, 96–99, 100; role in social structure of, 95; targeted for health care, 121; as volunteers in People's Army, 259
worker remittances. *See* remittances
World Bank, xxiv, 131
World Health Organization (WHO), 118
Writers' Association, 219

Yarmuk Brigade, 56, 264
Yarmuk River, 68, 154, 165, 227
Yarmuk University, 116, 231
Yemen Arab Republic (North Yemen), 214, 219
Young Turks, 18, 20
Yugoslavia, 160

Zayadin, Yaqub, 232
Zionist Congress, First, 17
Zionist General Council, 28
Zionist Organization, 17, 23
Zionists, 17, 22

# Published Country Studies

## (Area Handbook Series)

| | | | | |
|---|---|---|---|---|
| 550–65 | Afghanistan | 550–87 | Greece |
| 550–98 | Albania | 550–78 | Guatemala |
| 550–44 | Algeria | 550–174 | Guinea |
| 550–59 | Angola | 550–82 | Guyana and Belize |
| 550–73 | Argentina | 550–151 | Honduras |
| | | | |
| 550–169 | Australia | 550–165 | Hungary |
| 550–176 | Austria | 550–21 | India |
| 550–175 | Bangladesh | 550–154 | Indian Ocean |
| 550–170 | Belgium | 550–39 | Indonesia |
| 550–66 | Bolivia | 550–68 | Iran |
| | | | |
| 550–20 | Brazil | 550–31 | Iraq |
| 550–168 | Bulgaria | 550–25 | Israel |
| 550–61 | Burma | 550–182 | Italy |
| 550–50 | Cambodia | 550–30 | Japan |
| 550–166 | Cameroon | 550–34 | Jordan |
| | | | |
| 550–159 | Chad | 550–56 | Kenya |
| 550 77 | Chile | 550–81 | Korea, North |
| 550–60 | China | 550–41 | Korea, South |
| 550–26 | Colombia | 550–58 | Laos |
| 550–33 | Commonwealth Caribbean, Islands of the | 550–24 | Lebanon |
| | | | |
| 550–91 | Congo | 550–38 | Liberia |
| 550–90 | Costa Rica | 550–85 | Libya |
| 550–69 | Côte d'Ivoire (Ivory Coast) | 550–172 | Malawi |
| 550–152 | Cuba | 550–45 | Malaysia |
| 550–22 | Cyprus | 550–161 | Mauritania |
| | | | |
| 550–158 | Czechoslovakia | 550–79 | Mexico |
| 550–36 | Dominican Republic and Haiti | 550–76 | Mongolia |
| 550–52 | Ecuador | 550–49 | Morocco |
| 550–43 | Egypt | 550–64 | Mozambique |
| 550–150 | El Salvador | 550–35 | Nepal and Bhutan |
| | | | |
| 550–28 | Ethiopia | 550–88 | Nicaragua |
| 550–167 | Finland | 550–157 | Nigeria |
| 550–155 | Germany, East | 550–94 | Oceania |
| 550–173 | Germany, Fed. Rep. of | 550–48 | Pakistan |
| 550–153 | Ghana | 550–46 | Panama |

| | | | |
|---|---|---|---|
| 550-156 | Paraguay | 550-53 | Thailand |
| 550-185 | Persian Gulf States | 550-89 | Tunisia |
| 550-42 | Peru | 550-80 | Turkey |
| 550-72 | Philippines | 550-74 | Uganda |
| 550-162 | Poland | 550-97 | Uruguay |
| | | | |
| 550-181 | Portugal | 550-71 | Venezuela |
| 550-160 | Romania | 550-32 | Vietnam |
| 550-37 | Rwanda and Burundi | 550-183 | Yemens, The |
| 550-51 | Saudi Arabia | 550-99 | Yugoslavia |
| 550-70 | Senegal | 550-67 | Zaire |
| | | | |
| 550-180 | Sierra Leone | 550-75 | Zambia |
| 550-184 | Singapore | 550-171 | Zimbabwe |
| 550-86 | Somalia | | |
| 550-93 | South Africa | | |
| 550-95 | Soviet Union | | |
| | | | |
| 550-179 | Spain | | |
| 550-96 | Sri Lanka | | |
| 550-27 | Sudan | | |
| 550-47 | Syria | | |
| 550-62 | Tanzania | | |